"E. J. W. GIBB MEMORIAL"

SERIES.

VOL. XXI.

THE DĪWĀNS

OF

ʿABĪD IBN AL-ABRAṢ, OF ASAD,

AND

ʿĀMIR IBN AṬ-ṬUFAIL, OF ʿĀMIR IBN ṢAʿṢAʿAH,

EDITED FOR THE FIRST TIME, FROM THE MS. IN
THE BRITISH MUSEUM,

AND SUPPLIED WITH A TRANSLATION AND NOTES,

BY

SIR CHARLES LYALL

PUBLISHED AND DISTRIBUTED BY THE
TRUSTEES OF THE "E. J. W. GIBB MEMORIAL",
c/o SPICER AND PEGLER, LEDA HOUSE,
STATION ROAD, CAMBRIDGE, ENGLAND

ISBN 0 906094 13 5

Produced in association with
Book Production Consultants, Cambridge, England

Reprinted at the University Press, Cambridge

DEDICATED

TO

OUR MASTER

THEODOR NÖLDEKE

IN GRATITUDE AND AFFECTION.

PREFACE.

The MS. from which the two ancient Arabic *Dīwāns* contained in this book are now published was transcribed early in the 5th century of the Hijrah, and was acquired by the British Museum at Beyrout in 1907. [1] The MS. is, so far as is known, unique, and no other copy of the collections contained in it has come to light. The editing of them for the press has therefore been a work of some difficulty, since comparison with other texts was excluded. As explained in the Introductions, however, certain poems in each *Dīwān* are contained in other well-known collections, and the editor's work was so far facilitated; while for ʿĀmir the commentary, by a celebrated scholar of the 4th century, was a guarantee of the readings adopted in the text.

The Editor has to acknowledge kind assistance from several scholars in settling the text and collecting the passages contained in the Supplements: in particular from Mr. Fritz Krenkow, of Leicester, and Prof. Rudolf Geyer, of Vienna, the latter of whom placed at his disposal his *collectanea* for ʿAbīd and ʿĀmir. He has also to acknowledge the assistance he derived from Prof. Hommel's list of citations from ʿAbīd contained in his *Aufsätze u. Abhandlungen*, published at Munich in 1892. But of capital importance to the work was the generous and unfailing help afforded by Prof. Nöldeke, who not only looked through the first draft of the text with the photographs of the MS., but also insisted on seeing the proof-sheets as they were set up. Whatever merit the edition may possess is due to this most valuable cooperation of the acknowledged Master of all European scholars in this field of study.

The Editor begs those who may peruse the volume to turn first to the list of *Emendanda et Addenda* at pp. 129—134, and to make the corrections and note the additions there indicated before using the book. He hopes that the Index of Words will be found useful, and desires to explain that it was constructed with a double object, *viz.*, first, to afford a criterion for judging of the style of each poet by citing the characteristic words employed by him and noting the number of times that they occur; and secondly, as an assistance to lexicographers, by pointing to passages where words of interest are to be found.

---

[1] I understand that the importance of the MS. was first recognized by Mr. H. S. Cowper, through whose mediation it was obtained by the Trustees of the Museum.

It should be explained that the *Muᶜallaqāt* are cited from the edition with Tibrīzī's commentary published at Calcutta by the editor of this volume in 1891—94, and that the references to the *Mufaḍḍalīyāt* are to the edition (by the same hand) of this collection now in the press, which will (it is hoped) shortly be issued by the Clarendon Press among the *Anecdota Oxoniensia*. Where the *Dīwān* of Ṭufail is mentioned, the forthcoming edition by Mr. Krenkow is meant. Citations from Dhu-r-Rummah are also occasionally referred to the edition of this poet's *Dīwān* by Mr. C. H. H. Macartney, now in the press.

LIST OF ABBREVIATIONS.

Abkar.: Abkāriūs, *Nihāyat al-ʾArab fī Akhbār al-ʿArab*, Beyrout 1865.

Abū Ḥātim as-Sijistānī: *Kitāb al-Muʿammarīn*, ed. Goldziher, 1899.

Abū Zaid: *Nawādir*, ed. Beyrout, 1894.

Aḍdād: *Kitābo-l-Adhdād auct. Abū Bekr ibno-l-Anbārī*, ed. Houtsma, 1881.

Agh.: *Kitāb al-Aghānī*, ed. Cairo 1285 H.

Ahlw.: Wilhelm Ahlwardt, Prof. at Greifswald, editor of *Six Poets* (London 1870), *Aṣmaʿīyāt*, and *Dīwāns* of al-ʿAjjāj and Ruʾbah.

ʿAinī: *Kitāb al-ʿAinī*, on margin of *Khizānat al-Adab*, Cairo 1299 H.

ʿAjj., al-ʿAjjāj: *Dīwān*, ed. Ahlwardt, Berlin 1903.

Akhṭal: *Dīwān al-Akhṭal*, ed. Ṣālḥānī, Beyrout, 1891.

Altarab. Diiamb.: *Altarabische Diiamben*, ed. R. Geyer, Vienna 1908.

ʿAmr: *Muʿallaqah of ʿAmr b. Kulthūm* (ed. Lyall).

ʿAntarah: *Muʿallaqah*, ed. Lyall; *Dīwān*, ed. Ahlwardt.

Asās: *Asās al-Balāghah*, Lexicon, by az-Zamakhsharī, ed. Cairo 1299—1882.

Al-Aʿshà, poem beginning *Ma bukāʾu*, ed. Geyer (Vienna 1905). Poem in praise of the Prophet Muḥammad, ed. Thorbecke, in *Morgenländische Forschungen*, 1875. *Muʿallaqah*, ed. Lyall. *Dīwān*, MS. Escorial (numbering that of Geyer's forthcoming edition).

ʿAsk.: Abū Hilāl al-ʿAskarī, *Kitāb aṣ-Ṣināʿatain*, ed. Constantinople 1319 H.

Aṣm.: al-Aṣmaʿī, *al-Aṣmaʿīyāt*, ed. Ahlwardt, Berlin 1902.

  Kitāb al-Khail, ed. Haffner, Vienna 1895.

  Kitāb al-Ibil, ed. Haffner 1905.

Aus: *Dīwān of Aus b. Ḥajar*, ed. Geyer, 1892.

B = *Ibn*, son,

BA, BAthīr: *al-Kāmil fi-t-Tārīkh* by Ibn al-Athīr, ed. Tornberg, 1867 (Vol. I only cited).

Bakrī: *Kitāb Muʿjam ma-staʿjam: Geographisches Wörterbuch*, ed. Wüstenfeld, Göttingen, 1876.

BDur., BDuraid: the *Kitāb al-Ishtiqāq*, by Abū Bakr ibn Duraid, ed. Wüstenfeld, Göttingen 1854.

BHish., BHishām: *Das Leben Muhammad's, nach Muḥd. Ibn Isḥāḳ, bearbeitet von ʿAbd el-Malik Ibn Hischām*, ed. Wüstenfeld, Göttingen 1860.

BIsḥāḳ: see above, BHishām.

BQut.: Ibn Qutaibah, *Kitāb ash-Shiᶜr wa-sh-Shuᶜarā*, ed. De Goeje, Leiden 1904.
  id. *Adab al-Kuttāb*, ed. Grünert, Leiden 1901.

BSaᶜd: *Kitāb aṭ-Ṭabaqāt al-Kabīr*, by Muḥd. b. Saᶜd Kātib al-Wāqidī, ed. Sachau, Leiden (in progress).

Buḥt. Ḥam.: the *Ḥamāsah* of al-Buḥturī, MS. Leiden, reproduced in *fac-simile*, Leiden 1909.

Caetani, Annali: *Annali dell' Islam*, by Leone Caetani, Principe di Teano, Rome (in progress).

Caussin de Perceval: *Essai sur l'histoire des Arabes avant l'Islamisme, pendant l'époque de Mahomet, et jusqu'à la réduction de toutes les tribus sous la loi musulmane*, Paris 1847.

Damīrī: *Ḥayāt al-Ḥayawān*, ed. Bulak 1284 H.

Dh.R. Dhu-r-Rummah (Ghailān), *Dīwān*, ed. Macartney, in progress.

Dīw. = *Dīwān*.

Doughty: *Travels in Arabia Deserta*, by C. M. Doughty, Cambridge 1888.

Dozy, Suppl.: *Supplément aux Dictionnaires Arabes*, par R. Dozy, Leiden 1881.

Fāʾiq: the *Fāʾiq* of az-Zamakhsharī, ed. Haidarābād 1324 H.

Ḥam.: the *Ḥamāsah* of Abū Tammām, ed. Freytag, Bonn 1828.

Ḥassān: the *Dīwān* of Ḥassān b. Thābit, ed. Hirschfeld, London 1910.

Hudh.: the *Dīwān* of the Poets of Hudhail, ed. Kosegarten (1854) and Wellhausen (1884).

Ḥuṭaiʾah: the *Dīwān* of (Jarwal) al-Ḥuṭaiʾah, ed. Goldziher, Leipzig 1893.

I. Q.: The *Dīwān* of Imraʾ-al-Qais, ed. Ahlwardt (in *Six Poets*); *Muᶜallaqah*, ed. Lyall.

ᶜIqd: *al-ᶜIqd al-Farīd*, by Ibn ᶜAbd-Rabbihi, ed. Cairo 1293.

Iqtiḍāb: *Al-Iqtiḍāb fi Adab al-Kuttāb*, Beyrout 1901.

Jāḥ., Jāḥiḍh: *Kitāb al-Bayān wa-t-Tibyān*, ed. Cairo 1313 H.
  Kitāb al-Ḥayawān, ed. Cairo, 1323—4.

Jam., Jamh.: *Jamharat Ashᶜār al-ᶜArab*, ed. Cairo, 1308 H.

Jarīr: *Dīwān*, ed. Cairo 1313 H.

Khiz.: *Khizānat al-Adab*, by ᶜAbd al-Qādir al-Baghdādī, ed. Cairo 1299 H.

Kk: a MS. formerly belonging to Mr. Krenkow, and now the property of the India Office, containing a recension of the *Mufaḍḍalīyāt* and *Aṣmaᶜīyāt* differing from that generally known.

LA: *Lisān al-ᶜArab*, by Muḥammad b. al-Mukarram, ed. Cairo 1308 H.

Lab.: Labīd, *Dīwān*, ed. Khālidī (Vienna 1880) and Huber (Leiden 1891).

Lane: *Arabic-English Lexicon*, by E. W. Lane, London 1863—1893.

Maid. Freyt.: *Amthal alᶜ-Arab*, by al-Maidānī, ed. Freytag, Bonn 1838—43.

Majāni-l-Adab, edited by the Jesuit Fathers, St. Joseph's University, Beyrout 1884.

Majmūᶜat al-Maᶜānī, a miscellany of verses published by the *Jawāᶜib* Press, Constantinople 1301 H.

MbdKām.: the *Kāmil* of al-Mubarrad, ed. W. Wright, Leipzig 1892.

Mfḍt.: the *Mufaḍḍalīyāt, with the commentary of al-Qāsim al-Anbārī*, ed. Lyall (in progress).

Muʿall. = *Muʿallaqah.*

Mukht.: the *Mukhtārāt* of Hibat-allāh b. ash-Shajarī, lith. Cairo 1306.

Murtaḍà, Amālī: The *Amālī* of as-Sayyid al-Murtaḍà, ed. Cairo 1907—1325.

Nāb.: the *Dīwān* of an-Nābighah adh-Dhubyānī, ed. Ahlwardt (in *Six Poets*); *Muʿallaqah,* ed. Lyall.

Naq.: the *Naqāʾiḍ* of Jarīr and al-Farazdaq, ed. Bevan, Leiden 1905—12.

Naṣr.: *ash-Shuʿarāʾ an-Naṣrānīyah fi-l-Jāhilīyah,* ed. L. Cheikho. Beyrout 1890 ff.

Nöldeke: *Beiträge zur Kenntniss der Poesie der Alten Araber,* Hannover 1864.
Zur Grammatik des classischen Arabisch, Vienna 1896.
Gedichte des ʿUrwah b. al-Ward, Göttingen 1863.
Geschichte der Perser u. Araber zur Zeit der Sāsāniden, Leiden 1879.

Qālī: the *Amālī* of al-Qālī, ed. Cairo 1324 H.

Qur.: the *Qurʾān,* cited after the numbering of *Sūrahs* and verses in al-Baiḍāwī's text, ed. Fleischer, Leipzig 1878.

Quṭāmī: the *Dīwān* of al-Quṭāmī, ed. J. Barth, Leiden 1902.

Ruʾbah: the *Dīwān* of Ruʾbah b. al-ʿAjjaj, ed. Ahlwardt, Berlin 1903.

ash-Shammākh: *Dīwān,* ed. Aḥmad ash-Shinqīṭī, Cairo 1327 H.

Sībawaihi, *The Kitāb,* ed. H. Derenbourg. Paris 1881—89.

SSM., Sh.Sh.Mughni: *Sharḥ Shawāhid al-Mughnī,* by Jalāl ad-Dīn as-Suyūṭī, ed. Cairo 1322.

TA.: the *Tāj al-ʿArūs,* second ed., Cairo 1307 H.

Ṭab.: *Annales quos scripsit Abū Djaʿfar Muḥammad b. Djarīr aṭ-Ṭabarī,* ed. Leiden 1879—1901.

Ṭarafah: *Dīwān,* ed. Ahlw. in *Six Poets; Muʿallaqah,* ed. Lyall.

Tib.: *A Commentary on Ten Ancient Arabic Poems,* by Abū Zakarīyā Yaḥyà at-Tibrīzī, ed. Lyall, Calcutta 1891—94.

ʿUmdah: the *ʿUmdah* of Ibn Rashīq, ed. Cairo 1907—1325 H.

Wāqidī: the *Maghāzī* of al-Wāqidī, ed. von Kremer, Calcutta 1856.

Wellhausen, Heidenthum[2]: *Reste Arabischen Heidenthums,* von J. Wellhausen, Berlin 1897.

Wright, Opuscula: *Opuscula Arabica, collected and edited from MSS. in the University Library of Leyden,* by W. Wright. 1859.

Wüst. Tab.: *Genealogische Tabellen der Arab. Stämme u. Familien,* by Ferd. Wüstenfeld, Göttingen 1852. *Register zu den Genealog. Tabellen,* Gött. 1853.

Yāq., Yāqūt: *Jacut's Geographisches Wörterbuch,* (*Muʿjam al-Buldān*), ed. F. Wüstenfeld, Leipzig 1866—1870.

Yaʿq., Yaʿqūbī: *Ibn Wādhiḥ qui dicitur Al-Jaʿqūbī Historiae,* ed. Houtsma, Leiden 1883.

Zuhair: the *Dīwān* of Zuhair, ed. Ahlwardt (in *Six Poets*); the *Muʿallaqah,* ed. Lyall.

CONTENTS.

THE *DĪWĀN* OF ʿABĪD IBN AL–ABRAṢ OF ASAD.

INTRODUCTION.

ʿABĪD IBN AL-ABRAṢ of Asad was a contemporary of Ḥujr, the Prince of Kindah, whom his father al-Ḥārith, while supreme over the Northern Arab tribes, some time at the end of the fifth or in the first quarter of the sixth century, had placed at the head of the group of tribes consisting of Asad, Ghaṭafān, and Kinānah [1]. Byzantine annalists tell of raids led (it would seem) by Ḥujr and his brother Maʿdīkarib (who had, according to the tradition, similarly been made ruler of the neighbouring group of Qais or Hawāzin), whom they call ῎Ωγαρος and Βαδικάριμος, upon the Roman border in 497 and 501 A.D. [2]; and these dates may represent approximately the time at which the division of the tribes among al-Ḥārith's sons was made.

One of the sons of Ḥujr was the famous Imraʾ al-Qais, by common consent the greatest poet of the ancient time whose poems have come down to us. Of these compositions the number is, by comparison with those of other bards of the same age, very considerable; and the geographical details which are given in all the longer odes, not dealing with warfare and wandering, show that they were composed while the young prince dwelt with his father in the country of Asad [3]. We may assume, therefore, that the rule of Ḥujr in Asad lasted for several years, but how long it is impossible to determine.

Al-Ḥārith of Kindah, who appears at one time to have occupied al-Ḥīrah on the Euphrates, the capital of the Lakhmite kingdom, was expelled from it by his son-in-law the celebrated al-Mundhir ibn Māʾ-as-Samā, known to the Greek historians as Ἀλαμούν-δαρος ὁ Σακίκας (or Ζακίκης), the terror of the Roman border from 506 to 554. The Byzantines assert that al-Ḥārith was killed by al-Mundhir in 529, but this appears to

---

[1] See *Ibn al-Kalbī's account of the First Day of al-Kulāb* in Nöldeke-Festschrift (1906), p. 136.

[2] See original passages from Theophanes cited in Brünnow and Domaszewski's *Die Provincia Arabia*, III, 348—349. Theophanes says that Ogarus was killed (or had died) before Badikarimus' attack in 501; but this may not be correct.

[3] See BQut., *Shiʿr*, 37⁵.

be doubtful, as Arabian tradition alleges that he died, perhaps at some later date, at a place called Mushulān in the country of Kalb, while hunting [1]. After his death, whenever it occurred, the principalities in which he had established his sons among the tribes of Northern Arabia seem gradually to have fallen to pieces [2]. The rule of Ḥujr over the tribe of Asad was brought to an end by his sudden death at their hands. Of this event no less than four different accounts are given in the *Kitāb al-Aghānī* [3]:

(1) First, that related by Hishām ibn al-Kalbī († 204) on the authority of his father Muḥammad († 146), who claimed to have had it from à descendant of the Asadite *Kāhin* [4]. This version states that while Ḥujr was absent in Tihāmah, the men of Asad refused to pay the annual tribute which they had been in the habit of rendering, and beat and maltreated his tax-gatherers. Thereupon Ḥujr attacked them with an army drawn from Qais and Kinānah, and having seized their chiefs began to kill them by blows with cudgels, whence they were called "Slaves of the Stick", عَبِيد اَلْعَصَا [5]. After having devastated their country, he banished the tribe to the hot and unhealthy region by the Red Sea called Tihāmah or Low-land, and swore that they would never be allowed to return to Najd. Upon this he was approached by 'Abīd ibn al-Abraṣ, to whom, with some other leading men of Asad, he had shown favour and exempted them from the common penalty, who recited before. him a poem [6], offering the humble submission of the tribe, and entreating that they might be allowed to return. Ḥujr, moved by pity, permitted them to come back after they had gone three days' journey towards the coast. They set out on their way, and when they were one day's journey from the Upland their *Kāhin*, 'Auf son of Rabī'ah, speaking in the name of their tribal God, uttered a prediction that Ḥujr would be the first to be slain on the morrow. Thereupon the whole tribe rode tumultuously to the place where Ḥujr was encamped. He was surrounded there by his body-guard, the Banū Khaddān, belonging to the sub-tribe Banu-l-Ḥārith ibn Sa'd of Asad, whose father had been exempted from the maltreatment to which the other chiefs of Asad had been subjected; they offered no resistance to their fellow-tribesmen, and 'Ilbā son of al-Ḥārith of Kāhil (another sub-tribe), whose father had been killed by Ḥujr, burst through the guards, pierced him in their midst with a spear, and slew him. 'Ilbā then incited the men of Qais and Kinānah, who had been in the following of Ḥujr, to plunder his camp; and the body of the slain prince was wrapped in a sheet and cast forth to lie in the public highway. 'Amr ibn Mas'ūd [7], one of the

---

[1] *First Day of al-Kulāb*, 136.   [2] See *op. cit., passim*, and especially p. 153.
[3] Agh VIII, 65—67.   [4] Agh VIII, 68⁵.
[5] See Imra'al-Qais, Dīw. LI, 3.   [6] No XXIX of the *Dīwān*.
[7] This man is named as one of the two boon-companions of al-Mundhir of al-Ḥīrah, whose death the King ordered when drunken, and afterwards built over their graves the pillars called the *Gharīyāni*; see the legend of 'Abīd's death, and BQut., *Shi'r*, 144¹³.

chiefs of Asad whom Ḥujr had favoured, is said to have protected his women and to have conveyed them to a place of safety.

Ibn al-Kalbī observes that a large number of the sub-tribes of Asad claim the glory of having slain Ḥujr. Those not belonging to Kāhil say that ʿIlbā was not the actual slayer, though he was the chief of the conspiracy which compassed his death.

(2) The second version [1] is that of Abū ʿAmr ash-Shaibānī († 205), who relates that Ḥujr had news beforehand of the plot against him, and had sought the protection of ʿUwair ibn Shijnah of the Banū ʿUṭārid ibn Kaʿb ibn Zaid-Manāt of Tamīm for his daughter Hind and his family. He then received the Banū Asad when they gathered together, and announced to them that he was leaving them to themselves and departing. The men of Asad bade him farewell, and he then took his way to Khālid son of Khaddān, one of the Banū Saʿd ibn Thaʿlabah. There ʿIlbā ibn al-Ḥārith of Kāhil overtook him, and exhorted Khālid to slay him, saying that Ḥujr would surely bring disaster upon them all if allowed to go free. When Khālid refused, ʿIlbā picked up a broken piece of a lance with the spear-head on it, and with it pierced Ḥujr in the flank while he was off his guard, and so slew him. With reference to this the Asadī poet says:

"The broken spear-shaft of ʿIlbā son of Qais son of Kāhil was the death

of Ḥujr while he was under the protection of the son of Khaddān".

(3) The third version [2] is that of al-Haitham son of ʿAdī († 206), who says: After Ḥujr had placed his family in safety with ʿUwair ibn Shijnah, he returned to his own people, the Banū Kindah, and abode with them for some time. Then he gathered together a great host against the Banū Asad, and advanced in pomp to attack them. The men of Asad were exhorted by their leaders to resist to the utmost, and they marched to meet Ḥujr. When they drew near his host, they fought vigorously in self-defence, their leader being ʿIlbā ibn al-Ḥārith, who bore down on Ḥujr and pierced him with his spear and killed him. The Kindah were routed, among them being Imraʾal-Qais, who fled on his sorrel mare and escaped. The Asad captured several men of the family of Ḥujr and slew them, and they also gained much booty, as well as the women of Ḥujr's household.

(4) The fourth [3] narrative is that of Yaʿqūb ibn as-Sikkīt († 244), who says, on the authority of Khālid of Kilāb (a sub-tribe of ʿĀmir b. Ṣaʿṣaʿah), that Ḥujr had left the Banū ·Asad to visit his father al-Ḥārith, then sick of the illness of which he died; that he remained with him until his death, and then marched back again to Asad, sending on each day a camp ahead to make ready for him at the next halting-place. He had incurred the hatred of Asad by the severity of his rule and by his attacks on the honour of their women; and when news reached them of the death of al-Ḥārith they consulted together and resolved to make a venture for freedom. So when his advance

---

[1] Agh VIII, 66[20] ff.   [2] Agh VIII, 66[28] ff.   [3] Agh ut sup., p. 67[4] ff.

camp reached the place where they were, Naufal ibn Rabīʿah ibn Khaddān resolved to commit the tribe to a conflict by attacking the camp, which he did, plundering it, slaying its defenders, and taking possession of two of Ḥujr's slave-girls (singers). The whole tribe then made common cause, and met Ḥujr at a place known to this day [1] as *Abraqā Ḥujr*, lying between two tracts of rugged ground where black stones and white sand are mingled together. It was not long before they prevailed against him, put to flight his companions, and took himself prisoner. They bound him in his tent, and then consulted together as to what they should do with him. Their *Kāhin* advised them to wait until he had consulted the omens, and went away to do so; whereupon ʿIlbā, fearing lest Ḥujr should escape, induced his sister's son, a boy whose father had been killed by Ḥujr, to slay him with a dagger in revenge. The boy, hiding the dagger, crept into the tent with the rest of the folk who had come to gaze on the prisoner, and suddenly, watching his opportunity, sprang upon him and stabbed him to death. An outcry was raised, but the Banū Kāhil (whose prisoner Ḥujr was) admitted the right of the boy to take vengeance for his father.

Of these four accounts the third agrees best with the testimony of ʿAbīd in his *Dīwān*[2]: see Nos. II, 27, IV, 6—20, VII (the whole), XVII, 12—18, XXVI, 11—13, Frag. 1; these passages are altogether inconsistent with the second and fourth. As regards the first, the doubtful poem No. XXIX is in favour of it; but this piece of verse gives the impression of being a composition of later date than ʿAbīd's time (see the mention of the Resurrection in v. 11), and one cannot avoid a suspicion that it was the work of some enemy of the Banū Asad and favourer of the cause of Yaman (to which Kindah belonged) against Maʿadd (the ancestor of Asad). Such forgeries are frequently attributed to Ibn al-Kalbī in the case of stories dealing with Yamanite stocks and northern Arabs: *e. g.*, the forged verses [3] ascribed to him by the author of the *Aghānī* concerning the contest between ʿĀmir ibn aṭ-Ṭufail and Yazīd ibn ʿAbd al-Mádān of the Bal-Ḥārith; also the verses he is said [4] to have fabricated in order to cast discredit on Duraid ibn aṣ-Ṣimmah, another champion of Hawāzin against the Bal-Ḥārith.

After the death of Ḥujr, the task of exacting vengeance for him devolved upon his youngest son Imra’ al-Qais; and in the *Kitāb al-Aghānī*[5] there is a long account of the measures taken by him to this end. Seeking assistance in this pursuit of vengeance, in which he was opposed not only by his local enemies, but also by the gradually increasing influence over Northern Arabia of al-Mundhir, king of al-Ḥīrah, he wandered from tribe to tribe, and gained the name by which he is known in Arabian tradition, "the Wandering King", الْمَلِك الضِّلِّيل. At last in despair he betook himself to the court of the

---

[1] See Yāqūt I, 81[12].   [2] It is also supported by BQut., *Shiʿr*, p. 43.
[3] Agh. XVIII, 161, foot.   [4] Agh. IX, 19, foot.   [5] VIII, 67 ff.

Qaiṣar, whither — so the story tells — he was followed by an emissary from Asad, aṭ-Ṭammāḥ, who set the mind of the Emperor against him by tales of an intrigue with the Emperor's daughter. The Qaiṣar is said to have sent Imraᵓ al-Qais (who had been given a force to assist him against Asad, and had started on his return to Arabia) a robe poisoned like that of Nessus in classical story. He put it on, and was speedily stricken with ulcers, of which he died on his way southwards at Ancyra (called by the Arabs Anqirah)[1]. The manner of his death caused him to be called "the Man of the Ulcers", ذو القُروح, by which name he is referred to by the poet al-Farazdaq in the first century of Islām. Nothing can be stated with certainty as to the date of the death of Imraᵓ al-Qais, but, as Prof. Nöldeke conjectures[2], he probably died young, some time between 530 and 540 A. D. The Emperor of the time was Justinian I. We know from the Byzantine annals the dates of several events in the reigns of the contemporary Arabian Kings or Phylarchs, al-Ḥārith the Lame of Ghassān (529—569), and al-Mundhir of al-Ḥīrah (506—554), who held the northern borders respectively in the interests of Rome and Persia; but of events in the interior of the Peninsula we have information only from the tribal traditions, vague and confused, and chiefly connected with the poems composed by the tribal bards, which were collected, a considerable time after the establishment of Islām, by the humanists of the later Umayyad and early ᶜAbbāsid reigns. These investigators, being ignorant of the Byzantine records, and having only the traditions to work upon, have constructed from them a chronology which cannot be reconciled with the facts stated in the former.

The territory of Asad lay to the south of the important settlement of Taimā, to the east of the great south-north trade-route, now represented by the pilgrimage road from Maᶜān to Medīnah, and to the west and south of the westward termination of the parallel ranges of Ajaᵓ and Salmà, the mountains of Ṭayyiᵓ. The tribe[3] was the northernmost of Maᶜadd on the way from the south to Palestine and Syria; beyond it were the Yamanite tribes of ᶜUdhrah, Judhām, and Balī[4] along the trade-route, while to the east and north-east of them was the tribe of Kalb, also of Yamanite origin, in the depressions now known as the Wādī Sirḥān and the Jauf: from these Asad was separated by a wide belt of sand-dunes (the modern Nefūd). The territory of Asad has

---

[1] I. Q. Dīw. XXVIII.   [2] See article Moᶜallakāt in Encycl. Britan. 11th Edn., p. 634.

[3] The name Asad, אל אשׁדין, figures among the subjects of King Imraᵓ al-Qais, whose tomb, bearing an inscription dated 328 A.D., is at en-Nemārah in the Ruḥbah east of the Ḥaurān; see Dussaud, Les Arabes en Syrie avant l'Islam, pp. 34 ff. This however may be a different tribe of the name, as Nizār, Maᶜadd, and Madhḥij are also mentioned in the inscription, and these names belong to an earlier genealogical stratum than Asad b. Khuzaimah. This Imraᵓ al-Qais (or Marᵓ al-Qais) was apparently an early Lakhmite king.

[4] Lakhm is frequently mentioned by the old poets together with Judhām: e. g. in ᶜAbīd frag. 16. Balī lay partly to the west of the trade-route and the country of Asad, and still occupies the same region (see Doughty, Arabia Deserta).

been traversed by several European travellers. Doughty, in the spring of 1877, passed
through it on his way from Madāʾin Ṣāliḥ to Taimā and from Taimā to Ḥāʾil. Euting
and Huber journeyed through it in 1884. And quite recently Mr. Douglas Carruthers,
who visited Taimā from the north in the winter of 1908–9, has described his experiences
in the *Journal of the Royal Geographical Society* for March 1910. The scenery is varied.
In the east and north are the ranges of Ajaʾ and Salmà, running NE. and SW., great
granite masses; in the west are the upland sandstone and gravel regions adjoining the
Ḥajj road, bearing good pasture in the spring, and having many watering-places. In the
intermediate space are ridges and ranges of varying rocky heights, and to the south
the great *Ḥarraḥs,* or volcanic lava plains, not destitute of pasture or water; the largest
of these is the *Ḥarrah* of Khaibar, formerly called the *Ḥarrah* of Ḍarghad [1].

ʿAbīd belonged to the division of Asad called Saʿd ibn Thaʿlabah (b. Dūdān, b. Asad).
His full genealogy appears to be: ʿAbīd b. al-Abraṣ (b. ʿAuf [2]) b. Jusham b. ʿĀmir
b. Mālik b. Zuhair (or Hirr) b. Mālik b. al-Ḥārith b. Saʿd b. Thaʿlabah. The tract where
the Banū Saʿd dwelt is described in Bakrī [3] as 16 miles on the way from Faid towards
al-Kūfah, on the skirts of the hill ʿUnaizah. Numerous places in this region are men-
tioned in the poems [4]. The description given of it shows that the settlement was not
far from the modern Ḥāʾil, and that the Asad *dārs* were much intermixed with those
of branches of Ṭayyiʾ. The sub-tribe appears from No. XVIII to have suffered severe
losses from the attacks of Ghassān under the energetic king, well-known at Constantinople,
al-Ḥārith the Lame [5]. The opening of No. I speaks of their land as entirely desolate,
and No. XVIII, v. 2, of the survivors being dispersed among the other divisions of the
tribe. Contentions with al-Ḥārith are mentioned in other poems; and the geographical
situation was such that Asad was the first independent tribe not of Yamanite origin
which a ruler of Ghassān would encounter in an expedition sent to punish an invasion
of the Roman border. Perhaps this division of Asad was engaged in the attacks already
mentioned of Ḥujr and Maʿdīkarib on the *Limes* in 497 and 501.

But the main historical bearing of the poems relates to the slaying of Ḥujr and
the pursuit of vengeance by Imraʾ al-Qais. Of the thirty poems in the *Dīwān*, one
(No. XXIX) is addressed to Ḥujr himself; Nos. IV, XII, XVII and XXX are addressed
or refer to Imraʾal-Qais; in two besides those above specified, Nos. II (v. 27) and XXVI
(v. 11), the death of Ḥujr is mentioned. Among the fragments at the end of the *Dīwān*
there are three (Nos. 1, 8, 10) which refer to the same event.

---

[1] See Dīwān, XXX, 1.
[2] ʿAuf is perhaps the personal name of his father; *Abraṣ* means "suffering from *leucoderma*", and
is an epithet.
[3] p. 718[3] ff.   [4] See Geographical index.
[5] Prof. Littmann, in a paper published in the *Rivista degli Studi Orientali,* 1911, vol. IV, pp. 193—5,
has shown that we have an epigraphic record of a expedition by al-Ḥārith to Khaibar in 567 A.D. This,
of course, was long after ʿAbīd's time: but he may have raided the country many times before.

Not only is ᶜAbīd connected with Imraʾ al-Qais by these historical notices: there are evident signs in the compositions of the two poets that both handled the same subjects, and probably (before the feud arose) in friendly rivalry with one another. ᶜAbīd's most celebrated poem, No. I, agrees in phrase and measure, as Dr. Hommel pointed out in 1892 [1], with a poem by Imraʾ al-Qais, No. LV in Ahlwardt's edition. This is the more remarkable, as the metre of both, a form of the *Basīṭ*, is extremely rare, and so far as I am aware no other example of it has been found in the old poetry. There are other cases in which it is evident that both poets drew on the same stock of poetic phrases and subjects, or handled their themes in the same way; attention is drawn to these in the notes on the separate poems. It is scarcely necessary to point out that these historical references and coincidences of treatment furnish a very strong argument in favour of the genuineness of the poems, both those of the Asadite and those of the Prince of Kindah, in which they occur. We may well be sceptical as to the legendary details of the slaying of Ḥujr and the wanderings of Imraʾ al-Qais in his quest of vengeance, as handed down by tradition: but as to the main facts there does not appear to me to be any reason for doubt. Even the journey of Imraʾ al-Qais to ask the assistance of the Emperor at Constantinople, which at first sight seems improbable, is attested by a reference in ᶜAbīd's poem No. IV, v. 19; and other evidence in favour of the truth of the story is yielded by the tradition which tells how the Prince, when starting on his journey to the North, made over for safe keeping to the Jewish chief as-Samauʾal ibn ᶜĀdiyā a valuable stock of arms and armour, which the latter laid up in his castle of al-Ablaq near Taimā. When Imra ʾal-Qais died on his return journey, al-Ḥārith [2] king of Ghassān, as protector of the Roman border, appeared before al-Ablaq and demanded from as-Samauʾal the mail-coats of Imraʾal-Qais. The Jewish chief refused to surrender his trust, even though al-Ḥārith, who had captured his son when out hunting, threatened to put the boy to death before his father's eyes, and actually did so. The Ghassanide king, however, was unable to reduce the castle, and retired without accomplishing his purpose. The claim of al-Ḥārith was evidently founded on the fact that Imraʾ al-Qais had become a subject of Rome by seeking the Qaiṣar's help, and that he, as the representative of Rome, was entitled to his inheritance. This act of faithfulness on the part of as-Samauʾal was celebrated in a famous poem [3] addressed, some time early in the seventh century

---

[1] *Aufsätze u. Abhandlungen*, 52—92.

[2] According to BQut, 46[6], it was not the king himself, but his kinsman al-Ḥārith b. Mālik, who besieged al-Ablaq.

[3] The poem is in Agh. VIII, 82, BQut, *Shiᶜr*, 139—40, Maidānī (Freyt.), *Proverbs*, II, 829; see Nöldeke, *Beiträge*, 58—64. Prof. Nöldeke, in his paper on as-Samauʾal in the *Zeitschrift f. Assyriologie*, XXVII, 173, has expressed some doubt as to the story of the mail-coats, inasmuch as the Jewish chief is represented by the poet as replying to the summons to deliver إِنَّي مانِعٌ جارِى; but might not defence of the *jār's* property be spoken of as defence of the *jār* himself? See the analogous case of the arms and treasure of an-Nᶜumān in the hands of the Banū Bakr, previous to the battle of Dhū-Qār.

A.D., by al-Aᶜshà of Qais to Shuraiḥ, the descendant of as-Samauʾal, about the genuineness of which there can be no doubt.

None of the poems in the *Dīwān* refers to Imraʾ al-Qais as dead, and possibly ᶜAbīd did not survive him.

Concerning the details of ᶜAbīd's own life we have, outside of his poems, no information. The stories that are told about him are manifestly legendary, and carry no authority. His first appearance as a poet is said to have been due to a vision [1] which he had, while asleep under a tree in the wilderness, of a heavenly messenger who put into his mouth a rolled-up ball of poems, and predicted that he would become a famous poet and the glory of his tribe. He is credited with having lived to a fabulous age, even as much as 300 years being mentioned [2]. He is said to have visited the celebrated Ḥatim of Ṭayyiʾ in the company of Bishr ibn Abī Khāzim and an-Nābighah of Dhubyān, while journeying to the court of an-Nuᶜmān Abū Qābūs, the last Lakhmite king of al-Ḥīrah. This is totally inconsistent with the other and better supported story, that ᶜAbīd was put to death by al-Mundhir ibn Māʾ-as-Samā, grandfather of an-Nuᶜmān. Al-Mundhir met his death, as we know from the Byzantine and Syriac historians, in battle with al-Ḥārith of Ghassān in 554 A.D.; that year is, therefore, the latest possible date for the death of ᶜAbīd, though how long before it he died we cannot say. An-Nuᶜmān did not come to the throne till about 580 A.D. The picturesque legend of the slaying of ᶜAbīd by al-Mundhir [3] will be found at pp. 2—4 of the *Dīwān*; the best version of it is perhaps that in al-Qālī's *Amālī*. The two pillars built over the graves of the two Asadite boon-companions of the King, upon which al-Mundhir daubed the blood of the first person who met his eyes on his Evil Day, called the *Gharīyāni* or *Ṭirbālāni*, were both pointed out in Ibn Qutaibah's time [4] at al-Kūfah (adjacent to the ancient al-Ḥīrah). In Yāqūt's Dictionary [5] it is recorded that Maᶜn b. Zāʾidah, in the time of the grammarian Thaᶜlab, found one of them crumbled away, but the other still standing.

Most of ᶜAbīd's poems are composed from the point of view of old age, and look back upon a youth which the poet depicts as one of gallant deeds in which he bore a valiant part. This seems inconsistent with the story of his having been a poor man, grazing a little flock of sheep and goats, when he first received his inspiration as a poet; and our MS, it will be seen, inserts some words [6], not in the version of the tale as printed in *Ten Poems*, p. 159, to indicate that his poverty was due to his lavish generosity and the burdens he had borne on behalf of his kindred.

The rank accorded to ᶜAbīd among the ancient poets was high. Muḥammad b. Sallām classed [7] him in the fourth class of the *Fuḥūl*, together with Ṭarafah, ᶜAlqamah b. ᶜAbadah,

---

[1] See *Dīwān* p. 1.   [2] BQut, *Shiᶜr*, 144[5]; Abu Ḥātim, *Kitāb al-Muᶜammarīn*, 66.
[3] Ibn Qutaibah (144[4]) stupidly attributes the deed to an-Nuᶜmān.   [4] *Shiᶜr* p. 144[14].
[5] Yāq. III, 795[10] ff.   [6] *Dīw.* p. 2[2].   [7] Agh. XIX, 84.

and ʿAdī b. Zaid; but the same passage tells us that that writer only knew among his poems the first, اَفْقَرُ مِنْ اَهْلِهِ مَلْحُوبُ: on account of his antiquity his compositions were, it is said, in a state of disorder and confusion, and passing out of men's memories (شعرُه مضطرب ذاهب), in spite of his great fame. The first poem is said by Ibn Qutaibah [1] to have been counted as "one of the Seven", that is, of the *Muʿallaqāt*; the critics probably valued it most for its didactic and moralizing character, which to our apprehension is not its chief merit: this, no doubt, caused ʿAbīd to be classified with ʿAdī b. Zaid, the townsman, in all other respects a very different personality. ʿAbīd was famous as a depicter of storms and rain: Yūnus ascertained from Dhu-r-Rummah (who himself excelled in this subject) that he preferred Imraʾ al-Qais to him; but he is classed with Aus ibn Ḥajar as a master in this style [2]. Among his poems that survive are several dealing with storms [3]. Al-Farazdaq, in a celebrated passage enumerating his great forerunners in the art of poesy [4], mentions him as one of those who "gave over to him their *qaṣīdahs* when they passed away".

No information has reached us as to the scholar who first put together into a *Dīwān* the surviving poems of ʿAbīd. From the observations of Ibn Sallām († 231) referred to above it would seem that when he wrote the طَبَقَاتُ الشُّعَرَاءِ الجَاهِلِيِّينَ they had not yet been collected. Yet Abū ʿAmr ash-Shaibānī, that indefatigable gatherer-together of the old poetry, who died 20 or 25 years before (205, 206, or 213 are the dates mentioned), is referred to in our commentary no less than ten times [5] as acquainted with several of the poems; he is also the authority for the version of the story of ʿAbīd's inspiration as a poet with which the *Dīwān* opens. Al-Aṣmaʿī († 213) and Abū ʿUbaidah († between 208 and 211) are each cited in the scholia three times [6], Khālid b. Kulthūm twice, Abu-l-Ḥasan al-Athram once [7]. But the authorities most frequently mentioned in the scholia for the interpretation of the poems are Ibn Kunāsah and Abu-l-Walīd. The former, who is last cited by name in the scholion to v. 2 of No. III, seems to be the Muḥammad ibn Kunāsah whose biography is given in Agh. XII, 111—115. He was a man of Asad, belonging to the sub-tribe of al-Ḥārith b. Thaʿlabah (brother to ʿAbīd's ancestor Saʿd b. Thaʿlabah), and lived at al-Kūfah, where large portions of Asad appear to have settled in the Umayyad and early ʿAbbāsid period; he was a sister's son [8] of the celebrated early Ṣūfī Ibrāhīm ibn Adham, on whom he wrote a *marthiyah*. The date

---

[1] *Shiʿr*, 144[17]. [2] BQut. *Shiʿr*, 41[7] ff.

[3] Nos. VI, XXI 9—11, XXIII 1—7, XXVIII 6—15, Frags. 6 and 12.

[4] Naq. No. 39 vv. 51—62 (pp. 200—202); ʿAbīd is mentioned in v. 55 together with a contemporary, Abū Duʾād of Iyād.

[5] 9[14] (سَمِعَهُ حُبَيْد من أبي عمرو), 16[11], 25[4], 29[11], 31[6], 50[7], 51[14], 55[15], 56[9], 59[5].

[6] Al-Aṣmaʿī 11[7], 41[11], 52[1]: Abū ʿUbaidah 41[12], 52[1], 59[5].

[7] Khālid 41[3], 52[2]: al-Athram 37[2—3]. [8] Or first cousin: Agh. XII, 113[4].

of Ibn Adham's death is put by Jāmī in the *Nafaḥāt al-Uns* as 161 or 166. Ibn Kunāsah is also stated to have been a hearer of the traditionist al-Aʿmash, sometimes cited in the *Lisān al-ʿArab*, a client of the Banū Kāhil b. Asad at al-Kūfah, who died there in 147 (or 148 or 149). Abu-l-Walīd of the scholia, who is also mentioned in Hibat-allāh's commentary in the *Mukhtārāt* [1], has not been identified. He may possibly be the Abu-l-Walīd ʿĪsà b. Yazīd b. Bakr b. Daʾb of the Banu-sh-Shuddākh of Kinānah, mentioned in the *Fihrist* (p. 90[23]) [2] as a genealogist and traditionist; his father is there said to have been well acquainted with the traditions and poems of the Arabs. The many citations of ʿAbīd's poems in the works of Jāḥiḍh († 256) are good evidence of the existence of the *Dīwān* (or the poems composing it) early in the third century, while Ibn Qutaibah († 276) attests its currency later in the same century. Twelve of ʿAbīd's poems are contained in the collection called *Mukhtārāt Shuʿarāʾ al-ʿArab*, made by Hibat-allāh b. ash-Shajarī († 542), of which the autograph exists in the Khedivial Library at Cairo, and was lithographed there in 1306 H.

The commentary attached to the poems bears no name and has no preface explaining its *provenance*. It is evidently of *Kūfī* origin [3], and the authorities cited in it (Abū ʿAmr and Ibn Kunāsah) belong to that school. The notes contained in it (or some of them) appear to have been originally written in the margin of the verses; in binding the copy of which our MS. is a transcript some of these notes had had their ends pared away by the binder, and the scholia are thus, incomplete (see, *e. g.* II, 2, 3, III, 8, etc.). The author of the commentary sometimes makes serious mistakes, and cannot have been a scholar of any eminence: see, *e. g.*, as to grammar, the scholia to IV, 12, and V, 11; as to the meaning of words, the scholia to I, 29, VI, 1, and XII, 12; as to matters of fact, XX, 8. The notes are often insufficient, avoiding real difficulties, and contain many useless repetitions. On only five [4] occasions are verses from other poets cited in illustration of words explained. The last three poems of the MS, offering many problems for solution, have no commentary whatever.

This indifferent text, in what was probably a poor original, badly written and often destitute of vowels and diacritical points, has been transcribed in our MS. in a manner which frequently shows the grossest ignorance and carelessness. If one of the poems contained in the *Mukhtārāt* be compared with our text and the differences noted, this will be seen at a glance. The scribe was a Maghribī, probably of Spain, and as all the four *Dīwāns* are in the same hand, the date of the MS. was about 430 (see colophon to *Dīwān* of ʿĀmir b. aṭ-Ṭufail). The original of our MS. was also written in the Maghrib, as is plain from such corruptions as وَٱسْتَكَلَ عَنْهِنّ for وَٱسْتَظَلَّ تَحْتَهِنّ in p. 1, l. 5: only a

---

[1] See note to No. XIII, v. 11.   [2] He is also mentioned in BDuraid 106[11].
[3] See scholion to No. XXI, v. 12.
[4] al-Aʿshà 7[6], Zuhair 17[2], Labīd 10[11], 22[2], Kaʿb b. Zuhair, 20[16].

ظ with the *markaz* slanting backwards as in Maghribī writing could have been confused with ك. Our Maghribī transcript, frequently without diacritical points and almost always without vowels, passed into the hands of a possessor in the East, and was by him supplied with both in a fashion which shows that he had often not the faintest idea of the meaning. In the Maghrib ڡ indicates *qāf* and ڢ *fē*: the oriental arabist supplied wanting points after the fashion current in the East, using ڡ for *qāf* and ڢ for *fē*. The confusion which results is extraordinary [1].

With such a MS. only to work upon, it would have been hazardous in the highest degree to attempt a reconstitution of the text, but for the fact that a great portion of the poems included in the *Dīwān* occurs elsewhere. Of the 24 poems contained in the MS., no less than 23 are cited, in whole or part, in other works. The 24 poems contain 462 verses, and of these 279 are found elsewhere, so that for only 183 are we left unaided to the guidance of the MS. It is true that many of these present serious difficulties; but, with the help of parallel passages in ʿAbīd's other poems and the ancient poetry generally, it is possible to offer a text which seems plausible, and does not differ materially from the readings of the MS. In printing, I have not thought it necessary to mark trifling departures from the MS., such as the supply of wanting points, or the correction of obvious blunders in supplying them committed by the second possessor: if every change of the kind had been indicated the notes would have become intolerably bulky; but I believe that I have shown all important differences between the text adopted and the MS. For the last three poems, which are entirely without a commentary, and, out of 71 verses, contain only seven which are cited elsewhere, a photographic copy of the MS. is offered for comparison.

The question of the authenticity of the poems is one which will naturally be regarded by different persons from different points of view. It is quite certain that the poems of pagan nomadic Arabia were not transmitted in writing, but orally. The odes recording the triumphs of a tribe were its most precious possession, and were handed down from generation to generation. Besides this general knowledge, spread throughout the tribe, there was also the special institution of the *rāwī* or transmitter, whose business it was to guard the deposit of poetry committed to his memory. In an age when writing was not used except in towns and for special purposes, the art of memory was much more actively cultivated than it is in modern times; and there is nothing to surprise us in the transmission of poems in this manner for two or three hundred years [2].

---

[1] The four pages of *facsimile* included in the *Dīwān* enable these remarks to be verified.

[2] It has often been pointed out that the conservation of the ancient Indian literature, during the centuries before writing came into general use, affords a still more striking example of the achievements of human memory.

It is natural to suppose that in the process of such transmission the poems suffered some degree of change. Words of equivalent meaning would be substituted for others: infirmity of memory would lead to the dropping of verses, the shifting of arrangement of lines, the supply of parts forgotten by other phrases extemporised by the reciter; such phenomena are common everywhere. Yet, when we examine the poems themselves, we find sufficient evidence of individuality of character to warrant us in concluding that there is no difficulty in holding that they are in the main the work of the authors to whom they are ascribed. The seven *Muʿallaqāt*, for example, are all highly individual and characteristic poems, and set before us seven very distinct personalities. The same is the case with the remaining three poems (by al-Aʿshà, an-Nābighah, and ʿAbīd) which have by different judges been reckoned among the *Muʿallaqāt*. Characters like Imraʾal-Qais, Zuhair, Labīd, an-Nābighah, al-Aʿshà have communicated their own stamp to their poetry, and it would be a most fantastic view to take that the main part of the poems attributed to them was fabricated in a later age, by scholars who lived under totally different conditions, in a world which had radically changed from the days of the nomadic life of desert Arabia.

Another reason for holding that the ancient poetry is entitled to be received as, on the whole, genuine and not fabricated is that it is presupposed by the poetry of the first age under Islām. The famous poets of the first century, — al-Farazdaq, Jarīr, al-Akhṭal, Dhu-r-Rummah, — carried on without a break the tradition of the poets of the pagan time. Besides the personal references which they make to them, they use their poetical stock-in-trade over and over again, elaborating the same themes in the same way, improving, modifying, adapting, but still carrying on the same tradition [1]. There can be no question that we possess the genuine works of these poets, who lived in an age when writing was generally used for recording poetical compositions, though oral recitation was still the method of producing them to the public.

A third reason is that the ancient poems abound in words which were not intelligible to the scholars who first subjected them to critical examination; they belong to an older stratum of language, and had passed out of current use when the poems were written down and put together into *Dīwāns*. Any one familiar with the ancient commentaries (which form the material from which the great lexicons were afterwards compiled) must be aware that the commentators — who differ greatly among themselves — arrived at their explanations of difficulties by comparing one passage with another, by argument and discussion, and not to any great extent by reference to the living speech, which no longer contained the words of which the meaning was sought. The lexicographical literature is entirely founded upon the ancient poetry and the

---

[1] This point is very well illustrated by many passages in BQut's *Shiʿr wa Shuʿarā*.

language of the Qurʾān and the Traditions of the Prophet, and it assumes the genuineness of the former just as much as it does that of the latter.

Bearing these considerations in mind, let us examine the poems and fragments attributed to ʿAbīd. We find that they consist to a large extent of the preludes (*nasīb* or *tashbīb*) to longer odes, thus exhibiting the work of the professional and practised poet. These passages must have been preserved because they were admired. Twenty-three out of the thirty pieces of the *Dīwān* have the opening verse with its double rhyme, and the geographical indications which show the tribe and sub-tribe to which the poet belonged. These indications recur from one poem to another, and prove that the author was a man of Saʿd ibn Thaʿlabah, a sub-tribe of Asad, in whose territory the places named are found. The poems contain references to events of ʿAbīd's time — the slaying of Ḥujr, the great feat of arms of which the tribe made its boast, and the resistance to Ghassān and their king al-Ḥārith the Lame. All these are consistent with ʿAbīd's authorship. In some cases (as for instance the reference to the conflicts with ʿĀmir at an-Nisār and with Dārim at al-Jifār, in No. II, vv. 18, 19, if these events are correctly placed by tradition after the battle of Shiʿb Jabalah) verses referring to events subsequent to ʿAbīd's time have apparently been taken up into his poems from the compositions of other tribal bards.

The language of the poems displays a strikingly individual character. Below will be found a list of words which occur more than once, and seem to be favourites with the poet: —

أُلَّى, "those who": VII, 12; XX, 18; XXII 1.

أَهْلُ القِبَاب "owners of costly tents", of his tribe: XXV, 10; XXVII, 5; XXIX, 2.

أَهْلُ الجُرْد "owners of shorthaired horses": IX, 2; XXV, 10; XXIX, 3.

آنِيس "kind", of a woman friend: III, 4; أَوانِس, of women, VII, 24; X, 2; XV, 14; آنِسَة XXI, 5; XXIV, 11.

نَجَّ of rain, "to pour vehemently"; XI, 7; XXIII, 2.

الجَمِيع "the whole tribe dwelling together; V, 4; XV, 2; *id.* 5.

مُجَلْجِلٌ "a thundering cloud"; IV, 3; VI, 1.

خَرِقُ البَوارِق "glowing with lightning flashes": IV, 3; *v. l.* خَرِقُ البَوارِق "quick in its flashes": see بَرْقُها حَرِقٌ in XXI, 10, and commentary.

خُرْص "spear-head" (or "spear"): II, 21; V, 12; XIII, 16.

خَلَلٌ "sword-sheaths painted with patterns": tent-traces compared to them: III, 6; خِلالٌ *id.*, XI, 3.

دَاوِيَّةٌ "a desert": XXI, 12; also الدَّوُّ XXII, 12; الدَّوَّى XXI, 14.

دَيْمُومَةٌ "a desert": XII, 13; XXI, 12.

دُلَّحٌ (clouds) "bearing heavy burdens" (of rain): XXIII, 2; دَلاَّحٌ id., XXVIII, 4.

أَذَاعَ "he dispersed", "scattered": IV, 3; XVIII, 2.

شَنَانَةٌ رَجَبِيَّةٌ "a shower in Rajab" (winter): XVI, 3.

لَيْلَةٌ رَجَبِيَّةٌ "a winter night": XIX, 10.

رِيِّقٌ "firstling", of rain: XXI, 10; XXVIII, 9.

سَبْسَبٌ "desert": I, 38; XI, 33 (but سَبَاسِبُ, XV, 2).

مَسَارِبُ "pastures": IV, 4; XIX, 4.

مُشِيحًا "hastening": I, 27; read يُشِيحُ for يَسِيحُ in VIII, 10.

عَكَفَ, of horses treading on a dead warrior: IV, 10, 14; of lions standing at gaze, X, 19.

عُقَابٌ "eagle", for standard: II, 21; VII, 22.

عَوْمُ السَّفِينِ "ships sailing": VIII, 5; XIII, 3.

غَابٌ "thickets", or perhaps a proper name: I, 30; XXII, 18.

قَدْ أَتْرُكُ ٱلْقِرْنَ "I leave my antagonist" (lying): VIII, 12; XXV, 11.

قَلِّصِي "gird thyself", addressed to a she-camel: X, 7; تَقَلَّصَتْ, of the same XV, 11.

قَفَا "the back", of a place: قَفَا حِبِرٍّ I, 3; قَفَا شَرَافِ XII, 3; قَفَا نَبَالٍ XIII, 2.

لُجَيْنٌ "silver": XI, 7; XIII, 11 (footnote).

تَلُفُّهُ شَمْأَلٌ "the north-wind wraps him round": I, 31; تَلُفُّ ضِرَامَهَا بِضِرَامٍ, IV, 17.

أَمْثَالِي "those like me": V, 4; XI, 14; XV, 1.

مُرَّانُ ٱلْوَشِيجِ "spears": II, 5; XVI, 6.

مَطُّ حَاجِبَيْكَ "frowning": XI, 11; cf. XIII, 8.

مَهَاةٌ, مَهًا "gazelle, gazelles", for women: V, 15; XI, 10; XXI, 6; XXII, 1 (cf. سِرْبٌ مِن ظِبَاءٍ VIII, 14).

نَاعِمَةٌ "soft, gentle", epithet for a woman: V, 15; XII, 5; XXI, 6.

نَاهِلٌ, نَوَاهِلُ "thirsting" (spears): II, 27; VII, 10; XXVI, 14.

وَهَكَذَا, for a change of subject: V, 9; VII, 15; XXI, 12.

هِيِّ, Asadī idiom for هِيَ: I, 29; V, 16.

أَوْجَرْتُ "I pierced" (with a spear): V, 12; XXV, 12.

The themes in the several poems exhibit a uniform manner of dwelling upon the same subjects. Thus, No. XIII takes up the same theme as No. XI, and we find it again in No. XXVIII, vv. 1—5. In the *Mufaḍḍalīyāt* there is a poem (No. IV) by a fellow-tribesman of ʿAbīd's of the next generation, al-Jumaiḥ (otherwise called Munqidh) ibn aṭ-Ṭammāḥ, which deals with the same subject in a manner which recalls ʿAbīd's; al-Jumaiḥ, who speaks of himself as an old man (v. 3), was killed at Shiʿb Jabalah. His father aṭ-Ṭammāḥ is mentioned by Imraʾal-Qais (XXX, 13) as a contemporary enemy, and the worker against him with the Qaiṣar. Again, No. IV, 6 ff., is repeated in No. VII. The various passages describing storms have striking resemblances in treatment (see notes *in loco* against each).

Again, the poems contain passages which are not intelligible because the explanation has been lost, or lines have been omitted which would have made things clear; such cases are Nos. II and XIX, 16—17. A good many words are of doubtful or unknown meaning; but in view of the badness of the MS. it cannot be said in these cases exactly what the reading should be.

On the whole, there seems to be no reason to doubt that the majority of the poems are rightly ascribed to ʿAbīd. Questionable (for reasons indicated in the translation against each) are Nos. XX, XXIII, XXIV, XXIX, besides parts of No. II; while moralizing phrases having an Islamic colour, which appear in No. I and some other passages, may be additions by later hands. Of the fragments in the Supplement some are obviously fabricated or wrongly assigned to ʿAbīd, *e. g.* Nos. 3, 4, 5, 10, 11, and 16; the remainder may possibly be genuine.

The style of ʿAbīd is natural and easy, and does not exhibit the *curiositas* (*takalluf*) which later became fashionable. The poems for the most part (where not corrupt) present few difficulties in translation. In some of the renderings offered an attempt has been made to imitate the original metres; this has entailed a little freedom of handling, but it is hoped that it will be found that the sense has not been inadequately conveyed.

ʿABĪD.

TRANSLATION.

I.

The poem opens with a picture of desolation. The poet's tribe has been spoiled and scattered, many slain and others dispersed. The occasion may be the attack by al-Ḥārith the Lame, king of Ghassān, referred to in No. XVIII (where Madhānib = our adh-Dhanūb, and "the sides of Ḥibirr" = our Qafā Ḥibirr). The poet is already old (v. 11), and has seen the vicissitudes and vanity of things, on which he moralises (vv. 12—24). Among these reflections Tibrīzī's version of the poem interpolates, after our v. 23 (which itself may be an interpolation of Islamic times), the following two verses:

> In God is all good attained to:
> > the doctrine that He is made up of separate Persons (?) is foolishness.
> God has no partner:
> > He knows all that men's hearts hide.

The second hemistich of the first verse may perhaps be directed against the doctrine of the Trinity, if we understand بَعْضُهُ as equivalent to تَبْعِيضُهُ. On the other hand, it is possible to take the clause more simply, as meaning "in *certain statements* (that are made about God) is foolishness". In any case the passage is clearly polemical. تَلْغِيب is an unusual word. The absence of these verses from most versions of the poem, and their irrelevance to the subject, seem decisive against their authenticity; their case differs widely from that of the religious passage in Zuhair's *Muʿallaqah*, vv. 26—28, which is essential to the argument.

The poet then recurs to memories of his youth — journeys undertaken through dangerous regions (25, 26), on a she-camel, compared for swiftness to a wild ass (30) or a young oryx (31). Then he passes to expeditions on his war-mare (32—34), which is the subject of comparison in the last section of the poem (35—45), containing the famous description of the Eagle and the Fox. The proper termination of the ode has probably been lost, and there may be gaps elsewhere: *e.g.*, between vv. 24 and 25, or after vv. 30 and 31, where we should expect the similes to be further developed.

(1) Malḥūb is desolate, all its folk gone,
      and al-Quṭabīyāt and adh-Dhanūb,
(2) And Rākis and Thuʿailibāt,
      and Dhāt-Firqain and al-Qalīb,
(3) And ʿArdah and Qafā-Ḥibirr —
      no soul is left of them there.
(4) If they have gotten in exchange for their folk the wildings,
      and the things that have happened have changed their aspect,
(5) 'Tis a land to which Death has become the heir
      — all those who dwelt there have been spoiled and scattered,
(6) Either slain by the sword or dead and gone —
      and grey hairs are a shame to him who shows them.
(7) Thine eyes stream with the flowing tears,
      as though their tear-ducts were a waterskin full of holes,
(8) Old and worn out, or a torrent swiftly flowing,
      from [1] a hill which high cliffs gird round about,
(9) Or a brook at the bottom of a valley
      with water rushing along between its banks,
(10) Or a runnel under the shade of date-palms
      — its water murmuring as it hurries along.
(11) Thou thinkest of youth and love; and how canst thou dally —
      how, when grey hairs have already warned thee?
(12) If these lands be changed and their people vanisht,
      they are not the first, nor is there cause to marvel;
(13) Or if the broad strath be desolate of them,
      and Famine and Drought have come there to dwell —
(14) All that is pleasant must be snatched away,
      and every one that hopes must find his hope belied;
(15) Every master of camels hands them on to an heir,
      and every one that gathers spoil is spoiled in turn.
(16) Every one that is absent may come again,
      but the absent in death returns no more.
(17) Is the barren like to the fruitful womb,
      or the lucky raider like him that gets no spoil?
(18) Be happy with what thou wilt: ofttimes the weakling
      comes to his goal in spite of weakness, oft is the skilful cheated.
(19) Men cannot save by preaching him whom Time
      teaches not, and vain are all attempts to make wise;

---

[1] Adopting Tibrīzī's reading *min haḍbatin* instead of that of our MS.

(20) There help only natural gifts of judgement —
      how often has a friend become a hater!

(21) Help thou a land while thou dwellest therein,
      and say not — 'I am a stranger here';

(22) Ofttimes the stranger from afar becomes the nearest:
      often the nearest kinsman is cut off and becomes strange.

(23) Whoso begs of man, meets but refusals:
      but he that prays God is not rejected.

(24) Man as long as he lives is a self-deceiver:
      length of life is but increase of trouble.

          *   *   *   *

(25) Yea, many the water, long lonely [1], have I visited
      — the way to it perilous, through dry deserts;

(26) The feathers of doves lay about its borders:
      there the heart fluttered in its fear.

(27) I have passed on to it swiftly at dawn,
      my comrade a great she-camel, fleet of foot,

(28) Swift as a wild ass, strongly knit her back-bone,
      with withers rounded and smooth like a sand-hill;

(29) Her seven-year tooth has given place to a nine-year tush,
      she is not too young, nor yet too old;

(30) She is like one of the wild asses of Ghāb,
      dark-hued, with scars of fight on the sides of his neck;

(31) Or a young wild bull that digs up the *rukhāmà* [2],
      wrapped round by the North-wind blowing shrilly.

(32) Long since was that; and I see myself again
      borne along on a tall long-backed fleet mare,

(33) Her frame closely knit joint to joint,
      her fore-lock parting broadly to show her forehead,

(34) Smooth as oil in her motions, with veins unfevered,
      lithe in her build, her limbs moving easily.

(35) She is like an eagle, swift to seize her quarry —
      — in her nest are the hearts of her victims gathered.

(36) Night-long she stood on a way-mark [3], still, upright [4],
      like an old woman whose children all are dead;

---

[1] Literally, "altered for the worse, covered with slime and stinking, from long standing unvisited".

[2] Perhaps the wild narcissus: a bulbous plant with a white flower. The Arabs use words applicable to the bovine kind of the *Oryx beatrix*, the white antelope of the deserts.

[3] A cairn of stones, or (as otherwise explained) a small hill.

[4] Also rendered "fasting", which is perhaps the proper signification ("tormented" [by hunger]).

(37) And at dawn she was there in the piercing cold,
    the hoar-frost dropping from her feathers.

(38) Then she spied on the moment a fox far off —
    between him and her was a droughty desert:

(39) Then she shook her feathers and stirred herself,
    ready to rise and make her swoop.

(42) [1] He raised his tail and quailed as he saw her —
    so behaves his kind when fright possesses them:

(41) She rose, and swiftly towards him she sped,
    gliding down, making for him her prey.

(40) He creeps, as he spies her coming, on his belly:
    his eyes show the whites as they turn towards her.

(43) Then she swoops with him aloft, and casts him headlong,
    and the prey beneath her is in pain and anguish,

(44) She dashes him to earth with a violent shock,
    and all his face is torn by the stones.

(45) He shrieks — but her talons are in his side:
    no help! with her beak she tears his breast.

II.

This is a difficult poem, because we do not know the circumstances of its composition, and the text appears to be in places defective, corrupt, and interpolated. Jadīlah is a division of Ṭayyiʾ, and Asad, who lived closely intermixed with Ṭayyite tribes[2], were generally on good terms with them, though no doubt causes of quarrel arose from time to time. Later, their relations were embodied in a formal alliance, and Asad and Ṭayyiʾ were known as the *Aḥlāf,* or Confederates, Ghaṭafān being subsequently admitted to the league[3].

Jadīlah is depicted as assembling to attack Asad, in spite of unfavourable omens (1—4): in the attack three warriors of Asad were slain (vv. 5, 7). The meaning of v. 6 is obscure, and had probably been forgotten when the poem was written down. But if Asad had received these wounds, on a former occasion she had inflicted on Ṭayyiʾ severe loss (7, 8). The place of vv. 9—11 in the poem is uncertain, and the meaning doubtful: perhaps the text is corrupt. In vv. 12—17 the forces of Asad are described, and in vv. 18—26 former triumphs are recalled — at al-Jifār against Dārim, a sub-tribe of Tamīm, and at an-Nisār against ʿĀmir b. Ṣaʿṣaʿah. But these lines must be interpolations if the rest of the poem is

---

[1] Adopting the order of verses in Tibrīzī. In v. 42 read حَمِيسًا for حَشِيشًا, which is a misprint.

[2] Bakrī 718—19.

[3] See Zuhair, Muʿall. 26; BQut *Shiʿr,* 145[14]; Naq 238[13] ff.

by 'Abīd, as the battles of an-Nisār and al-Jifār were fought after the Day of Shi'b-Jabalah, and this was long after 'Abīd's time[1]. In v. 27 the slaying of Ḥujr is referred to. In v. 28 the "Confederates" are said in the scholion of the *Mukhtārāt* to be Fazārah, a sub-tribe of Ghaṭafān, but it seems more probable that Jadīlah is meant, as our commentary alleges; the second hemistich appears to imply that further prosecution of the quarrel will be disastrous, and lead to many funerals and the loss of many valiant defenders of the cause of their tribe.

(1) I have been told that the Sons of Jadīlah have been gathering together
    armed men from mount Salmà against us, and assembling for war;

(2) And yet there had appeared to them — though they took no omen from it —
    a buck-antelope coming from behind like a saddle-pad, having one horn
        broken;

(3) And the father of a brood[2], over his featherless black nestlings in a dry
        broken tree,
    bending in the direction of the north, croaked at them.

(4) Yet they passed on by all these (evil omens) towards us,
    galloping and ambling, and when they approached

(5) They assailed us with a forest of spears; and nought couldst thou see,
    after the spear-points, but the veins that spouted blood.

(6) And they took in exchange for their God, Ya'būb an idol —
    be still, Jadīlah, and restrain yourselves!

(7) If ye have slain of us three warriors,
    truly those slain at Sāḥūq[3] were a mighty host!

(8) And those that fought there gained praise and honour for their tribe and kin,
    when long was the day to them, and the blamers blamed them.

(9) As for me, I am a man who has no brother in mankind,
    to be glad with in his gladness, or angry when men anger me;

(10) And when thou desertest thy brother, or any man his (?),
    then thy brother perishes, and thou also art in danger of destruction.

(11) So let the singing women lament over their heads:
    of their wine but a remnant is left, and....[4]

---

[1] It appears, however, from Naq 239[6-7], that the Ribāb (Ḍabbah, etc.) asserted that the battle of an-Nisār preceded that of Shi'b-Jabalah. This does not, however, seem to be correct.

[2] *I.e.*, a raven.

[3] This cannot be the Day of Sāḥūq mentioned in the *Kāmil* of Ibn al-Athīr, I 483, which was long after 'Abīd's time, and between Dhubyān and 'Āmir b. Ṣa'ṣa'ah; it was probably the fight mentioned in a verse of al-Kumait's quoted in Bakrī 767[10], in which the two chiefs of Kindah called "the Two Falcons", *al-Ajdalāni* (see *post*, No. XVII, 7), were slain.

[4] The meaning of the word مُنَحَّب is not known: the reading may be corrupt.

(12) Nay, there is no avoiding the encounter of noble knights
    — when they are called to an alarm, at once they ride forth.

(13) High-nosed are they, and the sheen of their helmets' crests
    is like a fire kindled on a tall mountain top;

(14) There bear them white camels whose saddle-straps creak,
    with deep-sunken eyes, as walk forth a herd of white oryx.

(15) They have taken with them in their saddle-bags mail-coats of iron,
    and among them are steeds led alongside, with white patches in their
        sides (where the rider's heel smites),

(16) All of them with well-knit muscular backs, slender of leg,
    rendered lean and spare by long leading and weariness;

(17) And many a fleet mare, like a wolf spare and thin,
    bestridden by a lion with thick strong neck, and shoulders broad and stout.

(18) And truly in time gone by we have lighted in al-Jifār for Dārim
    a fire whereof the birds of ill-omen croak their rede.

(19) And long ago in an-Nisār we made ready for ῾Āmir
    a Day there for them most grievous, full of disaster;

(20) Yea, we gave them to drink of a bitter cup
    wherein was poison well steeped — they must quaff it!

(21) With a host full of clamour — the place was too strait for them:
    their eagle [1], on the head of a lance, fluttered like a tumbling bird.

(22) And in sooth news came to us from Tamīm that they
    were sore distrest and wrathful at the slain of ῾Āmir;

(23) Be thy father's nose rubbed in the dust! — I care not:
    a light thing is it to me that they are not content.

(24) And that morning that our horse came down on al-Jifār with lips drawn
        back for fight,
    their vanguard with forelocks flying, lean and spare of limb —

(25) When they saw us — and already the javelins were in their midst,
    and the horses now showed forth, now were hidden in the welter of dust —

(26) They turned and fled, and our steeds wheeled in their tracks,
    driving their rout, and we set upon them with the sword, and they
        came together again.

(27) Ask concerning us Ḥujr son of Umm Qaṭāmi, what time
    the thirsting tawny spears day-long made sport of him.

(28) Patience for what was done in the past by our confederates
    — musk [2] and washing of the heads with mallow mixed together.

---

[1] *I.e.* their standard.
[2] *I.e.* the perfumes used at funerals, and the washing of the corpses for burial.

(29) Let him bewail them whose women without ceasing
      on the day of battle cry — "Where is now our refuge"?

III.

A fragment, containing first the description of former abodes where the poet had companied with Mayyah. Notice the reference to painted parchment from al-Yaman in v. 6. Then follows (7—12) a description of a camel journey, ending in a watering-place at Līnah, a famous locality for wells and springs (Yāqūt IV, 375—6).

(1) Empty of Mayyah are the torrent-beds of Khabt,
      and Lubnà of Faiḥān, and the water-courses of the foot-hills,
(2) And al-Quṭabīyāt, and ad-Dakādik, and al-Haij,
      and the upper part of its hollow plain of soft sand,
(3) And al-Jumud that guards the path from crookedness [1],
      and the flats of the long sand-stretches, and the rolling dunes,
(4) And aṭ-Ṭalb, and the margin of Tabālah, — no sign
      of the Friend there — what have they done with her?
(5) What the burying winds have left of her traces,
      and the years now spent that have sped so swiftly away,
(6) Is like the finest painted parchment [2], whose makers spared no pains,
      on pictured boxes of al-Yaman, or the painted sheaths of swords.

               *   *   *   *   *

(7) Brave camel of mine! I arrayed her in saddle
      and girth-straps — spare her frame, great as a male;
(8) She speeds swiftly through deserts and waterless sands,
      what time Canopus glows, bursting suddenly on my sight.
(9) Good luck to her and her fellow [3] who bears her company!
      he hurries through the land, desolate as it is, and the way unknown.

---

[1] *I.e.* acts as a way-mark so that the traveller does not go astray.

[2] The word قَضِيم properly indicates the painting, or perhaps embroidery, in the parchment, rather than the parchment itself: see ʿAlqamah's verse in Bakrī 505⁵, and an-Nābighah XVII, 5 (Ahlw. reads حَصِير, but LA XV, 389¹² قَضِيم); the ṣawānīʿ are always women (Nöldeke).

[3] *I.e.* himself.

(10) He brought her down to drink at Līnah, but on the way thither
      no salt pasture did she find — mountain brooks feed its spring [1].

(11) God send blessings on its water, and on that
      which shines in the sun thereof as though it were honey:

(12) Water in an over-curving rock, that is safe from the well-picks [2]
      — a mountain defends it in the midst of a wilderness.

IV.

Vv. 1—5 are the usual introduction; the next section of the poem begins abruptly, and probably something has dropped out between vv. 5 and 6.

Vv. 6 to 20 are addressed to Imra᾽ al-Qais. Twice ‘Abīd refers to lamentations by Imra᾽ al-Qais over the slain *of Asad* — here (v. 7) and again in No. VII, 3; this point is not explained in the traditions regarding the death of Ḥujr and the pursuit of vengeance by his son. The death of the Prince is described (8, 9), and the host of the slayers (10—17); they have routed Kindah (18). Imra᾽ al-Qais has given out that he will seek help from Cæsar (19), at which the poet shouts his defiance (20).

(1) Now has Kubaishah gone to dwell in the hollow of Dhāt Ru᾽ām,
      and effaced are her camping-places in the lowland of Barām;

(2) All her landmarks are blotted out, and the tearing winds
      and the long lapse of days have swept away her traces

(3) Until they have dispersed them utterly — these, and the many thunder-clouds,
      gleaming with lightning flashes, their rumbling never still;

(4) An abode where now the large-eyed wild kine [3] graze quietly:
      they roam through its pasture-places together with the gazelles.

(5) Yet time was when there dwelt there one the moisture of whose lips
      was like a clear pool of water among rocks, the best of it mixed with wine.

      *   *   *   *   *

(6) O thou that threatenest us with terrors because of the slaying of thy Chief,
      Ḥujr — thy hope is but an empty dream!

(7) Weep not for us in thy folly, nor for our lords —
      turn thy cries and tears towards the son of Umm Qaṭāmi [4],

(8) Ḥujr — the morning that our spears pierced him one after another,
      in the low ground between the waterless plains and the hills;

---

[1] or — "between her and it are mountain-brooks".

[2] *I.e.* a natural spring, out of rock too hard to be dug with picks: its water therefore is pure and fresh.

[3] See *ante*, p. 19, note [2].   [4] See al-Ḥārith, Muʿall. 76.

(9) The shafts moved up and down in the thrust, all pointed at him,
     some aiming, others withdrawn, covered with blood;

(10) And the horses stood there over him, as though they were
     tall palm-trees, their fruit far out of the reach of the gatherers[1] —

(11) Horses that vie one with another in speed, bearing against the reins, with
     teeth displayed,
     carrying on their backs a company of champions great in stature,

(12) The vanguard of a host mountain-like, whose dust floats not away,
     helmeted all, bristling with steel, a mighty concourse.

(13) Therein are mail-coats of iron, and bows of *nabʿ* wood, kept with care
     for the time of need, straight spearshafts, and keen swords.

(14) Yea, verily they slew them[2]; and how many a lord
     and mighty chief have our horses trampled under foot!

(15) When the straightening-iron grips the shaft of our spear,
     it springs back — and then it pursues the best of purposes[3].

(16) We shield from harm all our weak ones, and defend the stranger,
     and provide for the needs of the widows with orphan children.

(17) And we march forth to war, the ever-renewed, whenso it threatens,
     and we add fresh fuel to its rising blaze.

(18) When thou[4] sawest the hosts of Kindah giving way
     before us — and no great nobleness is there in Kindah!

(19) Didst thou say that thou wouldst seek to Cæsar for help?
     — then shalt thou surely die a Syrian, (subject to Rome)!

(20) We refuse to all men submission to their leading
     till we lead them ourselves, yea, without reins!

V.

Vv. 1—5, the deserted dwellings, and memories of those who once lived there. The poet, old, recalls his youth — long journeys on a swift camel (6—8), deeds of valour in warfare (9—12), banqueting and wine-drinking (13—14), love (15—16); gone is youth, never to return! (17—18).

(1) O home of Hind! there have wrecked it showers continuous and heavy:
     in al-Jauw it lies like a precious stuff of al-Yaman, ragged and tattered;

---

[1] *cf.* Labīd, Muʿall. 66.
[2] *I. e.* the men of Kindah about King Ḥujr.
[3] *I. e.* it wounds him who attempts to straighten it: *cf.* ʿAmr, Muʿall. 50—51.
[4] *I. e.* Imraʾ al-Qais.

(2) The winds of summer have passed over it, following one on another,
  and have swept it clear of all traces by the trailing of their skirts.

(3) I stayed my companions there that I might enquire of it,
  and my tears, as I stood, soaked through the bosom of my tunic,

(4) In longing for the tribe, and the days when all of them were there together:
  but what right to emotion or longing have those that are like me?

(5) Already there has come upon my locks the silvering of old age,
  and thereon in disgust fair women have bidden me a final farewell.

(6) Yea, once did I soothe my cares, whenas they came upon me,
  with a stout camel, like an anvil in hardness, swift of pace;

(7) Lightly she travels with the saddle-trees, fleet of foot is she:
  straight goes she through the hot noontide, ambling and trotting on;

(8) Lumps of flesh have been cast upon her, as it were, on either side:
  she is like a lonely wild bull in al-Jauw that sweeps the ground with his tail.

(9) Enough of this! many the war wherein I have borne my part,
  until I have caused its fire to blaze up with my kindling,

(10) Beneath me a mare, strongly-built, short-haired, mighty of limb,
  swift as an arrow which a strong bowman sends forth from his hand.

(11) And many the captain of a closely-gathered host, bristling with teeth [1],
  bright with armour, in mail-coats, with many brave champions,

(12) Whose body I have pierced with my lance, and he has swayed and fallen,
  as bends and falls a bough cut through of a soft-wooded jujube tree.

(13) And ofttimes the wine, in fragrance like broken pieces of musk, —
  long time has it spent in the wine-jar, year after year passing by —

(14) Have I quaffed in the morning before the Dawn shone forth to our mirth,
  in the tent of a man rich in bounty, pouring it freely to all.

(15) And many the damsel, large-limbed, like a hind of al-Jauw, soft of skin —
  the dew of her lips was as though it had been mixed with potent wine —

(16) Have I dallied with for near half the night, and she with me,
  and then departed, with her love fixed deep within my heart.

(17) Ah! gone is Youth, and has sworn that ne'er will he visit me more,
  and hoariness has taken his place in the locks that fall on each side;

(18) And hoary hairs are a shame to the court where they come to dwell [2]
  — yea, goodly the full black locks that were mine in days gone by!

---

[1] *I. e.* weapons.   [2] *Cf.* No. I, 6.

VI.

A vivid picture of a storm. It is worth while to compare this, in its language and imagery, with the greatly-admired description in XXVIII, 6—15 (the latter disputed with Aus b. Ḥajar). In both the cyclonic movement of the air before and during the storm is noted; here the East-wind (صَبًا) rolls the clouds together, and the gusts are compared to the strokes of the herdsman's hands on the she-camel's udders to promote the flow of milk; till, when the clouds are full and ready to pour down, the South-wind (يَمَانِيَّة in v. 6: جَنُوب in XXVIII, 4) comes and gives the needed impulse (*cf.* v. 5 with XXVIII, 10: the phrases are the same). In both the image of the camels is brought in, but in the more elaborate piece, XXVIII, 12—13, they are connected with the thunder rather than the rain. The likeness in treatment is striking, and inclines us to believe that XXVIII is rightly ascribed to ʿAbīd. See more *in loco.*

(Original metre imitated)

$\smile\smile - \smile - \ |\ \smile\smile - \smile - \ \|\ \smile\smile - \smile - \ |\ \smile\smile - \smile - \ |\ \subset$

(1) May the cloud pour down on Rabāb its rain,
　　with the thunder rumbling amid the flashes!
(2) Black is its mass by the Eastwind rolled,
　　in the early night, and the strong gusts stroke it,
(3) As the herdsman strokes his she-camel's dugs,
　　till the gathered rain fills all the udders.
(4) And it draws anigh with its fringe of white [1]
　　lighting the scrub which its flashes kindle;
(5) Until no more can its strength uphold
　　the abounding burthen of pent-up waters.
(6) There blows behind it a gentle breeze
　　from al-Yaman, thrusting the mass before it;
(7) Then loosed the South all its water-spouts [2],
　　and it pours the flood from its rifts wide-opened.

VII.

Another poem of defiance addressed to Imraʾ al-Qais, in much the same terms as the first (No. IV). The same phrases recur (*cf.* IV 16 and VII 5). From the defeat of Kindah

---

[1] Reading with al-Qālī رَبَابُه.
[2] The word is that used for the spout of a water-skin.

the poet passes to other glories of his tribe — their resistance to Ghassān (8—9), and defeat
of Hawāzin (10—11). Again Imraʾ al-Qais is threatened (13—16), and boast is made of luxurious
wine-drinking and banqueting (17—18), not to be equalled by any other tribe (19). Vv. 20—25
are the same boasts over again, in general terms, no names being mentioned.

(1) O thou that threatenest us, for the slaying
      of thy Father, with vile abasement and death,

(2) Dost thou say that thou hast slain
      our Chiefs? a lie, a false deceit!

(3) Why dost thou not spend thy tears for Ḥujr [1]
      son of Umm Qaṭāmi, not for us?

(4) Yea, we, when the straightening-clip bites
      the head of our spear-shaft, back we spring [2];

(5) We defend our honour: and some there be
      that fall, weaklings, worthless, between this and that!

(6) Why askedst thou not the hosts of Kindah,
      the day they turned their backs — "Whither, whither away?"

(7) The days when we battered their skulls
      with our keen-edged swords till the blades were bent?

(8) And the hosts of Ghassān, the kings,
      our horses reached them, worn and spare with travel,

(9) With their flanks drawn in through want of food
      after toiling through long journeys and weariness.

(10) And in time past they have met in battle Hawāzin
      with spear-shafts athirst till they were sated;

(11) We lifted over them, under the dust of battle,
      our Mashrafite [3] swords, shouting name and lineage.

(12) Yea, these are we! Gather then thy hosts —
      gather them and hurl them on us!

(13) And know thou that our noble steeds [4]
      have sworn that they will not pay the debt thou claimest.

(14) Already have we plundered what thou hadst taken
      under shelter; but none robs what we keep safe.

(15) So far well! but if the spears of my kin
      could get power over thee, they would not be held back

(16) Until they reached to thee — a reaching!
      a custom of theirs when they shape a purpose!

                *   *   *   *

---

[1] *cf.* IV, 7.   [2] IV, 15.   [3] A standing epithet of swords, explained in different ways.
[4] Constantly in the old poetry the steeds are named where the riders are intended.

(17) We bid up the price of all old wine,

        strong and fragrant, whiles we are sober;

(18) And we hold of no account, in pursuit of its delights,

        the mass of our inherited wealth, when we are drunken.

(19) The builder cannot attain, although he raise

        his pillars high, to the height we build.

(20) How many a chieftain have we laid dead!

        how many a wrong have we hurled back with scorn!

(21) Yea, many a lord of a mighty clan,

        great in his bounty, have we dashed against;

(22) His eagles [1], under the shadow of other eagles [2],

        made for the battle-field whither we too wended;

(23) Till we left him lying, a mangled corse,

        the prey of wild beasts, after we had passed on.

(24) And many damsels, fair as statues,

        with large black eyes, have we taken captive.

(25) Yea, by thy life! our confederate

        suffers no wrong while he holds by us.

VIII.

A fragment containing the opening of an ode, with several phrases which, later, become the stock language of poetry; *cf.* v. 4 with No. X, 1, and with Zuhair, *Muʿall.* 7 and many other like passages; and the comparison of camels bearing ladies' litters to ships in v. 5 with Ṭarafah, *Muʿall.* 3. The mention of *Jewish* sailors in v. 6 is interesting. In the morning the poet (v. 7) rides forth, like Imraʾ al-Qais (*Muʿall.* 53) before the birds are astir. His steed in its swiftness is like an oryx (8—10), started at the best of its speed by hunters who beset it with their dogs (10—11). He recalls his feats of arms and the champions he has slain (12—14).

(Metre imitated, though not exactly followed)

ᴗ−ᴗ | ᴗ−−− | ᴗ−ᴗ | ᴗ−ᴗ− ‖ ᴗ−ᴗ | ᴗ−−− | ᴗ−ᴗ | ᴗ−ᴗ−

(1) Sulaimà has left thee, and thy heart bears an aching wound,

        and nothing there is to ease the longing that fills thy breast.

(2) Whenas thou tastedst her lips, thou wouldst say — the sweetest wine

        — wine ladled forth from the jar — men trail their skirts that drink —

(3) Mixed with the pure rain of heaven, in vessels of silver wrought:

        — high is the price men bid for it, gain to the merchants great.

---

[1] *I. e.* his banners: see II, 21.   [2] Here is meant the birds of prey: see Nābighah I, 10—12.

(4) Consider, O friend! dost thou see aught of ladies camel-borne?
of al-Yaman their race: at dawn they started or eventide;
(5) They show like to ships that sail the billows of stormy seas:
wind-smitten, they bend as they stem the waters of Tigris stream;
(6) Their sides overhang deep gulfs, and over their bulwarks lean
the sailors — of Jewry they, of fair skin, with ruddy hair.

* * * * *

(7) And oft did I go forth at dawn, or ever the sandgrouse drink,
my fellow a trusty steed, a strong swimmer, broad of breast;
(8) When stirred by the touch of my heel, he flies like an antelope
smooth-skinned, fed strong by the pastures started by early rain;
(9) Alone has he [1] grazed clay bottoms starred with the springing green:
when others would race with him, he leaves them all far behind.
(10) Then rises a band ambushed at dawn, and upon his track
they set on their dogs, well trained to follow the quarry [2] close.
(11) When fears he their fangs, forth puts he all his reserve of speed,
and flies on his slender shanks, his thighs built to bound amain.

* * * * *

(12) And oft did I leave on ground the champion who met my spear —
a wound in his breast spouts blood, above where the belt goes round:
(13) The red stream will not be stanched by fingers that strive to help:
though after the first full flood the oozing is slack and slow.
(14) When comes a pale crowd of gazelles [3] to tend him as prone he lies,
a cry of despair outbreaks from each as she sees his plight.

IX.

Like I and XVIII, the opening of this poem is not concerned with sentimental longings for departed loves, but with stern fact. The poet recalls his comrades of old who have fallen before the arms of Ghassān, and their wasted home. The place named is that of No. I, Malḥūb; dear friends and brothers dwelt there (2 and 7), maidens kind and fair (4); many were the revellings with music and song (5, 6). Then he praises the deeds of old: his horse (9—10), his mare (11), his camel (12—15). All is vanity (16). Vv. 8 and 16 repeat the language of I, 14, 24.

---

[1] *I.e.* the antelope.   [2] Read خشيـ for حسيـ; see 'Āmir, frag. 5³ (p. 154).   [3] *I.e.* his women.

(1) I pondered on thoughts of my people, the kind ones who dwelt at Malḥūb,
        and my heart was sore for them, overwhelmed with sorrow;

(2) I remembered the men of good deeds, liberal, generous givers,
        masters of short-haired thoroughbreds, men of piety and goodness.

(3) And as remembrance filled me, the tears streamed ceaselessly
        like a water-runnel watering the seed-plots of one who has come to decay.

(4) Yea, many the tent from whose chambers the scent of musk floated forth,
        have I entered, mayhap in secret, mayhap as an open wooer;

(5) And many the songstress whose voice the wine had rendered hoarse,
        who sings to the strings stretched over a hollow curvèd lyre,

(6) Have I listened to with companions, all men of noble race,
        who count themselves bound without stint to give to all seeking help.

(7) And many the generous youth, more sure in his stedfastness
        than a sword, one seemly of speech, have I taken as my brother.

(8) And now all these things are gone, and I am left to mourn
        — nay, what man on earth is there whose hopes are never belied?

(9) Time was I rode forth at dawn with a company, mounted on a fleet she-camel,
        with a thoroughbred horse by her side, swift as a wolf, short-haired,

(10) A bay, like an antelope of the sands, clear of skin,
        with wide rims to his hoofs, broad-breasted, no mean strain in him.

(11) And many the host of horse like flocks of sandgrouse have I captained,
        with a mare light of foot as a locust, tall in shank and hock.

(12) And many the desert wherein the owl hooted and the screech-owl shrieked
        — terrors beset it whenas the night lay dark thereon —

(13) Have I passed through on a camel light-red, fleet of foot,
        — the saddle-pads slip from her sides, so solid and firm are they;

(14) A hump she has, towering up, that opens wide the wood of the saddle,
        joined to withers that are firmly set, compact with her back-bone.

(15) When my leg stirs her to speed, thou wouldst think her an ostrich fleeing,
        and if she is chidden one day, no fluttered weakling is she.

*   *   *   *   *

(16) Thou seëst a man ever yearn and pine for length of life:
        but what is long life's sum but a burthen of grief and pain?

X.

Vv. 1—4 give a picture of a moving camp, with ladies who stir thoughts of love (2—4). But the poet is far away from those he thinks of: his camel, like himself, is moved to yearn after places where both once were happy by the sight of distant lightning, playing over the Ḥijāz (5—6). But other things have now to be done — crossing the desert instead of plenty of food and rest (7). The march is described (8—10). Perhaps a *lacuna* follows: v. 11, with its rhyme-word the same as that of v. 9, can scarcely have stood so near.

With v. 12 the poet turns abruptly to another theme — his contests with other poets, either on behalf of his tribe or for mastery in the art of verse. Several of the words here are doubtful, though the general sense is sufficiently clear. The passage terminates with a spirited comparison of the poet's self to a lion, whom other lions would like to engage, but, after experience of his prowess, dare not attack (18—20).

The rare rhyme of this poem recalls Imraʾ al-Qais XXXV, in the same metre and with several of the same rhyme-words; but there is no resemblance in the contents.

(1) Look forth, O Friend; canst thou see aught of ladies camel-borne
    that take their way through Ghumair, with hollows between us and them?
(2) And riding on the light-coloured camels are girls with swelling breasts,
    slender of waist, virgins, friendly in their manners, white.
(3) Yea, many the tent of maidens who toss the curtain to and fro [1]
    have I entered, when within was a woman unwed and sick with love;
(4) And I lent her my love that I might be paid it in turn; in sooth
    the incurring of debt hangs heavy on the hands of decent folk.

(5) And my young camel uttered her yearning cry when a third of the night
                                      was spent:
    — her longing was stirred by the distant gleam of lightning in the Ḥijāz:
(6) I said to her — "Grumble not thus: for verily an abode
    where Hind is far away is nought but hateful to me.
(7) "Thou hast at hand to plunge into the desert: so gird thyself thereto!
    not now as aforetime calls thee pasture and restful ease".

(8) So when they [2] had passed through the home-lands, they set them to face
                                     the toil
    of deserts unwatered, wide, with spaces of sand between.
(9) Already the saddle-girths loosened, and sides that streamed with sweat
    let slip the saddle-gear backward, for all that the foregirth held;
(10) And our troop were like swarms of sandgrouse whose flight to the water-springs
    is speeded by fierce hot winds in a morning of burning heat.

             *   *   *   *   *

---

[1] Or, perhaps, "shoot glances that assail the beholder from behind the curtain".

[2] "They" refers to the caravan of which the poet formed part; it is best to take the verb so, not of his camel only, in view of كُرَّ in v. 10. "Homelands" بِلادًا, the inhabited tracts.

(11) And many the stout young fighters above whom I have spread
      my cloak as a shelter in sleep when the day-long sun drooped low.

        *   *   *   *   *

(12) Am I not the man to break off a man's speech, when his bitter tongue
      spits forth odes, some of them insults, and all of them meant to wound?
(13) Then do I stay his clamour and choke him with his own spittle,
      and he speaks, after I have done with him, with words of humbleness.
(14) Yea, how many a raging adversary have I handled thus, and left him
      after I had spoken, with no power more to sharpen [1] a phrase!
(15) And I have returned with glory from the contest — for I was given a tongue
                                 sharp as a sword
      whereby the clamour of the antagonist is reduced to impotence [2];
(16) I cut therewith the sinews of thy feet, and they were severéd,
      and after my satire had sped thou hadst no more power to rise;
(17) I smote thee with notable verses, full of strange startling words,
      a blow thou didst cower beneath, and thy heart was well-nigh dead.
(18) Ye suffered scathe from a lion whose covert few care to seek,
      a father of whelps — after battle his teeth let the vanquisht heed!
(19) When he stalks forth, the lions his fellows stand still before him at gaze:
      none dares, for fear of sure death, to break against him the peace;
(20) Yea, one mayst thou see, broken-necked, lying there whelmed in death,
      and another, in fear for dear life, fleeing with a gaping wound [3].

XI.

    This interesting poem offers a very well-supported text (see the notes to the Arabic original). The locality indicated by the opening verses (ad-Dafīn, Dharwah, Uthāl, Dhiyāl), is the same as that of No. XIII, which in subject also agrees with this ode.

    Vv. 1—7, the usual introduction, from which the poet turns abruptly to a description of his wife's aversion from him (8—14), which he considers, doubtfully, may proceed either from real dislike, with divorce the object, or from coquetry. If real, it is presumably due to his age and infirmities (13—15). Yet time was when he was acceptable as a lover (16—18). Then he turns to his wife, and exhorts her to leave those who prompt her resentment against him, who, if she elects divorce, will not keep her in comfort, and desire only

---

[1] This sense of نَحَضَ is established by its use in *Mufaḍḍ.* 238²².

[2] Reading رَبِيضْ as suggested in the note.

[3] Lit., "with a morsel of his flesh bitten off".

to get hold of her property (19—21). The dispute seems to have been about a small herd of camels, claimed by a family called "Zaid's people", which he was in favour of letting go: they were not the spoil of warfare, and there was no reason in honour why they should not be relinquished (22, 23).

Then the poet passes on to a passionate rhapsody in praise of youth, recalling his rides on camel and horse, his delight in the chase, his captaining the tribe in battle on a war-mare, and journeys undertaken to distant and dangerous places (24—35); and ends (if the additional verse found in the *Mukhtārāt* is genuine) with a cry at the vanity and emptiness of life (*cf.* IX, 16).

(Metre imitated, with occasional divergences)

⏖ ⏑ – ⏖ | ⏓ – ⏑ – | ⏖ ⏑ – – || ⏖ ⏑ – ⏖ | ⏓ – ⏑ – | ⏖ ⏑ – –

(1) Still to see are the traces at ad-Dafīn, and
in the sand-slope of Dharwah, the sides of Uthāl;
(2) Al-Maraurāt and aṣ-Ṣaḥīfah [1] are empty,
every valley and meadow, once full of people:
(3) The abode of a tribe whom past time has smitten —
their dwellings show now like patterns on sword-sheaths [2] —
(4) Desolate all, save for ashes extinguisht,
and leavings of rubbish and ridges of shelters,
(5) Shreds of tethering-ropes, and a trench round the tent-place,
and lines plotted out, changed [3] by long years' lapse.
(6) Instead of their folk now ostriches dwell there,
red-shanked, driving on the troops of their younglings,
(7) And gazelles, that stand like ewers of silver,
bending downwards to tend their fawns by their side.

* * * * *

(8) This my wife, in her wrath [4] she seeks to be rid of me:
is it that she desires divorce, or is feigning?
(9) If thy mind be on feigning coyness, why didst thou
jest not thus in time past, the nights long vanisht?
(10) Fair wast thou as an oryx then, I thy bondsman,
drunk with love, trailing skirts, I sought thy bower.
(11) So now leave off thy frowning, live with me peaceably
— hope remains for us yet, yet may we be happy.
(12) But if severance be thy desire, then what more
needs it than to turn elsewhere the breasts of thy camels?
(13) She will have it that I am old and decrepid,
reft of wealth, and my cousins too stingy to help me,

---

[1] *V. l.* aṣ-Ṣafīḥah. [2] See *ante*, III, 6. [3] Reading غُيِّرْنَ [4] Reading غَيْرَى تُرِيدُ

(14) Youth's lightness all soured, my hair gone hoary,
      not a fit mate for her, the young and mirthful.

(15) If she finds me now pale, youth's colour vanisht,
      greyness spread over brow and cheek and temple,

(16) Time was when I entered a tent to find there
      one slender of waist, soft of skin, a gazelle.

(17) Round her neck went my arms, and toward me she bent her,
      as the sandhill slopes down to the sands below it.

(18) Then said she — "My soul be ransom for thy soul!
      "all my wealth be a gift from me to thy people!"

(19) Leave the censurers then, and get thee some wisdom:
      let not them weigh against me in thy affection,

(20) Or against all our life together, nor follow
      silly preachings intended to cause thee terror.

(21) Some there be of them niggards, and some mere paupers,
      others misers intent to grasp thy substance.

(22) Leave the herd then to fall to the share of Zaid's people,
      in Quṭaibāt be they or in Aurāl;

(23) They were not won in foray, nor did our war-steeds
      wear the points of their shoes in driving them homewards.

          *   *   *   *   *

(24) O how goodly is youth, the day of the black locks,
      when the camels step briskly under the harness!

(25) When the long-necked steeds, spare like arrows of *shauḥaṭ*, [1]
      bear the warriors, heavy with arms and armour!

(26) Oft of old did I fright herds of deer with a prancer
      like a young buck in swiftness, full of spirit,

(27) Not hump-nosed, nor wont to knock hocks together
      — no, his hoofs hammer mightily, quick are his changes;

(28) Foremost he of a thousand, bearing as burthen
      knight in armour and helm, comes home like a picture;

(29) Swift as straight-feathered shaft of *shauḥaṭ* his onset,
      shot with skill by an archer cunning in bow-craft,

(30) Cutting down deer and ostrich, reaving the camels
      of a herdsman who dwells far away from his people. [2]

---

[1] A wood used for making bows and arrows.

[2] The ancient poets boast of their herdsmen going far away from the protection of the tribal encampment in seeking for pasture for their camels; the implication is that their tribe is so great and powerful, and its prowess so terrible, that no one will venture to attack its herds however distant from

(31) Yea and time was I led the host on a war-mare,

     short of hair, good in hand, to wheel or to race:

(32) Me she shielded with throat, and I with my spear-play

     shielded her from the lances that men couched at us.

(33) Oft of old did I traverse deserts and sand-dunes,

     borne aloft on a camel noble and fleet,

(35)[1] Great of frame, strong and swift, like a wild bull roaming,

     whom a night full of rain has pent in a valley:

(34) All her flesh I wore down with journeyings ceaseless:

     at the end of our travel she was lean as the new moon.

        *   *   *   *   *

[(36) Such was life when I loved it: all now is vanisht

     — all our lives thus sink into ashes and emptiness!]

XII.

Vv. 1—6, the usual amatory prelude. Here the lady gives no encouragement, and the poet in her presence is too much abashed to urge his suit. Notice a simile for her limbs which recurs in the poetry of Imraʾ al-Qais (v. 6). As convention requires, the poet seeks forgetfulness by roaming far afield on a strong camel (7—10), whose reserve of strength (the fat of her hump) is exhausted by his long travel (10). Then he passes to his war-mare, described at length (11—18), his weapons (19, 19 a), and his fellows (vv. 20—22). Notice that Asad is here spoken of by the wider tribal name, Khuzaimah. Another point of contact with Imraʾ al-Qais is v. 17.

(1) Whose are the abodes in Ṣāḥah and Ḥarūs?

     worn are they by long desolation — how great a wearing!

(2) Only scraps left of tethering ropes, and the traces

     like lines of writing faded in a worn-out parchment.

(3) Fāṭimah's abode in the Spring was in Ghamrah,

     then Qafā Sharāfi, and the Hills of the many Heads,

(4) In the days when she was heedless of thee — though thou askedst no

                          grace of her

     through weakness of spirit: and the worst of all ails is the weakness

                       that relapses ever on itself.

---

head-quarters. Here the herdsman is described by an intensive form, مُعْزِئِبْ, indicating that he is a long way off from his tribal centre, and consequently an adventurous and valiant man. Our poet, by giving him this epithet of praise, enhances his own credit for attacking him and robbing him of his camels.

[1] Vv. 34 and 35 transposed, as in *Mukht.*

(5) Yet she led thee captive — a delicate one, the choicest of delicate beauties,
   white, shining clear of skin, like pale-coloured gazelles,

(6) Young and tender, dainty and perfect in all her limbs,
   like a papyrus-plant growing among off-sets of palms.

*　　*　　*　　*　　*

(7) Wilt thou not then seek forgetfulness of her love on a great she-camel,
   thick of cheek, tall as a plastered tower, nimble of pace?

(8) Long roaming in the rich spring-pasture has raised her hump high,
   and she has grown fat; and it has brought out her last tooth after the
   last but one.

(9) (So strong is she on her feet, that) she seems, when she is started on her way,
   to be crushing down the wood and the twigs of the thorny scrub with hoes.

(10) I have caused her cheerful spirit, and the fatness of her hump, to vanish
   by constant travel, and gone are all her pride and wantonness.

*　　*　　*　　*

(11) And many the captain of a host of horse whom I have disobeyed
   with a stout short-haired mare, compact of flesh, tall of stature,

(12) Shaped with legs like palm-branches, in the full age of vigour:
   for a year has she been trained, and no ill-luck has come.

(13) And when (the other horses) are toiling on the way, and the last drop of
   their water has been almost spent,
   and they push along through a waterless desert where is no herbage,

(14) She keeps the slow-going camels from the level part of the track,
   (and makes them travel) the road through the uplands, while they have
   no spirit of refractoriness left in them.

(15) When thou lookest at her from the front, she is like a straight spear-shaft
   from India, long and slender, pliant, not harsh and dry:

(16) But when thou viewest her from behind, then is she like
   a bottle of yellow glass (round and compact), filled with some perfume;

(17) And when we go hunting, the blazon of blood [1] (of the slain quarry) is
   never dry,
   and her breast is ever like the stone on which a bride grinds down her
   unguents;

(18) And when we dash into the herds of camels [2], her spoil
   is the nearest of the troops of camels covered with pieces of hair-cloth.

---

[1] The Arabs were accustomed to anoint the foreheads and the breasts of their horses, when they
had hunted game with them, with the blood of the slain quarry.

[2] Or, "the close thickets of trees, or scrub."

(19) This (mare of mine) shall carry me, and a bright keen blade,
  and a sharp spear-head set on a pliant shaft five cubits long —
[(19a) A trusty shaft from India, with the socket (of the spear-head) at the
                    upper end
  stuck upon a knot, like a date-stone, smooth and hard,]
(20) Among a band of kinsmen that draw sword on the day of battle
  like lions from whom none ventures to snatch the prey.
(21) Yea, the Children of Khuzaimah know well that we
  are of their best in all fortune, be it prosperous or evil;
(22) We bring woe to their foes, and our wether butts on their behalf
  with a thrust of his horns that is no mere scratch.

XIII.

As already noted, this poem is a doublet of No. XI, but in a different metre; it has also points of contact with other poems by 'Abīd: *cf.* v. 3 with VIII, 4, 5, and v. 5 with XXVIII, 1. The localities named in vv. 1—4 are all in the neighbourhood of Faid, the centre of the tribal settlements (Yāqūt II, 810), on the south-eastern slopes of Mount Salmà.

(1) Changed are the abodes in Dhu-d-Dafīn,
  and the valleys of al-Liwà, and the sands of Līn,
(2) And the two straits of Dharwah, and the back of Dhayāl,
  — the long lapse of years has outworn their traces.
(3) Look forth, O Friend — dost thou see aught of laden camels,
  led along as though they were ships sailing on the sea?
(4) To the left hand they have passed the defile of Rakak,
  and on the right they have turned away from at-Tawī.
     *   *   *   *   *
(5) Lo, to-day my wife spends her time in reviling me:
  she woke up while it was still night to pour out her complaints;
(6) She said to me — "Thou art old". I answered — "Truly!
  in sooth I have left behind me year after year."
(7) She shows me signs of aversion in her,
  and rude and rough of speech is she after smoothness;
(8) She knits her brows and frowns because she sees me
  an old man, with my locks all changed to white.
(9) I said to her — "Gently! spare a little of thy censure:
  I hold it not fitting thou shouldst treat me lightly.

(10) "Live with me as long as thou canst, until,
      whenas thou wilt begone, depart as likes thee.

(11) "If to my sorrow Youth has fled and left me,
      and my head now is but as withered leaves(?) [1] —

(12) "Time was when Pleasure was my sworn companion,
      though to-day the bond is cut between us.

(13) "Time was I entered in to tented maidens,
      whose eyes were full and black like those of wild kine;

(14) "They clung close to me now, and now my arms
      embraced necks white as robes of the finest linen.

(15) "And many the dun spear I have couched against
      one great in fame, who sees in me true valour;

(16) "He strives to rise: but there he lies all helpless,
      his body pierced through by the thirsty spear-shaft.

(17) "Whenso his women come to tend their master,
      their eyes gush forth with tears, and loud they wail.

(18) "And many the desert where I have scared the wild kine [2],
      mounted on a light-coloured camel, swift as a wild ass, neither
                                     fat nor lean."

XIV.

This spirited fragment seems to refer to some encounter between Ghassān and an ally of Asad, perhaps one of the Ṭayyite tribes, in which the leader of the latter had been slain. The poet asks why he had not sought the aid of Asad, as on a former occasion, at the battle on the skirt of Mount Shaṭib. He describes the host of Asad ready for war (a *lacuna*, apparently, between verses 6 and 7), and mentions a former battle, the Day of Murār, when Ghassān had retired discomfited before Asad.

(metre imitated, with occasional variations)

⏑–⏑– | ⏑⏑– | ⏑–⏑– | ⏑⏑–‖⏑–⏑– | ⏑⏑– | ⏑–⏑– | ⏑⏑–

(1) He called on kinsmen — but ears were stopt to his cry for help:
      woe's me — hadst thou only called the men of Asad to aid!

(2) Then hadst thou called on a folk, true helpers, none of them slack
      when blades in hands of the tribesmen glitter like burning brands;

. (3) Had they been thy helpers, good help in sooth had they given, and thou
      hadst not been left to a Day that has plunged thy people in woe:

---

[1] This is the interpretation given in the commentary: but the alternative *lujain*, silver, seems to suit the phrase better, though it involves a metrical anomaly.

[2] Or, with *Mukhtārāt*, "the ostriches;" the latter is more probable, as *jaun* more often means black, the colour of ostriches, than white, the colour of the oryx.

(4) As we shielded thee on the Day of the skirt of Mount Shaṭib,
   when our foes had the better in wind and in number above our strength;
(5) Then had they come to thy help with a host that has no peer,
   a folk that are famed among men to the furthest limit of fame,
(6) A host like the blackness of night when they wend to their enemy's land,
   that swallow all things on their way, in number beyond all count.

             *   *   *   *   *

(7) Alongside they lead steeds straining the rein and pawing the ground,
   like sand-grouse at noontide athirst coming down to a scanty pool:
(8) Strong-built mares, showing their back-teeth over bridle and bit,
   vying with the riding camels, froward, impatient,
(9) And short-haired horses, the saddles set on their backs awry,
   stout in the flanks, full of muscle, humped at the base of the mane:
(10) So laid they hold of the war Ghassān had raised in their land,
   there on the Day of Murār, nor turned for any aside.
(11) When Ghassān saw thee their chief[1], the bright swords shining aloft,
   and all the lances uplifted, as a well-rope straight of shaft,
(12) Then were they sick of the men of Asad, knowing not how
   to handle them; rarely does Ghassān choose the right way to go!

XV.

A poem that well illustrates ʿAbīd's mastery and charm of phrase, which no doubt led to the preservation of so many of his *nasīb* pieces. Vv. 1—7 describe in the usual way the deserted dwelling-places; then with v. 8 the poet assumes that another parting is impending, and exhorts his two companions to await a group of ladies who, escorted by two caravan-leaders, are journeying by (9—10). He joins them, putting his beast, and his companions theirs, to their best pace (11—13), and is rewarded by speech with the fair ones (14—15). The passage ends with two beautiful verses describing the result (16—17); v. 16 recalls Imraʾ al-Qais's language in *Muʿall.* 8.

(1) Dost thou weep for a vanisht abode, over traces of tents outworn?
   — and is weeping for love-longing the business of one like me?
(2) These were their camps when the tribe was gathered all together:
   now are they a wilderness, save for wildings in an empty land.
(3) No voices stir there now but the uncouth sounds of the wild,
   the cries of the male and female ostriches, dusky herds.

---

[1] Perhaps we should read رَأوْنا, "saw our array".

(4) Yea, if Ghabrā' al-Khubaibah has become desolate,
 and gained in exchange for our folk other dwellers not equal to those,

(5) Yet time was I looked on the whole kin dwelling there in content
 and happy: but what is the passing of days but change on change?

(6) After the children of ᶜAmr, my kinsfolk and my brethren,
 can I hope for smoothness of life? nay, life is a leader astray.

(7) But although they have gone, and departed on their way,
 — never will I forget them all my life long, or cease to mourn.

 * * * * *

(8) Will ye two not stay for a moment to-day, before we part,
 — before long distance, and cares, and variance, have sundered us,

(9) To await ladies borne on camels that travel between Tabālah
 and the high land of al-Khall, with the followers trailing after them?

(10) When I saw the two leaders of the caravan hasten briskly along,
 a pang seized my breast that they should depart with a heart so light.

(11) We raised our whips to our beasts, and they skimmed along with us
 — our camels with well-knit fore-legs, swift and fleet of pace,

(12) Plying briskly their hind-legs, as though behind them lay
 deserts trackless, forlorn, where they trotted in the fore-noon haze;

(13) And they brought us up to the caravan, our beasts the active and light,
 the breastgirth securing the saddle, thick of cheek, quick of step.

(14) Then we bent sideways, and entered on talk with women kind
 — above them were hangings of striped cloth of Jaishān, with broi-
 dered borders;

(15) And they turned to us their necks, and the jewels that thereon hung,
 with speech that dealt with such things as the careless loves to hear;

(16) Then was it as though the East-wind had wafted to us the scent
 of a bale of musk, so precious that none could pay its price,

(17) Or the fragrance of lavender by the brook-sides of a mead,
 where a plenteous shower in the night has washed away dust and grime.

XVI.

A lamentation over the disappearance from their land of the poet's kin, the Banū Saᶜd ibn Thaᶜlabah. It seems a little uncertain whether the poem is by ᶜAbīd or by a man of the Banū Saᶜd ibn Zaid-Manāt of Tamīm, since "the gravelly plain of Rauḥān", spoken of in v. 1, appears to have been in the country of Tamīm; it is mentioned by Jarīr (Bakrī 427[9] and 81[5]) and Aufā al-Māzinī (Yāq. I. 582[20]), poets of that tribe. Yāqūt says it was in al-Yamāmah (*l. c.*, line 15). Yet the poem is attributed to ʿAbīd by Bakrī, Yāqūt, and al-ʿAskarī, and criticized by the last-named in his *Kitāb aṣ-Sināʿatain* (p. 126). Notice شَنَانَةٌ رَجِيبَةٌ, "a shower in the month of Rajab" (v. 3), a month of winter (see XIX, 10): the months still had reference to the natural seasons of the year. The reading of v. 8, second hemistich, is uncertain: probably يَحْبُون (ʿAsk. يحدون) is not the original word, which must denote some act happening instantaneously on "*nazāli*" [1] being shouted.

(1) Whose are the abodes in the gravelly plain of Rauḥān?
    worn are they — the destroying hand of time has changed them.
(2) I stayed therein my camel that I might ask of the traces,
    and as I turned away, mine eyes gushed forth with tears —
(3) A copious stream, as though on a sudden burst from my lids
    a shower of rain, such as falls unawares from a winter cloud.
(4) I thought how had dwelt there my kin, the best of all men not kingly
    to the famine-stricken, the wretched, and the captive in sorest need,
(5) And goodly gamers over the slaughtered camel, what time
    the wintry wind was blowing, and the strangers were gathered in.
(6) But when spear-play was the business that they had in hand,
    then dyed they deep in blood the upper third of their shafts;
(7) And when it was time for the smiting of swords, behold them then
    like lions that bend above their whelps and repel the foe;
(8) And when men shouted — "Down to the foot-fight!" then did they do on
    the mail-coats ample, that fall in folds as far as the knees.
(9) Now I remain — they are gone: and I too must pass away:
    change upon change — that is life, and colour to colour succeeds!
(10) God knows how they came to their end — I know not: all that is left
    for me is remembrance of things lost — when and where, He knows!

XVII.

This poem is in a somewhat unsatisfactory condition, and its text has suffered from the long time during which it was transmitted orally. The accusative ذٰلِكا in v. 1 has no proper government. There is evidently a *hiatus* between v. 6 and v. 7. The rhymes in vv. 12, 13 and 14 (all the same word) are not possible. The brief *nasīb* (vv. 1—6) finished, the poet begins at once to boast of his tribe's prowess in war. The poem is addressed to Imraʾ al-Qais (v. 14), and the men whose slaying is mentioned in vv. 7, 8, and 9a were of Kindah; Quṛṣ, whose death is alluded to in 9 b, appears to have been a chief of Ghas-

---

[1] "Dismount to fight on foot!"

sān (see note in Arabic text). The defeat of ʿĀmir at an-Nisār (vv. 10—11) has been mentioned already (II, 19 ff., VII, 10, 11); where the Ribāb (12 a) were defeated is uncertain: at an-Nisār they were the allies of Asad. Again ʿAbīd returns to the slaying of Ḥujr and others of Kindah (12 b, 13). Then he taunts Imraʾ al-Qais with his addiction to wine, music, and song, which makes him unfit to follow after vengeance; while he is dallying, those whom he would smite have time to guard themselves (14—16). He only escaped by flight the fate of his father (17). He is but a poet, full of boastful words, but no fighter (18).

(1) The tent-traces of Sulaimà are all effaced in Dakādik
    and desolate: the violent tearing winds have swept them away;

(2) They have gotten in exchange for Sulaimà and her folk, since I dwelt there,
    ostriches that feed there together, and white gazelles lingering behind
        the herd.

(3) I stayed there my beast, and wept like a dove that mourns as she sits
    on a bough of *arāk*, and calls to her fellows that dwell in the grove;

(4) Whenas she thought on her pain, and moaned with a piteous voice,
    on a tree-top, straight from [1] mine eyes gushed forth the tide of tears.

(5) High noon was the time: then, when my passion had spent itself,
    I fastened the saddle on the back of a stout camel, high of hump;

(6) The saddle-trees topped, it seemed, a rough-skinned wild ass, driven forth
    by his fellows, who sees the herd coming nigh, and flies at full speed.

        *   *   *   *   *

(7) Yea, our hands it was that slew the twin Hawks, and Mālik, him [2]
    the dearer of them to thee in thy loss, the dearer in death:

(8) 'Twas we that pressed home the spear directed at his throat,
    and down did it cast him prone, his hips brought rudely to ground;

(9) And we it was slew among you him whom they called Murrah the good,
    and Qurṣ — yea, Qurṣ also was one of those we slew;

(10) And we it was gave ʿĀmir to drink for their morning wine,
    as they came on with pomp, keen swords, hung round us for time of need;

(11) We gripped, as a camel bites, their horsemen, and straight they fled
    in frantic rout, and the blood streamed down to their horses' hoofs.

(12) The day, too, we met the Ribāb, we slew their foremost man,
    and Ḥujr — we slew him too, and ʿAmr fell eke to our blades;

(13) And we it was slew Jandal in the midst of his gathered hosts,
    and earlier fell to our hand his elder, the ancient chief.

        *   *   *   *   *

---

[1] It is best to take أَذْرَت of the poet's eyes, as the dove does not weep.

[2] Perhaps we should read وَمالِكٌ أَعَزُّهُما, as Mālik was evidently one of the two "Falcons."

(14) But thou — a man of light pleasure, of timbrels and singing girls,
   thou drinkest the wine at dawn, at even thou liest drunk —

(15) Forgetful of vengeance thou, till those whom thou seekest guard
   their breaches, [1] and sore thou weepest for time and occasion lost;

(16) No man to win blood for blood art thou in thy daintiness:
   thou knowest not purpose firm, the hand that will help itself!

(17) And had it not been for thy riding, thou hadst met the fate of those:
   thy swift flight it was that saved thee from that which them befell.

(18) Day-long thou singest, if only thou canst get a girl to hear,
   as though all Maʿadd [2] had come within the cords of thy sway.

XVIII.

A fragment lamenting the destruction (according to the commentary, by Ghassān) of the poet's tribe, Saʿd ibn Thaʿlabah, and their scattering among the other·sub-tribes of Asad; v. 5 is often quoted as a proverb.

(1) To whom belong the remnants of camps not yet effaced in al-Madhānib?
   — then the sides of Ḥibirr, and Wāhib — in both they have been
           swept away;

(2) The abodes were they of the Children of Saʿd son of Thaʿlabah,
   whom Time has scattered far and wide, Time the destroyer of men.

(3) They have perished, as others before them have been brought to their end,
   by the teeth of wars, and the Dooms that dog the steps of all.

(4) How many a clan of our kin have we seen in these camping-grounds,
   before whose vanguard the bands of hostile scouts turned aside in fear!

    *   *   *   *   *

(5) Betake thyself now to thy business, and leave things too hard alone:
   thou art troubled about things vain — for all are passing away.

XIX.

The prelude of a poem addressed to Sharāḥīl (v. 16), whose bounty is sought. There are some abrupt changes of theme which suggest *lacunæ*, but on the whole the fragment seems fairly complete, and contains two similes (4—6 and 9—14) of great beauty. V. 2 appears to be intrusive, and the passage would be better without it. The transition in v. 3 *b* is very

---

[1] *I. e.*, their places open to attack.

[2] Maʿadd, the collective name of the northern Arabs not of Yamanite stock.

abrupt. In v. 5 supply الغيل as the nominative to خَلَ. The account of the bull-oryx in vv. 9—14 is perhaps incomplete, and may have been supplemented by the appearance of hunters with dogs (*cf.* VIII, 10—11) to cause him to put forth his full speed. Notice again rain in Rajab (v. 10), evidently under wintry conditions (*cf.* XVI. 3). The mention of snow in verse 14 is noteworthy: Doughty observed snow on the *ḥarrahs* enclosing the valley of Madāʾin Ṣāliḥ during his stay at that place, and snow is common in the winter in the Syrian Desert, though rare so far south as the land of Asad. In the MS. v. 15 of our text stands between vv. 12 and 13; it has been restored to what appears to be its proper place; but some verses have probably dropped out between it and v. 16.

The Sharāḥīl of the poem may possibly be the father of the two Kindite princes called *al-Jaunāni* (ʿAmr and Muʿāwiyah were their names), who were taken prisoners and slain at the battle of Shiʿb Jabalah (See *Naqāʾid*, 407²); this Sharāḥīl is described as son of ʿAmr son of Muʿāwiyah, called al-Jaun, son of Ḥujr ʿĀkil al-Murār; his father and al-Ḥārith, father of Ḥujr the Prince of the Banū Asad, were thus first cousins. The variants to v. 17 show that the reading is uncertain, and the comparison of generosity to lightning among the hills is an improbable one; if it is the right reading the lightning must be taken as the sign of plenteous rain; but the variant given in the commentary is preferable. Mr. Krenkow suggests reading حَمْلُهُ يَزِنُ الْجِبَالَ, which is possible, and has been adopted in our rendering.

Metre imitated.

∪∪–∪– | ∪∪–∪– | ∪∪–∪–‖∪∪–∪– | ∪∪–∪– | ∪∪–∪–

(1) Of a truth the morrow shall bring with it its happenings,
    and the morning light and the eventide are their time of tryst;

[(2) And mankind revile their leader when he has missed the way
    to attain success: but he that walks straight is not blamed.]

(3) And a man is ever the prey of Fate — unawares it comes
    and bears him down. But to Mahdad[1] how shall we say farewell?

(4) Like a fawn is she: by the thicket sides it plucks the fruit
    the *arāk*-twigs yield, and the herbage crops where the grove is clear;

(5) All alone is it as it seeks the water — no sound to fear,
    save only where some turtle moans, or a hoopoe calls;

(6) There calls the ringdove through the noon on its fledgling brood,
    and the youngling comes, now falling, now making good its flight.

*   *   *   *   *

(7) Our friends, they say that tomorrow's dawn will see them gone
    — yea, thus portended the raven's croak to us yester-eve;

(8) Cut short thy longing for loves departed, and mount a strong
    well-fleshed she-camel, one good to travel when others flag;

---

[1] A rare feminine proper name, perhaps of Persian origin (= Māh-dādh, "gift of the Moon-god": *cf.* Mihrdādh, Mithradāta).

(9) On her back it seems as it were beneath my saddle-tree

   there sped a bull of the Aurāl hills, going forth alone;

(10) O'er him a night of the bleakest winter had shed its gloom:

   as he stood, the rain poured on, a stream that had no surcease;

(11) From its icy blast he sought the shelter of friendly trees [1],

   but as dawn drew on cold shivering seized upon every limb.

(12) Lo! how his back shines in the mirk like a pearly [2] star:

   — with the cold and hunger his spine is bent, as it were a bow:

(13) In a meadow snowed in its hollow bights by the winter storm,

   soaked well by showers — no herdsmen venture to wander there;

(14) In its midst a lakelet, around, the earth with its fragrance sweet,

   like a gust of saffron the wind has swept over choicest nard [3].

* * * * *

(15) If the night be set for thy journey, safe upon her thy road:

   if the noon-tide heat be the toil to face, she basks therein —

(16) To the Lord Sharāḥīl, great in bounty to all who come,

   like palms fruit-laden, with runnels flowing about their stems;

(17) Euphrates-like he pours his gifts, and the burden bears

   like mountain-masses [4], unfailing ever his generous hand.

XX.

The form of this poem, in which all the 18 verses except one (No. 8) have the article الـ at the end of the first hemistich, is very strange if we suppose it to be the original work of ʿAbīd. This phenomenon occurs sporadically in the ancient poetry: e. g. ʿAntarah, Muʿall. 29: Zuhair, III, 38, XVIII. 7; but it is, in the longer metres, extremely rare. For this reason we cannot but doubt the genuineness of the piece. Apart from its metrical strangeness, however, and some grammatical artificialities, there is nothing in the contents of the poem to make us hesitate to ascribe it to ʿAbīd. The nasīb, vv. 1—5, is of the usual character. Then the poet proceeds to glorify his tribe's feats in war, against Ghassān under al-Ḥārith the Lame (vv. 6—8), ʿAdī, (9) and Quraṣ (10—11): for the last cf. No. XVII 9 b. The concluding

---

[1] The kind of tree called ʾalāʾah — species unknown.

[2] Reading ad-durrīyi.

[3] "Saffron", ʿabīr, or a mixture of saffron with other perfumes; "nard" is put for malāb, a Persian perfume also said to contain saffron as one of its ingredients. LA (see Arabic text, note) has another reading and interpretation of this verse, according to which (taking kaukab in the sense, not of a pool, but of bloom [see al-Aʿshà, Muʿall. 13]), it may be rendered:

"And a fragrance spreads from its wealth of bloom like saffron mixed
   by a cunning hand with a perfumed mass of absinthium."

[4] Reading حَمْلُهُ يَزِنُ الْجِبَالَ, which seems on the whole the best choice.

verses (14—18) contain vaunts of prowess generally; v. 16 resembles the saying of al-Akhnas b. Shihāb of Taghlib in *Mufaḍḍalīyāt* XLI, 18—19.

(1) O my two friends! stay a little while and question
    the abode that is fading away of the folk of al-Ḥalāl;

(2) It is like a worn-out robe of al-Yaman, effaced, since thou didst dwell there,
    by the rain and the sweeping thereover of the North-wind.

(3) Yet time was when there sojourned there thy fellows,
    the firm in holding to thee with the cords of comradeship.

(4) But then their love grew cold, when they resolved
    on parting from us; and the Days bring change after change.

(5) Now comfort thyself for their loss with a trusty camel
    swift as a lusty wild-ass with his mates, or a buck of the sands.

            *   *   *   *   *

(6) Time was we led, from the hills of al-Malà,
    horses like demons, linked to camels by head-ropes,

(7) Lean and spare, entering upon a land unknown,
    sand in which they sank, of plain and mountain.

(8) Then we sought out al-Ḥārith the Lame
    with a great host like the night, their spears quivering as they rode:

(9) The day that we left ʿAdī with the slender
    tawny spears piercing him, prone in the place of combat.

(10) Then we turned them [1] aside, with sunken eyes, swift as sand-grouse
    when they draw near to the drinking-place after weariness and travail,

(11) Towards Qurṣ, on the day that there galloped about him
    horses slender-waisted to right and left.

(12) How many a chief, leader of a thousand, who rode
    a swift swimmer [2], tall, unfailing in his speed,

(13) Have our swords spoiled, and destroyed his host
    — our swords the white, our spears the dun — how many a mighty tribe!

(14) Yea, a country is ours whose strength, the ancient,
    from far-off time we have inherited from father's and mother's kin:

(15) An abode in which our fathers have left their traces,
    and an inheritance of glory from the first of all days;

(16) No castles are ours therein, save only our steeds,
    the short-haired, at home in our tents, that gallop with us on their backs,

(17) Among the outliers of an ancient, high uplifted,
    mountain peak wherein is a heritage of glory and renown;

---

[1] The horses.   [2] *I. e.* a horse with an action like swimming.

(18) And we follow the ways of our forefathers, those
   who kindled wars and were faithful to the ties of kinship.

XXI.

A fragment consisting mainly of an elaborate *nasīb* (vv. 1—8), with many phrases that have passed into the general stock of poetic language; compare v. 2 with Zuhair, *Muʿall.* 9, and Labīd, *Muʿall.* 13. In v. 4 the ladies' litters, shrouded with broidered linen cloths, are compared to date-palms, the rich dark clusters of their ripening fruit swathed round with linen sheaths as a protection from birds and locusts. In v. 6 Hind's hands are not tattooed: only women of evil fame tattoo their palms. In v. 8 note the vintner "red of moustache and hair", perhaps a Jew from al-ʿIrāq (*cf.* the red-haired Jewish sailors in VIII, 6). In vv. 9—11 a storm in the distance is described; v. 10, رَبِّق, the firstling of the rain: *cf.* No. XXVIII, 9. If the poet could but taste its rain he would be in the company of his beloved (*cf.* No. X, 5); but (vv. 12—14) his way lies otherwhere. "Its tracks like stripes on a robe": the *burd* or striped stuff made in the Yaman. V. 14: for سَاعَة مَسْمُومَة, "a time of the *samūm* or poison-wind", *cf.* يَوْم مَسْمُوم in ʿAlqamah XIII, 45.

(Some approach to the rhythm of the original is aimed at)

(1) Whose are these camels, bridled for a journey before the dawn,
   about to start for regions to us unknown?
(2) Over their litters are drawn broidered cloths, and carpets twain,
   and linen veils pricked out with choicest needle-work —
(3) A glow of colour in the morning most wonderful to behold, [1]
   as though the canopies all were stained with circles of blood.
(4) High stand the litters to see like palm-trees laden with fruit,
   their bunches blackening to ripeness, swathed in linen sheaths.
(5) Within is Hind, she who holds my fevered heart in her thrall,
   a white one, sweet of discourse, a marvel of loveliness;
(6) A doe she seems of the wild, soft-skinned, of gentle breed:
   her veil she draws to her face with a hand that is not tattooed;
(7) Meseems the dew of her lips, whenas she rises from sleep,
   were a draught of pure pale wine, the flagon sealed with musk —
(8) Wine which a crowd bid against each other to buy, long stored
   by a vintner red of moustache and hair, most precious of brands.

*   *   *   *   *

(9) Ho! who will watch by my side the long night through, as I wake
   and gaze at flashes that pierce the mass of high-built cloud?

---

[1] An attempt to render ʿAbqarī, according to the explanation of *Mukht.*, *q. v.*

(10) The lightning flames, and the rain forth gushes swift on its track:

   below, the firstling, above, long-lasting waters are pent;

(11) Ah! if but once I could taste the flood that falls from those clouds,

   — a medicine it for a heart sore wounded, cloven with love!

    *   *   *   *   *

(12) Enough! ofttimes in a desert where the guides are astray

   — far are its borders away, its tracks like stripes on a robe —

(13) I crossed its wastes on a tall stout camel, good as a male,

   swift as a wild ass, and hard as an anvil, no mother[1] of young;

(14) I force her pace through the sand — no sound[2] hear'st thou from her lips,

   when e'en the chamæleon cowers, nigh slain by the burning glow.[3]

XXII.

This and the two following poems, placed at the end of the *Dīwān* without a word of commentary, naturally suggest doubt as to their authenticity. Of the first, all that can be said is that there is nothing in it to make it impossible that it should be by ʿAbīd, to whom it is ascribed by Ibn Rashīq in the *ʿUmdah*: if not by him, it is by a fellow-tribesman of later date. The geographical indications suit the tribe.

Vv. 1—17 contain a long and beautiful *nasīb*. Vv. 1, 2: the Arabs (like the Hebrews)[4] admired long necks in women, and v. 2 is a playful exaggeration. V. 5: the rendering is somewhat uncertain. In vv. 6—16 the journey of the departing friends is described. Vv. 8—10 tell of the *Qaṭas* or sand-grouse at the watering-place. Vv. 13—15 set forth a vigorous picture of the leader of the caravan. Vv. 18—27 give a fine outline of heroic character and conduct, the ideal which the poet attributes to his tribe. V. 26: notches in a sword are praised as evidence of use in fierce combat: *cf.* Nābighah I. 19. V. 27: *cf.* Nāb. I. 28.

Metre imitated (see the scheme prefixed to No. XIV).

(1) Gone are the comrades whose parting pained thy heart as they sped,

   and in the litters gazelles lay hidden, long in the neck;

(2) The earrings hang o'er a gulf so deep that, were one to fall,

   'twould break in pieces before it reached the ledge of the breast.

(3) Ah! will the days and the nights return again to our joy

   — the days when Salmà and we were neighbours, partners in love:

(4) When each was faithful and fain, and well content with his mate,

   nor thought of seeking another, and life was to all most sweet,

---

[1] Barren she-camels are the strongest. [2] Read ضَامِزَةٌ for ضَامِرَةٌ.

[3] Lit., "at a time when the *samūm* is blowing, and sends (even) the chamæleon (which ordinarily enjoys and basks in the heat) to take shelter."   [4] See Canticles, IV, 4.

(5) All things combined in delight — long time had hindered the day,
    which Fortune made it her aim to minish, hasten its end?

(6) My time with them was below the bend of Ramaq vale,
    and up the hill-side the litters swiftly sped on their road;

(7) The pale-hued camels that bore them glided on with their loads,
    even as ostriches fleeing, plying featherless legs.

(8) Then down they came to a water there below on their left,
    a waste and desolate spot, with clamouring sand-grouse red:[1]

(9) A noisy crowd as they rose or hopped by the water's brink,
    what time the travellers stayed to drink or send on a scout;

(10) Some, dark of hue[2], lie outworn by travel close to the pool,
    and others, dust-coloured, throng the place, too strait for their need.

(11) Al-Aṭwā rises above them as they mount to the right,
    and near they draw to the place where tents shall stand, or approach

(12) The Sand-grouse Meadows to south of the *sidrah*[3]-trees of Khiyam,
    and al-Mukhtabī: then they cross ad-Dauw, and downward they draw.

(13) Now lies a waterless waste before them, level and bare;
    and into it plunges a Leader, calm in his resolute way:

(14) His loins well girt, and his shirt upon him ragged and torn,
    rough and ungentle of speech, crisp-haired, a masterful man;

(15) He lays on each of his train the burden of desert and thirst
    — swift goers they after noon-tide, nimbly he leads the way.

(16) Day-long I followed their course, mine eye agaze in its grief,
    the eyeball swimming in tears, astrain to trace out their road.

(17) All things in peace brought together — Fate shall fling them apart!
    all life, how tender soever, prone shall lie in the dust.[4]

                    *   *   *   *   *

(18) Young men of Asad my tribe, like lions haunting the brake
    — no stint is known to their bounty, none goes poor from their hands;

(19) Fair-skinned, a smile on their face, their calmness[5] beats folly down:
    but when they burn with the flame of wrath, the Earth is afraid.

(20) Whom Pride uplifts in his fury, down they force him to bend:
    but bending falls not to them whenso they rise up in pride.

---

[1] As noted in the Arabic text, "red" is not an appropriate word for the sand-grouse: see v. 10; some other adjective must have originally stood here.

[2] The Arabs distinguish two kinds of sand-grouse, the *Jūnī*, of dark colour, and the *Kudrī*, or dust-coloured.

[3] *Sidrah*, a species of lote-tree, *Rhamnus spina-Christi*, Linn.

[4] Literally: "shall be wrapped in a shroud with spices and perfumes for burial."

[5] *Ḥilm* is a difficult word to render: it connotes a wise patience and forbearance joined with power; see Lane, *s. v.* The quality is ascribed to God in the Qur'ān.

(21) They clear away care and grief with counsel prudent and just,
> when minds are filled with distress, and ways are doubtful and dark.

(22) Their word decides all disputes: their nature knows not to change:
> their promise fails not when pledged: no crooked speech is theirs.

(23) The wretched finds in their tents a plenty freely bestowed:[1]
> most generous are they to him who wanders, waif of the Night:

(24) Bitter to meet in the battle: keepers they of their word,
> when many a covenant falls unheeded, unfulfilled.

(25) Grave are their tempers, and staid, when council gathers the tribe:
> their armour ever is ready, spears and ropes for the steeds,[2]

(26) And swords of price, in their edges notches, record of fame
> in battle, yea, and the hands in time of need quick to give.

(27) They deem not wealth will endure, nor lacking: each has its day,
> though headstrong short-sighted folk think thus in their foolishness.

XXIII.

This poem is of doubtful authenticity. The elaborate picture of a storm in vv. 1—7 contains, it is true, several words used elsewhere by ʿAbīd in a similar connexion, and this is probably the reason why the poem was attributed to him by those who recorded it; *e. g.* دُلَّج in v. 2; *cf.* XXVIII, 14, دَلَّج; تَثَّمَ id.: *cf.* ثَمَّ in VI, 7: مُكَفَّهِر in v. 3, *cf.* XXI, 9. But on the whole the picture wants the definiteness of the other passages, and it has no proper names to mark the locality as is customary; there is a heaping-together of high-sounding words which savours of over-elaboration. Some of the words used are (as not un-frequently happens with a difficult rhyme) of doubtful reading and application; see the note to vv. 6 and 7.

Then follows a curious and almost unique passage, vv. 8—16, in which the poet com-pares his dexterity in "swimming the seas of verse" to the movements of a great fish in transparent waters. This passage is old, because it was well-known to Jāḥiḍh (159—255 H), and most probably led to the choice of the word بَحَر, sea, to indicate metre in the language of prosody established by al-Khalīl (100—175 [or 190]).[3] Several of the words here also are of very doubtful meaning, and the alliteration in some of the lines (*e. g.*, v. 15) is not like the style of the ancient poetry.

Vv. 17—24 contrast the poet's care for his good name with the shameless greed ex-hibited by his competitors, some particular one of whom appears to be satirized in scathing language; on the other hand, it is possible to take the passage as of general application,

---

[1] Literally, "Mixing the destitute of them with the well-to-do."

[2] The Arabs on an expedition led their steeds by ropes alongside the camels on which they rode until the place of battle was reached, when they mounted the horses.

[3] See more on this subject in the *Zeitschrift f. Assyriologie*, XXVI, pp. 388—392, (Goldziher-Festschrift).

contrasting the honourable poet as a class with the parasite, also as a class. The situation depicted here seems to be that of town life: *cf.* v. 20 — "at rich men's gates a burden than lead more grievous", and the "gate-keeper" of v. 21; ʿAbīd was a nomad, though he may have frequented courts of great men in the settled country, beyond Bedouin Arabia, and received gifts from them. Yet see *contra* Zuhair IX, 27.

(Original metre imitated)

∪−∪∪− | ∪−∪∪− | ∪−− ‖ ∪−∪∪− | ∪−∪∪− | ∪−−

(1) I watched through the night the flashes that lit the towering
    high-piled cloud-masses filled to the full, nigh bursting:

(2) The heavily-burdened wombs of the fruitful waters,
    that spout forth rain from many a rift of blackness:

(3) The mists built up in darkness unfathomed, rain-drops
    that carve deep caverns [1] when they are cast to earth-ward.

(4) The mass grew one, compact in an even surface,
    and poured forth rain in streams from its clefts, unstinted;

(5) Like night in its gloom it swept over all the champaign,
    one blackness, or like the sea with advancing billows.

(6) It seemed, when the lightning clove it and flashed and flickered,
    as though in the smile of rain-bringing constellations

(7) One saw the white teeth flash forth in a sudden gladness
    from faces of black-eyed maidens that laugh in joyance [2].

        *   *   *   *   *

(8) Nay, ask thou the poets if they can swim as I swim
    the seas of the art of song, or can dive as I dive!

(9) My tongue, in the shaping deftly of praise, or banning, [3]
    and choosing of cunning words, is a nimbler swimmer

(10) Than is in the sea the fish that amid the billows
    swims bravely, and dives deep down to the depths of Ocean.

(11) When he darts forward, see how his sides flash brightly,
    and how when he turns the white scales shine and glitter;

---

[1] The deep holes made in the earth by the falling rain-drops are compared to the hollows (*afāḥīṣ*, sing. *ufḥūṣ*) made by the sand-grouse in which to lay its eggs.

[2] The translation offered of vv. 6 and 7 is tentative merely. "Smile", *tabassama*, is used of lightning in the clouds, and *inkalla* is also an appropriate word for lightning (L A XIV, 116[20]ff.); the *anwā'* (sing. *nau'*) are the asterisms the auroral rising of which is coincident with the season of rain. The literal rendering paraphrased above is — "(It seemed) as though the smile of the constellations therein, when it shone forth from the white (clouds) flashing with lightning, and played in them, were the smiling of white (teeth) that adorns the faces of black-eyed maidens."

[3] *Qarīḍ* is properly a laudatory ode, while the original meaning ef *qāfiyah* (pl. *qawāfī*) is a satire: see Goldziher, *Abhandlungen z. Arab. Philologie* I, 83 ff. Later Arabic uses *qarīḍ* for any form of verse other than *rajaz*, and *qāfiyah* for rhyme.

(12) And how, on the right and left, as he swims, the watching
        shoal of small fry keep close to the smooth rocks' shelter [1] —

(13) The brood of the sea — no life have they left, if only
        thou liftest them from the wave where they dart and circle.

(14) But he, if the hand goes forth in attempt to grasp him,
        he slips from beneath it, not to be caught with fingers!

(15) So swims he, advancing now and retreating smoothly, [2]
        — and black in the sea are slippery fishes ever,

(16) The sea's own colour, guarded by scaly armour
        set close as the scales on doublets of mail well woven.

              *   *   *   *   *

(17) And I — by thy life! — refraining myself from baseness,
        I shield with a generous hand the afflicted stranger;

(18) I honour my father's stock, and I guard my good name:
        I loathe to be counted one of the greedy beggars.

(19) While thou — at the doors a lick-dish, and yet a miser,
        a beggar before the great, and at home a skin-flint;

(20) Where victuals are spread more swift than an eagle swooping,
        at rich men's gates a burden than lead more grievous;

(21) The gate-keeper weeps to see thee approach — "Will no one
        rid me and the door from this unwelcome fellow"?

(22) And sooth, no wonder were it if he should meet thee
        with blows, and expel thee headlong from out the gateway.

(23) If I were to place my honour within my belly,
        what refuge were mine against the reproach of all men?

(24) Nay, were but my legs to hasten to still my hunger,
        "God smite them with palsy"! — thus would I pray, I swear it!

XXIV.

    This poem also is open to suspicion. No quotation from it has so far been traced.
It uses the rhyme-words of a very different piece, No. XXVIII, though its contents are in
no respect similar. Vv. 11—13 contain phrases plainly identical with those of Aus b. Ḥajar,

---

    [1] This rendering also is tentative, and does not pretend to be definitive; it is based on (1) the mea-
nings of مَوصَلَة as stated in L A VIII, 357⁵, and (2) the verse (13) supplied from the *Asās*, which clearly
seems to refer to *small* fishes, as opposed to the big fish described.

    [2] Rendering very uncertain.

IV, 2—4. V. 2 seems to be Qurᵃ̄nic in character. V. 4 appears to glance at a vice not prevalent among the nomad Arabs. Vv. 5—6 suggest the luxury of Persian banquets.

V. 7 turns abruptly to deeds of daring wrought in former days. Vv. 15—21 contain reflections upon death which may possibly be ancient: they do not appear to be Islamic. V. 18 makes a reference to the heathen notion (still prevalent among the Tigrē people of Abyssinia) that the souls of dead men became owls, which hooted from their graves so long as their desires (for vengeance or otherwise) remained unsatisfied. V. 19: "Branch of a *ben*-tree", غُصْنُ ٱلْبَانِ, is a frequently-used simile for youth and fresh vigour; the *ben* is a tree with a leafy crown, *Moringa pterygosperma*, grateful, like all verdure, in the Desert.

The poem contains two verses resembling other verses of 'Abīd's, viz:, 10 = XXI, 13, and 15 = XXVIII, 2; these resemblances may have led to its attribution to him.

(Metre imitated: see for scheme Nos. XIV and XXII)

(1) Nay, fellow mine, hold thy peace, and stay the tongue of reproach:
    let not reviling and evil speech be thy stock-in-trade.

(2) I swear — my witness is God, the bountiful Lord of good
    to whom He wills, and forgiving, full of mercy and grace —

(3) Mine eye looks not to the goods that are not mine with a glance
    wherein is covetousness, nor seeks to make them my own.

(4) I keep not company with one fair of face, nor desire
    converse with him unpermitted: no such thought is mine!

(5) When men recline, and their hands send round the circle in turn
    pure wine in bowls and in cups, and heads grow hot with the grape,

(6) I fear the violent man, the stubborn heart perverse,
    but shield myself from the pious and staid with nought but the hand.

* * * * *

(7) And ne'er, so long as I live, shall leave me a steed white of flank [1],
    stout-withered, fleet in his gallop, not soon yielding to thirst:

(8) Or else a filly of race, a swimmer, sprightly of mood,
    like to a strip of good cloth that flutters, held between spears. [2]

(9) And many wastes where no way-mark guides through waterless plains,
    — the pools we seek far away, dry hollows stretching for leagues,

(10) Have I sped through on a camel tall, strong, good as a male,
    as wild-ass swift, busy plier of forelegs, eager to go.

* * * * *

(Vv. 11—14 not translated).

* * * * *

---

[1] Having a white mark where the rider's heel strikes.

[2] The reference is to a temporary shelter made by stretching a cloak or cloth of *burd*, with the ropes of horses, over spears stuck in the ground. See Ṭufail, *Dīw*. I. 6—9.

(15) Nay, by thy Fortune, if I should deal too wisely with wealth,

>when I am dead, men would give, methinks, scant praise to my skill.

(16) I buy the praise of the guest by spending, lavish of hand,

>my goods, until on a day my corse shall rot in the grave:

(17) When sped my spirit, full swiftly shall the pillow be set

>beneath my head in a chamber deep, dark, ugly to see;

(18) Or may be on a high hill the owl shall hoot from my tomb,

>or may be in a low ground my grave shall look to the sky.

(19) How many a youth, fair of shape, straight, fresh as branch of the *ben*,

>of stock unsullied, of face bright, open, light-hued of skin,

(20) Have I stood by, I who loved him, yea and he loved me well,

>while there apart he was laid in the hollowed side of the grave.

(21) What are we men but as corpses strewn world-wide in the dust,

>whereso thou goest, and wind as vain as the passing breeze?

XXV.

This poem, being much quoted, has taken up a considerable variety of reading and arrangement. It is evidently a mere fragment, and as we do not know the circumstances which led to its composition, it is difficult to gather the precise sequence and import of the verses. It is addressed to ʿAmr, called Abū Karib, a prince of the house of Kindah, who according to the scholion on v. 4 was one of the sons of al-Ḥārith the king, and therefore brother to Ḥujr prince of Asad whom ʿIlbā slew. But the genealogies give only four sons to al-Ḥārith — Salamah, Shuraḥbīl, Ḥujr, and Maʿdī-karib. It seems probable that some collateral prince of the tribe is meant: *cf.* Sharāḥīl in No. XIX.

Vv. 1—3, the short *nasīb*, which has evidently lost some verses. The nightly phantom of the Beloved, a constant figure in old Arabian poetry, appears only here in the poems that remain of ʿAbīd. V. 2 *a* contains a phrase which has passed into the common stock of poetical language; *cf.* al-Ḥārith b. Ḥillizah, Mfḍt. LXII, 2. Vv. 4—12, the address to Abū Karib. V. 10 *b*: *cf.* IX, 2, and XXIX, 2, 3.

(Metre imitated: for scheme see No. XIV)

(1) The phantom glided among us while we lay in the Vale

>from Asmā's folk: but it came not pledged to visit us there.

(2) How didst thou trace out the way to men who had ridden far,

>through wastes where no water is, 'twixt plain and heaped sand-hills?

(3) Nightlong they journeyed and pushed their camels, ready and strong,

>to give the best of their speed, like fleet-foot kine of the wild.

*   *   *   *   *

(4) This message carry from me to Abū Karib and his kin —
  a word to spread through the low-land after its upland way:

(5) "O ʿAmr! no man there is goes forth at night or at dawn,
  but wends unseen in his train a Driver driving to Death![1]

(6) "And if thou seest in a vale a serpent coiled in thy road,
  pass on, and leave me to face that serpent as I may.[2]

(7) "Ay sooth! thy praise shall abound whenas I pass to my death,
  when never living I gained aught kind or good from thy hand!

(8) "In front, see, waits thee a day to which thou surely shalt come:
  escapes no dweller in towns, no wandering son of the wild.

(9) "See then the shadow of kingship which one day thou shalt leave
  — can one secure it with tent-ropes, fasten safe with pegs?

(10) "Nay, get thee gone to thine own! a man of Asad am I —
  the folk that gather for counsel in tents, lords of short-haired steeds.

(11) "I leave my enemy lying prone and paling to death,
  his raiment bloodied, as though stained through with mulberry-juice;

(12) "I pierced his body, the while our steeds with forelocks adrift
  bore down, and out from his back a cubit of spear-shaft showed."

*   *.   *   *   *

(additional verse in *Khizānah* and *Aghānī*).

(13) Good shall abide, though the time be long since kindness was done:
  wrong is the worst of all gear to store for journey's use.

XXVI.

Vv. 1—8, the *nasīb*; with v. 4 *cf.* No. V, 4—5. V. 8, ʿĀqil, a valley of which the upper
part belonged to Ghanī, and the lower to Asad, Ḍabbah, and the Banū Abān b. Dārim (of
Tamīm): see Yaq. III, 589, 17; several other places appear to have borne the name.

Vv. 9—21, a recital of the glories of Asad: 11—13, the slaying of Ḥujr and defeat
of Kindah: 14, the defeat of ʿĀmir b. Ṣaʿṣaʿah; 15, the encounter with Ghassān (*cf.* II,
19—27; VII, 1—11; XVII, 7—13; XX, 6—11). As indicated in the note to the Arabic
text, this poem is intimately related to Imraʾ al-Qais, No. LI.

(1) Is it at tent-traces whereof the trench round the tents has become thin,
  scarcely to be seen,
  and at vanisht abodes that thy tears are falling fast?

---

[1] The image is that of a driver of camels, *hādī*, who pushes them on with his voice, sometimes by
singing verses to them (*cf.* No. XXII, 13—15).

[2] This verse has given rise to an apocryphal anecdote about ʿAbīd and a serpent which will be
found in *Jamharah* p. 22.

(2) Over them the wind has drawn its trailing skirts

　　for a year, and the dark cloud full of heavy rain has swept them.

(3) Day-long I stood there (overcome), as though I had drunk

　　strong pale wine, of that which Babylon has matured.

(4) But what boots the weeping of an old man among tent-traces,

　　after that there has come upon him the white hair of old age?

(5) The place is empty of those who once dwelt there:

　　since they have gone, no hope is left there of return;

(6) And yet many times was it Sulaimà's abode —

　　she that was like a long-necked doe that had lagged behind the herd.

(7) Why dost thou not forget her by the help of a she-camel strong as a male,

　　light of colour, with a pad bleeding (through constant travel), of full growth,

(8) Emaciated by toil? The saddle upon her seems

　　as though it were set on a wild-ass with his mates, whose grazing-

　　　　　　　　　　　　　　　　　　　　　　　　ground is ᶜĀqil.

　　　　　*　　　*　　　*　　　*　　　*

(9) O thou that askest concerning our glory —

　　it seems thou hast not heard of our mighty deeds.

(10) If the tale of our Days [1] has not reached to thine ears,

　　ask, then — thou shalt be told, o asker!

(11) Ask concerning us Ḥujr and his hosts

　　— the day when his army turned their backs, fleeing in affright:

(12) The day that he came upon Saᶜd in the place of battle,

　　and Kāhil galloped after his flying horse;

(13) And they brought his herd down to drink of slender spears, [2]

　　(their heads) as though they were points of burning flame.

(14) And ask ᶜĀmir to tell how, when we met them,

　　there was uplifted over them the thirsty keen-edged sword.

(15) And the host of Ghassān — we encountered them

　　with a mighty army whose dust trailed far behind.

(16) My people are the sons of Dūdān, men of skill

　　what time War, long barren, becomes pregnant again:

(17) How many are there among them of mighty lords,

　　givers of gifts, the sayer also a doer —

(18) Men whose words are words (to pin faith upon),

　　their deeds (great) deeds, their gifts (true) bounty,

(19) Utterers of words the like of which

　　cause fruitfulness to spring from the droughty field!

---

[1] *I.e.*, battles.　　[2] A metaphor for a bloody fight: see note in Arabic text.

(20) Never did they disappoint the seeker who repaired to them,
    nor did the censurer ever hinder their generosity:

(21) Dealers of spear-thrusts on the day of battle,
    wherefrom the mightiest of champions forgets his prowess.

XXVII.

Vv. 1—10, the *nasīb*: al-Jināb is said to be a place near Faid, the centre of the settlements of ʿAbīd's sub-tribe Saʿd ibn Thaʿlabah.

Vv. 11—18, the prowess of his tribe described.

(1) Whose is the abode that has become desolate at al-Jināb,
    effaced all but a trench and traces like writing in a book?

(2) The East-wind has changed it, and the blowing of the South,
    and the North-wind that drives along the particles of dust —

(3) At eventide they visited it one after the other: — and every cloud that
                                    stayed over it,
    thundering continuously, with heavy masses compacted together.

(4) The place has become desert: once mightst thou have seen there horses
                                    trained spare, like demons,
    the offspring of al-Wajīh or Ḥallāb, [1]

(5) And (camels) brought home at evening and sent forth to pasture in the
                                    morning, and a whole tribe dwelling together,
    and tall gentle maidens, fair like statues, and sumptuous tents,

(6) And elders famed for bounty and wisdom,
    and young men, the noblest of warriors stout of neck.

(7) The well-known landmarks of it stirred in me longing,
    what time hoariness took up its abode in the house of youth.

(8) The dust-coloured gazelles have made their home there: it was
    aforetime the home of plump women, equal in age,

(9) Modest — among them one tender who took me captive
    with her dainty ways, and stirred the strings of my heart;

(10) A straight spear-shaft was she from the waist upwards:
    below her girdle her hips were round and full as a sand-hill.
    *   *   *   *   *

(11) As for us, we were all of us shaped for headship —
    who would ever equate the heads with the tails?

---

[1] Names of celebrated stallions.

(12) We defend not our wealth with the shield of our honour —
       nay, we make wealth the shield to save our honour;

(13) And we hold off our foes from us by smiting
       that cuts deep, and javelins that pierce all armour,

(14) When the horsemen [1] gird themselves in the blaze of battle,
       and the dust mounts up to above their side-locks.

(15) And with us the horsemen take shelter quickly,
       their steeds heavily laden on back and quarter,

(16) Hanging down their heads, unkempt their forelocks,
       dispersed on a raid, troop following troop,

(17) Coming hastening towards us, as if they were trained dogs
       that have heard the voice of their master calling:

(18) Light of belly, they whinny in pride as they come in,
       having captured booty after booty.

XXVIII.

A famous poem. The prelude may be compared with XIII, 5. V. 2 has the same phrase as XXIV, 15. Vv. 4, 5: "He will be sober — yes! when he is dead." V. 5: graves were dug in places where moisture kept the neighbourhood green: in a *wādī* or water-course this would be most so at a bend.

Vv. 6—15, a much-admired description of a storm, claimed as the work of ʿAbīd (against Aus b. Ḥajar) by the mention of Mount Shaṭib in v. 9, and by the resemblances to other passages of ʿAbīd dealing with storms (VI, XXI, 9, 10): v. 6 a is identical with v. 9 a of No. XXI. V. 15 anticipates the effect of the storm in starting the greenery everywhere: *cf.* Imraʾ al-Qais, *Muʿall.* 70. It is necessary to transpose v. 8 and to place it between vv. 14 and 15: probably its appearance where it is now placed is due to the frequency with which v. 7 and it are quoted together, as the most admirable verses of the poem.

(Metre imitated: for scheme see Nos. XIV and XXI)

(1) Night's rest she broke with her railing: no time that for her tongue!
       why didst thou not wait for dawn to ply thy trade of reproach?

(2) God's curse light on her! she knows full well, in spite of her blame,
       myself, not her, it concerns, my goods to waste or to keep.

(3) Youth brought us all its delight, and filled with wonder our life:
       we gave not gifts to be paid, nor bought to sell at a gain!

(4) If I drink wine, if I buy the costly juice at its price,
       the day shall come, never fear, that makes me sober again:

---

[1] Here and in v. 15 "horses" are used for both horses and riders: see p. 28, note 4.

(5) Yes, sure enough, in a grave, dug where the valley is bent,
　　and swathed in white [1] I shall lie — white like an antelope's back.

　　　　　*　　　*　　　*　　　*　　　*

(6) Ho! who will help me to watch the lightning flash through the night
　　from out a mountain of cloud that shines like whiteness of Dawn?

(7) Close down, with hardly a break, its mighty fringe sweeps the ground:
　　it seems as though he who stands could thrust it back with his hand.

(9) When first its opening rain enfolds Mount Shaṭib in mist
　　the flashes gleam like a piebald prancing steed in the fight;

(10) The roar begins at the top: then all below quakes again,
　　and straightway loosed is the flood — no more can the burthen be borne.

(11) Between the topmost and lowest parts one radiance spreads,
　　as though were stretched a great sheet, or shone a torch in the night.

(12) The thunder rolls, as if there she-camels great, of full age,
　　rough-haired, their dugs full of milk, yearned crying after their young;

(13) Hoarse-throated, moaning their cry — trembling their pendulous lips —
　　they lead their younglings to feed some stretch of plain in the sun.

(14) The South-wind blew on its van, and then the full mass behind
　　began to pour down the freight of waters pent in its womb.

(8) Before the rush of its rain high ground and low are all one,
　　and he who crouches at home as he who wades through the plain.

(15) And in the morning the meadows all were green in the light —
　　hollows where pools stood unstirred, or brooklets coursing the field.

XXIX.

　　This poem attaches itself to the story of the slaying of Ḥujr as related by Ibn al-Kalbī, who, in traditions where the Yaman and the Northern tribes come into conflict, is not to be trusted (*cf.* Introduction, p. 4). As noted in the Arabic, it is often quoted. Possibly some of the verses may be by ʿAbīd, while others have been inserted by a forger.

　　In v. 5 the extent of the area said to have been devastated by Ḥujr — the triangle between Yathrib [2] (al-Madīnah) in the South, "the Castles" — which must be the *Castella* marking the *Limes* of Roman jurisdiction, — in the North, and al-Yamāmah in the East — is far in excess of the region held by Asad, and includes the territory of many other tribes. The mention of the Resurrection in v. 11 points to an origin in Muslim times, while the word "slaves" in the same verse seems to be taken from Imraʾ al-Qais's expression عَبِيد
أَلْعَسَا in his poem LI, 3. The following is Prof. Nöldeke's observation in regard to the

---

[1] *I. e.*, his shroud: coffins are not used for burial in Arabia.
[2] The *v. l.* *Yatrab* seems impossible, as this is the name of a place in al-Yamāmah: Bakrī, 850.

piece, written quite independently of the editor's view stated above: "Ob dies Gedicht nicht von einem bitterbösen Gegner der Asad deren berühmtesten Dichter untergeschoben ist? القيامة v. 11 deutet auf einem Muslim als Verfasser."

(1) Weep, O mine eye, for Asad's sons!
  Sunk are they in anguish of heart.
(2) Once had they tents of leather red,
  vast herds of camels, and plenteous wine,
(3) And short-haired steeds of noble race,
  and spears well straightened in the clip.
(4) Give pause, O King! avoid the curse!
  stay! in thy sentence ruin falls.
(5) In every valley from Yathrib's town,
  and from the Castles to far Yamāmah,
(6) Sounds wailing of captives, or the shriek
  of fire-scathed wretch, or the death-bird's hooting. [1]
(7) Najd hast thou barred to them, and now
  in fear they dwell in low Tihāmah;
(8) Trembling the sons of Asad crouch,
  as the dove trembles o'er her eggs:
(9) A poor nest built she of two twigs
  of *nasham* [2] and of panic-grass.
(10) If thou leave them, it is thy grace;
  and if thou slay them, it is no wrong:
(11) Thou art the Lord and Master, thou,
  and they thy slaves till the Resurrection;
(12) Submissive under thy scourge are they
  as a young dun camel under the nose-ring.

XXX.

This poem, though so far only found in the modern collection made at second-hand by Abkāriyūs, has in favour of its genuineness the citation of v. 6 (with ʿAbīd's name) in LA IV, 322[7], with a reading containing a rare word [3] for which this passage is apparently the only authority. The *nasīb* (vv. 1—9) has many beauties. The didactic portion (10—28) suits well the conditions of tribal nomadic life in ʿAbīd's time; while the last part, in which

---

[1] See XXIV, 18, and remark in introduction to that poem.

[2] *Nasham*, a species of tree growing in the mountainous country, of which bows were made.

[3] Perhaps تَغَلَّدَ used of a snake may be related to the Persian غَلْطِيدَن.

Imraʾ al-Qais is contemptuously mentioned as a rival not yet dead, fixes the age of the poem, if genuine, as before 535 A. D. There are a number of expressions which coincide with Ṭarafah's *Muᶜallaqah* (the date of which falls between 554 and 569): v. 1, تَلُوحُ, *Muᶜall.* 1; *id.*, ضَرْغَد, *Muᶜall.* 79; v. 3, أُمُّ فَرْقَد, *Muᶜall.* 32; v. 4, الخَمائِل تُراعِى, *Muᶜall.* 7; *id.*, أَراك, *Muᶜall. id.*; البَرِير, v. 7, إِثْمِد, *Muᶜall.* 9; v. 8, *Muᶜall.* 8; v. 28, تَنَوَّرْ, *Muᶜall.* 104.

Either both poets drew upon a common stock of poetic images and turns of phrase, or one must have copied the other, or used his language as the established idiom of verse. V. 1: Ḍarghad is at the eastern end of the great *ḥarrah* or volcanic plateau now called the *ḥarrah* of Khaibar; it still bears the name (spelt by Doughty "Thurghrud"). V. 4, "in bosky shade": literally, "in the shade of the *arāk*, a shrub or small tree, *Salvadora persica*, and the *gharqad*, a thorny tree, *Lycium sp.*" V. 7: Arab women dust their gums with powder of antimony sulphide (*stibium*) in order to set forth the whiteness of their teeth.

The *nasīb*, 1—9, has been rendered in rhythm imitating the metre of the original (see No. VIII for the scheme). In the rest of the translation no close adherence to rhythm has been attempted.

(1) Whose are the traces of tents, outworn, in the black plain of Ḍarghad,
    that shine like the opening page of a book with its script new-limned?
(2) Of Suᶜdà [1] are they, what time she gave thee her love for thine —
    the days when, as oft as we met, the omens were fair and bright:
(3) The days when her deep black eyes beamed kind from a shape of grace
    like an antelope, perfect in race, a mother, whose fawn stands by.
(4) With it by her side she crops the herbage in early morn:
    with it, when the heat grows cruel, she shelters in bosky shade;
(5) She makes it, in all her herd, the point whereon dwells her eye,
    and over it bends her neck whenever they lie asleep.

(6) Yea, truly she fixed in my heart a pain that comes back to it
    again and again, as rankles a serpent's poisonous tooth:
(7) That morn when her face shone forth from out where the curtain hung
    — just then, methinks, had she drawn round her teeth lines of *stibium*.
(8) She smiled, and her lips disclosed white pearls set amidst the gums,
    as though they were camomile blowing on sand-mounds, moist in the sun.
(9) For Suᶜdà I yearn, how long soever the absence be:
    life-long for her love shall I thirst like the hovering bird o'er the spring.

*   *   *   *   *

(10) When thou art one that gives no heed to counsel, nor follows
    good advice, nor inclines to the voice of him who points out the right way,

---

[1] Called here Saᶜdah, but Suᶜdà in v. 9.

(11) And holds in no respect the blame of the whole tribe,

  nor defends it against its enemy both with his tongue and his arm,

(12) Nor shows clemency towards its foolish ones, nor guards it,

  nor strikes down in its defence the insolence of the threatening foe,

(13) Nor stands for it in the contest of praise, wherein is shown forth

  its superiority in the world against another who boasts himself[1] —

(14) Then art thou not, though thou cheat thyself with vain desires,

  one fit for chiefship preeminent, nor near to being a chief.

(15) By thy life! my partner fears no wantonness from me,

  and never do I desert him who gives his love to me;

(16) And I seek not the love of him who has in him little good,

  nor am I too proud to welcome the friend who would seek my side.

(17) Yea, and I quench the fire of warfare when it blazes up

  and has been kindled for nought but folly throughout the land;

(18) And, on the contrary, I light it up against the wrong-doer who warms himself thereat,

  when his intelligence holds him not back from active mischief.

(19) And I pardon my client[2] little offences that cause me anger,

  and, on the other hand, I use him with roughness so long as he recognizes not the claims (?) of my stock.

(20) And whoso among them thinks to do me a wrong, in sooth

  he is like one attempting to shatter the topmost peaks of Ṣindid.

(21) Yea, and I am a man whose counsel brings life to him who prizes it,

  nor am I one who is a novice in great affairs.

(22) When thou placest trust in a treacherous man

  verily thou restest it on the worst of all supports.

(23) I have found the treacherous man like the camel-plague, dreaded by all his folk,

  and never have I considered the trouble of my client as other than my own.

(24) Manifest not love towards a man before thou hast put him to proof:

  after thou hast tried a man thoroughly, blame him or give him praise.

(25) Follow not the counsel of him whose ways thou hast not tracked out:

  but the counsel of him whose wisdom is known — take that for thy guide!

(26) Be not slothful in admitting the claims of kinship on thee

  in order that thou mayst hoard wealth: but be slow to join thyself to strangers.

---

[1] This verse may also be taken as referring to contests for superiority *within* the tribe: one who would be a leader must know how to assert himself.

[2] Client: *i. e.* protected stranger, *jār*, for which *maulà* is here the equivalent.

(27) And if thou hast gotten a gain of glory and wealth of fame,
   repeat thine exploit, and add to that which thou hast gained.
(28) Stock thyself well with provision of this world's goods, for, sure,
   in every case such store is the best to make light the way.

*   *   *   *   *

(29) Poor Imra᾿ al-Qais longs for my death — and if I die
   verily that is a road in which I journey not alone.
(30) Mayhap he that longs for my destruction and sudden death
   in his folly and cowardice — shall himself be the first to die.
(31) The life of him who hopes for my passing hurts me not,
   nor does the death of him who has died before me prolong my life.
(32) The days of a man are numbered to him, and through them all
   the snares of Death lurk by the warrior as he travels perilous ways.
(33) His Doom shall spring upon him at its appointed time,
   and his way is towards that meeting, though he make no tryst therefor.
(34) And he who dies not to-day, yet surely his fate it is
   to-morrow to be ensnared in the nooses of Death's doom.
(35) Say thou to him who seeks things different from things gone by:
   "Be ready to meet the like: for lo! it is here at hand."
(36) We men who live and the dead of us are but as travellers twain:
   — one starts at night, and one packs his gear for to-morrow's morn.

FRAGMENTS.

1.

(1) Dost thou threaten my kin, while thou hast left Ḥujr
   with the raven digging his beak into the black of his eyes?

*   *   *   *   *

(2) They refused to be servants of kings, and never were ruled by any:
   When they were called on for help in war, they responded gladly.

*   *   *   *   *

(3) And if thou [1] hadst overtaken ῾Ilbā son of Qais,
   thou wouldst have been content with safe return instead of booty.

---

[1] *I. e.*, Imra᾿ al-Qais: the verse has reference to that poet's threats of vengeance: see note in Arabic text.

2.

So he[1] fails at one time, and brings gain at another,
 and joins the abused, reviled one to the skilful, clever (or, causes
 him to overtake him).

3.

This piece, like most others in the work of Abū Ḥātim where it is found, is a mani-
fest fabrication, destitute of poetic merit. V. 5. The "kingdom of Naṣr" is the royal house
of al-Ḥīrah: Sindād was one of its palaces overlooking the Euphrates, or a canal leading
from it. V. 6. Dhu-l-Qarnain: see Qurʾān XVIII, 82 ff.: Alexander the Great in the cha-
racter of Zeus-Ammon. V. 8 is taken straight from the Qurʾān.

(1) And there shall surely come after me generations unnumbered,
 that shall pasture the precipices of Aikah and Ladūd;
(2) And the sun shall rise, and the night shall eclipse it,
 and the Pleiades shall circle, bringing evil fortune and good:
(3) So long shall it be said to one who wears out the last flicker of his life:
 "O thou of long life's space — hast thou seen ʿAbīd?"
(4) Two hundred years in full and something over —
 twenty have I lived, brought to great age and praised;
(5) I reached back to the beginning of the kingdom of Naṣr at my birth
 and the building of Sindād: and long since has it fallen into ruin;
(6) And I followed after Dhu-l-Qarnain until he escaped me
 by galloping hard; and I almost saw David.
(7) After this no kind of life remains to be sought for
 save life for ever: but thou canst not attain to that.
(8) And surely both this and that (my life and yours) shall pass away —
 everything except God, and His Face, the worshipped.

4.

(1) Has Wudaik left its place since I dwelt there,
 and shifted to where delivers the torrent of Dhāt al-Masājid?
 * * * * *
(2) I have perished: Time has swept me away; the stars of the Wain[2]
 and the bright stars of the Lesser Bear have become my equals in age.

---

[1] His horse.
[2] The constellations *Ursa Major* and *Minor*.

5.

This is a patchwork of verses taken from XXV, 5 and XXIV, 21. V. 3 completely spoils the sense of the verse from which it is taken.

(1) O Ḥārith! never went forth a folk at night or at break of day
    but there travelled in their track a Driver driving to Death.
(2) O Ḥārith! never there rose the Sun and never it set,
    but the fated Dooms of men drew nearer the appointed day.
(3) What are we but as the winds — thou passest them lightly by
    below in the dust — and bodies like millions gone to decay?

6.

(1) O comrade! seest thou the lightning? I watch it through the night,
    as the darkness closes in, there in the shining clouds;
(2) It stayed over a pool below Dhū Raid,
    and scattered its rain over [the sides of] Dhu-l-ʿIthyar:
(3) Then [moved on to] ʿAns and al-ʿUnāb and the sides
    of ʿArdah, and the hollow of Dhu-l-ʾAjfur.

7.

This verse is interesting as a link between ʿAbīd and the comparison of lightning, in v. 72 of the *Muʿallaqah* of Imraʾ al-Qais, to the lamp lit by a Christian devotee (*rāhib*) as a guide to travellers by night in the Desert. It may be a verse of the poem to which No. 6 belongs.

It was (or, is) like the lamp of a hermit speaking Syriac,
    or the featherless arrow being shuffled by the hand of a player (at
                                                         Maisir) by night.

8.

(1) We gave to drink to Imraʾ al-Qais son of Ḥujr son of Ḥārith
    cups that choked him, till he became accustomed to defeat.
(2) There delighted him the drinking of luxurious wine and the voice of a
                                                         sweet singer,
    and the vengeance which he was seeking for Ḥujr became too hard
                                                         for him:
(3) And that — by my life! — was an easier way to take [1]
    for him than facing sharp swords, and the points of tawny spears.

---

[1] Or, drinking place to resort to (for watering camels).

9.

(1) And when griefs attend thee, [know that] some of them are debts to be paid at a future time, and some, debts to be paid at once.

             *   *   *   *   *

(2) And verily assemblies are made resplendent by thy presence: thou art not one whose beard covers nearly the whole of his face, nor one overwhelmed with fat:

             *   *   *   *   *

(3) But like the sharpened sword of India, brandished by a warrior who comes forth as the champion of his side.

10.

This exercise of ingenuity has of course no pretensions to be ancient. A similar contest in verse, said to have taken place between Imraʾ al-Qais and at-Tauʾam of Yashkur, will be found in the former's *Dīwān*, ed. Ahlwardt, No. XXII (*cf.* LA VIII, 98): other specimens of the style occur in later poetry. Qurʾānic wording is visible in v. 4 and v. 16, and modernity in v. 13.

ʿABĪD.

(1) What is that living thing that is dead, but revives life by means of its dead: toothless itself, what is that which causes to sprout teeth and fangs?

IMRAʾ AL-QAIS.

(2) That is the barley-corn: watered when it puts forth its ears, after long time it begets heaps of grain on the threshing-floors.

ʿABĪD.

(3) What are they that are black, and white, and yet both of one name: man cannot reach up to them to touch them with his hand?

IMRAʾ AL-QAIS.

(4) These are the clouds: when the Merciful sends them forth on their way, He waters with them the dry places of the deserts of earth.

ʿABĪD.

(5) What are they whose caravans move all freighted with hopes and fears: far do they wend to their goal, then return to their place again?

IMRAʾ AL-QAIS.

(6) These are the Stars, when their places of rising shift through the year: I have likened them to fire-brands breaking the blackness of night.

ʿABĪD.

(7) What are they that traverse a land — no fellow have they on their way: swiftly do they speed along, and return not the way they went?

IMRAʾ AL-QAIS.

(8) These are the Winds: what time their violent gusts sweep by,
         their skirts are sufficient, broom-like, to whirl the dust away.

ʿABĪD.

(9) What are the afflictions that openly bring to men grief and pain:
         more terrible they than a host on march with resistless might?

IMRAʾ AL-QAIS.

(10) These are the Dooms: none they spare among the tribes of earth;
         the fools they o'erthrow, and they leave not the wisest where they stand.

ʿABĪD.

(11) What are those ones that outstrip the swiftest of birds with ease:
         they will not be humble and mild, though thou bridle their mouths
                                                                       with steel?

IMRAʾ AL-QAIS.

(12) These are the steeds of pure race, on which men swim through the air:
         their constant comrades are they in days of strife and alarm.

ʿABĪD.

(13) What are those that with one bound leap over valley and hill
         before day dawns — yet they go no step on their way by night?

IMRAʾ AL-QAIS.

(14) These are the Hopes that possess man's heart and make him a king
         beneath the heaven, and yet they lift not at all his head.

ʿABĪD.

(15) What are the Judges that judge without or hearing or sight,
         or tongue of men to give sentence, words or eloquence fit?

IMRAʾ AL-QAIS.

(16) These are the Balances set by God Most High among men,
         the Lord of creatures, to weigh men's deeds whether evil or good.

11.

One of the pieces of verse inserted in the picturesque legend of the death of ʿAbīd
at the hands of King al-Mundhir of al-Ḥīrah.

(1) The King of evil intent on his evil Day gave me choice
         of cases to choose, each of which flashed death full sure to mine eyes:
(2) As once of old was the choice offered the Children of ʿĀd —
         yea, clouds wherein no delight or joy to the choosers was hid:

(3) Clouds fraught with tempest of wind, which, once let loose on a land,
    leave all therein like the night that comes before thirst quenched.[1]

12.

A beautiful fragment of a *nasīb*, in the shortened form of the *Basīt* metre called *Munsariḥ*: $-\smile\lor-|\smile\lor-|\lor-|\lor\lor-\|-\smile\lor-|\smile\lor-|\lor-|\lor\lor-$. The rendering imitates the rhythm of the original. Verse 2 is ascribed to Abū Duʾād of Iyād in B Qut. 123[2].

(1) No thunder came from the cloud nor lightning flash:
    it rose and spread, giving hope to us of the rain.
(2) The rain-drops fell from it one by one in a string —
    where water finds but a crevice, through it will fare.
(3) We passed the night, she and I, stayed there on her rugs;
    till spread the dawning, her eyen closed not their lids,
(4) For that 'twas said — 'After morning march we away,
    and all the folk gathered here shall scatter abroad'.

13.

Know this surely — truth it is, no empty word —
    only he who shares thy case can help thy need.

14.

Whether this fragment is rightly included in the collection is uncertain: "'Abdallāh ibn al-ʾAbraṣ" may be some other person.

(1) I become gentle when the creditor is gentle, and I put him off when he is
    insistent, until he that slays me will have to take the debt on himself;
(2) Evening and morning I postpone the date of payment, that he may be weary
    of me, and be satisfied with getting part of the debt without reaping any profit.

15.

(Metre of version like that of No. XI)

(1) Steel thy soul whensoe'er a trial approaches:
    Patience teaches the best of skill to the skilful.
(2) Be not straitened in heart before all thy troubles:
    they will clear, never fear, without much scheming.
(3) Often men are perplext and plunged in distresses:
    sudden comes a relief like loosing of shackles!

---

[1] A phrase of doubtful meaning: evidently here used for the torment of thirst.

16.

(1) Bear to Judhām and to Lakhm whenas thou passest their way
    — and sooth, to all men a good it is to hear of the truth —
(2) This word, that ye are our brothers (so stands it in God's book)
    when portioned out were the spirits and the kinships of men.

17.

And night-long the gazelles[1] of Rumāḥ about him were lamenting
    with bared heads, neither sleeping nor letting others sleep.

_____

[1] *I. e.* his women. *Cf.* No. VIII, 14.

THE *DĪWĀN* OF ʿĀMIR IBN AT-TUFAIL, OF ʿĀMIR IBN SAʿSAʿAH.

INTRODUCTION.

THE TRIBE of ʿĀmir ibn Ṣaʿṣaʿah, to which our poet belonged, was the most powerful member of the large group called Hawāzin, descended, according to the genealogists, from Muḍar (son of Nizār, son of Maʿadd, son of ʿAdnān) through Qais ʿAilān. ʿĀmir appears, during the time with which our history deals, to have held pretty strongly together, and its various sub-tribes to have acted as a unity in contentions with its neighbours. Its principal subdivisions were Hilāl [1], Numair, Suwāʾah, and the families said to be descended from Rabīʿah by his wife Majd, a woman of Quraish: from this marriage were sprung the powerful sections called Kilāb and Kaʿb; to the latter belong ʿUqail, Jaʿdah, Qushair, and other stocks with which we are not here concerned: to the former several houses, of which the most notable were Jaʿfar and Abū Bakr. Our poet was a member of the house of Jaʿfar, in which, during his life-time and that of the previous generation, the chiefship of the whole group called ʿĀmir ibn Ṣaʿṣaʿah appears, with a brief interregnum, to have resided. The following table shows his immediate genealogy: —

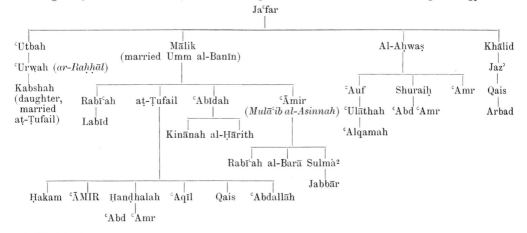

---

[1] This tribe, in the 11th and 12th centuries A. D., became famous for what has been described as the second Arab invasion of North Africa, which has furnished the matter for a popular romance.

[2] Also vocalized *Salmà*.

memorable battle of Shiʿb Jabalah al-Aḥwaṣ was the chief of the whole tribe of ʿĀmir. He was succeeded in this dignity by his nephew ʿĀmir Abū Barā, called "the Player with Lances", *Mulāʿib al-Asinnah*, and he by his nephew ʿĀmir son of aṭ-Ṭufail, our poet. Of the persons shewn in ʿĀmir's family tree the great majority died in battle. His uncle Rabīʿah, father of the poet Labīd, was slain at Dhū ʿAlaq, fighting the tribe of Asad[1]: his uncle ʿAbīdah was killed at Dhū Najab, a year after Shiʿb Jabalah, in conflict with the Banū Yarbūʿ of Tamīm[2]; his father aṭ-Ṭufail fell at Hirjāb[3]. Of his brothers, Qais and Ḥakam lost their lives on the Day of ar-Raqam[4], while Ḥanḍhalah fell at Hismà[5], and ʿAbdallāh was killed at al-Bathāʾah[6]; his cousins Kinānah and al-Ḥārith, sons of ʿAbīdah, were also slain at ar-Raqam; ʿAbd ʿAmr, son of Ḥanḍhalah, his nephew, died at Badwah[7]. The members of this illustrious family were fully conscious of its eminence; Labīd's first poem, the *Rajaz* verses with which he discomfited ar-Rabīʿ b. Ziyād of ʿAbs at the court of an-Nuʿmān king of al-Ḥīrah, claims the highest place for his stock[8]:

نَحْنُ بَنُو أُمِّ الْبَنِينَ ٱلْأَرْبَعَة

وَنَحْنُ خَيْرُ عَامِرِ بْنِ صَعْصَعَة

ٱلْمُطْعِمُونَ الْجَفْنَةَ الْمُدَعْدَعَة

وَالضَّارِبُونَ الْهَامَ تَحْتَ الْخَيْضَعَة

"We are the Sons of the Mother of the Four:[9]
We are the best of ʿĀmir son of Ṣaʿṣaʿah;
We feast our guests on platters ever full,
And smite the heads beneath the battle-din."

Although the various sections of the tribe of ʿĀmir appear generally to have acted together against external enemies, they were not always without variance among themselves. The traditions tell of quarrels between the house of Jaʿfar and that of Abū Bakr, the two principal branches of Kilāb. At the battle of Shiʿb Jabalah the tribe of ʿAbs were under the protection of the former, and fought with them in the great fight; but the position soon after became strained between ʿAbs and Jaʿfar, and the former withdrew from the protection of the latter, and put themselves under that of Abū Bakr. Not long afterwards, Jaʿfar appear to have seceded from the brotherhood of ʿĀmir in consequence of a quarrel with the Abū Bakr, and to have allied themselves with the Banu-l-Ḥārith b. Kaʿb of the Yaman: they were absent[10] from the tribe on the Day of

---

[1] See Labīd, Dīw. (Khālidī) p. 75.   [2] See Naq. 587[19].   [3] See Dīw. No. XXXII.
[4] See Mfḍt, pp. 30—34, and further on; also No. XXIX, vv. 5 and 6.   [5] See Dīw. No. XVI A, 6.
[6] See BAthīr, 485, foot.   [7] See Frag. 4.   [8] Labīd, Dīw. No. XXXIII 3—6; Agh. XIV, 95; L A IX, 427[18].
[9] Or "We are the four sons of Umm al-Banīn"; Umm al-Banīn, "Mother of the Sons", is a proper name, though no doubt originally implying a title of honour; but when Labīd spoke her four sons were no longer alive, and the second generation were more than four.   [10] Naq. 244[4]; Mfḍt. 366, top.

an-Nisār, fought not long after Shiʿb Jabalah, when Asad and the Ribāb inflicted on ʿĀmir a disastrous defeat, and took much plunder and many women captives. On another occasion, apparently, a feud with Abū Bakr led to a second exodus of Jaʿfar to the protection of the Banu-l-Ḥārith; the story of this is told in the *Naqāʾiḍ*, pp. 532—35. The dispute was eventually composed upon equitable terms, and the return of the Jaʿfarīs to the parent stock arranged, and ʿĀmir b. aṭ-Ṭufail [1] was a party to the composition. In the *Dīwān* there is one piece, No. IV, v. 2 ff, which speaks of Abū Bakr in very hostile language.

The tribe of ʿĀmir held very extensive lands in central Arabia. To the North and North-west were the great group of Ghaṭafān, consisting of ʿAbs, Dhubyān, Anmār, and Ashjaʿ; next to them eastwards were the Asad, then a portion of the Ṭayyiʾ, and then a corner of the Tamīm, belonging chiefly to the branch of Dārim. The country between the modern ʿUnaizah (ʿAneyza) and ar-Rass must be nearly the meeting-place of ʿĀmir's land with that of the last three stocks. To the East were Ḥanīfah, in al-Yamāmah [2] or Central Najd; to the West the kindred tribe of Sulaim, cantoned along the pilgrimage (formerly the main commercial) road from Mecca northwards, and occupying a wide *Ḥarrah* lying North and South which appears to correspond with the "*Ḥarrah* of Kisshub" [3] in Doughty's map. On the South of Sulaim began the *Ḥaram*, or sacred territory of Mecca, with which the lands of ʿĀmir were in direct contact. An enclave in their territory was formed by the oasis of aṭ-Ṭāʾif, a very fertile region held by the tribe of Thaqīf, and richly cultivated. The ʿĀmir pastures swept round this oasis, aud adjoined on the south the region held by the Yamanite tribes of al-Ḥārith b. Kaʿb, Khathʿam, and Hamdān. In this region — Tabālah [4] and Bīshah — the settlements of ʿĀmir were partly intermixed with those of the Yamanites, collectively called Madhḥij.

Mr. Doughty, in his journey from ʿUnaizah (ʿAneyza) to aṭ-Ṭāʾif, marched right through the northern portion of the territory of ʿĀmir, which is now occupied by the ʿUtaibah (ʿAteyba) Bedouins. Many of the names of places mentioned in his travels are the same as those of the sixth and seventh century A. D. The following extracts describe the features of the country (in its summer aspect):

"We are here [at ar-Rass] [5] on the border of the Nefūd; and bye and bye the plain is harsh gravel under our feet: we reenter that granitic and basaltic middle region of Arabia, which lasts from the mountains of Shammar [6] to Mecca" (Vol. II, p. 459).

---

[1] Naq. 535⁵.

[2] This name, on modern maps, bears a much more restricted signification than in the old geography: see Bakrī 5¹⁹⁻²⁰, 8⁵ff, etc..

[3] Perhaps the *Ḥarrah* of Hilāl may also be included in the modern *Ḥarrat al-Kisshub*.

[4] Tabālah was celebrated for its rich pastures: see Labīd, *Muʿall.* 75.

[5] Ar-Rass is a place in the Wādī ar-Rummah, the great water-course of Central Arabia which delivers into the Shaṭṭ al-ʿArab south of Baṣrah: it has cornfields and palm-groves. The name and the site are ancient; see Zuhair, *Muʿall.* 13.   [6] Formerly the mountains of Ṭayyiʾ.

"From this *mogyil* [*maqīl*, place of midday rest] we journeyed forth through a plain wilderness full of basaltic and grey-red granite bergs, such as we have seen in the Ḥarb and Shammar *dīras* westwards . . . . We journeyed on the morrow with the same high country about us, beset with bergs of basaltic traps and granite. The steppe rises continually from al-Qaṣīm to aṭ-Ṭāʾif" (p. 460).

Several villages were passed, and then — "On the morrow we journeyed through the same high steppe, full of sharp rocks, bergs and *jibāl*, of trap and granite. At noon we felt no more the fiery heat of yesterday, and I read in the aneroid that we were come to an altitude of nearly five thousand feet, where the bright summer air was light and refreshing. . . . . At our right was a considerable mountain of granite, Tokhfa [1]. Our *mogyil* [*maqīl*] was by the watering el-Ghrôl [2], in a hollow ground amidst trap mountains: that soil is green with growth of harsh desert bushes; and here are two-fathom *golbân* [3] of the ancients, well steyned; the water is sweet and light" (p. 461) [4].

"This high wilderness is the best wild pasture land that I have seen in Arabia: the bushes are few, but it is 'a white country', overgrown with the desert-grass, *nussy* [5] . . . . Everywhere we see some growth of acacias [6], signs doubtless of ground-water not far under" (p. 462).

[Mr. Doughty thought that this country lay "in the border of the monsoon or tropical rains, which fall heavily in the early autumn, and commonly last five or six weeks at aṭ-Ṭāʾif".]

"We rode in the afternoon through the like plain desert, full of standing hay, but most desolate: the basalt rocks now exceed the granites. And already two or three desert plants appeared, which were new to my eyes, — the modest blossoms of another climate" (p. 463).

"We removed an hour before dawn; and the light showed a landscape more open before us, with many acacia trees . . . . This land is full of *golbân* and water-pits of the Aarāb . . . The country is full of cattle-paths" (p. 464).

"ʿAfîf [7], where we rested, is a hollow ground like el-Ghrôl, encompassed by low basaltic mountains. . . . . Hereabout grows great plenty of that tall joint-grass (*thurrm*) [8] which we have seen upon the Syrian *Ḥajj* road" (p. 467).

---

[1] The ancient Ṭikhfah, site of a battle between the Ḍibāb and Jaʿfar b. Kilāb.

[2] Anciently Ghaul: see Labīd, *Muʿall.* 1. Scene of a battle with Ḥanīfah: *vide* Dīw. No. VII.

[3] Wells: *qulbān*, plural of *qalīb*.

[4] Doughty continues: "A day eastward from hence is a mountain, *Gabbily*; where rocks are said to be hewn in strange manner". If *g* could represent ج, it would be tempting to see here the site of the famous battle of Shiʿb Jabalah; but in Doughty's orthography *g* commonly represents ق.

[5] *Naṣī*, نَصى, also called طُرَيفَة.

[6] The *samurah*, *salam*, or *ṭalḥ*, Acacia gummifera (so called by the older botanists, but now differentiated into several species: it is uncertain to which the indigenous Arabian kinds belong).

[7] Perhaps العُقَيْف of Yāqut III 690.

[8] This word has not been identified in its literary form. It might be either *thaghām* ثَغام, or *ḍurm*,

"We set forward from ʿAfīf before the new day. When the sun came up, we had left the low mountain train of Aṭula [1] on our left hand, and the wilderness in advance appeared more open: it is overgrown with hay; and yet.... they have better pastures! The mountains are now few: instead of bergs and peaks, we see but rocks".

"Our *mogyil* was between the mountains ʿAjjilla and *eth-Thʿal*; the site is called *Shebrûm*, a bottom ground with acacia-trees, and where grows great plenty of a low prickly herb with purple blossoms of the same name" [2] (p. 468).

The caravan now entered upon a region "plain without bergs, of mixed earth and good pasture" (p. 469), and began to approach "That great vulcanic country, the *Ḥarrat el-Kisshub*. We pass wide-lying miry grounds, encrusted with *subbakha* [3]; and white as it were with hoarfrost: at other times we rode over black plutonic gravel.... In this desert landscape, of one height and aspect, are many (*sammar*) [4] acacia trees: but the most were sere, and I saw none grown to timber" (p. 470).

They proceeded between the edge of the *Ḥarrah* and the plain, where were various watering-places; but most of them giving bad water. They came to "*Hazzeym es-Seyd*, a grove of acacia-trees, very beautiful in the empty *khála*! and here are many cattle-pits of a fathom and a half to the water, which rises of the rain".... "The salt flats, reaching back to the vulcanic coast, lay always before us (p. 473)". Another water was "*el-Moy*, or *el-Moy Sheʾab*, or *Ameah Hakràn*, of many wells, a principal *maurid* [5] of the Aarâb" (*id.*).

Thus the journey proceeded, until the caravan (bound for Mecca) reached the edge of the plateau of Najd, where Mr. Doughty parted from them.

The extracts given above show that the country of ʿĀmir had good pasture, and was not deficient in water-supplies; grass and acacia timber were plentiful. Probably in the South, towards Tabālah, the conditions were even better. Mountains and volcanic rocks were numerous, and the surface was considerably diversified, with some variety of vegetation, even in the height of summer.

According to the most generally received account, ʿĀmir b. aṭ-Ṭufail [6] was born on the day of the Battle of Shiʿb Jabalah, the important victory won by his tribe over the combined forces of Tamīm (Dārim), Asad and Dhubyān; according to another tradition [1], he was then a

---

ضَرَم, according to Mr. Doughty's system of writing Arabic words; but neither is a grass. Perhaps نَوْمان (L A 14, 344[6]) may be connected with it: it is a plant fed upon by camels and sheep.

[1] Possibly a mis-writing for Aṭwaʾ (أَطْواع); see Yāqūt I, 312[2-3].

[2] *Shubrum* (شبرم) in L A XV, 210[10], is described as "a kind of *shīḥ* (wormwood); others say it is one of the *ʿiḍḍ* (the class of small thorny bushes): it has thorns and a red flower." The latter agrees with Mr. Doughty. In Aṣm. *Kit. an-Nabāt wa-sh-Shajar* Prof. Haffner identifies it with *Euphorbia pityusa*, Leclerc.

[3] Salt efflorescence, سَبَخَة.

[4] *Samur.*   [5] Watering-place.   [6] So Naq. 659[11ff]; Agh. X, 37[12ff].   [1] Naq. 229[14], 790[12].

babe in his mother's arms. His mother was Kabshah, daughter of ʿUrwah, called *ar-Raḥḥāl* because he was in the habit of escorting trading caravans from the King of al-Ḥīrah to the fair of ʿUkāḍh. The date of the battle is variously stated. Ṭabarī (I, 966[13]), following Abū ʿUbaidah[1], says that it was fought in the year of the Prophet's birth, the "year of the Elephant", generally reckoned as 570 A. D. On the other hand, it is put by others (probably following Ibn al-Kalbī) seventeen years earlier[2]. This second date is evidently deduced from the statement that ʿĀmir b. aṭ-Ṭufail, when he visited the Prophet in the year of the latter's death, was eighty years old. But various considerations make this extremely improbable. One is that ʿĀmir's uncle, ʿĀmir b. Mālik Abū Barā, "the Player with Lances", was still alive and in authority in A. H. 4, the year of the affair of Biʾr Maʿūnah[3]; he was one of the captains of ʿĀmir at the battle of Jabalah, and can scarcely have been less than 20 or 25 years old at the time; if his nephew was eighty when he died, Abū Barā must have been near 100 at the time of Biʾr Maʿūnah, which is unlikely. Again, the poet Labīd, who was ʿĀmir's first cousin, is said to have been 9 or 10 years old at the date of Shiʿb Jabalah[4]; if the battle took place eighty years before ʿĀmir's death, Labīd would then have been 89 or 90 when he embraced Islām. But he lived many years afterwards, and is related to have died at the beginning of the caliphate of Muʿāwiyah, A. H. 40[5]: he would then have been 120, an impossible age. Moreover, the story of Labīd's first appearance as a poet puts this event during the reign of an-Nuʿmān Abū Qābūs, the last king of al-Ḥīrah, who did not come to the throne till 580 A. D.[6]. Even if the visit of the Jaʿfarīs, with Labīd among them, to an-Nuʿmān's court happened in the first year of his reign, if the battle of Shiʿb Jabalah was fought in 553, the poet, if nine years old in that year, could hardly have been described as a boy (*ghulām*)[7] when he appeared before the king. If, however, Jabalah was fought in 570, he may have been a lad of 19 or 20 in the year of an-Nuʿmān's accession[8]. Lastly, ʿĀmir's activity as a warrior up to the end of his life certainly does not suggest that he was then an old man of 80, and is much more consistent with the statement that he was, like the Prophet, about 62 or 63 when he died.

During the life of ʿĀmir b. aṭ-Ṭufail an almost continuous condition of warfare appears to have existed between his tribe and the groups of Ghaṭafān to the North and Northwest, and of Madhḥij in the South. ʿAbs, which had been dependent upon ʿĀmir b. Ṣaʿṣaʿah at Jabalah, had long since made peace with Dhubyān, and was now an enemy like the rest of Ghaṭafān. Most of the poems of the *Dīwān* refer to this state of hostility. No. II, if it is rightly ascribed to our poet, depicts warfare with the Yaman and Tamīm

---

[1] Naq. 790[12].   [2] Naq. 676[2-3]. Agh. X 46[24] has nineteen, but نسع is probably a misprint for سبع.

[3] See below.   [4] Naq. 668[10, 11]: Agh X, 42[8].

[5] Agh. XIV, 97[21ff.] (tradition makes him 145 when he died!)   [6] Nöldeke, *Sasaniden*, 347.

[7] Agh. XIV, 95[5].   [8] See Agh. XIV, 98[23], where Ṭarafah is described as غلام ابن ثمان عشرة سنة.

as the main direction of the tribal activities, though it mentions also other tribes, Shaibān, v. 10, Asad, v. 11, Ḥanīfah, v. 13, and even distant ʿAbd al-Qais in Baḥrain, v. 17, as enemies. It is somewhat difficult to locate the relations of ʿĀmir with Tamīm (or rather with the sept of Dārim) set forth in vv. 28—29. It is clear that the military reputation of ʿĀmir b. Ṣaʿṣaʿah stood high in the time of the Prophet. The most formidable combination which Muḥammad ever had to face was that of Hawāzin at Ḥunain (A. H. 8), which nearly resulted in a disaster to his cause: but in this the Kilāb and Kaʿb divisions of ʿĀmir took no part; had they been present, the history of Islam might perhaps have been very different.

It would serve no useful purpose to attempt a record or a chronology of all the fights in which ʿĀmir b. aṭ-Ṭufail took part as the champion of his tribe. In the geographical index it will be seen how many of such combats are mentioned in the *Dīwān*. Arabian warfare has changed little in its characteristics through the course of centuries. We may safely conclude that the majority of these "Days" were mere skirmishes, that the number of slain and wounded was small, and that the language of the poems greatly exaggerates the importance of the affairs. This discount, as Mr. Doughty points out, has to be applied to all records of fighting in Arabia [1]. One striking incident in the history is the fact that the Banū Jaʿfar, when they fell out with their cousins the Abū Bakr b. Kilāb, repaired to the Banu-l-Ḥārith b. Kaʿb of Najrān [2] for protection; yet the Banu-l-Ḥārith were, one would conclude from the poems, their most deadly and hereditary enemies. Another is the fact that in the celebrated contest for preëminence in valour and prowess between ʿĀmir b. aṭ-Ṭufail and his cousin ʿAlqamah b. ʿUlāthah, the decision, after being refused successively by Abū Sufyān and Abū Jahl [3] of the Quraish, ʿUyainah b. Ḥiṣn of Fazārah, Ghailān b. Salamah of Thaqīf, and Ḥarmalah b. al-Ashʿar of Murrah, was eventually placed in the hands of Harim b. Quṭbah b. Sinān of Fazārah, a branch of Dhubyān concerning which language of the most violent hatred is used in ʿĀmir's odes. These two facts show that, apart from the exaggeration of numbers engaged or slain attaching to stories of conflict, we must make large deductions from the accounts given of the feelings of the combatants towards one another.

The ʿĀmir, as neighbours of the Holy Territory, were specially concerned in the celebrations connected with the annual feast at Mecca. Some sections of them belonged to the tribes called *Ḥums* (plural of *aḥmas*), who imposed on themselves special austerities when celebrating the Pilgrimage. Although not actually dwelling within the *Ḥaram*, like the other *Ḥums*, they acquired this character because Rabīʿah, son of ʿĀmir b. Ṣaʿṣaʿah, married Majd, daughter of Taim b. Murrah of Quraish [4], and became by her the father

---

[1] *Arabia Deserta*, Vol. I, 130.

[2] The position of Najrān indicated in modern maps seems to be much too far to the South, or else in ancient times the name included a much larger area to the North (Bīshah, Tabālah, etc.).

[3] Properly Abu-l-Ḥakam.   [4] See *Mufaḍḍalīyāt*, p. 259[11—20]

of Kilāb and Kaʿb, who thus counted among the *Ḥums* in virtue of their mother. Labīd,
a man naturally sensitive to religious influences, may have been helped by this practice
of austerities; his cousin ʿĀmir b. aṭ-Ṭufail shows no signs of a religious disposition [1].
But of course all the neighbouring tribes observed the truce of the three sacred months,
and visited the fair at ʿUkāḍh, which must have given opportunities for the meeting
in peaceful intercourse of those who were at other times divided by blood-feuds. One
of the first of the contests in which ʿĀmir b. aṭ-Ṭufail was engaged was the Sacrilegious
War, caused by a breach of the sacred peace. This occurred, it is said, when Muḥammad
was a youth [2] and when ʿĀmir was consequently about the same age. The occasion was
the murder, by al-Barrāḍ of the tribe of Kinānah, then in alliance with the Quraish,
of ʿUrwah ar-Raḥḥāl of Jaʿfar during the trucial season. ʿUrwah, who was the father
of ʿĀmir's mother Kabshah, had made himself responsible for the safe conduct of a
caravan of merchandise from an-Nuʿman king of al-Ḥīrah to the fair of ʿUkāḍh. The news
of his death was brought first to Quraish and Kinānah, and they immediately withdrew
from the fair. When it reached the men of ʿĀmir, they followed the retreating Quraish,
and came up with them at Nakhlah. In the battle there [3] ʿĀmir were commanded by
our poet's uncle Abū Barā, and Quraish by ʿAbdallah b. Judʿān, Hishām b. al-Mughīrah,
and Ḥarb b. Umayyah. In this fight Quraish were worsted, but succeeded in getting
within the Sacred Territory (*Ḥaram*), where they found an asylum which their enemies
feared to violate. The war was not terminated by this battle, but lasted for three years
more; the sections of Kilāb and Kaʿb, however, took no further part in it with their
brethren of ʿĀmir [4].

The next important affair in which ʿĀmir b. aṭ-Ṭufail was engaged appears to have
been the fight of ar-Raqam. Of this there is a long account, due to Ibn al-Kalbī, in al-
Anbārī's Commentary to No. V of the *Mufaḍḍalīyāt* [5]. This story appears to mix up two
different battles, that of ar-Raqam and that of Sāḥūq, which Abū ʿUbaidah treats of
separately [6]. According to the last-named traditionist, ʿĀmir b. aṭ-Ṭufail was then a youth,
not yet a leader in the tribe. The ʿĀmirites made a raid upon the Banū Murrah b.
ʿAuf and the Banū Fazārah of Ghaṭafān, and set upon them in the valley of ar-Raqam.
The horses of the ʿĀmirites were tired, and they were unable to get away with their
spoil before the main body of the Fazārites (under ʿUyainah b. Ḥiṣn) and Murrites (under
Sinān b. Abī Ḥārithah) were upon them. The men of ʿĀmir, not knowing the country,
took the way up the valley, hoping to emerge at the other end and escape: but the

---

[1] See Fragments 8 and 16.   [2] The age is differently stated, the lowest being 14 and the highest 20.
[3] The Day of ʿUkāḍh is referred to in Dīw. No. XXVII, 6.   [4] Agh. XIX, 77⁶.
[5] Pp. 30—34 of my edition.
[6] See BAthīr, *Kāmil* I 482—3. Sāḥūq is mentioned in Salamah's poem, v. 16. Perhaps there is
an omission in the commentary; for the end of the narrative (p. 34 l. 2—3) speaks of *two* battles
كان هذان اليومان اشدّ يومين مرّا على بنى عامر قطّ, although our text tells only of one.

valley was a *cul de sac*, and on returning they found their way blocked and the enemy awaiting them at the entrance. According to the story, both in Abū ʿUbaidah and Ibn al-Kalbī, ʿĀmir b. aṭ-Ṭufail had turned aside to visit the tent of a woman of Fazārah, Asmā, daughter of Qudāmah b. Sukain b. Khadīj, of Saʿd b. ʿAdī, whose acquaintance he had perhaps made at ʿUkāḍh [1]: she had just been married to Shabath b. Ḥauq b. Qais, of the same tribe. There he is said to have stayed till the ʿĀmirites, discovering their error, resolved to make a dash for escape through the opposing forces. As they passed by Asmā's tent, he rejoined them in the desperate effort for freedom. He and some of the band escaped; but he lost his horse [2], which broke down with him, and he had to be taken up by his cousin Jabbār behind him on his horse al-Aḥwà, after ʿĀmir's brother ʿAqīl, who was fleeing on his horse al-Wuḥaif, had refused to take him. Fazārah took 84 prisoners of ʿĀmir on that day, and delivered them one by one to a family in Ashjaʿ for safe keeping till the fight was over. The Ashjaʿī, Ḥulais b. ʿAbdallāh b. Duhmān, however, killed them all in revenge for a slaughter which ʿĀmir had previously perpetrated on his kin. In this fight were slain Kinānah and al-Ḥārith, sons of ʿAbīdah ʿĀmir's uncle, and Qais son of aṭ-Ṭufail his brother. Abū ʿUbaidah fixes the date of the battle [3] by saying that it occurred when an-Nābighah, the poet of Dhubyān, had fled from the court of an-Nuʿmān of al-Ḥīrah, and taken refuge with the kings of Ghassān. Nos. VIII and XXIX of our collection refer to this engagement. The men of Fazārah resented the choice by ʿĀmir of Asmā as the mistress to be celebrated in the preludes to his odes, and desired an-Nābighah to satirize him. Of this the *Dīwān* shows traces in Nos. XVI, XVI A, and XXIII.

Upon the disaster at ar-Raqam followed, according to Abū ʿUbaidah, the Day of Sāḥūq, when the Banū Dhubyān raided the Banū ʿĀmir and carried off a large number of camels. The ʿĀmirites followed, and a fierce fight ensued, in which the Banū ʿĀmir were defeated and put to flight. ʿĀmir's brother Ḥakam, who fled and with his companions lost his way in the desert, after suffering severely from thirst, hanged himself for fear of falling into the hands of his enemies and being put to torture. Reference to this is made by Salamah b. al-Khurshub of Anmār in *Mufaḍḍalīyāt* V, and by ʿUrwah b. al-Ward of ʿAbs (*Dīwān* No. X).

According to one story, embodied in Ibn al-Kalbī's account in the commentary [4] to the *Mufaḍḍalīyāt*, ʿĀmir was taken prisoner by Fazārah either at ar-Raqam or Sāḥūq, and his life was saved by Jabbār b. Mālik b. Ḥimār and his nephew Khidhām b. Zaid of that tribe, who took him under their protection when ʿUyainah, their chief, wished to kill him. To this refers the fragment forming No. XXVI of the *Dīwān*, in which ʿĀmir praises his protectors. This incident is involved in some doubt. The poem of Salamah

---

[1] See Frag. 16. [2] Al-Kalbī says the horse's name was al-Kalb; but see Frag. 13. ·
[3] BAthīr 482, foot. [4] P. 33.

b. al-Khurshub, to which the narrative is appended, distinctly represents ʿĀmir as having escaped by reason of the speed of his horse (vv. 6 ff.); and Salamah mentions as the scene of the engagement (v. 13) "the East of al-Maraurāt" (where Ḥakam is said to have hanged himself) and Sāḥūq (v. 16), where there is said to have been a great slaughter of the Banū ʿĀmir [1]. The fragment comes from a suspected source: not only is it put forward by Ibn al-Kalbī [2], whose good faith is doubtful: it is also said to have been copied by him from "the Book of Ḥammād ar-Rāwiyah", a man who is charged with much falsification of ancient poetry.

Another mishap was suffered by the Banū ʿĀmir at a place called al-Bathāʾah [3], where they had raided the Banū ʿAbs, but were repulsed and pursued. Here ʿĀmir is said to have hamstrung his horse al-Ward or al-Maznūq [4], when it broke down with him in his flight. Here also were killed ʿĀmir's cousin al-Barā, son of ʿĀmir b. Mālik the chief of the tribe, and ʿAbdallāh b. aṭ-Ṭufail ʿĀmir's brother.

To judge by the *Dīwān*, there must have been many other engagements between ʿĀmir and the tribes of Ghaṭafān, with results more favourable to the former than those here recorded; but our sources do not give the details of them.

On the side of al-Yaman also it is clear that ʿĀmir and Madhḥij were often in conflict; but we have the particulars of only one important fight, that of Faif ar-Rīḥ [5]. Here the whole of Madhḥij, under the command of al-Ḥusain b. Yazīd al-Ḥārithī, are said to have assembled together, including Nahd (to which several champions belonged), the Banu-l-Ḥārith, Juʿfī, Zubaid, Saʿd al-ʿAshīrah, Murād, and Ṣudāʾ, besides several divisions of Khathʿam, and to have attacked ʿĀmir b. Ṣaʿṣaʿah, then dispersed at their summer pastures in Faif ar-Rīḥ [6]. ʿĀmir was also represented by nearly all its divisions, including Kilāb, Numair, Jaʿdah, and al-Bakkā. Hilāl was not present, but ʿĀmir b. aṭ-Ṭufail is said to have bought from that tribe forty lances [7] and distributed them among his followers. The battle is said to have lasted three days, but little is told of it except the fights between particular champions. ʿĀmir b. aṭ-Ṭufail was the leader of ʿĀmir b. Ṣaʿṣaʿah, and is related himself to have received twenty spear-wounds between the throat and the navel. On the side of ʿĀmir was fighting one Mus-hir, son of Yazīd, son of ʿAbd-Yaghūth chief of the Bal-Ḥārith. Mus-hir had committed some crime in his own tribe which compelled him to leave it, and had claimed the protection of ʿĀmir. During

---

[1] The commy. to ʿUrwah X, like that to Salamah's poem, treats the Days of ar-Raqam and al-Maraurāt (or Sāḥūq) as the same.   [2] See *ante*, p. 4.

[3] See Bakrī 139²⁻⁵. This is the name misprinted in BAthīr 484 النبأة, and in the *ʿIqd* النتنة. See Frag. 13 in our *Dīwān*.

[4] This must be incorrect, as al-Maznūq carried him long afterwards, at the Battle of Faif ar-Rīḥ (Dīw. No. XI, 2).

[5] Narratives in Naq. 469 ff., BAthīr I, 474, and ʿIqd III, 102.

[6] The name means "The level waterless desert where the wind blows strongly."

[7] This very moderate number justifies us in suspecting exaggeration in the account of the battle.

the battle ʿĀmir b. aṭ-Ṭufail, while encouraging his men to distinguish themselves in fight, was examining their spear-heads to see if they bore blood-marks, when Mus-hir came up and held out his lance, calling on ʿĀmir to inspect it. ʿĀmir bent down to do so, when Mus-hir thrust forward the spear, and with it gashed ʿĀmir's cheek and pierced his eye. Having done him this injury, Mus-hir left his spear behind him and galloped away, rejoining his own tribe, with which he hoped to make his peace by the treacherous attack on ʿĀmir. The fight was inconclusive, each party withdrawing without obtaining booty: "but the greatest endurance and valour in battle were shown by the Banū ʿĀmir". [1]

To this battle refer Nos. X and XI of the *Dīwān*. We may estimate approximately its date by the facts that it was subsequent to the Day of al-Mushaqqar (XI, 6), and that Mus-hir was the grand-son of ʿAbd-Yaghūth, who led the tribes of Madhḥij at the fight of the Second Kulāb, and who must have been dead when the command fell to al-Ḥusain. Caussin de Perceval [2], with some probability, fixes al-Mushaqqar in 611 A. D., and Kulāb the year after; so that Faif ar-Rīḥ may have been fought in 613 or 614.

The *Dīwān* contains no reference, except in the Introduction prefixed to the poems, to the celebrated contest for preëminence in glory between ʿĀmir b. aṭ-Ṭufail and his cousin ʿAlqamah b. ʿUlāthah. The story will be found in the *Aghānī*, XV, 52—59, and is admirably translated in Caussin de Perceval's *Essai*, II, 564—69. The principals did not themselves compose the poems which play so great a part in such contests, but appeared with poets in attendance who recited compositions in their praise. On the side of ʿĀmir b. aṭ-Ṭufail was his cousin Labīd, and later on, more important still, Maimūn al-Aʿsha of Bakr b. Wāʾil; on the side of ʿAlqamah, Marwān b. Surāqah b. ʿAuf, Quḥāfah b. ʿAuf, as-Sandarī b. Yazīd b. Shuraiḥ (all of them his cousins), and Jarwal, called al-Ḥuṭaiʾah. As already mentioned, the matter in dispute was referred to Harim b. Quṭbah b. Sinān of Fazārah, who prudently decided that the two parties were equal in merit, "like the two knees of a camel, which touch the earth together when it kneels." Harim in due time embraced Islām, and was praised by the Caliph ʿUmar for his discretion in refusing to disclose which of the litigants he really preferred. ʿAlqamah also became a Muslim, but when is uncertain: he had succeeded to the chiefship of ʿĀmir b. Ṣaʿṣaʿah after the death of ʿĀmir b. aṭ-Ṭufail. On the Prophet's death he apostatized, like the leaders of most other nomad tribes. Khālid b. al-Walīd was sent against him by Abū Bakr, whereupon ʿAlqamah hastened again to declare his adherence to Islām and made his peace with the Caliph [3]. Another version is that after confessing Islām he apostatized

---

[1] Naq 472[13]. In the ʿIqd an account less favourable to ʿĀmir is given, though all three narratives profess to be drawn from Abū ʿUbaidah. Probably the Muslim conception of ʿĀmir as the "enemy of God" (see further on) has prejudiced the reporter. The *Dīwān*, however, appears to admit the loss of some spoil by ʿĀmir: see No. X, 3, and No. XI, 12.

[2] *Essai*, II, pp. 576, 579.   [3] Agh. XV, 57.

during the Prophet's life, and went away to Syria after the conquest of aṭ-Ṭāʾif. When Muḥammad died, he returned hastily to his tribe, and remained hesitating what to do. Eventually he decided again to accept Islām, and was taken into favour by Abū Bakr[1]. There is a story told of the poet al-Ḥuṭaiʾah in the *Aghānī*[2] which implies that ʿUmar made ʿAlqamah governor of the Ḥaurān, and that he died while holding that office. All these indications point to the contest being late in ʿĀmir's life, though before the death of his uncle ʿĀmir Abū Barā, who regarded it with great disfavour.

We now come to two events of which there is no mention in the *Dīwān*, but which, inasmuch as they connect ʿĀmir b. aṭ-Ṭufail with the Prophet, bring him into the general history of Islām and have, most probably, influenced tradition as to the occurrences of his life, and perhaps even the judgment of critics on his poetry.

The first of these is the affair of Biʾr Maʿūnah, where, in the month of Ṣafar of the 4th year of the Hijrah, four months after the battle of Uḥud, the cause of the Prophet sustained a severe disaster[3]. According to the received story, as related by Ibn Isḥāq, Abū Barā ʿĀmir b. Mālik, the old chief of ʿĀmir b. Ṣaʿṣaʿah, visited the Prophet in Madīnah with a present of valuable horses and camels. Muḥammad refused to receive a gift from an unbeliever, and invited Abū Barā to accept Islām. He did not do so, but did not reject it, and suggested that the Prophet should send some of his companions to Najd to preach the new faith to the people, adding that he hoped that the mission would largely be successful. Muḥammad said that he feared the risk the missioners would run from the people of Najd. Abū Barā promised to be their protector, and again urged the Prophet to send them. Thereupon Muḥammad despatched a party of forty[4] men, the most eminent of the believers, under the command of al-Mundhir b. ʿAmr, one of the Banū Sāʿidah of Madīnah, called "He that hastens to death," *al-Muʿniq liyamūt*. They had a guide of Sulaim, who took them to a water belonging to that tribe called Biʾr Maʿūnah, at the eastern edge of the *ḥarrah* of Sulaim, on the boundary of ʿĀmir, where they encamped. Thence they sent forward Ḥarām b. Milḥām as messenger to ʿĀmir b. aṭ-Ṭufail with a letter from the Prophet. ʿĀmir did not even read the letter, but fell upon the messenger and slew him. Thereupon he called on his tribe, the Banū ʿĀmir, to attack the little band of missionaries. They refused, alleging that to do so would be to violate the safe-conduct given by Abū Barā. ʿĀmir then sought the aid of the sub-tribes of Sulaim called ʿUṣayyah, Riʿl, and Dhakwān, who joined him in his attack on the band of Muslims. They found them encamped about their camel-saddles, having sent out their beasts to graze, and surrounded them. A fight ensued in which

---

[1] Ṭabarī I, 1899—1900.   [2] XV, 59, top.

[3] The authorities are BHishām 648 ff; BSaʿd, II, Part 1, 36 ff; Ṭabarī, I, 1441 ff; Wāqidī, *Maghāzī*, 337 ff; Yaʿqūbī, *Historiae*, II, 75.

[4] So BIsḥāq in BHishām and Ṭabarī 1442[18]; Wāqidī 337, seventy, and so BSaʿd 36[21]; Yaʿqūbī 75, foot, twenty-nine.

the Prophet's followers fought bravely until they were all slain except one man, Kaʿb b. Zaid, who, though grievously wounded, survived and recovered, to fall next year (A. H. 5) fighting at the Battle of the Trench. Two of their number, ʿAmr b. Umayyah aḍ-Ḍamrī and al-Mundhir b. Muḥammad b. ʿUqbah, [1] a man of Madīnah, were absent at the time, tending the camels of the party. From a distance they saw the birds of prey circling over the scene of the fight, and went towards the encampment, where they found their companions butchered, and the horsemen of their enemies standing by. ʿAmr b. Umayyah was for escaping, that he might carry news of the fate of the party to the Prophet: but the man of Madīnah, saying that he had no desire to live longer after the death of his friends, attacked the Sulamīs, and fought till he was slain. ʿAmr was taken prisoner and brought before ʿĀmir b. aṭ-Ṭufail, who, ascertaining that he belonged to Muḍar [2], released him, after cutting off his fore-lock, saying that he did so because of a vow his mother had made to release a captive [3]. ʿAmr then made his way towards Madīnah, and at Qanāt, a valley near the town, met two men of the Banū Kilāb of ʿĀmir, whose tribe he ascertained by questioning them. He waited until they were asleep, and then killed them both, in reprisal for his slain companions. These men, however, had been visiting the Prophet, and had received a safe-conduct from him, which ʿAmr did not know. When, therefore, he reached Madīnah and told the tale of the death of his fellows and the slaying of the two ʿĀmirites, Muḥammad decided that the price of blood must be paid for the latter to Abū Barā.

The Prophet was greatly distressed at the fate of his missioners — more so than at the death of any others who fell in his wars. He continued for fifteen days (others say forty) [4] after the morning prayer to invoke the curse of God upon their slayers, as well as upon the tribes of Liḥyān, ʿAḍal, and Qārah (branches of Hudhail [5]), who had put to death another small party of emissaries sent to them at ar-Rajīʿ, the news of which event reached him on the same day as that of Biʾr Maʿūnah. This continued until the verse Qur. III 123 [6] was sent down. Afterwards a message from the slain Muslims was delivered by Gabriel to the Prophet as a verse of the Qurʾān [7] in the following words: "Tell our people that we have met our Lord, and He is satisfied with us and we are satisfied with Him." This verse was, after it had for some time been recited as part

---

[1] So BHishām 649; Wāqidī calls the second man al-Ḥārith b. aṣ-Ṣimmah.

[2] And not to al-Yaman like the people of Madīnah.

[3] BHish. 650 قال عامر بـن الطفيل : قـد كان . BSaʿd 37^14 اعْتَقَهُ عن رَقَبَةٍ زَعَم انّها كانَتْ على أُمِّه على أُمّى نَسَمَة فَأَنْتَ حُرّ عنها.

[4] Wāqidī 341 (BSaʿd 38 foot says 30).

[5] ʿAḍal and Qārah are also said to be descended from Khuzaimah (father of Asad) through al-Haun (BDuraid 110).

[6] "Thou hast nought to do with the matter: it is for God to bring them to repentance or to punish them." [7] Wāqidī 341, BSaʿd 38.

of the Qurʾān [1], abrogated, and in its place Qur. III 163 was delivered: "By no means think ye that those who have been slain in the cause of God are dead: nay, rather, they are alive with their Lord, where they are nourished and are joyful."

This narrative has aroused considerable doubt among those who have examined it [2]. In the first place, it occurs in a record of warlike expeditions, *Maghāzī* [3], not of peaceful missions. It will be observed from the opening of the narrative in BHishām 648 that the expedition to Biʾr Maᶜūnah was sent in Ṣafar, just after the three months of peace, Dhu-l-Qaᶜdah, Dhu-l-Ḥijjah, and Muḥarram, had expired; this would seem to indicate that it was connected with warfare. For a preaching mission so large a number as 40 would scarcely be required, still less 70. We have, moreover, an account of the affair which makes no mention at all of ᶜĀmir b. aṭ-Ṭufail. In BSaᶜd, p. 385 ff., there is a short statement resting on the authority of Anas b. Mālik, which asserts that the sub-tribes Riᶜl, Dhakwān and ᶜUṣayyah [4] of Sulaim came to the Prophet and asked his help against the other sections of that group: that the Prophet gave them according to their request a body of seventy men of the *Ansār* called the *Qurrā* (because they collected wood and water for the Prophet during the day-time, and spent the night in prayer and reciting the Qurʾān): that when this band arrived at Biʾr Maᶜūnah, the sections of Sulaim named acted treacherously by them, and attacked and slew them: that when the news reached the Prophet, he prayed for a whole month in the morning prayers that the curse of God might rest upon Riᶜl, Dhakwān, and ᶜUṣayyah; and that the Prophet also recited as a verse of the Qurʾān the words already quoted, which were afterwards abrogated or forgotten (رُفِعَ أَوْ نُسِّىَ). With this agrees the statement made by Wāqidī that the guide of the party was a man of Sulaim. It should also be remembered that in the previous year, A. H. 3 [5], the Prophet had already attacked the Banū Sulaim, and that, owing to the dispersion of the tribe to its watering-places, he had not inflicted on it any serious loss. According to the genealogists, Sulaim was the brother of Hawāzin, but not more nearly connected with ᶜĀmir b. Ṣaᶜṣaᶜah.

As regards the guarantee of protection said to have been given by Abū Barā, the traditions also exhibit serious discrepancies. It is not probable that Abū Barā himself visited Muḥammad. The account in *Aghānī* XV [6] states that he was ill with an internal tumour [7], and that he sent his nephew Labīd to the Prophet with a present of camels

---

[1] Ṭabarī 1447 12.

[2] See Muir, *Life of Mahomet*, Vol. III, p. 208, note; Caetani, *Annali*, I, p. 580, note 3; Lammens, *Encyclopædia of Islam*, s. v. Biʾr Maᶜūna.

[3] Wāqidī, BSaᶜd, Yaᶜqūbī.

[4] The record adds Liḥyān, but this was a section of Hudhail, a quite different stock; the name seems to have crept in because this tribe was mentioned in the Prophet's curse: see above.

[5] In Jumādà I: see BSaᶜd 24; BHishām 544; Wāqidī 195. The expedition was led by Muḥammad in person, and consisted of 300 men.

[6] P. 137, foot. [7] دُبَيْلَة.

to ask his aid in effecting a cure. The Prophet refused the present, at the same time saying that if he could have accepted any gift from a polytheist, he would have taken one from Abū Barā; he sent, however, by the hand of Labīd a lump of clay which he had moistened with his spittle, and told him to dissolve it in water and give it to Abū Barā to drink. Labīd, it is added, stayed some time in Madīnah, reading the Qurʾān, of which he copied out the *Sūrat ar-Raḥmān* [1], and took it home with him. He gave the clay as directed to Abū Barā, who dissolved and drank it and recovered [2].

Finally, had ʿĀmir b. aṭ-Ṭufail been primarily responsible for the treachery which led to the slaughter of the mission, it is very strange that his name should not have been embodied in the formal curse which, for many days after hearing of the disaster, the Prophet recited in the morning prayers at Madīnah.

The strongest evidence that ʿĀmir b. aṭ-Ṭufail was concerned in the slaughter at Biʾr Maʿūnah, and that Abū Barā had given some sort of guarantee for the safety of the party, is contained in the fragments of contemporary poetry relating to the event which have been preserved in the *dīwān* of Ḥassān b. Thābit and elsewhere. In the *dīwān* [3] there are three pieces, No. XL, an elegy of 3 verses on Nāfiʾ b. Budail, who fell in the fight, No. XCIV, an elegy on the slain of Maʿūnah, mentioning the leader al-Mundhir by the name given to him by the Prophet, *al-Muʿniq liyamūt* [4], and No. CXI, addressed to Rabīʿah, son of Abū Barā. In the first of these (which is also attributed to ʿAbdallāh b. Rawāḥah) there is no mention of ʿĀmir; nor in the second, for the third verse, which speaks of treachery, would be equally or more applicable to the sections of Sulaim who are said to have invited the party [5]. In the third, (of which the verses are given in a different order in BHishām 650 and Ṭabari 1445) the poet says (following BHishām):

"Ye sons of Umm al-Banīn [6], are ye not stirred — and ye are among the foremost of the people of Najd —

"By the flouting by ʿĀmir of Abū Barā, that he might break his covenant? And a mistake is not the same thing as a crime deliberately committed.

"Carry this message to Rabīʿah, the man of enterprise — 'What hast thou accomplished in the passage of time since I saw thee?

"Thy father is the old warrior Abū Barā, and thy mother's brother the glorious Ḥakam son of Saʿd."

In the commentary to this piece [7] it is explained that the poem was addressed to

---

[1] Sūrah LV.   [2] For the rest of this story see below.

[3] Ed. Hirschfeld, London 1910.   [4] See v. 4 أَعْنَقَ فِى مَنِيَّتِه.

[5] Observe that the mission is spoken of in v. 2 by a warlike denomination, خَيْلُ الرَّسُولِ.

[6] See genealogy of the house of Jaʿfar, *ante* p. 73.

[7] Hirschfeld, Scholia and Annotations, p. 81.

Rabīʿah, urging him to take steps to punish ʿĀmir b. aṭ-Ṭufail for his treachery. When Rabīʿah heard the verses, he went to the Prophet and said: "O Apostle of God! Will a sword-blow or a spear-thrust that I inflict upon ʿĀmir wash away from my father the guilt of this act of treachery?" "Yes, God knows," said the Prophet. Rabīʿah then returned home and struck ʿĀmir a blow which did not wound him in a vital part. His fellow-tribesmen sprang upon him and seized him, and called out to ʿĀmir — "Retaliate upon him with the like!" ʿĀmir rescued Rabīʿah from their hands, and then dug a pit and said: "Bear witness, all of you, that I have put away his sin in this pit." Then he filled in the earth again, and let Rabīʿah go.

In the commentary to No. XL of Ḥassān's *Dīwān* [1] an elegy on al-Mundhir b. ʿAmr, the captain of the expedition, by his sister is cited, which is more explicit; vv. 4—8:

"Weep for the warriors who stood their ground, the noble in nature, the noble in stock!

"There joined together against them the wolves of the Ḥijāz, the sons of Buhthah and the sons of Jaʿfar;

"Their leader was ʿĀmir, the miserable wretch, the traitor, the man of violent, horrible deeds.

"If they had had but warning of that combination against them, the hosts of the adulterous one-eyed wretch [2],

"Their foes would have found them lions on the morning of battle: not strange to them was such a case of old!"

There is no possibility of misunderstanding this piece; but it rather gives the impression of being too conclusive, and is scarcely consistent with the next two extracts. Buhthah is the name of a subdivision of Sulaim. "Wolves of the Ḥijāz" is a strange name to give to the Banū Jaʿfar, who were a tribe inhabiting Najd, not the Ḥijāz.

Kaʿb b. Mālik the Anṣārī, one of the Prophet's poets, in a passage quoted by BHishām [3], says to the Banū Jaʿfar:

"Ye left your protected stranger [4] to the mercy of the Banū Sulaim, in cowardice and shame, for fear of an attack by them.

"If he had taken hold of a bond uniting him to Nufail [5], he would (in so doing) have stretched a cord which would have held securely;

"Or the Quraṭā [5] — they would not have deserted him: of old they have been faithful when ye have broken faith."

This last passage appears to be irreconcilable with the account of the affair given by Ibn Isḥāq. Another poem by Kaʿb b. Mālik is quoted by Ṭabarī [6], which seems, like

---

[1] Hirschfeld *ut sup.* pp. 57—8.

[2] *I. e.* ʿĀmir b. aṭ-Ṭufail, who lost one eye at Faif ar-Rīḥ.

[3] P. 652.   [4] Read *jārakum.*

[5] Nufail and al-Quraṭā are said to be the names of tribes or houses in Hawāzin.   [6] I, pp. 1445—6.

the piece just cited, to blame the Banū Jaʿfar, *including ʿĀmir b. aṭ-Ṭufail*, not for falling on the party of Muslims, but for not protecting them against Sulaim, and for not answering their call for help when they were beset by their enemies.

Lastly, BHishām [1] quotes a pair of verses by a man of Sulaim, Anas b. ʿAbbās, exulting over the slaying of Nāfiʿ b. Budail (one of the Muslims who fell) as an act of vengeance for the death of Ṭuʿaimah b. ʿAdī, his nephew, whom he calls Abū Zabbān.

The conclusion of the whole matter would seem to be that the mission to Biʾr Maʿūnah was a warlike expedition, sent by the Prophet to help one section of the Banū Sulaim against another, and that it was not a body of preachers sent for the conversion of the Banū ʿĀmir; at the same time the Prophet had reason to think, from his relations with Abū Barā, that the Banū ʿĀmir were friendly to him, and might be expected to help. In this he was disappointed; the Sulamīs proved to be treacherous, and ʿĀmir b. aṭ-Ṭufail perhaps joined them in the attack on the Prophet's party. At the same time it is unlikely that in so doing he violated an express pledge of protection given by Abū Barā; this seems probable from the fact that the Prophet paid the blood-wit for the two ʿĀmirites whom ʿAmr b. Umayyah slew when they were returning from Madīnah to their tribe.

Abū Barā did not live long after the affair of Biʾr Maʿūnah. There is a legend which says that grief for the treachery practised by ʿĀmir b. aṭ-Ṭufail on this occasion caused him to commit suicide by drinking strong wine till he died [2].

The second of the two events mentioned above is the visit of ʿĀmir b. aṭ-Ṭufail to the Prophet, probably in the year 9 [3], or perhaps 10 of the Hijrah. According to the account in BHishām (p. 939 ff.), Ṭabarī (I 1745—7), and the *Aghānī* (XV 137) [4], all of which draw the tale from the same source and tell it in practically the same words, a deputation of the Banū ʿĀmir b. Ṣaʿṣaʿah, headed by ʿĀmir b. aṭ-Ṭufail, Arbad b. Qais (half-brother to Labīd), and Jabbār b. Salmà, came to the Prophet. ʿĀmir, it is said, intended treachery. When urged by his tribe to accept Islām, he had answered — "I have sworn that I will not cease until the Arabs all become subject to me. Shall I then myself follow after this champion of the Quraish?" He arranged with Arbad that he, ʿĀmir, should occupy Muḥammad's attention by conversation, and that Arbad should then fall upon him and despatch him with his sword. When ʿĀmir reached the Prophet's dwelling he said — "O Muḥammad! grant me a private interview" [5]. "No," answered Mu-

---

[1] P. 651. [2] See Agh. XXI, 100[19]; BQut., 224[3] ff; Naq. p. 199, note.

[3] This is BHisham's date: Ṭabarī gives 10; others speak of the year as that in which the Prophet died (Naq. 676[4]). Caetani (*Annali dell' Islam*, Vol. II Pt. 2 p. 90) puts the visit in A. H. 8 (Jumāda II) but this appears to be doubtful; see below.

[4] Other versions are in BSaʿd (Wellhausen *Sk. u. Vorarb.* IV) § 96; Mubarrad, *Kāmil* 725[12ff]; Maidānī (Freyt.) II, 172. There is much discrepancy here.

[5] This is the only suitable translation of خالِنْنِى (not خالَّنِى): see Tab. 1746, note *d*, and glossary.

ḥammad, "until thou profess faith in the unity of God." The conversation went on, ʿĀmir expecting Arbad to carry out his instructions and attack the Prophet: but Arbad did nothing. At last, after again asking in vain for a private interview, ʿĀmir said to Muḥammad — "By God! I will fill the land against thee with horses and men." As he departed, the Prophet cried — "O God! be thou my helper against ʿĀmir b. aṭ-Ṭufail!" ʿĀmir, as he went away, said to Arbad: "Woe to thee, Arbad! Where was what I commanded thee to do? By God! there was not a man on the face of the earth whom I used to fear more than thee: but now I swear that I will never fear thee again.' "Prithee," said Arbad, "be not hasty against me. By God! whenever I attempted to do what thou badest me, thou camest between me and the man, so that I saw thee only. Should I then have smitten thee with my sword?" So they returned to their own land. And while they were journeying, God sent upon ʿĀmir a tumour in his neck, from which he died in the tent of a woman of Salūl; and as he was dying he said — "O ye sons of ʿĀmir! a tumour like the tumour of a young camel, and a death in the tent of a woman of Salūl!" [1] His companions buried him there, and passed on to their homes. When asked how they had fared at Madīnah, Arbad said: "It was nought! He called upon us to worship a Thing — would that it were here before me now, that I might shoot it with this arrow and slay it!" A day or two after this speech he went forth with a camel for sale, when God sent upon him and his beast a flash of lightning, which consumed them both.

This is the story of Ibn Isḥāq. But there is another version of the interview between ʿĀmir b. aṭ-Ṭufail and the Prophet [2], which makes no mention of his being accompanied by Arbad, and says nothing about a plot to assassinate Muḥammad. ʿĀmir, it is said, was received in a friendly way by the Prophet, who set a cushion for him to lean on, and invited him to accept Islām. ʿĀmir replied that he would do so on condition that he was given dominion over the nomads, while Muḥammad ruled over the towns and villages. The Prophet refused: whereupon ʿĀmir rose in anger and departed, saying — "Verily I will fill the land against thee with short-haired horses and youthful warriors"! On his way home ʿĀmir was attacked, as already related, by the bubonic plague, and died in the tent of a woman of Salūl.

There is also a quite different story of Arbad's death [3], which makes it happen in A. H. 4, after the return of Labīd from his mission to the Prophet on behalf of Abū Barā. As already stated [4], Labīd while at Madīnah became acquainted with the Prophet's teaching, and is said to have brought home with him a copy of the 55th Chapter of the Qurʾān. Arbad met him and said: "Brother, tell me about this man: for there is no one who has visited him whose word in regard to him I trust more fully than I

---

[1] The tribe of Salūl was held in contempt by the rest of ʿĀmir: see Dīw. No. XXV, transl., preamble.
[2] Agh. XV 138, lower half.
[3] Agh XV 138, upper half.   [4] See above, p. 87.

do thine." "Brother," said Labīd, "never did I see his like;" and he began to speak of his sincerity, his piety, and the beauty of his speech. "Hast thou anything with thee of his sayings?" "Yes," he answered, and he drew out the Chapter of "The Merciful," and read it to Arbad. When he had finished, Arbad said — "Would that I could meet ar-Raḥmān ('the Merciful') in this wilderness! Curses upon me if I smote him not with my sword!" A cloud gathered above the twain, and they went to seek for their camels. As Arbad reached his, a thunderbolt from heaven fell upon him and slew him.

Neither of these stories commands our confidence. But we have a piece of evidence, in the large number of elegies composed by Labīd on his half-brother Arbad, to whom he was passionately attached, which is conclusive as regards the fact that the latter did die by lightning [1], and that Labīd at the time had not accepted Islam [2]. It is quite improbable that Labīd, already a mind disposed to piety, would have lamented Arbad so deeply, and in so many beautiful poems, if the latter had really been a party to a treacherous attack on the Prophet, or spoken the blasphemy imputed to him; and the number of these poems indicates that they covered a considerable space of time, so that it is more probable that Arbad died about the time of Labīd's first visit, on Abū Barā's behalf, to Muḥammad, than that he died some years later, on returning from ʿĀmir's visit in A. H. 9 or 10. It is certain that Labīd, if not then already a Muslim, was disposed to accept the new Faith, and did so very soon afterwards. [3] It is significant that we have no marthiyah by him on the death of ʿĀmir b. aṭ-Ṭufail.

On the whole, therefore, it seems probable that we may dismiss as quite without foundation the story of ʿĀmir's project of assassinating the Prophet. That he used truculent language to him is possible; but we cannot, of course, place any confidence in the conflicting accounts of what actually passed at the interview. It is likely that he died soon after his return; but whether he really passed away among the Salūl, as his reported last words (which have become a proverb) would indicate, seems uncertain. The story told in Agh. XV, 139, and repeated in the preface to our Dīwān (p. 91¹ ff.), that the Banū ʿĀmir set up standing stones (anṣāb) enclosing a space of a square mile round his grave, within which the ground was a ḥimà, not to be violated by man or beast entering it, rather leads one to suppose that he died among his own people. "Never," says Abū ʿUbaidah [4], "was there seen a day with more men and women weeping, or more faces torn with nails, or more garments rent in mourning, than the

---

[1] Labīd Dīw. V, 2—3 (Khālidī p. 17).

[2] See Dīw. VI (Khālidī, p. 21), in the form in which it stands in Agh. XIV, 99 and XV 140, and in BQut. 151—2.

[3] One of the difficulties in the chronology of this series of episodes is the fact that in one list of the persons among whom the booty of Ḥunain was distributed (A. H. 8), called al-Muʾallafah qulūbuhum, appear the names of Labīd and ʿAlqamah b. ʿUlāthah (BHisham 883); their names are absent from the second list. See Caetani, Annali, Vol. II, Part 2, p. 185. It is apparently this fact that has induced Caetani to put the visit of ʿĀmir to the Prophet before the battle of Ḥunain.

[4] Agh. XV 139.

day when ʿĀmir son of aṭ-Ṭufail died." He left no son, though his *kunyah* Abū ʿAlī
shows that he had had at least one born to him, who probably died in infancy.

As in the case of ʿAbīd, we have no information regarding the person who first
collected the poems of ʿĀmir b. aṭ-Ṭufail; he may very possibly have been Abū ʿAmr
ash-Shaibānī. Our present *dīwān* is said to follow the readings of Abu-l-ʿAbbās Aḥmad
b. Yaḥyà, called Thaʿlab (200—291), a pupil of Ibn al-Aʿrābī and a celebrated doctor of
the Kūfī school of grammar. The author of the commentary, Abū Bakr Muḥammad b.
al-Qāsim al-Anbārī (271—327 or 328), was Thaʿlab's most distinguished pupil, and also
of the school of Kūfah. He is well-known as the editor of his father's great commen-
tary on the *Mufaḍḍalīyāt*, and as author of the *Kitāb al-Aḍdād* (ed. Houtsma, 1881), and
the *Kitāb az-Zāhir fī Maʿānī Kalimāt an-Nās* (MS. Köprülü 1280). A great commentary
on the *Muʿallaqāt* also goes by his name, and exists in MS. in Constantinople: of this the
commentary on Ṭarafah's *Muʿallaqah* was published by Dr. O. Rescher in 1910. The present
work is not mentioned by name in the list of compositions attributed to him in Ibn
Khallikān's *Biographies* or in the *Fihrist*, p. 75 [1], but there can be no doubt whatever of its
authenticity. The introduction, and the commentaries on the two poems (Nos. XI and XXIX)
which are included in the *Mufaḍḍalīyāt*, agree with the commentary on that work which
goes by his father's name and was revised by himself; No. XXVI is also, as noted on
p. ١۴١, taken from the same commentary. The scholia are deficient in information regarding
the historical bearing of the poems; perhaps it was in many cases no longer procurable.
They sometimes contain evident inaccuracies, as for instance in p. ۹۹¹³, p. ١٣٩², p. ١١٧⁷,
p. ١٣٣¹, and p. ١۴۹⁴. A curious slip of memory is the quotation of verses made up
of hemistichs taken from different parts of the same poem; *e.g.*: p. ١٣١¹², p. ١١٥³,
p. ١١٧⁶. Notwithstanding these defects, however, the commentary is useful, especially
as a guarantee of the accuracy of the text. The original from which our MS. was copied
was a good one, and the copyist has generally been faithful to it. All departures from
the text have been indicated in the notes. The case is very different from that of the
portion of the MS. (undoubtedly by the same hand) containing the *Dīwān* of ʿAbīd.

There may have been other collections of ʿĀmir's poetry in existence. In the com-
mentary to the *Mufaḍḍalīyāt*, p. 33, v. 2 of poem No. VIII is cited as in our MS,
and a marginal note alleges that the reading in ʿĀmir's *Dīwān* [2] is مِثْلَ خُشْبِ ٱلْغَرْقَدِ;
as the poem rhymes in ب, this would imply that a *dīwān* exists somewhere with a wholly
different recension of the poem. [3] Some of the pieces in the Supplement seem to be taken

---

[1] This work says that he prepared a number of *Dīwāns* of celebrated poets, including Zuhair, Nā-
bighah Jaʿdī, al-Aʿshà, and others.

[2] كذا فى ديوانه.

[3] As noticed on p. ١٣٩, note *d*, a verse ending in our recension in ٱلْأَجْسَمِ, occurs in the L A and

from such a collection; No. 1 has every appearance of being genuine; No. 2 is clearly a portion of No. VIII. Nos. 4, 5, 6 (very celebrated), 7, 8 (actually cited in commy. to *Mufaḍḍalīyāt*), 10, 11 (also from commy. *Mufḍt*), 13, 15, 16, 17, 20, 22 all seem to be probably the work of ʿĀmir, and to have been taken from some other collection of his poems. The other fragments included in the Supplement are either doubtful or clearly spurious. Of the pieces in the *Dīwān*, No. II (the only long *qaṣīdah*) is perhaps open to suspicion because of its insistence on the theme of the defeat of Tamīm at Shiʿb Jabalah; if ʿĀmir was born on the day of that battle, it may be thought hardly likely that he would speak of it as if it were a recent event. The verse (No. 18) which is said in the commentary to refer to the leader of the Banu-l-Ḥārith b. Kaʿb who was certainly a contemporary of ʿĀmir may possibly in reality refer to some other chief called Ḥuṣain; the battle of Dhū Najab, if it was the engagement referred to in Naq. 587 and 1079, was a *defeat* of ʿĀmir, not a victory: some other fight must be intended. Other pieces which appear to be doubtful are Nos. XVII (on account of its reference to ʿAntarah of ʿAbs) and XXVI (see *ante*, p. 81—82).

Only four pieces in the *Dīwān*, Nos. II, VII, XXVIII and XXXII, exhibit the double rhyme marking the commencement of an ode; in addition there are two in the Supplement (16 and 21), of which the second is certainly spurious. The other pieces are all mere fragments, and the theme is throughout what the Arabs call *fakhr*, boasting of warlike exploits and the glories of the tribe. ʿĀmir was esteemed by al-Aṣmaʿī [1] a good poet in this style. He says that he was called المُحَبِّر, "the adorner "or" beautifier" of verse. [2] Of himself he says repeatedly that he is a "Child of War" (XIV, 1; XXIII, 4; XXIX, 10), and it is of warfare only that he has to tell. We must not expect to find in him the variety and the poetic imagination displayed by ʿAbīd. A comparison with ʿAntarah, the other great warrior-poet, suggests itself; but of ʿĀmir we possess no *nasīb*, in which the resources of Desert minstrelsy were chiefly displayed, and are thus unable to set one poet against the other. For the rest, the reader of the *Dīwān* will judge for himself of the man and his work.

T A with the rhyme الأَحْمَسا. This may, however, be only an inaccuracy in the Lexicons, and it is possible that the note referred to above may also be due to a confusion of memory on the part of the annotator.

[1] Mbd Kämil 93[14].   [2] The same epithet is applied to Ṭufail of Ghanī: Mfḍt. p. 410[15].

ʿĀMIR.

TRANSLATION.

I.

These three verses belong to a poem the full text of which is given in the Supplement, No. 1, which see for other readings. They are very celebrated and often cited.

(1) As for me, though I be the son of the Chief of ʿĀmir, and the Knight of the tribe, called on for help in every adventure,[1]

(2) It was not for my kinsmen's sake that ʿĀmir made me their chief: God forbid that I should exalt myself on mother's or father's fame!

(3) But it was because I guard their peculiar land,[2] and shield them from annoy, and hurl myself[3] against him that strikes at their peace.

II.

An ode devoted to setting forth the glorious deeds of his tribe. In the *nasīb* the lady mentioned, Salmà, (diminutive Sulaimà, v. 5), is said (like Asmā, the mistress most frequently named) to belong to a hostile tribe. Vv. 1—2 are addressed to himself.

(1) Hast thou recognized, in the low land of ʿĀrimah, the place where Salmà halted, or known again the signs of her abiding

(2) In the nights when she took thee captive with her rows of pearly teeth, and her eyes like a fawn's that feeds on the balsam[4] bushes —

---

[1] Literally, "In every cavalcade that rides forth."

[2] *Ḥimāhā*, "their reserved land", that which they claim as their own peculiar.

[3] Lit.: "thrust at him with my shoulder."

[4] The balsam of Mecca (identical with the "Balm of Gilead" of the O. T.), *Commiphora opobalsamum* (formerly *Amyris commiphora*).

(3) What time my tribe were at enmity with her kin,[1] that she might create between her (and us) a cause of trouble and quarrel?

(4) And if thy people hold thee back that thou leave them not to join us — yet time was when we dwelt together in ʿĀrimah in sweet peace.

(5) Yet if Sulaimà knew what she might know of my deeds on the morning[2] of alarm, she would cast her lot with the noble.

(6) We left Madhḥij[3] like a tale of yesternight, and Arḥab, when (our horsemen) enveloped them with their troops;

(7) And we sold Shākir for the ancestral wealth of ʿAkk, and a band of our warriors faced Judhām;

(8) And we scattered Shanūʾah in every direction, and Ḥimyar met at our hands with trouble;

(9) And Hamdān[4] there — it matters not to me whether they be at war with me or at peace.

(10) And we met, in the valley of Dhū Zarūd, the Sons of Shaibān[5], and they were swallowed up utterly;

(11) And as for a tribe of the Sons of Asad, we left their women in mourning garb, widowed of their husbands;

(12) We cut to pieces their chiefs for all to see, and we fed the hyenas full with the flesh of the mighty;[6]

(13) And we gave Ḥanīfah[7] over to slaughter in their villages, and our attack utterly destroyed Hakam and Hām;[8]

(14) We slew their captain, and they fled, scattering hither and thither, as thou scatterest in flight the bands of ostriches;

(15) We returned home with their women captive behind us on our camel-saddles, and with booty of camels — they were our meat.

(16) And we fell upon Zubaid[8] in the middle of the night, and by dawn their abode was held by a clamorous mighty host;[9]

(17) And of ʿAbd al-Qais[10] we obtained captives, from far Baḥrain, and divided them amongst us;

---

[1] *Lit.*: "That she might bestow between her (and us) buckets of unwholesome water."

[2] Attacks were always made in the morning, just before dawn.

[3] The tribes named in vv. 6—9 are all of al-Yaman, or of Yamanic origin settled elsewhere (Judhām).

[4] See the contempt with which Hamdān is spoken of in No. XXXVII, *post*.

[5] A division of Bakr b. Wāʾil.   [6] Paraphrase.

[7] The most powerful division of Bakr b. Wāʾil, settled in the mountains of al-Yamāmah, about the site of the modern Riyāḍ: they were to a considerable extent cultivators, having a good water-supply.

[8] Again tribes of the Yaman.

[9] The omission of a proper subject to صبّح in this verse suggests that something has fallen out, and that a second hemistich of v. 16, with a first hemistich containing the missing subject, has disappeared.

[10] A Maʿaddic stock settled on the sea-coast of the Persian Gulf, about the peninsula of Qaṭar: this shore (not the islands now called by the name) is meant by *Baḥrain*.

(18) And at Dhū Najab we met Huṣain (of the Bal-Ḥārith [1]), and in the battle we destroyed Usāmah;

(19) And at al-Haumān Qais just escaped us, but left in our hands his bride a prisoner while safe himself:

(20) And sooth, if he had loved his wife as well as himself, he would have met there his death at the points of our spears!

(21) And the kin of al-Jaun [2] travelled to meet us [on the morning of the Defile [3]], and were cut off utterly;

(22) We slew of them a hundred in requital for an old man, and we put chains on a number of their people our prisoners.

(23) And on the Day of the Defile we met Laqīṭ [4], and made his head the raiment of a keen sword-blade;

(24) Ḥājib [5] we took captive, and he remained in bonds, until we had left his kinsfolk not a single camel;

(25) And the host of the Sons of Tamīm we left lying there, slain, with arms and heads lopped off;

(26) Yea, long was the Day to them there, as when thou pilest on a blazing fire fresh wood;

(27) Unlucky was the day we brought upon them in their own country, poison was the draught they were given there to drink.

(28) And if the changes of things do not hurry me out of life, they will go on paying tribute to us year after year;

(29) They will pay it, though they loathe it, abased beneath us, and will give into our hands the reins to guide them.

(30) But carry this message, if thou passest them, to the host of Saʿd [6] — 'Sleep soundly! Never shall we break your rest:

(31) 'Ye gave us secret tidings, and ye took no part in the attack upon us — verily ye were generous to us!

(32) 'If ye had joined the host with the Son of al-Jaun, ye would have been like those who perished and brought shame upon themselves.'

---

[1] The leading Yamanic tribe of Najrān, south of the territory of ʿĀmir. (See remarks on this verse *ante*, p. 93.)

[2] The two sons of a prince of Kindah, called al-Jaun, "the Black". See *post*, Frag. 15.

[3] Entered conjecturally in a break in the MS. These two princes were slain on the Day of Shiʿb Jabalah.

[4] Chief and leader of the tribe of Tamīm at the battle of Shiʿb Jabalah, where he was killed.

[5] Ḥājib was the brother of Laqīṭ: the verse means that his tribe had to pay in ransom for him all their herds.

[6] The sub-tribe of Tamīm called Saʿd b. Zaid-Manāt, which sent warning to ʿĀmir of the intended attack at Shiʿb-Jabalah. (They claimed Ṣaʿṣaʿah, the progenitor of the tribe of ʿĀmir, as one of their kin: see Naq. 657[8] and 1064[8ff]; Agh. X, 36[3]).

III.

Tells of a battle with the tribes of Najrān — Nahd, the Banu-l-Ḥārith b. Kaʿb, and Jarm — in al-Kaur (the name of a mountain-range in the Yaman).

(1) Why askest thou[1] not of us — for thou art kind and carest for our for-
tunes — how we fared in the hollow plain the day that Nahd blenched before us,

(2) And the tribe of Kaʿb and the whole of Jarm in the plain, the day when
they were driven to face us with the whip,

(3) In al-Kaur, the day that al-Ḥuṣain[2] lay there still, and ʿAbd al-Madān had
seen gallop our[3] horse

(4) Bestridden by stern warriors eager for battle, clad in ring-mail of iron, deftly
fashioned by the armourer?

(5) (Why askest thou not) which of the knights did most slaughter in the
mellay among our foes, when the toil of battle had changed their hue,

(6) When I singled out their captain, and then left him there, food for the wild
beasts, a mass of dead flesh,

(7) And Rabīʿah[4] fell there in the onset, flung to ground, and the cry of mour-
ning went up at that which Fate had brought to pass?

(8) That was *my* place — as thou askest, there stood I: how we came there,
ask further another time.

(9) Hast thou asked my people of Ziyād[5], when the spear-point scathed him,
and when ʿAbd did mischief to him?

(10) And the man Zaid — I left him leading him[6] towards the hills — but it
had not been in his mind that he should take refuge there!

IV.

(1) We went up with noble steeds against the tribe of Ward[7], and after our
onset ill was the luck they gained;

(2) We destroyed the tribe of Dhu-l-Bazarà,[8] and Kaʿb, and their Mālik, and
we brought to nought Bashīr;

---

[1] Addressed to a woman-friend.

[2] Al-Ḥuṣain and ʿAbd al-Madān, two chiefs of the Banu-l-Ḥārith.

[3] Lit., "their horse," but he means the horse of his tribe ʿĀmir.

[4] Rabīʿah here is not the father of Labīd, who was killed, before the battle of Shiʿb Jabalah, in a
fight with the Asad at Dhū ʿAlaq: it is the name of some enemy; a *v. l.* is Ḍubaiʿah: see No. XXI.

[5] The person meant is said in the commentary to be Ziyād son of al-Ḥārith, perhaps of the Banu-l-Ḥārith.

[6] *I. e.* Ziyād. [7] *I. e.* the tribe of ʿAbs; Ward was the father of ʿUrwah, a celebrated poet and hero.

[8] Dhu-l-Bazarà is said to be a name of the tribe of Abū Bakr b. Kilāb, a branch of ʿĀmir b. Ṣaʿṣaʿah:
see Introduction, pp. 74—5.

(3) And near did we bring ar-Ribābah to perdition on the Day of Fajj, and we captured in our noose ʿAshīr,

(4) And Sayyār, the champion of Saʿd son of Bakr; and we slew Baḥīr in requital for Mafrūq.

V.

A description of the cavalry of ʿĀmir ibn Ṣaʿṣaʿah.

(1) We led our noble steeds until we stalled [1] them in Thahlān by force, and there they abode.

(2) And I chid al-Maznūq [2] until he charged with me into the midst of a compact body of horse, and they were scattered.

(3) And we gave ʿAbs and Murrah [3] to drink of a cup in the borders of their country — and long was the draught!

(4) And as for our steeds, we accustom them to spring forward, whensoever a raid chances, or looms large before us —

(5) Tethered close to our tents, (eager) like camels maddened with thirst [4], rough in the forelocks, — we call on them for their best speed, and they answer fully,

(6) Bestridden by the youth of ʿĀmir, who smite the helms when the cavalry are wedged together in the strait of battle —

(7) In the strait wherein the spear-tops fly in splinters, when the bravest warriors shrink, and (slaughter) waxes hot;

(8) They smite the armed enemy in the rising dust of battle, what time their War shines forth and hurls herself upon them;

(9) And they raise up a heavy dust-cloud after a lighter one, and after neighing with a din like thunder, come on stern and fierce ···

(10) Steeds that go forth at dawn, a mighty strength, and fall on their foes and ravage them throughly.

VI.

(1) Of a truth the horsemen who ride on a foray know well that we, what time men vie one with another in deeds of valour, are their lions,

---

[1] Paraphrase.   [2] Name of his war-horse.
[3] Murrah, a sub-tribe of Dhubyān: Dhubyān, ʿAbs, Anmār, and Ashjaʿ together make up the great group called Ghaṭafān, with which ʿĀmir were constantly at war.
[4] *I. e.* Eager to spring upon their foes, as camels suffering from the disease called *huyām*, mad with thirst, rush to the water.

(2) Mounted on swift coursers, that gather ever more pace as they gallop along, when under the saddles the saddle-cloths have become loose;

(3) And already are the steeds bathed in moisture, until the black horses (by reason of the drying sweat) resemble in colour the bays.

(4) And it is we that have held Madhḥij out of their lands: they were slaughtered until their mightiest returned home vanquished;

(5) One body of them was at al-Maṣāmah, who fled, and another (stood their ground, but) their good fortune had been blotted out.

(6) What time an evil year presses, and long lasts its dreariness, and heaven's rain falls not, and the trees grow yellow,

(7) Then are we found to be the generous ones: our guest is not turned away when the hoar-frost lies crisp about all the tent-places.

(8) Yea, even this morning my wife has been railing at me from dawn: for no crime of mine does she shun me and show her aversion;

(9) When I have said my say, and have done with (my answer to her reproaches), she brings upon me another (burden of reviling) — a condition of things which I like not.

(10) There is no good in affection when its bond has become worn out: the best of bonds for those who are joined together is the newest of them[1].

VII.

Tells of fighting with Ḥanīfah at Ghaul, and with ʿAbd al-Qais at Mardā.

(1) Lo! Kanūd has visited thee by night[2] from Khabt: yet she severed our bond, and swore that she would return no more.

(2) Methinks thou[3] didst not see us on the Day of Ghaul, nor did the hosts bring thee tidings of our doings —

(3) What befell the chiefs of the Sons of Lujaim[4] — leathern thongs bite into their flesh, in bonds with us.

(4) And ʿAbd al-Qais[5] in al-Mardā — there overwhelmed them a morning of ruin such as fell upon Thamūd[6];

---

[1] Perhaps جَديد here may mean "that which is cut off"; see Labīd, Muʿall. 20.

[2] I. e. in a vision, khayāl.   [3] I. e.. Kanūd.

[4] Lujaim is the name of the father of Ḥanīfah: see No. II, 13.   [5] See No. II, 17.

[6] See Qurʾān, VII 71—77, etc.

(5) We came upon them at dawn with our tall steeds, lean and sinewy, and spears whose steel was as burning flame,

(6) And swords that reap the necks, keen and sharp of edge, kept carefully in the sheaths till the time of need,

(7) And war-mares, springing lightly, of eager heart, strongly knit together, not to be overtaken.

(8) We came upon their host in the morning, and they were like a flock of sheep on which falls the ravening wolf;

(9) And there were left there on ground of them ʿAmr, and ʿAmr, and Aswad — the fighters are my witness that I speak true!

(10) ʿAbdallāh too lay there, and the son of Bishr, and ʿAttāb, and Murrah, and al-Walīd.

(11) We fell upon them with white steel ground to keenness: we cut them to pieces therewith until they were destroyed;

(12) And we carried off their women on the saddles behind us, with their cheeks bleeding, torn in anguish by their nails [1].

VIII.

For the subject, see the note in the Arabic text, p. 111.

(1) As for me, what time the udder-strings of your mother are pulled tight, I am of those to whom the call goes out — 'Gird on thine armour and ride forth!' [2].

(2) No matter! before now has (War) pressed Murrah with the weight of her breast, and (the cavalry) have left Ashjaʿ lying like logs of *ath'ab* [3].

[Frag. 2. (1) Black are they, given to fattening their camels: when they lead them down to drink, the richest of them in milk comes up from the water without being milked [4].

(2) Bald are they, little-headed: their noses are (round and small) like pieces of dry camel's-dung which a boy strings together in play;]

---

[1] This rendering does not follow the commentary, which seems to be erroneous.

[2] The "udder-strings" are cords tied round the udders of camels, to prevent the young from sucking or the herdsman from stealing milk: the reference to their tightness carries a charge of niggardliness, and also implies that the people addressed are mean herdsmen, while he, the poet, is a warrior. The commentary, however, which speaks of "picking up" the udder-strings, suggests that the correct reading is أنتثرت, "are scattered about.". The reading of the MS. is clear.

[3] Murrah: see above, V, v. 3. Ashjaʿ, on the Day of ar-Raqam, showed particular cruelty to the prisoners of ʿĀmir, who were all slaughtered by this tribe. "Like logs of *ath'ab*", a tree: *i. e.* like dead corpses. *Ath'ab* is a species of fig.

[4] Again the charge of niggardliness, repeated: they allow their camels to grow fat by not being milked, instead of using their milk for hospitality.

(3) They ask not the noble to give them their daughters in marriage, and their own unwedded maid grows grey, while none seeks to wed her.

(4) Dost thou exult that Fortune has dealt treacherously with a knight? The yellow-toothed dogs! I was not the one overcome again and again!

(5) O Murrah! Time has dealt fiercely with you in the past, and I have reopened your bleeding wounds, myself unscathed:

(6) And I have left their host in the lava of Ḍarghad[1], the prey of wild beasts and vultures with long hanging feathers.

(7) Yea, many a time have I stalled[2] my horses in your camping-grounds, in the midst of your home-land, on their backs keen warriors skilled in battle;

(8) And I have assuaged my thirst for vengeance on Fazārah — verily they are folk of deeds and men of sturdy thick-necked glory;[3]

(9) And many a time hast thou gloried in trifles which thou hast counted up: — when thou comest to the tents of thy people, recount them there if thou darest!

(10) Then, surely, shall one bereaved (of husband or son) tell thee of her pain, with her eyelids that have lost their lashes from constant weeping!

(11) And many a time hast thou come upon our horse, and hast liked them not, and hast turned aside from their vanguard that seemed to thee dangerous!

(12) Yea, they have borne down with their breasts the Sons of Fazārah, and the tribe of Ashjaᶜ they have overthrown with a shoulder-thrust;

(13) They have left of them nine lying dead on the battle-field, and another three they have bound in bonds and destined for death.

IX.

(1) Fazārah pasture their camels in the very midst of their home-land[4], and the herds suffer torments of thirst between the long rugged strips clear of sand, and the sand-hills.

(2) They pay their tribute without any friendliness: — and Fortune is full of troubles and vicissitudes.

(3) We are the warriors to deal with him who brings War with its terrors: we are those who dye with heart's blood the mailcoat where it enfolds the breast.

(4) And Bakr passed upon you a fitting and right judgement; and the Sons of Fazārah turned tail and fled when the time for fleeing came.

---

[1] See ᶜAbīd, XXX, 1.   [2] Paraphrase,   [3] Sarcasm.
[4] I. e. through cowardice they do not venture to send them to feed far from their head-quarters: see note to ᶜAbīd XI, 30 (translation).

X.

These verses appear to be a fragment of a poem which was afterwards superseded by No. XI. The lines that have survived contain obscurities which are not cleared up in the commentary. They refer to the battle of Faif ar-Rīḥ, an inconclusive engagement in which ʿĀmir was opposed to Yamanite tribes collectively called Madhḥij, and in which our poet lost an eye by a treacherous thrust of a lance by a man of Khathʿam who professed to be fighting on his side; see Introduction, p. 82.

(1) They [1] came on with the whole of Shahrān of the broad plain [2], and Aklub thereof, the offspring of Bakr son of Wā'il [3];

(2) The Ancients of the tribe were busy between Suwaiqah and the south of Mount Qahr, with their left hands (holding their bows) aslant [4].

(3) And if there had been a host like us, they had not spoiled us: but those that came upon us were all *Jinn* and evil devils.

(4) And we spent the night — and whoso has alighting at his tent a guest such as ours, spends the night not unmindful of the entertainment of his guests.

[(5) [5] And Khathʿam are a tribe accounted equal with Madhḥij: and are we anything but as one of the tribes ourselves?]

XI.

Reflections on the fight at Faif ar-Rīḥ, and the wound he received there from the hand of Mus-hir, the man of Khathʿam (see note at beginning of No. X).

(1) Verily the Chiefs of Hawāzin [6] know well that I am the knight who defends the cause of the house of Jaʿfar [7];

(2) And al-Maznūq [8] knows well that I urged him again and again, on the evening of Faif ar-Rīḥ, to face the foe, as the blank arrow [9], denounced by the gamers, is put back again and again into the bag.

---

[1] *I. e.* Khathʿam.   [2] or, "of al-ʿArīdah", a proper name.

[3] What this means is not clear, since Bakr was not a Yamanite stock; *Mīlād* also properly means the time of birth, birthday, not offspring.

[4] Or, "taking the way towards the North."

[5] Additional verse not in our text.

[6] Or "Uplands of Hawāzin": that is, the large group of tribes of which ʿĀmir b. Ṣaʿṣaʿah, his own tribe, was the most powerful.

[7] His subtribe among the divisions of ʿĀmir.   [8] Name of his horse.

[9] In the game of *Maisir* the lots of the players are cast by shuffling arrows, of which there are seven that bear a name and carry a share in the prize (a slaughtered camel), while three are blank, carry no share, and are put in only to make up the number of ten. When one of these last is drawn, it is reviled by the gamers, and put back into the bag again.

(3) When he flinched and turned aside from the thrust of the spears, I urged him on and said to him — 'Get thee on, straight forward — never turn thy back!'

(4) And I admonished him that to fly were a disgrace to a man so long as he has not put forth his utmost strength — in which case he is to be held excused:

(5) 'Seest thou not that their spears are all couched straight at me? and thou art a charger of noble stock: so bear it bravely!'

(6) I desired that God might know that I endured patiently; and in truth I dreaded a day like that of al-Mushaqqar [1].

(7) By my life — and my life is no light thing to me! — verily the spear-thrust of Mus-hir has spoiled the beauty of my face;

(8) And an evil man shall I be if I be one-eyed, unsteady on my legs in fight, a coward — and what shall be my excuse in all assemblies?

(9) And sooth, they know full well that I dashed against them, on the evening of Faif ar-Rīḥ, as one circles the Pillar [2] again and again;

(10) And I ceased not until my breast and my charger's throat were covered with streaming blood like the fringe of a striped silken cloth.

(11) I said to a soul the like of which is not poured forth (in death) [3]: 'Cut short thine exulting: verily I fail not in carrying out my purpose!'

(12) And if they (the enemy) had been a host like ourselves in number, they had not spoiled us: but there came upon us a stock full of boastful words;

(13) They came upon us with all Shahrān of the broad plain, and the whole. of Aklub, clad in coats of mail of the best.

XII.

(1) We went forth, a party to treat, and repaired to the nobles of Dārim, on the morning when we repaid to al-Jaun a calamity for what had happened to al-Jaun [4];

(2) And there was not another tribe that could hold our place: we sought no help from aught but our spears, in the day of alarm or when bent on some violence.

(3) And never did I see a kin that carried their standard to the height of glory reached by us, of all men that use speech.

---

[1] The name of a fortress held by the Persian Governor in al-Baḥrain, where a number of the tribe of Tamīm met their death; see my *Translations of Ancient Arabian Poetry* (1885) pp. 87—89.

[2] This "Pillar" is the name of a standing stone to which reverence was done in the days of Arab heathenism by circumambulation, as the Kaʿbah is still circumambulated at the Pilgrimage; see Frag. No. 8, *post*.

[3] *I. e.*, his life is so precious that it should not be squandered.

[4] Dārim, an important branch of the great tribe of Tamīm; al-Jaun, name of a Kindite prince. The precise circumstances to which the poem refers are not explained.

(4) Who among men does not know that we are their betters in the noble handling of great affairs?

(5) We are they that led our noble steeds forth on a foray in spite of worn hoofs: (slender and muscular are they) like bows of *nabʿ* or *saʾsam* wood which the bow-maker heats in the fire (to bend them into shape)[1].

(6) And we fell upon the tribe of Asmā[2] with our lances in the dawning, and we left in the tribe of Murrah none but women lamenting their dead.

(7) We ripped up the women with child of Shanūʾah, after that (our horses) had trampled under foot in Faif ar-Rīḥ Nahd and Khathʿam[3],

(8) Led along by our side — the foray had rendered them lean and lank, as the vehement gallopers of them vied in speed with the straightened spear-shafts laid in rest[4];

(9) And we brought in the dawning upon the tribe of Najrān a raid which caused their women with child to give birth prematurely through fear of us[5].

XIII.

(1) Avoid Numair[6], and trample them not with thy cavalry,
    for among them are men of ʿĀmir settled.

(2) And verily the spears of the Sons of ʿĀmir
    drip from their points drops of red blood;

(3) They are the menders of the broken bones,
    when the breakings give no hope of mending;

(4) They are the men to smite, in the raid at dawning,
    the heavily-armed warrior in his *mighfar*[7] on the nose;

(5) They straighten what is crooked in the battle,
    what time the dust-clouds rise high in air;

(6) Warriors, defenders of the right, what time
    lips are parted perforce in the fierceness of fight.

---

[1] Lit., "as the bow-maker shapes (by heating) bows of *nabʿ* and *saʾsam*." *Nabʿ* is said to be the same as *shauhaṭ* (ʿAbīd XI 25, 29), a tree, *Zizyphus jujuba*; *saʾsam* (Hindī *shīsham*) is *Dalbergia sisu*, an Indian wood.

[2] *I. e.* Fazārah.   [3] All these are Yamanite stocks.

[4] The repetition of بَعَدَ مَا in v. 8 in the same place as in v. 7 suggests that the text of the former verse is corrupt; the idea in the second hemistich of course is that the horses race with the couched lances held by their riders.

[5] Paraphrase. The "tribe of Najrān" is the Banu-l-Ḥārith b. Kaʿb, which held that region.

[6] Numair, a tribe descended from ʿĀmir b. Ṣaʿṣaʿah and brothers of the Banū Hilāl.

[7] The *mighfar* is a skirt of mail depending from the helmet and shielding the neck; it corresponds to the original meaning of *hauberk* = *halsberge*.

(7) Long do they keep on foot warfare time after time,
      when strife blazes up in a burning flame.

(8) As for your boasts which ye put forth,
      he who knows the truth shall give you the lie;

(9) Then shall the troops of them, when they meet together
      weaponless, know which of them ye have sought to attack (?) [1]

(10) They [2] shine forth brightly when things are most doubtful —
      verily experience is preferred (before empty boasting).

(11) Truly in what is past there was an example,
      and he who is intelligent gains wisdom from knowledge.

(12) He is blamed who is remiss and neglectful in his business,
      when the task is clear and plain to him who exerts his full power.

XIV.

(1) Truly War knows that I am her child,
      and that I am the chief who wears her token in fight;

(2) And that I dwell on a mountain-top
      of glory in the highest honour;

(3) And that I render restive and distrest
      mail-clad warriors in the black dust stirred by battle;

(4) And that I dash upon them when they flinch before me,
      with an attack fiercer than the spring of the lion.

(5) With my sword I smite on the day of battle,
      cleaving in twain the rings of the strongest mail.

(6) This then is my equipment — would that the warrior
      could see length of days without thought of decay!

(7) And truly the folk of ʿĀmir know
      that we hold the peak of their mount of glory,

(8) And that we are the swordsmen of the day of battle,
      when the faint-hearts hold back and dare not advance.

XV.

(1) Our home-nurtured steeds are brisk in the morning when we gallop them
    and far do they carry us on a raid which stirs up the dust in clouds;

---

[1] The meaning of v. 9 is obscure, and the text seems to be corrupt.   [2] *I. e.* ʿĀmir.

(2) And al-Maznūq never leaves me, but is always ready saddled with the light saddle which constant training requires to be bound on his back.

(3) When the criers of War call her cry, then forth ride the Sons of ᶜĀmir, leading along steeds, each one of them the best of its stock;

(4) On them are the helms, and the mail-coats full and flowing; they dash their steeds into the fray as though the whole tribe were in the welter of dust.

(5) Sometimes they fall at dawn upon ᶜAbs with a sudden terror, and at others they mount up to the Son of al-Jaun by a rugged road.

(6) And the horsemen swoop down from the valley of adh-Dhināb, and they hold their lances inclined (for the thrust), red with the blood of the neck-veins.

(7) If thou askest the troop of our doings in their adventures on the day of al-Mushaqqar [1], when the bravest champions were in distress,

(8) They will tell thee that it was I who charged again and again among them, when the spears were shivered in the day of press and strain.

XVI.

A poem addressed by ᶜĀmir to an-Nābighah of Dhubyān, the veteran poet. His name was Ziyād, an-Nābighah being an epithet.

(1) Ho! who will carry for me a message to Ziyād, on the morning of the hollow plain, when the give and take of blows is near at hand —

(2) The morning when the horses of the Sons of Kilāb [2] come home with their breasts stained with fresh blood?

(3) And verily to us belongs the right of decision every day, when the right course is made plain in the matters for judgement.

(4) And I shall surely judge without going beyond the right, or using violent speech when an answer is sought by men:

(5) The judgement of one skilled and prudent, without a flaw, when the concourse is surfeited with much speaking.

(6) And verily the steed of weight and gravity is deliberation, that takes the needed time for thought: but youth is prone to headlong folly;

(7) Yet folly is not dependent only on age: the caravans disperse in all directions with the piercing arrows of things said.

(8) And as for the Sons of Baghīḍ [3], there has come to them the message of good counsellors, but they heeded not;

---

[1] It is not probable that the Mushaqqar mentioned here is the fortress in al-Baḥrain referred to in XI, 6.

[2] ᶜĀmir's house, the Banū Jaᶜfar, were sons of Kilāb.

[3] Baghīḍ, son of Raith, son of Ghaṭafān, was the father of ᶜAbs and Dhubyān.

(9) They returned no answer to their advisers, until the decision [1] came to us to deliver, and the veil was rent.

(10) And sooth, my sentence is what ye know well, and my cavalry — booty is lawful to them;

(11) When they take their way against other horsemen swiftly, the raven crosses the path of these, bearing evil omens;

(12) And if they pass on against a hostile people, in their forecourt, verily these shall lose and be disappointed.

XVIᴬ.

The answer of an-Nābighah to the foregoing [2]:

(1) Ho! carry this message from Ziyād to little ʿĀmir: 'Verily the appropriate place for folly is youth!

(2) 'And thou shalt surely attain to gravity, or be withheld (from folly), what time thou art grizzled, or the raven grows gray [3].

(3) 'Be thou like thy father, or like Abū Barā [4]: then shall judgement befit thee and right decision.

(4) 'Let not light-minded conceit fly away with thy wisdom, and land thee in a place which has no issue.

(5) 'So if there be an owner of camels in Ḥismà [5] — they brought to pass, when they met thee, the blow thou knowest;

(6) 'And certainly he was not of distant kinship to thee — nay, they reached thee (through him): and wrathful were they —

(7) 'The horsemen of Manūlah [6], not unsteady on their steeds, and Murrah, over their host the eagle standard [7].'

---

[1] Reading الحَكَم for الحِلْم, as suggested by Prof. Nöldeke.

[2] So our MS. But, as observed in the notes to the Arabic text, the previous poem seems rather to be the answer to this one.   [3] I. e., perhaps never at all.

[4] His uncle ʿĀmir b. Mālik, "the Player with Lances."

[5] So our text; but the Dīwān reads Ḥisy (حِسي): Ḥismà is the name of a tract far to the north, bordering on Syria, and seems unsuitable here. Ḥisy means a water-bearing *stratum* of sand with rock below, and several places are called by the name. According to the commentary Ḥanḍhalah, brother of ʿĀmir, was killed in the fight in Ḥismà or Ḥisy. أَصابُوا is an ambiguous word, and may mean either "they inflicted a blow or disaster" (as would be the loss of Ḥanḍhalah), or "they obtained booty" (as might be inferred from the mention of camels).

[6] The wife of Fazārah and mother of Shamkh and Māzin his sons.

[7] Or possibly the eagle itself, awaiting its prey as the result of their prowess: see Nābighah I, 10—12.

XVII.

Boasts of a victory gained over ʿAbs, and taunts ʿAntarah, the celebrated champion of that tribe, with fleeing and leaving his mistress ʿAblah behind. As noted in the Arabic, it is scarcely possible that this fragment can be by ʿĀmir, since ʿAntarah was much his senior in years, and was probably dead in old age before ʿĀmir became famous as a warrior.

(1) Ah many the champion I have left dead on ground, generous in his gifts, the chief of a numerous tribe!

(2) And I have left his women whelmed in sorrow, lamenting him at eventide with cries of bitter grief.

(3) I have slaked my burning thirst with the House of ʿAbs, and I have won all kinds of booty, though I grew not rich thereby[1].

(4) And al-Agharr[2] saved ʿAntarah from destruction, speeding away with him swiftly as a falcon darts on its prey;

(5) And thou didst leave ʿAblah there, in the midst of young warriors who had passed the night[3] on the backs of galloping steeds;

(6) They carried off Hind and al-Wajīhah by force, on the day of the disaster, on thoroughbred swiftly-trotting camels.

XVIII.

(1) We gave the tribe of ʿAbs to drink in the morning a cup in whose sides was poison steeping;

(2) And long did we make for Murrah the day of misfortune, and for their brothers; and truly our hot thirst was slaked;

(3) We left their camps full of pools of blood and dead corpses, and everywhere was raised the cry of anguish;

(4) And the proud and vainglorious was abased — we brought him down; and the humble was exalted by our means.

(5) We slew Mālik and Abū Razīn, on the morning of the hollow plain, when the scout signalled to us that they had come.

(6) Of us in the day of alarm are noble champions, when the horses neigh mightily at the coming fight,

---

[1] Because it was soon distributed in bounty to others.

[2] The name of his horse, meaning "having a white star (ghurrah) on the forehead."

[3] Because raids were made in the morning before dawn.

(7) Mounted on short-haired steeds, noble of stock, branded with our mark, that prance and curvet with knights young and old,

(8) What time galloping has caused their sides to stream with sweat, their pace the best, their shoes (made of double soles of leather) cut to pieces (by the stony ground).

(9) And on the Day of the Defile we left Laqīṭ lying slain by a gleaming, keen-edged, polished sword [1] —

(10) The morning that he purposed to go up to fight us with his kinsfolk: but his tribesmen left him without a backing;

(11) And we returned home, rich with plunder and captives, leading along white women crying and lamenting.

XIX.

Addressed to the tribe of ʿĀmir b. Ṣaʿṣaʿah, and recounting the achievements of his sub-tribe Jaʿfar b. Kilāb in the common service.

(1) Ye Sons of ʿĀmir, stay your reviling and give heed! Come, count up to-day my doings in your service.

(2) Be not thankless for our labours in times of misfortune, when there bit you sore distress, yea the sternest.

(3) Ask, and ye shall learn, of our deeds on the morning of Uqaiṣir, and the Days of Ḥismà [2], or the teeth fastened in Ḥāshid,

(4) And of al-Kaur [3], when the companies of Jaʿfar returned to your help, and Khathʿam came on, gathering mightily against you,

(5) That they might tear to pieces our substance, and eat it up: but my spear brought destruction to all their mightiest men.

(6) Then did I transfix ʿAbdallāh there with a sword-stroke before which blenched and quailed every champion and defender.

(7) I left overthrown on the bare earth, cast to ground, Ḍubaiʿah [4], what time there rescued Shatīr son of Khālid

(8) A swift steed; and Zaid of the Horse [5] too received a spear-thrust, what time the man Zaid dealt unjustly, and kept not the road of right.

---

[1] See No. II, 23.   [2] See No. XVIA, 5.

[3] See No. III, 3.

[4] See No. XXI, and for Shatīr id. v. 10.

[5] Zaid al-Khail, son of Muhalhil, a famous chief of Ṭayyi', subdivision Nabhān. He became a Muslim shortly before his death in 632 A. D.

(9) Yea, this is my equipment for every stress of warfare, and for every year
that presses heavily on the tribe.

XX.

(1) We slew Yazīd son of ʿAbd al-Madān [1], and no crime was it, nor did we
wrong to any:

(2) In Aʿwà, the day that we faced them with a mighty mountainous host,
full of clamour, giving no hold to attack.

XXI.

ʿĀmir son of aṭ-Ṭufail, with a band of horsemen, led a raid upon ʿAbs, among whom
Zaid al-Khail was at the time sojourning [2]. As ʿĀmir was driving away the captured camels,
Zaid came up with him. ʿĀmir, who was protecting the rear of his troop, called out: "What
dost thou want?" Zaid answered: "Thou knowest what I want." ʿĀmir said: "The men of
ʿAbs would not suffer thee to keep my spoils; and methinks thou wouldst not gain them
before I made thee taste somewhat thou wouldst not like." Zaid said: "Dost thou not see
that the upper end of thy spear is shattered?" "Yea", said ʿĀmir, "but my sword has
received no hurt." "Wouldst thou", said Zaid, "that I gave thee this my spear?" ʿĀmir
answered: "Yes: plant it in the ground, and stand apart from it thyself." Zaid did so; then
ʿĀmir took the spear, and as he did so, Ḍubaiʿah son of al-Ḥārith of ʿAbs galloped up.
"O Zaid", he cried, "have at the man!" Zaid answered: "Verily I think of him what thou
thinkest" (meaning — "I fear him as much as thou dost"). Then Ḍubaiʿah drove at ʿĀmir
with his spear, but missed him. ʿĀmir thrust at him, and pierced him through; then
said ʿĀmir:

(1) So, if thou escapest from it [3], O Ḍubaiʿah, as for me, by thy fortune, I,
tied on thee no amulets!

(2) I brought him down from his steed as the like of me does to the like of
him, with a wide-stretching [4] thrust that wetted with blood his back and his
buttocks;

---

[1] A celebrated chief of the Banu-l-Ḥārith ibn Kaʿb. In Agh. XIX, 141[10] he is said to have been killed
at the second Battle of al-Kulāb; if so, this fragment must be spurious.

[2] The word is مُجَاوِر, which implies living under the protection of another: but ʿĀmir's poem shows
that Zaid was a prisoner awaiting ransom; he is said in the *Aghānī* to have more than once attacked
Fazārah. It seems possible that this narrative is another (and very different) version of the anecdote
related in Agh. XVI 55 (authority Abū ʿAmr ash-Shaibānī).

[3] The spear-thrust.   [4] Causing a wide-extending gash.

(3) And I restored Zaid, after he had spent a long time (a prisoner), to his people safe and sound on the Day of the Pass;

(4) And ye did not become possessed of the camels that were to have been his ransom, while he, in Taimān, goes along jauntily at his ease;

(5) He drives his noble steeds towards your grazing-grounds — and time was when he was straitly bound among you with leathern bonds.

(6) Be not hasty then: expect a knight[1] in your land who wields a Rudainian[2] spear and a keen glittering blade;

(7) Every day he makes a foray, well known to men as his, when he leads his horses, the short-haired, the lean and sinewy, to (their work of) death.

(8) And the Slave of the Sons of Barshā[3] we left lying on ground, the morning that he fell among the riders, shrunken together;

(9) I reached to him, and the edge of my sword shore through the extremities of his ribs in his breast, and cut through his wrists;

(10) And thou wast near by, and sawest him where he lay, as thou calledst out for Shatīr[4] that day, and ʿĀṣim.

XXII.

(1) Our cavalry drove Madhḥij from the plain to take refuge in the mountain-tops, giving them in exchange (for the herbage, or crops, of the low country) *shathth*, *bān*, and *ʿarʿar*[5]:

(2) And they (the horse) left not for ʿĀmir any fortune among men that had not been attained and extracted to the last drop.

XXIII.

An answer to some attack made upon him by an-Nābighah (Ziyād), referring to the Day of al-Marāurāt, which is said by Ibn al-Kalbī to be the name by which the Ghaṭafān called the Day of ar-Raqam, when ʿĀmir met with a heavy disaster. (See No. VIII and No. XXIX, and Introduction, pp. 80—81).

---

[1] *I. e.* himself.

[2] A stock epithet of spears: said to mean spear-shafts straightened by Rudainah, a woman of al-Khaṭṭ in Baḥrain.

[3] Or, possibly, "ʿAbd (a proper name) of the Sons of B." The latter is a family group mentioned by an-Nābighah of Dhubyān.   [4] See No. XIX, 7.

[5] These are all names of shrubs or trees of the hills. *Shathth* is described as a shrub or tree growing in the mountains, of sweet odour but bitter to the taste, used in tanning; *bān* (or *ben*) is a tree, for which see *ante*, p. 54, l. 8, (where for *Moringa pterygosperma* read *M. aptera*); *ʿarʿar* is the juniper.

(1) By my life! verily Ziyād has put forth a lampoon against us; and though it be strong and well knit together, has it caused us any harm?

(2) Thou speakest shame of us in respect of the Day of al-Maraurāt — without deliberation; and on thy side also are evil chances from Days before when we were the victors.

(3) Now who will carry a message to Dhubyān from me, a message that shall be swiftly borne abroad — and excuses will profit nothing?

(4) The Chiefs of Hawāzin [1] know well that we are the Children of War: we weary not in entering thereon or in coming forth [2];

(5) We tie tight the thigh-cord [3] of War until we make her yield her milk abundantly, what time the souls of other men have come up into their throats.

(6) Thou mayst see the horses grazing hither and thither around our tents in companies, that come prancing about us in the evenings and the mornings.

XXIV.

An indignant remonstrance with his own sub-tribe, the Banū Jaʿfar ibn Kilāb, for blaming him for some evil fortune which had befallen them (see No. XXXIV).

(1) By thy life! the Sons of Jaʿfar cease not to revile me, as often as hatreds stir up men's minds in Jaʿfar.

(2) When I said — 'Now is the time when their love will return', the hatred that was in their breasts refused to do aught but harp upon old memories (of quarrel)

(3) For the death of horses that have been slain; and ofttimes did they too slay in requital for them the like number, yea and many more —

(4) People of the land, in addition to camels won, and clients. [4] They (our horsemen), with me as their captain, rendered continuous to them (our foes) the meetings of mourning women, bare of head.

XXV.

An expression of disgust at an expedition against Khathʿam that failed, owing to warnings carried to that tribe by Salūl, a tribe (so called from its mother) descended from

---

[1] Cf. No. XI, 1.   [2] A metaphor from watering camels.

[3] When a she-camel refuses to give milk, her thighs are bound round with a cord or thong, when the milk is said to come abundantly.

[4] The rendering of the first hemistich of v. 4 is somewhat uncertain. Probably something has fallen out which would have made the construction clear.

Murrah son of Ṣaʿṣaʿah, brother of ʿĀmir. They were settled in the neighbourhood of aṭ-Ṭaʾif, in lands that produced crops of fruit and grain, and were thus averse from the predatory life of the nomads. As neighbours of the Yamanite stocks of Najrān, they had an understanding with these that they would warn them of any attack projected by their kindred, ʿĀmir b. Ṣaʿṣaʿah.

(1) Alas me for my labour lost, and my travel in the noon-tide without a midday rest!

(2) For the men of Khathʿam were guarded by their spears, and Salūl had warned them

(3) Of our going-forth against them, so that we were not hidden from them, and the guide brought them tidings of our undefended places.

(4) But if I had been listened to, there had happened to Mudrik of Aklub [1] a day long and evil at my hands;

(5) But I was disobeyed: and folly it was on their part that gave no heed to what I said.

(6) There blame me those I left behind me (in camp), and there disobey me those I chose to make the attack with me.

XXVI.

ʿĀmir is said to have been taken prisoner at the Battle of Sāhūq (or al-Maraurāt), and to have owed his life to the protection given to him by Khidhām son of Zaid, a man of Fazārah, when ʿUyainah, the chief of the tribe, and other leading men wished to put him to death (see commy. to *Mufaḍḍalīyāt*, p. 33). This poem is in praise of his protectors. Its authenticity is somewhat doubtful: see Introduction, p. 81.

(1) When thou desirest to meet with a sure defence, seek the protection of Khidhām son of Zaid, if Khidhām will grant it thee.

(2) I called upon Abu-l-Jabbār [2], specially naming Mālik; and from aforetime he whom thou tookest under thy shield was never scathed;

(3) And Abu-l-Jabbār arose, joyful to do a generous deed, even as a sharp cutting two-edged sword rejoices to do its work;

(4) And thou art (by nature) the (camel's) hump [3] of Fazārah, high and firm; and in every people there is someone who is the topmost hump.

(5) And thou didst turn aside from me those who were plotting to do me mischief [4]; and for fear of the mischief of the plotters I had been unable to sleep.

---

[1] A branch of Khathʿam.   [2] The *kunyah* or byname of Khidhām.   [3] *I. e.*, the top or highest.
[4] Or, perhaps, "those who had couched spears at me to slay me."

XXVII.

A recital of the glorious deeds of his tribe.

(1) Are not we the people who lead along their slender-waisted steeds, with lips drawn back from the teeth (in fight), and who, on the day of alarm, dye their swords in blood?

(2) And we defend our dependants what time spears are locked together, and we turn away from the road [1] (of their owners: *i. e.* we carry off as plunder) the company of thorough-bred branded steeds;

(3) And we take as spoil the black [2] horses with fierce faces, slender like spears, shrunken with the toil of foray, that carry the straightened lances.

(4) And we have brought on the tribe of Asmā [3] a morning raid, the terror of which has caused the pregnant women thereof to cast their young [4].

(5) And in the dust of the valley of Abīdah (our horse) engaged face to face Unais [5], and had destroyed already the Chiefs of Khathʿam;

(6) And on the Day of ʿUkādh [6] — well do ye know — we were present, and brought up our kin to the front of the battle;

(7) And we wrought with the two Confederates [7] a work that stayed for ever the violent oppressor from us;

(8) And never in all time has there wanted a band of us to stand in defence of our honour against him that dealt perversely;

(9) They lead alongside the short-haired steeds, (lean and spare) like wolves, that race after the spear-heads, [some bay,] some black.

(10) And we destroyed the tribe of Ashjaʿ with our spears, and we left the tribe of Murrah a crowd of mourning women.

XXVIII.

Complains of the ingratitude of a fellow-tribesman, Sumaiṭ, whom he had saved from death in a fight.

(1) I feared — but it was not fear of death that disturbed me, and I strove with a besetting care — and I was ever disposed to anxiety

---

[1] Or, "from the herd."   [2] Or, "dark bay."   [3] Fazārah.   [4] Paraphrase.

[5] Unais, diminutive form of Anas, son of Mudrik, a chief of Aklub, a division of Khathʿam: *cf.* XXV. 4.

[6] A reference to the so-called "Sacrilegious" war between Kinānah, Quraish and Qais; ʿUkādh, above Mecca, was the market and meeting-place of the tribes during the sacred months of peace.

[7] Asad and Ghaṭafān: the reference is to the Battle of Shiʿb Jabalah.

(2) From a lad even until hoariness gathered over my head, and there clad me therefrom (as it were) the pulled-up stalks of *thaghām*. [1]

(3) Sumaiṭ called upon me that day in a cry for help, and I beat (the foe) back from him, while the spears were all pointing at us.

*   *   (a lacuna)   *   *

(4) And but for my defence of Sumaiṭ and my dash to his aid, he had had to endure the bonds of raw hide, that creak when the leather dries.

(5) And I swear that Sumaiṭ is not requiting me for the service I did to him — and how should a crop-eared ass requite thee?

(6) And there gave the enemy the advantage of me, on the day that I met them, four deep wounds that had pierced my body:

(7) Though, had I willed it, there had borne me far away from the field a fleet swimmer, that strains the reins against her cheeks and gallops unwearied on.

XXIX.

A piece (like No. VIII) dealing with the disaster that befell ʿĀmir on the Day of ar-Raqam.

(1) Yea, let Asmā ask — for [2] she is kind and cares for our fortunes — let her ask her counsellors whether I was driven away or not;

(2) They said to her — "Yea: we drove away and scattered his horsemen" — the yellow-toothed dogs! it was not I that was wont to be driven away!

(3) And I will surely seek you out at al-Malā and ʿUwāriḍ, and I will bring my horsemen down upon you at the lava of Ḍarghad —

(4) The horses that gallop with the riders on their backs, as though they were kites following one another in the straight way;

(5) And I will surely take vengeance for Mālik, and for Mālik, and for the man of al-Maraurāt [3] whose head was not propped (in his grave).

(6) And the man whom Murrah [4] slew I will surely avenge — truly he was a noble chief; and their brother was not slain outright.

(7) O Asmā, thou child of the House of Fazārah! verily I am a fighter, and no man can hope to live for ever:

(8) Get thee gone to thine own! No peace can there be between us, after the knights that lie dead in the place of ambush,

---

[1] Perhaps a kind of wormwood, or possibly a plant akin to *Edelweiss*, to which hoary hair is compared.
[2] *Cf.* No. III, 1.   [3] Probably his brother Ḥakam is meant; see *Mufaḍḍalīyāt* No. V and commentary.
[4] His brother Ḥandhalah (so commentary): see No. XVI A, *ante*; apparently he was put to death in retaliation for some one of the enemy who had been grievously wounded, but not killed.

(9) Save by help of black, tall, swimming steeds, and the comfort[1] that comes from the thrust of a tawny spear.

(10) Yea, a Son of War am I — continually do I heighten her blaze, and stir her up to burn whensoever she is not yet kindled.

XXX.

(1) Ho! who will carry from me a message to Asmā, though she dwell far away in Yumn or Jubār,

(2) How that her husband[2] — there have fallen upon him troubles that can no longer be hidden in darkness?

XXXI.

(1) Woe[3] to the horsemen, the flood of horse on a foray, that see an object of greed or of fear, while all are bridled

(2)   *   *   *lacuna*   *   *

the points of the spears: they all cried together "Forward"!

XXXII.

Verses on the death of his father aṭ-Ṭufail at Hirjāb.

(1) Alas, that all things on which the wind blows must pass away, and every warrior, after a life-time unscathed, must come to his end!

(2) Alas, that the best of men in gentleness and valour lies there at Hirjāb, with no camels tethered around his grave![4]

(3) Somewhat it assuages my grief to think that if I had seen a lion with bristling mane, filled with fury, spring upon him,

---

[1] This rendering takes علالة in the more usual sense of "something that diverts, or appeases the sense of pain or loss"; but the scholion interprets it as "something that comes after another," as a second draught after a first: if the latter is accepted, we might render "and the last (decisive) thrust of a tawny spear."

[2] The name of Asmā's husband was Shabath b. Ḥaut b. Qais, of the Banu Saʿd b. ʿAdī of Fazārah (Mufḍt. p. 30).

[3] *Wail*, "woe", does not necessarily mean an imprecation: it may be an expression of admiration.

[4] The heathen Arabs were accustomed to tether by a dead man's grave his riding-camel, with the sinews of its hind-legs cut so that it could not run away: there it was left without food or drink till it died. See Wellhausen, *Heidenthum*[2], 180—81, and references in notes.

(4) I had sprung to hold back from him the horsemen without a moment's delay —
by the life of my father! — if Death came not to stay my feet[1].

XXXIII.

'Āmir rode his horse al-Kulaib in a race, and was beaten: to this the verses refer.

(1) Methinks al-Kulaib betrayed me, or else I did him wrong, in the rugged
ground of Hillīt — yet he was not wont to fail me.
(2) Yea, I hold him excused: 'twas I myself was unskilful; I was matched with
a guileful man[2], and was found to be too heavy a weight.

XXXIV.

See *ante*, No. XXIV.

(1) I am told that my people attach blame to me: it seems that the deaths of
my fellows are to be laid to my charge;
(2) And if horses have been slain, and the men that rode them, it is I, forsooth,
that am their destroyer — I that am myself destroyed!

XXXIVᴀ.

A fragment by Dubai'ah of 'Abs[3], said to be an answer to some poem by 'Āmir: but
the part that has been preserved does not indicate the circumstances or the point of the
controversy. Vv. 1—4 are part of a *nasīb*: v. 5 is scarcely intelligible; v. 6 appears to be
part of the description of a horse.

(1) The tale-bearers say that Dūmah has come short of my thought of her, and
that her promised grace has all shrunk away.
(2) They spoke true: the deceitful shows of her have become plain to me, and
(a raven)[4], coming from behind, with featherless wings, has set forth her case:

---

[1] Vv. 3 and 4 do not seem to have stood thus in the original poem, as they do not cohere together:
v. 3 speaks of a lion besetting his father, v. 4 of horsemen attacking him.

[2] So our text. Prof. Nöldeke would read خَفّ for خِبّ, and would render "I was matched with a
man of lighter weight." This suggestion is supported by Yāq.'s false reading خَفّ, and by the anti-
thesis of بادنا.   [3] See No. XXI *ante*.   [4] A bird of ill omen: see 'Abīd II, 3.

(3) A bird with his beak set close, that croaks in the noon-tide, full of clamour,
looking as though his wings were bound.

(4) And I reviled him — "May all his eggs be addled, and may there hit him
an arrow with a rusty head tied on with a sinew, travelling straight!"

*   *   *   *   *

(5) Dost thou rejoice that a wound has befallen a knight? There is not left of
all whom thou ruledst except one subject (?)

*   *   *   *   *

(6) It seemed as though his neck, when thou didst look at it from the side,
were a palm-trunk bare, stripped of its covering of *lif*[1] and naked.

XXXV.

A satire.

(1) Thou art the son of a mother black in the wrists, woolly-haired, and a
hunch-backed father sprung from the offspring of slave-girls;

(2) A hanger-on of a tribe, he was not of their full blood, but of some outside
strain the stock of which has perished.

(3) Thy father was an evil sire, and thy mother's brother like to him; how
then canst thou resemble any but thy father and (maternal) uncle?

XXXVI.

(1) I left the women of Sāʿidah son of Murr[2] wailing loudly where the fight
was fought (and he lay dead):

(2) I grasped with both hands, to deal with him, a knotty lance — a long brown
shaft was topped by its sharp blade;

(3) I clove therewith the junction of his broad ribs, and his outer wrapper was
all defiled with blood.[3]

XXXVII.

(1) Ha! what a raid was ours, while all the country lay gasping with famine,
and the horizon was bare and naked,[4]

---

[1] *Lif* is the membranous fibres that grow at the base of the branches of palm-trees.
[2] A man of ʿAbs, slain by ʿĀmir.
[3] Or, according to the commentary, served as a plug to stanch the blood.
[4] Bare, that is, either of clouds or of greenery.

(2) Till we poured down upon Hamdān[1] in a whirlwind of dust — The leavings of dogs! — and yet they were not our business!

(3) And all day long in the hollow plain we left not a neck or a face or a skull but we rained blows upon it.

(4) Then we withdrew, and their wretched case had ceased not until we had stanched to the full the thirst of spearshafts and javelins.

(5) No, we had not them in mind: no excuse had we for falling on them: but what came to pass came to pass.

(6) We started, intending the Sons of Nahd and their brothers, Jarm: but God intended Hamdān.

END OF THE DĪWĀN.

SUPPLEMENT

OF VERSES FOUND ELSEWHERE AND ATTRIBUTED TO 'ĀMIR IBN AṬ-ṬUFAIL,
BUT NOT CONTAINED IN THE DĪWĀN.

1.

This is the poem in which is contained (vv. 8—10) the fragment forming No. I of the *Dīwān*; there seems to be no reason to doubt its genuineness.

(1) The daughter of the 'Amrite says — "What is the matter with thee, that thou lookest like one tortured by the bite of a snake, whereas but now thou wast strong and healthy?"

(2) I answered her — "The care that carks me thou knowest well: 'tis to get vengeance from the tribes of Zubaid and Arḥab.

(3) "If I assail Zubaid, I assail a mighty people: their stock and weight in their tribe are of the best;

(4) "And if I attack the two tribes of Khath'am, their blood will be medicine for my hurt; and he gets the best of vengeance who seeks it steadily:

(5) "Yea, none gets vengeance so well as he that seeks it earnestly, mounted on a short-haired steed, spare and lean like a palm-branch pruned of leaves and thorns,

(6) "With a brown spear of al-Khaṭṭ, and a bright keen sword, and a finely-woven mail-coat shining like a pool with glittering wavelets:

---

[1] See *ante*, II, 9.

(7) "The gear of a man of whom all men know well that he is a steady seeker of vengeance, himself the object of many another's quest.

(8) "And as for me, though I be the son of the Knight of ʿĀmir and born of their best, of their purest and most chastened stock,

(9) "Yet ʿĀmir has not made me its Lord because I inherited the place — God forbid that I should rise upon mother's or father's fame!

(10) "Nay, it was because I guard their peculiar land, and shield them from annoy, and hurl a troop of horse against him that strikes at their peace."

2.

See verses inserted in No. VIII, after v. 2.

3.

This verse, as indicated in the Arabic, properly belongs to a poem printed in the *Dīwān* of Labīd.

Give me not to drink with thy hands if I ladle not the water out with my own — (I mean) the camels of aḍ-Dajūʿ, with a raid in which many troops (of camels or horses) follow one after another in a string.

4.

A lamentation over the death of ʿAbd ʿAmr, son of ʿĀmir's brother Ḥandhalah ibn aṭ-Ṭufail.

(1) Is there any crier to shout the name of ʿAbd ʿAmr to the furthest line of the horsemen whom the spears hurl to ground?

(2) Nay, never, by thy father, shall I forget my friend who fell at Badwah, so long as the winds blow hither and thither!

(3) Thou wast the chosen of my soul from out of all my people, and my dearest out of all that carry arms!

5.

This short piece resembles some verses in ʿAbīd VIII, and contains the description of a bull-oryx.

(1) And there carries (me and) my weapons a steed that outstrips all others, swift as (an oryx) black-banded on the legs, black of eye-ball, a swimmer,

(2) Solitary in the plain of al-Yafāʿ, where he stalks after the herd that has passed on, himself thrust out (by some stronger fighter with his horns). [1]

(3) The hunters of a land have espied him, and have let loose their trained hounds: in each of the pursuing (hounds) is a striving to overtake him.

(4) When he fears that they may reach him, his slender shanks, wide in the space between the hind-legs, bear him swiftly away from the terror.

6.

A celebrated saying.

(1) No attack of mine brings fear to my uncle's son, nor do I blench before the attack of him that threatens me;

(2) And as for me, if I have threatened him (*i. e.* my cousin) or promised him aught, I leave unfulfilled my threat, but bring to pass my promise.

7.

(1) God has appointed for a man in some of his difficulties a straight way (of escape), and in some of his desires a warning to bid him pause;

(2) Knowst thou not that whensoever my fellow would lead me into wrong-doing, I refuse to be led, and let him go his evil way alone?

8.

(1) Would that my mother's kin, Ghanī [2], held a festival (*Duwār* [3]) whensoever evening draws in [4],

(2) In honour of their god, so that among them the days might be short (because full of delight) for the guest and the stranger!

9.

These verses are cited in connexion with the alleged intention of ʿĀmir b. aṭ-Ṭufail to

---

[1] This appears to be the sense of نَطِيحٌ, which occurs only in a passive signification; see ʾUrwah XXXIII, 2. The bull-oryx is solitary, because he has lost the fight for the possession of the herd of females: nevertheless his speed is still equal to outstripping any other enemy. Perhaps we should read نَطِيحَ for تَطْبِيحْ in the parallel passage of ʿAbīd VIII, 9.

[2] Ghanī (the stock of Ṭufail al-Ghanawī), a tribe closely associated with Jaʿfar b. Kilāb, probably on the mother's side, though not nearly related by male descent to ʿĀmir b. Ṣaʿṣaʿah.

[3] *Duwār*, the name of the "Pillar" mentioned before in No. XI, 9. Here the word seems to stand for a festival of some kind, involving sacrifice and feasting.

[4] Various reading "on every third day."

attack the Prophet at al-Madīnah: but it seems scarcely possible that they should be genuine. ʿĀmir would not have spoken of Yathrib by the Prophet's name of al-Madīnah, nor would he have spoken of its inhabitants as "Helpers", Anṣār, also an Islamic title. See Introduction, pp. 89—91.

(1) The Prophet sent what thou seest: and meseemeth we are deliberately leading an army against the companies (?);

(2) And verily they (the horses) have brought us down to al-Madīnah, lean of flesh, and verily they have slain in its open valley the Helpers.

10.

(1) Why dost thou not ask (what happens) when the pregnant camels come home at evening distressed (?) like young ostriches, without moistening their udder cords ? [1]

(2) Verily we hasten the entertainment of our guest by slaying a camel in a sound and healthy condition, before we provide for our own household: and we also seek vengeance for wrongs done to us;

(3) And we count up Days [2] and glorious deeds that are ours: of old do we surpass all men, whether of the Desert or of settled countries;

(4) And among them (the Days) were Khuwaiy, the Day of adh-Dhuhāb, and in aṣ-Ṣafā a Day of which the glory was made plain and manifest,. and went forth (in fame abroad).

11.

Praise of a warrior of ʿAmir, ʿAbs son of Ḥidhār, called by his *kunyah* of Abū Ubaiy, of the subtribe of Wā'ilah, for his valiant deeds on the disastrous Day of ar-Raqam: so at least says Hishām ibn al-Kalbī; but the tenor of the verses suggests some other engagement: they do not suit well the circumstances of ar-Raqam (see Introduction, pp. 80—81).

(1) And Abū Ubaiy — never did I see the like of him: goodly was he in the evening and in full daylight!

(2) Abū Ubaiy faced the host, springing forward to the fight, he of Wā'ilah, and spurned the thought of turning his back;

(3) He covered the rearguard, what time Salūl [3] and ʿĀmir began to give way on the day of battle before Fazārah.

---

[1] See for "udder-cords", No. VIII, 1; the meaning here is, "in times of cold and drought, when milk is scarce." The reading of the verse appears to be partly corrupt; هَرَّجَ الرِّئَالِ can hardly be right.

[2] *I. e.*, battles won.

[3] It is somewhat surprising to find Salūl mentioned here as taking part with ʿĀmir in the battle of ar-Raqam: see *ante*, No. XXV.

12.

And in al-Faifā of the Yaman the tribes that he had gathered together stirred up mutual boasting, clamouring against one another.

13.

'Āmir is said to have hamstrung his horse Qurzul [1] (which had previously been the steed of his father aṭ--Ṭufail) on the Day of ar-Raqam; the horse had broken down with him in the flight, and could carry him no further, and he left him thus to die in order to prevent his falling into the hands of the enemy; and he said:

A good companion for a homeless wanderer was he whom yesternight I left in Taḍrūʿ, beating the ground with his forefeet and breathing out his life!

14.

According to the traditionist Muʾarrij, a chief and famous warrior belonging to the tribe of Ṭayyiʾ named Duʾāb [2], who had taken a wife in Hawāzin, was treacherously killed while visiting his father-in-law. Thereupon Zaid al-Khail [3], with a body of horse belonging to his sub-tribe Nabhān and some of al-Ghauth, raided the tribe of 'Āmir b. Ṣaʿṣaʿah, and killed every man of that tribe who fell into his hands and admitted that he knew of the murder of the chief of Ṭayyiʾ. When he returned, his fellow tribesmen asked him about his doings; Zaid in reply declared that he had in no way obtained due vengeance for the death of Duʾāb, which could only be satisfied by the slaying of 'Āmir b. Mālik "the Player with Lances" (uncle of 'Āmir b. aṭ-Ṭufail and chief of the tribe of 'Āmir), and that 'Āmir son of aṭ-Ṭufail would not be an equivalent. To this arrogant claim 'Āmir is said to have replied in the following verses:

(1) Say to Zaid — 'Time was when thou wast preferred for thy balanced mind, when the minds of other men were marked by violence and folly.

(2) 'This slain man of yours was not one of your foremost — [Dhu-l]-Kalāʿ, or Yaḥsub, or ['Abd]-Kulāl, [4]

(3) 'Or the sons of the Eater of Murār [5], or the proud race of Jafnah [6], kings of exalted rank,

---

[1] This is the statement of LA XI, 151; but the same thing is said in BAthīr 485 of 'Āmir's horse al-Ward (also called al-Maznūq) on the Day called there يوم النباة (Caussin de Perceval's "Journée de Noubaa"; Essai II 538). In the ʿIqd the name is given as النتناة, but the correct spelling appears to be البَتْناءة: see Bakrī 138—9.

[2] So Agh.: perhaps we should read *Dhuʾāb*.   [3] For Zaid see Nos. XIX and XXI, *ante*.

[4] Names of Ḥimyarite princes.   [5] The ancestor of the Kindite kings of Northern Arabia.

[6] Ancestor of the Kings of Ghassān.

(4) 'Or the "Son of the Rain of the Heaven"[1] — well do men know it, and it boots not to use high boastful words.

(5) 'Were ye to slay ʿĀmir son of Ṭufail, well were Ṭayyiʾ of the mountains[2] repaid for any death of theirs.

(6) 'As for me, by Him to whom men go on pilgrimage, few there be in ʿĀmir that are like me,

(7) 'On the day when the wealth of the warrior in fight is in naught but the point of a tawny quivering spear,

(8) 'A bridle in the mouth of a short-haired steed, tall as a palm-stem, and a glittering keen-edged sword,

(9) 'And a mail-coat like a shining pool, with ample skirts — these, in the medley of fortune, these are my wealth;

(10) 'And my uncle has the dignity of headship and age, and a lofty fortune in all Hawāzin:

(11) 'Save that I have the command of Hawāzin in war, to smite down the crowned head that uplifts itself,

(12) 'And to drive home my lance through the warrior in the hot dust of battle, on the back of a great strong steed, that obeys my slightest touch.'

15.

A verse recalling the Day of Shiʿb Jabalah and events prior thereto.

We exacted the price of al-Jaun from ʿAbs[3], and Maʿbad[4] died among us a prisoner, starving himself to death.

16.

The passage is cited in the Lexicons in illustration of the special use of the verb

---

[1] Title of al-Mundhir, the most celebrated king of al-Ḥīrah (see *ante*, pp. 1, 4, 8).

[2] Referring to the two mountain ranges Ajaʾ and Salmā, on and between which Ṭayyiʾ were settled.

[3] Two Kindite princes, ʿAmr and Muʿāwiyah, called "Sons of al-Jaun," accompanied their mother's kin of Tamīm on the Day of Shiʿb Jabalah. Both were taken prisoners, ʿAmr by ʿAuf b. al-Aḥwaṣ, and Muʿāwiyah by Ṭufail, father of our poet ʿĀmir. ʿAuf released ʿAmr, after cutting off his forelock; some men of ʿAbs met him on his way homewards, and killed him. Thereupon ʿAuf made a claim upon ʿAbs, requiring them either to pay the blood-wit for ʿAmr, or to give a man to be slain in exchange for him. Qais b. Zuhair, the Chief of ʿAbs, applied to Ṭufail, and induced him to surrender his prisoner Muʿāwiyah, who was given up to ʿAuf, who killed him. The price Qais paid to Ṭufail for his captive was the famous horse Qurzul. (In Agh. X 42 this verse is ascribed to an Islamic poet of ʿĀmir's kindred, Nāfiʿ b. al-Ḥanjarah b. al-Ḥakim b. ʿAqīl b. Ṭufail b. Mālik, and the story is somewhat differently told.)

[4] Maʿbad son of Zurārah was the elder brother of Laqīṭ and chief of Tamīm; he was captured by ʿĀmir b. Ṣaʿṣaʿah at the battle of Raḥraḥān, a year before the Day of Shiʿb Jabalah. They demanded for him the ransom of a king, 1000 camels. This Laqīṭ refused to pay, and Maʿbad died a prisoner, as the verse relates.

نُزِّل in the sense of visiting Minà during the Pilgrimage season: it is the opening two verses of a *qaṣīdah*, and has every appearance of being genuine.

(1) Does Asmā intend to go down to Minà or not? Tell us, O Asmā, what is in thy mind to do.

(2) If thou goest down to Minà, I will go there too, and not visit the fair, even though Jasr and Bāhilah [1] journey thereto to sell their wares.

17.

Apparently a passage from a poem addressed to his tribe for failing to recognize his deserts (*cf.* No. XXIV).

(1) I am utterly worn out among you by your crookedness against me every day, though I myself be straight.

(2) Thick stubborn necks like bleachers' bats, and swelling rumps on the camel-saddles!

18.

Said in the *ʿUmdah* to have been uttered by ʿĀmir b. aṭ-Ṭufail at the court of an-Nuʿmān, the last Lakhmite King of al-Ḥīrah, when Bisṭām b. Qais of Shaibān (Bakr b. Wāʾil) was preferred before him for honour among the tribes visiting the King.

(1) The Tubbaʿs [2] in past time had the preeminence, and the Son of (the Eater of) Murār, and the Kings over Syria;

(2) Now at last the kingdom of Lakhm has come to a King whose spear-point bristles up, who attacks one who makes no attack upon him;

(3) He falls upon us with his claws, and seeks to put upon us the collar of the ring-dove, causing us to stumble and lie prone in the dust.

(4) If God grant a time to come when thou [3] art in evil case, we shall leave thee there alone, while thou callest on the house of Bisṭām!

(5) Look now on the proud ones of Muḍar [4] who protect thee not. Is there in Rabīʿah for thee any protector, if thou call not on us?

---

[1] Jasr, a Yamanite tribe sprung from Saʿd al-ʿAshīrah; Bāhilah, a sister-tribe of Ghanī, of Maʿaddic descent, who lived under the protection of branches of ʿĀmir b. Ṣaʿṣaʿah (Agh. IV, 140).

[2] *Tubbaʿ* was the title of the succession of later Ḥimyarite kings; for "the Eater of Murār" see *ante* No. 14, 3; by the kings over Syria is meant the House of Ghassān.   [3] Addressed to an-Nuʿmān.

[4] The expression Muḍar would include the great groups of Hawāzin, Ghaṭafān, and Tamīm, besides many other smaller units: the leading tribe of Rabīʿah would be Bakr b. Waʾil.

19.

Attributed in the commentary to the Ḥamāsah to ʿAbd ʿAmr b. Shuraiḥ, at the battle of Faif ar-Rīḥ (*ante*, No. XI).

(1) Be thou divorced if thou ask not what manner of knight thy husband showed himself when he faced Ṣudā' and Khathʿam!

(2) I dash against them Daʿlaj my steed, and his breast resounds with a murmurous sound as he plains to me of the impact thereon of the spears[1].

20.

Cited by Ibn Qutaibah as a fine passage in ʿĀmir's poetry.

(1) There is no land but the men of Qais ʿAilān are the lords thereof; to them belong both of its open spaces, (that is), its levels and its rugged uplands;

(2) And our glory has attained to the utmost horizons of the heaven: ours are the clear blue spaces, ours are the clouds thereof.

21.

See the note prefixed to the Arabic text: the verses below can scarcely be understood without reading the poem ascribed to Yazīd b. ʿAbd al-Madān to which they reply.

(1) I marvel at him that portrays the night-wanderer of the steppes, and at the charges which the Sons of ad-Dayyān bring against us;

(2) They exult against me because we paid tax to Muḥarriq[2], and because of the tribute (in camels) that was led to an-Nuʿmān;

(3) What hast thou to do with the son of Muḥarriq and his tribes, and the tribute paid to the Lakhmite among ʿAilān?

(4) Turn thy powers to the aid of thine own people, and leave alone the tribes of the sons of Qaḥtān[3].

(5) If among you aforetime any received tribute or not[4], your boast is that of every man of al-Yaman.

---

[1] *Cf.* ʿAntarah *Muʿall.* 73.

[2] Meaning (probably) ʿAmr b. Hind, son of al-Mundhir, king of al-Ḥīrah.

[3] Probably, if the reading is correct, by this is meant the Yamanite stocks which founded kingdoms in the North, Lakhm, Ghassān, and Kindah.

[4] Prof. Nöldeke would read أوْ لا instead of أوْلَى, and render as above.

(6) Boast thyself of the house of al-Ḥimās and Mālik and the sons of aḍ-Ḍibāb,
and Raʿbal and Qanān (?).

(7) As for me, I am accounted the illustrious, son of the rider of Qurzul, and
Abū Barā honoured and exalted me;

(8) And Abū Jarī[1] of the great deeds, and Mālik — these two protect our honour
on every morning of a contest with lances.

(9) And when severe troubles beset Hawāzin, I am the one whose name is
exalted, and the builder up (of their prosperity: or, of their fame).

22.

(1) Verily if thou hadst seen my people, O Umaimah, on the morning of Qurāqir,
it would have pleased thine eyes.

(2) (Their horse) came forth, having charged through the tribe of Kalb[2], and
their thirst (for blood) had been quenched and (their fever) cured.

(3) And on the day of ʿUwairiḍāt, a little before dawn, they gave a morning-
draught to al-Ḥusain in al-Yaman:

(4) And in al-Mardāt they lit upon spoil, and all that they sought from the
people of al-Yamāmah[3]. ʿ

23.

A fragment of a *nasīb* referring to the traces of an encampment.

They became (or, were) conspicuous in the upper parts of the waste, as though
they were the parchments of a scribe that are unfolded before a reader[4].

---

[1] Probably we should read *Ḥarī* for *Jarī*.

[2] Probably we should read Kaʿb (*i. e.*, the tribe of al-Ḥārith b. Kaʿb) for Kalb.

[3] See *ante*, No. VII, 3, 4.

[4] It is very unlikely that this v. is by ʿĀmir b. aṭ-Ṭufail. It is cited in the L A and T A as by
"Ibn Ṭufail", without ʿĀmir or the article, and appears to be the only authority for the (otherwise
unknown) word قلّوج in the sence of "a writer." Prof. Nöldeke suggests that *Fallūj* is a place-name:
see *Fallūjah*, said in Yāq. III 915—16 to be the name of two villages in the cultivated plain of Baghdād,
near ʿAin Tamr. The use of تَلا in the sense of "reader, cantillator," in itself almost certainly excludes
the possibility of our poet being the author; this sense, which the word does not possess in the old
poetry, is borrowed from Aramaic liturgical language, and appears for the first time in the Qurʾān.

EMENDANDA ET ADDENDA.

In printing an Arabic work in Europe (especially when vocalized) many accidents to the type are inevitable; fortunately the blemishes are generally such as can easily be corrected by the touch of a pen. In the following list only the more important cases of lost points or slipped vowels are noticed.

ARABIC TEXT.

Page line

I 7-8: see LA XIX, 225[10].

٢ notes, line 1: insert full stop after MS.

٧ 6 Read شَاخِصْ.

١١ 3 For حَشِيشِهَا read حَسِيسِهَا.

١٢ 3 Read جَرَبُوا.

4 This verse is also cited LA IV, 361, foot.

١٥ 17 Read بِمَعْضَلٍ.

١٨ 9 For تَأَنَّقَ read (with the MS) تَنَوَّقَ (identical in meaning).

١٩ 10 Read حَاجَنَاءٍ.

٢١ 12 In some copies خَاصَّةٌ has lost the dot of the خ.

٢٢ 10 Read عَضَّ.

٣٣ 1 For غِيَرْ read غَيَرْ.

4 *Cf.* the verse of Rabī'ah of Asad cited LA XVII, 356[14].

٢٩ 11 Read لِلضِّبَاءِ.

٣١ 9 Perhaps نَطْبِيَجْ should be read for تَطْبِيَجْ: *cf.* 'Āmir Frag. 5 (p. ١٥٤), l. 2.

10 For يَسِيبَجْ read يُشِيبَجْ: *cf. l. c.*, l. 3.

15 For 51 read 15.

٣٥ 1 Read خَضَّمَ.

Note *b*: the use of حَضَّ in the sense "to sharpen" is confirmed by Anbārī, *Mufaḍḍalīyāt*, 238[22], and scholion to Hudh. 18, 27 (ed. Kosegarten p. 49): the statement that it is unknown to the Lexx. should be cancelled; see LA IX, 103[21].

Page　line

٣٤　Note *b*: read الدَّمِين.

٣٧　11　For صُدُورًا read صُدُورَ.

٣٩　11　This verse, with غَالَتْ for مَالَتْ, and يَمِين for شِمَالُ, is cited LA X, 229[4] as by al-Aʿshà; it does not, however, as Prof. Geyer informs me, occur in Thaʿlab's recension of that poet's *Dīwān*, and the LA should no doubt be corrected to قال عَبِيد بن الأَبرص.

٤٠　14　Read ضَرْبٌ.

٤٤　7　For ٩ read ٧.

　　11　Read مَدَّتْهُ.

٤٥　1　Read تَنَّأَى.

٤٧　7　Read وَكُلُّ.

٤٩　10　Read مِذْنَبٌ.

٥٠　16　Read غِيَرٍ.

　　17　Read جَهِلْتُ.

٥٥　13　Read رِحْلَتَنَا.

　　14　Read الرِّكَابُ.

　　15　Read بُرَايَةٍ.

٥٦　8　Read خَرِصًا.

　　12　Read (the second time) بَطْنُهُ.

٥٧　6　Read الْهَوَاجِرَ.

　　12　For بَرْق الْجِبَالِ read يَزِنُ الْجِبَالَ (see translation p. 45, end of argument, and p. 46, note [4]).

٥٩　Note *f*: read يَوْمَئِذ.

٦١　4　Read بِالْحَمْلِ (see Lane 648 *c*).

　　Note *f*: read عِنْدُ.

٦٢　10　Read سَاعَةَ, ضَامِزَةً, and مَسْمُومَةَ, and cancel the last seven words of note *h*.

٦٣　10　and note *d*: The reading of the MS, فَالْمِحَا, suggests فَالْمُحْتَبَى (instead of فَالْمُخْتَبَى) as the right version: this would mean "a place where one sits at ease": Naq. 712[3]; but no proper name of this form is given in the Lexx.

٦٤　6　Read خَمَطُوا.

Page line

٦٥ 4 Perhaps in place of مَتْقِبه (MS مَتْقِفَة) we should read مَتْعِبه; see LA I, 229[17 ff.]

11 Read الْمَحَاص.

٦٧ 16 For بَعْد انْتِقال we should perhaps put بَعْد الظَّلَال as the more probable reading of the MS; *cf.* ʿAbīd XV, 6.

٧٠ 9 Read مُقْلِتٌ مِنْه.

٧٣ 2 Read عُطْبُولَةٌ.

10 Read أَبِيها.

11 Read أَجْنَادَه.

٧٦ 9 Delete the *e* before رَبْط.

14 Read صَاحْصَم.

٧٩ Note *a*, line 2, end: read يَعُدّه.

5 Read تُطْع.

15 Read صِنْدِد.

٨٠ 8 Read لَعَلّ.

9 Read هَلاكِى.

٨١ 2 Read يُرِبغ.

11 Read جَمَّة.

٨٣ 1 Read ں – for – ں.

2 Read ں – –, and فَجَنْبَى.

٨٤ 13 The phrase سِيْرًا وَأمْرَأسَا is perhaps an allusion to I. Q. Muʿall. 48.

٧٩ Fragment 12: vv. 1 and 2 are cited in LA XX, 239[6,7], with other readings (poet not named). In BQut. *Shiʿr* 123 v. 2 is ascribed to Abū Duʾād.

id. Fragment 15: this piece appears to be by Umayyah b. Abi-ṣ-Ṣalt; vv. 2 and 3 are cited as by him in LA III, 166[1,2]. See also Schulthess, Umayyah, p. 34, ll. 25—26, and p. 33, v. ٣١. Read in v. 3 فَرْجَة for فُرْجَة.

٩٠ 13 Read الطفيل.

٩٢ 10 Delete the *kasrah* below الْمُناقَرة.

٩٣ 4 Read عَرَفْت.

٩٤ Note *g*: add "but *cf.* v. 9 on opposite page."

٩٩ 6 Read الشاعِر.

Note *f*: read أُخْرِج.

Page	line	
٩٧	14	Read نَجَبِ.
٩٨	13	Verses 23 and 24 of this poem are cited in Naq. 678[1,2], with slight differences of reading, and a third verse, not in our version, is added:

وَجَمْعُ الْجَوْنِ إِذْ دَلَفُوا إِلَيْنَا صَبَحْنَا جَمْعَهُمْ جَيْشًا لُهَامَا

	16	Read فَتَوَى.
١..	15	Read الْجَوْنِ.
١.٢	13	Read السِّنَانُ.
١.٥	10	Read نُشَكُّ.
	13	Read الْخَيْلُ.
	18	Read كَأْسَهُ.
١.٨	17	Read رَتَّ.
١١.	16:	the statement that سِيدٌ, "wolf", has no plural من هذا اللفظ is incorrect; see ʿAbīd IX, 9, السِّيدَانُ, Ibn Athīr, *Kāmil*, I, 484, last v. of poem. LAN, 217[22] has the word.
١١١	7:	انْتَتَرَتْ is clear in the MS., and yields a possible sense; but the commentator appears to have read انْتَتَرَتْ.
١١٢	11	Read كُلِّ.
١١٣	line 8	فَلَتَنَخْبِرَنَّكَ should have been shown as an alternative reading.
„	10:	the name of Muʿaqqir's father (or grandfather) was undoubtedly حِمَارٌ.
„	11:	for وَضَنَتْ read وَضَتْ (LA XI, 189[6]), or أَوْضَتْ (LA II, 205[7]).

This citation is another example of Ibn al-Anbārī's defective memory, noticed in the Introduction, p. 92, and a very curious one; for the two hemistichs of the verse do not cohere together in the original, and relate to quite different things. The passage is fully explained in Khiz. II, 289, and is there given as follows:

وَذُبْيَانِيَّةٌ أَوْصَتْ بَنِيهَا بِأَنْ كَذَبَ الْقَرَاطِفُ وَالْقُرُوفُ

تُنَجِّزُهُمْ بِمَا اسْطَاعَتْ وَقَالَتْ بَنِيَّ فَكُلُّكُمْ بَطَلٌ مُسِيفُ

فَأَخْلَقْنَا مَوَدَّتَهَا فَقَاظَتْ وَمَأْقِى عَيْنِهَا حَذِلٌ نَطُوفُ

The poet (originally from al-Yaman) was an adherent of ʿĀmir (section Numair) on the great Day of Jabalah, and the poem is one of those he made to celebrate that victory. He imagines a mother of sons in the tribe of Dhubyān (one of those who were routed): —

"Many the mother in Dhubyān who enjoined her sons — 'Be sure to bring back plunder of blankets with heavy nap and bags of leather tanned with pomegranate-skin!'

"She fitted them out with all she could scrape together, and said — 'Sons of mine! surely each one of you is a needy [1] hero.'

"But we disappointed her affection, and she spent the summer with the rims of her eyes bare of lashes through constant weeping [2]."

The first verse is frequently quoted in Dictionaries and other linguistic works for the remarkable use of the verb كَذَبَ in exhortation or instigation: see the Khiz. *l. c.*, LA II, 205, Lane 2598 *c*, and Howell, Grammar I, pp. 661 and 102-3 A. The third verse, as noted, is in LA XIII, 158[10].

١١٧ 10 Read بِمَوْضِع.

١١٩ 9 Read عَشِيَّةَ.

١٢٠ 8 Read الْعَوَانِ.

١٢١ 4 This verse of an-Namir's and the poem to which it belongs will be found in *Mukhtārāt*, p. 20.

13 Read وَخَثْعَمَا.

١٢٢ 7 Read ٱلدَّمُ.

8 The verse of ʿUjair's to which the fragment سَلَالِيمَ الْعَلَقْ belongs will be found in Anb. *Mufaḍḍt.* 402[6].

١٣٤ 14 The two words ascribed to الْغَنَوِيِّ look like a fragment from the poem in *Mukhtārāt* 27—30, *Aṣmaʿīyāt* 11 and 12, by Kaʿb b. Saʿd al-Ghanawī: but they do not actually occur in the poem; perhaps the commentator's memory has again played him false.

١٣٥ 9 For شَتِيرَ read شُتَيْرَ; see Naq. 387[6] and 388[6]: this is not however the same person as mentioned there, who was a Kilābī, of ʿĀmir's own tribe: this is an enemy.

١٣٦ 13 *Cf.* al-Mubarrad, *Kāmil* 564[6].

١٣٧ 20 Read شُتَيْرًا.

١٤٧ 1 Read نَجِّدُ.

١٤٨ 3 Read فَأَجَابَهُ.

١٤٩ 3 Read نَسِّلْ.

١٥٤ 12 Yāqūt reads الْبَقَاعِ, not الْبَغَاعِ: but no root يقع appears to exist in the Arabic

---

[1] Literally, one who has lost all his camels by murrain (*suwāf*).

[2] *I. e.*, for her sons all slain.

Page   line

language, while يفاع is common in the sense of "an elevated region", and
may have been used as a proper name; it seems to be so used in v. 35
of al-Marrār's poem, Mfḍt XVI (p. 150⁸), cited in Bakrī 782¹⁶. Yāqūt himself
seems to regard the spelling with ة as suspicious.

١٥٨   9   This verse, in LA XVII, 335⁶, is ascribed to عامر بن عُقَيْل السَّعْدىّ, and in Abū
Zaid, *Nawādir*, 161, both are attributed to عَلِىّ بن طُفَيْل السَّعْدىّ الجاهلىّ;
probably the last is the correct name of the poet.

15   Read بأَظْفارِ.

١٩.   5   Read كَعْب for كَلْب: see *ante*, No. IV, 2.

١٩٥   Against أُمّ قَطام, for 16²³ read 16¹³.

ENGLISH PORTION.

P. 10 l. 9. The date of the death of Jāḥiḍh is 255, not 256.

P. 13 l. 22. The first word of the list should be الأَلَى. The index of words appended
to the Arabic text enables this list of words special to ʿAbīd to be considerably extended.

P. 24 l. 1. The springs of Līnah were recently (March 1910) visited by Capt. G. E.
Leachman: see Journal of Royal Geographical Society, March 1911, p. 272.

P. 54 l. 9. For *pterygosperma* read *aptera*: see p. 112, note ⁵.

P. 63, verse (19): read "my".

P. 81 l. 6. For Ḥauq read Ḥauṭ: the genealogy is correctly given on p. 117, note 2.

P. 92 l. 13. For 1910 read 1911.

كِتَابُ دِيوَانِ شِعْرِ

عَـبِـيـدِ بْـن الْأَبْـرَصِ السَّعْدِيّ الْأَسَدِيّ

[MS. Brit. Mus. Or. 6771, Fol. 60b ff.]

بِسْمِ اللهِ الرَّحْمٰنِ الرَّحِيمِ

كَانَ مِنْ شَأْنِ a عُبَيْدِ بْنِ الْأَبْرَصِ بْنِ جُشَمَ بْنِ عَامِرِ [بْنِ هِرٍّ] بْنِ مَالِكِ بْنِ الْحٰرِثِ [بْنِ سَعْدِ]

ابْنِ ثَعْلَبَةَ [بْنِ دُودَانَ] بْنِ أَسَدِ بْنِ خُزَيْمَةَ بْنِ مُدْرِكَةَ بْنِ الْيَاسِ بْنِ مُضَرَ بْنِ نِزَارِ بْنِ مَعَدِّ بْنِ

عَدْنَانَ b أَنَّهُ كَانَ رَجُلًا مُقِلًّا لَا مَالَ لَهُ. فَأَقْبَلَ ذَاتَ يَوْمٍ وَمَعَهُ غُنَيْمَةٌ لَهُ وَمَعَهُ أُخْتٌ لَهُ تُدْعَى بِمَاوِيَّةَ

لِيُورِدَ غَنَمَهُ: فَمَنَعَهُ رَجُلٌ مِنْ مَالِكِ بْنِ ثَعْلَبَةَ وَجَبَهَهُ. فَانْطَلَقَ حَزِينًا مَهْمُومًا لِلَّذِي صَنَعَ الْمَالِكِيُّ بِهِ

حَتَّى أَتَى شَجَرَاتٍ وَاسْتَظَلَّ تَحْتَيْهِنَّ فَنَامَا هُوَ وَأُخْتُهُ. فَزَعَمُوا أَنَّ الْمَالِكِيَّ نَظَرَ إِلَيْهِ وَإِلَى أُخْتِهِ c [إِلَى 5

جَنْبِهِ فَقَالَ]

ذَاكَ عُبَيْدٌ قَدْ d أَصَابَ مَيَّا   يَا لَيْتَهُ أَنْقَحَهَا صَبِيَّا

فَحَمَلَتْ فَوَلَدَتْ ضَاوِيَّا

فَسَمِعَهُ عُبَيْدٌ فَرَفَعَ يَدَيْهِ إِلَى السَّمَاءِ ثُمَّ ابْتَهَلَ فَقَالَ: اللّٰهُمَّ إِنَّ فُلَانًا قَدْ ظَلَمَنِي وَرَمَانِي بِالْبُهْتَانِ:

فَأَذِلَّنِي مِنْهُ وَانْصُرْنِي عَلَيْهِ. ثُمَّ e رَفَعَ رَأْسَهُ إِلَى السَّمَاءِ ثُمَّ ابْتَهَلَ ثُمَّ قَالَ: اللّٰهُمَّ ذَاكَ يَقُولُ الشِّعْرَ. [ثُمَّ نَامَ.] 10

---

a) The genealogy here given, with the additions in square brackets, agrees with that in Kk fol. 131r and Mukht. 86, and also with that (due to Abū ʿAmr ash-Shaibānī) in Ten Poems 159, except that the latter has حَنْتَم for جُشَم and فِيْر for هِرّ; Agh XIX 84 has the same, with حنتم and زهير: سعيد is misprinted for سعد; so also Yaʿqūbī I 305 (MS جشم, print حنتم). Khiz. I, 323 (like the second genealogy given at head of poem No. I) inserts عوف before جشم, and has like Agh. زهير for هِر. As between حَنْتَم and جُشَم, MS. authority is generally in favour of the latter; and TA VIII, 229[31] indicates that it should be adopted.

b) The story that follows is said in Mukht. 83 to be due to Abū ʿUbaidah; Tibrīzī attributes it to Abū ʿAmr ash-Shaibānī; Agh. ascribes it to the latter and Ibn al-Aʿrābī (through Muḥammad b. Ḥabīb).   c) Added from other versions.   d) Mukht. أَتَى مَاوِيًّا; Agh. and Tib. as our text.

e) Compare Agh. XIX, 84, line 5 from foot; this awkward sentence and needless repetition of ثم ابتهل appear to be due to corruption of the reading in Agh.

فزعموا اَنَّه اَتاه آتٍ فى منامه بِكُبَّةٍ مِنْ *a* شِعْرٍ فَاَلْقاها فى فيه وقال: قُلْ ما يُذْلِكَ فَاَنْتَ اَشْعَرُ الْعَرَبِ واَمْجَدُ الْعَرَبِ: اِنْ صِرْتَ مُقْلًّا فَلَمّا بَسَطْتَ يَدًا ووَصَلْتَ رَحِمًا. فَاَنْتَبَهَ وَهُوَ *b* يَرْتَجِزُ بِبَنى مالِكٍ (وكان يقال لهم بَنُو الزِّنْيَةِ) وَهُوَ يقول

يَا بَنى الزِّنْيَةِ ما غَـرَّكُـمْ   لَكُمُ الْـوَيْـلُ بِسِرْبالٍ *c* حُجْرُ

5 فَلَمْ يَزَلْ فَضْلُه فى قَومِه يُعْرَفُ حَتّى قُتِلَ ☙

d وكان مِن [حديثِ] قَتْلِه اَنَّ الْمُنْذِرَ بن ماءِ السَّماءِ بَنى الْغَرِيَّيْنِ. فَقِيلَ له: ما ذا تُريد بِهِما. (وكان بِناؤُهُما على قَبْرَى رَجُلَيْنِ مِن بَنى اَسَدٍ كانا نَديمَيْهِ اَحَدُهُما خالِد بن *e* نَضْلَةَ الْقَقْعَسِىُّ *f* وكان اُسِرَ يَومَ جَبَلَةَ: والآخَرُ عَمْرُو بن مَسْعودٍ.) فَقال: *g* ما اَنَا بِمَلِكٍ اِن خالَفَ النّاسُ اَمْرى: لا يَمُرُّ اَحَدٌ مِن وُفودِ الْعَرَبِ اِلّا بَيْنَهُما. وكان [له] فى السَّنَةِ يَومانِ مَعْروفانِ بِيَومِ بُؤْسٍ ويَوم *h* نَعْمَةٍ: فكان اِذا خَرَجَ يَومَ بُؤْسِه 10 يَذْبَحُ فيه اَوَّلَ مَنْ (61a) يَلْقاه كائِنًا مَنْ كان: واِذا خَرَجَ فى يَوم نِعْمَتِه يَصِلُ اَوَّلَ مَن يَلْقاه ويَحْبُوه ويُحْسِنُ اِليه. فَبَيْنا هُوَ يَسيرُ فى يَوم بُؤْسِه اِذ اَشْرَفَ لَه عَبيدٌ. فَقال لِرَجُلٍ مِمَّنْ كان مَعه: مَنْ هذا الشَّقِىُّ. فَقال له: هذا عَبيد بن الاَبْرَصِ. فَاَتَى بِه. فَقال له الرَّجُلُ: اَبَيْتَ اللَّعْنَ اتْرُكْه: فَاِنَّ عِنْدَه مِن *i* حُسْنِ الْقَريضِ اَفْضَلَ مِمّا تُدْرِكُ فى قَتْلِه: مَعَ ما اَنَّه مِن رُؤَساءِ قَومِه واَهْلِ النَّجْدَةِ والشّاَنِ فيهِم.

---

a) So vocalized in MS Mukht. and Tib. have شَعَرٌ, which agrees better with كُبَّةٌ (a ball of thread or string rolled up), and is probably right; the tale evidently turns upon the fact that the radical of شَعَرٌ and شِعْرٌ is the same.

b) The lines that follow are not metrically a *rajaz*; all versions here agree, otherwise we might read يَرْتَجِلُ.   *c*) So all other versions. MS بِرِيبالٍ; with this reading (which Prof. Nöldeke prefers) حُجْر would apparently be a place-name.

d) This account of ʿAbīd's death is taken from Hishām b. al-Kalbī: see Agh. XIX 88 [5] ff.; Mukht. has the same version. Other forms of the legend are in Agh., *l.c.*, Khiz. I, 324, al-Qālī, *Amālī*, *Dhail* 199 ff., Yāqūt III, 792 ff., etc. The legend contains many proverbial phrases which are explained in Maidānī.   *e*) Agh. Qālī, الْمُضَلَّل.

f) No other version has this statement, which involves an anachronism; al-Mundhir was killed in 554 A.D., while the earliest alleged date of the battle of Shiʿb Jabalah is 551, and it is certainly in fact to be placed much later.   *g*) MS omits ما.   *h*) Other versions نَعيمٍ.   *i*) MS حُسْنٍ.

فَاسْمَعْ مِنْهُ وَأَدْعُهُ إِلَى مَدْحِكَ: فَإِنْ سَمِعْتَ ما يُعْجِبُكَ a كُنْتَ قَدْ عَقَتْ لَهُ المِنَّةَ: b فَإِنَّ مِدْحَتَهُ

التَّبِيعَةُ: فَإِنْ لَمْ يُعْجِبْكَ قَوْلُهُ كان هَنِيئًا عَلَيْكَ قَتْلُهُ. قال فَنَزَلَ المُنْذِرُ فَطَعِمَ

وشَرِبَ: وبَيْنَهُ وبَيْنَ النّاسِ حِجابٌ يَراهُمْ مِنْهُ ولا يَرَوْنَهُ. فَدَعا بِعَبِيد مِنْ وَراءِ السِّتْرِ. فقال لهُ رَدِيفُهُ:

ما تَرَى يا أَخا أَسَد. قال: أَرَى c الحَوايا عَلَيْها المَنايا. قال: فَعَلَيْكَ بِالخُرُوجِ لَهُ لِيُقَرِّبَكَ ذاكَ مِنَ الخَلاصِ.

قال: تَكَلَّتْكَ التَّواكِلُ d إِنِّي لا أُعْطِى بِاليَدِ ولا أُحْضِرُ البَعِيدَ والمَوْتُ أَحَبُّ إِلَيَّ. قال [لهُ المَلِكُ]: أَفَقُلْتَ 5

شَيْئًا. قال: e حالَ الجَرِيضُ دُونَ القَرِيضِ. قال لهُ المُنْذِرُ: أَنْشِدْنِى مِنْ قَوْلِكَ *أَقْفَرَ مِنْ أَهْلِهِ مَلْحُوبُ*

قال عبيد

أَقْـفَـرَ مِـنْ أَهْـلِـهِ عَـبِـيـدُ   فَلَيْسَ يُبْدِى ولا يُعِيدُ f

قال أَنْشِدْنا أَيْضًا. فقال

g الْخَمْرُ تُكْنَى الطِّلا   كَما الذِّئْبُ يُكَنَى أَبا جَعْدَةِ 10

فقال: قُلْ فِى مَدِيحًا h يَسِيرُ فِى العَرَبِ. [قال]: أَمّا والصَّبّارُ فِى ما تَجِلَ فَلا. قال: نُطْلِقُكَ وَنُحْسِنُ إِلَيْكَ.

قال: أَمّا وأَنا أَسِيرٌ فِى يَدَيْكَ فَلا. قال: نَرُدُّكَ إِلَى أَهْلِكَ وَنَلْتَزِمُ رَفْدَكَ. قال: أَمّا عَلَى شَرْطِ المُدْحِ فَلا.

قال عَـبِـيـد

---

a) This passage is difficult, and the reading probably corrupt.   b) MS التبيعة مختده فان.

c) For this proverb see Lane 679b, LA XVIII, 228⁶ ff., and Maid. (Freyt.) I, 185; and for a similar phrase see BHish. 441, 7.   d) The text is here corrupt, reading انا اى لا اعطى باليد ولا اخضر المعبد.   e) Maid. (Freyt.) I 340.

f) Agh. XIX 87 adds another verse: عَقَّتْ لَهُ عَقْةً نَكُودُ   وَحانَ مِنْها لَهُ وُرُودُ; see also Yāqūt III, 793⁹. The first verse is quoted in LA VI, 422²⁴ with فَالْيَوْمَ لا يُبْدِى ولا يُعِيدُ, and so Asās, I, 25.

g) The verse is almost always cited in this imperfect form, or with هِىَ prefixed to الخَمْرُ. The defect is cured by different persons in different ways; LA IV, 96 reads: وقالوا هِىَ الخَمْرُ الخ; Agh XIX, 88: هِىَ الخَمْرُ تُكْنَى بِأُمِّ الطِّلا; the latter seems a probable form, as أُمُّ الطِّلا is a suitable parallel to أَبُو جَعْدَةَ: wine-jars were closed with pitch or bitumen. A third attempt at amendment is that of the Muḥkam — هِىَ الخَمْرُ يَكْنُونَها بِالطِّلا: see al-Kumait, Hāshimīyāt (Horovitz), 118¹⁰. A fourth is in Yāqūt III, 79³: هِىَ الخَمْرُ بِالنِّزْلِ تُكْنَى الطِّلا.   h) MS سام: a perfect is here inadmissible.

a أَوْصَى بَنِيَّ وَأَعْمَامَهُمْ   بِأَنَّ ٱلْمَنَايَا لَهُمْ رَاصِدَهْ

لَهَا مُدَّةٌ فَنُفُوسُ ٱلْعِبَادِ   إِلَيْهَا وَإِنْ جَهَدُوا قَاصِدَهْ

فَوَٱللّٰهِ إِنْ عِشْتُ مَا سَرَّنِى   وَإِنْ مُتُّ مَا كَانَتِ ٱلْعَائِدَهْ

فَقَالَ بَعْضُ ٱلْقَوْمِ: أَنْشِدِ ٱلْمَلِكَ. قَالَ: b لَا يُرْجَى لَكَ (61b) مَنْ لَيْسَ مَعَكَ. قُلْ بَعْضُهُم مِنَ ٱلْقَوْمِ:

5 أَنْشِدِ ٱلْمَلِكَ. قَالَ: وَأُمِرَّ دُونَ عَبِيدِهِ ٱلْوَذَمُ. قَالَ بَعْضُ ٱلْقَوْمِ: أَنْشِدِ ٱلْمَلِكَ. فَقَالَ: حَالَ ٱلْجَرِيضُ دُونَ

ٱلْقَرِيضِ. وَكَانَ مِمَّا أَنْشَدَهُ عَبِيدُ بْنُ ٱلْأَبْرَصِ:

c مَهْلًا أَبَيْتَ ٱللَّعْنَ [مَهْـــلًا إِنَّ] فِيمَا قُلْتَ آمَهْ

فِى كُلِّ وَادٍ بَيْـــنَ يَثْـــرِبَ فَٱلْقُصُورِ إِلَى ٱلْيَمَامَهْ

تَطْرِيبُ عَانٍ أَوْ صِيَا ح مُحَرَّقٍ أَوْ [صَوْتُ] هَامَهْ

بَرِمَتْ بَنُو أَسَدٍ كَمَا   بَرِمَتْ بِبَيْضَتِهَا ٱلْحَمَامَهْ 10

مَهْمَا تَرَكْتَ تَرَكْتَ عَفْـــوًا أَوْ قَتَلْتَ فَلَا مَلَامَهْ

ذَلُّوا فَأَعْطَوْكَ ٱلْمَقَا دَهْ كَٱلْأَحِيمِرِ ذِى ٱلْخُزَامَهْ

قَالَ لَهُ ٱلْمُنْذِرُ: يَا عَبِيدُ أَىُّ قِتْلَةٍ أَحَبُّ إِلَيْكَ أَنْ أَقْتُلَكَ. قَالَ: أَيُّهَا ٱلْمَلِكُ رَوِّنِى مِنَ ٱلْخَمْرِ وَٱقْصِدْنِى

وَشَأْنَكَ وَشَأْنِى. [فَسَقَاهُ ٱلْخَمْرَ ثُمَّ] أَقْطَعَ لَهُ ٱلْأَكْحَلَ: فَلَمْ يَزَلِ ٱلدَّمُ يَسِيلُ حَتَّى نَفَدَ ٱلدَّمُ وَسَالَتِ

15 ٱلْخَمْرُ فَمَاتَ ☼ تَمَّ حَدِيثُهُ ثُمَّ ٱبْتَدَأْنَا بِشِعْرِهِ ☼

---

a) These verses are variously quoted: Khiz. IV, 165 and Qālī, *l.c.* have them thus:

لَا غَرْوَ مِنْ عِيشَةٍ نَافِدَهْ   وَقَلْ غَيْرَ مَا مِينَةٍ وَاحِدَهْ

فَأَبْلِغْ بَنِىَّ وَأَعْمَامَهُمْ   بِأَنَّ ٱلْمَنَايَا هِىَ ٱلرَّاصِدَهْ

لَهَا مُدَّةٌ فَنُفُوسُ ٱلْعِبَادِ   إِلَيْهَا وَإِنْ كَرِهَتْ قَاصِدَهْ

فَلَا تَجْزَعِى لِحِمَامٍ دَنَا   فَلِلْمَوْتِ مَا تَلِدُ ٱلْوَالِدَهْ

So also in Yāq. III, 793, except that the first verse there is:

وَٱللّٰهِ إِنْ مُتُّ مَا ضَرَّنِى   وَإِنْ عِشْتُ مَا عِشْتُ فِى وَاحِدَهْ

b) See Supplt. Frag. No. 13; MS reads مَعَكَ مِن لَيْسَ لَكَ يُوجِحَل لَا.   *c)* See Appendix, No. XXIX. The text of the MS is here exceedingly corrupt.   *d)* In the MS part of the preceding phrase is repeated, and some words inserted which have been marked as cancelled.

I.

قَالَ عَبِيدُ بْنُ الْأَبْرَصِ بْنِ عَوْفِ بْنِ جُشَمَ بْنِ سَعْدِ بْنِ ثَعْلَبَةَ بْنِ دُودَانَ بْنِ أَسَدِ بْنِ خُزَيْمَةَ:

وَكَانَ اسْمُ أُمِّ عَبِيدٍ أُمَامَةَ:

١   a أَقْفَرَ مِنْ أَهْلِهِ مَلْحُوبُ   فَالْقُطَبِيَّاتُ فَالذَّنُوبُ

٢   فَرَاكِسٌ فَثُعَيْلِبَاتُ   فَذَاتُ b فِرْقَيْنِ فَالْقَلِيبُ

٣   فَعَرْدَةٌ فَقَفَا حِبِرٍّ   لَيْسَ بِهَا مِنْهُمْ عَرِيبُ

٤   c إِنْ بُدِّلَتْ أَهْلَهَا وُحُوشًا   وَغَيَّرَتْ حَالَهَا الْخُطُوبُ

مَلْحُوبٌ وَالْقُطَبِيَّاتُ وَالذَّنُوبُ وَرَاكِسٌ وَثُعَيْلِبَاتٌ و[ذَاتُ] فِرْقَيْنِ وَالْقَلِيبُ وَقَفَا حِبِرٍّ هَذِهِ كُلُّهَا مَوَاضِعُ . أَنْ

بُدِّلَتْ: مَنْ فَتَحَ الْأَلِفَ فَتَحَهَا عَلَى كَلَامٍ مَحَلُّهَا وَجَعَلَ أَنْ اسْمًا كَقَوْلِكَ: لَكَذَا وَكَذَا صَارَتْ هَذِهِ الْأَرْضُ

وُحُوشًا . وَمِنْ كَسَرَ الْأَلِفَ جَعَلَهَا أَدَاةَ جَزَاءٍ كَقَوْلِكَ: إِنْ كَانَ كَذَا فَلَكَذَا . وَقَوْلُهُ: * إِنْ بُدِّلَتْ أَهْلَهَا

وُحُوشًا * الرُّوَاةُ يَرْوُونَ (62a): بُدِّلَتْ مِنْ أَهْلِهَا وُحُوشًا: فَمِنْ زَائِدَةٌ فِي الْوَزْنِ . وَقَالَ ابْنُ كُنَاسَةَ فِي هَذَا   10

I. This celebrated poem, which is said by BQut. (*Shiʿr* 144¹⁷) to have been included by some among «the Seven», that is, the *Muʿallaqāt*, has been printed in Tibrīzī, *Ten Poems*, pp. 159—164; Cheikho, *Shuʿarā Naṣrānīyah*, pp. 606—611; *Jamharah* (Cairo ed.) pp. 100—2; and Hommel, *Aufsätze u. Abhandlungen* (München 1892) I, 54—61. Several verses are cited in BQut. *Shiʿr*, pp. 144—5, and often elsewhere; there is much diversity of readings. The metre is a shortened form of the *Basīṭ*, which also appears in a poem, probably contemporary, by Imra' al-Qais (Ahlw. No. 55 [p. 155]); its scheme is:

$$\overset{\smile}{\overline{}}\smile\smile - \mid \smile\smile - \mid \overset{\smile}{\smile} \smile \equiv \parallel \overset{\smile}{\overline{}}\smile\smile - \mid \smile\smile - \mid \smile \smile -$$

The rarity and unfamiliarity of the metre have probably led to some of the differences of reading; many ancient critics speak of the metre as so irregular that the poem cannot be considered to be verse; a MS of the *Jamharah* in the Brit. Mus. (Or. 3158, fol. 56v) expresses this judgment:

لِكَثْرَةِ مَا دَخَلَهَا مِنَ الزِّحَافِ وَالْقَطْعِ كَادَتْ أَنْ لَا تَكُونَ شِعْرًا . It is cited by Ibn Sīdah in the *Muḥkam* (TA VII, 351¹⁷; LA XIII, 315⁹), apparently on the authority of al-Khalīl (Lane 1160a), as an example of شِعْرٌ مَيْزُولٌ غَيْرُ مُوتَلِفِ الْبِنَاءِ , "meagre, incongruous in structure." On this subject see the valuable note with which Prof. Nöldeke has favoured me (printed at the end of the poem).

    a) The poem in the Jamh. begins with vv. 7, 8, 10, 9: then follow vv. 1, 2 etc.

    b) The name is given with both *kasr* and *fatḥ* in Yāq. III, 882⁴ and Bakrī 409.

    c) Tib. <div dir="rtl">وَبُدِّلَتْ مِنْ أَعْلَيَا وُحُوشًا</div>, where <div dir="rtl">مِنْ</div> is unmetrical.

البيت (يعنى* إِنْ بَقِيتَ مِنْ أَهْلِهَا وُحوشًا* وَغَيَّرَتْ حَالَهَا الْخُطُوب*) قال: فإذا أَدْخَلْتَ مِنْ صار نِصْف

البيت رَجَزًا. قال: وَلَمْ أَرَ أَحَدًا يُنْشِد هذه القصيدة على إِقَامَة الْعَرُوض. وقوله *وَغَيَّرَتْ حَالَها الْخُطُوب*

يقول حال هذه الأَرْض. والْخُطُوب واحدها خَطْبٌ ☙

٥ أَرْضٌ تَوَارَثَـهَا شَعُـوبُ   وَكُلُّ مَـنْ حَلَّهَا مَحْرُوبُ

٦ إِمَّـا قَتِيلًا وَإِمَّـا هَالِكًا   وَالشَّيْبُ شَيْنٌ لِمَنْ يَشِيبُ

الشَّعُوب الْمَنِيَّة: يقال شَعَبَتْهُ شَعُوب غَيْرَ مَصْرُوفة. قال أبو الوليد: الْمَحْرُوب الذى قد ذهب ماله

وجمعهم مَحروبون. ويروى *إِمَّا قَتِيلٌ وَإِمَّا هَالِكٌ* بالرفع: ومن نَصَبَه فعَلَى الْحَال ☙

٧ عَيْنَاكَ دَمْعُهُمَا سَرُوبُ   كَأَنَّ شَأْنَيْهِمَا شَعِيبُ

الشَّعِيب الْقِرْبَة الْخَلَقَة: شبّه دُموعه بما يَسِيل منها. وسَرُوب فَعُولٌ من السَّرْب: يقال: سَرِبَ مَزَادَتك اذا

كانت جَديدَةً: اى اجْعَلْ فيها ماءً حتى يَنْسَرِب الماء وتُمْسِك الْخُرَز اذا ابْتَلَّتْ: والسَّرْب الماء السائل.

وقوله كَأَنَّ شَأْنَيْهِمَا واحدها شَأْنٌ والجمع شُؤون: وهى عُروق تكون فى الرَّأْس يجرى منها الدمْوع

الى الْعَين ☙

٨ وَاهِيَةٌ أَوْ مَعِينٌ [مُمْعِنٌ]   أَوْ هَضْبَةٌ دُونَهَا لُهُوبُ

واهِيَة نعت للشَّعِيب وهى قِرْبَةٌ [بَالِيَةٌ] ضَعُف مواضع الْخُرَز منها فالماء سَرِيع السَّيَلان. (62b) وقوله

أو مَعِينٌ [مُمْعِنٌ]: فالمَعِين الماء الظاهر على وَجْه الارض: والمُمْعِن الذاهب: يقال قد أَمْعَن فلان فى

السَّفَر اذا باعَدَ فيه وذَهَبَ. واللُّهُوب واحدها لَهْبٌ وهو الْمَهْوَى بين الْجَبَلَيْن: وقِل غير الشِّقّ بَيْن

جَبَلَيْن. والهَضْبة دون الجبل ☙

٩ أَوْ فَلَـجٍ مَّـا بِبَطْنِ وَادٍ   لِلْمَاءِ مِنْ بَيْنِهِ سَكُوبُ

١٠ أَوْ جَدْوَلٍ فى ظِلَالِ دَخْـلٍ   لِلْمَاءِ مِنْ تَحْتِهِ قَسِيبُ

١١ تَصْبُو فَأَنَّى لَكَ التَّصَابِى   أَنَّى وَقَدْ رَاعَكَ الْمَشِيبُ

١٢ إِنْ تَكُ حَالَتْ وَحُوِّلَ أَهْلُهَا   فَـلَا بَدِىٌّ وَّلَا عَـجِيبُ

_____

a) So Tib.   b) MS broken away.   c) MS والمعين.

d) Tib. تخدّ. Vv. 9 and 10 differ considerably in the different texts, and the hemistichs are

often transposed: see LA III, 171²⁵.

قال ابْنُ كُنَاسَة: الفَلَجُ a البِئْرُ الكَبِيرَة: وما صِلَتْ. والجَدْوَلُ النَهَرُ الصَغِيرُ. فلا بدىء: البَدِيءُ البَدِيعُ:
يقول لَيْسَتْ أُولَى أَرْضٍ حَوْلَ أَهْلِهَا فَعَجِبْتَ لِذلك ۞

١٣ أَوْ يَكُ أَقْفَرَ مِنْهَا جَوُّهَا b وَعَادَهَا المَحْلُ وَالجُدُوبُ

الجَوُّ ما اتَّسَعَ من الارض غير مهموز: والجَوُّ أيضًا غير مهموز ما بَيْنَ السَماءِ والارضِ: والجَوُّ أيضًا غير
مهموز قَصَبَةُ اليَمامة: قال الأَعْشَى

c فَاسْتَنْزَلُوا أَهْلَ جَوٍّ مِنْ مَساكِنِهِمْ وَقَدَّمُوا شَاخِصَ البُنْيانِ فَاتَّضَعا

ويُروى فَاخْتَضَعا. وعادَها يقول عاد على هذه الارضِ بعد تَفَرُّقِ أَهْلِها المَحْلُ: والمَحلُ القَحْطُ.
والجُدُوبُ القَحْطُ أيضًا ۞

١٤ d فَكُلُّ ذِى نَعْمَةٍ مَخْلُوسٌ وَكُلُّ ذِى أَمَلٍ مَكْذُوبُ

١٥ e وَكُلُّ ذِى إِبِلٍ مَوْرُوثٌ وَكُلُّ ذِى سَلَبٍ مَسْلُوبُ

١٦ وَكُلُّ ذِى غَيْبَةٍ يَؤُوبُ وَغَائِبُ المَوْتِ لَا يَؤُوبُ

١٧ (63a) أَعَاقِرٌ مِثْلُ ذَاتِ رِحْمٍ أَمْ غَانِمٌ مِثْلُ مَنْ يَّخِيبُ

ضرب مَثَلًا للعاقِر [وهى] التى لا تَلِدُ. يقول لا يَسْتَوِيانِ مَنْ يُغِير فَيَغْنَمُ ومَن لا يُغِير ولا يَغْنَمُ ۞

١٨ f أَفْلِحْ بِما شِئْتَ فَقَدْ يُبْلَغُ بِالـــضَّعْفِ وَقَدْ يُخْدَعُ الأَرِيبُ

١٩ لَا يَعِظُ النَّاسَ مَنْ لَمْ يَعِظِ الــــدَّهْرُ وَلَا يَنْفَعُ التَّلْبِيبُ

٢٠ g إِلَّا سَجِيَّاتِ مَا الـقُلُوبُ وَكَمْ يَصِيرَنَّ شَانِئًا حَبِيبُ

٢١ h سَاعِدْ بِأَرْضٍ إِذَا كُنْتَ بِهَا وَلَا تَقُلْ إِنَّنِى غَرِيبُ

---

a) This explanation of Ibn Kunāsah's is cited in TA II, 87¹⁹; all other interpreters explain
فَلَجٌ as meaning running water in some form, and that is clearly its sense here.

b) MS جَوُّكَ.　　　　c) LA XVIII, 173¹².

d) Tib. Hom. BQut. Jamh. مَخْلُوسُهَا.　　　　e) Hom. BQut. مَوْرُوثُهَا; Tib. and Jamh. as text.

f) This verse is often quoted unmetrically, with يُبَخْدَعُ for يُخْدَعُ; so Lane 2438c; LA III,
271¹³; aud Hom.　　　　g) Hom. has two couplets in place of this:

لَا يَنْفَعُ اللُّبُّ عَنْ تَعَلُّمٍ إِلَّا السَّجِيَّاتِ وَالـقُلُوبُ
فَقَدْ يَعُودَنَّ حَبِيبًا شَانِئِى وَيَرْجِعَنَّ شَانِئًا حَبِيبُ

h) Vv. 21 and 21 in Buḥt. Ḥam., p. 254, with a different text of v. 22.

٢٢   قَدْ يُوصَلُ النَّازِحُ [النَّائِى] وَقَدْ   يُقْطَعُ ذُو السَّهْمَةِ القَرِيبِ

٢٣   مَنْ يَسْأَلِ النَّاسَ يَحْرِمُوهُ   وَسَائِلُ اللهِ لَا يَخِيبُ   a

٢٤   وَالمَرْءُ مَا عَاشَ فِى تَكْذِيبِ   طُولُ الحَيَاةِ لَهُ تَعْذِيبُ

٢٥   b بَلْ رُبَّ مَاءٍ وَرَدْتُ آجِنٍ   سَبِيلُهُ خَائِفٌ جَدِيبُ

5 قال ابن كُناسة: ويروى c [يَأَرُبَّ مَاءٍ] صَرًى وَرَدْتُهُ: والصَّرَى المَاء المُتَغَيِّر الذى لا يَكَاد يَمُرُّ بِهِ أَحَدُ
المُحْتَبِس فى المكان: ويقال d شَاةٌ مُصَرَّاةٌ اذا احْتَبَسَ لَبَنُها وجُمِعَ فى ضَرْعِها. والآجِنُ المُتَغَيِّر.
والجَدِيب الذى لا شَجَر فيه ولا نَبْتَ ۞

٢٦   رِيشُ الحَمَامِ عَلَى أَرْجَائِهِ   لِلْقَلْبِ مِنْ خَوْفِهِ وَجِيبُ

الوَجِيب الخَفَقان. أَرْجَاوُهُ نَوَاحِيهِ: وواحد الارجاء رَجًا مقصور ۞

٢٧   e قَطَعْتُهُ غُدْوَةً مُشِيحًا   وَصَاحِبِى بَادِنٌ خَبُوبُ   10

قَطعْتُه خَلَّفْتُه. مُشِيحًا مُجِدًّا فى السَّيْر. وصاحِبى يريد ناقته. خَبُوب ذاتِ الخَبَب
فهو [ضَرْب] من السَّيْر ۞

٢٨   عَيْرَانَةٌ f مُوجَّدٌ فَقَارُهَا   كَأَنَّ حَارِكَهَا كَثِيبُ

عيرانة مأخوذ من اسم العَيْر: شبَّهها بالحِمار فى سرعتها. مُوجَّد فَقَارُها يريد مُوثَّقَة الخَلْقِ كأنّ (63b)
15 عَظْم [فَقَارِها] واحدٌ من صَلابته. والكثيب رَمْلَةٌ لَيِّنَة لَيِّسَتْ بالعظيمة يُشَبَّهُ بها أَعْجَازُ النساء كثيرًا ۞

---

a) After this v. Tib. and Hom. have two couplets:

بِاللهِ يُدْرَكُ كُلُّ خَيْرٍ   وَالْقَوْلُ فِى بَعْضِهِ تَلْغِيبُ

وَاللهُ لَيْسَ لَهُ شَرِيكٌ   عَلَّامُ مَا أَخْفَتِ الْقُلُوبُ

verse 23, with these additions, is put by Tib. immediately after v. 17; then follow v. 18—22,
then v. 24.   b) Aḍḍād 82, 3—4 expands this v. into two:

بَلْ إِنْ أَكُنْ قَدْ عَلَتْنِى ذِرْأَةٌ   وَالشَّيْبُ شَيْنٌ لِمَنْ يَشِيبُ

فَرُبَّ مَاءٍ وَرَدْتُ آجِنٍ   سَبِيلُهُ خَائِفٌ جَدِيبُ

See ante, v. 6, the second hemistich of which seems more appropriate here.

c) Words added from Tib.: omitted in our MS.   d) MS مَصرَّةٌ سَدَّه.

e) Aḍḍād 177[3] with بَازِلٌ for بادِن, and so Hommel.

f) MS مُوَحَّدٌ, and so also in scholion.

٢٩ *a* أَخْلَفَ مَا بَازِلًا سَدِيسُهَا ⁣ ⁣ لَا حِقَّةٌ هِيَّ وَلَا نَـيُـوبُ

أَخْلَفَ: يقول سَقَطَ السَّدِيسُ وطَلَعَ البَازِلُ. والسديس السِّنُّ التى تَأْتى بعد سبع سنين لِلْبَعِير: فإذا تَمَّ له ثَمانى سنينَ واشْتَمَلَ التاسِعَ بَزَلَ له نابٌ وهو آخِرُ أَسْنانِه: والبازِل من الإبل كالقارِح من الخيل. والحِقَّة التى يَأْتى عليها *b* سبع سنين. والنَّيوب النّابُ: وذلك اذا أَتى على الجَمَلِ والناقةِ سبع عشرة [سَنَةً] قيل للناقة بعد ذلك نابٌ وقيل للجَمَل *c* قَلُوبٌ ويقال له شارِفٌ: ثمّ لا يَـزال بعد هذه السنّ ٥ شارِفًا حتى يَمُوتَ. ولم يَكُن هذا [lacuna] *d*

٣٠ *e* كَأَنَّهَا مِنْ حَمِيرِ غَابٍ ⁣ ⁣ جَوْنٌ بِصَفْحَتِهِ نُـدُوبُ

واحد الغاب غابَة والغابَة الأَجَمَة: وفى هيهنا موضع لأنّ الحَمِيرَ *f* [الا] تكون فى الإجام. جَوْنٌ أَسْوَدُ يريد الحِمارَ: والجَوْنُ الأَبْيَضُ عن ابى عمرٍو: قال والشَّمْسُ يقال لها جَوْنَةٌ وذلك لأنّها ليست بخالصَةِ البَياض: والجَوْنُ الأَسْمَرُ ايضا. بصَفْحَتِه اراد بعُنُقِه: اراد من كَدْم الحَمِير. نُدُوب آثار واحدها نَدَبٌ ☙ ١٠

٣١ أَوْ شَبَبٌ *g* يَحْفِرُ الرُّخَامَى ⁣ ⁣ تَلُقُّهُ شَمْأَلٌ هَبُوبُ

٣٢ *h* [فَذَاكَ عَصْرٌ وَقَدْ أَرَانِى ⁣ ⁣ تَحْمِلُنِى نَهْدَةٌ سُرْحُوبُ]

اى ذلك دَهْرٌ قد ذَهَبَ. وقوله أَرَانى اى قد كُنْتُ [أَرْكَبُ] نَهْدَةً ضَخْمَةَ الوَسَطِ. والسُّرْحُوب الماضِيَة. قال ابو عمرٍو يقال عَصْر وعِصْر وعُصْر ثلث لُغات يعنى الدهرَ: سمعَه حميد من ابى عمرٍو ☙

٣٣ مُضَبَّرٌ خَلْقُهَا تَضْبِيرًا ⁣ ⁣ يَنْشَقُّ عَنْ وَجْهِهَا السَّبِيبُ ١٥

مُضَبَّر مُدَمَّجٌ. السَّبِيب الناصِيَة: يقول تُنْشَر ناصِيَتُها (64a) على وجهِها لِسَعَةِ جَبْهَتِها وكَثْرَةِ ناصِيَتِها. قال ابن كُناسَة السبيب الناصيَة ☙

---

a) MS بَازِلٌ. We must read هِيَّ, not هِيَّ: this is a peculiarity of the dialect of Asad; LA XX, 254². *b*) This is evidently incorrect; see Lane 608*b*: Aṣma῾ī, Ibil 76⁶; and Mbd Kām. 566¹³; read *three* instead of *seven*. *c*) This sense of قَلُوب is not in the Lexx.

d) MS broken: the letters (?) السطو can be distinguished.

e) Tib. حَمِير عَانَةٍ; Hom. حَمِير عَائذ. *f*) لا accidentally omitted in MS.

g) MS حَمْعِر: this is given as a *v. l.* in Tib., whose text has يَرْتَعِى; it is however unmetrical. يَحْفِر is also given as a *v. l.* by Tib, and is the reading of Jamh. and Hom.

h) Verse accidentally omitted in the MS, which has the commentary to it; the scholion to v. 31 has also fallen out.

٣٤   زَيْتِيَّةٌ نَاعِمٌ عُرُوقُهَا   وَلَيِّنٌ أَسْرُهَا رَطِيبُ

a زَيْتِيَّةٌ [مِن] الزَّيْتِ. [ويروى] نَائِمٌ: فمن قال نائمٌ عروقُها اى لَبِسَتْ بِمُنْتَشِرَة: ويقال نائِمٌ عروقها

ساكِنَةٌ عروقُها اى لصحَّتِها. وناعِمٌ لَيِّنَةٌ عروقها. والأَسْرُ الخَلْقُ: قال الله: b وَشَدَدْنَا أَسْرَهُمْ. وقولُه

رَطِيبٌ [اى] لَيْسَ غُصْنُها [يبايِس] ☙

٣٥   كَأَنَّهَا لِقُوَّةٍ طَلُوبٍ   c تُخَزَّنُ فِي وَكْرِهَا الْقُلُوبُ

اللِّقْوَةُ الْعُقَابُ تُشَبَّهُ فَرَسٌ بها لسرعتها: ويقال للذى بوَجْهِهِ الْقَلَهُ [لَهُ] اللَّقْوَةُ بفتح اللام. والقلوبُ

أراد قلوبَ الطَّيْرِ: وذلك أن العُقابَ والصَّقْرَ والبازِى وما أَشْبَهَهُمْ (sic) تاكل جميعَ الطير إلّا الْقَلْبَ

فإنها لا تأْكُلُه d ☙

٣٩   بَاتَتْ عَلَى إِرَمٍ عَذُوبًا   كَأَنَّهَا شَيْخَةٌ رَقُوبُ

الْعَذُوبُ الْمُنْتَصِبَة. كَأَنَّها: يقول: كَأَنَّ هذه الْعُقابَ امرأةٌ عَجُوزٌ. والرَّقُوبُ التى لا يعيشُ لها وَلَدٌ.

ويروى: عَلَى إِرَمٍ رَابِئَةً. الإِرَمُ الْعَلَمُ وهو الجَبَلُ الصغير مثل العلم الطويل وجماعُه الآرَامِ: قل لبيد:

e خَوَّفْيِها آرَامُهَا: اى أَعْلامُها. وقال ابن كِناسَةَ: الْعَذُوبُ الْمُنْتَصِب: وقال غير ابن كِناسة: العَذوبُ f القائِم

لا باكل ولا يَشْرَبُ ☙

٣٧   فَأَصْبَحَتْ فِي غَدَاةِ قِرَّةٍ   يَسْقُطُ عَنْ رِيشِهَا الضَّرِيبُ

الضَّرِيبُ والصَّقِيعُ والجَلِيدُ واحِد وهو ما سقط بالليل من النَّدَى بالشَّجَرِ فيَجْمُدُ عليه أو كما كان

ذُرَرٌ من السماء ☙

٣٨   فَأَبْصَرَتْ ثَعْلَبًا مِّنْ سَاعَةٍ   وَدُونَهُ سَبْسَبٌ جَدِيبُ

(64b) السَّبْسَبُ الأرض الْمُسْتَوِيَة وجمعها سَباسِب. الجَدِيبُ الذى لا يَنْبُتُ فيه شَجَرَةٌ ولا مَرْعًى ☙

٣٩   فَنَفَضَتْ رِيشَهَا g وَأَنْتَفَضَتْ   وَهِىَ مِنْ نَهْضَةٍ قَرِيبُ

---

a) الزَّيْتِيَّة and الزَّيْت are mentioned in the TA (*s. v.* زيت) as proper names of horses. In the corresponding poem of Imra' al-Qais (55,5) ناعمة and نائم أبَاجَلِهَا are *both* applied to a *camel*.

b) Qur. LXXVI, 28.   *c)* For تُخَزَّنُ Hom. has تَيْبَسُ, Tib. تَخَرُ (with تَيْبَسُ as *v.l.*); *cf.* I. Q. 52, 56.   *d)* But *cf.* I. Q. 55, 13—14.   *e)* Mu'all. 27.   *f)* Perhaps we should read الصائم.

g) Tib. وَلَمْ تَطِرْ وَهِىَ; Hom. وَوَلَّتْ فَذَاكَ. Tib. and Hom. arrange the verses thus: 39, 42, 41, 40, 43, 44, which gives a better sequence.

٤٠ وَّالْعَيْنِ حِمْلَاقُهَا مَقْلُوبُ   يَدِبُّ مِنْ حِسِّهَا دَبِيبًا

٤١ وَحَرَّدَتْ حَرَّةً تَسِيبُ   فَنَهَضَتْ نَحْوَهُ حَثِيثَةً

٤٢ وَفِعْلَهُ يَفْعَلُ الْمَدْرُوبُ   فَاشْتَالَ وَارْتَاعَ مِنْ حَشِيشِهَا

٤٣ وَالصَّيْدُ مِنْ تَحْتِهَا مَكْرُوبُ   [a فَأَدْرَكَتْهُ فَطَرَّحَتْهُ

٤٤ فَكَدَّحَتْ وَجْهَهُ الْجَبُوبُ]   فَجَدَّلَتْهُ فَطَرَّحَتْهُ

كَدَّحَتْ اى جَرَّحَتْ والكَدْحُ الجِرَاحُ. والجَبُوبُ b واحدُها جَبُوبَةٌ: قل ابى كِنَاسَةَ: الجَبُوبُ

وَجْهُ الأَرْضِ: ويُقَال الأَرْضِ الصُّلْبَةِ. قل الاصمعى: الجَبُوبُ المَدَرُ والجَبُوبَةُ القِطْعَةُ مِنَ المَدَرِ. قل ابو

الوَلِيد: c [أَعْطَى رسولُ اللهِ صلّى اللهُ عليه وسلّم لَبِيدًا] بـن رَبِيعَةَ الشاعِرَ جَبُوبَةً يُدَاوِى بها عَمَّهُ d أبا

بَرَاءٍ يُذوفِيها فى المَاءِ ويَشْرَبِها [ويَشْتَفِى] مِن دُبَيْلَةٍ كانت بـه ☙

١٠

٤٥ يَضْغُو وَمِخْلَبُهَا فِى دَفِّهِ   لَا بُدَّ حَيْزُومُهُ مَنْقُوبُ

الدَّفُّ الجَنْبُ والحَيْزُوم الصَّدرُ ☙

---

a) vv. 43 and 44 omitted in MS, entered from Tib.; our MS has a scholion on v. 44.

b) MS حَبُو (sic).   c) A line had apparently fallen out in the original of our MS; the words in brackets have been supplied from Agh. XV. 138[1-2].

d) MS أنا مرك. For يُذوفيها the MS has دسيا, which I am unable to read.

NOTE BY PROF. NÖLDEKE ON THE METRE OF THE ABOVE POEM.

Die metrischen Anstösse dieses Gedichtes sind meines Erachtens nicht etwa darauf zurückzu-führen, dass zu der Zeit des alten Dichters die Metrik überhaupt noch nicht streng durchgeführt worden wäre, denn in den anderen Gedichten ʿAbīd's, wie sonstiger alter Dichter, herrscht volle metrische Regelmässigkeit. Und gerade die Eigenthümlichkeit, die in diesem Gedichte zunächst befremdet, findet sich auch bei امرو القيس, dem Zeitgenossen des Dichters, in einem Gedichte desselben Metrums (siehe unten).

Diese Eigenthümlichkeit besteht darin, dass der letzte Fuss (namentlich des *ersten* Halbverses) statt ⌣ − − (oder gar ⌣ − ⌣, v. 20), auch ⌣ − ⌣ − resp. ⌣ ⌣ ⌣ − sein darf. (So eben auch bei Imra'al-Qais 55,10 − − ⌣ −, was freilich durch die Vocalisation رَبِيعَ صَيْفٍ vermieden werden könnte, und auch 55,5 − ⌣ ⌣ −). Der Fuss, welcher das Reimwort enthält, ist fast stets ⌣ − −, nur v. 20 auch mit der Verlängerung ⌣ − ⌣ − −.

(Eine ganz ähnliche Freiheit ist im Metrum *Kāmil* gar nicht selten, wo für den letzten hyper-katalectischen Fuss ⌣ ⌣ − manchmal der volle Fuss ⌣ ⌣ − ⌣ eintritt, z. B., Agh. 15,4, 1 und 3; ʿUmar b. Abī Rabīʿa [Schwarz] 37, 2, 12f; 39, 4, 13; 106, 5f; 109,9; 200, 7, und sonst bei Dichtern; auf Wunsch kann ich mehr Fälle geben).

Ich möchte annehmen, dass unser Gedicht ursprünglich weiter keine metrischen Licenzen auf-

II.

١ a أُنِبِّئْتُ أَنَّ بَنِى جَدِيلَةَ أَوْعَبُوا   نَفَرَاء مِـــنْ سَلْمَى لَنَا وَتَكَتَّبُوا

بنو جديلة حى من طَيّ. وأَوْعَبوا جَمَعوا. وسَلْمَى أحدُ جَبَلَىْ طَيّ. نَفَرَاء ونَفَرٌ ونَفَرٌ واحد وهٌ

b الحُماة. وتَكَتَّبوا اى صاروا كَنائبَ. ويروى نُبِّئْتُ وجُرِّبوا ۞

٢ c وَلَقَدْ جَـــرَى لَهُمْ فَلَمْ يَتَعَيَّفُوا   تَيْسٌ قَعِيدٌ كَالْوَرِيئَةِ أَعْضَبُ

٥ جرى لهم: يقول: جرى لهم هـذا النبيس (والنبيس من الظِباء) بالشُوم اى عَرَضَ لهم الظَّبْىُ d بالتَّلاتل:

يقول: جرى لبنى جديلة تَيْسٌ قَعِيدٌ بالشُوم. والقعيد الـذى بأَنى من خَلْفِكَ: (65a) والناطِح الـذى

بأَنى من بَيْن يَدَيْكَ: والسانِح الذى بأَتيك عـن يَمينك: والبارِح الـذى بأَتيك عـن يَسارِك الى يَمينك.

---

gewiesen hat als solche. Da dies Metrum in der *classischen* arabischen Poesie aber sehr selten ist, so haben sich die Ueberlieferer wohl nicht recht hineingefunden, die Grenze der erlaubten Freiheit überschritten, und solche Entstellungen hineingebracht, wie wir sie v. 18 finden (in v. 12 lässt sich das Metrum vielleicht herstellen durch وَحَوِّلْ أَهْلَهَا).

Dass das Gedicht durch lange mündliche Ueberlieferung mancherlei Veränderungen erfahren hat, ergiebt sich schon aus den Varianten und aus einigen Wiederholungen: vv. 9 und 10, so wie vv. 43a und 44a, können *so* nicht neben einander gestanden haben. Und v. 23 ist dem alten Heiden überhaupt nicht zuzuschreiben.

Ich füge noch hinzu, dass später (ich glaube bis auf den heutigen Tag) eine Modification dieses Metrums sehr beliebt geworden ist. Da ist aber anders abzutheilen, nämlich ⏑⏑–⏑|⏑|⏑⏑–⏑|–⏑. Dass der *Basīṭ*-Rhythmus hier verlassen ist, zeigt sich doch dadurch, dass die 6 und 7 silbe ⏑⏑ sein durfen: أَسْتَغْفِرُ اللَّهَ وَأَقْبِلُهُ Muslim b. al-Walīd 281, pænult.

II. From v. 12 to the end this poem is in the *Mukhtārāt* of Hibat-allāh, pp. 106—108; of the first eleven verses several are quoted elsewhere. Metre *Kāmil*.

a) LA II, 300[13] as text, and III, 222[6], with نُبِّئْتُ; Jāḥiẓh, Ḥayawān, III, 31 (vv. 1, 3, 5, 6); Fā'iq II, 311.   b) Probably we should read الكُماة.

c) LA III, 222[3], with كَالوَشِيجَةِ, and explanation: الوشيجة عِرْق الشَّجَرِ: شَبَّهَ النَّبِيسَ من ضُمْرِه بها.

d) MS بالبيابل; I owe this correction to Prof. Bevan.

والوَلِيّةُ البَرْذَعةُ سُمِّيَتْ وَلِيّةً لأنّها تَلى الجِلْدَ. وأَعْضَبُ المكسورُ القَرْنِ. ولم يتعيّقوا يقـول لم يَتَجَرّءوا

طائرَهُم. ويروى: كُلْوَشيجَةٍ أَعْضَبُ: والوَشيجَةُ [عِرْقُ الشَّجَرِ] ☙

٣ وَأَبُو الفِرَاخِ عَلَى خَشَاشِ هَشِيمَةٍ   *a* مُتَنَكِّبًا إِبْطَ الشَّمَائِلِ يَنْعَبُ

أبو الفِراخِ هو الطَّيْرُ وهو الغُرَابُ: يقول: فى وَكْرِهِ *b* يَنْعَبُ على فِراخِه. والهَشيمةُ الشَّجَرَةُ اليابِسَةُ. قوله

على خَشَاشٍ: قال ابنُ كُناسةَ: واحدُ الخَشاشِ خَشاشةٌ: وهى دَوابُّ أَمْثالُ الخَنافِسِ. قال أبو الوليد:

الخَشاشُ كلُّ ما لا عَظْمَ له من الدَّوابِّ مثل الحَيّاتِ والعَظايا وما أَشْبَهَهُما. قال ابنُ كُناسةَ: شَبَّهَ فِراخَ

الطَّيْرِ *c* لِمَعْطِها بالخَنافِسِ. وقال غيرُهُ: *d* للخَشاشِ اليابِسِ. وقوله: إِبْطَ الشَّمَائِلِ يُريدُ جَنْبَ الشَّمائلِ وفى

الرِّيحِ: يقول: قد مالَ عنها. يَنْعَبُ يَصيحُ. وقوله الشمائل الناحِيَةُ التى تَهُبُّ منها الرِّيحُ. وقل (sic)

٤ وَتَجَاوَزُوا ذَاكُمْ إِلَيْنَا كُلَّهُ   عَدْوًا *e* وَمَرْقَصَةً فَلَمَّا قَرَّبُوا

قال وسَأَلْتُ أبا عمرٍو عن العَدْوِ والمرقصةِ فقال: ضَرْبٌ من السير. *f* وقال غيرُهُ: [المَرْقَصَةُ] دون العدوِ

الشديد. يُريدُ بنى جَديلةَ اى جاءوا بجميع ما ذَكَرْنا البِنا. فلمّا قَرّبوا اى قَرّبوا خَيْلَنا لِقِتالِنا ☙

٥ طَعَنُوا بِمُرّانِ الوَشِيجِ فَمَا تَرَى   خَلْفَ الأَسِنّةِ غَيْرَ عِرْقٍ يَشْخَبُ

قال: مُرّانُ الوَشيجِ *g* الرِّماحِ (65b) لأنَّ القنا يدخل بعضُها على بعض. خَلْفَ الأَسِنّةِ اى بعد الأَسِنّةِ.

٦ *h* وَتَبَدَّلُوا اليَعْبُوبَ بَعْدَ إِلَاهِهِمْ   صَنَمًا فَقَرُّوا يَا جَدِيلُ وَأَعْذِبُوا

٧ إِنْ تَقْتُلُوا مِنَّا ثَلَاثَةَ فِتْيَةٍ   فَلَمَنْ بِسَاحُوقَ الرَّعِيلِ المُطْنِبُ

اليَعْبُوبُ صَنَمٌ لِعَبِيدٍ. قال ابنُ كُناسةَ أَعْذِبُوا كُفّوا. الرَّعيلُ رَعْلَةٌ وهى لِلجماعةِ من كلِّ شىءٍ. قال ابنُ

كُناسةُ: *i* المُطْنِبُ الكبيرُ ☙

---

a) Jāh. مُتَنَكِّبْ. MS حَشَاش, and so in scholion.   *b)* MS معك (!)

c) MS دلمعطها; مَعَطَ appears to be properly used of absence of *hair*, not, as here, of feathers.

d) Here we must read حشاش with unpointed ح.   *e)* MS وقريصَة, and so in scholion;

مَرْقَصَةَ does not occur in the Lexx.; but رقَص, رقَصان, is common in the sense of *ambling*.

f) Here in the MS the preceding words (from وسألت) are repeated.   *g)* MS الرَّمَل!

h) Cited Khiz. III, 246 and Fāʾiq II, 64, as text; Jāh. واوعبوا. Prof. Nöldeke notes: "Zu v. 6
hätte man gern einen ausführlichen Sachcommentar; aber die alten Erklärer wussten von diesen
Dingen selbst nichts Rechtes mehr. صَنَمًا ist vielleicht nicht ursprünglich."

i) LA II, 50²² explains مُطْنِب (of a stream) as بعيد الذهاب.

٨ فَيَحْمَدِ حَيَّهُمْ وَحَمْدِ قَبِيلِهِمْ   إِذْ طَالَ يَوْمُهُمْ وَعَابَ الْعُيَّبْ

يقول فيحمد حيَّهم وحمد قبيلهم اى يَحْمَد مَن كان منهم وعاب [الْعُيَّبْ]. وطال يومهم لأنَّهم قُتِلوا

وأُسِر منهم من أُسِر ☙

٩ إِنِّى آمْرُؤٌ فِى النَّاسِ لَيْسَ لَهُ أَخٌ   إِمَّا يُسَرُّ بِهِ وَإِمَّا يُغْضَبْ

١٠ وَإِذَا أَخُوكَ تَرَكْتَهُ وَأَخَا آمْرِئٍ a   أَوْدَى أَخُوكَ وَكُنْتَ أَنْتَ تَتَنَبْ

١١ فَلْتَعْرِفِ الْقَيْنَاتُ فَوْقَ رُؤُوسِهِمْ   وَشَرَابُهُمْ ذُو فَضْلَةٍ وَمُحَنَّبْ

فلتعرِف فلتنجِّ على مَن كان مثل هؤلاءِ. والقَيْنَة المُغَنِّيَة: وكلّ عامل بيدِه فهو قَين. وشرابهم يعنى الخمر.

وفَضلة بَقِيَّة. والمُحَنَّب من الشوائيَّة عن ابن كناسة: b لم يعرف المُحَنَّب: ويقال المُحَنَّب من الشواءِ

الذى لم يَنْضَج ثم أُعيد فتَدخَّن ففَسَدَ ☙

١٢ بَلْ لَا مَحَالَةَ مِنْ لِقَاءِ فَوَارِسٍ c   كَرَمٍ مَّتَى يُدْعُوا لِرَوْعٍ يَّرْكَبُوا

١٣ شُمٍّ كَأَنَّ سَنَا الْقَوَانِسِ فَوْقَهُمْ d   نَارٌ عَلَى شَرَفِ الْيَفَاعِ تَلَهَّبْ

قوله كأنَّ [سنا] القَوانِس يعنى قَوانِس البَيْض وهى أوساطها فى أعلاها: وقَونِس الانسان وَسَط رأسه:

وقَونِس البعير موضعُ الفَراغ حيث يُشَقّ العِذار من وَسَط رأسه. شبَّه بريق القَوانِس على رؤوس الفرسان

بنارٍ على شَرَفٍ مُرتَفِع من الارض: واليفاع كلُّ ما ارتفع من الارض ☙ (66a)

١٤ تَمْشِى بِهِمْ أُدْمٌ تَنِطُّ نُسُوعُهَا e   خُوصٌ كَمَا يَمْشِى الْهِجَانُ الرَّبْرَبْ

قوله أُدْمٌ إِبِلٌ بِيض. تَنِطُّ نُسُوعُها تَصيح. ولا يكون الأطيط إِلّا للرَّحْل اذا كان جديدًا والجِلْد

الجديد والخُفّ. خُوصٌ غائرةُ العُيون. والهِجان الابِل البيض. والرَّبْرَبْ جماعةُ البَقَر: f [شبَّهها بالبَقَر

لِبَياضِها] ☙

١٥ وَهُمْ قَدِ اتَّخَذُوا الْحَدِيدَ حَقَائِبًا   وَحِلَالَهُمْ g أُدْمُ الْمَرَاكِلِ تُجْنَبْ

a) MS أوذى and تَتَنَبْ. The words وَأَخَا آمْرِئٍ in this verse are not intelligible; possibly two half-verses may have accidentally dropped out.

b) Some word has apparently dropped out. مُحَنَّب as here explained is not in the Lexx.

c) Here begins the text of Mukht., which has مِنَّا in place of كَرَمٍ.

d) Mukht. أَعْلَى الْيَفَاعِ, and فَوْقِيم for مِنْهُمْ.   e) Mukht. تَمْشِى.

f) Added from scholion of Mukht.   g) Mukht. نَيْدُ الْمَرَاكِلِ (sic).

قوله للحديد يعنى الدروع. حقائبًا قد أَحْقَبُوها على الركائب. وقوله أُدْم المَراكل يقول قد أَبْيَضَّ موضع

عَقِب الفارِس من الفَرَس ممّا يَرْكُلُه برِجْله. وخِلالَهم بَيْنهم: ويروى خِلالَهم يعنى خَلَقَهم ۞

١٩   مِنْ كُلِّ مَمْسُودِ السَّرَاةِ مُقَلِّصٍ   قَدْ شَفَّهُ طُولُ القِيَادِ *a* وَالغَبُوا

قوله مَمْسُود يعنى مُوَثَّق الخَلْق. والسَّراة الظَّهْر. والمُقَلِّص المُشَمِّر. قد شَفَّهُ أَضْرَنَهُ وغَبَّرَهُ ۞

١٧   وَطِمِرَّةٍ كَالسِّيدِ *b* يَعْلُو فَوْقَها   ضِرْغَامَةٌ *c* عَبْلُ المَنَاكِبِ أَغْلَبُ

من كُلِّ طِمِرَّة يريد من كُلِّ فَرَسٍ أُنْثَى. والطِمِرَّة الكريمة السريعة شَبَّهها فى خِفَّتها بالسِّيد والسِّيد الذِّئب.

والضِّرْغامَة الاسد. عَبْلُ المَناكِب يعنى غليظ المَنْكَب [وهو] غليظ المَنْكَب. أَغْلَبُ غليظ الرَّقَبَة ۞

١٨   وَلَقَدْ *d* شَبَبْنَا بِالْجِفَارِ لِدَارِمٍ   نَارًا *e* بِهَا طَيْرُ الأَشَائِمِ يَنْعَبُ

ويروى: *وَلَقَدْ شَبَبْنَا *f* لِلرِّبَابِ إِذَا أَقْبَلُوا* نَارًا [بِهَا] الطَّيْرُ الأَشَائِمُ تَنْعَبُ*. وقوله شَبَبْنا أَوْقَدْنا يقال

شَبَبْتُ النار وحَشَشْتُها بمعنًى واحد أى أَوْقَدْتُها. والجِفار ماءٌ لبنى تميم تُدَّعيه بنو ضَبَّة: ودارِمٌ من

بنى تميم. وقوله طَيْرُ الأَشائِمِ يعنى طير الشُّوم وهى الغِرْبان ۞ (66b)

١٩ *g* وَلَقَدْ تَقَادَمَ بِالنِّسَارِ لِعَامِرٍ   يَوْمٌ لَهُم مِنَّا هُنَاكَ عَصَبْصَبُ

ويروى: *وَلَقَدْ مَضَى مِنَّا هُنَاكَ لِعَامِرٍ* يَوْمٌ عَلَيْهِم بِالنِّسَارِ عَصَبْصَبُ*. [عَصَبْصَبُ] شديد. والنِّسار

موضع وكان لهم فيه قتالٌ. وقوله تَقادَم يريد تَقَدَّم ۞

١٥   ٢٠   حَتَّى سَقَيْنَاهُمْ بِكَأْسٍ مُرَّةٍ   فِيهَا المُثَمَّلُ *h* نَاقِعًا فَلْيَشْرَبُوا

المُثَمَّل بكسر الميم ونَصْبها: وهو السَّمّ ويقال السُّكْر أيضا. ويروى: *حَتَّى جَبَيْنَاهُم بِكَأْسٍ مُرَّةٍ* ۞

٢١   بِمُعَضِّلٍ لَجِبٍ كَأَنَّ عُقَابَهُ   فِى رَأْسِ خُرْصٍ طَائِرٌ يَتَقَلَّبُ

قوله بمُعَضِّلٍ يقول الجَيْش منهم كثير يَضيق بهم موضعهم من كثرتهم؛ يقال قد عَضَّلَت المَرأة اذا

نَشَبَ وَلَدُها فى بَطْنِها ولم يَخْرُج من ضِحْكه. وعُقابُهُ رَأيَتُهُ. والخُرْص سِنانُ الرُّمْح ۞

---

a) So Mukht.: MS وَأَنْعَبُ.   *b)* Mukht. يَسْمُو.   *c)* Mukht. ضِحْكُم.   *d)* MS سَبَقْنَا.

e) Mukht. الطَّيْرُ الأَشَائِمُ تَنْعَبُ. The order in Mukht. after v. 17 is 19, 21, 18, 20, 22 etc.

f) MS لِلذِّيَابِ.   *g)* Mukht. as in scholion. In Naq. 245[8] and Bakrī 591[22] the reading is

وَلَقَدْ تَطَاوَلَ بِالنِّسَارِ لِعَامِرٍ   يَوْمٌ تَشِيبُ لَهُ الرُّؤُوسُ عَصَبْصَبُ

h) Mukht. as in scholion, end. In Mukht. this verse follows v. 18, being thus made to refer
to Dārim, instead of to ʿĀmir as here.

٢٢ a وَلَقَـــدْ أَتَانَا عَـنْ تَمِيمٍ أَنَّهُمْ ذَئِــرُوا لِقَتْلَى عَامِـرٍ وَتَغَضَّبُوا

ذَئِرُوا ذَعِرُوا وَفَزِعُوا. قال ابو الوليد: ذَئِرُوا غَضِبُوا وَنَفِرُوا: ويقال ذَئِرُوا b أَنْكَرُوا ☙

٢٣ c رَغْمٌ لِآنْفِ أَبِيكَ عِنْدِى ضَائِعٌ إِنِّى يَهُونُ عَلَىَّ أَنْ لَّا يَعْتِبُوا

٢٤ d وَغَدَاةَ صَبَّحْنَ الْجِفَارَ عَوَابِسًا يَهْدِى أَوَائِلَهُنَّ شُعْثٌ شُرَّبُ

5 ٢٥ e لَمَّا رَأَوْنَا وَالْمَغَاوِلُ وَسْطَهُمْ وَالْخَيْلُ تَبْدُو تَارَةً وَتَغِيَّبُ

رَغْمٌ غَيْظٌ: يقول انه مُسْتَهِينٌ [له]. شُعْثٌ يريد للخيل. وشُرَّبٌ ضُمَّرٌ. الْمَغَاوِلُ واحدها مِغْوَلٌ وهو

الذى يكون فى السَوْطِ شِبْهُ السَيْفِ. وتارةً مَرَّةً. تَبْدُو اذا خَرَجَتْ من الغُبار وَتَغِيَّبُ اذا دَخَلَتْ فيه.

ويقال الْمَغَاوِلُ فى حِرَابٌ صِغَارٌ مِثْلُ النَبْلِ ☙

٢٦ f وَلَّوْا وَهُنَّ يَجُلْنَ فِى آثَارِهِمْ شَلَلًا وَبِالطَّمَاهُمْ فَتَكَبْكَبُوا

10 (67a) وَلَّوْا [وَهُنَّ] يعنى للخيل. يَجُلْنَ اى يَرْمِينَ. شَلَلًا طَرْدًا. بِالطَّمَاهُمْ قال ابن كُنَاسَة جَالَدْنَاهُمْ

بالسيوف: قال ابو عمرو قَاتَلْنَاهُمْ وَنَازَلْنَاهُمْ: وقال غيرها غَاشَيْنَاهُمْ مُغَافَصَةً اى مُفَاجَأَةً. فَتَكَبْكَبُوا اى اجتمعوا:

وروى ابن كُنَاسَة فَتَكَتَّبُوا: وهما واحد ☙

٢٧ g سَائِلْ بِنَا حُجْرَ بْنَ أُمِّ قَطَامِ إِذْ ظَلَّتْ بِهِ السُّمْرُ النَّوَاهِلُ تَلْعَبُ

حُجْرٌ ابو امرئ القيس. السُّمْرُ الرماح. النَوَاهِلُ ههنا العطاش الى الدَمِ: والنَوَاهِلُ التى قد رَوِيَتْ من الدم

15 وانما أُخِذَ من النَهَلِ وهو الشُرْبُ الثانى: والعَلَلُ الشُرْبُ الأَوَّلُ. تَلْعَبُ يريد هذه الأَسِنَّةَ تَلْعَبُ فيهم

لأَنَّها تَخْرِقُ جلودَهُمْ بالطَعْنِ ☙

٢٨ h صَبْرًا عَلَى مَا كَانَ مِنْ حُلَفَائِنَا مِسْكٌ وَغِسْلٌ فِى الرُّؤُوسِ يُشَيَّبُ

---

a) LA V, 387²², with أَتَانِى لَمَّا; Mukht., Naq. 245⁹, and Bakrī 591²³ وَلَقَدْ أَتَانِى; 2nd hemistich

cited in Lane 950a.   b) MS (apparently) انغروا.

c) Mukht. and Naq. لَعَمْرُ أَبِيكَ, and هَيِّنٌ for ضَائِعٌ.   d) Mukht. صَبَّحْنَا and تَبْدِى.

e) Mukht. وَالْمَعَابِلُ (الْمَعَابِلُ السِهَامُ واحدها مِعْبَلَةٌ).

f) The MS has وَهُنَّ, but later on, before يَجُلْنَ.

g) Cited Murtaḍā Amālī I, 41, with الدَّوَابِلُ.   h) Mukht. transposes vv. 28 and 29,

which seems to give a better sequence. Mukht.'s scholion on v. 28:

حَلَقَاوُهُمْ يعنى قَرَابَةً (sic) وَأَنَّهُمْ قُتِلُوا فكان هذا حَنُوطُهُمْ: والغِسْلُ الخِطْمِى وَوَرَقُ السِدْرِ.

يقول للذى ذَكَرَهُ لَهُ: صبرًا على ما كان من خُلَفائنا: وحلفاؤكم هينا بنو جَديلَةَ. ثم قال: *مِسْكٌ

وغِسْلٌ فى الرُّوس يُشَيَّبُ*: يقول لم يكُنْ بَيْننا وبَيْنكم الّا الحَنوط: كَما قال زهير: a وَدَقُّوا بَيْنَهُم عِطْرَ

مَنْشِم: وذلك أنّ العرب اذا أرادت الحرب جَعَلَت معها للحنوط وانْتَسَلوا للموت. b وقولُه يُشَيَّبُ يَخْتَلطُ.

والغِسْل الخِطْمِيُّ ☙

٢٩ فَلْيَبْكِهِمْ مَـنْ لَا يَـزَالُ c نِسَاؤُهُ   يَوْمَ الْحِفَاظِ يَقُلْنَ أَيْنَ الْمَهْرَبُ

III.

١ أَقْفَرَ مِـنْ مَيَّةَ الـدَّوَافِـعُ مِنْ d خَبْتٍ فَلُبْنَى فَيْحَانَ فَالرَّجَلُ

الدوافِع دوافِعُ الماءِ من الجَبَل الى الرَّوْضِ. وقولُه: e انْتَنَى هـذا الـوادى اى انْفَرَجَ وانْقَطَع.

وفَيْحانُ وادٍ فَوْقَ f زُبالةَ بنَحْو من مِيلٍ شمائلَ المَغْرِب. والرِّجَلُ (67b) مجارى الماءِ من الجَبَل الى

الرَّوْضِ واحدها رِجْلَة ☙

٢ فَالْقُطَبِيَّاتُ فَالـدَّكَادِكُ فَـالْ   هَيْجُ فَـأَعْلَى هَبِيرِهِ السَّهَلُ

القُطَبِيَّاتُ هـذه مواضع بناحية زُبالَةَ. والدَّكادكُ مـوضع. والهَيْجُ مـوضع. والهَبِير مُطْمَئِنّ الارض: ومنه

المهمول مثلُه ايضًا: قال ابن كِناسة الهَبِير g المُطْمَئِنّ فى الرَّمْل ☙

٣ فَالْجُمُدُ الْحَافِظُ الطَّرِيقَ مِنَ آلِ   زَّيْغِ فَصَدْحَنُ الشَّقِيقِ فَـالْأُمُلُ

a) Mu'all. 19.   b) So also Mukht.; the verb meaning to mix is شوب, and this form with ى is not mentioned in the Lexx; but مَشِيب is cited in the meaning of مَشُوب in LA I, 493[17].   c) Mukht. نِسَاؤُكُمْ.

III. Of this poem vv. 1—3 are cited in Bakrī 722, and vv. 5—6 in LA XV, 389. Metre Munsariḥ.

d) Bakrī حَبْتٍ تَغْشَى (sic); Lubnà is the name of a ḥarrah between the lands of Asad, Taiyi' and 'Amir: Bakrī, 487 and 595.   e) MS انسى.

f) Zubālah, a village described in Yāq. II, 912. A well named Zibālah is in the latest map of Arabia (G. 4), but it cannot be the place meant here: it is on the Darb Zubaidah, about midway between Ḥā'il and the Baḥr Najaf (see Sprenger, Post- und Reiserouten, 112).

g) MS المطرف; see LA VII, 108[2] (and 107[22]).

الجَمْدُ مكانٌ يقال له السَّلَبُ: قال هو مكانٌ صُلْب من الارض فيه ارتِفاع. وقوله للحافظ الطريق من

الزَّبغ قال هذا الحَجَرُ مرتفعٌ من الارض وهو [من ال]طريق كأنّه الشِّراك: ما عن يمينه وشماله مُنتظافِرٌ:

والزبغ الميل. والشقيق طَرائِقُ فى الرَّمْل مستطيلة. والأُمْل جمع أَميل: والأَميل ما أَشْرَف من الرَّمل ✿

٤ فَالطَّلْبُ فَالأَحَدُّ مِنْ تَبَالَةَ لَا عَهْدَ لَـهُ بِالْأَنِيسِ مَا فَعَلُـوا

٥ كَأَنَّ مَا أَبْقَت الرَّوَامِس مِنْـهُ وَالسِّنُـونَ الـذَّوَاهِب الْأَوَّلُ

ما ههنا فى معنى الذى: يريد كأنّ الذى أبقت. الرَّوامِس التى تأتى فتَدْفِن كُلّ شئ: وإنّما أَخْذُه من

الرَّمس والرمس الدفن ✿

٦ فَرْعُ قَضِيمٍ غَلَا صَوَانِعُـهُ a فِى يَمَنِّى الْعِيَابِ أَوْ خَلَـلُ

غلا صوانعُه بالَغَ b وتأنّق صَوانِعُ هذا القَصيم. c فى يَمَنِّى العِياب يعنى به فى وَسَط العِياب وحَوْلَها مَواضِعُ

النَّقْش. والقَصيم الصَّحيفة. وفَرعُها خيرُها وأَجْوَدُها بالمكان: وفَرعُ كُلّ شئ رأسُه وأوّلُه. والخَلَلُ خِلَل

السيوف وهى أَجْفانُها وما عليها من النَّقْش من الحُمْرة d والصُّفْرة والخُضْرة كانوا يَتَّخِذُونَهُ قبل اليوم:

فشبَّه (68a) ما بَقِىَ من هذه الدار بنُقوش أَخِلَّة السُّيوف ✿

٧ يَا نَاقَةً مِّمَا كَسَوْتُهَا الرَّحْلَ وَالْ أَنْسَاع رَهْبًا كَأَنَّـهَا جَمَـلُ

قولُه يا ناقةً تعجُّبٌ اى ما لها [من] ناقةٍ. فقولُه كَسَوْتُها الرحل والأَنْساع يقول جَعَلْتُ الرحل والانساع

كِسْوَة [لها]. والرهب المَهْزُول الضّامِر: ويقال الضَّخْم ✿

٨ e تَخْتَرِق الْبِيدَ وَالْفَيَافِى إِنْ لَاحَ سُهَيْـلٌ كَأَنَّـهُ قَبَـلُ

تختَرِق البِيدَ اى تَقْطَعُها. والبِيد الصَّحارَى. والفَيافِى مِثْلُها وواحدها فَيْفاةٌ. لاحَ سُهَيْلٌ يقول فى

الساعة التى يَطْلُع فيها سُهَيْلٌ رَحَلْتُها وأَسِيرُ عليها. f والقَبَل ههنا يريد النار على جَبَلٍ عن ابى عَمْرو:

---

a) So LA; MS فى يُمْنَى العِقاب: see commy. b) MS ويدوبُ. c) MS العِماب.

d) MS العِبرة.   e) MS تغتَرِق (in scholion apparently تخزق).

f) Prof. Nöldeke writes: »Dass قَبَل das heisse, glaube ich dem Scholiasten nicht: auch andre

specielle Bedeutungen, die قَبَل haben soll, sind fraglich. Es ist hier wohl nur — als ob es etwas

plötzlich Erscheinendes wäre.« In LA XIV, 59[10ff.] the meanings of قَبَل are discussed, and a verse

of Nābighah Jaʿdī is quoted: إِنَّما ذِكْرى كَنارٍ بِقَبَلْ. This does not justify the scholion, since نار

والقَبَلُ فى غير هذا ايضًا ما قَبَلَكَ: يقال رَأَى الهِلالَ قَبَلًا اذا رَآهُ نَلَيْلَتِه فانَّهُ (sic) a

٩   وَيْلٌ آمِّهَا صَاحِبًا يُصَاحِبُها   مُعْتَسِفُ الأَرْضِ مُقْفِرٌ جَهِلُ

ويل آمِّها تَعَجُّبٌ. وقوله صاحبًا يعنى نفسَه. جَهِلٌ يقول هو غَيرُ عالِم بها فيَجِبُ ان يَقْطَعَها سَرِيعًا.

ويروى وَيْلٌ آمِّها: ويروى وَيْلٌ بِها: كُلُّه تَعَجُّبٌ. قولُه مقفرٌ فى أرضٍ قفرٍ ۞

١٠   أَوْرَدَها شَرْبَةً بِلِينَةَ لَمْ   تُحْمِضْ عَلَيْها مِنْ دُونِها رجَلُ

لِينَةُ أرضٌ: قال بعضُ الأَعْراب فيها [أَكْثَرُ] من مسائلِ بِئْرٍ: ولِينَةُ ايضًا بِئْرٌ. وقوله لم تُحْمِضْ يقول هذه

الرجَلُ (مَسائِلُ الماءِ) لم تُنْبِتِ الحَمْضَ: ويقال لم تَأْكُلْ حَمْضًا. عَلِيها يريد على شَرْبَتِها ۞

١١   بَارَكَ فى مَائِها الإِلاهُ فَمَا   يَبِضُّ مِنْهُ كَأَنَّهُ عَسَلُ

١٢   مِنْ مَّاءِ حَجْمَاءَ فى مُمَتَّعَةٍ   أَحْرَزَها فى تَنُوفَةٍ جَبَلُ

من ماءِ حَجْمَاءَ فى مُمَتَّعَةٍ [اى] صَخْرَةٌ تَمْنَعُ المَعاوِلَ ان تَحْفِرَها. فى تَنُوفَةٍ جَبَلٌ أَحْرَزَ هذه البِئْرَ: 10

يعنى لِينَةَ هذه (68b) والتَنُوفَةُ الصَحْراءُ التى حول هذه البِئْرِ ۞

IV.

حَلَّتْ كُبَيْشَةُ بَطْنَ ذَاتِ رُوَامِ   وَعَفَتْ مَنَازِلُها بِبَجِّوِ بَرَامِ c

رُوَامٌ موضِعٌ عن يَسارِ النَقْرَةِ d وانت مُصْعِدٌ الى مَكَّةَ: ويقال النَقْرُ والنَقْرَةُ. وجَوُّ بَرَامَ موضِعٌ فيما هُناكَ ۞

٢   أَقْوَتْ مَعَالِمُها وَغَيَّرَ رَسْمَها   هُوجُ الرِّيَاحِ وَحِقْبَةُ الأَيَّامِ e

---

is expressed. Prof. Nöldeke's interpretation is borne out by LA XIV, 54[5-7], of the *sudden* appearance of the new moon. *Cf.* Quṭāmī, 1, 27, قَبَلُ نَظْرَةٍ.

a) As elsewhere, the end of the scholion had been cut off in the original text from which the copy was made; perhaps we should supply طالِعٌ.

b) MS أُوْرَتُها. For Līnah see Yāq. IV, 375, and Sprenger, *Post- u. Reiserouten*, 114.

IV. Of this poem vv. 1, 2, 5, 6, 7 are cited elsewhere; metre *Kāmil*.

c) Yāq. II, 827[8]: Bakrī 148[8] and 390[13].

d) النَقْرَة, a place on the *Ḥajj* road from al-Kūfah to Mekka: see Yāq. IV, 804[6]; perhaps the "Naqrat-Rakham" of Capt. Hunter's map (F, 5).   e) Yāq. بادَتْ.

اى دَرَسَتْ وَأَقْفَرَتْ يقال a أقوت القوم اذا فنى زادُهم: ويقال أَقْوَتْ بادَتْ. المَعالِم مَعالِم الدار مثل الرَماد

والأَثافى وَمَربِط الفَرَس والمَسْجِد ومَراح الابِل والغَنَم. والحِقْبَة الدَّهْر ☙

٣ حَتَّى أَنَعْنَ بِهِ وَكُلُّ مُجَلْجِلٍ   حَرِقِ الْبَوَارِقِ دَائِمِ الْإِرْزَامِ

قوله أَنَعْنَ بِهِ اى تفرّقت هذه الريّاح به اى المَنْزِل. وقوله كُلُّ مُجَلْجِلٍ اى كل سَحاب مُصَوِّت يَرعُد.

٥ وقوله حَرِقِ البَوَارِق اى كأنّه نارٌ تُوَقَّد يعنى السَحاب. ويروى خَرِق البوارق اى b سريع البوارق بمنزلة

الانسان يَخْتَرِق فى المَشْيِ اى يُسْرِع فيه. والإرزام صوت الرَعْد ☙

٤ دَارٌ بِهَا عِينُ النِّعَاجِ رَوَاتِعًا   تَعْدُو c مَسَارِبَهَا مَعَ الْآرَامِ

قوله عِينُ النِعاج يريد البَقَر: وانما سُمِّيَتْ عِينًا لِعِظَم أَعْيُنِها. تَعْدُو تَتْبَع مَسارِبَها: والمَسارِب المَراعى

وبُطون الأَوْدِيَة. والْآرَام الظِباء البِيض واحدُها رِئْم وهى لِخالِصَة البَياض وهى التى تكون بالرَمْل: والأُدْم

١٠ الظِباء التى لَيْسَتْ بخالِصَة البَياض وهى التى تَسْكُنُ الجِبال ☙ (69a)

٥ وَلَقَدْ تَحُلُّ d بِهِ كَأَنَّ مُجَاجَهَا   e تَغْبٌ يُصَفِّقُ صَفْوَةٌ بِمُدَامِ

قوله ولقد تَحُلُّ بِهِ يعنى كُبَيْشَة بهذا المنزل. وقوله مُجاجها رِيقَتها. والتَغب مَنْقَع ماءٍ فى قَلعِ صَلْد

تكون فيه اسْتِطالة ورِقَّةٌ كالرَقّاق. وقوله يُصَفِّق يَمْزِج. والمُدام الخَمْر: وانما سُمِّيت الخَمْر مُداما f لأنّه

على شربها ☙

٦ g يَا ذَا الْمُخَوِّفِنَا بِمَقْتَلِ شَيْخِهِ   حُجْرٍ تَمَنَّى صَاحِبَ الْأَحْلَامِ   15

حُجْر أبو امْرِئ القيس. يقول تَتَمَنَّى صاحبَ الاحلام باطِلٌ: والاحلام باطِلٌ وتَضْلِيلٌ: قال الشاعر: h * إِنَّ

الْأَمَانِيَّ وَالْأَحْلَامَ تَضْلِيلُ * ☙

---

a) MS أقوت الرجل والقوم.

b) This sense of خَرِق does not appear to be mentioned in the Lexx: perhaps the reading is incorrect. For فى المَشْى the MS has فى الشى.

c) MS مراسبها; the commy. has (twice) مَشارِب, but مَسارِب has been substituted in view of LA I, 448[8].   d) MS بيا, but بِه in commy.

e) MS نعف, but نعب in commy. LA I, 232[16] has the v. with بيا and تَغْب.

f) Some words have dropped out here, which may be some of those in LA XV, 104[15ff] or TA VIII, 296[15ff].   g) Vv. 6—7 cited Khiz. I, 321.

h) Bānat Suʿād of Kaʿb b. Zuhair, v. 11.

٧   لَا تَبْكِنَـا سَفَهًـا وَّلَا سَـادَاتِنَـا   وَّاجْعَلْ بُكَـاءَكَ لِابْـنِ أُمِّ قَـطَامِ

٨   حُجْرٍ غَـدَاةَ تَعَـاوَرَتْـهُ رِمَاحُنَـا   بِالْقَاعِ بَـيْـنَ صَفَـاصِفٍ وَّإِكَامِ

تعاورَتْهُ يريد تَـدَاوَلَتْه طَعْنَةً مرّةً هـذا ومرّة هـذا. والقاع ما مَلَسَ من الارض واستَوَى وجمعه قِيعانٌ. والصَفَاصِف أرضُونَ مُسْتَوِيَة لا نَبْتَ فيها ولا عِلْم واحدها صَفْصَفٌ. والإكام ما ارتفع من الارض لم يَبْلُغْ أن يكون جَبَلًا واحدتها أَكَمَةٌ ۞

٩   حَتَّى خَطَرْنَ بِهِ وَهُـنَّ شَوَارِعٌ   مِّـنْ بَـيْـنِ مُقْتَصِدٍ وَّآخَـرَ دَامِ

خَطَرْنَ يعنى الرماح: اى a يقعنه. من بَيْنِ مُقْتَصِدٍ: ويروى مُنْتَصِدٍ وهو الْمُنْكَسِر. وقوله وهُنَّ شَوَارِعٌ اى قَصَدَتْ ومالَتْ إليه ۞

١٠   b وَالْخَيْلُ عَاكِفَةٌ عَلَيْهِ كَأَنَّهَا   سُحُقُ النَّخِيلِ نَأَتْ عَنِ الْجُرَّامِ

قال ابو الوليد: يقال سُحُقٌ وسُحْقٌ بِرفع للحاء وسكونِها والرفع أَفصَحُ وأَعْرَبُ: والسُحُق الطِّوال من النَخيل. وقوله نَأَتْ عن الجُرَّام يقول طالت عن الذين يَجْرُمُونَها لا تنالها (69b) الأَيْدِى. واحد الجُرَّام جَارِم: والصُرَّام والجُرَّام والجُدَّاد والقُطَّاع واحد وهم الذين يَصْرِمون النَخْلَ خاصَّةً: وواحد الجُدَّاد جادّ وواحد القُطَّاع قاطع وواحد الصُرَّام صارم ۞

١١   مُتَمَارِيَاتٍ فِى الْأَعِنَّةِ قُطَّبًـا   يَّحْمِلْنَ كُلَّ مُـنَازِلٍ قَمْقَامِ

قوله مُتَمَارِيَات يعنى الخيل تَبَارَى بَعْضُها بَعْضًا لِـئَـلَّا تَسْبِقَ إِحْـدَاهُـنَّ صَاحِبَها. والقَاطِب العَابِس. والمُنَازِل المُقَاتِل. والقَمْقَام العَظِيم من الرجال ۞

١٢   سَلَفًا لِّأَرْعَنَ مَـا يَخَـفُّ ضَبَابُهُ   مُتَقَنِّسٍ بَادِى الْحَدِيدِ أُهَـامِ

قوله سَلَفًا يريد هذه الخيل سَلَف لِأَرْعَنَ اى مُتَقَدِّمَةً لِأَرْعَنَ. الارعن الجَيْش. وضَبابُهُ سَحَابُهُ. قوله مُتَقَنِّس c نَعْتُ المُنَازِل: يَحْمِلْنَ كُلَّ مُنَازِلٍ [مُتَقَنِّس]: فبناه مُتَقَنِّسًا أَخَذَهُ من القَوْنُس: والقَوْنُس العَمُود القائم فى وَسَطِ البَيْضَة. وبادِى الحَديد ظاهِرُ الحَديد يعنى المُتَقَنِّس. واللُّهام الكَثير العَدَد: يقال لِلجمع

---

a) So MS: apparently there is some mistake: or we may read يَقَعْنَ عَلَيْهِ.

b) For the first hemist. cf. ʿAmr Muʿall. 24, and post, v. 14; for the second, Labīd Muʿall. 66.

c) This interpretation is clearly erroneous; مُتَقَنِّس and بَادِى الْحَدِيد are both epithets of أَرْعَن "the mountain-like mass of armed men", as is also لُهَام.

الكَتِير نِهَامْ: a والباب الكبير الذى يَدْخُلُ منه راكبُ البعير والفوس نِهَام. وَإِن لم تَكُن البيضةُ ذاتَ

قَوْنَسٍ فهى الـتَّرْكُ: قال لبيد: b وَتَرَكَا كَانْبَصَلْ: يقول مُسْتَديرَةً مَلْسَاءَ. قل ابو الوليد: البَصَلُ

رُوُوسُ الرجال ☙

١٣   فِيهِ الْحَدِيدُ وَفِيهِ كُلُّ مَصُونَةٍ   نَبْعٍ وَكُلُّ مُـثَـقَّفٍ وَّحُسَامِ

يقول في هذا الجَيْش الحَديد يريد السلاح وفيه كُلُّ مَصُونَةٍ اى كل c قَوْسٍ وَدعَت لِيَوْم الحاجة

البِها: والمَصُون الثوب الذى لا يُلْبَس إلّا في يَوْم عيد. والمُنتَقِف الرُمْحِ الـمُثَلَّحِ. والحُسام السَّيْف القاطِع

الذى يقطع كل شئ. ويقول الرجُلُ 70a للرجل: احْسِم الأَمْرَ بَيْنى وبَيْنَك اى اقْطَعْهُ ☙

١٤   وَلَقَدْ قَتَلْنَهُمْ وَكَمْ مِنْ سَيِّدٍ   عَكَفَت عَلَيْهِ خُيُولُنَا وَهُمَامِ

قوله قتلنهم يريد لخيل قَتَلَت كِنْدَة. والهُمام السَّيّد. ويروى جُمِعَتْ عَلَيْهِ خُيُولُنَا ☙

١٥   d إِنَّا إِذَا عَضَّ الثِّقَافُ قَنَاتَنَا   حَالَت وَرَامَت ثُمَّ خَيْرَ مَرَامِ

الثِقاف يُقَوَّم به الرُمْح. حالت ويروى جالت ومعناها e انْقَلَبَت. وقوله رامت خَيْرَ مَرَامٍ اى طَلَبَت

فَأَدْرَكَت بِخَيْرِ مَطْلَبٍ لأَنّها غَلَبَت: ولو لم تَغْلِبْ لقد رامت شَرَّ مَرَامٍ ☙

١٦   نَحْمِى حَقِيقَتَنَا وَنَمْنَعُ جَارَنَا   f وَنَلُفُّ بَيْنَ أَرَامِلِ الْأَيْتَامِ

الحقيقة ما يَحِقُّ عليه [أَنْ يَحْمِيَهُ]. وقوله جارَنا اى مَنْ لَجَأَ البِنا. ونَلُفُّ نَجْمَعُ ☙

١٧   وَنَسِيرُ لِلْحَرْبِ الْعَوَانِ إِذَا بَدَت   حَتَّى نَلُفَّ ضِرَامَها بِـضِرَامِ

العَوَان التى قد قُوتِلَ فيها مَرَّةً بعد مَرَّة. ونَلُفُّ نَجْمَعُ. وضِرامُها نارُها ☙

١٨   لَمَّا رَأَيْتَ جُمُوعَ كِنْدَةَ أَحْجَمَت   عَنَّا وَكِنْدَةَ غَيْـرُ جِدٍّ كِرَامِ

١٩   أَزَعَمْتَ أَنَّكَ سَوْفَ تَأْتِى قَيْصَرًا   فَلَتَهْلِكَنَّ إِذًا وَّأَنْتَ شَآمِى

٢٠   ذَابَى عَلَى النَّاسِ الْمَقَادَةَ كُلِّهِمْ   حَتَّى نَقُودَهُمْ بِـغَيْـرِ زِمَامِ

---

a) This use of نِهَامْ in the sense of "a great gate" does not appear to be recorded in the Lexx., and seems to be doubtful.   *b)* Labīd Dīw. 39, 59.

c) MS رفع قَوْسٍ (although البِها follows!)   *d)* Cf. ʿAmr. Muʿall. 50, 51.

e) MS الملس.

f) This word is supported by the commentary, but seems to be doubtful in view of its recurrence in the next verse; نَلُمّ would make good sense.

قل ابو الوليد. قوله [غيرا] جدٍّ كرامٍ اى غيرِ كبيرٍ جدًّا اى مُشرِفٌ. شَأمٌ: يريد a تَيَمُّلَك فى الشَّام قَبْلَ
اَن تَصِلَ الى قَيْصَر. وقولُه نَأْبَى على النَّاس اى نَأْبَى اَن نَقادَ لأَحَدٍ حتى يَتْبَعَنا النَّاسُ مِنْ غَيْرِ اَن
نَـسُـوقَـهُـم ۞

V.

١ يَا دَارَ هِنْدٍ عَفَاهَا كُلُّ هَطَّالِ   بِالْجَوِّ مِثْلَ سَحِيقِ الْيُمْنَةِ الْبَالِى

الهَطَّال السَّحابة التى تَنْطِل بالمَطَر. والسَّحِيق الثَّوب (70b) الخَلَق. والجَوّ موضع: والجَوّ قصر اليمامة ﻩ

........c واليه النِّسبة اليَمانى وجمعه يُمْنٌ ۞

٢ جَرَتْ عَلَيْهَا رِيَاحُ الصَّيْفِ فَاطَّرَدَتْ   وَالرِّيحُ فِيهَا تُعَقِّيهَا بِأَذْيَالِ

ويروى e حالَتْ عليها. اطَّرَدَتْ اى جاءَتْ f [وذَهَبَتْ]. تُعَقِّيها تَدْرُسها. اراد g وتَجْرِى هذه الرِّياحُ على
هذه الدار التراب كما تَجُرُّ المرأةُ ذَيْلَها ۞

١٠

٣ حَبَسْتُ فِيهَا صِحَابِى كَىْ أُسَائِلَهَا   وَالدَّمْعُ قَدْ بَلَّ مِنِّى جَيْبَ سِرْبَالِى

٤ شَوْقًا إِلَى الْحَىِّ أَيَّامَ الْجَمِيعِ بِهَا   وَكَيْفَ يَطْرَبُ أَوْ يَشْتَاقُ أَمْثَالِى

٥ وَقَدْ عَلَا لِمَّتِى شَيْبٌ فَوَدَّعَنِى   مِنْهَا الْغَوَانِى وَدَاعَ الصَّارِمِ الْقَالِى

) MS كيهلك الى الشام.

V. This poem is in the *Mukhtārāt*, pp 97—99; vv. 5—7, 10, 18, 17, 16, 11—14, are in the
Kitāb as-Sināʿatain of al-ʿAskarī, pp. 124—6; vv. 1—4 in Agh. XIX, 84 (copied Naṣr. 615);
vv. 9, 10, 13a, 14b in Jamh. 8; vv. 12 and 16 in LA; and vv. 17—18 in Buḥt. Ḥam. pp. 266—7.
Metre *Basīṭ*.   b) Agh. بالجَوّ for بالخَبْتِ.

c) Evidently there is a *lacuna* here, though there is no trace of it in the MS.

d) Mukht. and Agh. ممّا for فيها; Agh. has the first hemist. thus: أَرْبَ فِيهَا وِلْىٍ مَا يُغَيِّرُهَا;
in the following scholion Agh. cites our reading, with فَاطَّرَقَتْ for فاطردت, and explains اطَّرَقت
by تلبَّدت.   e) So in MS: the word may be حالَتْ, as points are often omitted.

f) Supplied from schol. of Mukht.   g) So MS; perhaps we should read تَجُرُّ.

h) First hemist. in Agh. دَارٌ وَقَفْتُ بَيا صَحْبِى أُسَائِلُهَا.

i) Mukht., ʿAsk., مِنْهُ, which seems preferable (referring to لِمَّة): شَيْبٌ منها would refer to .

القالى الْمُبْغِض. واللَّمَّة دون الْجُمَّة. والصارم القاطع. والغوانى اللواتى قد غنينَ بالأزواج عن الرجال �™

٦ وَقَدْ أُسَلِّى هُمُومى حِينَ تَحْضُرُنى   بِجَسْرَةٍ كَعَلَاةِ الْقَيْنِ شِمْلَالِ

لجسرة الماضية ويقال الجَسِيمَة. والعلاة سِنْدان الْحَدَّاد. وكل صانع بيده فهو قَيْن. والشمْلَال الخفيفة ☙

٧ زَيَّافَةٍ بِقُتُودِ الرَّحْلِ نَاجِيَةٍ   تَفْرِى الْهَجِيرَ بِتَبْغِيلٍ وَّإِرْقَالِ

5 زَيَّافَة a تَزَيَّفَتْ فى سيرها: وهو ضَرْب من السَّيْر فى خِفَّةٍ وذكاءً. والقتود عيدان الرَّحْل واحدها قَتَدٌ. والناجية السريعة التى تَنْجُو فى سَيْرِها. تَفْرى تقطع. والهَجير أنصاف النهار. والتَّبْغيل ضرب من السير شبيه بالهَمْلَجة وليس بها: هو بين الهَمْلَجة والمَشْى. الإرْقال فوق الهَمْلَجة وهو الخَبَبُ ☙

٨ مَقْذُوفَةٍ b بِلَكِيكِ اللَّحْمِ عَنْ عُرُضٍ   كَمُفْرَدٍ وَّحَدٍ بِالْـجَوِّ دَيَّالِ

مَقْذُوفَة قُذِفَ فيها اللَّحْم. واللَّكِيك بَضَع اللحم. c عَنْ عُرُضٍ اى عن جِزَافٍ: يقول: لَم يُقَدَّر اللَّحْمُ
10 لها: ويقال رماهُ بِكَلامٍ [عن] عُرُضٍ اى جِزَافًا بغير قَدَرٍ اى جَاوَزَ الْحَدَّ. والمُفْرَدُ الثور يَرْعَى وَحْدَهُ ☙ (71a)

٩ d هَذَا وَرُبَّتَ حَرْبٍ قَدْ سَمَوْتُ لَهَا   حَتَّى شَبَبْتُ لَهَا نَارًا بِإِشْعَالِ

١٠ تَحْتِى e مُصَبَّرَةٌ جَرْدَاءُ عِجْلِزَةٌ   كَالسَّهْمِ أَرْسَلَهُ مِنْ كَفِّهِ الْغَالِى

سَمَوْتُ ارْتَفَعْت. شَبَبْتُ أوْقَدْتُها. المصبَّرة المُدَمَّجة. ويروى تَحْتِى مَسْوَمَةٌ: وِهى الْمُعْلَمة. والجَرْدَاء القصيرة
15 الشَّعر. والعِجْلِزَة الشديدة ويقال التى لم تَحْمِل قَطُّ شَيْئًا وهو اشدُّ لها. والغالى الذى [يَغْلُو] بالسهم اى يُباعد ☙

١١ وَكَبْشٍ مَلْمُومَةٍ بَادٍ f نَوَاجِذُهُ   شَهْبَاءَ ذَاتِ سَرَابِيلٍ وَّأَبْطَالِ

الكبش صاحب الجَيْش ورئيسُهم. الملمومة الكتيبة المجتمعة. والنواجذ نَواجِذُ الكَبْش: يقول هذا

---

a) MS مربعب.   b) MS باكيد: in commy. والكيد.

c) Mukht. schol. explains differently: عن عُرُضٍ اى من أَىِّ عُرُضٍ اسْتَعْرَضْتها رَأَيْتَها لَحِيمَةً.

d) Mukht., Jamh. لها نَارًا for نَوَاحِيْبَا, and سَمَوْتُ for نَهَضْتُ Jamh. هَذَا وَحَرْبٍ عَوَانٍ.

e) Mukht., ʿAsk. مُسَوَّمَةٌ (with our text as v.l.): and so Jamh., with قَوْدَاءُ for جَرْدَاءُ.

f) Mukht. and ʿAsk. have نَواجِذُها, making the description to apply to the ملمومة, not to the كَبْش; and this, in spite of our commentary, is the only possible grammatical construction. A similar confusion has been noticed above in the commentary to No. IV, v. 12.

كانَّتِ في الحرب أبدًا لأنّه أبدًا مُستعِدّ للحرب. ويروى باد نَواجِدُها: يريد المَلمومة. شَهْباء يريد بَيْضاء من الحديد. وقوله ذات سرابيل السرابيل الدروع ☆

١٢ a أَوْجَرْتُ جُفْرَتَهُ خُرْصًا فَمَالَ بِهِ   كَمَا انْثَنَى مُخْضَدٌ مِّنْ نَاعِمِ الضَّالِ

الخُرْصُ سِنانُ الرُّمحِ: b يقال خُرْص [وخِرْص وخَرْص]. كما انثَنَى مُخْضَد: قال ابو عمرو: المُخْضَد ما قد قُطِع: قال لا يكون مُخْضَد c [إلّا] بفتح الصاد: وقال غيره المُخْضَد الغُصن الرَّيّان المُمتَلئ ماءً ٥ وهو الذى يُكسَر غيرَ أن يُقطَع وهو رَطْب: ويروى خَضَد وهو الغُصن [المَقطوع]. ويروى ايضا مُحَضَّد بالحاء والصاد وهو d الأَمْلَس. وقوله أَوْجَرْتُ جُفْرَتَهُ: يروى ثُغْرَتَهُ e وهى ثُغْرَة نَحْرِهِ وهى f [اليَزَمَة] التى [بَيْنَ] g التَرْقُوَتَيْنِ. الجُفْرَة لخاصِرة. والضال السِّدْر الصِّغار التى تكون فى الباديَة وإحدُها ضالَة ☆

١٣ h وَلَهْوَةٍ كَرُضَابِ الْمِسْكِ طَالَ بِهَا   [فِى] دَنِّهَا كَرُّ حَوْلٍ بَعْدَ أَحْوَالِ

اللهوة i الخمر: وإنما قيل لها لَهْوَة لأن الانسان اذا شَرِب (71a) اشْتَهَى عليها الطعام. وقوله z كرُضاب ١٠ المِسْكِ يريد كَفِنات المِسْك فى طِيب ريحِها. ويروى وقَيْوَة كَرُضاب المِسْك ☆

١٤ k بَاكَرْتُهَا قَبْلَ مَا بَدَا الصَّبَاحِ لَنَا   فِى بَيْتِ مُنْهَمِرِ الْكَفَّيْنِ مِفْضَالِ

قال ابو الوليد المِفْضال الذى يَعْظُم فَضلُه إن شاء الله. l [مُنْهَمِر الكَفَّيْنِ سَخِىّ سائِلُ الكَفَّيْنِ بالعَطاء: شبّه جُودَه بمُنْهَمِر المَطَر] ☆

١٥ m وَعَبْلَةٍ كَمَهَاةِ الْجَوِّ نَاعِمَةٍ   كَأَنَّ رِيقَتَهَا شِيبَتْ بِسَلْسَالِ

ويروى: وَثَفْلَةٍ n كَمَهَاة. المَهَاة البَقَرة. العَبْلة المرأة الحَسَنة الذِّراع o المُمَلَّس لَحْمُها. شِيبَتْ خُلِطَتْ.

---

a) LA IV, 142¹⁴ and VIII, 287¹⁸, with خَضَد for مُخْضَد; Mukht مُخْضَد.

b) MS فقال اخْرُص.   c) This correction seems certain.

d) No such meaning of مُحَضَّد is mentioned in the Lexx., and there must be some mistake.

e) MS ويروى for وهى.   f) Entered from LA V, 173⁵,⁶.   g) MS الرووس.

h) Mukht. وقَيْوَة كَرُضاب, with وَلَهْوَة as v. l. in scholion; 'Ask. كَرُضاب; Jamh. 8³ has a verse compounded of the first hemist. of v. 13 and the second of v. 14, and reads وقَيْوَة كَمَذَاجِيع الْجَوِفِ صَافِيَةٍ

i) MS جَمْع (!)   j) MS كفراب.

k) Mukht and 'Ask. قبل ما يَبْدَأُ الصباح; MS قَبْلَ أَنْ يَبْدُو الصَّبَاحِ.

l) Added from scholion of Mukht.   m) Mukht وَغِبْلَة (see LA XIV, 25¹⁴).

n) MS لحميا.   o) MS الملمسيا.

والسلسال الخَمْر: a ويقال انّما سمّى سَلْسالًا لأنّه يَتَسَلْسَلُ فى الحَلْقِ: ويقال الصافية [من الخمر] ✧

١٩ b قَدْ بِتُّ الْعَبُهَا وَهْنًا وَّتُلْعِبِنِى   ثُمَّ اَنْصَرَفْتُ وَهِىْ مِنِّى عَلَى بَالِ

١٧ c بَانَ الشَّبَابُ فَاَلَى لَا يُلِمُّ بِنَا   وَاَحْتَلَّ بِى مِنْ مُلِمِّ الشَّيْبِ مِحْلَالِ

١٨ d وَالشَّيْبُ شَيْنٌ لِمَنْ d يَّحْتَلُّ سَاحَتَهُ   لِلّٰهِ دَرُّ سَوَادِ اللِّمَّةِ الْخَالِى

VI.

١ سَقَى الرَّبَابَ مُجَلْجِلٌ ال e اَكْنَافِ لَمَّاحٌ بُرُوقُهْ

٢ جَوْنٌ f تُكَرِّكُرُهُ الصَّبَا وَهْنًا وَّتَمْرِيهِ خَرِيقُهْ   5

g الرَّبَابُ السحابُ الرَّقيقُ. والمُجَلْجِلِ المُصَوّت: يريد السحابَ فيه رَعْدٌ. والاكنافِ الجَوانِب. واللمّاح الذى يَلْمَحُ [ويقال] لَمَحَ الرجُلُ بِثَوبِه اذا اشارَ به. والجَوْن الأَسْوَدُ من السحاب. تُكَرْكِرُهُ تردُّدُه. وَهْنًا بعد رَقْدَةٍ. وتَمْرِيه تُنَزِّلُ مَطَرَه. h والخَريق الريحُ الجَنُوب ✧

---

a) Before this sentence the following words appear in the MS: يقال الماءُ فى سلسال ; I take them to be a blundering attempt to write the words which follow, left uncancelled by oversight.

b) Cited LA II, 236²⁵; 'Ask. طُورًا, قَبِتُّ. Observe هِىْ for هِىَ (see ante, No. I. v. 29).

c) Mukht. مِحْلَال. ; وَاَحْتَلَّ بِى مِنْ مَشِيبٍ اَىْ مِحْلَال; 'Ask., the same, with كُلَّ مِحْلَال. Buḥt. (266—7) has vv. 17 and 18, with مِحْلَالِى.

d) Mukht., 'Ask., Buḥt. أَرْسَى بِسَاحَتِهِ (explained as ثَبَّتَ وَأَقَامَ). Buḥt. الخَالِى; Mukht. explains خَالِى as ماضى =. It is used by I. Q. in this sense: e. g. 52,1.

VI. The whole of this poem is in the *Amālī* of al-Qālī I, 180; v. 7 is cited Asās I, 60. Metre *Kāmil muraffal.*   e) Qālī لَمَّاعٌ.

f) Qālī تُكَفْكِفُهُ. The MS wrongly inserts لَه between وَ and تَمْرِيه, spoiling metre, sense and grammar. *Iqtiḍāb* 413 has the verse, with بَاتَتْ in place of جَوْنٌ. For the use of مِرى in the same way as here see I. Q. 18, 6.

g) This must be wrong: a cloud cannot be said to water a part of itself. الرَّبَابُ is a proper name, either of a place, a tribe, or a person. Yāq. II, 746²⁰ mentions a mountain of this name between Faid and al-Madīnah, which would suit the context; for الرباب as a personal (woman's) name see I. Q. 63, 2.

h) This explanation conflicts with the Lexx, and with vv. 6 and 7 of the poem (يَمانِيَة); perhaps we should read والخريق الريحُ [الشديدة] الهَبُوب: LA XI, 360⁹.

٣ مَرْعَى الْعَسِيفِ عِشَارَهْ   حَتَّى إِذَا دَرَّتْ عُرُوقُهْ

٤ وَدَنَا يُضِىءُ a صُبَابُهُ   غَابًا يُضَرِّمُهُ حَرِيقُهْ

العَسِيفُ الحُرّ ويقال العَبْد: والأَسِيف العبد. والعِشار اللقاح: فى التى تُحْلَب. والغاب الإجام. يُضَرِّمُهْ
حَرِيقُهُ يُوقِدُهُ ۞ (72a)

٥ حَتَّى إِذَا مَا ذَرْعُهْ   بِالْمَاءِ ضَاقَ فَمَا يُطِيقُهْ

٦ هَبَّتْ لَهُ مِنْ خَلْفِهِ   رِيحٌ b يَمَانِيَةٌ تَسُوقُهْ

٧ c حَلَّتْ عَزَالِيَهُ الْجَنُو   بُ فَثَجَّ وَاهِيَةً خُرُوقُهْ

ذَرْعُه حِيلَتُه. ويروى شَامِيَة. واليَمانِيَة الجَنُوب لأنها من قِبَل d القِبلَة. عَزالِيه أَفْواهُه واحدها عَزْلَاء.
وثَجَّ سال وصَبّ. واهِيَة ضعيفة مُنْشَقَّة ۞

VII.

١ يَا ذَا e الْمُخَوِّفُنَا f بِقَتْـلِ أَبِيهِ g إِذْلَالًا وَحَيْنَا

٢ أَزَعَمْتَ أَنَّكَ قَدْ قَتَلْـتَ h سَرَاتَنَا كَذِبًا وَمَيْنَا

٣ i هَلَّا عَلَى حُجْرِ بْنِ أُمْ   مِ قَطَامِ تَبْكِى لَا عَلَيْنَا

٤ j إِنَّا إِذَا عَضَّ الثِّقَا   فُ بِرَأْسِ صَعْدَتِنَا لَوَيْنَا

٥ k نَحْمِى حَقِيقَتَنَا وَبَعْـ   ضُ الْقَوْمِ يَسْقُطُ بَيْنَ بَيْنَا

---

a) Qālī رِبَابُهْ, a much better reading.

b) Qālī شَامِيَة. *Cf.* a similar passage from al-Kumait (also of Asad), cited in LA XIII, 470[1],
Lane 2036c.   c) Cited Asās I, 60, *s. v.* ثَجَّ.   d) MS القبيلة.

VII. In Mukht. pp. 90—92; Agh. XIX, 85—86 (copied Naṣr. 599—600); Khiz. I, 322 (vv.
1—8 and 12—14); ʿAinī I, 490 (1—8, 12); S. S. Mughnī 91 (vv. 1—6, 12, 19, 20); BQut. 39
(vv. 1—2) and 143—4 (vv. 1—7); Yaʿqūbī I, 249 (vv. 1—5). Metre *Kāmil muraffal*.

e) Yaʿq. الْمُعَيِّرنَا.   f) MS لعل; see *ante*, No. IV, 6.

g) Mukht. إِذْلَالَ (misprint).   h) Mukht. سُرَاتَنَا.   i) SSM لَوْ لَا, Mukht. لَوْ مَا.

j) *Ante*, No. IV, 15.

k) Agh. النَّاس; v. cited Lane 288a, LA XVI, 214[6], Howell Grammar I, 815..

٦   هَلَّا سَأَلْتَ جُمُوعَ كِنْدَةَ a يَوْمَ وَلَّوْا أَيْنَ أَيَّنَا

٧   أَيَّامَ نَضْرِبُ هَامَهُمْ   بِبَوَاتِرٍ حَتَّى انْحَنَيْنَا

٨   b [وَجُمُوعَ غَسَّانَ الْمُلُو كَ أَتَيْنَهُمْ وَقَدِ انْطَوَيْنَا]

٩   لَحِقًا أَبَاطِلُهُنَّ قَدْ عَالَجْنَ أَسْفَارًا وَأَيَّنَا

٥ لَحِقًا أَبَاطِلُهُنَّ اى قَدْ لَحِقَتْ الخَوَاصِرُ بِالْأَصْلَابِ: واحدها إِطْلٌ وَأَبْطَلَ. وَالْأَيْنُ الاعياءُ ☆

١٠   c وَلَقَدْ صَلَقْنَ هَوَازِنًا   بِنَوَاهِلٍ حَتَّى ارْتَوَيْنَا

١١   نُعْلِيهِمُ تَحْتَ الضِّبَا بِ الْمَشْرَفِيَّ إِذَا اعْتَزَيْنَا

يقول هذه الخيل صَلَقْنَ اى نَقَيْنَ هَوَازِنَ: ويقال d صَلَقْنَ اى عَضَضْنَ: ويقال للخيل اذا عَضَّ e بَعْضُها بَعْضًا قَدْ صَلَقَ f بِنَابِهِ: ويقال لِأَنْيَابِ البعير اذا كانت حِدَادًا طِوَالًا عُضُلٌ مَصَاليقُ. وَقوله بِنَوَاهِلٍ

١٠ يعنى بِأَسِنَّةٍ كانت عِطَاشًا فَرَوِيَتْ من الدَّمِ. حتى ارْتَوَيْنَا يريد الاسنة من الدَّم. الاعْتِزَاءُ أَنْ يَنْتَسِبَ الرجلُ عند الضَّرْبَةِ. الْمَشْرَفِيَّةُ نُسِبَتْ الى مَشَارِفَ g قُرًى بالشَّامِ: ويقال إِنَّمَا سُمِّيَتْ مَشْرَفِيَّةً لِأَنَّهَا بِيعَتْ بِالمَشَارِفِ من سَرَاةِ الْيَمَنِ ☆

١٢   نَحْنُ الْأُولَى h جَمَعْ جُمُو عًا ثُمَّ وَجَّهْهُمْ إِلَيْنَا

١٣   وَاعْلَمْ بِأَنَّ جِيَادَنَا آلَيْنَ لَا يَقْضِينَ دَيْنَا

١٤   وَلَقَدْ أَبَحْنَا مَا حَمَيْتَ وَلَا مُبِيحَ لِمَا حَمَيْنَا

١٥   هَذَا i وَلَوْ قَدَرَتْ عَلَيْكَ رِمَاحُ قَوْمِى مَا انْتَهَيْنَا

١٦   حَتَّى تَشُوشَكَ نَوْشَةً عَادَاتِهِنَّ إِذَا j انْتَوَيْنَا

١٧   نُغْلِى الشَّمُولَ بِكُلِّ عَا تِقَةٍ شَمُولٍ مَّا صَحَوْنَا

١٨   وَنُهِينُ فِى k لَذَّاتِهَا عِظَمَ التِّلَادِ إِذَا انْتَشَيْنَا

         15

---

a) SSM اِنْ تَوَلَّوْا, Mukht. (*sic*) اِنْ تَوَلَّوْا, BQut. 43, 16 هَارِبِينَا (against rhyme), but p. 144 as our text.   *b)* This verse, omitted in MS, is found in Mukht. Agh. and Khiz., and is required by the context; scholion of Mukht.: يعنى للخيل انْطَوَيْنَ من الضُّمْرِ.

c) Agh. omits vv. 10 and 11.   *d)* MS صُلِبْنَ   *e)* Instead of بعضها بعضًا MS has احمر   *f)* MS بِنَابِهِ.   *g)* MS مُوازِ السَّلَمِ.

h) Mukht., Agh., Howell Gram. I, 601 فَاجْمَعْ جُمُوعَكَ.

i) MS وَقَدْ for وَلَوْ.   *j)* MS ابدينا (given correctly in scholion).   *k)* Agh. لَذَّاتِنا.

١٩ لَا يَبْلُغُ الْبَانِى وَلَوْ   رَفَعَ الدَّعَائِمَ مَا بَنَيْنَا

(**72**b) قال ابو الوليد: يروى: فَاجْمَعْ جُمُوعَكَ. انْتَوَيْنَا الْتَحَقْنَا وأَتَيْنَاهم من بُعْدٍ. وسُمّيت الخَمْرُ شَمُولًا لأَنّ رِيحَها تَشْمَلُ القومَ اذا فُتِحَتْ. انْتَشَيْنا شَرِبْنا. التِلاد المال القديم. تَنُوشُكَ تُناوِلُكَ ۞

٢٠ كَمْ مِنْ [a]رَئِيسٍ قَدْ قَتَلْنَاهُ   وَضَيْمٍ قَدْ أَبَيْنَا

٢١ وَلَرُبَّ سَيِّدِ مَعْشَرٍ   ضَخْمِ الدَّسِيعَةِ قَدْ رَمَيْنَا

٢٢ عِقْبَانُهُ بِظِلَالِ عِقْبَانٍ   [b]تَيَمَّمُ [c]مَا نَوَيْنَا

٢٣ حَتَّى تَرَكْنَا شِلْوَهُ   جَزَرَ السِّبَاعِ وَقَدْ مَضَيْنَا

٢٤ [d]وَأَوَانِسٍ مِثْلِ الدُّمَى   حُورِ الْعُيُونِ قَدِ ٱسْتَبَيْنَا

٢٥ إِنَّا لَعَمْرُكَ [e]لَا يُضَا   مُ حَلِيفُنَا أَبَدًا لَدَيْنَا

الدَّسِيعة الحَسَبُ والشَرَفُ والدسيعة [f]الجِرَّة والدسيعة الجَفْنَة. الأَوانِس اللواتى يأْنَسْنَ فى الحديث. والحُور التى قد فَضَلَ سَوادَها بياضُها: قال ابو عمرو: الحَوَرُ عِنْدى سَوادُ المُقْلةِ لأنّه مَثَلٌ للظّباء والبَقَرِ: ولا يَكُون ذلك لانْسانٍ فى الدُّنْيا ۞

VIII.

١ نَأَتْكَ سُلَيْمَى فَالْفُؤَادُ قَرِيحُ   وَلَيْسَ لِحَاجَاتِ الْفُؤَادِ مُرِيحُ

٢ إِذا [g]ذُقْتَ فَاهَا قُلْتَ طَعْمُ مُدَامَةٍ   مُشَعْشَعَةٍ تُرْخِى الْإِزَارَ قَدِيحُ

القديح الذى يُقْدَحُ منه بالقَدَحِ: ويقال قديح مَبْزول. والمشعشعة الرقيقة المِزاجِ ۞

٣ بِمَاءِ سَحَابٍ فِى أَبَارِيقِ فِضَّةٍ   لَهَا ثَمَنٌ فِى الْبَايِعِينَ رَبِيحُ

٤ [h]تَأَمَّلْ خَلِيلِى هَلْ تَرَى مِنْ ظَعَائِنٍ   يَمَانِيَةٍ قَدْ تَغْتَدِى وَتَرُوحُ

---

a) MS نفيس, against all other texts.

b) Agh. corruptly تتمّم.   c) Mukht. مَنْ نَوَيْنَا.

d) Agh. and Mukht. transpose vv. 24 and 25.   e) Agh., Mukht. مَا يُضَامُ.

VIII. Four vv. of this poem are cited in Naṣr. 614 (vv. 7 and 12—14), and one (4) in Sh. Sh. Mughnī. Metre *Ṭawīl*.

f) MS الجزله.   g) MS ذُقْتُ.   h) Cited SSM 35, with تَبَصَّرْ.

٥ a كَعَوْمِ السَّفِينِ فِى غَوَارِبِ لُجَّةٍ   تُكَفِّئُهَا فِى مَاءِ دِجْلَةَ رِيحُ

قوله تُكَفِّئُها b مهموز اى تُميلها: شبّه c الظُّعْنَ لعَوْمِ السَّفِينِ: ويروى تُكَفْكِفُها. والغَوَارِبُ الأَمْواجِ واحدها

غارِب: والغارِبُ من الجَمَلِ يَتقدّم السَّنامَ. واللُّجّة المَاء الكثير. والظعائِن النساء سُمّينَ d بدَ لأَنّهنّ

يُظْعَنَّ [بِهِنَّ] ☙

٦ e جَوَانِبُهَا تَغْشَى الْمُتَالِفَ أَشْرَفَتْ   عَلَيْهِنَّ صُهْبُ مِّنْ يَهُودَ جُنُوحُ   ٥

(73a) أَشْرَفَتْ عليهِنَّ على الجَوانِبِ. والصُّهْبُ المَلّاحون: صُهْب اى الشُّعور: يريد انّهم نَبَطٌ ☙

٧ وَقَدْ أَغْتَدِى قَبْلَ الْغَطَاطِ وَصَاحِبِى   أَمِينُ الشَّظَا رَخْوُ f اللَّبَانِ سَبُوحُ

الشَّظَا g عُظَيْمٌ رقيقٌ فى وظِيفِ الفرس: اذا انْكَسَرَ ذلك العُظَيْم أو زال h انْتَشَرَ [عَصَبُ] الفَرَس مِنه:

ويقال الشَّظا عُظَيْمٌ رقيقٌ صغيرٌ i مُسْتَكِنّ بوظِيفِ الفرس: والوظِيف فوق k الرُّسْغِ: واذا انكَسر أو زالَ   ١٠

شَظَى l الفَرَس فَعَتَرَ m يقال: فُلِقَ شَظاهُ. وقوله رَخْوُ اللَّبَان الصدر اى واسِع الصَّدْرِ: واللَّبان

ما بَيْنَ المَنْكِبَيْنِ: ويُسْتَحَبّ للفرس ان يكون كذلك. والسَّبوح الخَلِيق فى سَيْرِ. والغَطَاط يقال الصُّبْح

يقال الغَطاط السُّودُ بطونِ الأَجْنِحَة من القطا: والكُدْرِيُّون n من القطا بيضُ بطونِ الأَجنِحَة: وما كان

من أَبْيَضَ بطْنِ الجَناحِ فهو كُدْرِيّ وما كان من أَسْوَدَ بطنِ الجَناحِ فهو o جُونِىّ: يقال كُدْرِيُّ القطا وجُونِىّ

ويقال للكُدْرِيّ أيضًا p غَطاطٌ ☙

٨ إِذَا حَرَّكَتْهُ السَّاقُ قُلْتَ مُجَنَّبٌ   غَضِيضٌ q غَذَتْهُ عَهْـدَةٌ وَسُرُوحُ   ١٥

اذا حرّكتْهُ الساق يريد الفرس. والمُجَنَّب هاهنا الظَّبْى r الظَّبْى لشدّة خَلْق الظَّبْى وأَنّ قوائمه

---

a) This verse has been imitated by the poet's fellow-tribesman Bishr b. Abī Khāzim (LA I, 135²³):

وَكَأَنَّ ظُعْنَهُمْ غَدَاةَ تَحَمَّلُوا   سُفُنٌ تَكَفَّأُ فِى خَلِيجِ مُغْرِبِ

b) MS مَهْمُوزَة اى مَثلِها.   c) MS الغُصْنَ كَعُومٍ.   d) MS بِها.

e) MS تَغْشَى.   f) Naṣr. اللسان (!)

g) The MS in this scholion is very corrupt: the first part has been set right with the help
of LA XIX, 162, and Aṣmaʿī, Khail (Haffner) 62—5.   h) MS بنسر.

i) MS مسكس.   j) MS الدمع.   k) MS و.   l) MS فعمر.

m) MS فَوْق شَظا (!)   n) MS والكدرين.   o) MS حودى und later حُورَى.

p) MS غطى.   q) MS عدده عبده فَسُروحٌ.   r) MS الطَّبْير (!)

a نَبَسَتْ بِمُنْبَسِطَة: فاذا كان كذلك فيهو مجنّب. واذا كان منبسط القوائم فيهو b قاسط: يقال قاسط

القوائم والتخلّف اذا كان مُسْتَقيمًا وهو عَيْب في الفرس. والغَضِيض السَّمين الأَمْلَس ويريد الظَّبْيَ. وقوله

c غذَتْهُ عَيْهَدة d وسُروح والعَيْهَدة المَطْرة تأتى في الارض أثَر من أُخْرَى كانت قَبْلَها والجماع العِهاد. ويروى

e غَذاه وَحْدَهُ: اى رَعَى ذلك المكان وَحْدَهُ. ويقال العِهاد الأَمْطار (73b) المُتَقَدِّمة تكون من فَرْغ

الدَّلْو الآخِر والنَّحوت والشَّرطَيْن والبُطَيْن والثُّرَيَّا: فكلّ مَطَر كان بهذه الأَنْواء فيهو عِهادٌ: والقول الأَوَّل قول 5

اى عَمْر وهو وَسْمِى وهو خَطَأٌ. وهو f رَصَد وهو بَدْرِى ايضا. والسُّروح المَراعِى واحدها سَرْح: وواحد

المَسارِح مَسْرَح وهى مَراعِى الابل والغَنَم. يقول له في هذا المكان عِهادٌ وله رِعْىٌ: والرِّعْىُ الاسم والرَّعْىُ

المَصْدَر ☙

إِذَا مَا تُمَاشِيهِ الظِّبَاءُ g تَطِيحُ	٩ مَرَاتِعُهُ الْقِيعَانِ فَرْدٌ كَأَنَّهُ
كِلَابًا فَكُلَّ الضَّارِبَاتِ يَسِيحُ	١٠ فَهَاجَ لَهُ حَى غَدَاةً فَأَوْسَدُوا
قَوَائِمُ حَمْشَاتُ الأَسَافِلِ زُوحُ	١١ إِذَا خَافَ مِنْهُنَّ اللِّحَاقَ نَمَتْ بِهِ
مُشَلْشِلَةٌ فَوْقَ h النِّطَاقِ تَفُوحُ	١٢ وَقَدْ أَتْرُكُ الْقِرْنَ الْكَمِىَّ بِصَدْرِهِ
لَهَا بَعْدَ j إِشْرَافِ k الْعَبِيطِ نَشِيحُ	١٣ دَفُوعٌ لِأَطْرَافِ الأَنَامِلِ i ثَرَّةٌ
تَبَادَرْنَ شَتَّى كُلُّهُنَّ m تَمُوحُ	١٤ إِذَا جَاءَ سِرْبٌ مِنْ l ظِبَاءٍ يَعُدْنَهُ

IX.

فَقَلْبِى عَلَيْهِمْ هَالِكٌ جِدَّ مَغْلُوبِ	١ تَذَكَّرْتُ أَهْلِى الصَّالِحِينَ بِمَلْحُوبِ	51
وَأَهْلَ عِتَاقِ الْجُرْدِ الْبِرِّ n وَالطِّيبِ	٢ تَذَكَّرْتُ أَهْلَ الْخَيْرِ وَالْبَاعِ وَالنَّدَى	

---

a) MS لِيْبَسَت تلك الْمُنْبَسِطَة.   b) In LA IX, 254 أَقْسَطُ is given in this sense.

c) MS عمده عيهد.   d) MS الْعِيْد (this also has the same meaning).

e) MS عده.   f) MS رسد,   g) MS تَطِيح.   h) Naṣr. السِّنَان.

i) MS تارة; the reading adopted is that of Naṣr.   j) Naṣr. إِنْزَاح.

k) MS نَسِيح; Naṣr. as text.   l) Naṣr. نَسَاء.   m) Naṣr. يَبُوحُ.

IX. vv. 1 and 3 in Bakrī 537[9]; vv. 2, 8, 16 in Khiz. I, 323; vv. 7 and 15 in LA. Metre *Ṭawīl*

n) Khiz. وَأَهْلَ عِتَاقِ الْخَيْبِلَ وَالْخَمْرِ.

٣   تَذَكَّرْتُهُمْ مَا إِنْ تَجِفُّ مَدَامِعِى   كَأَنَّ ^aجَدْوَلَ يَّسْقِى مَزَارِعَ مَكْرُوب

٤   وَبَيْتٍ يَّفُوحُ الْمِسْكُ مِنْ حُجُرَاتِهِ   تَسَكَّيْتُهُ ^bمِنْ بَيْنِ سِرٍّ وَّمَخْطُوب

٥   وَمُسْمِعَةٍ قَدْ أَصْحَلَ الشَّرْبُ صَوْتَهَا   تَأَوَّى إِلَى أَوْتَارِ أَجْوَفَ مَخْفُوب

٦   شَهِدْتُ بِفِتْيَانٍ كِرَامٍ عَلَيْهِمُ   جِبَاءٌ لِّمَنْ يَّنْتَابُهُمْ غَيْرُ مَحْجُوب

٥   ٧   وَخِرْقٍ مِّنَ الْفِتْيَانِ أَكْرَمَ مَصْدَقًا   مِّنَ السَّيْفِ قَدْ آخَيْتُ لَيْسَ بِمَذْرُوب

الخِرْقُ الظَّرِيفُ السَّخِىّ. وَالمَذْرُوبُ السَّيِّئُ الخُلُقِ لِخَبِيثِ ^dاللِّسَانِ: وَيُقَالُ ^eسَاءَ بِالدَّرَبِى أَى أَسَاءَ

عَلَيهِ النَّثَا وَعَابَهُ: وَالذَّرَبَى السَّمُّ أَيضًا: يُقَالُ سَيْفٌ مَذْرُوبٌ وَمُذَرَّبٌ إِذَا كَانَ مَسْمُومًا: (74a) وَرَجُلٌ

ذَرِبُ اللِّسَانِ إِذَا كَانَ سَيِّئَ اللَّفْظِ كَثِيرَ الفُحْشِ: وَيُقَالُ المَذْرُوبُ المَسمُوم. أَكْرَمَ مَصْدَقًا هُوَ أَصْدَقُ مِنَ

السيفِ إِذَا ضَرَبْتَ بِهِ فَصَدَقَ ☙

١٠   ٨   فَأَصْبَحَ مِنِّى كُلُّ ذَلِكَ ^fقَدْ مَضَى   فَأَىُّ فَتًى فِى النَّاسِ لَيْسَ بِمَكْذُوب

٩   وَقَدْ أَغْتَدِى فِى الْقَوْمِ تَحْتِى شِمِلَّةٍ   بِطِرْفٍ مِّنَ السِّيدَانِ أَجْرَدَ مَنْسُوب

الشِّمِلَّةُ السَّرِيعَةُ: يُرِيدُ نَاقَتَهُ. الطِّرْفُ الفَرَسُ ^g[الكَرِيمُ الاطراف يعنى الآباء وَالأُمَّهَاتِ]. وَالسِّيدَانُ الذِّئَابُ

وَاحِدُهَا سِيدٌ: وَإِنَّمَا شَبَّهَ الذِّئْبَ بِالفَرَسِ ^hالجَوَادِ وَيُقَالُ الطَّوِيلُ ☙

١٠   ⁱكُمَيْتٍ كَشَاةِ الرَّمْلِ صَافٍ أَدِيمُهُ   مُفِجِّ الْكَوَامِى جُرْشُعٍ غَيْرِ مَكْشُوب

١٥   قَالَ أَبُو الوَلِيدِ المَكْشُوبُ المَخْلُوطُ الفَرَسُ يَدْخُلُ فِيهَا ^jالهَجْنَةَ. وَغَيْرَهُ: المَكْشُوبُ ^kالمُقْرِفُ. وَالشَّاةُ

^lالظَّبْىُ وَيُقَالُ البَقَرَةُ. وَالمُفِجِّ المُفَرِّجِ. الكَوَامِى جَوَانِبُ الحَوَافِرِ الَّتِى تَحْمِى النُّسُورَ [أَنْ] يُصِيبَهَا الرَّمْضُ ☙

١١   وَحَيْلٍ كَأَسْرَابِ الْقَطَا قَدْ ^mوَزَعْتُهَا   بِخَيْفَانَةٍ تَنْمِى بِسَاقٍ وَّعُرْقُوب

---

a) MS. جَدْوَلُ السَّقِى مَزَارِع. Bakrī as text.

b) See this rare word in a similar context in I. Q. 19, 16.

c) LA I, 372¹⁷ as text.   d) MS الشَّانُ.   e) MS ماوه بالدرى.

f) Khiz. I, 333 قد خَلَا.   g) Added from LA XI, 117⁷.   h) MS. الجُوف.

i) Cf. a similar collocation of epithets in al-Aʿshà's v. (LA XIV, 80³):

قَافِلٍ جُرْشُعٍ تَرَاهُ كَتَيْسِ الــــرَّمْلِ لَا مُقْرِفٍ وَّلَا مَكْشُوب.

(misprinted LA I, 342²⁵ كَبِيْسِ الرَّمْلِ).   j) MS الهَجر.

k) MS الحروف.   l) MS الصى.   m) MS وَدَعْتُهَا, and so in scholion.

قال وَزَعْنَها اى قد *a* كَفَفْنَها. خَيْفَانَةٍ [وهى الجَرَادَة] يقال *b* لها هذا اذا *c* اسْتَخَفَّتْ وطارت. تنمى بِسَاقٍ

وعُرْقُوب يريد تَرْتَفِع ☆

١٢   وَحَرْقٍ تَصيحُ الْهَامُ فيهِ مَعَ الصَّدَى   مَخُوفٍ إِذَا مَا جَنَّهُ اللَّيْلُ مَرْهُوب

الْهَامَةُ ذَكَرُ الْبُوم: والصَّدَى ذَكَرُ البوم ايضًا. وقوله جَنَّهُ الليل اى غَطَّاهُ الليل وسَتَرَهُ ☆

١٣   قَطَعْتُ بِصَهْبَاءِ السَّرَاةِ شِمِـلَّـةٍ   تَرِلُّ الْوَلَايَا عَـنْ جَوَانِب مَكْرُوب

١٤   لَهَا قَمَعٌ تَـذْرى بِـهِ الْكُورَ تَـامِـكٌ   إِلَى حَارِك تَأْوى إِلَى الصُّلْب مَنْصُوب

الْقَمَعُ السَّنَام واحدها قَمَعَةٌ وهى أَعْلَى السنام. تَذْرى بـه الْكُور اى يَبِرُّ سنامُها الْكُور يَرْمى به. التامِك

السنام الصَّخُم ☆

١٥   *d* إِذَا حَرَّكَتْهَا السَّاقُ قُلْتَ نَعَامَةٌ   وَإِنْ *e* زُجِرَتْ يَوْمًا فَلَيْسَت بِرُعْبُوب

١٩   (74*b*) تَرَى الْمَرْءَ يَصْبُو *f* لِلْمَحَيَاةِ وَطُولِهَا   وَفِى طُولِ عَيْشِ الْمَرْءِ *g* الْمَرْءِ *h* أَبْرَحُ تَعْذِيب

يصبو يميل. ويروى: *أَعَشَّ إِلَى طُولِ الْحَيَاةِ وَعَيْشِها*. وقوله أَبْرَحُ تَعْذِيب اى أَشَدُّ تَعْذِيب: يقال

قد بَرَّح به اى عَذَّبَهُ: والتَّبَارِيحُ منذ *i* وهى ما بَرَّح به اى اى قد أَضَرَّهُ عليه. وقولهم: بَرَّحَتْ بِيَدَى طَلَحِ

نَقَالٌ: والنقال هاهنا الرِّقَاعُ التى على خُفِّها *k* والنقال ايضًا الخِفَاف الْخُلْقَانُ: والنقال المَخْصُوفَة واحدها

نَقْلٌ [وتَقْبِلَة وهى] *l* الرُّقْعَة وجمعها نَقَائِلُ ☆

---

a) MS كَشَفْنَها.

b) MS لَهُ انه اذا.

c) MS اسحب.

d) Cited LA I, 406[7], TA I, 272.

e) MS جُرِّدَت.

f) Khiz. لِلْحَيَاة وَطِيبِهَا.

g) MS الَّذى.

h) Khiz. بَرِّح بِتَعْذِيب.

i) وهو ما بَرَّح لَهُ اى قد ضَرَّه علمه MS; perhaps صرَّه may represent صَبَرَهُ.

j) MS وقوله برحت يدى يُقَال طَلْحٍ. The phrase means "The niqāl (rags wrapped round the pad) caused pain to the forefeet of the wearied camel".

k) MS والمِقَال ايضا لْحَاف.

l) MS والرِّتعه جمعيا نقايل.

X.

١   سَلَكْنَ غُمَيْرًا دُونَهُنَّ غُمُوضُ   تَبَصَّرْ خَلِيلِى هَلْ تَرَى مِنْ ظَعَائِنٍ

الظعائن النساء فى الهوادج. والغمير موضع. والغموض أرض مستوية مطمئنة واحدها غمض ☙

٢   مَخَامِيضُ أَبْكَارٌ أَوَانِسُ بِيضُ   وَفَوْقَ الْجِمَالِ النَّاعِجَاتِ كَوَاعِبٌ

٣   دَخَلْتُ وَفِيهِ عَانِسٌ وَمَرِيضُ   ^a وَبَيْتِ عَذَارَى يَرْتَمِينَ بِجَخْدَرِه

٤   تَدِقُّ أَيَادِى الصَّالِحِينَ قُرُوضُ   ^b فَأَقْرَضْتُهَا وُدِّى لِأَجْزَاهُ إِنَّمَا   5

٥   مَعَ الشَّوْقِ يَوْمًا بِالْحِجَازِ وَمِيضُ   ^c وَحَنَّتْ قَلُوصِى بَعْدَ وَهْنٍ ^d وَهَاجَهَا

٦   نَأَتْنِى بِهِ هِنْدٌ إِلَىَّ بَغِيضُ ^g   فَقُلْتُ لَهَا لَا ^f تَضْجَرِى إِنَّ مَنْزِلًا

٧   بِمَا قَدْ طَبَاكِ رِعْيَةٌ وَحُفُوضُ   دَنَا مِنْكِ تَجْوَابُ الْفَلَاةِ فَقَلِّصِى

تجواب الفلاة قطع الفلاة. طباك دعاك. وقوله ^h ... فى موضع رب (sic). ⁱ قلّصى شمّرى

10   والرعيّة المرعى. والخفوض الدعة والسكون ☙

٨   مَهَامِهَ رُبِيدًا بَيْنَهُنَّ عَرِيضُ   إِذَا جَاوَزَتْ مِنْهَا بِلَادًا تَنَاوَلَتْ

٩   مَعَ الْغَرْزِ أَحْنَاءٌ لَهُنَّ دُحُوضُ   وَقَدْ مَاجَتِ الْأَنْسَاعُ وَاسْتَأْخَرَتْ بِهَا

١٠   مَعَ [^kالصُّبْحِ فِى] يَوْمُ ^lالْحَرُورِ ^mرَمِيضُ   وَكُنَّ كَأَسْرَابِ الْقَطَا هَاجَ وِرْدَهَا

١١   رِدَائِى وَفِى شَمْسِ النَّهَارِ دُحُوضُ   (75a) وَفِتْيَانِ صِدْقٍ قَدْ ثَنَيْتُ عَلَيْهِمْ

١٢   قَصَائِدَ مِنْهَا آبِنٌ وَهَضِيضُ   أَلَسْتَ أَشُقُّ الْقَوْلَ يَقْذِفُ غَرْبُهُ   15

١٣   فَيَنْطِقُ بَعْدِى وَالْكَلَامُ خَفِيضُ   ⁿ أُغِضُّ إِذَا شَغُبَ الْأَلَدُّ بِرِيقِهِ

X. The only verses of this poem which have been found elsewhere are 1, 2, 5, 6 in Yāq. III, 816 (copied Naṣr. 613). For a similar rhyme see I. Q. 35. Metre *Ṭawīl*.

a) MS عَانِسٌ (sic), ترتمين, روبيت.

b) MS فاقصرتها: the correction is clearly indicated by قروض (Nöldeke).

c) MS. وخبّت ; Yāq. وجبّت.   *d)* Yāq. بعد هدّ.

e) Yāq. برق.   *f)* Yāq. تعجّلى.   *g)* MS. ثأت.

h) Unintelligible.   *i)* MS قلوصى.   *j)* MS بيد.

k) MS broken away: supplied conjecturally.

l) MS الخلود.   *m)* MS ربيض, but رميض in scholion lower down.

n) MS (sic) أُغِضُّ انّا الشعبُ الألدّ بَريقُه.

١٤ وَكَمْ مِنْ a أَخِى خَصْمٍ تَرَكْتُ وَمَا بِهِ   إِذَا قُلْتُ فِى أَىِّ الْكَلَامِ نَخُوضُ

b النَّحْسُ ضَرْبُ الرَّجُلِ لِلْحَدِيدِ . c غَرَبَهُ حَدَّهُ . آبَنَ يُقَالُ أَبَنْتُهُ فَأَنَا آبِنُهُ أَبْنًا [أَتَيْمَتْهُ وَعِبْتُهُ] . وَالرَّمِيضُ

الحَرُّ . وَالدُّحُوصُ الزَّلَقُ وَالزَّوَالُ . وَالبَضِيضُ الْمُوجِعُ . الأَلَدُّ الشَّدِيدُ الْخُصُومَةِ ☆

١٥ فَوَلَّيْتُ ذَا مَجْدٍ وَأُعْطِيتُ مِسْحَلًا   حُسَامًا بِهِ شَغْبُ الْأَلَدِّ d نَهُوضُ

١٦ قَطَعْتُ بِهِ مِنْكَ الْحَوَامِلَ فَانْبَرَتْ   فَمَا بِكَ مِنْ بَعْدِ الْهِجَاءِ d نَهُوضُ

١٧ صَقَعْتُكَ بِالْغُرِّ الْأَوَابِدِ e صَقْعَةً   خَضَعْتَ لَهَا فَالْقَلْبُ مِنْكَ جَرِيضُ

صَقَعْتُكَ رَمَيْتُكَ . وَالْغُرُّ الْقَوَافِى الْمَشْهُورَةُ . وَالأَوَابِدُ الدَّوَالِى . وَالجَرِيضُ الْمَائِتُ : يُقَالُ هُوَ يَجْرِضُ بِرِيقِهِ اذا

كَانَ [يَغَصُّ عِنْدَ مَوْتِهِ] ☆

١٨ f صَلِيتُمْ بِلَيْثٍ مَّا يُرَامُ عَرِيسُهُ   أَبِى أَشْبُلٍ بَعْدَ الْعِرَاكِ g عَضُوضُ

١٩ اذَا مَا بَدَا ظَلَّتْ لَهُ الأُسْدُ عُكَّفًا   فَهُنَّ حِذَارَ الْمَوْتِ مِنْهُ رُبُوضُ

٢٠ تَرَى بَيْنَ مَوْقُوصٍ تَغَطْمَطَ فِى الرَّدَى   h وَذِى رَغْبَةٍ يَرْجُو الْحَيَاةَ نَجِيضُ

الْمَوْقُوصُ الْمُدَقَّقُ الْعُنُقِ : وَجَاءَ بِالحَدِيثِ أَنَّ فُلَانًا وُقِصَ (مُخَفَّفًا) اى سَقَطَ فَانْدَقَّتْ عُنُقُهُ . تَغَطْمَطَ

اى غَرِقَ فِى الرَّدَى : يُقَالُ قَدْ i تَغَطْمَطَ الْمَاءُ اذا غَرِقَ فِيهِ : وَيُقَالُ بَحْرٌ غَطْمَطٌ غَطِيمٌ وَغُطَامِطٌ اى غَمْرٌ كَثِيرُ

الْمَاءِ . وَالرَّدَى الْهَلَاكُ . وَذِى رَغْبَةٍ يَقُولُ رَغِبَ فِى الحَيَاةِ فَفَرَّ بِنَفْسِهِ فَجَبُنَ عَنْ قِتَالِ هَذَا الْأَسَدِ بَعْدَ مَا

_____

a) MS اين خَصْمٍ .

b) This sense of نحس appears to be unknown to the Lexx.; perhaps it is inferred from I. Q. 35, 13: كَصَفْحِ السِّنَانِ الصُّلْبِىِّ النَّحِيضِ (LA كَحَكِّ). — The MS of the scholion reads المعس, but the spelling is clear in the verse.

c) MS الابن يقال اتيته فانا اتيمه ابنا . — MS عربه حدب : the words within brackets are supplied from LA XVI, 139¹⁷.   d) The recurrence of نَهُوضٌ as a rhyme-word in two consecutive verses is impossible, and in one of them something else must be the true reading; perhaps in v. 15 we should read رَبِيضٌ , "quiet, inactive".   e) MS صَقْقَةً .

f) MS مَلِيتُمْ ; for صَلِيتُمْ see Ḥam. 385⁷.   g) MS عَضُوضٌ .

h) MS وَذَا رَغْبَةٍ and نَحِيضٌ , which it appears impossible to justify. The scholion also (line 14) has اذا in the MS.

i) So in MS: probably we should read تَغَطْمَطَ فِى الماءِ : the senses of this verb as given in the Lexx. do not agree with the explanation in the scholion.

قد نُحِصَ مِن لَحْمِهِ: اى [قد] عَقَرَهُ [الأَسَدُ: والنَّحْضُ] قِطَعُ اللَّحمِ الذى قد قُطِّعَ: ونَحَصَ على

العظم: وقولُه حَصِّ كَسِف ... lacuna

XI.

۱ [b لَيْسَ رَسْمٌ عَلَى الدَّفِينِ بِبَالِي   فَلَوَى ذَرْوَةٍ فَجَنْبَىْ أُثَالِ

۲ c فَالْمَرُّورَاةُ فَالصَّحِيفَةُ قَفْرٌ   كُلُّ وَادٍ وَرَوْضَةٍ مِحْلَالِ

۳ d دَارُ حَيٍّ أَصَابَهُمْ سَالِفُ الدَّهْـ   ـرِ فَأَضْحَتْ دِيَارُهُمْ كَالْخِلَالِ

٥ الخِلَالُ أَجْفَانُ السُّيُوفِ واحدُها خِلّة وخِلَالٌ وللجمع خِلَل كما قال: *إِذَا السُّيُوفُ جُرِّدَتْ مِنَ الخِلَلْ*.

شَبَّه الدار بنُقُوش الخِلَلِ☞]

٤ مُقْفِرَاتٍ إِلَّا رَمَادًا e غَبِيًّا   وَبَقَايَا مِنْ دِمْنَةِ الْأَطْلَالِ

75b مُقْفِرَات دَارِسَات. والغَبِيُّ الخَفِيُّ وهو ايضا الخَامِل. والدِّمْنَة الكُنَاسَة والدِّمْنَة السِّرْقِين وهو الزِّبْل

والدِّمْنَة ايضا العَذِرَة. والاطلال ما أَشْرَفَ مِن الدِّيار: والرسوم ما بَقِيَ مِن آثَار الدار ☞

٥ وَأَوَارِيَّ قَدْ عَفَوْنَ وَنُؤْيًا   وَرُسُومًا f غُبْرِيــنَ مُذْ أَحْوَالِ   10

---

a) From here to the end of the scholion the text is very corrupt, and terminates in a *lacuna* which goes back to the MS from which our text is copied, as the latter shows no break; at least one leaf, and probably more, must have fallen out.

XI. This poem is contained in Mr. Krenkow's MS of Selections from the *Mufaḍḍalīyāt* and *Asmaʿīyāt*, fol. 131a to 132b (cited as Kk.); it is in the Mukhtārāt, pp. 102—4; ʿAinī IV, 461—2, has 1—5, 8, 12, 9—11, 22, 23, 13; Sh. Sh. Mughnī 317 has vv. 8—16 and 29—30, and so Jāḥiḍh, *Bayān*, I, 95—6; Agh. XIX, 90, has vv. 24, 25, 1, 8; Naṣr. 605 has vv. 1—2, then three verses not in our text (see Supplement, No. 15), then v. 3. Other verses occur in Yāq., LA, etc., as noted in their places. In consequence of the *lacuna* noticed above the first three verses are wanting in the MS, and have been supplied from other texts. Metre *Khafīf*.   *b)* Kk. and ʿAinī الدِّمَيْنِ, otherwise as text: Agh. as text; Yāq. II, 579 and III, 402 ذَيَالٍ فَجَنْبَىْ, and so Mukht.

c) So text of Kk. Yāq. III, 402¹⁸ has فالْمَرُّوْراتُ فالصَّفِيحَـةُ and كُلِّ قَفْرٍ (and so Naṣr.); ʿAinī فالمروراتُ فالصفيحة; Mukht. كَالصَّحِيفَةِ.

d) This v. is wanting in Mukht. It is given after Kk., with the scholion. LA XIII, 233²³ has it, with بِهِمْ مَضَى for أَصَابَهُمْ, and so Naṣr.   *e)* ʿAinī عفيّا (misprint).

f) This is Mukht.'s reading: Kk. and ʿAinī have غُبَّرٍ: MS عَفِينَ, which is impossible with عَفَوْنَ in the same verse. Kk. ʿAinī and Mukht. عَنْ أَحْوَالٍ.

٩   a) بُدِّلَتْ مِنْهُم الدِّيَارُ نَعَامًا   خَاضِبَاتٍ يُزْجِينَ خَيْطَ الرِّئَالِ

الخاضب من النعام الذى قد أكل الربيع فاحمرّت سوقُه. والخيط للجماعة من النعام. وحُكى عن ابى

الحَسَن الأثرَم أنّه حَكَى خِيطٌ من وَخِيطٍ ووَخْطٌ ☙

٧   b) وظِبَاءَ كَأَنَّهُنَّ أَبَارِيقٌ لُجَينٍ تَحْنُو عَلَى الأَطْفَالِ

٨   c) تِلْكَ عِرْسِى تَرُومُ قِدْمًا زِيَالِى   أَلبَيْنِ تُريدُ أَمْ لِدَلَالِ

٩   d) إِنْ يَكُنْ طِبُّكِ الدَّلَالَ فَلَوْ فِى   سَالِفِ الدَّهْرِ e) واللَّيَالِى الخَوَالِى

١٠   f) أَنْتِ بَيْضَاءُ كَالْمَهَاةِ وَإِنْ آ   تِيكِ نَشْوَانَ مُرْخِيًا أَذْيَالِى

شبّة الظبآء بأباريق الفِضّة لطول أعْناقِها وحُسنِها وبَياضِها. واللُجَين الفِضّة. عِرْسى امرأتى. والغَيْرَى الغَيُور.

g) وشبابك يقول: لَوْ كانَ هذا فى شبابى وشبابك ☙

١١   h) فَاتْرُكِى مَطَّ حَاجِبَيْكِ وَعِيشِى   مَعَنَا بِالرَّجَاءِ وَالتَّأَمَّالِ

١٢   i) أَوْ يَكُنْ طِبُّكِ الزِّيَالَ فَإِنَّ الْبَيْنَ أَنْ تَعْطِفِى صُدُورَا الْجِمَالِ

---

a) v. 6 is wanting in Kk.

b) v. 7 wanting in Kk.

c) In Kk. this verse runs: تِلْكَ عِرْسِى غَيْرَى تُرِيدُ زِيَالِى   أَلبَيْنِ تَقُولُهُ أَمْ دَلَالِ ; ᶜAinī (misprinted) has the same reading; and the scholion to v. 10 shows that this was probably the original text of our MS; قِدْمًا does not suit v. 9, where he asks why she did not act thus long ago. Mukht. reads الحَلَال الفِراش اعْتَنزَلْتُه فى المَضْجَع : وقيل للحَلال ، أَمْسَتْ تَمِيزُ حِلَالِى with note: — Jāḥ. and SSM have غَضْبَى تُرِيدُ زِيَالِى; Agh. قَدْ عَيَّرَتْنِى خَلَالِى. — After this v. Kk., هنا المناع, ᶜAinī, SSM and Jāḥ. have v. 12 in a different form (see further on).

d) Kk., ᶜAinī, أَوْ يَكُنْ (following on v. 12 inserted).

e) Kk., ᶜAinī, SSM, Jāḥ. والسِّنِينَ الخَوَالِى.

f) Kk. and ᶜAinī have this v. thus: إِنْ أَرَاهَا مِثْلَ الْمَهَاةِ وَإِنْ أَغْدُو كَجَذْلَانَ مُرْخِيًا أَذْيَالِى. SSM and Jāḥ. كَالمَهاة; ذاك إِنْ أَنْتِ كَالْمَهاة Mukht.: كُنْتِ بَيْضَاءَ.

g) This scholion indicates some reading of v. 10 not in our text or in the parallel versions.

h) Kk., ᶜAinī, فَدَعِى, Mukht. (which puts the v. lower down) وَدَعِى. MS والآمَال, all others as text.

i) Kk., ᶜAinī, SSM and Jāḥ. read إِنْ يَكُنْ طِبُّكِ الْفِرَاقَ فَلَا أَحْفِلُ أَنْ تَعْطِفِى صُدُورَ الْجِمَالِ; Mukht. as text.

١٣ ‏ ^a زَعَمْتُ أَنَّنِى كَبِرْتُ وَأَنَّى   قَلَّ مَالِى وَضَنَّ عَنِّى الْمَوَالِى

١٤ وَصَحَا بَاطِلِى وَأَصْبَحْتُ ^b كَهْلًا   لَا يُوَاتِى أَمْثَالَهَا أَمْثَالِى

١٥ ^c إِنْ رَأَتْنِى تَغَيَّرَ اللَّوْنُ مِنِّى   وَعَلَا الشَّيْبُ مَفْرِقِى وَقَذَالِى

١٦ ^d فِيمَا أَدْخُلُ الْخِبَاءَ عَلَى مَهْضُومَةِ الْكَشْحِ طَفْلَةٍ كَالْغَزَالِ

١٧ فَتَعَاطَيْتُ جِيدَهَا ثُمَّ مَالَتْ   مَيَلَانَ الْكَثِيبِ بَيْنَ الرِّمَالِ   5

١٨ ثُمَّ قَالَتْ فِدًى لِنَفْسِكَ نَفْسِى   وَفِدَاءٌ ^e لِّمَالِ أَهْلِكَ مَالِى

١٩ ^f فَأَرْفُضِى الْعَاذِلِينَ وَأَقْنِى حَيَاءً   لَا يَكُونُوا عَلَيْكِ حَظَّ مِثَالِى

٢٠ ^g (76a) وَبِحَظٍّ مِّمَّا نَعِيشُ فَلَا تَذْ   هَبْ بِكِ التُّرَّهَاتُ فِى الْأَهْوَالِ

٢١ ^h مِنْهُمْ مُمْسِكٌ وَمِنْهُمْ عَدِيمٌ   وَبَخِيلٌ عَلَيْكِ فِى بُخَّالِ

٢٢ ⁱ وَأَتْرُكِى صِرْمَةً عَلَى آلِ زَيْدٍ   بِالْقُطَيْبَاتِ كُنَّ أَوْ أَوْزَالِ   10

٢٣ لَمْ تَكُنْ غَزْوَةَ الْجِيَادِ وَلَمْ يُنْقَبْ بِآثَارِهَا صُدُورُ النِّعَالِ

^j لم تكن غزوة الجياد: يقول لم يقاتل عليها أحدٌ بغير قتال. ولم ينقب بآثارها: يقول لم يسافر ^r عليها ☙

٢٤ ^k دَرَّ دَرُّ الشَّبَابِ وَالشَّعَرِ الْأَسْوَدِ وَالرَّانِكَاتِ تَحْتَ الرِّحَالِ

---

^a) Kk. runs together the صدر of v. 13 and the عجز of v. 14, omitting the rest. ʿAinī زعمت أنّى، زَعَمْتِ أَنَّنِى our MS has رَأَيْتِنِى قَدْ كَبِرْت ,Mukht. After v. 14 the order of Kk. differs considerably from that of our text.   ^b) Jāḥ., SSM, شَبِيبًا.

^c) Wanting in Kk.; in Mukht. as text. Jāḥ. and SSM إِنْ تَرَيْنِى.

^d) In our MS vv. 16 and 17—18 are separated by 12 verses: In Kk. and Mukht. they are put together, as they clearly should be, the former placing the three early in the poem, as here, the latter later, in the place which vv. 17—18 occupy in our MS. I have preferred the former. Kk. and Mukht. in place of فِيمَا, read وَلَقَدْ.   ^e) MS لِأَهْلِ مَالَكَ مَالِى (sic).

^f) Not in Kk.; Mukht. as our text: MS الْعَاذِلَات. Scholion of Mukht: الَّذِى لَا تَأْخُذِى بِمِثَالِهِمْ.   ^g) Kk. فَبِحَظٍّ. يَمْثُلُونَ لَكَ مِنَ الْقَطِيعَةِ وَلَا تَقْبَلِى أَقَاوِيلَهُمْ.

^h) Wanting in Kk.; Mukht. as text.

ⁱ) Mukht. omits vv. 22 and 23: Kk. and ʿAinī as text. — MS أَوْزَالٍ, a name not mentioned in the dictionaries; I have substituted أَوْزَالٍ in view of No. XIX, 9. ʿAinī misprints مِنْ أَدْوَالٍ.

^j) Kk.'s scholion: — أى لم تكن هذه الصرمة عن غزوة الجياد ولكنّها تركت رجال أَوْزَالٍ (read أَوْزَالٍ).

^k) Kk. دَرْ لاه دَرْ. Agh. XIX, 90¹¹, with وَالصَّامِرَاتِ تَحْتَ الرِّجَالِ: we should probably read وَالصَّامِزَاتِ (see al-Aʿshà, Ma bukāʾu, v. 49).

الراتكات يريد الابل فى سيرها: وهو ضرب من السير شبيهٌ بالخبب ☸

٢٥   a وَالْعَنَاجِيجِ كَالْقِدَاحِ مِنَ الشَّوْ   حَطِ b يَحْمِلْنَ شِكَّةَ الْأَبْطَالِ

واحد العناجيج عُنْجُوجٌ وهى الطِوَال الاعناق من الخيل. والقِداح السِهام. والشَوْحَط شَجَرٌ تتخَذ
منه القِسِىُّ والسِهام. والشِكّة السلاحِ ☸

٥   ٢٦ وَلَقَدْ أَذْعَرُ c الـسَّـرُوبَ بِـطِـرْفٍ   d مِثْلِ شَاةِ الْإِرَانِ غَيْرِ مُذَالِ

الشاة التَيْس. والإران عاصَنا النَشاط. ويقال ايضا الإران لِتَابوت الموتَى. والمُذال الذَليل المُهان ☸

٢٧   غَيْـرِ أَقْـنَـى e وَلَا أَصَكَّ وَلٰكِنْ   مِّـرْجَـمٌ ذُو كَرِيـهَـةٍ وَّنِـقَـالِ

الأصَكّ الذى يَصِطَكُّ عُرْقُوباه. والمِرْجَم السريع. النِقال المُناقَلَة. f والاَقْنَى الطَويل الاَنَف: ولِلخيل توصَف
g بالقَطوسة وسعَةِ المَنْخَرين. والكريهة شِدّة نَفَس الفرس ☸

١٠   ٢٨ h يَسْبِقُ الْأَلْفَ بِالْمُدَجَّجِ ذِى الْقَوْ   نَـسِ حَتَّـى يَـؤُوبَ كَالتِّمْثَالِ

٢٩   فَهْوَ i كَالْمِنْزَعِ الْمَرِيشِ مِنَ الشَّوْ   حَطِ مَالَتْ بِـهِ رِشمَالُ الْمُغَالِى

المِنْزَع المَرِيش سَهمٌ خَفِيف فيه رِيشٌ. والمُغالى الذى يباعِد فى رَمْيِه اذا رمَى ☸

٣٠   يَعْقِرُ الظَّبْيَ وَالظَّلِيمَ k وَيَـلْـوِى   بِلَبُونِ l الْمِعْزَابَةِ الْمِـعْـزَالِ

m المِعزال الرجل [الذى] يبِيت عن أهلِه ☸ (76b)

١٥   a) Agh. (l.c.) فَالْخَمَاذِيذ.
    b) Mukht. schol. mentions v.l. بِشِكّة الأبطال تَرْدى.

c) Kk. الْوُحُوش, Mukht. السَّراب (sic).

d) Kk. الإران or الاَان must be the name of a place, and the scholion
is incorrect. مِثْلِ تَيْسِ الاَان ;   e) Kk. ولا أَقَبّ.

f) Our gloss agrees with LA s.v. قنا; but Kk. glosses as follows:

يقال فرَسٌ أقْنَى يَبِين القَنَا اذا كان فى عِظامِه انْحِناء وفى أَضْلاعه. والاَقَبّ اللاحِق البَطْنُ بالظهر: واذا
كان ذلك مِن ضَرٍّ فهو عيب ☸

g) This form is not found in the Lexx., which give قَطِسَ instead (LA VIII, 45.)

h) LA XI, 22¹⁵, with يَرْعِف for يَسْبِق and يَعُود for يَؤوب; Kk. and Mukht. as text.

i) MS كالمُربع.   j) Kk. يُبِين الْمُغَالِى.   k) Kk. وَيُودِى بِحَلُوب.

l) So Mukht. and Kk.: MS الْمِعْزى, in which another reading may possibly be concealed.

m) Gloss of Mukht.: يَلْوى يَذْهَب بها. والمِعزابة والمِعزال واحد وهو الذى قد عَزَب بإِبِلِه خَوْف
الغارة: وقِيل المِعزال الذى لا يَحمِل السلاح: وقِيل الذى لا يُحْسِن رُكوب الخيل ☸

٣١   وَلَقَدْ أَقْدُمُ الْخَمِيسَ عَلَى الْجَرْ   دَاءَ ذَاتِ الْجِرَاءِ a وَالتَّنْقَالِ b

٣٢   فَتَقِينِى بِنَحْرِهَا وَأَقِيهَا   بِقَضِيبٍ c مِّنَ الْقَنَا غَيْرِ بَالِى

٣٣   وَلَقَدْ أَقْطَعُ السَّبَاسِبَ d وَالشُّهْبَ عَلَى e الصَّيْعَرِيَّةِ الشَّمْلَالِ

التَّنْقَالِ الْمُنَاقَلة. ويروى ذات الْجَرَاءِ وَالنَّبْغَالِ: والنَّبْغَال ضَرْبٌ من الجَرْى. الْخَمِيس الجَيْش. والجِرَاء

الجَرْى. غير بالٍ غير صُلْب. السباسب أَرَضُون مُسْتَوِيَةٌ لا شىءَ فيها واحدها سَبْسَبٌ f [والصَّيْعَرِيّة ضَرْبٌ من

الابل النجائب لها سِمَةٌ] فى أعناقها. والشَّمْلَال لِلخَفِيفة. والشُّهْب g الفَلَوات ☼

٣٤ h   ثُمَّ أُبْرِى نِحَاضَهَا فَتَرَاهَا   ضَامِرًا بَعْدَ بُدْنِهَا كَالْهِلَالِ

٣٥ i   عَنْتَرِيسٍ كَأَنَّهَا ذُو وُشُومٍ   أَخْرَجَتْهُ j بِالْجَوِّ إِحْدَى اللَّيَالِى

نِحَاضَها لَحْمُها. وذو وُشُومٍ يريد الثور وفيه تَوْلِيع سَوادٍ وبياضٍ. أَخْرَجَتْهُ k اى حبسَتْهُ ☼

---

a) MS الجَرَّد.

b) Kk. النَّبْغَال, with التَّنْقَال as *v.l.* in scholion.

c) MS بنصيب,

d) Kk. and Mukht. بالرَّكِب.

e) MS الصَّغِيرَة.

f) A lacuna here (not indicated in MS): the words in brackets added from LA VI, 127[5ff]; the word صَيْعَرِيّة is the subject of a celebrated anecdote relating to Ṭarafah when a young boy: see Agh. XXI, 203.

g) MS الفلاه.

h) Cited LA IX, 103[17]. Mukht. transposes vv. 34 and 35, which seems evidently to be the right order; Kk. however has the same order as our text.

i) MS عندليس.

j) Kk. أَخْدَرَتْهُ.

k) Gloss of Mukht.: أَخْرَجَتْهُ أَلْجَأَتْهُ الى شَجَرَة. والجَوُّ ما اتَّسَع من الأرض. أراد احدى اللَّيَالِى الموصوفات بالبَرْد: وإنما يقال احدى اللَّيَالِى لَلَّيْلَةَ الَّتِى يُنْعَمُ فيها أو الشديدة. Mukht. has an additional verse:

ذَاكَ عَيْشٌ رَضِيتُهُ وَتَوَلَّى   كُلُّ عَيْشٍ مَصِيرُهُ لِهَبَالِى

For the last word are should no doubt read لِهَبَالِ, from هَبَلَ in the sense of vanishing, passing away (Heb. הֶבֶל).

The order of the verses of this poem in Kk. is as follows: 1—5, 8, 12, 9—11, 22, 23, 13a+14b, 20, 24—30, 16—18, 31—35.

In Mukht. the order is: 1, 2, 4—10, 12—15, 19, 11, 20, 21, 24—30, 16—18, 31—33, 35, 34, addl. v.

XII.

١ a وَلِمَنِ الدِّيَارُ بِصَاحَةٍ فَحَرُوسِ ‌ ‌ دَرَسَتْ مِنَ الْإِقْفَارِ أَىَّ دُرُوسِ

٢ b إِلَّا أَوَارِيًّا كَأَنَّ رُسُومَهَا ‌ ‌ فِى مُهْرَقٍ خَلَقٍ c الدَّوَاةِ لَبِيسِ

٣ دَارٌ لِفَاطِمَةَ الرَّبِيعَ بِغَمْرَةٍ ‌ ‌ فَقَفَا d شَرَافِ فَهَضْبِ ذَاتِ رُوُوسِ

نصب الربيع على الظرف على معنى فى الربيع. [وغَمْرَة] وقفا شَراف وهَضْب ذات رؤوس كلّها مواضع ☙

٤ أَزْمَانَ e غَفْلَتِهَا وَإِنْ لَّمْ تَجْدِهَا ‌ ‌ نَكْسًا وَّشَرُّ السَّدَاءِ دَاءٌ نُكُوسِ

٥ وَسَبَتْكَ نَاعِمَةٌ صَفِىٌّ نَوَاعِمٌ ‌ ‌ بِيضٌ غَرَائِرُ كَالظِّبَاءِ الْعِيسِ

٦ خَوْدٌ مُبَتَّلَةُ الْعِظَامِ g كَأَنَّهَا ‌ ‌ h بُرْدِيَّةٌ نَبَتَتْ خِلَالَ غُرُوسِ

صفىّ نَوَاعِم صَفْو نَوَاعِم i مُتَخَفِّرات خَرِيدات. الخَوْد الشابّة. (77a) والمُبَتَّلة الحَسَنَة الخَلْق التى تراها وكلّ شىءٍ منها على حِدَته: وحِدَتُه ناحِيتُه ☙

٧ أَفَلَا تُنَاسِى حُبَّهَا بِبِجْلَاَةٍ ‌ ‌ وَجْنَاءَ كَالْأُجْمِ الْمَطِينِ وَلُوسِ

الجِلالة الناقة الضَّخْمَة. وقال ابو عمرو الوَجْناء الكثيرة لَحْم j الوَجَنات: وقال الاصمعى انّما أُخِذَ من وَجِين الارض وهى الناقة الصُّلْبَة: والوَجِين من الارض ما غَلُظَ منها وصَعُبَ: وهو قول ابى عُبَيْدَة ايضًا: قال خالد بن كُلْثوم الوَجْناء الضَّخْمَة. والأُجْم البُيوت المرتفعة. والمَطِين قد طِين. [وَلُوس اى] فى سَيْرِها وَلَسَتْ تَلِس ولَقَنْت تَلَقُ ووَخَدَتْ تَخِدُ: وهو ضَرْبٌ من السَّيْر ☙

٨ رَفَعَ k الْمَرَادُ مِنَ الرَّبِيعِ سَنَامَهَا ‌ ‌ فَنَمَتْ وَأَرْدَفَ نَابَهَا لِسَدِيسِ

XII. Of this poem only vv. 1, 15, and 19, with an additional verse belonging to it, have been found cited elsewhere. — Metre *Kāmil*.

a) Yaq. II, 247⁴, as text; Bakrī 597¹⁶, with بِصَاحَةٍ. MS مِنَ الْأَقْوَاءِ كُلَّ دُرُوسِ.

b) MS الاوارىا. ‌ ‌ *c*) MS الدَّوَا ملبيس.

d) MS شُراب (but شَراف correctly in commy.)

e) MS عفلها. ‌ ‌ *f*) MS حده.

g) The MS carelessly repeats نواعم from the verse above. ‌ ‌ *h*) Cf. I.Q. Muʿall. 36.

i) MS محمرات. ‌ ‌ *j*) MS الوجين. ‌ ‌ *k*) MS المراز.

٩ فَكَأَنَّمَا a تَحْمُو إِذَا مَا أُرْسِلَتْ   عُودَ الْعُضَاهِ وَدِقَّةُ بِـفُـؤُوس

١٠ أَفْنَيْتُ بَهْجَتَهَا وَنَىَّ سَنَامِهَا   بِالرَّحْلِ بَعْدَ مَخِيلَةٍ وَشَرِيس

مَخِيلَةٌ مِن الْخُيَلَاءِ. وَالشَّرِيسُ النَّشَاطُ وَالصُّعُوبَةُ وَشِدَّةُ نَفْسٍ وَسُوءُ خَلْقٍ ۞

١١ وَأَمِيرِ b خَيْلٍ قَدْ عَصَيْتُ بِمَهْدَةٍ   جَرْدَاءَ خَاظِيَةِ السَّرَاةِ جَلُـوس

النهده الضاخمة. وَالْجُرْدَاءُ الْقَصِيرَةُ الشَّعِرِ. وَالْخَاظِيَةُ الشَّدِيدَةُ. c وَجَلُوس هُوَ مَا ارْتَفَعَ مِن الارض يَصِفُهَا

بِالْعِظَمِ ۞

١٢ خُلِقَتْ عَلَى عُسُبٍ وَتَمَّ ذَكَاؤُهَا   d وَاحْتَالَ فِيهَا الصَّنْعُ غَيْرَ نَكِيس

الْعُسْبُ الْقَوَائِمُ وَاحِدُهَا عَسِيبٌ أُخِذَ مِن عَسِيبِ النَّخْلِ: يَصِفُهَا بِطُولِ الْقَوَائِمِ: وَالْعَسِيبُ اذا لم يكن

عَلَيْهِ خُوصٌ: وَاذَا كَانَ عَلَيْهِ خُوصٌ فَهُو e الْجَرِيدُ. وَتَمَّ ذَكَاؤُهَا اى تَمَّ f سِنُّهَا. وَاحْتَالَ فِيهَا الصَّنْعُ يَقُولُ

حَالَ عَلَيْهَا الْحَوْلُ وَفِى تَصْنَعُ. g وَالنَّكِيسُ الْغَرِيزَةُ ۞ (77b)

١٣ وَإِذَا جُهِدْنَ وَقَلَّ مَصُّ نِطَافِهَا   وَصَلَقْنَ فِى دَيْمُومَةٍ إِمْلِـيـس

النطاف بقايا الماءِ واحدها نُطْفَة. وجمع دَيْمُومَة دَيَامِيم. ويروى وشَرِسْنَ. وَالصَّلْقُ الْجَرْى ۞

١٤ تَنْفِي الأَوَائِمَ عَنْ سَوَاءِ سَبِيلِهَا   شَرَكَ الأَجِرَّةِ وَهْىَ غَيْـرُ شَمُوس

الأَوَائِمُ الابِلُ الْمُبْطِّئَاتُ فِى السير. h وَالشَّرَكُ الطَّرِيقُ. وَالأَجِرَّةُ وَاحِدُهَا جَرِيرٌ وَهُو مَا خَشُنَ مِن الأَرْضِ

وَصَلُبَ ۞

١٥ i أَمَّا إِذَا اسْتَقْبَلْتَهَا فَكَأَنَّـهَا   ذَبُلَتْ مِن الْهِنْدِىِّ غَيْرُ يَبُوس

---

a) MS حموا without points.   b) MS خَيْلِى.

c) This sense is attributed in the Lexx. to جَلَسَ (LA VII, 341[1]).

d) MS in the v. has وَاحَالَ, in the scholion وَاحْتَالَ: both are possible, but the commentary is generally more correct than the text.

e) This is incorrect: جَرِيدٌ (as the word implies) is a palm-branch stripped of its leaves; with the leaves on it is called سَعَفَة.   f) MS نسبها.

g) This also is an error; غَرِيزَة ("nature, natural disposition") is a synonym of نِحَاسٌ, not of نَكِيس, which means „unlucky, unprosperous".

h) شَرَك is plural of شَرَكَة: see LA XII 336[10ff].

i) Cited (with ʿAbīd's name) LA VIII 148[17], with explanation: اراد عَصًا ذَبُلَتْ أَوْ قَنَاةً ذَبُلَتْ فَحُذِف الموصوف.

١٩ أَمَّـا إِذَا اسْتَدْبَرْتَهَا فَكَأَنَّهَا   قَارُورَةٌ صَفْـرَاءُ ذَاتُ a كَبِيسِ

شبَّهها بالقارورة فى استدارة أوراكها. والكَبِيس ما كُبِس فيها من الطيب من المَلاب: والملاب ضَرْبٌ من الطيب من الزَّعْفَران وغيره ۞

١٧ b وَإِذَا اقْتَنَصْنَا لَا يَجِفُّ خِضَابُهَا   وَكَأَنَّ بِرْكَتَهَا مَـدَاكُ عَـرُوسِ

لِخضاب الدَّم. والبِرْكة الصدر. والمَدَاك الصَّلاية النى يُسْحَقُ فيها الطيب ۞

١٨ وَإِذَا دَفَعْنَـا لِلْـحِـرَاجِ فَنَهْبُهَا   أَدْنَى سَوَامِ الْجَامِلِ الْمَحْلُوسِ

الحِرَاج جماعة الشجر واحدها حَرَجَة: ويقال الحِرَاج جماعة النَّعَم ۞

١٩ c هَاتِيكَ تَحْمِلُنِى وَأَبْيَضَ صَارِمًا   وَمُحَـرَّبًـا فِى مَـارِنٍ مَخْمُوسِ

المُحرَّب السنان. والمارِن القناة اللَّينة. المَخْمُوس رُمْحٌ طوله خَمْس [أَذْرُع] d ۞

٢٠ e فِى أُسْرَةٍ يَـوْمَ الْحِفَاظِ مَصَالِتٍ   كَالْأُسْدِ لَا يُنْمَى لَـهَا بِفَرِيسِ

الأُسْرة الجماعة. والحِفاظ المحافظة على القتال [و]الى الحَمِيّة: والأُسْرة ايضًا العشيرة: والحِفاظ ايضًا الغَضَب. مَصَالِتٌ اى أَصْلَتوا سيوفهم وشَهَروها وأخْرَجوها من أغْمادها. والفَرِيس ما افتَرَسْتَه: وهو دَقُّ العُنُق ۞ (78a)

٢١ وَبَنُو خُزَيْمَةَ يَعْـلَـمُـونَ بِأَنَّـنَا   f مِـنْ خَيْرِهِمْ فِى غِبْطَةٍ وَتَمِيسِ

٢٢ نُبْكِى عَدُوَّهُمْ وَيَنْطَحُ g كَبْشَنَا   لَهُمْ وَلَيْسَ النَّطْحُ بِالْمَوْمُوسِ

---

a) MS كنبيس, and so in scholion.   b) *Cf.* I. Q. Muʿall. 62.

c) MS صانمك. This verse is in LA VII, 371¹⁵ and XVII 290²⁵, where wrongly stated to refer to a camel; in both places مُذَرَّبًا for our مُحَرَّبًا. It is also found, without the name of the poet, in Jāḥiḍh, *Bayān*, II, 55⁹, where the reading is مُحَرِّبًا.

d) An additional verse, LA VIII, 106⁵, would fit in between vv. 19 and 20;

صَدْقٍ مِنَ الْهِنْدِى أَلْيَسَ جُبَّةً   لَحِقَتْ بِكَعْبٍ كَاسْتِـوَاءِ مَلِيسِ

(LA misprints جَنَّة for جُبَّة).

e) MS فى أسر سوم.   f) MS من غيرِمْ فى عطبه ونبيس.

g) MS حبينا. This word may possibly be حِيَنَا, but probably the old form of ك, without a *markaz*, has been mistaken for ح; one certain case of this will be found in the scholion to v. 9 of No. XXI below. كَبْش is indicated by the verb ينطح.

XIII.

۱ a تَغَيَّرَتِ الدِّيَارُ بِذِى الدَّفِينِ   فَأَوْدِيَةِ اللِّوَى فَرِمَالِ لِينِ

۲ b فَحَرْجَى ذَرْوَةٍ فَقَفَا ذَيَالٍ   يُعَقِّى آيَهُ سَلَفُ السِّنِينِ

يُعَقِّى يَدْرِس. آيَهُ عَلَامَتُهُ واحِدُها آيَةٌ. والسَّلَف ما تَقَادَم. ويروى آيَهُ c مَرُّ السِّنِينِ ☙

۳ d تَبَصَّرُ صَاحِبِى أَتَرَى حُمُولًا   e تُسَاقُ كَأَنَّها عَوْمُ السَّفِينِ

۴ جَعَلْنَ f الْفَجَّ مِنْ رَكَكِ شِمَالًا   g وَنَكَّبْنَ الطَّوَى عَنِ الْيَمِينِ   5

۵ أَلَا h عَتَبْتَ عَلَى الْيَوْمَ عِرْسِى   i وَقَدْ هَمَّتْ بِلَيْلٍ تَشْتَكِينِى

۶ فَقَالَتْ j زِلَى كَبِرْتَ فَقُلْتُ حَقًّا   لَقَدْ أَخْلَفْتُ حِينًا بَعْدَ حِينِ

أَخْلَفْتُ كما يقال للجمل أَخْلَف عامًا: اى مَضَتْ له سُنُون. ويروى لَقَدْ خَلَفْتُ حِينًا: اى مَضَتْ له سَنُون بَعْدَ سِنِينِ ☙

۷ تُرِينِى آيَةَ الْإِعْرَاضِ مِنْهَا   k وَفَظَّتْ فِى الْمَقَالَةِ بَعْدَ لِينِ

۸ وَمَطَّتْ حَاجِبَيْها أَنْ رَأَتْنِى   كَبِرْتُ وَأَنْ قَدِ l ابْيَضَّتْ قُرُونِى   10

آيَةُ الْإِعْرَاضِ علامة الاعْتِراض. m وَفَظَّتْ عَتَبَتْ. وَمَطَّتْ حَاجِبَيْها اى تَنَتَّهُ. قُرُونُهُ ذَوَائِبُهُ ☙

۹ فَقُلْتُ لَهَا رُوَيْدَكِ n بَعْضَ عَتْبِى   فَإِنِّى لَا أَرَى أَنْ o تَرْدَهِينِى

XIII. Mukht. pp. 92—94. Vv. 1—4, 11, 13 are in Naṣr. 612; other verses are cited as mentioned in the notes. Metre *Wāfir*.

a) Yāq. II, 726¹² and 810⁹, as text.

b) Omitted in Yāq. II, 810, but given in II, 726; wanting in Mukht. Yāq. فَلِوَى ذَيَالٍ.

c) MS مِنَ السِّنِينِ; Naṣr. reads مَرُّ السِّنِينِ.

d) Mukht., Yāqūt II, 810, Naṣr., تَبَيَّنْ.

e) Mukht. يُشَبَّهُ سَيْرُها عَوْمُ; Yāq. *id.* with تَشَبَّهَ; Naṣr. *id.* with يشبه; see *ante*, No. VIII, 5.

f) MS الفَجَّ مِن رَكَب; Mukht. as text. Yāq. (II, 810) and Naṣr. الفَلْجَ.

g) MS ونكسا.   h) MS عتب علب.   i) MS حب بليل تسكين.

j) MS فِى كَثرت.   k) Mukht. incorrectly وقَظَّتْ.

l) MS انتصب.   m) MS وقطعت عسن.   n) So Mukht. MS بعد.

o) So MS; Mukht. تَرْهَدِينِى in text, but تَردهينِى in scholion.

١٠   [وَعِيشِى بِالَّذِى يُغْنِيكِ حَتَّى]   إِذَا مَا شِئْتِ أَنْ تَنْأَى فَبِينِى

١١   فَإِنْ يَكُ فَاتَنِى أَسَفًا شَبَابِى   وَأَضْحَى الرَّأْسُ مِنِّى كَاللَّجِينِ b

١٢   وَكَانَ اللَّهْوُ حَالَفَنِى زَمَانًا   فَأَضْحَى الْيَوْمَ مُنْقَطِعَ الْقَرِينِ

١٣   فَقَدْ أَلِجُ الْخِبَاءَ c عَلَى الْعَذَارَى   كَأَنَّ عُيُونَهُنَّ عُيُونُ عِينِ

١٤   يَمِلْنَ عَلَىَّ بِالْأَقْرَابِ طَوْرًا   وَبِالْأَجْيَادِ كَالرَّيْطِ الْمَصُونِ

١٥   وَأَسْمَرَ قَدْ نَصَبْتُ لِذِى سَنَاءٍ   يَرَى مِنِّى مُحَافَظَةَ الْيَقِينِ

١٩   (78) يُحَاوِلُ أَنْ يَقُومَ وَقَدْ مَضَتْهُ   مُغَابِنَةً بِذِى خُرْصٍ قَتِينِ

قال ابو عمرو: القتين الزهيد الذى لا يُحَاوِلُ بِأَكْلٍ ولا يشرَب: d والقتين عهنا السِّنان. يُحَاوِل [أَنْ] يَقُومُ

اى يقوم الرَّجُل [من] e طَعْنَةٍ أَمَاتَتْهُ. وقد مَضَتْهُ اى f تَنَفَّذَتْ مِنْهُ الطَّعْنَةُ. والمُغَابِنَةُ التى

تَغْبِنُ g من لَحْمِهِ ويَغْبِنُ الثَّوْبُ [اى h يُثْنَى   ۞

١٧   إِذَا مَا i عَادَهُ مِنْهَا نِسَاءٌ   صَفَحْنَ الدَّمْعَ [مِنْ] بَعْدِ الرَّنِينِ

١٨   وَحَرْفٍ قَدْ ذَعَرْتُ الْجُونَ فِيهِ   عَلَى أَدْمَاءَ كَالْعَيْرِ الشَّنُونِ

الشنون الذى ليس بالسَّمِين [ولا] الْمَهْزُول بَيْنَ ذَلِكَ. j والجُون البَقَر والظباء: وإنما اراد بَيَاضَها ۞

---

a) Added from Mukht.; cf. ante, No. XI, 11, 12.

b) Scholion of Mukht.: اى فَاتَنِى وأنا أَسَفٌ عليه. واللَّجِينُ الْخَبَطُ وهو وَرَقُ الطَّلْحِ يُدَقُّ

ويُرَشُّ بالماء ويُطْعَم للابل: وقال ابو الوليد اللجين ورق يُخْلَط إمَّا بِدَقِيق وإمَّا بِنَوًى: وقال الاصمعى

اللجين الزَّبَد على الشىء اذا جَفَّ شبه لُغَام الابل مثل بياض شَعَره: واللجين ورق الشجر يُخْبَط

فهو لَوْنَانِ رَطْبٌ ويَابِسٌ فشبَّه الشَّيْبَ بالبابس والسواد بالرطب. ويروى كَاللَّجِينِيْن (so Naṣr. reads)

يريد الفِضَّة: فذلك عَيْبٌ من عُيوب القافية يُسَمَّى السناد   See LA XVII, 262 ۞

c) Naṣr. reads: على مُلُوكٍ *كَأَنَّ دِيَارَهُمْ أَمَلُ الْحَزِينِ; it is not stated where this version is found.

d) MS والقبس.   العدارى كهن MS

e) MS اماده طعن.   f) MS بعدت.   g) MS دعمر (twice).

h) سبا. Mukht.'s scholion: — اى طَعْنَتْهُ مُغَابِنَةً تَغْبِنُ من لَحْمِهِ اى تَثْنِيه: ويروى مُعَابِنَةً اى وهو

يرى ذاك ويُعَايِنُه. ويروى مُعَانَدَةً. والخُرْص السنان وقتِين مُحَدَّدُ الرَّأْس: والقتين ايضا

القليل الطُّعْم الَّخِ.   V. 16 is cited LA XVII, 208[12] as in text; see discussion there. ۞

i) MS عادته contra metrum.

j) Mukht.: — والجُون الظِّلْمَان وتَكُون البَقَر ايضًا والظباء لِبَيَاضِهِنَّ.

XIV.

١ *a* دَعَا مَعَاشِرَ فَاسْتَكَّتْ مَسَامِعُهُمْ   يَا لَهْفَ [نَفْسِيَ] لَوْ تَدْعُو بَنِى أَسَدِ

اسْتَكَّتْ اى انْسَدَّتْ: يقال انْسَدَّتْ واسْتَدَّتْ بمعنًى واحدٍ ۞

٢ تَدْعُو إِذَا حَامَى الْكُمَاةُ لَا *b* [كَسِلًا]   إِذَا السُّيُوفُ بِأَيْدِى الْقَوْمِ كَالْوَقَدِ

٣ لَوْ هُمْ حُمَاتُكَ *c* بِالْمَحْمَى حَمَوْكَ وَآمَ   تُتْرَكْ لِيَوْمٍ أَقَامَ النَّاسَ فِى كَبَدِ

٥ ٤ *d* كَمَا حَمَيْنَاكَ يَوْمَ النَّعْفِ مِنْ شَطِبٍ   وَالْفَضْلُ لِلْقَوْمِ مِنْ رِيحٍ وَمِنْ عَدَدِ

شَطِبٌ جَبَلٌ. والنَّعْفُ أَسْفَلُ لِلجبل. والفضل للقوم: يقول الرِيحُ مَعَهُمْ والعَدَدُ لهم. ويُروى مِنْ صَوْتٍ

ومِنْ غَرَدٍ: [والغَرَدُ] يريد الصوتَ هٰهنا ۞

٥ *e* أَوْ لَاتَوْكَ بِجَمْعٍ لَّا كِفَاءَ لَـهُ   قَوْمٌ هُمُ الْقَوْمُ *f* فِى الْأَنَى وَفِى الْبُعُدِ

٦ بِجَحْفَلٍ كَبَهِيمِ اللَّيْلِ مُنْتَجِعٍ   أَرْضَ الْعَدُوِّ لُهَامٍ وَافِرِ الْعَدَدِ

١٠ الْأَنَى مِن أَنَأَى يَنْأَى اى بَعُدَ. البهيمُ الأَسْوَدُ. الجَحْفَلُ للجيش: وَإِنَّما شبَّهَهُمْ بالليل لأَنَّ اللَّيْل يُغَطِّى

كُلَّ شىءٍ. *g* واللُّهامُ الذى يَلْتَهِمُ كُلَّ شىءٍ يَذْهَبُ به. والمُنْتَجِعُ الطالبُ ۞ (79a)

٧ *h* الْقَائِدُ الْخَيْلَ تَرْدِى فِى أَعِنَّتِهَا   وِرْدَ الْقَطَا هَجَّرَتْ ظِنًّا إِلَى الثَّمَدِ

XIV. Vv. 1, 3 and 4 of this poem are cited elsewhere. Metre *Basīṭ*.

a) LA XII, 324[20]: Fā'iq I, 301; Ḥam. (commy.) 395[23], all with يَدْعُو; Naṣr. 612, Yāq. III, 289, as text.

b) Inserted conjecturally: MS reads unmetrically لا تدعوا اذا حام الكماه ولا اذا أنّم.

c) Yāq. *l. c.* and Naṣr. بِالْمَحْمَى حَمِيتَن.

d) Yāq. *ut sup.* and Bakrī 811[20]. Yāq. vocalizes شَطَب and Bakrī شَطْب. The Battle of the Skirt of Mount Shaṭib is also referred to in a poem of Bishr b. Abī Khāzim, quoted in Yāq. *l. c.*; the antagonist of Asad was Numair, a branch of ʿAmir b. Ṣaʿṣaʿah.

e) MS او لا أتوك بجمعِم (this suggestion is due to Prof. Nöldeke).

f) In view of the identity of meaning of انْأَى and بعد, the original reading was probably فِى الْأَدْنَى.   *g*) MS carelessly والبهيم.

h) "Dieser Vers ist ohne Verbindung. Vorher muss etwas ausgefallen sein, worauf sich القائد bezieht" (Nöldeke).

٨ مِنْ كُلِّ عِجْلِزَةٍ بَادٍ نَوَاجِذُهَا ۞ عَلَى اللِّجَامِ تُبَارِى الرَّكْبَ فِى عَمَدِ

الرَّدَيَانِ ضَرْب مِن عَدْوِهَا. والعِجْلِزَة الشَّدِيدَة. تُبَارِى الرَّكْبَ تُعَارِضُهِم. عَنَد اى تَذْهَب عَلى الْمَرِج ۞

٩ وَكُلِّ أَجْرَدَ قَدْ مَالَتْ رِحَالَتُهُ ۞ نَهْدِ الْمَرَاكِلِ نَعْمِ نَاتِئِ الْكَتَدِ

[نهد] الْمَراكِل يريد ضَخْم الْوَسَط حيث يَرْكُلُه الرَّاكِب. ونَاتِئُ الْكَتَد مرتفع الكَتَد: [والْكَتَدُ] للحارك

من البعير وموضع a النَّبَج من الفرس [اى] مُنْقَطَع الْعُذْرَة مِمَّا يَلِى الحارك ۞

١٠ حَتَّى تَعَاطَيْنَ غَسَّانًا فَحَرَّبَهُم ۞ يَوْمَ الْمُرَارِ وَلَمْ يَلْوُوا عَلَى أَحَدِ

١١ لَمَّا رَأَوْكَ [وَ]أَبْلَجَ الْبِيضِ وَسْطَهُم ۞ وَكُلِّ مُطَّرِدِ الْأُنْبُوبِ كَالْمَسَدِ

بُلْج شَبَّهَا c بِالصُّبْحِ فِى بياضها]. مُطَّرِدِ الْأُنْبُوب طويل مُقَوَّم. والمَسَد الحَبْل من اللِيف ۞

١٢ غَوَتْ بَنُو أَسَدٍ غَسَّانَ أَمْرَهُم ۞ وَقَلَّ مَا وَقَفَتْ غَسَّانُ لِلرَّشَدِ

XV.

١ أَمِنْ مَنْزِلٍ عَافٍ وَمِنْ رَسْمِ أَطْلَالِ ۞ [بَكَيْتَ وَهَلْ] e يَبْكِى مِنَ الشَّوْقِ أَمْثَالِى

٢ دِيَارُهُمُ إِنْ هُمْ جَمِيعٌ فَأَصْبَحَتْ ۞ بَسَابَسَ إِلَّا الْوَحْشَ فِى الْبَلَدِ الْخَالِى

٣ قَلِيلًا بِهَا الْأَصْوَاتِ إِلَّا عَوَارِفًا ۞ عَرَارًا [زِمَارًا] f مِّنْ غَيَاهِيبَ آجَالِ

الْآجَال الْأَقْطِيع بَقَر أَوْ ظِباء: واحد الْآجَال إِجْل: والْإِجْل لا يكون إِلَّا من البقر والظباء فقد جَعَلَ

---

a) MS الهسج (no such root exists): see **LA IV.** 380[17].

b) MS لما راونك تلج. *Cf.* No. II, 25, *ante;* perhaps we should read رَأَوْنَا.

c) Added conjecturally.

d) MS عَبَّتْ. "عبت ist schwerlich richtig. Aber was? zur Noth غَبَّتْ, als Causativ von غَبِىَ das transitiv sein darf (Lisān XIX, 349 pænult.), aber doch kaum recht passt. غَوَتْ gäbe einen passenden Gegensatz zu لِلرَّشَد, und da غَوَى = أَغْوَى sein kann (Lis. XIX 378[11]), so könnte auch غَوَى doppelt transitiv sein. Aber misslich ist das auch!" (Nöldeke).

XV. Of this poem vv. 1, 2, 4, 5 are in Yāq. III, 772, and v. 14 in Bakrī 258. Naṣr. has reproduced them at p. 611. Metre *Ṭawīl.*

e) Carelessly omitted in MS. Yāq. and Naṣr. بَكَيْتُ, but usage is generally in favour of the second person.

f) Added conjecturally to fill metrical *lacuna*: see end of scholion.

هَيِّنا للنعام مُسْتَعارًا. وقوله قليلًا يقول أَصْبَحَتْ بها قليلًا الأَصْوَاتُ. والعِرار اصوات الظّلمان والغَبَاغِيب المُسَوّد واحدها غَبْغَبٌ يريد النعام السُودَ والرُمْدَ. ويروى قليلٌ بالرفع. والعِرار للظلمان والزِمار اصوات إِناث النعام ☆ (79b)

خَلَتْ مِنْهُمْ وَٱسْتَبْدَلَتْ غَيْرَ أَبْدَالِ	۴ a فَإِنْ تَكُ غَبْرَاءُ الْخُبَيْبَةِ أَصْبَحَتْ
بِهَا وَاللَّيَالِى لَا تَدُومُ عَلَى حَالِ	۵ b بِمَا قَدْ أَرَى الْحَىَّ الْجَمِيعَ بِغِبْطَةٍ
أُرَجِّى لَيَانَ الْعَيْشِ [وَالْعَيْشُ] c ضَلَالُ	۶ أَبَعْدَ بَنِى عَمْرِو وَرَهْطِى وَإِخْوَتِى
بِمَاسِيهِمْ طُولَ الْحَيَاةِ وَلَا سَالِى	۷ فَلَسْتُ وَإِنْ أَضْحَوْا مَضَوْا لِسَبِيلِهِمْ
وَنَأْىِ بَعِيدٍ وَٱخْتِلَافٍ وَأَشْغَالِ	۸ أَلَا تَقِفَانِ الْيَوْمَ قَبْلَ تَفَرُّقٍ
وَبَيْنَ أَعَالِى الْحَلِّ لَاحِقَةِ التَّالِى	۹ إِلَى ظُعْنٍ يَّسْلُكْنَ بَيْنَ تَبَالَةٍ

10 يقول كلَحِقها الذى يَتْلُوها. ويروى بَيْنَ أَعَالِى الرَّوْضِ d. والحَلّ الطريق الصَّغير فى الرمال ☆

نَدِمْتُ عَلَى أَنْ يَذْهَبَا نَاعِمَى بَالِ	۱۰ فَلَمَّا رَأَيْتُ الْحَادِيَيْنِ تَكَمَّشَا

الحادِيان السائقان. ان يَذْهَبَا ناعِمَى بال: يريد أَنْ يَذْهَبَا بهذه المرأة وهَنا ناعِما البال ☆

بِمَا كُلُّ فَتْلَاءَ الذِّرَاعَيْنِ شِمْلَالِ	۱۱ e رَفَعْنَا عَلَيْهِنَّ السِّيَاطَ فَقَلَّصَتْ
فَيَافِى سُهُوبٍ حَيْثُ تَحْتَتُّ فِى الْآلِ	۱۲ خَلُوجٍ بِرِجْلَيْهَا كَأَنَّ فُرُوجَهَا

15 خَلُوجٍ يَدْفَعُ بَيْنٍ. والقَيافِى الصَّحارى واحدها فَيْفَاء. والسُّهُوب الصَّحارى التى لا شىء فيها واحدها سُهْبٌ. والآلُ مثل السَّراب إلَّا أن الآلَ ضَحْوَةً والسَّراب نِصْفَ النهار ☆

مُصَدَّرَةٍ بِالرَّحْلِ وَجْنَاءَ مِرْقَالِ	۱۳ فَأَلْحَقَنَا بِالْقَوْدِ كُلُّ f دِفَقَّةٍ

---

a) See Yāq. V 334—5 for corrections of text in III, 772.

b) Yāq. فَقِدْمًا أَرَى (Naṣr. misprinted أَتَى): our reading (MS clear) is more in accordance with ʿAbīd's usage; see ante, No. XI, 16.

c) Another careless *lacuna* in the MS, filled on the assumption that it is due to *homoioteleuton*. We might read ضَلَالِى and so avoid the إِقْوَاء; but Nöldeke observes: «Ich würde lieber ضَلَالٍ, mit إِقْوَاء, lesen. Ich weiss nicht, ob für ein solches Intensiv   Adj. das Personal-suffix passt.»

d) الحَلّ seems here to be a place-name; see Yāq. II, 464, Bakrī 316.

e) MS رَفَعْنَ.   f) MS دڡعه (but دفعه in scholion).

الدِّقَّةِ الّتِى تَنْدَفِعُ فِى سَيْرِها كانْدِفاقِ الماءِ فِى السُّرْعَةِ ۞ والإرْقالُ ضَرْبٌ مِن السَّيْرِ ۞

١٤ b فَمِلْنا وَنازَعْنا الْـحَـدِيـتَ أُوانِـسًـا   عَلَيهِـنَّ جَيْـشانِـيَّـةٌ ذَاتُ أَغْـيـالِ

الأوانِسُ اللواتِى يُؤنَسُ بِهِنَّ مِن غَيْرِ ذَنْبٍ. والجَيْشانِيَّةُ بُرُودٌ حُمْرٌ وسُودٌ. ذاتُ أَغْيالٍ ذاتُ سَعَةٍ وطُولٍ : ويقال ذاتُ خُطُوطٍ ۞

١٥ وَمِلْنَ إِلَيْنَا بِـالسَّـوَالِـفِ وَالْحُلَى   وَبِالْقَوْلِ فِيمَا يَشْتَهِى الْـمَـرْحُ الْخَالِى

١٦ (80a) كَأَنَّ الصَّبَا جَاءَتْ بِرِيحِ لَطِيمَةٍ   مِّنَ الْمِسْكِ لَا تُسْطَاعُ بالثَّمَنِ الْغَالِى

١٧ وَرِيحِ خُزَامَى فِى مَذَانِبِ رَوْضَةٍ c جَلَا دِمْنَها سَارٍ مِّنَ الْمُزْنِ هَطَّالِ

اللَّطِيمَةُ القِطْعَةُ مِن الْمِسْكِ وجمعها لَطائِم. يقول لا تُشْتَرَى هـذه اللطيمة إلّا بالثمن الغالِى. ويُروَى كَأَنَّ صَبًا. والمَذَانِب مَجارِى الماءِ من التِّلاعِ الى الـروضِ. والتِّلاعُ مَجارِى الماءِ d من أَعْلَى الجبلِ واحدها تَلْعَةٌ : والمَذانِب مَجارِى الماءِ فِى أَسْفَلِ الجَبَلِ واحدها مَذْنَبٌ. والدِّمْنَة الأَبْعار والأَبْوَالُ. سارٍ من المُزن سَحابَةٌ جاءَتْ لَيْلًا [اى] سَرَتْ. هَطَّالٌ تَهْطِلُ الصَّبَّ ۞

XVI.

١ لِمَنِ الدِّيَارُ بِبُرْقَةِ الرَّوْحَانِ   دَرَسَتْ وَغَيَّرَهَا صُرُوفُ زَمَانِ

البُرْقَةُ حِجارةٌ ورَمْلٌ او حِجارةٌ وطِينٌ : وكلّ لَوْنَيْنِ فهِى بُرْقَةٌ وتُجْمَعُ بُرَقٌ : ويقال جَبَلٌ أَبْرَقُ اذا كان فيه سوادٌ وبياضٌ وكِساءٌ أَبْرَقُ اذا كان فيه سوادٌ وبياضٌ وحُمْرَةٌ وغير ذلك. وصروفُ الزمان تَقَلُّبُه بأَهْلِه حالًا

---

a) MS والرِّجل .

b) Cited Bakrī 258[9]; second hemistich in Yāq. II, 177[20] (with اعسال misprinted for اَغْيَال).
Bakrī فَأبْنَا for فَمِلْنا , and so Naṣr.   Jaishān is a *Mikhlāf* in al-Yaman.

c) MS دفنها ; but see scholion.

d) MS فِى .   e) MS ذات .

XVI. Vv. 1—2 of this poem are in Yāq., Bakrī, Naṣr.; v. 5 in LA; vv. 8, 9, 10 in ʿAskarī,
Kitāb aṣ-Ṣināʿatain, 126. Metre *Kāmil.*

f) Bakrī 427[7] as text: Yāq. I, 582[16] دَرَسَتْ لِطُولِ تَقَادُمِ الْأَزْمَانِ .

بعد حالٍ: والتَصْريفُ ايضًا تقلُّبُ الطائرِ جناحَيْهِ اى إطارتُهُ [إيّاهما]. ويُروى: * دَرَسَتْ لِطُولِ تَرَاوُحِ الأَزْمانِ * ☙

٢ a فَوَقَفْتُ فيها ناقَتى لِسُؤالِها   فَصَرَفْتُ وَالْعَيْنَانِ تَبْتَدِرَانِ

٣ سَجْمًا كَأَنَّ شُنَانَةً رَجَبِيَّةً   سَبَقَتْ إِلَى بِمائِهَا الْعَيْنَانِ

٥ سَجْمًا صَبًّا والسَجْمُ الصَبُّ. رَجَبِيَّةٌ جَاءَتْ فى رَجَبٍ ☙

٤ أَيَّامَ قَوْمى خَيْرُ قَوْمٍ سُوقَةً   لِمُعَصِّبٍ b وَلِبَائِسٍ وَّلِعَانِى

يقول كان فى ايام قومى. وقوله سُوقةً قال ابو عمرو الناس كُلُّهم سُوقةٌ إلّا c مَن كانت فى يَدَيْهِ شُعْبةٌ من سُلْطان. والْمُعَصِّب الذى يُعَصِّب على بَطْنِه الحَجَرَ من الجُوع ☙ (80b)

٥ d وَلَنِعْمَ أَيْسَارُ الْجَزُورِ إِذَا زَهَتْ   رِيحُ الشِّتاءِ وَمَأْلَفُ الْجِيرَانِ

١٠ الأَيْسَارُ الذينَ يَضْرِبُون بالقِداح يُقامِرُون ويَنْحَرُون [الجَزُورَ] ويُطْعِمُونها واحِدُهُم يَسَرٌ. وقوله اذا زَهَتْ رِيحُ الشِّتاءِ يقول [اذا] ارْتَفَعَتْ ☙

٦ أَمَّا إِذَا كَانَ الطِّعَانُ فَإِنَّهُمْ   قَدْ يَخْضِبُونَ عَوَالِيَ الْمُرَّانِ

واحِدُ العَوالى عاليةٌ وهى دون السِّنان بِشِبْرٍ او ذِراع حَيْثُ يُعْقَد f اللِّواءُ. والمُرَّانُ القَنا ☙

٧ أَمَّا إِذَا كَانَ الضِّرَابُ فَإِنَّهُمْ   أُسْدٌ لَدَى g أَشْبَالِهِنَّ حَوَارِنى

٨ أَمَّا إِذَا دُعِيَتْ نَزَالِ فَإِنَّهُمْ   يَحْجُبُونَ لِلْمُرَكَّبَاتِ فِى الْأَبْدَانِ

٩ فَخَلَدْتُ i بَعْدَهُمْ وَلَسْتُ بِخَالِدٍ   فَالدَّهْرُ ذُو غِيَرٍ وَّذُو أَلْوَانِ

١٠ j اللَّهُ يَعْلَمُ مَا جَهِلْتُ بِعَقْبِهِمْ   وَتَذَكُّرى مَا فَاتَ أَىَّ أَوَانِ

15

---

a) Yāq, *l. c.*, as text.   b) MS وكمادِس.   c) MS أن.

d) Cited LA XIX, 81²⁴, where the 2nd hemist. is رِيحِ الشِّتنا وَتَأْلَفُ الْجِيرانْ, with إِقْواء. In our MS the first hemist. is corrupt (probably from defects in the original from which the copy was made) and reads ولنعم السر الجوى ريح: the scholion however shows that the true text is that of LA.   e) MS ضب.

f) MS اللوى والمران القناه.   g) MS أشبالِهِم.

h) ʿAsk. يحدون; the author criticises the verse as رَدِىُّ الرَّصْفِ.

i) MS بعضهم; for the converse (د for ض) see *ante* No. XIII, 9.

j) ʿAsk. reads إِلّا لَأَعْلَمُ مَا جَهِلْتُ, and describes the verse as مُخْتَلُّ النَّظْمِ; he proceeds: ومعناه لَسْتُ بِخَالِد إِلّا لَأَعْلَمُ ما جَهِلْتُ وتَذَكُّرى ما فات أَىَّ أَوانٍ كان ☙

XVII.

١ ‏a‏ تَعَقَّفْتْ رُسُومٌ مِّنْ سُلَيْمَى دَكادِكَا   خَلَاءٌ تُعَقِّيهَا الرِّيَاحُ سَوَاهِكَا

‏b‏ يروى: *أَقْوَتْ رُسُومٌ مِنْ سُلَيْمَى دَكادِكَا*. ويروى *تُحَاوِلُ رَسْمًا من سُلَيْمَى دَكادِكَا*. والرسوم ما بَقِىَ

من الديار. والدَّكادِكُ ‏c‏ أرَضُونَ مُسْتَوِيَة. ويروى قِفَارًا. والسَّوَاهِكُ الرِّياحِ التى تَمُرُّ مَرًّا شديدًا وتأتى بالتُّراب

واحِدُها سَاهِكَة ☆

٥ ٢ ‏d‏ تَبَدَّلْنَ بَعْدِى مِن سُلَيْمَى وَأَهْلِهَا   نَعَامًا تَرَاعَاهَا ‏e‏ وَأُدْمًا تَرَائِكَا

تَرَاى هٰذه النعمُ الرسومَ. والأُدْمُ الظباء التى ليست بخالِصَة البياض: والآرَامُ الظباء البِيضُ وهى التى

تَسْكُنُ الرمال واحِدُها رِئْم ☆

٣ وَقَفْتُ بِهَا أَبْكِى بُكَاءَ حَمَامَةٍ   أَرَاكِيَّةٍ تَدْعُو حَمَامًا أَوَارِكَا

يقول وقفتُ فى هٰذه الرسوم. والأراكِيَّة التى فى شَجَرِ الأراك ☆

١٠ ٤ إِذَا ذَكَرَتْ يَوْمًا مِنَ الدَّهْرِ شَجَوُهَا   عَلَى فَرْعِ سَاقٍ أَذْرَتِ الدَّمْعَ سَافِكَا

(‏81a‏) يقول اذا ذكرَتِ الحَمامَةُ شَجَوُها يريد حُزْنَها والشَّجوُ الحُزْن: وفى لِلحُزن أَرْبَعُ لُغات: ‏f‏ الحَزْن

والحُزْن والحِزْن والحَزَن. والسَّاقُ عُودُ الشَّجَرِ الذى يقوم عليه. أَذْرَتْ صَبَّتْ. سَافِكًا صَابًّا ☆

٥ سَرَاةَ الضُّحَى حَتَّى إِذَا مَا عَمَايَتِى   تَجَلَّتْ كَسَوْتُ الرَّحْلَ وَجْنَاءَ تَامِكَا

سَرَاةَ الضُّحَى ‏g‏ [أَوَّلَ الضُّحَى]. عمايتى غَفْلَتى. تَجَلَّتْ تكَشَّفَتْ. والوَجْناء العَظِيمَة الوَجَنات: عن ابى

XVII. Mukht. pp. 87—88. Metre *Ṭawīl*.

In Mukht. the order of verses differs from that of the text, as follows:

1—8, an additional verse in place of 9, 12, 17, 18, 14, 15, 16, 13, 10, 11.

‏a‏) Mukht. تُحَاوِلُ رَسْمًا مِنْ and تَعَقِّيه.

‏b‏) „Den Accus. دَكادكا kann ich mir weder bei der Lesart تَعَقَّتْ noch bei أَقْوَتْ erklären. Die Lesart تُحَاوِلُ رَسْمًا sieht aber aus wie eine Correctur, um eine Construction hinein zu bringen; da wäre دَكادكا ein بَدَل zu رَسْمًا. Vermuthlich sehr alte Corruptel." (Nöldeke).

‏c‏) Dakādik is a place-name: see *ante*, III, 2 and Bakrī, 346.

‏d‏) Mukht. تَبَدَّلَ and تَرْعَاهُ (*sic*).   ‏e‏) MS وأدم.

‏f‏) The MS has no vowels to any of these forms; the last two are not mentioned in Lane.

‏g‏) Supplied from Mukht. scholion.

عمرو: وقال ابو عبيدة والأصمعيّ: أُخِذَت من الوَجِين [وهو] ما غَلُظَ من الارض وصَعُبَ السَّيْرُ فيها. وقال

خالد الوَجْناء الصَّخِمة. والتَّنامُك العظيمة السَّنام ۞

٩   كَأَنَّ قُتُودِى فَوْقَ جَأْبٍ مُّطَرَّدٍ   رَأَى عَانَةً تَهْوِى فَوَّلَّى a مُوَاشِكَا

القُتود عِيدان الرَّحْل واحدها قَتَدٌ. [الجأب] الحمار الغليظ. والمُطَرَّد الذى قد طَرَدَه للحمير. والعانة جماعةُ

٥ حُمُرٍ. تَهْوِى تُسْرِع فى عَدْوِها. مُوَاشِكًا اى سريعًا. شبّه ناقته فى مَضِيها وسُرعتها [بحمار الوَحْش] ۞

٧ bوَنَحْنُ قَتَلْنَا الْأَجْدَلَيْن وَمَالِكًا   أَعَزَّهُمَا فَقْدًا عَلَيْكَ cوَهَالِكَا

الأَجْدَلانِ رجلان من كِنْدَة. يريد نحن قتلنا أعزَّهُما عليك: وهالك الأَجْدَلَيْن مالكٌ ۞

٨ وَنَحْنُ جَعَلْنَا الرُّمْحَ قِرْنًا لِنَحْرِهِ   فَقَطَّرَهُ كَأَنَّمَا كَانَ وَارِكَا

٩ dوَنَحْنُ قَتَلْنَا مُرَّةَ الْخَيْرِ مِنْكُمْ   وَقُرْصًا وَقُرْضًا مِمَّا كَانَ fأُولَاذِكَا

١٠ gوَنَحْنُ صَبَحْنَا عَامِرًا يَوْمَ أَقْبَلُوا   سُيُوفًا عَلَيْهِنَّ النِّجَادُ بَوَاتِكَا

١١ عَطَفْنَا لَهُم عَطْفَ الضَّرُوسِ فَأَدْبَرُوا   hشِلَالًا وَقَدْ بَلَّ النَّجِيعُ السَّنَابِكَا

الضَّرُوس الناقة التى تَعْذِم مَن دَنا منها. شِلَالًا عِرابًا. والنَّجِيع الدم. وواحد السنابك سُنْبُك وهو

مُقَدَّمُ الحافِر ۞

١٢ وَيَوْمَ الرِّبَابِ قَدْ قَتَلْنَا iهُمَامَهَا   وَحُجْرًا قَتَلْنَاهُ وَعَمْرًا كَذَلِكَا

------

a) MS موامكا, and so in scholion; no such root exists; text follows Mukht.

b) Evidently verses have dropped out between v. 6 and v. 7; it is impossible that the transition from the *nasīb* to the main subject of the poem should be as abrupt as here. Mukht. reads أَعَزَّهُم.   c) MS مهالكا (but see scholion).

d) Mukht. has an entirely different verse here:

وَنَحْنُ الْأُولَى إِنْ تَسْتَطِعْكَ رِمَاحُنَا   تَفِدْكَ إِلَى نَارِ لَعَمْرُ إِلهِكَا

e) Quṣ is named again in No. XX, v. 11; and in a note at p. 79 of Prof. Hirschfeld's edition of the Dīw. of Ḥassān b. Thābit the name is cited as that of a king of Ghassān who had a conflict with the Banū Asad.   f) MS اوالكا.

g) Cited LA V, 63[17], with عَلَيْهِنَّ الْأَنْوُر. Mukht. has النّجَار (explained as العِنْف والكَرَم).

h) Mukht. سِراعًا (with شِلَالًا as v. l. in scholion).

i) Mukht. هُمَاعِمًا.

(81b) الرِّبابُ جماعةٌ أَحياءٍ: زَعْكُلٌ ومَرَّةٌ وثَورٌ وضَبَّةٌ. والهُمامُ السَّيّدُ. وحاجَّ أبو امرِئِ القيسِ الشاعرَ ☙

١٣ وَنَحْنُ قَتَلْنَا جَنْدَلًا فِى جُمُوعِهِ   وَنَحْنُ قَتَلْنَا شَيْخَهُ قَبْلَ ذَالِكَا

١٤ وَأَنْتَ آمِرُو الْهَاكَ b دُقَّ وَقَيْنَةٌ   فَتُصْبِحُ مَخْمُورًا وَتُمْسِى c كَذَالِكَا

ويروى تُمْسِى مُتَارِكًا ☙

٥ ١٥ d عَنِ الوِتْرِ حَتَّى أَحْرَزَ الوِتْرَ أَهْلُهُ e وَأَنْتَ تَبَكَّى إِثْرَهُ مُتَهَالِكَا

[الوِتْرُ] مِثْلُ الذَّحْلِ وهو الحَقُّ يكون للرَّجُلِ من دَمٍ أو غيرِ ذلك ☙

١٩ فَلَا أَنْتَ بِالْأَوْتَارِ أَدْرَكْتَ أَهْلَهَا   وَلَمْ تَكُ إِنْ لَمْ تَنْتَصِرْ مُتَمَاسِكَا

يقول لم تَكُنْ مُتَماسِكًا بِطَلَبِ الأَوْتَارِ إِنْ لَمْ تَنْتَصِرْ ☙

١٧ وَرَكْضُكَ لَوْلَاهُ f لَقِيتَ الَّذِى لَقُوا   فَذَاكَ الَّذِى أَنْجَاكَ مِمَّا هُنَالِكَا

١٠ ١٨ ظَلِلْتَ تُغَنِّى إِنْ g أَصَبْتَ وَلِيدَةً   كَأَنَّ مَعَدًّا أَصْبَحَتْ فِى حِبَالِكَا

XVIII.

١ لِمَنْ طَلَلٌ لَـمْ يَعْفُ مِنْهُ الْمَذَانِبُ   فَجَنْبَا h حِبِرٍّ قَدْ تَعَفَّى فَوَاهِبُ

ويروى الذَّنائِبُ والمَذانِبُ وهما واحِدٌ. وسَمِعْتُ أَعرابِيًّا من قيسٍ وهو يقول: إِنَّ لِكُلِّ وادٍ مِذْنَبًا. ومِذْنَبُ الوادِى أَسْفَلُهُ: وأَعْلَى الأَوْدِيَةِ تلاعُها واحِدُها تَلْعَةٌ ☙

―――――

a) This list is defective: the five tribes forming the confederacy called the *Ribāb* were Taim, ʿAdī, ʿAuf (ʿUkl) and Thaur, sons of ʿAbd-Manāt son of Udd, and Ḍabbah son of Udd; Mukht.'s scholion gives the names correctly.

b) Mukht. زِقٌّ.

c) Mukht. مُتَارِكًا (schol. فانت مُتَارِكٌ لِمَنْ عادَاكَ); the latter reading seems to be demanded by the next verse, and the repetition of ذلك in rhyme is objectionable.

d) Mukht. عَلَى الوِتْرِ.   e) Mukht. فَأَنْتَ.   f) MS لولاهو.

g) Mukht. أَخَذْتَ. Schol. of Mukht: يقول من إِنْجَابِكَ بِوَلِيدَةٍ أَخَذْتَها ظَنَنْتَ أَنَّكَ مَلَكْتَ مَعَدًّا كُلَّها.

XVIII. Of this fragment vv. 1—2 in Bakrī 409 (copied Wüst. *Register* 394 and Naṣr. 614) and v. 5 in Fā'iq, Asās, and TA. — Metre *Ṭawīl*.

h) MS واهِب and جَنْبا حِبِرٍّ are collocated in a verse of Ibn Muqbil's cited Yāq. II, 194[19].

٢ دِيَـارُ بَنِى سَعْدِ بْـنِ تَعْلَبَةَ الأُولَى *a* أَذَاعَ بِهِمْ دَهْرٌ عَلَى النَّاسِ راتِبُ *b*

بنو سَعْد بن أَنَس *c*: وهم الذين أبادُهم غَسَّان. أذاع بهم اى فرَّقَهم. وراتب شديد ☙

٣ فَأَذْهَبَهُمْ مَا أَذْهَبَ النَّـاسَ قَبْلَهُمْ ضِرَاسُ الْحُرُوبِ وَالْمَنَايَا الْعَوَاقِبُ

الاذهاب ههنا الفَنَاء والهلاك. ضراس الحروب يريد عِضاص للحروب: يقال رجلٌ مَضْروس ومُجرِس ومُجرَّد

٥ ومُقتَّل وهو المُجَرَّب. والعواقب التى تَعقُب مرّة بعد مرّة ☙ (82a)

۴ أَلَا رُبَّ حَيٍّ قَدْ رَأَيْتَـمَا هُنَـالِكُمْ لَهُمْ سَلَفٌ تَـزْوَرُّ مِنْـهُ الْمَقَانِبُ

هنالكم يريد فى هذه المواضع التى ذكرها. لهم سَلَف ههنا الجَيش المُتقدِّم. والسُّلَاف الذين

يتَقدَّمون الناس فى المنازل: ومنه قولهم: اجْعَلْهُ لنا سَلَفًا واجْعَلْهُ لنا فَرَطًا: اى اجْعَلْهُ [من] يَتَقَدَّم

لنا بِخَبَر. تزوَرُّ تَعدِلُ عنه خَوفًا: يعنى من الجَيش. وواحد المَقانب مقنَبٌ والمقْنَب ما بَين العشرين

١٠ فارسًا الى أَكْثَر من ذلك ☙

٥ فَأَقْبِلْ عَلَى أَفْوَاقٍ مَا لَكَ إِنَّـمَا *d* تَكَلَّفْتَ مِـلْ أَشْيَاءَ مَا هُوَ ذَاهِبُ *e*

واحد الأَفواق فُوق وهو الموضِع الذى يُجْعَلُ فيه [الوَتر من السَّهْم] ☙

XIX.

١ إِنَّ الْحَوَادِثَ قَدْ يَجِيءُ بِهَا الْغَدُ وَالصُّبْحُ وَالإِمْسَاءِ مِنْهَا مَوْعِدُ

٢ وَالنَّاسُ يَلْحَوْنَ الْأَمِيرَ إِذَا غَوَى خَطْبَ الصَّوَابِ وَلَا يُلَامُ الْمُرْشَدُ

١٥ يَلْحَوْنَ الامير يَلُومُونَه. معناه يَلْحَوْن الامير اذا غوى الصَّوَاب ولا يُلام المُرْشَد ☙

---

a) Bakrī (Wüst., Naṣr.) أَضَاعَ. b) Wüst. راتِب.

c) This *Anas* is not in the genealogies; probably we should read *Asad*.

d) Cited Fā'iq II, 150, with سَيْمَك for ما لَكَ, and من أَشْيَاءَ. Asās II, 144, with نَبْلَكَ and

بِلاشِياءَ. TA VII, 53³², with سَيْمَك and مِلْ أَشْيَاءَ.

e) MS من الأَشْيَاءَ.

XIX. Of this poem vv. 9—10 are in Yāqūt, and vv. 9, 13, 14 in LA; v. 9 also in Asās.
Metre *Kāmil*.

٣ وَالْمَرْءُ مِنْ رَيْبِ الْمَنُونِ بِغِرَّةٍ   وَعَدَا الْعَدَاءُ وَلَا تُوَدِّعُ *a* مَهْدَدُ

عَدَا العَدَاءُ اى صَرَفَتْنا الصوارِفُ : وكلّ ما *b* جاءك من شىء فقد عداك اى شغلكَ الشُّغْلُ ✿

٤ أُدْمَانَةٌ *c* تَرِدُ الْبَرِيرَ بِغِيلِهَا   تَقْرُو *d* مَسَارِبَ أَيْكَةٍ وَتَرَدَّدُ

الادمانة الظَّبْيَةُ: يقول *e* مَهْدَدُ فى *f* الحُسْنِ هذه الظَّبْيَةُ. والظباءُ على ثَلٰثَةِ أَلْوانٍ: منها الرئم ومنها الأُدْم ومنها العُفْر: وأمّا الآرام من الظباء فهى لخالصَةُ البياض وهى تَسْكُن الرمال: واما الأُدْم فالتى لَيْسَتْ بخالصة البياض وهى تَسْكُنُ الجبال: وأمّا العُفْر فالتى لَوْنُها لون التراب (82*b*) وهى التى تَسْكُن الصحارى: عن ابى حَفْصَةَ الشاعر. [البرير] ثَمَرُ الأَراك. والغِيل جماعةُ الشَجَرِ بِغِيلِها يريد تَوارَتْها. وتَقْرُو مَسارِبَ يقول *g* تَرْتَعِى المَسارِبَ: والمَسارِبُ المَرَاعِى واحدها مَسْرَبٌ. والأَيْكَةُ الغَيْضَةُ ✿

٥ وَخَلَا عَلَيْهَا مَا يُفَزِّعُ وِرْدَهَا   إِلَّا الْحَمَامُ *h* دَعَا بِهِ وَالْهُدْهُدُ

٦ فَدَعَا هَدِيلًا سَاقُ حُرٍّ *i* ضَحْوَةً   فَدَنَا الْهَدِيلُ لَهُ يَصُبُّ وَيَصْعَدُ

الهديل الفَرْخ. وساقُ حُرٍّ الذَكَرُ من القَمارِىّ. يقول دعا الساق الفَرْخَ فدنا الهديلُ اى الفَرْخ يَصُبُّ ويَصْعَدُ: اى يَنْحَطُّ مرّةً ويصعد أُخْرَى ✿

٧ *j* زَعَمَ الْأَحِبَّةُ أَنَّ رِحْلَتَنَا غَدًا   وَبِذَاكَ خَبَّرَنَا الْغُدَافُ الْأَسْوَدُ

٨ فَاقْطَعْ لُبَانَتَهُمْ بِذَاتِ بُرَايَةٍ   أُجُدٍ إِذَا وَنَتِ الرِّكَابُ تَزَيَّدُ

ذات بُراية يريد ذات لحمٍ وشحمٍ وقوّة. والأُجُد المُوثَّقة الخَلْق التى كأنّ فَقارَها عَظْمٌ واحد: قال ابو عمرو: رأيتُ ثلٰثَ فِقرٍ عَظْمًا واحدًا. وقوله اذا وَنَتِ الرِكابُ اى اذا فَتَرَتْ وأَعْيَتْ ✿

٩ *k* وَكَأَنَّ أَقْتَادِى تَضَمَّنَ نِسْعَهَا   مِنْ وَحْشِ أَوْرَالٍ هَبِيطٌ مُفْرَدُ

---

a) For this unusual name see LA IV, 419[19], and v. 2 of al-Aʿshà's poem in praise of the Prophet.

b) MS حسك.   *c*) MS نزل (but points added by a later hand).

d) MS مشارب, and so once in commy.: but the second time مسارب.

e) MS مَهَدَّد.   *f*) MS حُسْنِ.

g) MS منع(!)   *h*) MS دعاه for دعا به.   *i*) MS قوة.

j) See Nābighah 7, 3 for a similar verse.

k) So LA IX, 300[24], Yāq. I, 400[15]; Asās II, 349[3] reads وَكَأَنَّ أَنْسَاعِى تَضَمَّنَ كُورَهَا. Our MS has اوزال, but it is doubtful if the point is by the original hand; the name is *Aurāl* (so all the citations); see I.Q. 52, 55, and Bakrī 130; also *ante*, No. XI, 22.

أوْرَال موضع. والهبيط الثور الـذى يَهْبِط من مكانٍ الى مكانٍ مثل الناشط. ويروى: *مِنْ وَحْشِ أوْرَالٍ شَبُوبٌ مُقْرُدٌ*: فالشَّبُوب الذى تَمَّتْ أَسْنانه من المَسانّ. ومُقْرد يرَوَى وَحْدَهُ ۞

١٠ aبَاتَتْ عَلَيْهِ لَيْلَـةٌ رَجَبِيَّـةٌ   نَصْبًا تَسُحُّ الْمَـاءَ أوْ هِـىَ أَسْوَدُ

١١ يَنْفِى بِـأَطْرَافِ الْأَلَاءِ شَفِيفَهَا   فَغَدَا وَكُلُّ خَصِيلِ عُضْوٍ يُرْعَدُ

٥ ينفى هذا الثورُ اى يُنَّحِى عَنْهُ شفيف هذه الليلة. والشفيف الريحِ الباردة التى كأنها تَنْضَحُ الماءَ. والأَلاء الشَّجَرُ واحدها أَلَاةٌ مثل (83a) bعَلَاةٌ. فغَدا هذا الثـور: الخَصِيلَةُ كُلّ لَحْمٍ مجتمع ۞

١٢ كَالْكَوْكَبِ الـدِّرّىِّ يَشْرَقُ مَتْنُهُ   خَرْصًا خَمِيصًا صُلْبُهُ يَتَأَوَّدُ

قال ابو عمرو: كُلّ كوكب له اسمٌ مَعْروفٌ فهو دِرّىٌّ مهموز مثل دِرّيعٍ: ويروى دُرّى أُخِذَ من الـدُّرِّ. ١٠ وقوله كالكوكب يعنى الثور كالكوكب فى بَياضه: ويقال فى سُرْعَـته بَحَطٍّ. يَشْرَقُ مَتْنُ الثور من البياض. والخَرِص لِلجائع المَقْرور ولا يكون خَرِصٌ جائعًا إلّا وهو مقرور ايضًا. والخميص الضامر. صُلْبُهُ يتأوّد اى يَتَأَوَّج. ويروى *خَرْصًا خَمِيصًا بَطْنُهُ cيَتَأَوَّدُ* بريد خَميصًا بَطْنُهُ: ثم قال cيتناوّد النّـثورُ dۙ۞

١٣ eفِى رَوْضَةٍ ثَلَجَ الرَّبِيـعُ قَرَارَهَا   مَوْلِيَّةٍ لَـمْ يَسْتَطِعْهَا الرَّوَّدُ

ثَلَجَ fخَضَّرَ. قَرارُها وَسَطُها. ويروى: ثَلَجَ الرَّبِيعُ [قَرَارَهَا]: اى gأَبْدَت الربيع بالثَّلَجَانِ. [ويقال] hاذا ١٥ صار الى الطين قبل ان يَخْرُجُ الماءُ: قد أَثْلَجَ: فاذا iصار الى الماءِ: قد أَنْبَطَ. مَوْلِيَّةٍ اصابها مَطَرُ الوَلِىِّ: وهو

---

a) Yāq. I, 400[16], with أوْ هِىَ أَبْرَدُ, which is probably the right reading, as الْأَسْوَدُ occurs as an ending in v. 7, and would not be repeated so soon afterwards; أسود is moreover not an appropriate epithet for the night. For the stormy character of the month of Rajab see *ante*, XVI, 3.

b) MS علاله.

c) MS in both places دماول.

d) The MS gives, after v. 12, v. 15 with its scholion: in our text this v. has been restored to its proper place.

e) See LA III, 45[15], where text agrees: our MS has قلالها, which may represent a reading قَلَاتَيَا: the scholion however has قرارها, and قلات is an unsuitable word in describing a روضة.

f) MS حسر.   g) MS بدت.

h) اخا سار الى الطى.   i) صاروا.

المطر الثانى والوَسمىّ الأوّل. لم يستطعها a الرَّوْد اى لم يَبْلُغْها b الرَّوْد والناس فيَذْعَمونها ويَرْعَوْن فيها

فيكون فيها السَّرْقِين قد بَعَرَ: فهى أُطْيَبُ اذا لم يَقْدِرْها الناسُ ۞

١٤ c وَبَـلَـدًا لِكَوْكَبِها صَعيدٌ مِثْلَ مَـا   ريحَ الْعَبِيرُ عَلَى الْمَلَابِ الْأَصْفَدُ

كَوْكَبُها ماؤُها الذى فى وَسَطِها. والصَّعيد التَّرى وهو التُّراب النَّدِى. ريحَ نَفَحَ. ويُروى: مِثْلَ ما d كِيسَ

العَبِيرُ: شبّه التّرى بالمِلابِ (٨٣b) لطيب ريحِه. الأصْفَد نَعْت العَبِير وهو الجَيِّدُ ۞

١٥ وَإِذَا سَرَيْتَ سَرَتْ e أَمُونًا رَسْـلَـةً   وَّإِذَا تُكَلِّفُهَا الْـهَـوَاجِرَ تَصْخَدُ

الامون التى قد أمِنْتَ عِثارَها. والرَّسْلَة التى تُعْطِيكَ أَسْرَها عَفْوًا. ويروى: f أَمُونًا جَلْدَةً. ويروى تَكْنُفها

الهَواجِرَ بالنُّون: اى تَكَلَّفُها السَّيْرَ فى الهواجِرِ. تَصْخَدُ اى تَجِدُّ. ويروى g تَحْصَدُ: والأوْلَى أَجْوَدُ ۞

١٦ h وَإِلَى شَرَاحِيلَ الْهُمَامِ بِـمَـنْـصَـرِهِ   نَصَرَ الْأَشَاءَ سَرِيَّةٌ مُسْتَـرْغَدُ

الهُمام السَّيّد. بِنَصْرِه بحَمْلِه. نَصَرَ الأَشاءَ اى كحَمْل الأَشاءِ: والأَشاءُ النَّخْل الصِّغار واحدها أَشاءَةٌ.

والسَّرِيّ النَّهْر الذى ليس بالعَظيم. والمُسْتَرْغَد الكَثير ۞

١٧ مَنْ سَيْبُهُ سَحُّ الْفُـرَاتِ وَحَمْلُهُ   i بَـرْقُ الْجِبَالِ وَنَيْلُهُ لَا يَـنْـفَـدُ

سَيْبُهُ عَطاؤُه. سَحُّ الفُرات مَدُّ الفُرات. ويروى *مَنْ حَدُّهُ حَدُّ السِّنانِ وسَيْبُهُ* جَرَى الْعُرَابِ: حَدُّهُ

حَدُّ السِّنانِ فى الغَضَبِ ۞

---

a) MS الروب, after which the following words are written: ورِيها يأتُونَها, which seem to make
no sense.   b) MS المرود.

c) Cited LA IV, 244[11], with ريحَ for صَعيدٌ and كِيسَ for صَعيدٌ (قال إنّما أراد الْأَصْفَنْطَ).

d) MS حس; see, for cases in which our MS has mistaken ك for ح, *ante* No. XII, 22, and
No. XXI, 9 scholion. The reading كِيسَ is established by LA, and the word occurs in No. XII,
16 and scholion.   e) MS أمُونْ.   f) MS حلده أمُونْ.

g) This word seems to yield no appropriate sense; perhaps we should read تَصْيَدُ, a synonym
of تَصْخَدُ (Nöldeke).

h) The و before الى suggests that something has dropped out before this verse. The MS care-
lessly repeats the word مُسْتَرْغَد (written مسرغد) at the end.

i) MS برن الجمال: the expression is obscure, and the reading doubtful; possibly the first word
may be مَزْن. The alternative reading in the scholion makes good sense.

XX.

١ يَا خَلِيلَيَّ أَرْبَعَا وَٱسْتَخْبِرَا آلْ　مَنْزِلَ الدَّارِسَ a مِنْ أَهْلِ الْحَلَالِ

أَرْبَعَا قِفَا. وَالْحَلَالُ ٱمْرَأَتُهُ. وَيُرْوَى الْحَلَالُ: وَالْحَلَالُ جَمْعُ حِلَّةٍ وَالْحُلَّةَ وَالْحَلَّةَ وَاحِدٌ ☆

٢ b مِثْلَ سَحْقِ الْبُرْدِ عَفَّى بَعْدَكَ آلْ　قَطْرُ مَغْنَاهُ وَتَأْوِيبُ الشَّمَالْ

السَحْقُ أَخْلَاقُ الثَّوْبِ. عَفَّى دَرَسَ. مَغْنَاهُ مَوْضِعُهُ يَعْنِى مَوْضِعَ هَذَا الْمَنْزِلِ الَّذِى كَانُوا c يَسْكُنُونَهُ.

5 وَالتَّأْوِيبُ الرُّجُوعُ: يَقُولُ كَانَتْ d رِيحُ الشَّمَالِ تَأْتِى مِنَّا عَلَى هَذَا الْمَوْضِعِ ☆

٣ وَلَقَدْ يَغْنَى بِهِ e أَصْحَابُكَ آلْ　مُمْسِكُو مِنْكَ بِأَسْبَابِ الْوِصَالِ

٤ ثُمَّ f أَكْدَى وُدُّهُمْ g أَنْ أَزْمَعُوا آلْ　بَيْنَ وَالْأَيَّامُ حَالٌ بَعْدَ حَالِ

٥ h فَٱسْأَلْ عَنْهُمْ بِأَمُونٍ كَالْوَأَى آلْ　جَأْبٍ ذِى الْعَانَةِ أَوْ i تَيْسِ الرِّمَالِ

يَقُولُ فَٱسْأَلْ هَمَّكَ عَنْهُمْ. وَالْأَمُونُ النَّاقَةُ الَّتِى قَدْ أَمِنْتَ عِثَارَهَا. وَالْوَأَى (مِثْلُ الْوَعَى) لِلْحِمَارِ الشَّدِيدِ.

10 وَالْجَأْبُ j [الْغَلِيظُ مِنَ الْحَمِيرِ الْمُوَثَّقُ الْخَلْقِ. وَالْعَانَةُ الْقِطْعَةُ مِنَ الْحَمِيرِ] ☆

٦ نَحْنُ قُدْنَا مِنْ أَهَاضِيبِ الْمَلَا آلْ　خَيْلَ فِى الْأَرْسَانِ أَمْثَالَ السَّعَالِى

٧ شُرَّبًا k يَغْشَيْنَ مِنْ مَجْهُولَةِ آلْ　أَرْضٍ وَعْثًا مِّنْ سُهُولٍ l وَجِبَالِ

XX. This remarkable poem, with each verse except one broken in the middle by an article and noun divided between the two hemistichs, is in Mukht. 88—90, ʿAinī I, 511, and Khiz. III, 233, 237; and several verses of it are cited elsewhere and collected in Naṣr. 611—12. Prof. Nöldeke considers that this metrical anomaly makes it very improbable that the poem is the genuine work of ʿAbīd. Metre *Ramal muraffal*.

a) Mukht. عَنْ; both Mukht. and Khiz. الْحَلَالِ.

b) Cited Faʾiq I, 273. Naṣr. بَعْدَهَا.

c) MS نَكدون.　　*d)* MS الريح.

e) MS أَصْحَابُكَ; Mukht., Khiz., Naṣr. جِيرَانُكَ.

f) Khiz. أَوْدَى.　　*g)* Khiz., Mukht., إِنْ.

h) Mukht., Khiz. فَٱنْصَرِفْ عَنْهُمْ بِعَنْسٍ كَالْوَأَى.　　*i)* Mukht. شَاءَ.

j) Scholion completed from Mukht.

k) MS لعلسن, Khiz. يَغْسَفْنَ, Mukht. as text.　　*l)* Khiz., Mukht. أَوْ رِمَالِ.

الملا a الصحراء. والسعالى الغيلان واحدها b سِعْلَاةً اى غُولٌ. (84a) الوعْث c ما غَلُظَ من الارض وصَلُبَ ومنه قبل أَوْعَثَ البعيرُ ☜

٨   d فَأَنْتَجَعْنَا الْحَارِثَ الْأَعْـرَجَ فِى   جَحْفَلٍ كَالـلَّيْلِ خَطَّارِ الْـعَـوَالِى

للحارث e جدّ امرئ القيس. والْجَحْفَلُ الجَيْشُ الكَثِير. وواحد العوالى [عالِيَة]: وهو

دون السنان بذراع او نَحْوِهِ او شِبْرٍ عن أَبِى عَمْرٍو: وقال ابو عبيدة: عالِيَةُ الرُمْحِ من الثُّلُثِ الأَوَّلِ ☜   5

٩   f يَوْمَ غَادَرْنَا عَدِيًّا بِـالْـقَـفَـا آلْ   ذُبَّـلِ السُّمْرِ صَرِيعًا فِى الْمَجَالِ

١٠   ثُمَّ عَجَّنَاهُنَّ خُوصًا كَالْقَطَا آلْ g   قَارِبِ الْمَنْهَلَ مِنْ أَيْـنِ h الْكَلَالِ

الخُوص الضامِرَة الغائرة العيون كالقَطَا. للخيل مُتَواتِرة يَتْبَع بَعْضُها بعضًا. والْقَارِب الذى يطلُب [الماءَ] ☜

١١   ذَكَوْ i قُرْصٍ j يَوْمَ جَالَتْ k حَوْلَهُ آلْ   خَيْلُ قُبًّا عَـنْ يَـمِـينٍ l وَّشِـمَـالِ

١٢   كَمْ رَئِيسٍ يَّقْدُمُ الْأَلْفَ عَلَى m الْ   أَجْوَدِ السَّابِحِ ذِى الْعَـقْبِ الطُّوَالِ

١٣   قَدْ أَبَاحَتْ جَمْعَهُ أَسْيَافـنَـا n آلْ   بِيضُ وَالسُّمْرُ وَمِـنْ حَيِّ حِـلَالِ

---

a) MS (!)المُحرى.   b) MS سفل جمع قَوْلٌ(!)

c) This is the exact opposite of the fact: وَعْث is soft soil — sand or earth — into which the foot sinks as one treads it.

d) Cited Yāq. IV, 57, with بالليل, and so Naṣr. 611.   e) Sic!!

f) Khiz. omits. Mukht. ثُمَّ for يَوْمَ. Scholion of Mukht.: عَدِىّ بن مالك ابن أُخْت للحارث بن شَمِر (sic) فُتِلَ يَوْمَئَذٍ ☜

g) Mukht. الْقَارِبَاتِ أَلْمَاءَ عَلَى. Yāq. IV, 57, Khiz. الْقَارِب أَلْمَاءَ مِنْ.

h) MS ان؛ Yāq. Naṣr. إِثْر.

i) MS قوم؛ Khiz. قوص؛ Mukht. Yāq. as text: see ante, No. XVII, 9.

j) Yāq. ثُمَّ.

k) Khiz., Yāq. جَوْلَةَ الْخَيْلِ.

l) Khiz. قُرص بن مالك من غَسَّان: ويقال هو رجلٌ من بنى كعب بن. Schol. Mukht.: أَوْ شِمال. قُرْص تَلٌّ بِأَرْضِ غَسَّان؛ Yāq.: رَبيعة بن عامر بن صعصعة: و يقال هو من كنده.

m) Mukht. الْعَقْب الْعَدْو الثانى: قال ابو عمرو: أَجْوَد. Khiz. السابِح الأَجْوَد. Schol. of Mukht.: العقب الجَرْى بعد الجَرى: قال البُدَاعَنْ أَوّل جرى الفرس والعَلالَة والعقب آخِرُهُ ☜

n) Mukht. الْبِيض فى الرَّوْع وَمِنْ. Khiz. الْبِيض فى الرَّوْعَة مِن.

١٤ a وَلَنَا دَارٌ وَرِثْنَا عِزَّهَا آلْ　　　　أَقْدَمَ الْقُدْمُوسَ عَنْ عَمٍّ وَخَالِ

١٥ b مَنْزِلٌ دَمَّنَهُ آبَاؤُنَا آلْ　　　　مُورِثُونَا الْمَجْدَ فِى أُولَى اللَّيَالِ

١٩ مَا لَنَا c فِيهَا حُصُونٌ غَيْرَ مَا d آلْ　　　　مُقْرَبَاتِ الْجُرْدِ e تَرْدِى بِالرِّجَالِ

الْمُقْرَبَاتِ لِلْخَيْلِ الَّتِى f يُقْرِبُونَهَا إِليهم فِى الْبُيُوتِ وَاحِدَتها مُقْرَبَةٌ ☙

٥ ١٧ فِى رَوَابِى عَنْدُمُلِيٍّ شَامِخٍ آلْ　　　　أَنِفٍ فِيهِ g إِرْثُ وَمَجْدٍ وَجَمَالِ

الْعَنْدُمُلِيُّ الْقَدِيمُ. وَالْإِرْثُ الْأَصْلُ ☙

١٨ h فَاتَّبَعْنَا ذَاتَ أُولَانَا الْأُولَى آلْ　　　　مُوقِدِى الْحَرْبَ وَمُوفِى بِالْحِبَالِ

XXI.

١ لِمَنْ جِمَالٌ قُبَيْلَ الصُّبْحِ مَزْمُومَةْ　　　　مُيَمِّمَاتٍ i بِلَادًا غَيْرَ مَعْلُومَةْ

٢ j عَالَيْنَ رَقْمًا وَأَنْمَاطًا مُظَاهَرَةً　　　　k وَكِلَّةً بِعَتِيقٍ l الْعَقْلِ مَقْرُومَةْ

١٠ الرَّقْمُ مَا كَانَ مِنَ الْوَشْىِ مُسْتَدِيرًا. وَالْعَقْلُ مَا كَانَ مُسْتَطِيلًا. (84b) مَقْرُومَةٌ قُرِمَتِ الْمَقْرَمَةْ ☙

---

a) LA VIII, 52[14] reads : وَلَنَا دَارٌ وَرِثْنَاهَا عَنِ الْأَقْدَمِ الْقُدْمُوسِ مِنْ عَمٍّ وَخَالِ: Mukht. as text,
except مِنْ for عَنْ.

b) MS الْمُورِثُوهَا; Mukht. and Khiz. as text; Naṣr. الْمُورِثُونَ.

c) Mukht. فِيهِ.　　　　*d*) Khiz. لِلْخَيلِ تَعدو (sic) الْمُفرِدَاتِ.

e) MS نردى.

f) Words taken from LA II, 158[23] in place of the very corrupt reading of the MS.

g) MS محمد!!

h) LA XIV. 242[3], as text, with وَمُوفِ for مُوفٍ بِالْحِبَالِ). Khiz. داب for وَمُوفِى (أراد ومنهم مُوفٍ بِالْحِبَالِ) وَمُوفٍ. ذات, and ومروى for مُوفِى. دَأْبَ " scheint mir besser. مُوفٍ (wofür مُوفٍ nicht angeht, da ein Plural nöthig) sieht mir auch nach Grammatiker-Künstelei aus". (Nöldeke.) — Mukht. omits the verse.

XXI. Mukht. pp. 96—7. Naṣr. 614—15 has vv. 1, 3, 4; Agh. XIX, 90 vv. 1 and 5. —
Metre *Basīṭ*.

i) MS باد　　　　*j*) MS عالمن.　　　　*k*) Mukht. وَكَلَّلَ.

l) MS النعل مرقومه, but correctly in scholion.

٣   *a* لِلْعَبْقَرِيِّ عَلَيْهَا إِذْ غَدَوْا صَبَحٌ   كَأَنَّهَا مِنْ نَجِيعِ الجَوْفِ مَدْمُومَهْ

[العَبْقَرِيُّ] ضَرْبٌ مِن الثِّياب ويقال مِن الوَشْىِ. والصَّبَحُ بَياضٌ وحُمْرَةٌ: ومنه رَجُلٌ أَصْبَحُ. *b* والنَّجِيعُ الدَّم

الطَّرِىُّ: ويقال الدِّمامُ لِلطِّيب الذى تجعله النساء على رُوؤسِهِنّ: وكُلُّ شىءٍ مَلَسْتَهُ فهو مَدْمُوم ☿

٤   كَأَنَّ *c* أَظْعانَهُمْ نَخْلٌ مُوَسَّقَةٌ   سُودٌ ذَوَائِبُها بالحَمْلِ *d* مَكْمُومَهْ

أَظْعانَهُمْ أَجْمالُهم عليها النساء. والنَّخْلُ المُوَسَّقَة [سُودٌ]: خُضْرَتُها مِن الرِّىِّ. والكِمام يعنى سَعَفُها *e* مستورٌ

مِن شِدّةِ ما غُطِّيَت به ☿

٥   فِيهِنَّ *f* هِنْدٌ الَّتِى هامَ الفُؤادُ بها   بَيْضاءُ آنِسَةٌ بالحُسْنِ مَوْسُومَهْ

٦   *g* وَإِنَّها كَمَهاةِ الجَوِّ ناعِمَةٌ   تُدْنِى النَّصِيف بِكَفٍّ غَيْرِ مَوْشُومَهْ

٧   كَأَنَّ رِيقَتَها بَعْدَ الكَرَى اغْتَبَقَتْ   صَهْباءَ صافِيَةً بالمِسْكِ *h* مَخْتُومَهْ

٨   مِمَّا يُغالِى بِها البَيّاعُ عَتَّقَها   ذُو شارِبٍ أَصْهَبٍ يُغْلَى بِها *i* السِّيمَهْ

٩   يا مَنْ لِبَرْقٍ أَبِيتُ اللَّيْلَ أَرْقُبُهُ *j*   فِى مُكْفَهِرٍّ وَفِى سَوْداءَ مَرْكُومَهْ

المُكْفَهِرّ السحاب المتراكب بعضها على بعضٍ فى سَحابٍ كثيرةِ الظُّلْمَة. والمركومة التى تَراكَمَت ظُلْمَتُها

بَعْضُها على بَعْضٍ ☿

---

a) Mukht. Naṣr. مِثْلُ عَبْقَرِىٍّ. LA VI, 207٢٠: عَبْقَرٌ موضعٌ بالبادية كثيرُ الجنّ. Mukht. scholion:
كُلُّ شىءٍ كَرُمَ فهو عبقرى: وأراد رقمًا عَبْقَرِيًّا: ورجلٌ عَبْقَرِىٌّ اى كريم ☿

b) MS والجمع.

c) Mukht. ظُعَنَهُمْ. Naṣr.'s text conflates vv. 4 and 5, and has بالحُسْنِ موسومةٌ at end.

d) MS carelessly repeats مَدْمُومَهْ from preceding verse: but the commentary indicates the
correct reading.

e) MS مَكْمومة مُعَطَّلات مَخافَةَ الجَراد والطَّيْر. Schol. of Mukht: نُسِرَ من سده ما عطيب به.

f) Mukht., Agh. هِنْدٌ وَقَدْ هامَ.

g) Mukht. تُدْنِى النَّصِيف فتستر. Schol. of Mukht. مَكْمورة امرأة منكوحة (LA مَكْمورة تُدْنِى النَّصِيف كَمَهاةٍ
جمالها للعقة. وقوله بِكَفٍّ غيرِ مَوْشُومه انّما تَشِمُ الأَكَفَّ البَغايا ☿

h) "Hat Muḥammad خِتامُهُ مِسْكٌ, Sūr. 83,26, aus Stellen wie dieser, oder hat ein Späterer
die Qurʾānstelle hier benutzt?" (Nöldeke).

i) Schol. of Mukht. السِّيمَة الاسم (sic) من سام يَسُوم سَوْمًا وسِيمَةً: والبَيّاع الَّذين يَشْتَرُون والذين
البَيّاع; Mukht. therefore read البُيّاع, though the print has البَيّاع; Prof. Nöldeke prefers يَبِيعون ايضا
with يُغالِى: "sells at a high price."   *j*) MS نراحمت, where it is evident that ح has been
miscopied for ك; see No. XII v. 22, and XIX, 14, *ante*.

١۰   فَبَرَقْتُهَا حَرِقٌ وَمَاؤُهَا دَفِقٌ   وَتَحْتَهَا رَيِّقٌ وَّفَوْقَهَا دِيمَهْ

حَرِقٌ سَرِيعٌ. وَالدَّفِقُ السَّائِلُ. وَالرَّيِّقُ الكَدَرُ: وَيُقَالُ الرَّيِّقُ أَوَّلُ المَطَرِ: وَالدِّيمَةُ المَطَرُ الدَّائِمُ اليَوْمَ

وَاللَّيْلَةَ أَوِ اليَوْمَيْنِ وَاللَّيْلَتَيْنِ أَوِ الثَّلَاثَةَ ☙

١١   فَذَلِكَ المَاءُ لَوْ أَنِّى شَرِبْتُ بِهِ   إِذًا شَفَى كَبِدًا a شَكَّاءَ مَكْلُومَهْ

٥   ١٢   هَذَا b وَدَاوِيَّةٍ يَعْمَى الهُدَاةُ c بِهَا   نَاءٍ مَسَافَتُهَا كَالبُرْدِ دَيْمُومَهْ

الدَّاوِيَّةُ الصَّحْرَاءُ الوَاسِعَةُ. وَمِثْلُهَا الدَّيْمُومَةُ [وَجَمْعُهَا] d الدَّيَامِيم. يَعْمَى وَيَعْيَى وَاحِدٌ. الهُدَاةُ بِهَا يَقُولُ

يَعْمَى الهُدَاةُ لِطُرُقِهَا: وَالهُدَاةُ (85a) الأَدِلَّاءُ. وَالمَسَافَةُ مَا بَيْنَ الأَرْضَيْنِ: يُقَالُ كَمْ مَسَافَةُ مَا بَيْنَنَا وَبَيْنَ

الكُوفَةِ: فَيُقَالُ كَذَا وَكَذَا ☙

١٣   e جَاوَزْتُهَا بِعَلَنْدَاةٍ مُّذَكَّرَةٍ   [عَيْرَانَةٍ] f كَعَلَاةِ القَيْنِ g مَلْمُومَهْ

١۰   ١٤   [أَرْمِى بِهَا عُرْضَ الدَّوِّىِّ ضَامِرَةً   فِى سَاعَةٍ تَبْعَثُ الحِرْبَاءَ مَسْمُومَهْ] h

XXII.

١   بَانَ الخَلِيطُ الأُولَى شَاقُوكَ إِذْ شَحَطُوا   وَفِى الحُدُوجِ مَهًا أَعْنَاقُهَا عِيطُ

٢   i نَاطُوا الرِّعَاتَ لِمَهْوًى لَّوْ يَزِلُّ بِهِ   لَآنْدَقَّ دُونَ تَلَاقِى اللَّبَّةِ القُرْطُ

---

a) Mukht. شَكَّاءَ وَهِىَ الَّتِى شَكَّتْ أَىْ طَعَنَتْ فَانْتَظَمَهَا الطَّعْنُ (scholion: هَيْمَاءَ وَيُرْوَى).

b) Mukht. وَدَوِّيَّةٍ يَعْيَى الهُدَاةُ.   c) MS بِهِ.   d) MS وَهِىَ.

e) Mukht. reads the first hemist. thus: جَاوَزْتُ مَهْمَهَ يَهْمَاهَا بِعَيْهَمَةٍ.

f) Carelessly omitted in MS.

g) MS مملومه: Mukht. مَعْقُومَهْ,

h) This verse, wanting in the MS, has been added from Mukht.; for ضَامِرَةً we should perhaps
read هَاجِرَةً.

XXII. Metre Basīṭ. As photographic reproductions of the MS text of this and the two fol-
lowing poems are appended, it is not necessary to note every trifling variation in the text adopted.

Only two verses of this poem have so far been found cited elsewhere: v. 2 in the ʿUmdah
of Ibn Rashīq, I, 218, and v. 20 in LA IX, 168[13]; ʿAbīd is named in the first case: in the
second no poet's name is given.

i) The text in the ʿUmdah as printed is corrupt, reading مَاطُوا for نَاطُوا, and بِنَهْدٍ for لِمَهْوًى
(MS المهرى).

٣	هَلِ اللَّـيَـالِـي وَالْأَيَّـامُ رَاجِـعَـةٌ	أَيَّـامُ نَـدْمَـنُ وَسَلْمَى جِـيـرَةٌ خُـلُـطُ
٤	إِذْ كُلُّـنَـا رَاضٍ وَمَـقٌ بِـصَـاحِـبِـهِ	لَا يَبْتَغِى بَـدَلًا فَالْعَيْشُ مُغْتَـبِـطُ
٥	وَالـشَّمْـلُ مُجْتَمِعٌ فَـاعْتَـاقَـهُ قَـدَمٌ	وَالـدَّهْرُ مِنْـهُ عَلَى التَّخْيِيفِ وَالْـفُـرُطِ
٦	عَهْدِى بِهِمْ يَوْمَ جِزْعِ الْقَاعِ مِنْ رَمَقٍ	وَالـصَّفْحُ قَـدْ زَالَ بِالْأَحْـدَاجِ وَالْغِبْطِ
٧	وَالْعِيسُ مُـدْبِـرَةٌ تَـهْـوِى بِـأَرْكِبِها	كَأَنَّـهُنَّ نَـعَـامٌ نُـفْـرٌ مُـعَـطُ
٨	a فَـوَرَدَتْ مَـاءَ جِـزْعٍ عَـنْ شَمَائِلِهَا	فِى سَبْسَبٍ مُقْـفِرٍ b حُمْرٌ بِـهِ اللَّغَطُ
٩	تَـرَى لَهُنَّ عَـزِيـفًـا فِى مَـوَاثِـبِـهِ	إِذَا هُـمُ لَـبِـثُـوا لِلْـمَـاءِ وَآفْـتَـرَطُوا
١٠	وَتُصْبِحُ الْجُونُ حَسْرَى فِى مَنَـاهِلِهَا	وَالْكُدْرُ قَـدْ قَصَرَتْ عَـنْ وِرْدِهَا الْوُقَطُ
١١	وَعَـنْ أَيَامِنِهَا c الْأَطْـوَاءُ مُصْعِدَةٌ	قَـدْ شَارَفُـوا فَـرَحَ الْأَوْتَـادِ أَوْ وَسَطُوا
١٢	d رَوْضُ الْقَطَا مِنْ جَنُوبِ السِّدْرِ مِنْ خِيَمٍ	فَالْمُخْتَبِى فَـأَجَازُوا الـدَّوَّ أَوْ هَبَطُوا
١٣	يَجْتَابُ مَهْمَهَةً يَهْمَاءَ صَـمْـلَـقَـةً	e سَكَنُ الْخَلَائِقِ حَادِى الْأُدْمِ مُقْتَسِطُ
١٤	مُشَمِّـرٌ خَـلَـقٌ سِرْبَالُـهُ مَشِقٌ	قَـاذُورَةٌ f فَـائِـلٌ مُـغْـذَمِـرٌ قَـطَطُ

---

a) The first word is very doubtful: the sense seems to require فَاعْتَمَدَتْ or some such word: possibly we may read فَأَدْرَكَتْ.

b) حَمُرٌ is clear in the MS, yet hardly seems an appropriate word. The vocalisation of اللغط is uncertain; Ru'bah (LA IX, 244² and 268⁵) calls the sandgrouse اللُّغَط, pl. of لاغط; a singular لَغُوط, pl. لُغَط, is not cited, but may have existed.

c) This place is mentioned in Yāq. I, 312, "a water of 'Amr b. Kilāb in a mountain called الشَّرَاء (see Yāq. II, 267)". Note the س for ص in مسعدة for مصعدة. فرح الأوتان, "the joy of the tent-pegs," as an expression for a halt after a long journey, seems rather improbable, though the MS is clear.

d) Many places in Arabia bore the name of رَوْض الْقَطَا or رَوْضَة الْقَطَا; see Yāq. II, 856: one of them (*l.c.* line 12) was in the territory of Asad. Khiyam is mentioned Yāq. II 510; it was a part of the mountain called 'Amāyah, opposite Mount Yadhbul (Asad country). The reading الْمُخْتَبِى is unsatisfactory in view of the MS, الجما: this place is named Yāq. III, 908²: or we may suppose the name to be the الْمَجَنِّبى of Bakrī 507¹⁷.

e) سَكَنٌ may perhaps stand for سَكَّنٌ; see Lane *s. v.* حادى الأدم مقتسط is a somewhat violent conjecture, but appears to agree well with the context.

f) The transposition of فَائِلٌ and مُغْذَمِرٌ is necessary to preserve the metre; for مُغْذَمِرٌ see Labīd Mu'all. 79. فَائِلٌ = "morose". No such root as قطط exists, and clearly the scribe has accidentally omitted the *markaz* of the first ط: for قَطَطٌ see LA IX, 255²¹.

بَعْدَ ٱلْهَجِيرِ بِإِرْقَالٍ وَّيَبْتَبِيطِ	١٥	يُكَلِّفُ ٱلْغَوْلَ مِنْهَا كُلَّ نَاجِيَةٍ
إِنْسَانُهَا غَرِقٌ فِى مَاءِهَا مَغْطِ	١٩	فَظَلَّتْ أَتْبِعُهُمْ عَيْنًا عَلَى طَرَبٍ
وَكُلُّ ذِى عُمُرٍ يَّوْمًا a سَيَخْتَنِطِ	١٧	وَكُلُّ مُجْتَمِعٍ لَّا بُدَّ مُفْتَرِقِ
مَّا لِلنَّدَى عَنْهُمْ نَزْحٌ وَّلَا شَطَطِ	١٨	b وَفِتْنَةٍ كَلُيُوثِ ٱلْغَابِ مِنْ أَسَدٍ
وَتَفْزَعُ ٱلْأَرْضُ مِنْهُمْ إِذْ هُمُ سَخِطُوا	١٩	بِيضٌ بَهَالِيلُ c يَنْفِى ٱلْجَهْلَ حِلْمُهُمُ
مَا يَشْتَهُونَ وَلَا يُثْنَوْنَ إِنْ خَمِطُوا	٢٠	d (85b) إِذَا تَخَمَّطَ جَبَّارٌ تَنَوَّهَ إِلَى
إِذَا تَشَابَهَتِ ٱلْأَهْوَاءُ وَٱلشُّرُطِ	٢١	وَٱلْفَارِجُو ٱلْكَرْبِ وَٱلْغُمَّى بِرَأْيِهِمِ
وَمَا لِقَوْلِهِمُ خُلْفٌ وَّلَا مَيَطِ	٢٢	وَٱلْقَائِلُو ٱلْفَصْلِ لَا e تَنْآدُ طِينَتُهُمْ
وَأَكْرَمُ ٱلنَّاسِ مَطْرُوقًا إِذَا ٱخْتَبَطُوا	٢٣	وَٱلْخَالِطُو مُعْسِرٍ مِّنْهُمْ بِمُوسِرِهِمْ
إِذَا أَضَاعَ مِنَ ٱلْمِيثَاقِ مُشْتَرِطِ	٢٤	مُرُّو ٱللِّقَاءِ وَمُبْقُو ٱلْعَقْدِ إِنْ عَقَدُوا
وَفِيهِمُ ٱلزَّغْفُ وَٱلْخَطِّىُّ وَٱلرُّبُطِ	٢٥	رُجْحٌ إِذَا حَضَرَ ٱلنَّادِى حُلُومُهُمُ
يَوْمَ ٱللِّقَاءِ وَأَيْدٍ بِٱلنَّدَى f سَبِطِ	٢٩	وَٱلْمَشْرَفِيَّةُ مَفْلُولٌ ضَوَارِبُهَا
إِذَا رَأَى ذَاكَ مِنْهُمْ مَعْشَرٌ فُرُطِ	٢٧	g لَا يَحْسَبُونَ غِنًى يَّبْقَى وَلَا عَدَمَا

---

a) This is suggestion of Prof. Nöldeke's: the word might be سَيَخْتَبِطِ, but that this verb comes lower down, in v. 23, in a different sense.

b) If we read وَفِتْنَةٌ, with the وَاو رُبّ, we must suppose some verse containing the apodosis to have dropped out.

c) MS يسعى: perhaps we may read يُشْغَى, "opposes, disagrees with".

d) So LA IX, 168[13].

e) MS بعناد: it may be supposed that the reader dictated يَنْآد as if it were spelt تَنْعَاد; *hamzah* is often strengthened into ع in giving the measure of words containing it; *cf.* scholion to XIX, 11, 12, and XX, 5, *ante.* "«Vielleicht يَنْقَاد, 'lässt sich nicht gängeln'»" (Nöldeke).

f) The masc. form of the adjective, with أَيْدٍ, a plural of a feminine singular, is irregular, though not without parallel; (رَيْذٍ يَدَاءَ in ʿAntarah, Muʿall. 54 is not strictly analogous, as the adjective precedes). If we could assume a plural سُبْطِ the irregularity would be cured: but no singular سَبُوطِ is known to the Lexx.

g) *Cf.* Nābighah I, 28.

XXIII.

١ a أَرِقْتُ لِضَوْءِ بَرْقٍ فِي نَشَاصِ   تَلَأْلَأَ فِي مُمَلَّأَةٍ غِصَاصِ

٢ لَوَاقِحَ دُلَّحٍ بِالْمَاءِ سُحْمٍ   b تَثِجُّ الْمَاءَ مِنْ خَلَلِ الْخَصَاصِ

٣ سَحَابٍ ذَاتِ أَسْحَمَ مُكْفَهِرٍّ   تُوَحِّى الْأَرْضَ قَطْرًا ذَا افْتِحَاصِ

٤ تَأَلَّفَ فَاسْتَوَى طَبَقًا دُكَاكًا   مُحِيلًا دُونَ c مَثْقَبِهِ نَوَاصِ

٥ كَلَيْلٍ مُظْلِمٍ الْحَجَرَاتِ دَاجٍ   بَهِيمٍ أَوْ كَبَحْرٍ ذِى بَوَاصِ

٦ كَأَنَّ تَبَسُّمَ الْأَنْوَاءِ فِيهِ   إِذَا مَا انْكَلَّ عَنْ لَهَقٍ d هُصَاصِ

٧ وَلَاحَ بِهَا تَبَسُّمُ وَاضِحَاتٍ   يُزَيِّنُ صَفَائِحَ الْحُورِ e الْقِلَاصِ

٨ f أَسَلِ الشُّعَرَاءَ هَلْ سَبَحُوا كَسَبْحِى   بُحُورَ الشِّعْرِ أَوْ غَاصُوا مَغَاصِى

٩ لِسَانِى g بِالْقَرِيضِ وَبِالْقَوَافِى   h وَبِالْأَشْعَارِ أَمْهَرُ فِى الْغَوَّاصِ

١٠ مِنَ الْحُوتِ الَّذِى فِى لُجِّ بَحْرٍ   i يُجِيدُ السَّبْحَ فِى j اللُّجَجِ الْقُمَاصِ

١١ إِذَا مَا بَاصَ لَاحَ بِصَفْحَتَيْهِ   وَبَيَّضَ فِى الْمَكَرِّ وَفِى الْمَحَاصِ

١٣ تُلَاوِصُ فِى الْمَدَاصِ مُلَاوِصَاتٍ   لَهُ مَلَصَى دَوَاجِنَ بِالْمِلَاصِ

XXIII. Metre *Wafir.* Of this poem LA has vv. 1, 2 and 8 (VIII 365[20-22]), and Jāḥiḍh, *Bayān* I, 73—4, cites vv. 1, 2, 8—10 and 17, both anonymously; v. 13 occurs (with ʿAbīd's name) in *Asās* I, 190[2], and evidently belongs to the poem.

a) So LA and Jāḥ.   b) LA and Jāḥ. تَمُجُّ الْغَيْثَ.

c) MS مُثَقَّفَ نواص: right reading and meaning obscure.

d) Not found elsewhere: but هَصِيصٌ is used for the flashing or flickering of fire = تَلَأْلُوْ, بَرِيقٌ.

e) قِلَاص is here perhaps the plural of قُلُصٌ in the sense of young girls (Lane 2560a).

f) LA and Jāḥ. read بُحُورَ الْقَوْلِ and الْخُطَبَاءَ.

g) Jāḥ. بِالنَّثْرِ.   h) Jāḥ. وَبِالْأَسْجَاعِ.

i) Jāḥ. يُجِيدُ الْغَوْصَ.

j) Jāḥ. لُجَجِ الْمَغَاصِ: the latter word seems unlikely after مَغَاصِى two verses before. The MS reads الْعَمَّاصِ, which makes no sense; the verb قَمَصَ is used of the restless waves of the sea, and seems appropriate here: this particular form does not occur except as a *maṣdar*, but as such it may be used adjectivally.

إِذَا أَخْرَجْتَهُنَّ مِنَ الْمَدَاصِ]	١٣ ‪a‬ [بَنَاتُ الْمَاءِ لَيْسَ لَهَا حَيَاةٌ
تَنَاعَصَ تَحْتَهَا أَيَّ انْتِعَاصِ	١٤ إِذَا قَبَضَتْ عَلَيْهِ الْكَفُّ حِينًا
وَحُوتُ الْبَحْرِ أَسْوَدُ أَوْ مِلَاصِ	١٥ ‪b‬ وَبَاصٍ وَلَاصٍ مِنْ مَّلَصٍ مَّلَّاصِ
نُسِجْنَ تَلَاحُمَ السَّرْدِ الدِّلَاصِ	١٦ (86a) كَلَوْنِ الْمَاءِ أَسْوَدُ ذُو قُشُورِ
وَأَسْتُرُ بِالتَّكَرُّمِ مِنْ خَصَاصِ	١٧ ‪c‬ لَعَمْرُكَ إِنَّنِي لَأَعِفُّ نَفْسِى	5
وَأَكْرَهُ أَنْ أُعَدَّ مِنَ الْحِرَاصِ	١٨ وَأَكْرُمُ وَالِدِى وَأَصُونُ عِرْضِى
سَؤُولًا لِلْمُطَاعِ وَذَا ‪d‬ عِقَاصِ	١٩ إِذَا مَا كُنْتَ لَحَّاسًا بَخِيلًا
وَعِنْدَ الْبَابِ أَثْقَلَ مِنْ رَصَاصِ	٢٠ لِزَادِ الْمَرْءِ ‪e‬ آبَصَ مِنْ عُقَابِ
وَهَلْ لِلْبَابِ مِنْ ذَا مِنْ خَلَاصِ	٢١ بَكَى الْبَوَّابُ مِنْكَ وَقَالَ هَلْ لِي	10
عَدَاوَةَ مَنْ يُّلَاطِمُ أَوْ يُنَاصِى	٢٢ فَيُوشِكَ أَنْ يَّرَاكَ لَهُ عَدُوًّا
فَأَيْنَ مِنَ [أَنْ] أُسَبَّ بِهِ مَنَاصِى	٢٣ إِذَا مَا كَانَ عِرْضِى عِنْدَ بَطْنِى
فَدَقَّ اللَّهُ ‪f‬ رِجْلِى بِالْمَعَاصِ	٢٤ فَإِنْ خَفَّتْ لِجُوعِ الْبَطْنِ رِجْلِى

XXIV.

١ يَا صَاحِ مَهْلًا أَقِلِّ الْعَذْلَ يَا صَاحِ   وَلَا تَكُونَنَّ لِى بِاللَّائِمِ اللَّاحِى

---

a) Inserted from *Asâs, l. c.*; this seems to be its appropriate place.

b) The exact force of the three words from the root ملص in this v. is obscure, and the alliteration is unlike the ancient style.

c) "Das rectionslose أَسْتُرُ ist mir bedenklich — oder darf man übersetzen: 'und schütze (Andere) durch Hochherzigkeit vor Armuth'? das ist wohl das Richtige" (Nöldeke).

d) عِقَاص here seems to be a verbal noun from عَقَصَ "he was niggardly or close-handed".

e) آبَصُ is أَفْعَل of أَبِصَ, "nimble, agile".

f) This form does not appear to be recorded in the Lexx.; but فُعَال is the regular formation for maladies, and مَعِصَ is used in the sense of having a pain or weakness in the legs from too much walking.

XXIV. Metre *Basît*. So far no citation from this poem has been found elsewhere; but in its metre, in some of its phrases, and especially in its rhymes, it has many points of contact with No. XXVIII, which is also attributed to Aus b. Ḥajar, as well as with the verses, not contained in that poem, in Aus Dîw. No. IV.; vv. 11—14 are evidently closely allied to the vv. 2—4 with which Aus's poem opens.

٢ حَلَفْتُ بِاللَّهِ إِنَّ اللَّهَ ذُو نِعَمِ   لِّمَنْ يَشَاءُ وَذُو عَفْوٍ وَتَصْفَاحِ

٣ مَا الطَّرْفُ مِنِّى إِلَى مَا لَسْتُ أَمْلِكُهُ   مِمَّا بَدَا لِى بِبَاغِى اللَّحْظِ طَمَّاحِ

٤ a وَلَا أُجَالِسُ صُبَّاحًا أُحَادِثُهُ   حَدِيثَ لَغْوٍ فَمَا جِدِّى بِضَبَّاحِ

٥ إِذَا اتَّكَوْا فَأَدَارَتْهَا أَكُفُّهُمُ   صِرْفًا تُدَارُ b بِأَكْوَاسٍ وَأَقْدَاحِ

٦ إِنِّى لَأَخْشَى الْجَهُولَ الشَّكْسَ شِيمَتَهُ   وَأَتَّقِى ذَا التُّقَى وَالْحِلْمَ بِالرَّاحِ

٧ وَلَا يُفَارِقُنِى مَا عِشْتُ ذُو حَقَبٍ   c نَهْدُ الْقَذَالِ جَوَادٌ غَيْرُ مِلْوَاحِ

٨ أَوْ مُهْرَةٍ مِّنْ عِتَاقِ الْخَيْلِ سَابِحَةٍ   كَأَنَّهَا سَحْقُ بُرْدٍ بَيْنَ أَرْمَاحِ

٩ وَمَهْمَهٍ مُّقْفِرِ الْأَعْلَامِ مُنْجَرِدٍ   نَائِى الْمَنَاهِلِ جَدْبِ الْقَاعِ d مِنْزَاحِ

١٠ أَجَزْتُهُ بِعَلَنْدَاةٍ مُذَكَّرَةٍ   كَالْعَيْرِ مَوَّارَةِ الضَّبْعَيْنِ مِمْرَاحِ

١١ e وَقَدْ تَبَطَّنْتُ مِثْلَ الرِّئْمِ آنِسَةً   رُؤْدَ الشَّبَابِ كَعَابًا ذَاتَ أَوْضَاحِ

١٢ تُدْفِى الضَّجِيعَ إِذَا يَشْتُو وَتُخْصِرُهُ   فِى الصَّيْفِ حِينَ يَطِيبُ الْبَرْدُ لِلصَّاحِ

١٣ (86b) f تَخَالُ رِيقَ ثَنَايَاهَا إِذَا ابْتَسَمَتْ   وَكِمْزِجِ شَهْدٍ بِأُتْرُجٍّ وَتُفَّاحِ g

١٤ كَأَنَّ سُنَّتَهَا فِى كُلِّ دَاجِيَةٍ   حِينَ الظَّلَامُ بَهِيمٌ ضَوْءُ مِصْبَاحِ

١٥ إِنِّى وَجَدِّكَ لَوْ أَصْلَحْتُ مَا بِيَدِى   لَمْ يَحْمَدِ النَّاسُ بَعْدَ الْمَوْتِ إِصْلَاحِى

١٦ أَشْرِى التِّلَادَ بِحَمْدِ الْجَارِ أَبْذِلُهُ   حَتَّى أَصِيرَ رَمِيمًا تَحْتَ الْوَاحِ

١٧ بَعْدَ h انْتِقَالٍ إِذَا وُسِّدْتُ حَثْحَثَةً   فِى قَعْرِ مُظْلِمَةِ الْأَرْجَاءِ مِكْلَاحِ

١٨ أَوْ صِرْتُ i ذَا بُومَةٍ فِى رَأْسِ رَابِيَةٍ   أَوْ فِى قَرَارٍ مِّنَ الْأَرْضِينَ قِرْوَاحِ

---

a) This seems to be an allusion to a vice not known to have been prevalent in Arabia in the Days of the Ignorance.

b) This form (which is quite clear in the MS) is not known from any example in classical Arabic, though it appears in Dozy Suppl. II, 435 as a post-classical form. بَأْكُوسٍ, an allowable form, would satisfy the metre.

c) A conjecture of Mr. Krenkow's for the unmeaning words of the MS: نهد المراكل is the more usual phrase.

d) A conjecture for the مِنْسَاح of the original, which makes no sense.   *e*) *Cf.* Aus IV, 2.

f) MS حَال, which may also stand for كَأَنَّ.

g) كِمْزِج is a not altogether satisfactory conjecture (for the ك is superfluous) for the reading of the MS, apparently كسع; it would perhaps be better to read boldly مِزَاجٌ (or مِزَاجَ if كَأَنَّ is adopted). For the verse *cf.* Aus IV 3—4.

h) Word uncertain.   *i*) MS apparently ذو.

١٩ كَمْ مِّنْ فَتًى مِّثْلِ غُصْنِ الْبَانِ فِي كَرَمٍ   مَّحْضِ الضَّرِيبَةِ صَلْتِ الْخَدِّ وَضَّاحِ

٢٠ فَارَقْتُـهُ غَيْـرَ قَـالٍ لِّي وَلَسْتُ لَـهُ   بِالْقَالِ أَصْبَحَ فِي مَلْحُودَةٍ نَّاحِى

٢١ هَلْ نَحْنُ إِلَّا كَأَجْسَادٍ تَمُرُّ بِـهَا   تَحْـتَ الـتُّـرَابِ وَأَرْوَاحٍ كَأَرْوَاحِ

تَمَّ شِعْرُ عُبَيْدِ بن الأَبْرَصِ بِحَمْدِ الله وَعَوْنِهِ

وَصَلَّى الله على مُحَمَّدٍ وَآلِهِ وَسَلَّم

5

---

a) So MS: there are other examples of the shortening of the final ى in verse; or we might read بِقَالِ أَصْبَحَ with *waṣl*.

b) This seems the most probable conjecture for the ساح of the MS: *cf.* the use of نَحَا for burial in Ḥam. 477, line 7 from foot: نَحَاهُ لِلَحْدٍ زِبْرِقَانُ وَحَارِثُ. (The verb in this phrase is transitive, but نَحَا may also be used intransitively, in the sense of اِنْتَحَى.)

إذا أخصبتم فأرسلوا الرسول وما تستهووا وكا يسمون جميط
والعار حوز الطرب والعماء وان سرخ أن أصابت بلاء ما وللمس ط
والعاملوا الفصل القط ن عاد طبيعتهم وما العول ملحق وكاظهـ
وللناطقوا محشر مس بموسر هم واكرم الفادن سكر وماك الحسط
مرو اللعا وسع والمعدا ن عفروا إحد اضاع موا لبسا وميط ـف
دع إذا أخصر الماد ي حلو مهم وبهم الرعف ولتخ ولا وله
اكسر فد سعلوا صوار عها انوم اللقاء واد بالندى لـ
لتسون عامعا وهم ما اذا انى ي انتسيهم مسهر هـ
وهاك سبد ير لا حسى

ارفت لصو رو ي لشاص زافه سلام عـ
القاع ح ج دلنا سر مع القا ومن جلل الـ
ما ن اسر حكنهم روح لار فوكط الخلاص
للعه ما سرى طمعاد هاها عا لاد ون نعفه
خا ل مطلبـ لخران دا ج غبر او كر دير
ان نصر الاودا هنه اذا لماكله سكو ن هـ
عمـ جنا محشر واعلا رب صمائ المو ا الـ
سلل العمـ اد هر لتصوا كنب سور الشر غاصوا
لسار لمحرف الملوه والسهاد بهير ا العـ
سلحوا بالحد ه ي جكيم السخ ي فالي العـ

اذا ماد اهـ كلا مصلـصعو وبصـ ف الكر وغاصـ
بلا وص ن الش دامر ملا وماد له ملط دوانـ بالـ
اذا فبضت علي الكف حت نتلاعـ لنها بالانتطـ
وبامرو ه مر ملص و ضون الجرا سود وملا

علىٰ الشوك ... وفشو ... لاحم السرحان ...

لعزّ لديٰ لمعف ...بالنعم من ...

واكرم والدين ... فاصون حره واكده إذ لعبد من ...

اذ لما كنت كماصا ... بلا سوىٰ للمطاع ...

رياد السرايم من عقاب وعند الباب انفس من ...

نحاالسواب منا ... وهلك من ...

فنفوس دان ... له عزوك لغزاة من ...

اذا ما كان حرصه عند يبط وابن من ...

فارغبت لجوع البطن ... وله طا باسع

وما العسد برىٰ لا نوص ...

يا حاج منفذًا اقل الغزاة يا حاج وكذ ... يا الدرا الاخ

جلفت بالله ان الله ... ونصر من ... ومغو وتضاح

ظالطلو ف حجة إلى بالسك املكه ... الا ساع الحفظ

واجالس صلاحا الخادمه ... حرز العو ... فملحرى ...

اذا التكو ... فاداريها اكلم ... صرفًا راكنوا ...

اني لاحب الجهول الشكس شيمته ... واليه ... نا والحلو بالح

ولا زلت في ملشد ... وهقب بعد ... النهلمل جوا صفو ولوح

او صفره منهنا ولتغنيل ملحة كانها ... يود برارة

ومحبه مقفر الاعلام بمجرد ... الشامل لحرب القلع يسناح

لحرنه ... علند لا مذكرة كالعصر ... والصعبين ملا ح

وقد ... بنا الا ير السه ... و ... الشباب كعا ... اوط

نزيه الجيم إذا يشنواو تخصر ... في السنه ... زيه ...

APPENDIX

ODES ATTRIBUTED TO ʿABĪD IN THE *MUKHTĀRĀT* OF HIBAT-ALLĀH,
THE *AGHĀNĪ*, AND ELSEWHERE. *

XXV.

١ طَافَ الْخَيَالُ عَلَيْنَا لَيْلَةَ الْوَادِى *a* لِآلِ أَسْمَاءَ لَمْ يُلْمِمْ *b* لِمِيعَادِ

اى الْتَقَيْنَا على غَيرِ ميعاد ۞

٢ أَنَّى اهْتَدَيْتِ *c* لِرَكْبٍ طَالَ *d* سَيْرُهُمُ   فِى سَبْسَبٍ بَيْنَ دَكْدَاكٍ وَأَعْقَادِ

وبروى: طَالَ لَيْلُهُمْ. والسَّبْسَب ما اسْتَوَى من الارض. والدَّكْدَاك السُّهُولَة. والأَعْقَاد رِمالٌ مُنْتَراكِمَة

واحِدُها عَقْدٌ ۞

5

---

*) In our MS there is a *lacuna*, as indicated in the text, between Odes X and XI, which covers at least one leaf, and probably more; and it is likely that some of the poems contained in this Appendix, if not all, may originally have formed part of the *Dīwān*. There is good authority for attributing most of them to ʿAbīd, and some are celebrated.

XXV. Metre *Basīṭ*. This poem is printed as contained in the *Mukhtārāt*, pp. 99—100; the scholia are those of Hibatallāh. In the Khiz., IV, 500—1, another version is given, consisting of vv. 1—3, 10, 11, 7, an additional verse, 9, and a final verse; and it is said that the poem occurs in the *Aṣmaʿīyāt*. It is not, however, in that collection as printed by Ahlwardt from the Vienna MS, nor in Mr. Krenkow's MS of Selections from the *Mufaḍḍalīyāt* and *Aṣmaʿīyāt*. Agh. XIX, 89, has vv. 1, 2, 10, 4, 7, 8, 9, and the final v. of Khiz., and on the same page a variant of v. 7 is given separately. Naṣr. 597 has the same vv. as Agh. The *Sharḥ Shawāhid al-Mughnī*, p. 169, has vv. 1—3, 4, addl. v. of Khiz, 7, 10, 11, 12. The *Jamharah*, in Introduction p. 17, has vv. 1—4, 7, 8, and the poem is referred to as well-known and the work of ʿAbīd. Other vv. are cited elsewhere.

a) Khiz., SSM., مِنْ آلِ سَلْمَى وَلَمْ; Agh. (Naṣr.) مِنْ آلِ عَمْرٍو وَلَمْ; Jam. مِنْ آلِ.

b) Khiz., Jam. بِمِيعَادِ.

c) Jam. إِنَّى مَنْ، طَالَ نَيْلُهُمْ.   *d)* Khiz., SSM. نَيْلِهِمْ.

٣ ^a يُكَلِّفُونَ ^b سُرَاهَا كُلَّ يَعْمَلَةٍ   ^c مِثْلَ الْمَهَاةِ إِذَا مَا ^d اَحْتَتَّهَا الْحَادِى

البَعْمَلَة الْقَوِيَّة على العَمَل فى سيرها. والمهاة البقرة. ويروى ٭ يُكَلِّفُونَ فَلَاهَا كُلَّ نَاجِيَةٍ٭ مِثْلَ الْقَنِيقِ ۞

٤ أَبْـلِـغْ أَبَـا كَرِبٍ عَنِّى ^e وَأُسْرَتَـهُ   قَوْلًا سَيَذْهَبُ غَوْرًا بَعْدَ إِنْجَادِ

ابو كَرِب عمرو بن الحارث بن عمرو بن حُجْرٍ آكِل المُرار. والغَوْر ما تَطامَنَ من الارض والنَجْد ما ارتفع

٥ منها: اراد غَوْر تهامَةَ ونجْدَها: وأَنْجَد الرجل أَخَذَ الى نَجدٍ ۞

٥ ^f يَا عَمْرُو مَا رَاحَ مِنْ قَوْمٍ وَّلَا ابْتَكَرُوا   إِلَّا وَلِلْمَـوْتِ فِى آثَارِهِـمْ حَادِى

٦ فَاِنْ رَأَيْـتَ بِـوَادٍ حَيَّـةً ذَكَـرًا   فَامْضِ وَدَعْنِى أُمَارِسْ حَيَّةَ الْـوَادِى

٧ ^g لَأَعْرِفَنَّكَ بَعْدَ ^h الْمَوْتِ تَنْدُبُنِى   وَفِى حَيَاتِىَ مَا زَوَّدْتَنِى زَادِى

٨ ⁱ إِنَّ أَمَامَكَ يَوْمًا أَنْتَ مُدْرِكُهُ   لَا حَاضِرٌ مُفْلِتٌ مِنْهُ وَلَا بَادِى

٩ ١٠ فَانْظُرْ إِلَى رَفْيِ مُلْكٍ أَنْتَ تَارِكُهُ   هَـلْ تُرْسَـيَـنَّ أَوَاخِيـهِ بِأَوْتَـادِ

فِى مُلْكٍ ظِلِّ مُلْكٍ. وترْسِيَنَّ تُثْبَتَنَّ ۞

١٠ اذْهَبْ إِلَيْكَ فَإِنِّى مِـنْ بَنِى أَسَـدٍ   أَهْـلِ الْقِبَابِ وَأَهْـلِ ^k الْجُودِ وَالنَّادِى

اذْهَبْ إِلَيْكَ زَجْرٌ. اِنما ذكر النادِى لأنَّ لهم سادات يَجْتَمِعُون فيه: ولا للقَوم نادٍ إِلَّا ولهم سَيِّدٌ: وللجمع أَنْدِيَةٌ ۞

---

a) Khiz. يُطَوِّفُونَ الْفَلَا فِى كُلِّ هَاجِرَةٍ; SSM. *id.*, with يُكَلِّفُونَ.

b) Jam. فَلَاهَا.   *c*) Khiz. مِثْلَ الْقَنِيقِ إِذَا مَا حَتَّهُ; SSM. *id.*, with اَحْتَتَّها.

d) Jam. حَتَّهَا.   *e*) Khiz., Agh. وَإِخْوَتَهُ.

f) Vv. 5 and 6 are wanting in the other versions.

g) Mukht. and Khiz. have لَا أَعْرِفَنَّكَ; but BQut. 145[11], Agh., Jam., SSM all as text.

h) BQut., Khiz., Jam. بَعْدَ الْيَوْمِ.

i) Not in Khiz. or SSM.; Agh., Naṣr., as text; Jam. أَمَّا حِمَامَكَ. In place of v. 8 Khiz. and SSM have the following v.:

فَإِنْ حَيِيتُ فَلَا أَحْسِبْكَ فِى بَلَدِى   وَإِنْ مَرِضْتُ فَلَا أَحْسِبْكَ عَوَّادِى

In Ham. 637[6] this verse is quoted, with ʿAbīd's name, as follows:

فَإِنْ قُتِلْتُ فَلَا تَرْكَبْ لِتَثْأَرَ بِى   وَإِنْ مَرِضْتُ فَلَا تَحْسِبْكَ عَوَّادِى

j) Khiz., Agh. (Naṣr.) ظِلِّ مُلْكٍ.

k) Khiz. الْمَجْدِ; SSM, Jāḥiḍh *Ḥayawān* V, 143, الجُودِ; Howell, *Gram.* I, 669, التَّخَيُّلِ.

١١ a قَدْ أَتْرُكُ الْقِرْنَ مُصْفَرًّا أَنَامِلُهُ   كَأَنَّ أَثْوَابَهُ مُجَّتْ بِفِرْصَادِ

اراد كَأَنَّما مُجَّ عليها فِرْصادٌ لانها مُخْضَبَةٌ بالدماء. ومُصْفَرًّا أَنامِلُه: يقول طَعَنْتُهُ فَنَزَفَ حتى أَصْفَرَّ.

والفِرْصاد النَّوت وهو افصح من التَّوت ☙

١٢ b أَوْجَرْتُهُ وَنَوَاصِي الْخَيْلِ شَاحِبَةٌ   سَمْرَاءَ عَامِلُهَا مِنْ خَلْفِهِ بَادِى

العامل أَسْفَل من السِنان بذِراعٍ او شِبْرٍ حَيْثُ يُعْقَد اللِواءُ ☙

XXVI.

١ أَمِنْ رُسُومٍ نَأْيُهَا نَاحِلُ   وَمِنْ دِيَارٍ دَمْعُكَ الْهَامِلُ

٢ أَجَالَتِ الرِّيحُ بِهَا ذَيْلَهَا   عَامًا وَجَوْنٌ مُسْبِلٌ هَاطِلُ

أَجالَتْ جَرَّتْ. والجَوْنُ يعني السَّحاب. والمُسْبِل الدانى من الارض: يقال c أَسْبَلَ الحَرْبُ للمَطَرِ اذا لَزِم الأَرْضَ ☙

٣ ظَلْتُ بِهَا كَأَنَّنِى شَارِبٌ   صَهْبَاءَ مِمَّا عَتَّقَتْ بَابِلُ

ظَلْتُ مَكَثْتُ نَهَارِى ☙

٤ بَلْ مَا بُكَاءُ الشَّيْخِ فِى دِمْنَةٍ   وَقَدْ عَلَاهُ الْوَضَحُ الشَّامِلُ

الوَضَحُ الشَّيْبُ وكلُّ أَبْيَضَ وَضَحٌ ☙

٥ أَقْوَتْ مِنَ اللَّائِى هُمُ أَهْلُهَا   فَمَا بِهَا إِنْ ظَعَنُوا آمِلُ

---

a) Cited LA IV, 346⁴; first hemistich in Lane 2491a.

b) Wanting in Khiz.; SSM مُعْلَمَةٌ for شَاحِبَةٌ. The final verse in Khiz., Agh., Naṣr. is as follows:

الْتَخْيِيرُ يَبْقَى وَإِنْ طَالَ الزَّمَانُ بِهِ   وَالشَّرُّ أَخْبَثُ مَا أَوْعَيْتَ مِنْ زَادِ

This verse also occurs in Agh. XIX, 86, and Jam. Introd. 22, in connection with an apocryphal story about ᶜAbīd and a snake, related by Ibn al-Kalbī; it is quoted ᶜUmdah I, 191, and in many other places.

XXVI. Metre *Sarīᶜ*. Poem printed from Mukht. 94—96, whence the scholia are taken. Vv. 9—21 are in Naṣr., 604; vv. 9—13 in Yaᶜqūbī, History, I, 249; *Iqtiḍāb* (commy on BQut. *Adab al-Kuttāb*), p. 361, has vv. 16—18 and 21. The poem is intimately connected with Imra' al-Qais's poem No. 51 (Ahlw. p. 151), which is perhaps an answer to it.

c) I have not found this phrase in the Lexx.: perhaps there is some mistake.

أَقْوَتْ خَلَتْ ۞

٦ وَرُبَّـمَا حَلَّـتْ سُلَيْمَى بِهَا كَـأَنَّـهَا عُطْبُولَةٌ خَاذِلُ

الْعُطْبُولَةَ الظَّبْيَةَ الطَّوِيلَةَ الْعُنُقِ الْحَسَنَتُهَا. وَالْخَاذِلُ الَّتِى تَتَخَذَّلُ الظِّبَاء لَا تَرْعَى مَعَهَا وَتُقِيم عَلَى وَلَدِهَا ۞

٧ لَوْلَا تُسَلِّيكَ جُمَالِيَّةٌ أَدْمَاء دَامَ خُفُّهَا بَازِلُ

الْجُمَالِيَّةِ تُشْبِهُ الْجَمَلَ فِى عِظَمِ خَلْقِهَا. تُسَلِّيكَ تُنْسِيكَ هٰذَا اللَّهْوَ ۞

٨ حَرْفٌ كَأَنَّ الرَّحْلَ مِنْهَا عَلَى ذِى عَانَةٍ مُّرْتَبِعُ عَاقِلُ

الْحَرْفُ الضَّامِرَةُ مِنَ الْإِبِلِ. عَلَى ذِى عَانَةٍ اى عَلَى حِمَارٍ مَع قِطْعَةٍ مِنَ الْأُتُنِ. وَعَاقِلُ أَرْضٌ ۞

٩ a يَا أَيُّهَا السَّائِلُ عَنْ مَّجْدِنَا إِنَّكَ عَنْ مَسْعَاتِنَا جَاهِلُ

أَرَادَ بِمَسْعَاتِنَا فَأَدْخَلَ عَنْ مَكَانَ الْبَاء: وَمَسْعَاتُهُم فِعْلُهُم وَفَضْلُهُم ۞

١٠ b إِنْ كُنْتَ لَمْ تَأْتِكَ أَيَّامُنَا فَاسْأَلْ تُنَبَّأْ أَيُّهَا السَّائِلُ

١١ سَائِلْ بِنَا حُجْرًا c وَأَجْنَادَهُ d يَوْمَ تَوَلَّى جَمْعُهُ الْجَافِلُ

لِلْجَافِلِ الْهَارِب الْمَذْكُورِ ۞

١٢ يَوْمَ أَتَى e سَعْدًا عَلَى مَأْقِطٍ وَجَاوَلَتْ f مِنْ خَلْفِهِ كَاهِلُ

الْمَأْقِط وَالْمَأْزِق مَضِيق الْحَرْب. سَعد بن ثعلبة بن كاهل بن أسد بن خزيمة رَهْط الكُمَيْت ۞

١٣ فَأَوْرَدُوا g سِرْبًا لَّـهُ ذُبَّـلًا كَـأَنَّهُنَّ اللَّهْب الشَّاعِلُ

الذُّبَّل الْقَنَا الْيَابِس ۞

١٤ وَعَامِرًا أَنْ كَيْفَ يَعْلُوهُم إِنْ الْتَقَيْنَا h الْمُرْهَفُ i التَّـاهِلُ

---

a) Cited Yaᶜq. (l. c.) with second hemist. thus: إِنَّكِ مُسْتَغْبٍ بِنَا جَاهِلٌ; but the second and third words are editorial conjectures; the MS had مستغبنا (corruptly).

b) Yaᶜq. إِنْ كُنْتَ لَمْ تَسْمَعْ بِآبَائِنَا فَسَلْ الخ; Naṣr. إِنْ كُنْتَ لَمْ تَأْتِكَ أَنْبَاؤُنَا وَاسْأَلْ بِنَا يَا أَيُّهَا السَّائِلُ.

c) Yaᶜq., Naṣr. غَدَاةَ الْوَغَى.   d) Yaᶜq., Naṣr. الْحَافِلُ.

e) Yaᶜq., Naṣr. لَقُوا سَعْدًا.   f) Yaᶜq., Naṣr. وَحَاوَلَتْ.

g) Yaᶜq. سَرْبًا; for the metaphor cf. Zuhair, Muᶜall. 36.

h) Mukht. has إِنَا: "Ich vermuthe, dass hier إِذْ zu lesen, da es sich wahrscheinlich nur um *ein* Treffen handelt, dasselbe, das auch II, 19, VII, 10ff. und XVII, 10 gemeint ist" (Nöldeke).

i) Naṣr. النَّائِلُ.

الْمُرْهَفِ السيف المُحَدَّد. والناهِل العَطْشان ☙

١٥ *a* وَجَمْعَ غَسَّانَ ٱلقِيسَمَاهُمْ   بِجَحْفَلٍ قَسْطَلُهُ ذَائِلُ

القَسْطَل الغبار. والذائل الطويل الذَّيْل لا ينقطع ☙

١٦ قَوْمِى بَنُو دُودَانَ *b* أَهْلُ النُّهَى   يَوْمًا إِذَا أُلْقِحَتِ *c* الْحَائِلُ

الحَائِل التى أتى عليها حَوْلٌ ولم تَحْمِل وجمعها حُولٌ. وألْقِحَت الناقة اذا تَحْمِل ☙

١٧ كَمْ فِيهِمُ مِنْ سَيِّدٍ أَبْيَدٍ   ذِى نَفَحَاتٍ قَائِلٍ فَاعِلُ

١٨ مَنْ قَوْلُهُ قَوْلٌ وَمَنْ فِعْلُهُ   فِعْلٌ وَمَنْ نَائِلُهُ نَائِلُ

١٩ الْقَائِلِ الْقَوْلَ الَّذِى مِثْلُهُ *d*   يَنْبُتُ مِنْهُ الْبَلَدُ الْمَاحِلُ

٢٠ لَا يَحْرِمُ السَّائِلَ إِنْ جَاءَهُ *e*   وَلَا يُعَقِّى سَيْبَهُ الْعَاذِلُ

لا يُعَقِّى سَيْبَهُ لا يَحْبِسُه: يقال عَقّاه وٱعْتَقاه حبسه. ويروى يُعَقِّى يَمْحُو ☙

٢١ *f* وَالطَّاعِنُ الطَّعْنَةَ يَوْمَ الْوَغَى   يَذْهَلُ مِنْهَا الْبَطَلُ الْبَاسِلُ

XXVII.

١ لِمَنِ *g* الدَّارُ أَقْفَرَتْ *h* بِالْجِنَابِ   غَيْرَ نُؤْيٍ وَدِمْنَةٍ كَالْكِتَابِ

٢ غَيَّرَتْهَا الصَّبَا وَنَفْحُ جَنُوبٍ   وَشَمَالٍ تَذْرُو دُقَاقَ التُّرَابِ

---

a) Omitted in Naṣr.

b) Naṣr. أَهْلُ النَّدَى, Iqtiḍāb 361 أَهْلُ الحِجَى.

c) Naṣr. الْحَامِلُ.   *d*) Naṣr. يَمْرَعُ.

e) Mukht. text has يُعَقِّى with ف, and so in scholion عَقَّاه and ٱعْتَفَاه; but the last words of the scholion show that ق should be read throughout.

f) BQut. Adab and Iqtiḍāb read the second hemist. يَنْهَلُ مِنْهُ الْأَسَلُ النَّاهِلُ; and with this reading the v. is also attributed to an-Nābighah: see Frag. 45 (Ahlw. p. 174), where يَعُلُّ مِنْهَا for يَنْهَلُ مِنْهُ.

XXVII. Metre *Khafīf*. Poem in Mukht, 105—6; so far citations have not been found elsewhere.

g) Mukht. incorrectly الدِّيَارُ.

h) Mukht. الْجَنَابِ; see Yāqūt II, 120, and Bakrī 248.

٣   فَتَرَاوَحْـنَـهَا وَكُلُّ مُـلِـتٍّ   دَائِمِ الرَّعْدِ مُرْجَحِنِّ السَّحَابِ

مُرْجَحِنٌّ تقيل: يقال أَرْجَحَنَّ اذا اهْتَزَّ: وأَرْجَحَنَّ السَّرَابُ ارتفع ☙

٤   أَوْحَشَتْ بَعْدَ ضُمَّرٍ كَالسَّعَالَى   مِن بَنَاتِ الْوَجِيهِ[a] أَوْ حَلَّابِ

٥   وَمُرَاحٍ وَمُسْرَحٍ وَحُـلُـولٍ   وَرَعَابِـيـبَ كَالدُّمَى وَقِبَابِ

٥ الرُّعْبُوبَة من النساء الشَّطْبَة: والرُّعْبُوبَة القِطْعَة من السَّنام ☙

٦   وَكُـهُـولٍ ذَرِى نَـدًى وَحُـلُـومٍ   وَشَبَابٍ أَنْجَادِ غُلْبِ الرِّقَابِ

٧   هَيَّجَ الشَّوْقَ لِى مَعَارِفُ مِنْهَا   حِينَ حَلَّ الْمَشِيبُ دَارَ الشَّبَابِ

٨   أَوْطَنَتْهَا عُفْرُ الظِّبَاءِ وَكَانَتْ   قَبْلُ أَوْطَانَ بُدَّنٍ أَتْـرَابِ

٩   خُرَّدٌ بَيْنَهُنَّ خَوْدٌ سَبَتْنِى   بِـدَلَالٍ وَهَـيَّـجَـتْ أَطْـرَابِى

١٠ جَارِيَةٌ خَرُودٌ خَفِرَةٌ وجمعها خُرَّدٌ: يقال لكلّ عَذْرَاء خَرِيدة: والخَرِيدة اللُّوْلُوَة لم يُثْقَب. والخَوْد المرأة

الناعمة ☙

١٠   صَعْدَةٌ مَّا عَلَا الْحَقِيبَةَ مِـنْـهَـا   وَكَثِيبٌ مَّا كَانَ تَحْتَ الْعِقَابِ

يقول [هى] طويلة كالرُّمْحِ. والكَثِيب الرَّمْلُ الْمُجْتَمِع شبّه عَجُزَها به ☙

١١   إِنَّمَا إِنَّمَا خُـلِـقْـنَـا رُءُوسًا   مَّنْ يُّسَوِّى الرُّءُوسَ بِالْأَذْنَابِ

١٢   لَا نَقِى بِالْأَحْسَابِ مَالًا وَلَٰكِنْ   نَجْعَلُ الْمَالَ جُنَّةَ الْأَحْسَابِ

١٣   وَنَصُدُّ الْأَعْـدَاءَ عَـنَّـا بِضَرْبٍ   ذِى خِدَامٍ وَطَعْنِـنَـا بِالْحِرَابِ

الْخِذَام والتَّخْذِم القَطْع وسيفٌ مِخْذَمٌ قاطعٌ ☙

١٤[b]   وَإِذَا الْخَيْلُ شَمَّرَتْ فِى سَنَا الْحَرْ   بِ وَصَارَ الْغُبَارُ فَوْقَ الذَّوَابِ

١٥   وَاسْتَجَارَتْ بِنَا الْخُيُولُ عِجَالًا   مُّثْقَلَاتِ الْمُـتُـونِ وَالْأَصْلَابِ

١٦   مُصْغِيَاتِ الْخُدُودِ شُعْثَ النَّوَاصِى   فِى شَمَاطِيطَ غَارَةٍ أَسْرَابِ

الشَّمَاطِيط الفِرَق: جَاءَت الخَيْل شَمَاطِيط. والسِّرْب والسُّرْبَة الجماعة من القطا والظباء والشاء والنساء:

ويقال سُرْبَة من الخيل ☙

a) Al-Wajīh and Ḥallāb, names of celebrated stallions: the former belonged to Ghanī, the latter to Taghlib; for the former see Tufail I, 22, for the latter LA I, 324²⁻³.

b) The long protasis vv. 14—18 has no apodosis; probably a verse (or verses) containing it has (or have) fallen out.

١٧ مُسْرِعَاتٍ كَأَنَّهُنَّ ضِرَاءٌ   سَمِعَتْ صَوْتَ هَاتِفٍ كَلَّابِ

١٨ لَاحِقَاتِ الْبُطُونِ يَصْهِلْنَ فَخْرًا   قَدْ حَوَيْنَ النِّهَابَ بَعْدَ النِّهَابِ

XXVIII.

١ هَمَّتْ تَلُومُ وَلَيْسَتْ سَاعَةَ اللَّاحِى   هَلَّا انْتَظَرْتِ بِهَذَا اللَّوْمِ إِصْبَاحِى

٢ قَاتَلَهَا اللَّهُ تَلْحَانِى وَقَدْ عَلِمَتْ   أَنَّ لِنَفْسِىَ إِفْسَادِى وَإِصْلَاحِى

٣ كَانَ الشَّبَابُ a يُلْهِينَا وَيُعْجِبُنَا   فَمَا وَهَبْنَا وَلَا بِعْنَا بِأَرْبَاحِ

٤ b إِنْ أَشْرَبِ الْخَمْرَ أَوْ c أُرْزَأْ لَهَا ثَمَنًا   فَلَا مَحَالَةَ يَوْمًا أَنَّنِى صَاحِى

٥ وَلَا مَحَالَةَ مِنْ قَبْرٍ بِمَحْنِيَةٍ d   وَّكَفَنٍ كَسَرَاةِ الثَّوْرِ وَضَّاحِ

مَحْنِيَةٌ مَا انْعَطَفَ مِنَ الْوَادِى. كَسَرَاةِ الثَّوْرِ فِى بَيَاضِهِ: وَوَضَّاحٍ يَتَوَضَّحُ يَلْمَعُ ☙

٦ e يَا مَنْ لِبَرْقٍ أَبِيتُ اللَّيْلَ أَرْقُبُهُ   مِنْ عَارِضٍ كَبَيَاضِ الصُّبْحِ لَمَّاحِ

٧ دَانٍ مُسِفٍّ فُوَيْقَ الْأَرْضِ هَيْدَبُهُ   يَكَادُ يَدْفَعُهُ مَنْ قَامَ بِالرَّاحِ

مُسِفٌّ شَدِيدُ الدُّنُوِّ مِنَ الارْضِ. وَهَيْدَبُهُ مَا تَدَلَّى مِنْهُ ☙

XXVIII. Metre *Basīṭ*. This poem is printed as contained in the *Mukhtārāt*, pp. 100—101; it is variously attributed to ʿAbīd and to Aus b. Ḥajar of Tamīm: according to Agh. X, 5, the latter was al-Aṣmaʿī's opinion and that of some of the scholars of al-Kūfah, while others ascribed it to ʿAbīd; for a discussion of the question see notes to the translation. The poem is celebrated, and vv. 7 and 8 occur in a great number of citations; it has been printed in Geyer, Dīw. of Aus (pp. 3—4 Arabic text, pp. 27—31 translation); reference should be made to that work for a list of the places where verses of it are found. To this list may now be added the *Risālat al-Ghufrān* of Abu-l-ʿAlāʾ al-Maʿarrī, pp. 66—67 (ed. Cairo, 1907).

a) Mukht. wrongly يُلْهِينَا.

b) Mukht. wrongly أَنْ.

c) Agh. X, 5 أُغْلِى بِهَا.

d) LA X, 219[17], and Geyer, Aus: أَوْ فِى مَلِيعٍ كَظُهُورِ التُّرْسِ وَضَّاحِ.

e) Agh. X, 5 has instead: إِنِّى أَرِقْتُ وَلَمْ يَأْرَقْ مَعِى صَاحِ   لِمُسْتَكِفٍّ بُعَيْدَ النَّوْمِ لَوَّاحِ.

Geyer gives both this and our v. 6: both do not seem to be required. Yāq. III, 289 has vv. 6, 7, 9, 8, with ʿAbīd's name; in v. 6 Yāq. reads كَمُضِىِّ for كَبَيَاضِ, and so Geyer.

٨ a فَمَنْ بِنَجْوَتِهِ كَمَنْ بِمَحْفِلِهِ ۞ وَالْمُسْتَكِنُّ كَمَنْ يَمْشِي بِقِرْوَاحِ

النَّجْوَةُ مَا ارْتَفَعَ مِنَ الأرضِ. وَالْمَحْفِلُ مُسْتَقَرُّ الْمَاءِ. وَالْقِرْوَاحُ أرضٌ مُسْتَوِيَةٌ ظَاهِرَةٌ. وَالْمُسْتَكِنُّ الَّذِى

فِى بَيْتِهِ ۞

٩ b كَأَنَّ رَيِّقَهُ لَمَّا عَلَا شَطِبًا ۞ أَقْرَابُ أَبْلَقَ يَنْفِى الْخَيْلَ رَمَّاحِ

يَنْفِى لِلخيلِ يَطْرُدُهَا: شَبَّهَ تَكَشُّفَ بياضِ البَرْقِ بِتَكَشُّفِ الأَبْلَقِ عَنْ أَرْفَاغِهِ ۞

١٠ c فَالْتَجَّ أَعْلَاهُ ثُمَّ ارْتَجَّ أَسْفَلُهُ ۞ وَضَاقَ ذَرْعًا بِحَمْلِ الْمَاءِ مُنْصَاحِ

التَّجُّ صَوْتٌ وَهُوَ مِنَ اللَّجَّةِ. وَيُرْوَى فَتَجَّ أَعْلَاهُ. وَمُنْصَاحٍ مُنْشَقٌّ بِالمَاءِ. وَيُقَالُ انْصَاحَ البَرْقُ اذا انْصَدَعَ

وَكَذَلِكَ الثَّوْبُ ۞

١١ d كَأَنَّمَا بَيْنَ أَعْلَاهُ وَأَسْفَلِهِ ۞ e رَيِّطٌ مُنَشَّرَةٌ أَوْ ضَوْءُ مِصْبَاحِ

١٢ e كَأَنَّ فِيهِ عِشَارًا جِلَّةً شُرُفًا ۞ شُعْثًا لَهَامِيمَ قَدْ هَمَّتْ بِإِرْشَاحِ

العِشَارُ الَّتِى أَتَى عَلَيْهَا عَشَرَةُ أَشْهُرٍ مِنْ حَمْلِهَا. وَالجِلَّةُ المَسَانُّ مِنَ الإبلِ. وَالشُّرُفُ الكِبَارُ مِنْهَا. وَاللَّهَامِيمُ

الغِزَارُ. وَيُقَالُ أَرْشَحَتِ النَّاقَةُ اذا اشْتَدَّ فَصِيلُهَا وَقَوِيَ وَهُوَ فَصِيلٌ رَاشِحٌ: وَإِنَّمَا ذِكْرُهَا بِذَلِكَ لَأَنَّهَا تَحِنُّ ۞

١٣ f بُكًّا حَنَاجِرُهَا هُدْلًا مَشَافِرُهَا ۞ f تُسِيمُ أَوْلَادَهَا فِى قَرْقَرٍ ضَاحِى

يُرْوَى *تُرْجِى مَطَافِلَهَا فِى صُحْصُحٍ [ضَاحِى]*. وَتُسِيمُ تُرْعِى. وَضَاحٍ بَارِزٌ ۞

١٤ هَبَّتْ جَنُوبٌ بِأُوَلِهِ وَمَالَ بِهِ ۞ أَعْجَازُ مُزْنٍ يَسُحُّ الْمَاءَ دَلَّاحِ

---

a) LA III, 396¹⁸ (ʿAbīd) كَمَنْ بِعَقْوَتِهِ; Agh. X, 7, transposes بِمَحْفِلِهِ and بِنَجْوَتِهِ in the first hemist.; Yāq. reads فَمَنْ بِجَوْزَتِهِ كَمَنْ بِعَقْوَتِهِ. This verse appears to be out of place; see translation.

b) Mukht. غَلَا; but Khiz. I, 76, Bakrī 811¹⁸, Yāq. all with عَلَا, which seems to be the right reading; cf. عَلَا قَطَنًا in I. Q. Muʿall. 74. Mount Shaṭib is said by Bakrī to be in the country of Tamīm; but it occurs in ʿAbīd's poetry (ante, XIV, 4), and that of Bishr b. Abī Khāzim (Yāq. III, 289⁵) and Imraʾal-Qais (XXV, 1), which points to the territory of Asad rather than Tamīm.

c) Fāʾiq I, 225, with فَتَجَّ.

d) Agh. X, 7¹, as text.

e) Cited Labīd Diw., Khālidī p. 87¹, with بِيضًا for شُعْثًا.

f) Yāq. IV, 49¹ تُرْجِى مَرَابِعَهَا (ʿAbīd).

١٥ فَـأَصْبَحَ الـرَّوْضُ وَالْقِيعَانُ مُمْرِعَةً   مِنْ بَيْنِ مُرْتَفِقٍ فِيهِ a وَمُنْطَاحِ

الْمُرْتَفِقُ مَاءٌ رَاكِدٌ قَدْ حَبَسَهُ شيءٌ يَرْتَفِقُ بِهِ. وَالْمُنْطَاحُ سَائِلٌ لَمْ يَكُنْ لَهُ مَا يَحْبِسُهُ فَسَالَ: وَمَكَانٌ

مُرْتَفَقٌ فِيهِ وَمُنْطَاحٍ فِيهِ ☆

XXIX.

١ يَا عَيْنِ قَـاَبْكِى مَا بَنـى   أَسَدُ فَـهُمْ أَهْلُ الـنَّـدَامَهْ b

٢ أَهْلَ الْـقِبَابِ الْـحُمْرِ وَآلْ   نَـعَمِ الْـمُـوَبَّلِ c وَالْمُدَامَهْ

٣ وَذَوِي الْـجِيَـادِ الْـجُـرْدِ وَآلْ   أَسَلِ الْمُثَقَّفَةِ الْمُقَامَهْ

٤ حِـلًّا أَبَـيْتَ الـلَّـعْنَ حِـلًّا إِنَّ فِـيمَا قُـلْتَ آمَهْ d

٥ فِـى كُـلِّ وَادٍ بَيْنَ e يَثْـرِبَ فَالْقُصُورِ إِلَى الْـيَمَامَهْ

٦ تَـطْـرِيبُ عَـانٍ أَوْ صِـيَا   حْ مُـحَـرَّقٍ f أَوْ صَوْتُ هَامَهْ

٧ وَمَـنَـعْـتَـهُمْ نَـجْـدًا فَـقَـدْ   حَـلُّوا عَلَى وَجَلٍ تِـهَامَهْ

---

a) The print of Mukht. has مُنْطَاحٍ, but the word appears to be a participle, VII, from طَاحَ

(ى or و). This verse has been much discussed; see Lane 1127b, LA III, 352² and 354⁵, and

XI, 411²⁵; the alternatives for the last word are given in Lane as مِنْ طَاحِى and مُنْطَاحٍ: other

variations are مِنْ بَيْنِ for مَا بَيْنَ, مُرْتَفِقٍ for مُرْتَفِقٍ (LA III 352) and مِنْها for فِيه (LA XI 411).

LA III, 354 has another form of the first hemist.: وَأَمْسَتِ الْأَرْضُ وَالْقِيعَانُ مُثْرِيَةً.

XXIX. Metre *Kamil muraffal* (or *majzū'*). This is a celebrated poem; the text is taken from
Agh. VIII, 65, which has been copied in Naṣr. 598. BQut. 37 has vv. 1, 2, 4—6, 11; and verses
are often cited elsewhere; see some quoted in the Introduction, p. 4, *ante*.

b) BQut. 37 يَا عَيْنِ مَا قَاَبْكِى.   c) Naṣr., MSS of Agh., الْمُوَمَّلِ.

d) LA XIV 304²² and BQut. have مَهْلًا in both places for حِلًّا (and so *ante*, Introduction).

e) Yāq. IV 1008 يَتْـرَبَ وَالْقُصُورِ. BQut. وَالْقُصُورِ.

f) BQut. وَزُقَاءِ. In Yāq. *l. c.* the verse is differently given: عَـانٍ يُسَاقُ بِـهِ وَصَوْتُ مُحَرَّقٍ

وَزُقَاءِ هَامَهْ.

٨ a بَرِمَتْ بَنُو أَسَدٍ كَمَا بَرِمَتْ بِبَيْضَتِهَا الْحَمَامَهْ

٩ b جَعَلَتْ لَهَا عُودَيْنِ مِنْ نَشَمٍ وَآخَرَ مِنْ ثُمَامَهْ

١٠ إِمَّا تَرَكْتَ تَرَكْتَ عَفْوًا أَوْ قَتَلْتَ فَلَا مَلَامَهْ

١١ c أَنْتَ الْمَلِيكُ عَلَيْهِمْ وَهُمُ الْعَبِيدُ إِلَى الْقِيَامَهْ

١٢ d ذَلُّوا لِسَوْطِكَ مِثْلَ مَا ذَلَّ الْأُشَيْقِرُ ذُو الْخِزَامَهْ

XXX.

١ e لِمَنْ دِمْنَةٌ أَقْوَتْ بِجَرَّةِ ضَرْغَدِ تَلُوحُ كَعُنْوَانِ الْكِتَابِ الْمُجَدَّدِ

٢ لِسُعْدَةَ إِنْ كَانَتْ تُثِيبُ رِبُوَدَّهَا وَإِنْ هِيَ لَا تَلْقَاكَ إِلَّا وِبِأَسْعُدِ

٣ وَإِنْ هِيَ حَوْرَاءُ الْمَدَامِعِ طَفْلَةٌ كَمِثْلِ مَهَاةٍ حُرَّةٍ أُمِّ فَرْقَدِ

٤ ثُرَاعِى بِهِ نَبْتَ الْخَمَائِلِ بِالضُّحَى وَتَأْوِى بِهِ إِلَى أَرَاكٍ وَغَرْقَدِ

٥ وَتَجْعَلُهُ فِى سِرْبِهَا نَصْبَ عَيْنِهَا وَتَثْنِى عَلَيْهِ الْجِيدَ فِى كُلِّ مَرْقَدِ

---

a) Maidānī (Freyt.) I, 459 has vv. 8 and 9 as text. BQut. Adab, 70, Jāḥ. Ḥayawān III, 31, Damīrī I, 229, all read عَيُّوا بِأَمْرِهِم كَمَا عَيَّتْ آلخ.

b) BQut. Adab, Damīrī, ll. cc., as text; Jāḥ. misprints شمٍ for نَشَمٍ.

c) BQut. Shiʿr, Khiz. I, 160, Iqtiḍāb 314, all as text.

d) See a different reading in Introduction, p. 4 ante.

XXX. Metre *Tawīl*. This poem is taken from Abkāriyūs, *Nihāyat al-'Arab fī Akhbār al-'Arab* (Beyrout 1865), pp. 114—115, who appears to have derived it from some recension of the *Jamharah* of which MSS do not exist in Europe (Geyer's statements on this subject in *Zwei Gedichte v. al-A'šā* I, p. 2, note, require correction). It was reprinted in the *Majāni-l-Adab*, VI, 239, without any change. In Naṣr. 602—4 (where vv. 2—9 are omitted) many errors of the original have been set right, though some are still left. One verse, No. 6, is cited in the LA with 'Abīd's name.

e) Abkar. Naṣr. أَمِنْ دِمْنَةٍ أَقْوَتْ بِجَرَّةِ صَرْغَدِ: the correction of the first two words shown in the text is certain: it is rendered necessary by v. 2 لِسُعْدَةَ. The *Ḥarrah* or volcanic plain of Ḍarghad (which appears still to bear that name: see Doughty's map) is very frequently mentioned in the old poetry: Yāq. II, 249; Bakrī 619—20, 'Āmir Dīw. VIII, 6, XXIX, 3, etc.

f) Abkar. بُورِدَّهَا.

g) Abkar. بِأَسْعُدِ.

عِيَادًا كَسُمِّ الْحَيَّةِ الْمُتَوَرِّدِ	٦ a فَقَدْ أَوْرَثَتْ فِى الْقَلْبِ سُقْمًا يَعُودُهُ
تَحَفَّ ثَمَايَاهَا بِحَالِكِ إِثْمِدِ	٧ غَدَاةَ بَدَتْ مِنْ سِتْرِهَا وَكَأَنَّمَا
أَقَاحِى الرَّبَى أَضْحَى وَظَاهِرُهُ نَدِ	٨ b وَتَبْسِمُ عَنْ عَذْبِ اللِّثَاتِ كَأَنَّهُ
إِلَى نَيْلِهَا مَا عِشْتُ كَالْحَائِمِ الصَّدِى	٩ فَإِنِّى إِلَى سُعْدَى وَإِنْ طَالَ نَأْيُهَا
لِنُصْحٍ c وَلَا تُصْغِى إِلَى قَوْلِ مُرْشِدِ	١٠ إِذَا كُنْتَ لَمْ تَعْبَأْ بِرَأْيٍ وَّلَمْ تُطِعْ
وَتَدْفَعُ عَنْهَا بِاللِّسَانِ وَبِالْيَدِ	١١ فَلَا تَتَّقِى ذَمَّ الْعَشِيرَةِ كُلِّهَا
وَتَقْمَعُ عَنْهَا نَخْوَةَ الْمُتَهَدِّدِ	١٢ وَتَصْفَحُ عَنْ ذِى جَهْلِهَا وَتَحُوطُهَا
يُرَى الْفَضْلُ فِى الدُّنْيَا عَلَى الْمُتَحَمِّدِ	١٣ وَتَنْزِلُ مِنْهَا بِالْمَكَانِ الَّذِى بِهِ
بِذِى سُودَدٍ بَادٍ وَّلَا كُرْبِ سَيِّدِ	١٤ فَلَسْتَ وَإِنْ عَلَّلْتَ نَفْسَكَ بِالْمُنَى
عَلَيْهِ وَلَا أَنْأَى عَلَى الْمُتَوَدِّدِ	١٥ لَعَمْرُكَ مَا يَخْشَى d الْخَلِيطُ تَفَحُّشِى
وَلَا أَنَا عَنْ وَصْلِ الصَّدِيقِ بِأَصْيَدِ	١٦ وَلَا أَبْتَغِى وُدَّ امْرِئٍ قَلَّ خَيْرُهُ
وَقَدْ أُوقِدَتْ لِلْغَيِّ فِى كُلِّ مَوْقِدِ	١٧ وَإِنِّى لَأُطْفِى الْحَرْبَ بَعْدَ شُبُوبِهَا
إِذَا لَمْ يَزَعْهُ e رَأْيُهُ عَنْ تَرَدُّدِ	١٨ فَأَوْقَدْتُهَا لِلظَّالِمِ الْمُصْطَلِى بِهَا
فَأَظْلِمُهُ مَا لَمْ f يَنَلْنِى بِمَحْقِدِى	١٩ وَأَغْفِرُ لِلْمَوْلَى هَنَاةً تُرِيبُنِى
تَوَقَّصَ حِينًا مِّنْ شَوَاهِقِ g صِنْدِدِ	٢٠ وَمَنْ رَامَ ظُلْمِى مِنْهُمْ فَكَأَنَّمَا
وَمَا أَنَا مِنْ عِلْمِ الْأُمُورِ بِمُبْتَدِى	٢١ وَإِنِّى لَذُو رَأْيٍ يُعَاشُ بِفَضْلِهِ
فَإِنَّكَ قَدْ أَسْنَدْتَهَا شَرَّ مُسْنَدِ	٢٢ إِذَا أَنْتَ حَمَّلْتَ الْخَوُونَ أَمَانَةً

---

a) LA IV, 322[7] has this v. with the following reading: تَعُدُّهُ عِدَادًا كَسَمِّ الْحَيَّةِ الْمُتَغَلِّدِ; we should apparently read يَعُدُّهُ, which may be used in the sense of يُعَادُهُ: or the reading may be يَعُدُّهُ or يُعَادُهُ, either of them permissible variations for يُعَادُّهُ, which is inadmissible in verse. The verb تغلّد appears from LA to be a ἅπαξ λεγόμενον. (So also TA).

b) أَقَاحٍ construed with a singular is strange: cf. *ante*, XXII, 26.

c) Abkar. Naṣr. وَلَمْ تُصْغِى (but both have فلا تَتَّقِى in next v.).

d) Abkar. Naṣr. الْتَجَلِيدُ, which has no suitable meaning.

e) Abkar. Naṣr. read إِذَا لَمْ يَرِعْهُ رَأْيُهُ عَنْ تَوَدُّدِ, which appears to have no sense.

f) Some error seems to lie hid in يَنَلْنِى. Naṣr. changes the مَحْقِد of Abkar. to مَحْتِد; but both words have the same meaning.

g) Ṣindid, a mountain in Tihāmah: Yāq. III, 420.

وَمَا خِلْتُ b غَمَّ الْجَارِ إِلَّا بِمَعْهَدِى	وَجَدْتُ خَوُّونَ الْقَوْمِ a كَالْعَرِّ يُتَّقَى	٢٣
وَبَعْدَ بَلَاهُ الْمَرْءَ فَاذْمُمْ أَوِ احْمَدِ	وَلَا تُظْهِرَنْ حُبَّ امْرِئٍ قَبْلَ خُبْرِهِ	٢٤
وَلَكِنْ بِرَأْىِ الْمَرْءِ ذِى اللُّبِّ فَاقْتَدِ	c وَلَا تَتْبَعَنَّ رَأْىَ مَنْ لَّمْ تَقُصَّهُ	٢٥
لِلْخُرِّ وَفِى وَصْلِ الْأَبَاعِدِ فَازْهَدِ	وَلَا تَزْهَدَنْ فِى وَصْلِ أَهْلِ قَرَابَةٍ	٢٦
فَعُدْ لِلَّذِى صَادَفْتَ مِنْ ذَاكَ وَازْدَدِ	وَإِنْ أَنْتَ فِى مَجْدٍ أَصَبْتَ غَنِيمَةً	٢٧
عَلَى كُلِّ حَالٍ خَيْرُ زَادِ الْمُزَوِّدِ	تَزَوَّدْ مِنَ الدُّنْيَا مَتَاعًا فَإِنَّهُ	٢٨
فَتِلْكَ سَبِيلٌ لَّسْتُ فِيهَا بِأَوْحَدِ	تَمَنَّى امْرُؤُ الْقَيْسِ مَوْتِى وَإِنْ أَمُتْ	٢٩
سَفَاهًا وَجُبْنًا أَنْ يَكُونَ هُوَ الرَّدَى	لَعَلَّ الَّذِى يَرْجُو رَدَاىَ وَمِيتَتِى	٣٠
وَلَا مَوْتُ مَنْ قَدْ مَاتَ قَبْلِى بِمُخْلِدِى	فَمَا عَيْشُ مَنْ يَّرْجُو d هَلَاكِى بِضَائِرِى	٣١
حِبَالُ الْمَنَايَا لِلْفَتَى كُلَّ مَرْصَدِ	وَلِلْمَرْءِ أَيَّامٌ تُعَدُّ وَقَدْ رَعَتْ	٣٢
مُلَاقَاتُهَا يَوْمًا عَلَى غَيْرِ مَوْعِدِ	مَنِيَّتُهُ تَجْرِى لِوَقْتٍ وَقَصْرُهُ	٣٣
سَيَعْلَقُهُ حَبْلُ الْمَنِيَّةِ فِى غَدِ	فَمَنْ لَّمْ يَمُتْ فِى الْيَوْمِ لَا بُدَّ أَنَّهُ	٣٤
تَهَيَّأْ لِأُخْرَى مِثْلِهَا فَكَأَنْ قَدِ	فَقُلْ لِلَّذِى يَبْغِى خِلَافَ الَّذِى مَضَى	٣٥
يَرُوحُ وَكَالْقَاضِى الْبَتَاتَ e لِيَغْتَدِى	فَإِنَّا وَمَنْ قَدْ بَادَ مِنَّا فَكَالَّذِى	٣٦

a) Abkar. كَالْغَرّ (ويروى كَالْغَرّ); Naṣr. كَالْغَرّ; the correction to الْعُرّ is certain.

b) Abkar. Naṣr. عَمَّ: "Vielleicht غَمَّ für عَمَّ zu lesen — 'was den Schützling bekümmert, seine Sorgen'. 'Volk' heisst ja im Arabischen عَمّ aber nur ganz ausnahmsweise; und auf das Volk des Mannes, dem von einem Mächtigen Schutz zugestanden ist, bezieht sich der Schutz auch gar nicht: er gilt nur dem Individuum" (Nöldeke).

c) Naṣr. وَلَا تَتْبَعَنَّ الرَّأْىَ مِنْهُ تَقُصْهُ: Abkar. *id.* with تَقُصْهُ: the construction seems impossible.

d) Abkar. Naṣr. خَلَافِى. "Diese Verbesserung ist mir ziemlich wahrscheinlich" (Nöldeke).

e) Abkar. Naṣr. لِيَعْتَدِى.

SUPPLEMENT

OF FRAGMENTS ATTRIBUTED TO ʿABĪD BY VARIOUS WRITERS, BUT
NOT CONTAINED IN THE *DĪWĀN*.

1.

Khiz. II, 403:

١ أَتُوعِدُ أُسْرَتِى وَتَـرَكْتَ حُجْرًا   يُـدِيغُ سَوَادَ عَيْنَيْهِ الْـغُـرَابُ

Jāḥiḍh III, *Opuscula* 62[15]:

٢ *a* أَبَوْا دِينَ الْمُلُوكِ فَهُمْ لَقَاحٌ   إِذَا نُدِبُوا إِلَى حَـرْبٍ أَجَـابُـوا

5 *ʿUmdah*, I, 65:

٣ *b* فَلَوْ أَدْرَكْتَ عِلْبَاءَ بْنَ قَيْسٍ   قَنِعْتَ مِنَ الْغَنِيمَةِ بِالْإِيَابِ

2.

Aḍdād 176, 12:

قال عبيد يَذْكُرُ فرسَه:

c فَيَنْحَفِقُ مَرَّةً وَيُفِيدُ أُخْـرَى   وَيُلْحِقُ ذَا الْمَلَامَةِ بِـالْأَرِيـبِ

3.

10 Abū Ḥātim as-Sijistānī, *Kitāb al-Muʿammarīn* (ed. Goldziher) p. 66; Khiz. I, 323:

١ وَلَتَأْتِيَنْ بَعْدِى قُرُونٌ جَمَّةٌ   تَـرْعَى مَحَارِمَ أَيْكَةٍ وَلَـدُودَا

٢ فَالشَّمْسُ طَالِعَةٌ وَلَيْلٌ كَاسِفٌ   وَالنَّجْمُ تَجْرِى أَنْحَسًا وَسُعُودَا

---

a) For a similar verse, with a different rhyme, see LA III 419[23].

b) Cf. I. Q., V. 9 and VII, 3.

c) A similar verse is attributed to ʿAntarah, (Ahlw. p. 178) Frag. 4, and see LA XI 369[19].

٣ حَتَّى يُقَالَ لِمَنْ تَعَرَّقَ دَهْرَهُ   يَا ذَا الزَّمَانَةِ هَلْ رَأَيْتَ عَبِيدَا

٤ مِائَتَيْ زَمَانٍ كَامِلٍ a وَنَصِيَّةً   عِشْرِينَ عِشْتُ مُعَمَّرًا مَحْمُودَا

٥ أَدْرَكْتُ أَوَّلَ مُلْكِ نَصْرٍ نَاشِئًا   وَبِنَاءَ b سِنْدَادٍ وَكَانَ أَبِيدَا

٦ وَطَلَبْتُ ذَا الْقَرْنَيْنِ حَتَّى فَاتَنِي   رَكْضًا وَكِدْتُ بِأَنْ أَرَى دَاوُودَا

٧ مَا تَبْتَغَى مِنْ بَعْدِ هَذَا عِيشَةٌ   إِلَّا الْخُلُودُ وَلَنْ تَنَالَ خُلُودَا   5

٨ وَلَيَقْنِيَنَّ هَذَا وَذَاكَ كِلَاهُمَا c   إِلَّا الْإِلَهَ وَوَجْهَهُ الْمَعْبُودَا

4.

Yāq. IV, 916[16]:

١ وَهَلْ رَامَ عَنْ عَهْدِى وُدَيْكَ مَكَانَهُ   إِلَى حَيْثُ يُفْضِى سَيْلُ ذَاتِ الْمَسَاجِدِ

Khiz. I, 323[21]; *Mu‘ammarīn*, 67[2]:

٢ فَنِيتُ وَأَفْنَانِى الزَّمَانُ وَأَصْبَحَتْ   لِدَاتِى بَنُو نَعْشٍ وَزُهْرُ الْفَرَاقِدِ   10

5.

Naṣr. 605:

قَالَ يَرْثِى نَفْسَهُ:

١ يَا حَارِ مَا رَاحَ مِنْ قَوْمٍ وَلَا ابْتَكَرُوا d   إِلَّا وَلِلْمَوْتِ فِى آثَارِهِمْ حَادِى

٢ يَا حَارِ مَا طَلَعَتْ شَمْسٌ وَلَا غَرَبَتْ   إِلَّا تَقَرَّبَ آجَالٌ لِمِيعَادِ

٣ هَلْ نَحْنُ إِلَّا كَأَرْوَاحٍ نَمُرُّ بِهَا e   تَحْتَ التُّرَابِ وَأَجْسَادٍ كَأَجْسَادِ   15

6.

Bakrī 409[11]; Naṣr. 613; Wüstenfeld, Register 394 (vv. 1 and 2 only, and very corruptly):

١ صَاحِ تَرَى بَرْقًا بِتُّ أَرْقُبُهُ   ذَاتَ الْعِشَا فِى غَمَائِمٍ غُرِّ

---

a) A suggestion of De Goeje's: Khiz. وَيَضَعُهُ; Mu‘am. وَنَصِيَّةً.

b) Khiz. شَدَّادٍ.

c) *Cf.* Qur. LV, 26—27: كُلُّ مَنْ عَلَيْهَا فَانٍ * وَيَبْقَى وَجْهُ رَبِّكَ ذُو الْجَلَالِ وَالْإِكْرَامِ *.

d) See No. XXV, 5.

e) See No. XXIV, 21: this latter is intelligible, while our text here (أرواح تحت التراب) is not.

٢   *a*   فَحَلَّ [فِى] بِرْكَةٍ بِأَسْفَلِ ذِى   رَيْدٍ فَشَنَّ فِى [–⌣–] ذِى الْعَثْيَرِ

٣   فَعَنَّسَ [–––⌣] فَالْعُنَابَ فَجِنْــــــــــبَى عَرْدَةٍ ثُمَّ بَطْنِ ذِى الْأَجْفُرِ

7.

LA VI, 43[12] and IX 71[5]; TA V, 68[36]:

b   فَهْوَ كَنِبْرَاسِ النَّمِيطِ أَوِ الْـــــــفَرْضِ بِكَفِّ اللَّاعِبِ الْمُسْمِرِ

8.

5   Ya'qūbī, *Historiae*, I, 250:

١   سَقَيْنَا امْرَأَ الْقَيْسِ بْنَ حُجْرٍ [بْنِ حَارِثٍ]   كُوُوسَ الشَّجَا حَتَّى تَعَوَّدَ بِالْقَهْرِ

٢   *c*   وَأَلْهَاهُ شُرْبٌ نَاعِمٌ وَقَرَاتِرُ   وَأَعْيَاهُ ثَأْرٌ كَانَ يَطْلُبُ فِى حُجْرِ

٣   وَذَاكَ لَعَمْرِى كَانَ أَسْهَلَ مَشْرَعًا   عَلَيْهِ مِنَ الْبِيضِ الصَّوَارِمِ وَالسَّمْرِ

9.

Lane 2770*b*; LA VII, 281[11]; TA I, 111[31]; al-Qālī, I, 229:

10   ١   وَإِذَا تُبَاشِرُكَ الْهُمُو   مُ فَإِنَّهَا كَالٍ وَنَاجِزْ

LA VI, 318[20]:

٢   وَلَقَدْ تُزَانُ بِكَ الْمَجَا   لِسُ لَا أَغَرُّ وَلَا عُلَاكِزْ

LA VII, 281[17]:

٣   كَالْهُمْنُدُوَانِىِّ الْمُهَنَّدِ هَزَّةَ الْقِرْنِ الْمَنَاجِزْ

---

a) These lines are unmetrical (metre *Munsariḥ*). The wanting syllables are indicated. In v. 3*b* ثُمَّ بَطْنِ has been substituted for Bakrī's فَبَطْنِ.

b) See Lane 2374*c*. The verse is a description of lightning; it is compared to the lamp of an Aramaic-speaking devotee (*cf.* I. Q. Muʻall. 72), or the gaming arrow being shuffled in the hands of a player at *Maisir* by night.

c) For the sentiment see *ante*, XVII, 14—18; قَرَاتِرُ here apparently means "a sweet-voiced singer"; see LA VI 399[22].

10.

Majāni-l-Adab VI, 144—146; LA VIII, 98¹³ff. has the story and the first four verses, and it is mentioned that the verses are sixteen in all:

لَقِىَ عبيدُ بن الأبرَصِ امرأَ القَيسِ فقال لَه عبيد: كَيفَ مَعرِفَتُكَ بالأوابِد. فقال: أَلْقِ ما أَحبَبتَ.

فقال عبيد

١ a مَا حَيِّـةٌ مَيْتَـةٌ أَحْـيَـتْ بِمَيِّتِهَا   دَرْدَاءُ مَا أَنْبَتَتْ سِنًّا وَأَضْـرَاسَا   5

فقال امرُؤ القَيس

٢ تِـلْكَ الشَّعِيرَةُ تُسْقَى فِى سَنَابِلِهَا   فَأَخْرَجَتْ بَعْدَ طُولِ الْمُكْثِ أَكْدَاسَا

فقال عبيد

٣ مَا السُّودُ وَالْبِيـضُ وَالْأَسْمَاءُ وَاحِـدَةٌ   لَّا يَسْتَطِيعُ لَهُنَّ النَّـاسُ تَمْسَاسَا

10 فقال امرُؤ القَيس

۴ تِلْكَ السَّحَابُ إِذَا الرَّحْمَانُ b أَرْسَلَهَا   رَوَّى بِهَا مِـنْ مَحُولِ الْأَرْضِ c أَيْبَاسَا

فقال عبيد

٥ مَا مُرْتَجَاتٌ عَـلَـى هَـوْلٍ مَّرَاكِبُهَا   يَقْطَعْنَ طُـولَ الْمَدَى سَيْرًا وَأَمْرَاسَا

فقال امرُؤ القَيس

٦ تِلْكَ النُّجُومُ إِذَا حَـالَـتْ مَطَالِعُهَا   شَبَّهْتُهَا فِـى سَوَادِ اللَّيْلِ أَقْبَاسَا   15

فقال عبيد

٧ مَا الْقَـاطِعَـاتُ لِأَرْضٍ لَّا أَنِيسَ بِـهَـا   تَأْتِى سِرَاعًا وَّمَا يَـرْجِعْنَ أَنْكَاسَا

فقال امرُؤ القَيس

٨ تِلْكَ الـرِّيَـاحُ إِذَا هَبَّتْ عَـوَاصِفُهَا   كَفَى بِـأَذْيَالِـهَا لِلتُّرْبِ كَنَّاسَا

20 فقال عبيد

---

a) The readings of LA have been chosen for the first hemist.; the *Majānī* prints it thus: مَا حَبَّةٌ مَيْتَةٌ قَامَتْ بِمَيِّتِهَا. In the second hemist. LA has دَرْدَاءُ, and نَبَأً for سِنًّا.

b) LA أَنْشَأَهَا.

c) LA أَنْفَاسًا.

٩   مَا الْفَاجِعَاتِ جِهَارًا فِى عَلَانِيَةٍ   أَشَدُّ مِنْ فَيْلَقٍ مَمْلُوءَةٍ بَاسَا

فقال امرؤ القيس

١٠ تِلْكَ الْمَنَايَا فَمَا يُبْقِينَ مِنْ أَحَدٍ   يَكْفِتْنَ حَمْقَى وَمَا يُبْقِينَ أَكْيَاسَا

فقال عبيد

١١   مَا السَّابِقَاتِ سِرَاعَ الطَّيْرِ فِى مَهَلٍ   لَّا تَسْتَكِينُ وَلَوْ أَلْجَمْتَها فَاسَا

فقال امرؤ القيس

١٢ تِلْكَ الْجِيَادُ عَلَيْهَا الْقَوْمُ قَدْ سَبَحُوا   كَانُوا لَهُنَّ غَدَاةَ الرَّوْعِ أَحْلَاسَا

فقال عبيد

١٣   مَا الْقَاطِعَاتِ لِأَرْضِ الْجَوِّ فِى طَلَقٍ   قَبْلَ الصَّبَاحِ وَمَا يَسْرِينَ *a* قِرْطَاسَا

فقال امرؤ القيس

١٤ تِلْكَ الْأَمَانِىُّ يَتْرُكْنَ الْفَتَى مَلِكًا   دُونَ السَّمَاءِ وَلَمْ تَرْفَعْ بِهِ رَاسَا

فقال عبيد

١٥   مَا الْحَاكِمُونَ بِلَا سَمْعٍ وَّلَا بَصَرٍ   وَّلَا لِسَانٍ فَصِيحٍ يُعْجِبُ النَّاسَا

فقال امرؤ القيس

١٦ *b* تِلْكَ الْمَوَازِينُ وَالرَّحْمَانُ أَنْزَلَهَا   رَبُّ الْبَرِيَّةِ بَيْنَ النَّاسِ مِقْيَاسَا

11.

Khiz. I, 324; Agh. XIX, 87[16]; al Qālī, *Dhail* 200; Yāqūt III, 794; Naṣr. 602:

١ وَحَيَّرَنِى ذُو الْبُؤْسِ فِى يَوْمِ بُؤْسِهِ   خِصَالًا أَرَى فِى كُلِّهَا الْمَوْتَ قَدْ بَرَقْ

٢ كَمَا خُيِّرَتْ عَادٌ مِّنَ الدَّهْرِ مَرَّةً   سَحَائِبَ مَا فِيهَا لِذِى خِيرَةٍ أَنَقْ

٣ سَحَائِبَ رِيحٍ لَّمْ تُوَكَّلْ بِبَلْدَةٍ   فَتَتْرُكَهَا إِلَّا كَمَا *c* لَيْلَةَ الطَّلَقْ

---

a) قِرْطَاسَا, if the reading is correct, seems to have the sense of "a bit, a scrap"; this must be modern, referring to times when paper had become cheap, long after the foundation of Islām. The word is not assigned this sense in the Lexx.

b) See Qur. XLII, 16.

c) See Lane 1873*b*.

12.

Agh. VI, 77:

١ a مَا رَعَدَتْ رَعْدَةً وَلَا بَرَقَتْ   لَكِنَّهَا أَنْشَمَتْ لَمَّا خَلِقَهْ

٢ اَلْمَاء يَجْرِى عَلَى نِظَامٍ لَّهُ   لَوْ يَجِدُ الْمَاءَ مَحَدْرَقًا خَرَقَهْ

٣ بِتْنَا وَبَاتَتْ عَلَى نَمَارِقِهَا   حَتَّى بَدَا الصُّبْحُ عَيْنُهَا أَرِقَهْ

٤ أَنْ قِيلَ إِنَّ الرَّحِيلَ بَعْدَ غَدٍ   وَّالدَّارُ بَعْدَ الْجَمِيعِ مُفْتَرِقَهْ   5

13.

Jāḥiḍh, *Bukhalā*, 206:

وَاَعْلَمَنْ عِلْمًا يَّقِينًا أَنَّهُ   لَيْسَ يُرْجَى لَكَ مَنْ لَّيْسَ مَعَكْ

14.

Buḥturī, *Ḥamāsah*, p. 378:

قال عَبْدُ الله (sic) بن الابرص الأَسَدِيّ

١ أَلْبِينُ إِذَا آلَانَ الْغَرِيمُ وَأَلْتَوَى   إِذَا أَشْتَدَّ حَتَّى يُدْرِكَ الدَّيْنَ قَاتِلِى   10

٢ وَأُمْطِلُهُ الْعَصْرَيْنِ حَتَّى يَمَلَّنِى   وَيَرْضَى بِبَعْضِ الدَّيْنِ فِى غَيْرِ نَائِلِ

15.

Naṣr. 605: *Majmū'at al-Ma'ānī*, p. 135, has vv. 1 and 3:

١ b صَبِّرِ النَّفْسَ عِنْدَ كُلِّ مُلِمٍّ   إِنَّ فِى الصَّبْرِ حِيلَةَ الْمُحْتَالِ

٢ لَا تَضِيقَنَّ فِى الْأُمُورِ فَقَدْ تُكْشَفُ غَمَّاؤُهَا بِغَيْرِ احْتِيَالِ

٣ رُبَّمَا تَجْزَعُ النُّفُوسُ مِنَ الْأَمْـــرِ لَهُ فُرْجَةٌ كَحَلِّ الْعِقَالِ   15

---

a) Cited LA XI, 378¹⁸ (poet not named); for خَلِقَهْ see Lane 801b, LA XI, 378⁷.

b) *Majmū'ah* مِّيمٍ, أَصْبِرِ. These verses are given in Naṣr. as part of the poem No. XI in the *Dīwān*, but they do not fit in to that.

16.

Ya'qūbī, I. 264:

قال عَبِيدُ بن الْأَبْرَصِ فى شِعْرٍ لَه طَويلٍ

١ أَبْلِغْ جُذَامًا وَّلَخْمًا إِنْ عَرَضْتَ بِهِمْ   وَالْـقَوْمُ يَنْفَعُهُمْ عِلْمٌ إِذَا عَلِمُوا

٢ بِـأَنَّكُمْ فِى كِتَابِ اللَّـهِ إِخْـوَتُنَا   إِذَا تَـقَـسَّـمَـتِ الْأَرْحَامُ وَالنَّسَمُ

ويقال إِنَّ هذا الشِّعْرَ لِسَمْعَانَ بن هُبَيْرَةَ الْأَسَدِىّ ✾

17.

Bakrī, 412[19]:

قال عُمَارَةُ ورُمَاحٍ فى غير هذا الموضع نَقًا بِبِلاد رَبِيعَةَ بن عبد الله بن كِلاب يُقَال له نقا رُمَاح: ولكثرة
المَهَا بِرُمَاحٍ قال الشاعر يعنى النساء وهو عبيد بن الابرص

[a] وَقَدْ بَاتَتْ عَلَيْهِ مَهَا رُمَاحٍ   حَـوَاسِـرَ مَـا تَنَامُ وَلَا تُنِيمُ

---

a) Cf. No. VIII, 14.

كِتَابُ دِيوانِ شِعْرِ

عَامِرِ بْنِ الطُّفَيْلِ الْعَامِرِيّ

رِوَايَةُ أَبِى بَكْرٍ مُحَمَّدِ بْنِ الْقَاسِمِ الْأَنْبَارِيّ

عَنْ أَبِى الْعَبَّاسِ أَحْمَدَ بْنِ يَحْيَى ثَعْلَبٍ

رَحِمَهُمَا اللّٰهُ ٭

[MS. Brit. Mus. Or. 6771, Fol. 29a ff.]

بِسْمِ اللهِ الرَّحْمنِ الرَّحِيمِ

قال ابو بَكْرٍ مُحَمَّدُ بن القَاسِمِ الْأَنْبَارِيّ: قَرَأْتُ شِعْرَ عَامِرِ بن الطُّفَيْلِ عَلَى أَبِي الْعَبَّاسِ ثَعْلَبٍ وَزَادَنِي أَشْيَاءَ لم تَكُنْ فِي نُسْخَتِي وَأَنَا. أُبَيِّنُهَا فِي مَوَاضِعِهَا إِنْ شَاءَ اللهُ ☙ وهو عامرُ بن الطُّفَيْلِ بن مالِكِ بن جَعْفَرِ بن كِلابِ بن رَبِيعَةَ بن عامِرِ بن صَعْصَعَةَ بن مُعَاوِيَةَ بن بَكْرِ بن قوَازِنَ بن مَنْصُورِ بن عِكْرِمَةَ

5 ابن خَصَفَةَ بن قَيْسِ بن عَيْلانَ بن مُضَرَ بن نِزارِ بن مَعَدِّ بن عَدْنَانَ ☙ وأُمُّهُ كَبْشَةُ بِنْتُ عُرْوَةَ الرَّحَّالِ بن عُتْبَةَ بن جَعْفَرٍ. وأُمُّ أَبِيهِ أُمُّ الْبَنِينَ بنت رَبِيعَةَ بن عَمْرٍو: وقال ابنُ حَبِيبٍ: أُمُّ الْبَنِينِ بِنْتُ عَمْرِو بن عامِرٍ فارِسِ الضَّحْيَاءِ ابنِ رَبِيعَةَ بن عامِر بن صعصعةَ. وكان ابو عَلِيّ عامرُ بن الطفيلِ من أَشْهَرِ فُرْسَانِ العَرَبِ بَأْسًا وشِدَّةً ونَجْدَةً وأَبْعَدِهَا اسْمًا حَتَّى بَلَغَ بِهِ ذلك أَنَّ قَيْصَرَ كان إذا قَدِمَ عليه قادِمٌ من العرب قال: ما بَيْنَكَ وبَيْنَ عامرِ بن الطفيلِ. فإِنْ ذَكَرَ نَسَبًا عَظُمَ بِهِ عِنْدَهُ: حتى قَدِمَ

10 عليه عَلْقَمَةُ بن عُلَاثَةَ فانْتَسَبَ لهُ: فقال: أنْتَ ابنُ عَمِّ عامرِ بن الطفيلِ. فَغَضِبَ عَلْقَمَةُ وقال: أَرَانِي لا أُعْرَفُ إِلَّا بِعامرٍ. فكان ذلك مِمَّا أَوْحَرَ صَدْرَهُ عَلَيْهِ وقَيَّجَهُ إِلَى أَنْ دَعَاهُ إِلَى a الْمُنَافَرَةِ. وكان عَمْرُو ابنُ مَعْدِي كَرِبَ وهو فارِسُ اليَمَنِ يقول: ما أُبَالِي أَيَّ ظَعِينَةٍ لَقِينَ عَلَى ماءٍ من أَمْوَاهِ مَعَدٍّ ما لم يَلْقَنِي دُونَهَا حُرَّاقَا b أَوْ عَبْداها: يعني بالحُرَّتَيْنِ عامرَ بن الطفيلِ وعُتَيْبَةَ بن الحُرْثِ بن شِهَابٍ (30a) الْبَرْبُوعِيّ: والعَبْدانِ عَنْتَرَةُ العَبْسِيّ والسُّلَيْكُ بن السُّلَكَةِ وهو c [ابنُ] عامِرِ بن يَثْرِبِيِّ السَّعْدِيِّ ☙ قال

─────────────

a) For this celebrated contest see Agh. XV, 52—58.

b) MS وعَبْدَاها.

c) The word ابن is supplied from the commy. to Mfḍt CVI. The genealogy of as-Sulaik in Agh. XVIII, 133 is as follows:

هو السُّلَيْكُ بن عُمْرٍو وقِيلَ ابنُ عُمَيْرِ بن يَثْرِبِيّ أَحَدِ بنى مُقَاعِسٍ وهو الحَارِثُ بن عمرو بن كعب بن سَعْدِ مناةَ بن تميم.

وَلَمَّا مات عامر a [بعد] مُنْصَرَفِه عن النَبِيِّ صَلَّى اللهُ عليه وسَلَّم نَصَبَتْ عليه بنو عامر أَنْصابًا مِيلًا فى

مِيلٍ حِمًى على قَبْرِه: لا تَدْخُلُهُ مـاشِيَةٌ ولا b تَنْشُرَ فيه راعِيَةٌ ولا تَرْعَى ولا يَسْلُكُهُ راكِبٌ ولا ماشٍ.

وكان c جَبَّارُ بن سَلْمَى بن عامر بن مالك بن جعفر غائبًا: فَلَمَّا قَدِمَ قال: ما هذه الأَنْصاب قال: d قالوا:

نَصَبْناها حِمًى على قَبْرِ عامر. قال: ضَيَّقْتُم على أبى عَلِيٍّ: إِنَّ أَبا عَلِيٍّ بانَ مِنَ الناس بِثَلْثٍ: كان لا

يَعْطَشُ حتى تَعْطَشَ e الإِبِلُ: ولا يَصِلُّ حتى يَصِلَّ النَجْمُ: ولا يَجْبُنُ حتى يَجْبُنَ f اللَيْلُ: ولا .يَقِفُ 5

حتى يَقِفَ السَّبِيلُ (والحَرْفُ الرابِعُ زِيادة ابى العَبّاس) ۞ وله وَقائِعُ فى مَذْحِجٍ وغَطَفانَ وخَثْعَمَ وسائِرِ

العَرَبِ. وكان عامرٌ مـعَ شَجاعَتِه سَخِيًّا حَلِيمًا: مِمّا يُذْكَرُ من ذلك أَنَّ أَبا بَراءٍ عامر بن مالك بن جعفر

ابن كلاب رجع من غَزْوَةٍ غَزاها اليَمَنَ بِقَبائِلِ بنى عامر بن صعصعة: فقال: إِنَّ اللهَ قـد أَثْرَى عَدَدَكم

وكَثَّرَ أَمْوالَكُم وقد ظَفِرْتُم: ومن النـاسِ البَغْىُ والحَسَدُ: ولم يَكْثُرْ قَطُّ قـومٌ إِلّا تَباغَوْا: ولَسْتُ آمَنُهـا

عَلَيْكم وبَيْنَكم حَسائِفُ g وأَضْغانٌ: فَتَواعَـدوا ماءَ النَّظِيمِ يـومَ كذا وكذا: فأَعْطِى بَعْضَكم من بَعْضٍ 10

وأَسْتَلَّ ضِغْنَ بَعْضِكم من بَعْضٍ. قالوا: ما تَعَقَّبْنا من أَمْرِكَ قَطُّ إِلّا يُمْنـًا وحَزْمًا: نَحْنُ مُوافُوكَ بالنَّظِيمِ

فى اليوم الذى أَمَرْتَ بِمُوافاتِكَ فيه. قال فاجْتَمَعَتْ بنو عامرٍ لم يَفْقِدْ منهم أَحَدٌ غَيْرَ عامر بن الطفيل.

فأَقامُوا على ماءٍ (30b) [h النَّظِيمِ] ثَلْثًا يَنْحَرُونَ الجُزُرَ. فقال عَلْقَمَةُ بـنُ عُلاثَةَ: ما يَحْبِسُ النـاسَ ان

يَفْرُغُوا مِمّا اجْتَمَعُوا له. قيل له: يَنْتَظِرُونَ عامر بن الطفيل. فقام مُغْضَبًا وكان فيه حَدٌّ: i [فأَقْبَلَ] على

نـادِيهم فـقال: ما تَنْتَظِرُونَ مِنْهُ: فواللهِ إِنَّهُ لَأَعْوَرُ البَصَرِ عاهِرُ الذِّكْرِ قَلِيلُ النَفَرِ. فقال له عامر بن 15

مالكٍ: احْبِسْ ولا تَقُلْ فى ابن عَمِّكَ إِلا خَيْرًا: فَلَوْ شَهِدَ وغِبْتَ لم يَقُلْ k [فِيكَ] مَقالَتَكَ فِيه. فأَقْبَلَ

---

a) So in Agh. XV, 139⁷; MS مُنْصَرِفِه (sic).

b) MS تَنْشُرَ; "Ich denke, تَنْشُرَ ist das Richtige: ich würde dann auch تَرْعَى (activ) lesen;
das Vieh meidet *von selbst* den geweihten Bezirk" (Nöldeke).

c) So MS and Mfḍt commy.; Agh. حِبّان.

d) MS قال. e) Agh., Mfḍt., الجَمَلُ.

f) Agh., Mfḍt السَّيْلُ (omitting the fourth clause and the parenthesis), which is plainly the
reading to be preferred.

g) MS أَضْغانٌ. h) So Mfḍt.
i) Added from Mfḍt. k) So Mfḍt.

عامر بن الطفيل على ناقة له فتَلَقَّاهُ بَعْضُ مَنْ غَضِبَ لَهُ من فتيان بنى مالك فأخبَرَهُ بِمَقالَة عَلْقَمَة. قال:

قَهَلْ قال غَيْرَ هذا. قال: لا. قال: فقد واللّه صَدَقَ: ما لى وَلَدٌ وإنّى لَعامِرُ الذَّكَرِ وإنّى لأَعْوَرُ البَصَرِ

a) وخَبَرُ ذَهابِ عَيْنِه فى قَيْفِ الرِّيحِ). وقال للذى أخبَرَهُ: فهل رَدَّ عليه أَحَدٌ. قال: لا. قال: أَحْسَنُوا.

وجاءَ حتى وَقَفَ b على ناديهم فحَيّاهُم وقال: لِمَ c تَتَفَرَّونَ شَتْمِى بَيْنَكم: فواللّه ما أنا عن عَدُوِكُمْ بِجَبَانٍ

5 ولا أنا فيما نَابَكم بِخَاذلٍ ولا الى أَعْراضكم بِسَريعٍ: وما حَبَسَنى عنكم إلّا خَمْرٌ قُدِّمَ بها فَسَبَأْتُها

وجَمَعْتُ d لها شَبابَ الحَيِّ e فخَشيتُ أن أَدَعَهُمْ فيَتَفَرَّقوا حتى أَنْفَدَتْها. وقد عَلِمْتُ f لأَيِّ شَىْءٍ

جَمَعكم أبو بَرَاءَ: فأَصْلَحَ اللّهُ g تآكُم ولَمَّ شَعَنَكُمْ h: وكلُّ قُرامَةٍ او خَدْشٍ او ظُفرٍ تَطْلُبُه بنو عامرٍ كُلِّها

فى أَموالِ بنى مالكٍ: ومالى أوَّلُ ذلكِ: وكلُّ شىءٍ هو لنا i فهو لَكُمْ. فقال أَعْمامُهُ: قد رَضِينَا ما فَعَلَ

وحَمَلْنا ما j حَمَّلَ. فتَصَدَّعَ الناسُ على ذلك. فكان ذلك مِمّا زادَ صَدْرَ عَلْقَمَةَ وَحْرًا حتى دَعاهُ ذلك

10 الى المُنافَرَةِ ۞

وقال عامر بن الطفيل

I.

١ إنّى وإنْ كُنْتُ ابْنَ k سَيّدِ عامرٍ   وَّفارسَها المَنْدُوبِ فى كُلِّ مَوْكِبِ

٢ (31a) فَما سَوَّدَتْنى عامرٌ عَنْ l قَرَابَةٍ   أَبَى اللّهُ أَنْ أَسْمُوَ بِأُمٍّ وَّلا أَبِ

---

a) See *post*, No. XI.

b) Mfḍt inserts راحِلَتَهُ.

c) So MS; Mfḍt تَتَفَرَّونَ بِشَتْمى.

d) Mfḍt عَلَيْها.

e) Mfḍt فَكَرِهْتُ.

f) Mfḍt فى أَىّ.

g) MS تآكُمْ وَلا شَعَنَكُمْ (*sic!*).

h) Mfḍt adds وَكَثَّرَ أَمْوالَكُمْ.

i) Mfḍt inserts فيكُمْ.

j) So Mfḍt; MS حَمَلَ.

I. *Ṭawīl*. These verses are the last three of a poem of which the whole is contained in the Supplement, No. 1, *q. v.* for more variant readings. The vv. are cited BQut. (*Shiʿr*) 192, ʿUmdah II, 117, SSM. 322, ʿAskarī, Ṣināʿat. 298.

k) BQut المَنْدُوبِ for المَشْهُورِ; *Umdah* as text, with فارسِ عامرٍ وَسَيّدَها المَشْهُورِ.

l) BQut, *Umdah*, وِرَاثَةٍ; LA XIV, 113²³, and TA VIII, 102², كَلَالَةٍ.

أَسْمُو أَرْتَفِع فِى الشَّرَف: يقال سَمَا بَصَرُ فُلَانٍ وَسَمَا فِكْرُهُ يَسْمُو سُمُوًّا والسَّامِى الرَّافِع: قال الخُطَيْئَةُ a

يَسْمُو بِهَا أَشْعَى طَرْفُهُ سَامِى

٣ وَلٰكِنَّنِى أَحْمِى حِمَاهَا وَأَتَّقِى   أَذَاهَا وَأَرْمِى مَنْ رَمَاهَا بِمَنْكِبِ

II.

١ عَرَفْتَ بِجَوٍّ b عَارِمَةَ الْمُقَامَا   لِسَلْمَى أَوْ عَرَفْتَ لَـهَا عَلَامَا

الجَوّ ما اطْمَأَنَّ مِن الارض وأنْخَفَض: والجَوّ الهَوَاء: والجَوَّاء: مكان: وفَرَسٌ أَجَّى يَضْرِب إلى الجُوَّةِ 5 وهى السَّوَاد. وعَارِمَةُ موضع. وعَلَامٌ جمع عَلَامَةٍ كما قال القُطَامِىُّ فى جَمْعِ ساعَةٍ ساعٌ *c فَيَخْبُو سَاعَةً وَيَهُبُّ سَاعَا* ☽

٢ لَيَالِىَ تَسْتَبِيكَ بِـذِى غُـرُوبٍ   وَّمُقْلَةِ جُؤْذَرٍ يَّرْعَى بَـشَامَا

ويروى بِجِيدٍ رِثْمٍ. تَسْتَبِيك من السَّبْى: يقال سَبَاهُ يَسْبِيهِ سَبْيًا بلا هَمْزٍ: وَسَبَأْتُ الخَمْرَ d أَسْبَوُهَا سِبَاءً 10 أَىْ اشْتَرَيْتُهَا: ولا يقال سَبَأْتُ اشْتَرَيْتُ فى شىءٍ غَيْرِ الخَمْرِ. والسَّابِيَاء ما يَخْرُجُ مع الوَلَد وهو ماءٌ رَقِيقٌ. ومُقْلَةُ العَيْنِ تَجْمَعُ السَّوَادَ والبَيَاضَ والحَدَقَةَ والطَّرْفَةَ. ويقال جُؤْذَرٌ وجُؤْذُرٌ مِثْلُ جُنْدَبٍ وجُنْدُبٍ: ويقال للجُؤْذَر e البُرْغُزُ والبُرْغُزُ والجمع البَرَاغِزُ. وبَشَامٌ شَجَرٌ تُتَّخَذُ مِنْـهُ المَسَاوِيكُ: ومِمَّا ذَكَرَهُ شُعَرَاؤُمْ فى البَشَام قول جَرِير بن عَطِيَّة

f أَتَنْسَى أَنْ تَوَدِّعَنَا سُلَيْمَى   بِعُودِ بَشَامَةٍ سُقِىَ الْبَشَامْ

ومن الاسْحِل: قال امْرُؤُ الْقَيْس: g أَوْ مَسَاوِيكُ إِسْحِل. ومن الضَّرْوِ وهو شَجَرُ الحَبَّةِ الخَضْرَاءِ: والعُثْمِ وهو 15

---

a) Dīwān XI, 14.

II. Wāfir; vv. 1, 19, 23—25, and 30—32 are found elsewhere.

b) MS عَامِرَة (and again in commy.), but correctly in v. 4. MS also الْمَقَامَا. The v. is cited in Bakrī 651¹⁵, as text; in LA XV, 314⁵ and TA VIII, 406 with الْمُقَامَا بِسَلْمَى and بِهَا.

c) Dīwān XIII, 19.

d) MS incorrectly أَسْبَوُه and اشْتَرِينَهُ.

e) MS incorrectly has ر for ز in these three words.

f) Jarīr, Dīw. II, p. 99.   g) Muʿall. 38.

زَيْتُونُ الْبَرِّ: قال الجَعْدِيّ

a تَسْتَنُّ بِالضَّرْوِ مِنْ بَرَاقِشَ أَوْ   هَيْلَانَ أَوْ يَانِعٍ مِنَ الْعُتُمِ

قال (31b) اسْتَنَّ الرَّجُلُ وتَسَوَّكَ وَاسْتَاكَ وتَشَوَّصَ: وفى الحديث: النَّشُوصُ بِالأَصَابِع يُغْنِي عَنِ السِّوَاكِ:

يقال شَاصَ يَشُوصُ شَوْصًا وتَشَوَّصَ تَشَوُّصًا. وبِالأَرَاكِ: قال

5 b إِذَا هِىَ لَمْ تَسْتَكْ بِعُودِ أَرَاكَةٍ   نَخِيرٌ فَاسْتَاكَتْ بِهِ عُودَ إِسْحِلِ

٣ c وَإِنْ قَوْمِى لِأُسْرَتِهَا عَدُوُّ   لِتُبْلِىَ بَيْنَهَا سَجْلًا وَخَامَا

أُسْرَتُها قومها الأَدْنَوْنَ منهم: ومنه أُسْرَةُ النَّبِيّ صَلَّى اللهُ عليه وسَلَّم الحَسَنُ والحُسَيْنُ صَلَوَاتُ اللهِ عَلَيْهِما.

يقول عَلَّقْتُها وَأَنَا عَدُوُّ قَوْمِها: ومثله قول طُفَيْلٍ الغَنَوِىّ

d أَبَى الْقَلْبُ إِلَّا حُبَّها عَامِرِيَّةً   تُجَاوِرُ أَعْدَائِى وَأَعْدَاؤُهَا مَعِى

10 وقوله وَخَاما اى وَخِيمَةَ الغِبِّ: ومنه كَلَأٌ وَخِيمٌ اذا كان غَيْرَ مَرِىءٍ. وَأَخْرَجَ سَجْلًا e وَخَامَا مَخْرَجَ الجَمِيع

كما يقال: هَلَكَتِ الشاةُ والبَعِيرُ: ومثله: f إِنَّ الإِنْسَانَ لَيَطْغَى: أَرَادَ النَّاسَ ☸

٤ فَإِنْ يَمْنَعْكِ قَوْمُكِ أَنْ تَبِينِى   فَقَدْ نَغْنَى بِعَارِمَةٍ سِلَامَا

تَبِينِى تُفَارِقِى والبَيْنُ الفِرَاق: يقال بَانَ يَبِينُ بَيْنًا وبَيْنُونَةً: ويقال بَيْنَهُما بَيْنٌ وبَوْنٌ. وعَارِمَةُ أرضُ لبنى

عامرٍ. وسِلَامًا اى سِلْمًا والسِّلْمُ الصُّلْحُ: وقال أيضًا: g *فَإِنْ حَرْبًا ضَبِيعَةَ أَوْ سِلَامَا*. ونَغْنَى اى نَبْقَى يقال

15 غَنِينَا بِمَكَانِ كذا وكذا اى بَقِينَا فِيه وتَمَتَّعْنَا بِه ☸

٥ فَلَوْ عَلِمَتْ سُلَيْمَى عِلْمَ مِثْلِى   غَدَاةَ الرَّوْعِ وَاصَلَتِ الْكِرَامَا

ويروى: عِلْمَ قَوْمِى. والرَّوْعُ الفَزَعُ. يقال رَاعَ الفُؤَادُ اى فَزِعَ: وَارْتَاعَ مثلُه: قال النابغَةُ الذُّبْيَانِىُّ

---

a) LA XV, 276²⁴ and XIX, 218¹¹; Bakrī 151⁸; all with نَاضِر for يَانِعٍ: the latter in Yāq. I.

535¹⁶; corruptly in Agh. IV, 138¹.

b) Ṭufail, Dīw. VI, 15, and Sībawaihi I 30, both with تُنُخِّلَ: the latter incorrectly attri-

butes the v. to ʿUmar b. Abī Rabīʿah (see his Dīw. No. 410 and Schwarz's note).

c) MS وَإِذَا.   d) See Ṭufail, Dīw. No. 24, 5.

e) وَخَامَا apparently stands for وَخَامَى, pl. of وَخِيمٌ, so written to make the rhyme symmetrical;

it may also be a singular: أرضٌ وَخَامٌ in LA XVI, 117³, Abū Zaid 84⁴.

f) Qur. XCVI, 6.   g) This v. is not in ʿĀmir's Dīw.

a فَارْتَاعَ مِنْ صَوْتِ كِلَابٍ قَبَّاتٍ لَهُ   طَوْعُ الشَّوَامِتِ مِنْ خَوْفٍ وَمِنْ صَرَدِ

٦ تَرَكْنَا مَذْحِجًا كَحَدِيثِ أَمْسِ   وَأَرْحَبَ إِنْ تَكَفَّفْنُهُمْ فِثَامَا

(32a) مَذْحِجٌ فِى الْيَمَنِ وَأَرْحَبُ مِنْ هَمْدَانَ. وَتَكَفَّفْهُمْ أَرَادَ الْخَيْلَ فَأَضْمَرَ وَلَمْ يَجْرِ لَهَا ذِكْرٌ: قَالَ الْأَخْطَلُ

b ٭هَدَجَ الرِّثَّالُ تَكُبُّهُنَّ شَمَالًا٭ فَأَضْمَرَ الرِّيحَ. وَمِثْلُهُ مَا يُقَالُ: أَصْبَحَتْ بَارِدَةً: وَلَا يَذْكُرُونَ الدُّنْيَا. وَفِثَامٌ

جَمَاعَةٌ: قَالَ نَهْشَلُ بنُ الْحَرِّيِّ:

c تَرَى الْفِثَامَ فُعُودَا يَأْحُونَ لَهَا   دَأْبَ الْمُعَضِّلِ إِذْ شَتَّتْ مَلَاقِيهَا

قَوْلُهُ يَأْحُونَ اى يَرْحَرُونَ. وَالْمُعَضِّلُ الَّتِى قَدْ ضَاقَ مَخْرَجُ وَلَدِهَا. وَالْمَلَاقِى حَلْفُ الرَّحِمِ الْوَاحِدَةُ مَلْقَاةٌ ✿

٧ وَبِعْنَا شَاكِرًا بِتِلَادِ عَكٍّ   وَلَاقَى مَنْسِرٌ مِنَّا جُذَامَا

مَنْسِرٌ مِنَ الْخَيْلِ مَا بَيْنَ السِّتِّينَ الَى السَّبْعِينَ: *d* وَمِثْلُهُ الْمِقْنَبُ فِى السَّفَرِ وَالْمَوْكِبُ وَأَقَلَّ وَأَكْثَرَ: وَمِثْلُهُ فِى

السَّفَرِ بِغَيْرِ حَرْبٍ *e* مُجَلَّدٌ: قَالَ الْعَجَّاجُ يَمْدَحُ ابْرَاهِيمَ بنَ عَرَبِيٍّ أَخَا بَنِى عُبَيْدِ الرِّمَاحِ بنِ مَعَدٍّ

(وَعَدَدُهُمْ فِى بَنِى كِنَانَةَ) حِينَ وَفَدَ الَى الْوَلِيدِ بنِ عَبْدِ الْمَلِكِ عَامِلِ الْيَمَامَةِ

f بِمُجَلَّدٍ وَنِعْمَ رَأْسُ الْمُجَلَّدِ   عَلَيْهِ بِاللهِ بَلَاغُ الرُّحَّلِ

٨ وَطَحْطَحْنَا شَنُوءَةَ كُلَّ أَوْبٍ   وَلَاقَتْ حِمْيَرٌ مِنَّا غَرَامَا

شَنُوءَةُ يَعْنِى الْأَزْدَ: مَنْ أَقَامَ بِالْيَمَنِ فَهُمُ السَّرَاةُ: وَمَنْ سَارَ مِنْهُمْ فَتَخَلَّفَ بِمَكَّةَ فَهِىَ خُزَاعَةُ لِاخْزِرَاعِهِمْ

عَنْهُمْ: وَمَنْ أَقَامَ بِالْمَدِينَةِ مِنْهُمْ فَهُمُ الْأَوْسُ وَالْخَزْرَجُ حَتَّى أَكْرَمَهُمُ اللهُ بِالنُّصْرَةِ: وَمَنْ نَزَلَ مِنْهُمْ بِالشَّامِ

g فَهُمْ غَسَّانُ: وَمَنْ نَزَلَ مِنْهُمْ عُمَانَ فَهُمْ شَنُوءَةُ. وَالْغَرَامُ الْعَذَابُ ✿

٩ وَهَمْدَانٌ هُنَالِكَ مَا أُبَالِى   أَحَرْبًا أَصْبَحُوا لِى أَمْ سَلَامَا

١٠ وَلَاقَيْنَا بِأَبْطَحِ ذِى زَرُودٍ   بَنِى شَيْبَانَ فَالْتَهَمُوا التِّهَامَا

كُلُّ بَطْنِ وَادٍ أَبْطَحُ وَبَطْحَاءُ. وَزَرُودٌ *h* حَبْلُ رَمْلٍ. وَبَنُو شَيْبَانَ بنِ ذُهْلٍ. الْتَهَمُوا اى ابْتَلَعُوا ابْتِلَاعًا ✿

---

a) Nāb. Muʿall. 12.   *b)* Dīw. p. 43.   *c)* See Ḥam. 200¹², with الرِّجَالَ for الفِثَام and

شَتَّتْ for ضَاقَتْ.   *d)* So in MS; but probably the words وَأَقَلَّ وَأَكْثَرَ (so vocalized in MS)

should be transferred to the end of the previous sentence, after السَّبْعِينَ.   *e)* So MS, and

Ahlwardt in ʿAjjāj; LA XIII, 111¹² vocalizes مُجَلَّدٌ.   *f)* ʿAjj. Dīw. XXXI, 41—42; LA *ut sup.*

g) MS فَهُوَ.   *h)* So MS; Bakrī 436⁹ has جَبَلُ رَمْلٍ.

١١ (32ᵇ) وَحَيًّا مِّنْ بَنِى أَسَدٍ تَرَكْنَا   نِسَاءَهُمْ مُسَلِّبَةً أَيَامَا

يعنى اسد بن خُزَيْمَةَ بن مُدْرِكَةَ بن اِلْياس بن مُضَرَ بن نِزار. مُسَلِّبَةً اى تَرَكْتِ الزِّينَةَ وهى السَّلُوب:

وهى a لِلْحادِّ خاصَّةً التى تَتْرُك الصِّبْغَ والكُحْلَ على مبْتِنها. والأَيَامَى b اللَّواتى لا أَزْواجَ لَهُنَّ الواحدة أَيِّمٌ:

قال الشَّمَّاخ

c يَقُرُّ بِعَيْنِى أَنْ أَنَبَّأَ أَنَّها   وَإِنْ لَمْ أَنَلْها أَيِّمٌ لَمْ تَزَوَّج   5

وتكون الأَيِّمُ بِكْرًا وثَيِّبًا: قال الساعر: d *وَتَشِببُ أَيِّمهُمْ وَلَمَّا تُخْطَبْ:* فهذه بِكْرٌ: والأُولَى ثَيِّبٌ ۞

١٢ وَقَتَّلْنَا سَرَاتَهُمْ جِهَارًا   وَأَشْبَعْنَا الضِّبَاعَ خُصَى عِظَامَا

سَرَاةُ القوم e رُؤَساؤُهم وخِيارُهم: يقال اسْتَرَيْتُ المَتاعَ اى اخْتَرْتُه: ومنه يقال امْرَأَةٌ مُسْتَرَاةٌ اى مُخْتارَةٌ:

ومنه قول الأَعْشَى

f فَقَدْ أُخْرِجُ الكَاعِبَ المُسْتَرَا   ةَ مِنْ خِدْرِها وَأُشْبِعُ القِمَارَا   10

١٣ وَقَتَّلْنَا حَنِيفَةَ فِى قُرَاهَا   وَأَفْنَى غَزْوُنَا حَكَمًا وَّحَامَا

حَنِيفَةُ ابن لُجَيْم بن صَعْب بن عَلِيّ بن بَكْر بن وَائِل. g وحَامٌ اراد حَا وحَكَمَ ابْنَى سَعْد العَشِيرة

فزادَ ما صِلَةً له. وقالت h أُمُّ قَرارةَ وهى بِنْتُ لُجَيْمٍ لِابنها قَرارةَ وهى i تُرَفِّنُه:

إِنْ تَشْبِهِ الأَوْقَصَ أَوْ زُلَهَيْمَا   أَوْ عِجْلَ أَوْ حَنِيفَ أَوْ لُجَيْمَا

---

a) See Lane 524*c*.   *b*) MS التى.   *c*) Dīwān p. 7 l. 4.

d) See *post*, No. VIII, v. 3.   *e*) MS رتِيسهُمْ.

f) LA XIX, 100¹² , with أُطْبَى for أُخْرِجُ (latter as *v. l.*).

g) No such name as حام or حاء occurs among the descendants of Saᶜd al-ᶜAshīrah mentioned in Wüst. Tab. 7; حام is found as the name of one of the tribes of Khathᶜam in Tab. 9, 17. On the other hand, in Naq. 472⁵ a verse is quoted, relating to the Day of Faif ar-Rīḥ, by Abū Duᵓād of Ruᵓās (a sept of Kilāb), as follows:

ظَلَّتْ بُحَاِبرُ تُدْعَى وَسْطَ أَرْحُلِنَا   وَالْمُسْتَمِيتُونَ مِنْ حَاءٍ وَمِن حَكَمِ

A gloss to this verse says that Ḥaᵓ is a subtribe of Ḥakam. The explanation given in the scholion, that حامًا represents حا *plus* ما as صِلَة, may be frankly rejected as impossible.

h) The MS carelessly writes أمْرَةَ.

i) MS تُرَفِّيه: the word is equivalent to تُرَقِّصُ, «dandle». For the names that follow see Wüst. Tab. B.   *j*) MS لُجَيْمَا.

بَنَّيْنَا فَزَارَ تُشْبِهُ قَوْمًا   بِيضَ ٱلْوُجُوهِ يَمْنَعُونَ ضَيْمَا

١٤ قَتَلْنَا كَبْشَهُمْ فَنَجَوْا شِلَالًا   كَمَا نَفَّرْتَ بِٱلطَّرْدِ ٱلنَّعَامَا

ٱلْكَبْش ٱلرَّئِيس هُنا: وقال لِلْحَارِث بن وَعْلَةَ ٱلْجَرْمِيُّ

ٱلضَّارِبُونَ ٱلْكَبْش صَاحِبَةً   a كَٱلْكَوْكَبِ ٱلْمُتَوَقِّدِ ٱلْفَخْمِ

وَشِلَالًا طَرَدًا يقال شَلَّهُ يَشُلُّهُ شَلًّا اى طَرَدَهُ ورَجُلٌ مِشَلٌّ طَارِدٌ. b [وَلَيْسَ شَى]؟ أَنْفَرُ مِن ٱلنَّعَم ومِنه ٥
ٱلْمَثَل (33a) أَشْرَدُ مِنْ نَعَمٍ ☙

١٥ وَجِئْنَا بِٱلنِّسَاءِ مُرَدَّفَاتٍ   وَأَذْوَادٍ فَكُنَّ لَنَا طَعَامَا

مُرَدَّفَات اى سَبَيْنَاهُنَّ فَهُنَّ مُرَدَّفَات. وٱلذَّوْد (تُجْمَعُ أَذْوَادًا) بَيْنَ ٱلثَّلْثَةِ الى ٱلْعَشَرَةِ ☙

١٩ [وَبَيَّاتِنَا] زُبَيْدًا بَعْدَ هَدْءٍ   فَصَبَّحَ دَارَهُمْ لَجِبًا لُّهَامَا

زُبَيْد فى ٱلْيَمَن. وٱلْهَدْء وٱلْهُدُوء قِطْعَة تَمْضِى من ٱللَّيْل. وٱللَّجِب ٱلْجَيْش ٱلْكَثِير ٱلصَّوْت: ولم يَذْكُرِ ١٠
ٱلْجَيْش وجاءَ بِٱللَّجِب: وٱللَّجَب ٱلصَّوْت وٱللَّجِب ذو الصوت. وٱللُّهام ٱلْجَيْش ٱلصَّخْم ٱلْكَثِير يَلْتَهِمُ كُلَّ
شىءٍ مَرَّ عليه: لا واحِدَ له مِن لَفْظِه ☙

١٧ وَقَدْ نِلْنَا لِعَبْدِ ٱلْقَيْسِ سَبْيًا   مِّنَ ٱلْبَكْرَيْنِ يُقْتَسَمُ ٱقْتِسَامَا

١٨ وَلَاقَيْنَا بِذِى نَجَبٍ حُصَيْنًا   فَأَهْلَكْنَا بِمَقْلَتِنَا أُسَامَا c

يَعْنِى ٱلْحُصَيْنِ بن لِلْحَارِث بن كَعْب. [ذو] نَجَب مَوْضِع كانت لَهُمْ به وَقْعَةٌ. وأُسَامَةُ رَجُلٌ ☙ ١٥

١٩ وَأَفْلَتَمَا عَلَى ٱلْحَوْمَانِ قَيْسٌ d   وَأَسْلَمَ عِرْسَهُ ثُمَّ ٱسْتَقَامَا

ٱلْحَوْمَان فى طَرِيقِ ٱلْيَمَامَةِ من ٱلْبَصْرَةِ. وٱلْعِرْس اراد ٱلْمَرْأَة: اى أَسْلَم إِلَيْنَا عِرْسَهُ وأَفْلَتَ: يُعَيِّرُهُ بِقِلَّةِ
ٱلْوَفَاء وضِيَاعِ ٱلْحَرِيم e [وعَدَم] حِفْظ ما يَجِبُ عليه حِمَايَتُهُ وحِفْظُهُ ☙

٢٠ وَلَوْ آسَى حَلِيلَتَهُ لَلَاقَى   f [هُنَالِكَ] مِنْ أَسِنَّتِنَا حِمَامَا

---

a) MS, unmetrically and against the sense, إِذَا ٱلْكَوْكَب فَخْم; for a similar use of كَوْكَب فَخْم for
an army see the verse in LA II, 216[15]. The verse seems to belong to the poem in the same
metre from which the extract in Ḥam. 97—99 is taken; if so, the author is of Dhuhl b. Shaibān,
not of Jarm. There was a Waʻlah b. al-Ḥārith of Jarm, who was present at the second battle
of al-Kulāb, and was the author of a poem in the Mfḍt, No. XXXII (see Naq. 154—6).
b) MS broken. c) So MS; we should expect this unusual word to be noticed in the
scholion: perhaps the correct reading may be بِمَقْتَلِنَا. For قَلَتُ = هَلَكُ see LA II, 377[4] ff.
d) Bakrī 300[10]. e) omitted in MS; conj. f) carelessly omitted in MS; added conjecturally.

آسَى وَوَاسَى واحِدٌ مِن المُوَاسَاةِ: اى لو قَاتَلَ عَنْها وصَبَرَ على القِتال لَقِىَ الحِمامَ وهو القَدَرُ والمَوْتُ: يقال

حُمَّ عَلَيْهِ وقُدِّرَ وقَدَّرَ a بِمَعْنًى واحد. والأَسِنَّةُ] جمع سِنان ۞

٢١   وَآلَ الْـجَـوْنِ قَدْ سَـارُوا إِلَـيْـنَـا   b [غَدَاةَ الشِّـعْبِ] فَاصْطُلِمُوا اصْطِلَامَا

(33b) يريد ابْنَىْ أَبِى الجَوْنِ اللَّذَيْنِ كانا مع لَقِيط يَوْمَ جَبَلَة وحاجِب بن زُرارَة بن عُدَّسِ بن زَيْد

5 ابن عَبْدِ الله بن دَارِم. والجَوْنُ الأَبْيَضُ والأَسْوَد c وهى الجَوْنَةُ. ويقال للشَّمْسِ جَوْنَةٌ: قال طَرَفَةُ

d أَنْتَ الْهُمَامُ إِذَامَا جَوْنَةٌ طَلَعَتْ   وَأَنْتَ بِاللَّيْلِ طَلَّابُ الْمَوَا[عِيـ]ـسِ

واصْطُلِمُوا اى أُجْتِيحُوا اجْتِيَاحًا. ويقال صَلَمَ واصْطَلَمَ اذا قَطَعَهُ عن e [أَصْلِه: و]اسْتَوْعَبَ قَطَعَ الأَنْفَ:

ويقال نَعَامَةٌ مُصَلَّمَةٌ وكُلُّ النعام f صُلْمٌ لا آذانَ لها: ويقال رَجُلٌ أَصْلَمُ اذا كان مَقْطُوعَ الأُذُنَيْنِ ۞

٢٢   قَتَلْنَـا مِنْهُمْ مِائَـةً بِشَيْخٍ   وَصَفَّدْنَـاهُمْ عُصَبًا g قِيَامَا

10 قوله صَفَّدْنَا اى قَيَّدْنَا: يقال صَفَّدْتُ الرجُلَ أُصَفِّدُهُ اى h [أَكْثَرْتُ] قَيْدَهُ وهو الصِّفاد: قال الله تبارك وتعالى:

i مُقَرَّنِينَ فِى الأَصْفادِ: ويقال أَصْفَدْتُ بالأَلِف أُصْفِدُ إِصْفَادًا اى أَعْطَيْتُهُ. والعُصَبُ جمع عُصْبَة وهى الجَماعَة:

ويقال عَصَبَ عِمامَتَهُ على رَأْسِه اذا لَوَاها: ويقال هذا شَرٌّ يُعْصَبُ بِه رَأْسُ فلانٍ اى يُعْتَمُ بِه ۞

٢٣   j وَيَـوْمَ الشِّعْبِ لَاقَيْنَـا لَقِيطًا   كَسَوْنَـا رَأْسَهُ عَضْبًا حُسَامَا

يعنى يومَ شِعْبِ جَبَلَة. والعَضْبُ والحُسام واحدٌ وهُما السَيْفُ: والعَضْبُ القاطِع ومثْلُه الحُسام: يقال

15 حَسَمْتُ ما بَيْنَ فلانٍ وما بَيْنَ فلانٍ اى قَطَعْتُه: ويقال فى مَثَلٍ: ألْكَىُّ للدَّاءِ أَحْسَمُ ۞

٢٤   أَسَرْنَـا حَاجِبًا k فَثَوَى أَسِيرًا   وَلَمْ نَتْرُكْ l لِأُسْرَتِـهِ سَوَامَا

ثَوَى أَقَام فى m الأَسْرِ والثَاوِى المُقِيم والثَوَاءُ الاقامة: يقال ثَوَى فلانٌ فى مكانِ كذا وكذا وأَثْوَى: قال

---

a) MS broken away: conj.   b) MS broken away: conj.

c) MS وَهُو; perhaps we should read وَاسْمُهُ هُوَ الْجَوْنَةُ.

d) Not found in Ṭarafah's *Dīwān*, Ahlw. or Seligsohn; last word uncertain owing to decay

of MS. For مَوَاعِيسُ, pl. of مِيعَاسٌ, see LA VIII, 143^{10} ff.

e) Carelessly omitted in MS: conj.   f) MS صُلْمٌ لا الآذانِ لَهَا.

g) So MS: probably we should read فَقَامَا.

h) Word omitted: conj.   i) Qur. XIV, 50, and XXXVIII, 37.

j) Agh. X, 47^{26} has vv. 23—25. Agh. وَيَوْمَ الْجَمْعِ.

k) Agh. فَثَوَى بِقَيْدٍ.   l) Agh. لِنِسْوَتِهِ.   m) MS الأَسْرَةِ.

الْأَعْشَى: (34a) a *أَنْوَى وَأَقْصَرَ لَيْلَهُ لِيَزُوَّدَا*: وَأُمُّ الْمَثْوَى امْرَأَةُ الرَّجُلِ. وَالسَّوَامُ مَا رَعَى مِنَ الْمَالِ:

يُقَالُ سَامَتْ تَسُومُ وَالْمُسِيمُ الرَّاعِي: قَالَ الشَّاعِرُ: b *وَقَدْ الْمُسِيمِ [وَا]هَلَّكَ السَّوَامِ* ☙

٢٥ c وَجَمْعُ بَنِى تَمِيمٍ قَدْ تَرَكْنَا   نُبِيِّنُ سَوَاعِدًا مِّنْهُمْ وَهَامَا

يَعْنِى تَمِيمَ بْنَ مُرٍّ. نُبِيِّنُ نُفَرِّقُ أَى نَقْطَعُ وَنَفْصِلُ مِنْهُمْ. وَهَامَةٌ وَهَامٌ لِأُمِّ الدِّمَاغِ مِثْلَ قَارَةٍ وَقَارٍ:

5 وَالْهَامُ ذَكَرُ الْبُومِ ☙

٢٩ وَكَانَ لَهُمْ بِهَا يَوْمٌ طَوِيلٌ   كَمَا أَجَّجْتَ بِاللَّهَبِ الضِّرَامَا

يَوْمٌ طَوِيلٌ لِأَنَّهُ يَوْمُ حَزْنٍ وَغَمٍّ فَقَدْ طَالَ عَلَيْهِمْ: وَيَوْمُ الْفَرَجِ قَصِيرٌ. وَأَجَّجْتَ أَوْقَدْتَ يُقَالُ أَجِّجْ نَارَكَ d أَى أَذْكِهَا. وَاللَّهَبُ النَّارُ: قَالَ ذُو الرُّمَّةِ: e *كَأَنَّهُ حِينَ يَعْلُو عَاقِرًا لَهَبُ*. وَالضِّرَامُ مَا دَقَّ مِنَ الْحَطَبِ

وَضَمَرَ: وَالْجَزْلُ الْغَلِيظُ مِنَ الْحَطَبِ. وَقَوْلُهُ بِهَا أَى بِالْخَيْلِ وَلَمْ يَذْكُرْهَا: وَمِثْلُهُ: قَبِيتُ شِمَالًا: وَمِثْلُهُ

10 فِى الْقُرْآنِ: f حَتَّى تَوَارَتْ بِالْحِجَابِ: وَلَمْ يَأْتِ بِذِكْرِ الشَّمْسِ: وَمِثْلُهُ: g وَمَا تَرَكَ عَلَى ظَهْرِهَا مِنْ دَابَّةٍ ☙

٢٧ بِدَارِهِمْ تَرَكْنَا يَوْمَ نَحْسٍ   لَّدَى أَوْطَانِهِمْ تُسْقَى السِّمَامَا

يَوْمُ نَحْسٍ أَى شَرٍّ وَشُؤْمٍ: وَيُقَالُ يَوْمُ نَحْسٍ أَى يَوْمُ رِيحٍ فِى غَيْرِ هَذَا الْمَوْضِعِ. وَالْأَوْطَانُ جَمْعُ وَطَنٍ.

وَالسِّمَامُ جَمْعُ سَمٍّ: وَيُقَالُ سَمٌّ وَسُمٌّ: وَالسَّمُّ الثَّقْبُ: قَالَ الْفَرَزْدَقُ

h فَنَفَسْتُ عَنْ سَمَّيْهِ حَتَّى تَنَفَّسَا   وَقُلْتُ لَهُ لَا تَخْشَ شَيْئًا وَرَائِبَا

15 وَمِنْهُ: i يَلِجُ الْجُمَلُ فِى سَمِّ الْخِيَاطِ: وَالسَّامُ عِرْقُ الذَّهَبِ بِالتَّخْفِيفِ: قَالَ قَيْسُ بْنُ الْخَطِيمِ

زلَوْ أَنَّكَ تُلْقِى حَنْظَلًا [فَوْقَ بَيْضِنَا   تَدَحْرَجَ] عَنْ ذِى سَامِهِ الْمُتَقَارِبِ

---

a) LA XVIII, 136[10] (with قَصَّرَ): the form is disputed; see the discussion which follows in LA.

b) The insertion of وَ before هَلَّكَ is necessary to bring the phrase into metre: without the extra syllable it complies with no metrical scheme.

c) Agh. differs greatly: — وَجَمْعُ الْحَزْمِ إِذْ دَلَفُوا إِلَيْنَا   صَبَحْنَا جَمْعَهُمْ كَجِبَالٍ هَامَا

d) MS أَذْكَّهُ.   *e)* See Dh. R.'s *Bā'iyah* in Jamharah, p. 183, middle.

f) Qur. XXXVIII, 31.

g) Qur. XXXV, 44; in this verse عَلَى ظَهْرِهَا = عَلَى ظَهْرِ الْأَرْضِ.

h) Naq. 169[10] (سَمَّاهُ = "his nostrils").

i) Qur. VII, 38.

j) LA XV, 205[21], and Lane 1475c; middle of verse broken away in MS.

٢٨ فَإِنْ لَا يُرْهِقِ الْحَدَثَانِ نَفْسِى * يُؤَدُّوا الْخَرْجَ لِى عَامًا فَعَامَا[a]

(٣٤b) يُرْهِقْ اى يُعْجِلْ: يقال أَرْهَقَتْنَا الْحَرْبُ: ويقال فى غير هذا الموضع أَرْهَقْنَا أَخَّرْنَا: وغُلَامٌ مُرْهَقٌ[b]

اى بَالِغٌ: قال ابن قَرْمَةَ

خَيْرُ الرِّجَالِ الْمُرَهَّقُونَ كَمَا * خَيْرُ تِلَاعِ الْبِلَادِ أَوْطَؤُهَا[c]

يقول: إِنْ لَمْ يَأْخُذْنِى الْموتُ أَذَلْتُهُم حتى يَنْقَادُوا لِى وِيؤُدُّوا خَرْجَهُمْ إِلَىَّ ۞

٢٩ يُؤَدُّوهُ عَلَى رَغْمٍ صِغَارًا * وَيُعْطُونَا الْمَقَادَةَ وَالزِّمَامَا[d]

يُؤدُّوهُ يعنى الْخَرْجَ. والرَّغْمُ اراد الذُّلَّ: يقال أَرْغَمَ اللهُ أَنْفَهُ اى أَلْزَقَهُ بِالرَّغَامِ وهو التُّرَابُ: ويقال:

أَفْعَلُ ذلك وَإِنْ رَغِمَ أَنْفُكَ ۞

٣٠ فَأَبْلِغْ[e] إِنْ عَرَضْتَ جَمِيعَ سَعْدٍ * قِبِيتَهُمُ لَنْ نَهِيجَكُمْ نِيَامَا

تَشَكَّرَ لِبَنِى سَعْدٍ إِنْذَارَهُمْ كَرِبَ بن صَفْوان بن شَجْنَةَ بن عطارد بن عَوْف بن كَعْب بن سَعْد بن

زَيْد مَنَاةَ بن تميم بنى عامر يوم جَبَلَةَ ۞ وعُلَمَاءُ بنى تميم لا يَقْبَلُون من هذه الْأَرْبَعَةِ الْأَبْيَاتِ التى

فى آخِرِهَا شَيْئًا ۞ ويروى: *فَأَبْلِغْ مَا أَقُولُ جَمِيعَ سَعْدٍ* وشَجْنَةَ: [شَجْنَةَ] ابن عطارد بن عوف بن

كعب بن سعد بن زيد مناة بن تميم ۞

٣١ نَصَحْتُمْ بِالْمَغِيبِ[f] وَلَمْ تُعِينُوا * عَلَيْنَا إِنَّكُمْ كُنْتُمْ كِرَامَا

٣٢ فَلَوْ كُنْتُمْ مَعَ ابْنِ الْجَوْنِ كُنْتُمْ[g] * كَمَنْ أَوْدَى وَأَصْبَحَ قَدْ أَلَمَّا ١٥

ويروى: *كَمَنْ أَمْسَى وَأَصْبَحَ قَدْ أَلَمَّا*[h] أَلَمَّ أَتَى إِيدَاءً. أَوْدَى هَلَكَ يُودِى. أَلَامَ أَتَى مَا يُلَامُ عليه: يقال

---

a) Words broken away in MS supplied from the sense of the commy.

b) So MS; but in LA XI, 422[12], and Lane s. v., this sense is assigned to مُرَاهِقٌ.

c) LA XI, 422[2], with أَكَلُوهَا; in this verse الْمُرَهَّقُونَ is explained as "those at whose abodes suppliants and guests often apply", and it has nothing to do with بَالِغٌ = مُرَاهِقٌ.

d) MS وَيُعْطُونَ.

e) Agh. X, 38[11] has vv. 30—32. Agh. أَلَا أَبْلِغْ لَدَيْكَ جُمُوعَ تَيْمٍ.

f) Agh. بِالْمَغِيبِ تَغِيبُوا.   g) Agh. وَلَوْ.

h) In the MS part of this scholion is misplaced and put at the end of the commy. on v. 30. MS has كَمَا for كَمَنْ in the alternative reading given.

أَلَامَ الرَّجُلُ يُلِيمُ إِلَامَةً: ومنه قول الله تبارك وتعالى: a فَالْتَقَمَهُ الْحُوتُ وَهُوَ مُلِيمٌ: ويقال رَجُلٌ لَوَّامٌ اذا كان

لا يَزَالُ يلوم الناس. وابن الجَوْن الذى كان مع لَقِيط بن زُرَارَةَ ☆ (35a)

III.

١   هَلَّا سَأَلْتِ بِمَا وَأَنْتِ b حَفِيَّةٌ   بِالْقَاعِ يَوْمَ تَوَرَّعَتْ نَهْدُ

حَفِيَّة مُشْفِقَة بَارَّة. والْقَاعُ c والْقِيعَة الْمُسْتَوِى من الْأَرْض وجمعها قِيعَان. وتَوَرَّعَتْ جَبُنَتْ وتَأَخَّرَتْ

وهَابَتْ. نَهْدُ ابن زَيْد بن لَيْث بن سُود بن أَسْلَمَ بن الْحَافِ ☆

٢   d والْحَىُّ مِنْ كَلْبٍ وَجَرْمٍ كُلِّهَا   بِالْقَاعِ يَوْمَ يَحُتُّهَا الْجَلَدُ

ويروى *والْحَىُّ مِنْ جَرْمٍ وَأَكْلُبُ كُلُّهَا*. وجَرْمٌ ابن e رَيَّان بن حُلْوَان بن عِمْرَان بن الْحَافِ بن

قُضَاعَة. يَحُتُّهَا الْجَلَدُ اى يَجْلِدُهَا بِالسَّوْطِ: وهو مَصْدَرُ جَلَدْتُهُ: اى يَحُتُّونَها بِالسِّيَاطِ ☆

٣   f بِالْكَوْرِ يَوْمَ ثَوَى الْحُصَيْنُ وَقَدْ رَأَى   عَبْدُ الْمَدَانِ خُيُولَهَا تَعْدُو

الْكَوْرُ أرض بِنَاحِيَة نَجْرَانَ. g والْحُصَيْنُ هو ذو الغُصَّة من بَلْحَارِث بن كَعْب. ويروى: يَوْمَ دَعَا. وثَوَى

أَقَامَ. وعَبْدُ الْمَدَانِ ابن الدَّيَّانِ من بَلْحَارِث ايضًا ☆

٤   بِالْبَاسِلِينَ مِنَ الْكُمَاةِ عَلَيْهِمْ   حَلَقُ الْحَدِيدِ يَزِينُهَا السَّرْدُ

الباسِلُون الأشِدَّاء الواحد باسِل والبَسَالَة الشِّدَّة وهم الشُّجْعَان: والباسِل الكَرِيه الْمَنْظَر ايضا: يقال تَبَسَّلَ

فلانٌ اذا تَكَرَّهَ: وانشد

---

a) Qur. XXXVII, 142.

III. *Kāmil.* Vv. 2, 3 found elsewhere.

b) MS حَفِيْنَة; see *post*, No. XXIX, 1, and LA XVIII, 205⁵ ff.

c) LA X, 179² notes that some grammarians (Abū ʿUbaid is mentioned) hold قِيعَة to be a

singular; it is generally considered to be a plural of paucity.

d) Bakrī 482¹¹ reads مِنْ كَلْبٍ for مِنْ كَعْبٍ, and this must be the correct reading (unless, as is

probable, we should prefer the alternative in the scholion), as all the other names are of tribes in

Northern Yaman. The MS. gives the first hemistich corruptly thus: والْحَىُّ مِنْ جَرْمٍ كَلْبٍ وَجَرْمٍ كُلِّهَا.

e) MS زَبَّان.   f) So Bakrī, *l. c.* MS corruptly عَبْدُ الْمَدَامِ, but correctly in scholion.

g) See Wüst. Register 231; BDur. 240¹⁰.

a وَكُنْتُ ذَنُوبَ ٱلْبِئْرِ لَمَّا تَبَسَّلَتْ　　　وَسُرْبِلْتُ أَكْفَانِى وَوُسِّدْتُ سَاعِدِى

ولِكُمَاةِ الواحِدُ كَمِىٌّ اى يَكْمِى عَدْوَةً يَقْمَعُهُ: وانشد: *لَوْلَا تَكْمِى عَامِرٌ مَنْ جَارَا*: ويَرْوِى: b *لَوْلَا تَكْمِيكَ ذُرَى مَنْ جَارَا* اى لَـوْلَا قَمْعَكَ [lacuna: MS broken] ٱلْأَرْض لِأَنَّ الْأَرْض تَكْمِيها اى تَسْتُرُها. والكُمُّ منه أُخِذَ كَأَنَّهُ ما يَسْتُرُ الْيَدَ والسَّاعِدَ: ويقال: كَمَى شَهَادَتَهُ يَكْمِيها c [إذا كَتَمَها] وسَتَرَها . (35b)

٥ والسَّرْدُ تَتَابُعُ عَمَلِ الدِّرْعِ: ومِنْهُ: d وَقَدِّرْ فِى السَّرْدِ ✿

ه اَىُّ الْفَوَارِسِ كَانَ أَنْهَكَ فِى الْوَغَى　　　لِلْقَوْمِ لَمَّا لَاحَهَا الْجَهْهُدُ

أَنْهَكَ أَشَقَّ. ومنه نَهَكَتْهُ الْحُمَّى اشْتَدَّتْ عليه: ومنه شُجَاعٌ نَهِيكٌ اى شديدٌ. والْوَغَى والْوَعَى واللَّجَبُ الصَّوْتُ فِى الْحَرْبِ: فَكَثُرَ ذلك حَتَّى قيل للْحَرْبِ وَغًى. وَلَاحَها أَضْمَرَها وغَيَّرَ لَوْنَها: يقال لاحَـهُ يَلُوحُهُ ولَوَّحَ يُلَوِّحُ تَلْوِيحًا: قال رُوبَةُ

e لَوَّحَ مِنْهُ بَعْدَ بُدْنٍ وَسَنَقْ　　　مِنْ طُولِ تَعْدَاءَ الرَّبِيعِ فِى الْأَنَقْ

٩ لَمَّا رَأَيْتُ رَئِيسَهُمْ فَتَرَكْتُهُ　　　جَزَرَ السِّبَاعِ كَأَنَّهُ لَهْهُدُ

جَزَرُ السِّبَاعِ لَحْمٌ f لَهُمْ يَجْزَرُونَهُ. واللَّهْدُ واللُّهْدُ بِفَتْحِ اللام وكسرها الوَرَمُ: قال الْأَغْلَبُ الْعِجْلِىُّ g *تَطَّلَعُ مِنْ لَهْدٍ بِهَا وَلُهْدٍ*. ويروى: فَتَرَكْتُهُ* فِيهِ السِّنَان كَأَنَّهُ لَهْدٌ*. واذا طَعَنَهُ فَتَرَكَ الرُّمْحَ فيه فقد أَجَرَّهُ يُجِرُّهُ إِجْرَارًا: وقال: h *أَجَرَّهُ الرُّمْحَ وَلَا تِهَالَهُ*: وهو من أَجْرَرْتُ الْفَصِيلَ اللَّاهِجَ بِاللَّبَنِ وشَرَبِهِ: ١٥ وهو أن يُخَلَّ لِسَانُهُ بِخِلَالَةٍ حتى يَمْتَنِعَ عَنِ الْمَصِّ: ومنه قول امرئ الْقَيْسِ: *i كَمَا جَرَّ ظَهْرَ اللِّسَانِ الْمُجِرُّ* يعنى لِسَانَ الْفَصِيلِ ✿

٧ وَثَوَى رَبِيعَةُ فِى الْمَكَرِّ مُجَدَّلًا　　　فَعَلَا النَّعِيَّ بِمَا جَدَا الْجَدُّ

ثَوَى أَقَامَ ولم يَبْرَحْ. فِى الْمَكَرِّ يعنى موضع القِتَالِ والكَرِّ وهو مُعْتَرَكُهُمْ فِى الْحَرْبِ. مُجَدَّلًا اى مَصْرُوعًا مُلْقًى فى الْجَدَالَةِ وهى الْأَرْض وقال الراجز

---

a) LA I, 378¹; Qālī, *Amālī* I, 103¹⁵; poet Abū Dhu'aib.

b) This is the reading in 'Ajjāj, Dīw. XII, 68.

c) MS broken; conj.　　　d) Qur. XXXIV, 10.

e) Dīw. Ru'bah XL, 17—18.　　　f) So MS, for تَجْزِرُّها.

g) LA IV, 399¹¹, with أَنْهُد.　　　h) LA XIV, 236²⁴.

i) Dīw. XIX, 23 (Ahlw. p. 127); LA V, 196¹⁸; both with خَلَّ for جَرَّ.

a قَدْ أَرْكَبُ الْآلَةَ بَعْدَ الْآلَةْ   وَأَتْرُكُ الْعَـاجِزَ بِالْجَدَالَةْ

وجَدَا كَسَبَ: يقال b [ما يُجْدِى] عَنْكَ فلانٌ اى ما يُغْنِى عَنْكَ. والجَدُّ الْحَظُّ: ويقال b [رَجُلٌ] جَدِّيٌّ اذا كان ذا حَظٍّ. ويقال جَدَّا جَلَبَ. 36a ويروى: ضُبَيْعَةُ فِى الْمَكَرّ ☙

٨ هَذَا مَقَامِى قَدْ سَأَلْتَ وَمَوْقِفِى   وَعَـنِ الْمَسِيرِ فَسَائِلِى بَعْدُ

يقـال اراد مَوْقِفَهُ فِى الْحرب ويقال ايضًا فى الْمُنافَرة: اى انا شُجاعٌ شَرِيفٌ لا يُنافِرُنِى أَحَدٌ إِلّا غَلَبْتُهُ. ٥ ويروى *هَذَا مَقَامِى قَدْ عَرَفْتَ وَمَوْقِفِى* ☙

٩ أَسَأَلْتَ قَوْمِى عَنْ زِبَادٍ c إِنْ جَنَى   فِيهِ السِّمَانِ وَإِنْ جَنَى عَبْدُ

يريد زِبادَ بنَ الْحارث. وعَبْدُ اسمُ رجُلٍ. ويروى وَإِنْ هَوَى عَبْدُ: اى خَرَّ فِى القِتال: يقال d هَوَى يَهْوِى هُوِيًّا اذا سَقَطَ وهَوِى يَهْوَى هَوًى اذا أَحَبَّ ☙

١٠ وَالْمَرْءَ زَيْدًا قَدْ تَرَكْتُ يَقُودُهُ   نَحْـوَ الْهِضَاب وَدُونَهَا الْقَصْدُ

الهِضاب الأَكَمُ دُونَ الجَبَلِ والواحِدة هَضْبَةٌ ☙

IV.

١ سَمَوْنَا بِالْجِيَادِ لِـحَـيّ وَرْدٍ   فَلَاقَوْا بَعْدَ وَقْعَتِنَا النَّكِيرَا

سَمَوْنَا رَفَعْنا والسُّمُوّ الرِّفْعَة والسامِى الْمُرْتَفِع. وأراد بن ناشِبٍ أبا عُرْوَةَ الصَّعالِيكِ وحَبَّهُ يعنى بنى عَبْسٍ لأَنّ وَرْدًا عَبْسِىٌّ. اراد حرب عَبْسٍ وذُبْيانَ ☙

١٥ ٢ أَبَدْنَا حَيَّ ذِى الْبَزَرَى وَكَعْبًا   وَمَالِكَهَا وَأَهْلَكَنَا بَشِيرَا

الْبَزَرَى لَقَبٌ لِبَنِى اى e [بَكْرِ بنِ] كِلابٍ: قال الْقَتَّال وهو عبد الله بن f مُجِيبٍ [ڧ] اى بَكْرِ بنِ كِلاب

---

a) LA XIII, 41[7] and 109[19], and often elsewhere: poet Saʿīd b. Aus al-Anṣārī.

b, b) MS broken; conj.

c) MS إِذَا جَنَى: we might read زِبَادٍ آذَا جَنَى, with waṣl; but إِنْ in the second hemistich points to a copyist's error; the sense also requires إِنْ and not إِذَا, as only one definite act is referred to.

d) MS هَوَى.   IV. Wāfir. No citations found.

e) Omitted in MS, but given in the next line.

f) Acc. to Agh. XX, 158, al-Qattāl's father was named الْمَصْرَحِىّ, but this is no doubt an epithet.

a إِذَا مَا تَجَعْفَرْتُمْ عَلَيْنَا [فَإِنَّا   بَنُو الْبَزَرَى مِنْ عِزِّهِ نَتَبَزَّرُ

اى نَنْتَسِبُ إِلَيْهِ. أَبَدْنَا أَهْلَكْنَا: يقال أَبَادَهُ اللهُ يُبِيدُهُ. ويروى أَبَرْنَا فَالبَوَارُ الْهَلَاكُ ايضًا ⁕

۳ وَقَرَّبْنَا الرِّبَابَةَ يَوْمَ فَجٍّ   إِلَى [هُلْكٍ] b وَأَعْلَقْنَا عَشِيرَا

الرِّبَابَةُ الْجَمَاعَةُ مِنَ النَّاسِ: b[ويقال الرِّبَابَةُ] لِلْخِرْقَةِ الَّتِى (36b) يُجْمَعُ فِيهَا الْقِدَاحُ: وَرُبَّمَا كَانَتْ مِنْ

5 جِلْدٍ: قال ابو ذُؤَيْبٍ

c وَكَأَنَّهُنَّ   رِبَابَةٌ   وَكَأَنَّهُ   يَسَرٌ يُفِيضُ عَلَى الْقِدَاحِ وَيَصْدَعُ

كَأَنَّهُنَّ يعنى الْحَمِيرَ اذا اجْتَمَعُوا كَاجْتِمَاعِ الْقِدَاحِ فِى الرِّبَابَةِ: وَالْيَسَرُ الَّذِى يَضْرِبُ بِالْقِدَاحِ وَيُقَامِرُ: ويقال

أَفَاضَ بِسَهْمِهِ اذا ضَرَبَ بِهِ وَالْمُفِيضُ الضَّارِبُ. وَعَشِيرٌ رَجُلٌ ⁕

۴ وَسَيَّارًا فَتَى سَعْدِ بْنِ بَكْرٍ   وَأَقْعَصْنَا بِمَفْرُوقٍ بَعِيرَا

10 ذَكَرَ الْحِرْمَازِىُّ أَنَّهُ لَا يَعْرِفُ مَفْرُوقًا وَلَا بَعِيرًا. وَقَوْلُهُ أَقْعَصْنَا قَتَلْنَا وَالْقَعْصُ الْمَوْتُ الْوَحِىُّ: وَمِنْهُ قَوْلُ

الرَّاجِزِ d* بِالْقَعْصِ الْقَاصِى وَيَبْعَجْنَ الْجُفَرْ * ⁕

V.

١ نَحْنُ قُدْنَا الْجِيَادَ حَتَّى أَبَلْنَا   هَا بِثَهْلَانَ عَنْوَةً فَاسْتَقَرَّتْ

اى قُدْنَاهَا إِلَى الْعَدُوِّ حَتَّى وَطِئَتْ أَرْضَ ثَهْلَانَ (وهو جَبَلٌ) وَبَالَتْ فِيهَا. وَعَنْوَةً مِنْ غَيْرِ أَنْ يُنَازِعَنَا

أَحَدٌ e وَلَا اعْتِرَاضٍ مِنْ أَحَدٍ. فَاسْتَقَرَّتْ بِهَا لَمْ تَرَعْ وَلَا خَافَتْ إِنْسَانًا لِعِزِّهَا وَكَثْرَتِهَا ⁕

۲ وَزَجَرْتُ الْمَزْنُوقَ حَتَّى رَمَى بِى   وَسْطَ خَيْلٍ مَلْمُومَةٍ فَابْذَعَرَّتْ   15

الْمَزْنُوقُ اسم فَرَسِ عامر بن الطفيل. مَلْمُومَةٍ جَيْشٍ مُجْتَمِعٌ: قال النابغة الذُّبْيَانِىُّ

f فَلَسْتَ بِمُسْتَبْقٍ أَخًا لَا تَلُمُّهُ   عَلَى شَعَثٍ أَىُّ الرِّجَالِ الْمُهَذَّبُ

---

a) LA V, 121²⁵ (with عِزِّ corruptly).   b) MS broken; conj.

c) Mfḍt CXXVI, 23; LA IX, 78¹⁹, Lane 2473d.

d) ʿAjjāj, XI, 167.

V. *Khafīf.* No citations found.

e) MS وَلَا اعْتِرَاضٍ.   f) Nab. Dīw. III, 11.

اى تَجْمَعُ أَمْرَهُ عَلى انْتِشَارٍ. انْدَعَرَتْ اى تَفَرَّقَتْ والمُبْذَعِرُّ المُتَفَرِّقُ: ومثله المُشْفَتِرُّ: قال طرفةُ:

a كَالْجَرَادِ المُشْفَتِرِّ: يعنى الخَيْلَ b تَقَطَّرَتْ على الغَبِـ[يطِ]: وإِنَّما تَفَرَّقَتْ لِلْغَارَةِ والنَّهْبِ ☙

٣   وَصَبَّحْنَا عَبْسًا [وَمُرَّةَ] c كَأْسًا   فِى نَوَاحِى دِيَارِهِمْ فَاسْبَطَرَّتْ

(37a) يعنى عَبْسَ بن بَغِيضِ بن رَيْثِ بن غَطَفَانَ بن سَعْدِ بن قَيْسِ بن عَيْلَانَ: ومُرَّةُ ابنُ عَوْفِ

ابنِ سَعْدِ بن ذُبْيَانَ بن بَغِيضٍ: وهُمْ بنو أَعْمَامٍ. واسْبَطَرَّتْ اى انْتَشَرَتْ وامْتَدَّتْ ☙

٤   وَجِيَادًا لَمَّا نُعَـوِّدُهَا الإِقْـدَامَ إِنْ غَـارَةٌ بَـدَتْ وَازْبَـأَرَّتْ

الجِيادُ جمع جَوَادٍ من الخَيْلِ: ورجُلٌ جَوَادٌ من قومٍ أَجْوَادٍ: ويقال جادَتِ السَّماءُ تَجُودُ جَوْدًا والجَوْدُ

المَطَرُ: وسُمِّىَ من الخَيْلِ الجَوَادُ كأنَّهُ يَجُودُ بما عِنْدَهُ من الجَرْىِ. وازْبَأَرَّ انْتَفَشَ وتَكَبَّرَ وتَعَظَّمَ ☙

٥   مُقْرَبَاتٍ كَالْهِيمِ شُعْثَ النَّوَاصِى   قَدْ رَفَعْنَا مِنْ حُضْرِهَا فَاسْتَقَدَّرَتْ

المُقْرَبَةُ من الخَيْلِ التى تُشَدُّ عند بُيُوتِهِمْ لا تُتْرَكُ تَسْرَحُ: كأنَّها كَرِيمَةٌ عليهم فهم يُدْنُونَها منهم. والهِيمُ

اراد العطاشَ: أراد أنَّ هذه الخَيْلَ نُنَازِعُ d أَنْفُسَها أَصْحَابَها كما نُنَازِعُ هذه الظَّماءَ من الإِبِلِ أَنْفُسَها

[أَصْحَابَها] فى شُرْبِ الماءِ. والحُضْرُ والإِحْضَارُ الإِسْراعُ. فاسْتَقَدَّرَتْ جادَتْ بِقَدْرَتِها فى السَّيْرِ ☙

٦   بِشَبَابٍ مِّنْ عَـامِرٍ تَضْرِبُ الْبَيْـضَ إِذَا الْخَيْلُ بِالْمَضِيقِ اقْشَعَرَّتْ

البَيْضُ جمع بَيْضَةٍ: e والبَيْضُ شِدَّةُ الحَرِّ فى غير هذا الموضِعِ: والبَيْضُ عَيْبٌ فى قوائمِ الفَرَسِ.

واقْشَعَرَّتْ وازْبَأَرَّتْ بمعنًى ☙

٧   بِمَضِيقٍ تَطِيـرُ فِيـهِ الْعَـوَالِى   حِيـنَ هَرَّتْ كُمَاتُهَا وَاسْتَحَرَّتْ

العَوَالِى جمع عالِيَةٍ وهى ما دون السِّنانِ بِذِراعٍ: والسافِلَةُ ما دون الزُّجِّ من أَسْفَلِ الرُّمْحِ: يقال شابٌّ

كأنَّهُ عالِيَةُ رُمْحٍ. وقَرَّتْ كَرِهَتْ والهَرِيرُ هنا الكَرَاهِيَةُ: يقال: f فلانٌ هَرَّ كَأْسَهُ: قال الأَعْشَى

---

a) Ṭarafah Dīw. V, 31, where Ahlw. reads كَالْفُرَاشِ; LA VI, 89[14], has our reading.

b) MS broken: the first three letters of تَقَطَّرَتْ are beyond doubt, and the last two, with the vowel, of الغَبِيطِ: "The horse were dispersed like drops of rain over the hollow plain".

c) MS broken away: supplied from commy.

d) MS here, and further on, أَنْفُسَها; the insertion of أَصْحَابَها after the second أَنْفُسَها appears necessary.

e) In LA VIII, 396[21] and Lane 283*a* this sense is attributed to بَيْضَةٌ.

f) LA VII, 121[6].

a وَتَشْرَقُ بِالْقَوْلِ الَّذِى قَدْ أَذَعْتَهُ   كَمَا شَرِقَتْ صَدْرُ الْقَنَاةِ مِنَ الدَّمِ

(37b) b لَيَسْتَدْرِجَنَّكَ الْقَوْلُ حَتَّى تَهِرَّهُ   وَتَعْلَمَ أَنِّى عَنْكُمْ غَيْرُ مُلْجَمِ

وَالْكُمَاةُ الْأَبْطَالُ وَالشُّجْعَانُ الْوَاحِدُ كَمِيٌّ. وَقَوْلُهُ تَطِيرُ اى تَشَقَّقُ: قَالَ الْأَعْشَى c صَدْعًا عَلَى

نَأْيِهَا مُسْتَطِيرًا

٨   يَضْرِبُونَ الْكُمَاةَ فِى ثَوْرَةِ النَّقْـــعِ إِذَا حَرْبُهُمْ بَدَتْ وَاسْجَهَرَّتْ   ٥

ثَوْرَةُ النَّقْعِ مَا ثَارَ يَثُورُ مِنْهُ. وَالنَّقْعُ هَاهُنَا الْغُبَارُ. وَالنَّقْعُ أَيْضًا الصُّرَاخُ: قَالَ لَبِيد

d فَمَتَى يَنْفَعْ صُرَاخٌ صَادِقٌ   يَحْلُبُوهُ بَعْدَ جَرْسٍ وَزَجَلْ

يَحْلُبُوهُ يُعَاوِنُوهُ: الْإِحْلَابُ هُوَ الْمَعُونَةُ يُقَالُ أَحْلَبَنِى فُلَانٌ اذَا أَعَانَنِى وَالْمُحْلِبُ الْمُعِينُ. وَقَالَ عُمَرُ بْنُ

الْخَطَّابِ رَحِمَهُ اللهُ: مَا عَلَى نِسَاءِ بَنِى الْمُغِيرَةِ أَنْ يُفِضْنَ مِنْ دُمُوعِهِنَّ عَلَى e ابِى سُلَيْمَانَ مَا لَمْ يَكُنْ نَقْعٌ

١٠ وَلَا لَقْلَقَةٌ. فَالنَّقْعُ مَدُّ الصَّوْتِ فِى الصُّرَاخِ وَاللَّقْلَقَةُ بِاللِّسَانِ: وَيُقَالُ لِلِّسَانِ اللَّقْلَقُ وَلِلْبَطْنِ الْقَبْقَبُ f

٩   وَأَثَارَتْ عَجَاجَةً بَعْدَ نَقْعٍ   وَصَهِيلٍ مُسْتَرْعِدٍ فَاكْفَهَرَّتْ

الْعَجَاجَةُ الْغَبَرَةُ. وَنَقْعُ التُّرَابِ الدَّقِيقِ. وَمُسْتَرْعِدٌ كَأَنَّهُ صَوْتُ رَعْدٍ. وَاكْفَهَرَّتْ غَلُظَتْ وَتَغَيَّرَتْ: وَمِنْهُ

سَحَابَةٌ مُكْفَهِرَّةٌ. وَمِنْهُ أَيْضًا لِلْحَدِيثِ g أَلْقُوا الْكَافِرَ وَالْمُنَافِقَ بِوَجْهٍ عَابِسٍ مُكْفَهِرٍّ اى كَرِيهٍ بَاسِلٍ

---

a) LA XII, 44[17].

b) LA III, 93[3], with تَـهُـزَّهُ (corruptly).

c) Dīw. Escorial MS fol. 48a; the complete verse is

وَبَانَتْ وَقَدْ أَوْرَثْتَ فِى الْفُؤَا d صَدْعًا عَلَى نَأْيِهَا مُسْتَطِيرًا

d) Labīd XXXIX, 58; LA X, 241[8] (with يَحْلُبُوهَا); MbdKam. 320[8], all with ذَاتَ جَرْسٍ.

e) i. e. Khālid b. al-Walīd; see LA X, 241[11] ff.; for يُفِضْنَ LA has يُهْرِقْنَ or يَسْفُكْنَ. Our MS has incorrectly نَقْعًا and لَقْلَقَةٌ.

f) The scholion does not explain اسْجَهَرَّتْ; LA VI, 11[13] gives its meaning as اسْجَهَرَّتِ النَّارُ اتَّقَدَتْ وَالْتَهَبَتْ, but this appears to be incorrect. According to Prof. Nöldeke the meaning always implies quick motion to and fro; so Labīd, Khālidī p. 44, of the sun-mist; so Akhṭal 187, 2; of the clouds, Wright, *Opuscula*, 24[15]; of a shower of rain JRAS 1900 665[4]; of a hot wind, حَرُور, Kuthaiyir in Bakrī 467[14]; of the twinkling of the stars, Qālī, *Amālī* II, 123[13].

g) See LA VI, 467[21—22].

١٠ بِجِيَادٍ غَدَتْ بِجَمْعٍ عَزِيزٍ   وَأَصَابَتْ عُدَاتَهَا فَأَضَرَّتْ

VI.

١ لَقَدْ تَعْلَمُ الْخَيْلُ الْمُغِيرَةُ أَنَّنَا   إِذَا ٱبْتَدَرَ النَّاسُ الْفَعَالَ أُسُودُهَا

يعنى أَصْحَابَ الْخَيْلِ: ويقال سُمِّيَت الْخَيْلُ خيلًا لِخُيَلَائِهَا ۞

٢ عَلَى رَبِذٍ يَّزْدَادُ جَوْدًا إِذَا جَرَى   وَقَدْ قَلِقَتْ تَحْتَ السُّرُوجِ لُبُودُهَا

رَبِذ سَرِيع: قال عَنْتَرَةُ

a رَبِذٍ يَدَاهُ بِالْقِدَاحِ إِذَا شَتَا   هَتَّاكِ غَايَاتِ التِّجَارِ مُلَوَّمِ (38a)

والجَوْد هَاهنا الجَرْى: يقال جَادَت السَّمَاء بِالمَطَرِ تَجُود جَوْدًا. وإِنَّما قَلِقَتْ لُبُودُهَا اى مَاجَتْ لِأَنَّها تَضْمُرُ فى الغَزْوِ وللحَرْب فَيَقْلَق لُبُودُهَا وضِفَارُهَا ۞

٣ وَقَدْ حُضِبَتْ بِالْمَاءِ حَتَّى كَأَنَّمَا   تَشَبَّهُ كُمْتَ الْخَيْلِ مِنْهُنَّ سُودُهَا

الماء ارادَ العَرَق: وذلك انّ عَرَق لِلخيل اذا جَفَّ b اسْوَدَّ ۞

٤ وَنَحْنُ نَفَيْنَا مَذْحِجًا عَنْ بِلَادِهَا   تُقَتَّلُ حَتَّى عَادَ فَلًّا شَدِيدُهَا

مَذْحِجٌ فى اليَمَن: ويقال إِنَّما سُمِّيَتْ مَذْحِجًا لِأَنَّ أُمَّهُم وَلَدَتْ على أَكَمَة يقال لها مَذْحِجٌ فَسُمُّوا بِاسْمِ تِلْكَ الأَكَمَةِ. والفَلُّ المُنْهَزِمُون: يقال قَوْمٌ فَلٌّ بِفَتْحِ الفاء اى مُنْهَزِمُون: وَأَرْضٌ فَلٌّ اى لا نَبَاتَ فيها ۞

فَأَمَّا فَرِيقٌ بِالْمَصَامَةِ مِنْهُمُ   فَفَرُّوا وَأُخْرَى قَدْ أُبِيرَتْ جُدُودُهَا

المَصَامَة أَرْضٌ. وأُبِيرَتْ أُهْلِكَتْ: يقال أَبَارَهُم اللهُ يُبِيرُهُمْ إِبَارَةً اى أَهْلَكَهُم. والجُدُود جمع جَدٍّ وهو الحَظّ: والجَدّ الأَبُ الكَبِيرُ: والجَدّ ضِدّ الهَزْلِ: ويقال جَدَّ فى الارض سَيْرًا وأَجَدَّ وهو جَادٌّ ومُجِدٌّ فى ذلك الأَمْرِ: والجُدّ بضَمّ الجِيم البِئْر القَدِيمَة. وجَدَّ السَّيْرَ يَجُدُّهُ جَدًّا اذا قَطَعَهُ: وحَبْلٌ c [مَجْدُودٌ] اى مقطوع: واذا أَمَرْتَ من القَطْع قُلْتَ جُدَّ وأَجْدِدْ. والجُدُد جمع جَدِيد والجَدَد جمع جُدَّةٍ وه

VI. *Ṭawīl*: no citations found.

a) Muʿall. 54.

b) *sic!* evidently we should read أَبْيَضَّ.

c) Omitted in MS.

الطريقة التى على مَتْنِ الحمارِ: وناقةٌ جَدُودٌ وأتانٌ جَدُودٌ اذا انْقَطَعَ لَبَنُها وللجمع الجِدَادُ: قال

الشَّمَّاخ: a الجِدَادُ الغَوارِزِ: وأيّامُ الجِدادِ أيّامُ الصِّرامِ لِصِرامِ النَّخْلِ: وامرأةٌ جَدّاءُ لا ثَدْىَ لها ☙

٦   إذا سَنَةٌ عَزَّتْ وطالَ طِوالُها   وأقْحَطَ عَنْها القَطْرُ وآصْفَرَّ عُودُها

عَزَّتْ غَلَبَتْ: ومنه: مَنْ عَزَّ بَزَّ: اى مَنْ غَلَبَ سَلَبَ: ويقال أصابتْهُم (38) سَنَةٌ اى جَدْبٌ وقَحْطٌ:

5 وبنو فلانٍ قد أسْنَتُوا وهم مُسْنِتُونَ وأجْدَبُوا وقَحَطُوا بمعنًى. ويقال طالَ طَوالُهُ وطِيالُهُ وطَوْلُهُ وطِيلَهُ: قال

القُطامىّ: b وإنْ طالَتْ بكَ الطِّيَلُ ☙

٧   وُجِدْنا كِرامًا لا يُحَوَّلُ ضَيْفُنا   إذا جَفَّ فَوْقَ المَنْزِلاتِ جَلِيدُها

الجَلِيد والصَّقِيع c والحَبِيتُ (sic) بمعنًى واحدٍ ☙

٨   وقَدْ أصْبَحَتْ عِرْسِى الغَداةَ تَلُومُنِى   على غَيْرِ ذَنْبٍ هَجْرُها وصُدُودُها

10 عِرْسُ الرجلِ امرأتُهُ: ويقال قد عَرِسَ خُلُقُ الرجلِ اذا سَاءَ: وربّما سُمِّىَ اللَّبُوَة d أنْثَى السَّبْع عِرْسًا:

ويقال أعْرَسَ الرجلُ بأهلِهِ يُعْرِس إعْراسًا: وعَرَّسَ القومُ السَّفَرَ e اذا نَزَلُوا للتَّرْوِيحِ وللنَّوْمَةِ الخَفِيفَةِ

ثم يَرْتَحِلُونَ ☙

٩   f[فإذا] إذا ما قُلْتُ قَوْلى فَانْقَضَى   أتَتْنِى بأُخْرَى خُطَّةً لا أُرِيدُها

خُطَّةً اى حالةٌ أُخْرَى: وتكون الخُطَّةُ الأمْرَ: يقال: أقْدَمَ فلانٌ على خُطّةٍ عظيمةٍ اى على أمْرٍ عظيمٍ:

15 والخُطَّةُ هى الفاعِلَةُ ☙

١٠   فَلا خَيْرَ فى وُدٍّ إذا رَثَّ حَبْلُهُ   وخَيْرُ حِبالِ الواصِلِينَ جَدِيدُها

رَثَّ الحَبْلُ اى أخْلَقَ: ومنه حالُهُ حالٌ رَثَّةٌ اى خَلِقَةٌ: g والرَّثُّ الإصلاحُ فى غيرِ هذا الموضعِ: ويقال

---

a) Dīwān p. 43[7]; Jamharah p. 154.

b) Dīwān, I, 1.

c) The third word for hoar-frost is ضَرِيبٌ; the word in our MS. is not in the Lexx, and may
possibly stand for ضريب, or perhaps for جَلِيت, a bye-form of جَلِيد (LA II, 325[11]); حَلِيت is
also, in LA II, 329[9], said to have the same meaning in the dialect of Ṭayyi'.   *d)* MS الأُنْثَى.

e) Corrected by a later hand to فى السَّفَرِ.

f) Beginning of line broken: may be وإنّى.

g) The Lexx. do not give this sense, and it is not in the *Aḍdād*.

رَثَثْتُ مَتَاعِى اى أَصْلَحْتُهُ: وَآرْثَتْ فُلَانٌ اى ثَجَا جَرِيحًا: h والْمُرِثَّةُ لَبَنٌ يُنْصَبُ عَلَيْهِ ماءٌ او حَارُّ

على بَارِدٍ: وَمِنْهُ قَوْلُ الشاعرِ وهو بَعْضُ غِلْمَانِ العربِ

اذا شَرِبْتُ خِلْتِنِى صَبُوبًا   مُرِثَّةً تَتْرُكِنِى خَبِيثًا

فالصَبُوتُ الأَسَدُ. والْحَبْلُ العَهْدُ ✿

VII.

١ أَلَا طَرَقَتْكَ مِنْ h خَبْتٍ كَنُودُ   فَقَدْ فَعَلَتْ وَآلَتْ لَا تَعُودُ

الطُّرُوقُ لا يكونُ إلّا بالليلِ: يقال طَرَقَنِى فُلَانٌ اى أَتَانِى لَيْلًا (39a) الطَّارِقُ الفاعلُ والمطروقُ المفعولُ

بِهِ: وقال أُمَيَّةُ بنُ أَبِى الصَّلْتِ

c كَأَنِّى أَنَا الْمَطْرُوفُ دُونَكَ بالَّذِى   طُرِقْتَ بِهِ دُونِى وَعَيْنِى تَهْمُلُ

وأَصْلُ الطَّرْقِ الضَّرْبُ والْمِطْرَقَةُ العَصَا. وكَنُودُ اسمُ امرأةٍ. وقولُهُ فَعَلَتْ اى أَمْضَتِ الْهِجْرَانَ ولم تَتَقَلَّبْتْ.

وقد آلَتْ حَلَفَتْ من الأَلِيَّةِ: يقال آلَى فلانٌ يُولِى إِيلَاءً اذا أَقْسَمَ: قال الاعشى

d فَآلَيْتُ لا أَرْثِى لَهَا مِنْ كَلَالَةٍ   وَلَا مِنْ وَجَا حَتَّى تُلَاقِى مُحَمَّدَا

صلى الله عليه: يُخَاطِبُ نَاقَتَهُ يقول: اذا شَكَتِ الْكَلَالَ والفُتُورَ لم أَرِقَّ لها حتى تُوَدِّينِى الى النَّبِىِّ صلى

الله عليه، والْكَلَالُ والْكَلَالَةُ واحدٌ وهو الضَّجَرُ والاعْيَاءُ من سَيْرٍ أو عَمَلٍ ✿

٢ كَأَنَّكِ لَمْ تَرَيْنَا يَوْمَ غَوْلٍ   وَلَمْ يُخْبِرْكِ بالْخَبَرِ الْجُنُودُ

٣ بِمَا لَاقَتْ سَرَاةُ بَنِى لُجَيْمٍ   e تَعَضُّ سَرَاتَهُمْ فِيمَا الْقُيُودُ

---

a) Perhaps this word may be the origin of the modern "mereesy" of Doughty (*Arabia Deserta*).

VII. *Wāfir*. Vv. 1, 4 and 5 cited elsewhere.

b) Yāq. II, 139[19] reads جَوْبٍ; as خَبْتٍ appears, from Bakrī 305, to be in the lands of Kalb, far distant from those of ʿĀmir, Yāq.'s reading seems more probable.

c) See Ḥam. 355[8], Agh. III, 191[4]; Schulthess, Umayyah, No. VIII, 3, where إِذَا misprinted for أَنَا.

d) See al-Aʿshà's poem in Morg. Forschungen (1875), p. 253, verse 12, where Thorbecke reads حَفَا and تَزُورُ; other readings and citations are mentioned there.

e) MS تَعَضُّ.

٤ وَعَبْدُ الْقَيْسِ بِالْمَرْدَاهِ لَاقَتْ   صَبَاحًا مِثْلَ مَا لَقِيَتْ ثَمُودُ

عبد القيس ابن أَفْصَى بن دُعْمِيّ بن جَدِيلَةَ بن أَسَدٍ. والمَرْدَاهُ أَرْضٌ بِهَجَرَ. وبَنُو لُجَيْمٍ حَنِيفَةُ

وعِجْلٌ: b [وهو] ابن صَعْب بن عَلِيّ ۞

٥ صَبَّحْنَاهُمْ بِكُلِّ أَقَبَّ نَهْدٍ   وَمُطَّرِدٍ لَّهُ يَقِدُ الْحَدِيدُ

٥ أَقَبُّ فرسٌ ضامِرٌ والْقَبَبُ الضُّمُورُ: يقال فرسٌ أَقَبُّ وفرسٌ قَبَّاءُ وخيلٌ قُبٌّ. والنهد الضَّخْم المُشْرِف.
والمُطَّرِدُ الرُّمْحِ يطَّرِدُ فى اهْتِزازِهِ ۞

٦ وَأَبْيَضَ يَخْطِفُ الْقَصَرَاتِ عَضْبٍ   رَقِيقِ الْحَدِّ زَيَّنَهُ غُمُودُ

يَخْطِفُ يَسْتَلِب يقال خَطَفَهُ يَخْطِفُهُ خَطْفًا ولِلخاطِف السَّالِب: قال عَدِيُّ بن زَيْدٍ

c خَطِفَتْهُ مَنِيَّةٌ فَتَرَدَّى   وَلَقَدْ كَانَ يَأْمُلُ التَّعْمِيرَا

١٠ والقَصَرات جمع قَصَرَةٍ وهى أَصْلُ العُنُق. والعَضْبُ القاطِع (39b) والغُمُود جمع غِمْدٍ: اى انّه سَيْفٌ
مَصُونٌ لا مُبْتَذَلٌ فهو فى غِمْدِهِ صَقِيلٌ إلى وَقْتِ الْحاجَةِ إِلَيْهِ ۞

٧ وَكُلِّ طِمِرَّةٍ حَفِقٍ حَشَاهَا   مُلَمْلَمَةٍ تَلَاقِيهَا بَعِيدُ

الطِّمِرَّة الفرس الوَثَّابَة والطِّمْر الوَثْب والطامِر الوَثَّاب. وخَفِقُ حَشاها تُرْعَدُ من الحِدَّةِ. ومُلَمْلَمَة مُجْتَمِعَةُ
الخَلْقِ مُلَزَّوزَتُه. وقوله تَلاقِيها بعيدٌ اى إِدْراكها بعيدٌ اى لا تُلْحَقُ فى السَّبْقِ والعَدْو ۞

٨ لَقِينَا جَمْعَهُمْ صُبْحًا فَكَانُوا   كَمِثْلِ الضَّأْنِ عَادَاهُنَّ سِيدُ

السِّيدُ الذئبُ ولا جَمْعَ له من هذا اللَّفْظِ. وعاداهُنَّ من العَدْوِ اى نَفَرُوا وتَشَرَّدُوا كالضَّأْنِ الذى عاثَ
فيهنّ الذئبُ ۞

٩ فَغُودِرَ مِنْهُمْ عَمْرٌو وَعَمْرٌو   وَأَسْوَدُ وَالْكُمَاةُ بِهَا شُهُودُ

هؤلاء قومٌ قَتَلَهم. وغُودِرَ تُرِكَ فى المَعْرَكَةِ لأنّه مَقْتُولٌ. والكُماةُ الأبطال الواحد كَمِيٌّ. وقوله والكُماةُ بها
٢٠ شُهُودٌ: اى لى بما أَقُول من قَتْلِ هؤلاء القوم تِبْيانٌ وقوم حَضَرُوا هذه الوَقْعَةَ ۞

---

a) Bakrī 529⁴ has vv. 4 and 5 as text. الْمَرْدَاءُ appears in Frag. 22, 4 as الْمَرْدَات.

b) The MS has وعِجْل بن صعب; see Wüst. Tab. B for the necessity of the correction.

c) See Naṣr. p. 468, with v. l. وَهْوَ فِى الْمُلْكِ يَأْمُلُ; the reference is to King Shāpūr. Other
verses of the same poem in Buḥt Ham. p. 147, and in many other places.

١٠ وَعَبْدُ اللَّهِ غُودِرَ وَابْنُ بِشْرٍ   وَعَتَّابٌ وَمُرَّةُ وَالْوَلِيدُ

١١ لَقِينَاهُمْ بِبِيضٍ مُرْهَفَاتٍ   نُقَتِّلُهُمْ بِهَا حَتَّى أُبِيدُوا

البيضُ السيوفُ جمعُ أبيضَ: ومنه قولُ الشاعر: *وأبيضَ بَاتِرٍ ذَكَرِ حُسَامٍ*. أُبِيدُوا اى أُهْلِكُوا يقال بادَ

يَبيدُ بَيْدًا وبُيُودًا والبائِدُ الهالِكُ ۞

١٢ وَأَرْدَفْنَا نِسَاءَهُمْ وَجِشْنَا   وَقَدْ دَمِيَتْ مِنَ a الْخَمْشِ الْخُدُودُ

اى صَرَعْنَاهُم فتكَدَّحَتْ خُدُودُهُم. ويُرْوَى: من الجِبْسِ الخُدُودُ: الجِبْسُ الجَبَانُ الهَيُوبُ ۞

VIII.

١ (40a) إِنِّى إِذَا ٱنْتَتَرَتْ أَصِرَّةُ أَمْكُمْ   مِمَّنْ يُقَالُ لَهُ تَسَرْبَلْ فَٱرْكَبِ

اى اذا نَدِبْتُم لِلَقْطِ أَصِرَّةِ النُّوقِ: وهى أن تُصَرَّ الناقةُ حتى لا يَشْرَبَ الفَصِيلُ ولا يَحْلُبَها الراعى

لِبُخْلِ القَوْمِ باللَّبَنِ وقِلَّةِ الشَّىْءِ عِنْدَهُم: والواحد الصِّرَارُ وهو أيضًا مَصْدَرٌ: يقال صَرَّهُ يَصُرُّ صَرًّا وصِرَارًا.

يقول: أنا مِمَّنْ يُدْعَى لِلحَرْبِ ولِقَاءِ الأبْطَالِ والرُّكُوبِ لِحِفْظِ الحَقِيقَةِ: وأَنْتُمْ رُعَاةٌ لا غَنَاءَ عِنْدَكُم 10

ولا كِفَايَةَ ۞

٢ لَا ضَيْرَ قَدْ حَكَّتْ بِمُرَّةَ بَرْكَهَا   وَتَرَكْنَ أَشْجَعَ b مِثْلَ خُشْبِ ٱلْأَثْأَبِ

حَكَّتْ أرادَ لِلحَرْبِ فَأَضْمَرَها ولم يَأْتِ لها بِذِكْرٍ. وقولُه بَرْكَها اى مَصْدَرَها: كأنَّها أَلَمَّتْ بِه وَنَزَلَتْ عليه:

والبِرْكَةُ والبَرْكُ الصدرُ: وكان زيادٌ أَشْعَثَ بَرْكًا: وإنَّما أرادَ بالبَرْكِ الثِّقَلَ: كما يقال: أَلْقَى عليه كَلْكَلَهُ:

وهو مَثَلٌ. ومُرَّةُ هو ابنُ عَوْفِ بنِ سَعْدِ بنِ ذُبْيَانَ: وأَشْجَعُ ابنُ رَيْثِ بنِ غَطَفَانَ. وتَرَكْنَ يعنى 15

لِلخَيْلِ. والأثْأَبُ شَجَرٌ الواحدةُ أَثْأَبَةٌ: كأنَّه قال: قَتَلْنَهُ لا حَرَاكَ بِه كالخُشْبِ: اى مُلْقًى مَقْتُولٌ ۞

٣ c لَا يَخْطُبُونَ إِلَى الْكِرَامِ بَنَاتِهِمْ   وَتَشِيبُ أَيِّمُهُمْ وَلَمَّا تُخْطَبِ

VIII. *Kāmil.* This poem, of which v. 2 is cited in the commy. to v. 1 of No. V of the *Mufaḍḍalīyāt* (ed. Lyall, p. 33), appears to have been composed in reply to the songs of triumph of Fazārah and other branches of Ghaṭafān after the disaster suffered by ʿĀmir on the Day of ar-Raqam: see the Mfḍt, *l. c.*, and LA I, 306[18]. See *post*, No. XXIX, for another poem on the same occasion. See also Frag. 2 in Supplement for other vv. which may belong to this poem.

b) See note above; for a similar phrase see LA I, 227[22] (Kumait).

c) See Frag. 2, v. 3.

الأيِّم الّتى لا زَوْجَ لها قد مات عَنْها زَوْجُها: يَصِفُهم بالخُمُول والضَّعْف: اى ليس فيهِم مَرْغَبٌ لأنّهم نَبَطٌ

والصَّريحُ لا يَتزوّجُ إِلَيْهم ۞

٤ أفرِحْتَ أن غَدَرَ الزَّمانُ بِفارِسٍ   قُلْحَ الكِلابِ وكُنْتَ غَيْرَ مُغَلَّبِ

القَلَحُ صُفْرَةٌ تَعْلُو الأسْنانَ: يقال رجل أقْلَحُ وامرأة قَلْحاءُ وقوم قُلْحٌ: ونَصَبَ قُلْحَ على السَّبِّ والشَّتْمِ:

٥ ويَجُوزُ أن يكون نِدَاءً مُضافًا ۞ (40b)

٥ يا مُرَّ قد كَلِبَ الزَّمانُ عَلَيْكُمُ   وَنَكَأْتُ قَرْحَتَكُمْ وَلَمَّا أَنْكَبِ

كَلِبَ الزّمانُ اى اشْتَدَّ وأَظْهَرَ تَغَيُّرًا وعُبُوسًا: ومنه كَلْبٌ كَلِبٌ وقد كَلِبَ عَلَى فلانٍ اى ضَرِىَ. وقولُه

نَكَأْتُ قَرْحَتَكُمْ مَثَلٌ: ويقال نكَأْتُ القرحةَ اى قَشَرْتُ عنها الجِلْبَةَ الّتى تَعْلُوها a لِلْبُرْءِ. وقولُه لَمَّا أَنْكَبِ

اى لم يُغَضَّ مِنّى ولا لَحِقَتْنِى نَكْبَةٌ: ويقال رجل أَنْكَبُ وامرأة نَكْباءُ اذا كان بِهِما مَيَلٌ وقوم نُكْبٌ:

١٠ ومنه قول الأخْطَلِ: b كَالْقَيِّمِ النُّكَبِ ۞

٦ وَتَرَكْتُ جَمْعَهُمْ بِلَابَةِ ضَرْغَدٍ   جَزَرَ السِّباعِ وكُلَّ نَسْرٍ أَهْدَبِ

قولُه بِلَابَةِ [ضَرْغَد] موضِعٌ. واللَّابَةُ الحَرَّةُ وجَمْعُها لابٌ: ويقال للحَرَّةِ لَوبَةٌ وجمعها لُوبٌ: قال

الشاعر: c بَيْنَ الأَباطِحِ فالرَّحْواءِ فاللُّوبِ. وضَرْغَدٌ يقال إِنّه بَلَدٌ. وجَزَرَ السِّباعِ لَحْمٌ لها كما يُجْزَرُ

البَعِيرُ. والنَّسْرُ الرَّخَمُ وجمعه النُّسُورُ: ومنه نُسُورُ لُقْمانَ بن عادٍ: أعْطِىَ عُمْرَ سَبْعَةِ أَنْسُرٍ فَسُمِّىَ السابعُ

d لُبَدًا: ومنه قول النابغة: e أَخْنَى عَلَى القَوْمِ ما أَخْنَى عَلَى لُبَدِ: وله قِصّةٌ طَوِيلةٌ. والأَهْدَبُ الطويلُ

الرِّيشِ وهو بِمَنْزِلةِ هُدْبِ الثَّوْبِ وهو حاشِيَةُ الثوبِ ۞

٧ وَلَقَدْ أَبَلْتُ الخَيْلَ فى عَرَصاتِكُمْ   وَسْطَ الدِّيارِ يِكُلِّ خِرْقٍ مِحْرَبِ

قولُه أبَلْتُ الخيلَ فى عَرَصاتِكم اى قُدْتُها إِلَيْكُم حتّى f داسَتْ دِيارَكم وبالت فيها. وكُلُّ جَوْبَةٍ مُنْفَتِقَةٍ

فهى عَرْصَةٌ وللجمع عِراصٌ: والعَرَصُ بفتحِ العَيْنِ والرّاء النَّشاطُ: يقال عَرِصَ يَعْرَصُ عَرَصًا اذا نَشِطَ.

٢٠ والخِرْقُ (41a) بِكَسْرِ الخاءِ الّذى يَتَخَرَّقُ بالمَعْرُوفِ: والخَرْقُ بفتحِ الخاءِ القَفْلَةُ الواسِعَةُ الّتى تَنْخَرِقُ فيها

الرِّياحُ وجمعه خُرُوقٌ. والمِحْرَبُ صاحِبُ حَرْبٍ ۞

---

a) MS لَلبُرْوِ.   b) Dīw. p. 17, v. 2.   c) See a similar verse by al-Jumaiḥ, Mfḍt. IV, 10 (p. 29).

d) This anomalous form is also found in LA IV, 390¹⁸.   e) Nab. Muʿall. 6 (with vv. ll.).

f) MS حاسَتْ; cf. ante, No. V, 1.

٨ وَشَفَيْتُ نَفْسِي مِنْ فَزَارَةَ إِنَّهُمْ أَهْلُ الْفَعَالِ وَأَهْلُ عِزٍّ أَغْلَبُ

الْأَغْلَبُ الْغَلِيظُ الصَّخْمُ: وَيُقَالُ أَسَدٌ أَغْلَبُ اذا كَانَ غَلِيظَ الرَّقَبَةِ وَأَسْدٌ غُلْبٌ وَرَجُلٌ أَغْلَبُ وَامْرَأَةٌ غَلْبَاءُ:

وَرَجُلٌ أَرْقَبُ وَامْرَأَةٌ رَقْبَاءُ وَقَوْمٌ رَقْبٌ مِثْلُ أَغْلَبَ: وَمِنْهُ قَوْلُ أَعْشَى بَنِى قَيْسٍ فِى صِفَةِ الرُّمْحِ: b *وَأَرْقَبَ

مُطَّرِدٍ كَالشَّطَنْ* وَالشَّطَنُ الْحَبْلُ وَجَمْعُهُ أَشْطَانٌ ۞

٩ وَلَقَـدْ فَخَرْتَ بِبَاطِلٍ عَدَّدْتَهُ فَإِذَا أَتَيْتَ بُيُوتَ قَوْمِكَ فَاحْسُبِ

اى أَنْتَ تَفْخَرُ بِمَا لَا أَصْلَ لَهُ لِأَنَّكَ مُلْصَقٌ لَسْتَ مِنْ قَلْبِ الْقَوْمِ وَلَا مِنْ سَرَوَاتِهِمْ: فَإِذَا فَخَرْتَ عِنْدَهُمْ

بِمَا يُفْتَخَرُ بِهِ فِى الْمَوَاضِعِ الَّتِى يَغِيبُ عَنْهَا قَوْمُكَ رَدُّوا عَلَيْكَ وَلَمْ يَقْبَلُوهُ مِنْكَ ۞

١٠ فَلْتُخْبِرَنَّكَ فَاقِدٌ عَنْ شَجْوِهَا حَذِلٌ مَّدَامِعُهَا بِدَمْعٍ سَيْكَبِ

الْحَذَلُ سُقُوطُ الشَّعَرِ مِنْ جَفْنِ الْعَيْنِ مِنَ الْبُكَاءِ: يُقَالُ قَدْ حَذِلَتْ عَيْنُهُ تَحْذَلُ حَذَلًا: وَمِنْهُ قَوْلُ

d مُعَقِّرِ بْنِ جِعَارِ الْبَارِقِىِّ

وَذُبْيَانِيَّةٍ وَصَنَتْ بَنِيهَا وَمَأْقِى دَمْعِهَا حَذِلٌ نَطُوفُ

نَطُوفُ اى يَقْطُرُ: وَقَالَ الْعَجَّاجُ e *وَالشَّوْقُ شَاجٍ لِلْعُيُونِ الْحُذَّلِ*. وَالشَّجْوُ الْحُزْنُ وَرَجُلٌ شَجٍ اى

حَزِينٌ: وَمِنْهُ الْمَثَلُ: f وَيْلٌ لِلشَّجِى مِنَ الْخَلِىِّ: يُشَدَّدَانِ يَآءَا الْجَمِيعِ: وَرُبَّمَا خُفِّفَتْ يَآءُ الشَّجِى

وَثُقِّلَتْ يَآءُ الْخَلِىِّ فَيُقَالُ: وَيْلٌ لِلشَّجِى مِنَ الْخَلِىِّ ۞

---

a) MS أَغْلَبُ with *iqwā'*, undoubtedly a blunder.

b) So MS: we should however read مُطَّرِدًا, as the nouns are in the accusative; the complete verse (Escorial MS, fol. 17b) is — وَذَا هَبَّةٍ خَامِصًا كَلْبُهُ وَأَجْرَدَ مُطَّرِدًا كَالشَّطَنْ أَرْقَبَ for أَجْرَدَ is said by Thaʿlab to be Abū ʿUbaidah's reading.

c) MS يَسْكَبُ; Prof. Nöldeke prefers يَسْكَبُ (neut.) or يُسْكَبُ, with *iqwā'*.

d) The name (or nickname) of this poet's father (or grandfather) is variously given. The poet's name was سُفْيَانُ بْنُ أَوْسٍ (Agh. X, 47²²); he was called الْمُعَقِّر on account of a verse made by him. His grandfather is called حَمَّاد in Agh. X, 37⁸, جِمَاز in Agh. X, 46²⁷, and (father) حِمَار in LA XIII, 158¹⁰. This verse is cited at the last mentioned place as follows: — فَأَخْلَفَنَا مَوَدَّتَهَا فَقَاظَتْ وَمَأْقِى عَيْنِهَا حَذِلٌ نَطُوفُ (Our MS, corruptly, وَذُبْيَانِةٍ, وَصَنَتْ, وَمَا فِى). e) Diw. ʿAjj. XXIX, 2; LA XIII, 157¹⁶.

f) MS in both places وَيْلٌ الشَّجِى; see LA XIX, 150²⁵.

١١ وَلَقَـدْ لَحِقْتَ بِخَيْلِنَا a فَكَرِهْتَهَا   وَصَدَدْتَ عَنْ خَيْشُومِهَا الْمُسْتَكْلِبِ

(41b) خَيْشُومُهَا أَنْفُهَا وَلِلْجَمِع الْخَيَاشِيمُ: وَخَيْشُومُ كُلِّ شَيْءٍ مَا تَقَدَّمَ مِنْهُ: فَأَرَادَ: لَحِقْتَ اوَائِلَ الْخَيْلِ

فَوَلَّيْتَ عَنها وَفَرَرْتَ ۞

١٢ فَبَنِى فَزَارَةَ قَدْ عَلَوْنَ بِكَلْكَلٍ   وَالْحَىَّ أَشْجَعَ قَـدْ رَمَيْنَ بِمَنْكِبِ

5 الكلكل الصدر وهو مُعْظَم القوم: اى أَلْقَوْا عليهم أَثْقَالَهم. والمَنْكِب اراد ناحِيَةً من النَّواحِى ۞

١٣ غَادَرْنَ مِنْهُمْ تِسْعَةً فِى مَعْرَكٍ   وَّثَلاَثَةً قَرَّنَّهُمْ فِى الْمِشْعَبِ

غَادَرْنَ تَرَكْنَ وخَلَّفْنَ. فِى مَعْرَكٍ فِى موضِع اعْتِراكٍ وهو الازْدِحام يعنى موضِع القِتال: قُتِلوا هُناك

بعد ثلاثةً أُسِروا فقُرِنوا فى حَبْلٍ. والمِشْعَب b الموت التى تَشْعَبُ: واسم الموت شَعُوبٌ بِلا الِف ولام

ولا صَرِفٍ: كأنَّهُ قال شُدُّوا فى حَبْلٍ فَأُسْلِموا الى الموت ۞

IX.

١ تَرْعَى فَزَارَةُ فِى مَقَرِّ بِلادِهَا   وَتَهِيمُ بَيْنَ شَقَائِقٍ وَّرِمَالِ 10

يقول فَزارةُ ليس لها أنْبَعاثٌ ولا عِزٌّ فيَسْرَح مالُها فى المَراعِى لقلَّتِها وضَعْفِها: فهى تَرْعَى دِيارها خَوْفًا

من الغارةِ اذا انْتَشَرَتْ فى المَرْعَى. والشقائق جمع شَقِيقَة من الرَّمْل قِطَعٌ غِلاظٌ بَيْنَ جَبَلَىْ رَمْلٍ۞

٢ يُعْطَونَ خُرْجَهُمْ بِغَيْرِ هَوَادَةٍ   وَّالـدَّهْـرُ ذُو غِيَرٍ وَّذُو بَلْبَالِ

الخُرْج الخَراج: اى لَيْسوا بِأَعِزَّةٍ ولا لَهُمْ قَبْضٌ ولا بَسْطٌ فى الأمور: اى هم أَنَّلاءِ يُسامُونَ الضَّيْمَ

15 فَيَقْبَلُونَه. والهَوادة المُحاباة: يقال لَيْسَ بين البَرْد c وبين الحَرِّ هَوَادَةٌ اى مُحاباةٌ. والبَلْبال الغُموم والهُموم

والجمع البَلابِل: قال ذو الرُّمَّةِ (42a)

d لَعَلَّ انْحِدَارَ الدَّمْع يَعْقُبُ رَاحَةً   مِنَ الوَجْدِ أَوْ يَشْفِى نَجِىَّ الْبَلابِلِ

٣ نَحْنُ الْكُمَاةُ لِذِى الْوَغَى فِى هَوْلِهِ   وَّالْخَاضِبُونَ مُجَوَّبَ السِّرْبَالِ

a) MS وَكَرَهْتَها.

b) Notice المَوْت treated as fem. because of the neighbourhood of the equivalent شَعُوب.

IX. Kamil: no citations found.

c) MS وبِينَ أَحَدٍ وَهَوَادَةٍ!   d) Dh. R., Dīw. LXVI, 2; MbdKam. 52¹⁵.

الكُماةِ الأشدّاءُ. والوَغَى أرادَ لِلحربِ. والمَحَوبُ الذى له جَيْبٌ. اى *a* يُقْتَلونَ فيُخْضَبُ بالدّمِ سَرابيلُهم

وهى الدروعُ: وقال أوْسُ بن حَجَر

سَرابيلُنا فى الرَّوْعِ بِيضٌ كأنّها   *b* أضا اللُّوبِ هَزّتْها مِن الرِّيحِ شَمْألُ

٣ وَقَصَدْتُكُم بَكْرٌ قَضَاءً واجِبًا   وَبَنُو فَزارَةَ جُلَّسٍ حِينَ مَجْجَالِ

X.

١ *c* جاءُوا بِشَهْرانِ *d* العَريضةِ كُلَّها   وَأَكْلُبِها *e* ميلادَ بَكْرِ بْنِ وائِلِ

شَهْرانُ مِن *f* خَثْعَم وأَكْلُبُ مِن شَهْرانَ. يقولُ هم ميلادُ بَكْرِ بنِ وائلٍ فنحنُ دونَهم بآباءٍ نحو مِن عَشَرةٍ ۞

٢ وَسَعَّتْ شُيوخُ الحَيّ بَيْنَ سُوَيْقَةٍ   وَبَيْنَ جَنُوبِ القَهْرِ مِيلَ الشَّمائِلِ

القَهْرُ جَبَلٌ وسُوَيْقَةُ موضعٌ. وقولُه ميلَ الشمائل اى *g* أمالوها بالرَّمْى: ويقال بَلْ يأخُذون ذات الشمال ۞

٣ *h* فَلَوْ كانَ جَمْعٌ مِثْلُنا لَمْ يَبِزَّنا   وَلٰكِنْ أتانا كُلُّ جِنٍّ وَخايِلِ

قولُه لم يَبِزّنا اى لم يَسْلُبْنا والبَزُّ السَّلْبُ: قال امرؤُ القيس

i إذا ما الضّاجِعُ ابْتَزَّها مِن ثِيابِها   تَميلُ عليه هَوْنَةً غَيْرَ مِجْبالِ

---

a) MS يُقْتَل.

b) MS أضاءَ اللَّبوب. This verse is not in Geyer's edn. of Aus; it may perhaps belong to No. XXIX of that collection.

X. *Ṭawīl.* Vv. 1, 4 and 3 of this poem are quoted, with an additional verse, in BAthīr Kām. I, 475—6, and Naq. 472[9]; for vv. 1 and 3 *cf.* vv. 13 and 12 of No. XI, *post.*

c) BA, Naq. أتَوْنَا; *cf.* XI, 13.

d) MS الغُرَيْبِضَةِ here, but as text in XI, 13, and so BA, Naq.

e) MS مِيلادُ; Naq. ميلادِ, BA فى مِثْلِ; the scholion shows that the commentator read the second.

f) According to Wüst., Tab. 9, Aklub is not a branch of Shahrān, but a brother's son.

g) MS أمالوها والرَّمْى.

h) BA and Naq. أعاذِلُ لَوْ كانَ البِدَادُ لَقُوتِلوا (BA false reading لَقُوبِلوا); see LA IV, 457. For another verse in which جِنّ and خَايِل are collocated see LA XIII, 210[8].   *i)* Dīw. LII, 16.

وللخايل الحَجنُ ۞

٤ *a* فَمِتْنَا وَمَنْ يَنْزِلْ بِهِ مِثْلُ ضَيْفِنَا   يَبِتْ عَنْ قِرَى أَضْيَافِهِ غَيْرَ غَافِلِ

XI.

وقال عامر بن الطفيل يَوْمَ قَيْفِ الرِّيحِ الذي أُصِيبَتْ فيه عَيْنُهُ:

١ لَقَدْ عَلِمَتْ *b* عُلْيَا هَوَازِنَ أَنَّنِي   أَنَا الْفَارِسُ الْحَامِى حَقِيقَةَ جَعْفَرِ

٢ وَقَدْ *c* عَلِمَ الْمَزْنُوقُ أَنِّى أَكُرُّهُ *d*   عَشِيَّةَ قَيْفِ الرِّيحِ كَرَّ الْمُشَهَّرِ

المَزنوق فَرَسه. وقَيفُ الريح مكانٌ كانت الوَقعةُ فيه. و يروى: *على جَمعِهم كَرَّ الْمُنَبِّهِ الْمُشْهَرِ.*

والمُنَبِّهُ يعنى القِدْحَ الذى يُكَثَّرُ به القِدَاح لَيْسَ له غُنْمٌ ولا عليه غُرْمٌ: كُلّما خَرَجَ رُدَّ حتى يَخْرُجَ

(42b) آخِرُ القِدَاحِ ۞

٣ إِذَا ازْوَرَّ مِنْ *f* وَقْعِ الرِّمَاحِ زَجَرْتُهُ   وَقُلْتُ لَهُ ارْجِعْ مُقْبِلًا *g* غَيْرَ مُدْبِرِ

ازْوَرَّ عَدَلَ ومَالَ الى ناحِيةٍ أُخْرَى: يقال فلانٌ مُزْوَرٌّ عن صَدِيقِه اى عادِلٌ عَنْهُ: اى اذا مالَ عـن

الطَّعْنِ رَدَدْتُهُ اليه ۞

٤ وَأَنْبَأْتُهُ أَنَّ الْفِرَارَ خَزَايَةٌ   على الْمَرْءِ مَا لَمْ يُبْلِ *h* عُذْرًا فَيُعْذَرِ

---

a) So BA and Naq. The additional verse in these is as follows: —

وَخُتِّعَمْ حَىَّ يَعْدَلُونَ بِمَذْحِجِ   وَهَلْ نَحْنُ إِلَّا مِثْلُ إِحْدَى الْقَبَائِلِ

XI. *Ṭawīl.* This celebrated and much quoted poem is No. CVI of the *Mufaḍḍaliyāt*; as the citations and various readings are given there, they are not repeated here, except where our text differs from that of al-Mufaḍḍal. For the Day of Faif ar-Rīḥ see BAthīr, I, 474 ff., and Naq. 469—472.

b) MS عَلْيَا.   *c)* MS وَلَقَدْ.

d) Bakrī 721[17] has our text; Mfḍt, BQut. 191, and LA XII, 12[5], have the alternative reading mentioned in the scholion. Buḥt. Ḥam. 61 reads عَلَيْهِمْ بِقَيْفِ الرِّيحِ كَرَّ الْمُقَدَّرِ by confusion with v. 9 below.

e) In the MS the parts of the scholion have suffered dislocation, but have now been replaced in their proper order.

f) Buḥt. Ḥam. كَرِّ الرِّمَاحِ, apparently a copyist's error.   *g)* MS غَيْرُ.

h) Mfḍt جَهْدًا فَيُعْذَرِ; our reading is al-Athram's.

خَزَايَةٌ اسْتَحْيَاءٌ: يقال فلانٌ قد خَزِيَ اذا اسْتَحْيَا يَخْزَى خَزَايَةً: قال ذو الرُّمَّةِ

a خَزَايَةً أَدْرَكَتْهُ عِنْدَ جَوْلَتِهِ   مِنْ جَانِبِ الْحَبْلِ مَخْلُوطًا بِهَا الْغَضَبُ

وخَزِيَ يَخْزَى خِزْيًا اذا *b* تَبَاعَدَ. وخَزَا يَخْزُو اذا سَاسَ: قال لَبِيدٌ: *c* ‏*وَأَخْزُهَا بِالْبِرِّ لِلّٰهِ الْأَجَلْ*‏ ☙

ه أَلَسْتَ تَرَى أَرْمَاحَهُمْ فِىَّ شُرَّعًا   وَأَنْتَ حِصَانٌ مَاجِدُ الْعِرْقِ فَاصْبِرِ

يُخَاطِبُ فرَسَهُ: يقول: أَنَا صَابِرٌ على ما يَرِدُ عَلَىَّ مِن الرِّمَاحِ الْمُشْرَعَةِ نَحْوِي. يقال أَشْرَعْتُ الرُّمْحَ قِبَلَهُ ٥
اى فى وَجْهَتِهِ نَحْوَهُ. وأنتَ حِصَانٌ [اى] فَرَسٌ كَرِيمٌ شَرِيفُ الْعِرْقِ ما ضَرَبَ فيه *d* هَجِينٌ: فَاصْبِرْ مَعِى ☙

٩ أَرَدْتُ *e* لِكَيْمَا يَعْلَمَ اللّٰهُ أَنَّنِى   صَبَرْتُ وَأَخْشَى مِثْلَ يَوْمِ الْمُشَقَّرِ

الْمُشَقَّرُ مَدِينَةٌ وَهِى مَدِينَةُ هَجَرَ. وكَانَتْ بنو تَمِيمٍ وألْفَافُ *f* فيها قَطَعُوا على لَطِيمَةٍ لِكِسْرَى
جاءَتْ مِن قِبَلِ بَاذَانَ مِن الْيَمَنِ: فلَمَّا صَارَتْ فى أرضِ تَجِدُ حَقَّهَا قَوْذَةُ بن عَلِيٍّ الْحَنَفِىِّ. فَعَرَضَتْ
لهَا بنو تَمِيمٍ بمَوْضِعٍ يقال له نَطَاعٍ فَأَخَذُوا مِنْها سُيُوفًا وآنِيَةً ومَنَاطِقَ وجَوْهَرًا وعِطْرًا. وكَان الزِّبْرِقَانُ ١٠
فيهِمْ فهو قَوْلُهُ (43a)

اللّٰهُ أَعْطَانِى قَـنْــــعَمَ يَوْمَ زَوْمَلَةَ الْأَعَاجِمْ

فادَّعَى الْفَرَزْدَقُ ان صَعْصَعَةَ بن نَاجِيَةَ جَدَّهُ كَان رَأْسَ النَّاسِ فيها فى قوله:

g وَرَئِيسِ يَوْمِ نَطَاعِ صَعْصَعَةُ الَّذِى   حِينًا يَضُرُّ وَكَانَ حِينًا يَنْفَعُ

فمَضَى الْأَسَاوِرَةُ الذِينَ كَانُوا فيها وقَوْذَةُ مَعَهُمْ فَأَخْبَرُوا كِسْرَى الْخَبَرَ. فَكَتَبَ الى *h* جُوَانَابَةَ يَأْمُرُهُ أن ١٥

---

a) Dh. R., *bā'iyah*, v. 96.

b) This sense of خَزِيَ is not found in the Lexx; Mfḍt ‏وَقَعَ فِى الهَلاك‏; LA XVIII, 247¹⁹
‏وقع فى بَلِيَّةٍ وشَرٍّ وشُهْرَةٍ فَدَلَّ بذلك وهان‏; perhaps تَبَاعَدَ is used euphemistically.

c) Labīd XXXIX, 22.   *d*) MS هَجِينٍ.

e) Mfḍt (Abū 'Ikrimah's text) ‏نَكَى لا يَعْلَمُ‏ (Aḥmad as our text). Al-Kilābī (see commy. Mfḍt)
read ‏صَبَرْتُ حِفَاظًا يَعْلَمُ اللّٰهُ أَنَّنِى أُحَاذِرُ يَوْمًا مِثْلَ يَوْمِ الْمُشَقَّرِ‏.

f) فيها not in Mfḍt; seems superfluous. This account of the Day of al-Mushaqqar is identical
with that in al-Anbārī's Commentary on the Mfḍt; it rests on the authority of al-Ḥirmāzī.

g) Naq. 959¹³.

h) So our MS; Mfḍt has ‏جُوَانَبُوذَانَ‏; Agh. XVI, 79²⁵ ‏جـوارِبـوذار‏; Ṭabarī I, p. 985
‏ازانفـروز‏. Our form perhaps stands for the hypocoristic ‏جُوَانَتُوَيْة‏ (Nöldeke, *Sasaniden* 92). ‏بن جُشْنَس‏.

يَتَّفِقُ عَلَى مُضَرَ: وَوَافَقَ ذلِكَ جَدْبًا مِنَ الزَّمانِ: وَكَتَبَ اِلَى a عُمّالِهِ عَلَى b عِذَارِ العَرَبِ جَمِيعًا

(وَهُوَ فَضْلُ ما بَيْنَ العَرَبِ والعَجَمِ) اَنْ يَمْنَعُوهُمْ مِنَ المِيرَةِ. فَفَتَحَ جَوَانَبَةُ c بَابَ المُشَقَّرِ واَذِنَ لِلعَرَبِ فِى

المِيرَةِ: فَجَعَلَ يُدْخِلُهُمْ خَمْسَةً [خَمْسَةً] وَعَشَرَةً عَشَرَةً مِنْ بابِ السُّوقِ عَلَى اَنْ يُخْرِجَهُمْ مِنْ بابِ d جَبّارٍ

فِى اَنْفُسِهِمْ. eفَلَمّا دَخَلَتْ قِطْعَةٌ كَعَبَرَ رُؤُوسَهُمْ اَىْ قَطَعَها. فَلَمّا طالَ ذلِكَ عَلَيْهِمْ وَيَدْخُلُ النّاسُ وَلا

5 يَخْرُجُونَ بَعَثُوا فَنَظَرُوا اِلَى الاَبْوابِ f [فاذا هِىَ] مَأْخُوذٌ بِها ما خَلا البابَ الَّذِى يَدْخُلُونَ مِنْهُ. فَشَدَّ

رَجُلٌ مِنْ بَنِى عَبْسٍ فَضَرَبَ السِّلْسِلَةَ بِسَيْفِهِ فَقَطَعَها: فَخَرَجَ مَنْ كانَ يَلِيهِ. واَمَرَ المُكَعْبِرُ وَهُوَ جَوَانَبَةُ

بِاِغْلاقِ البابِ: ثُمَّ قَتَلَ مَنْ بَقِىَ فِى المَدِينَةِ.   وَكانَ كِسْرَى قَدْ g قَدِمَ عَلَيْهِ هَوْذَةُ واَوْجَهَهُ ونادَمَهُ واَلْبَسَهُ

تاجًا مِنْ تِيجانِهِ وحُلَلًا مِنْ حُلَلِهِ: فَزَعَمَتْ بَنُو حَنِيفَةَ اَنَّهُ كانَ لا يَراهُ اَحَدٌ مِنَ العَجَمِ اِلّا سَجَدَ لَهُ

لِذلِكَ التاجِ لِصُورَةِ كِسْرَى الَّذِى كانَ فِيهِ: فَقالَ الاَعْشَى

10

مَنْ يَرَ هَوْذَةَ يَسْجُدْ غَيْرَ مُتَّئِبٍ h   اِذا i تَعَمَّمَ فَوْقَ التّاجِ اَوْ وَضَعا

لَهُ اَكانِيلُ بِالْياقُوتِ j فَصَّلَها k   صَوّاغُها لا تَرَى عَيْبًا وَلا طَبَعا

مَنْ يَلْقَ هَوْذَةَ اَوْ يَنْزِلْ بِساحَتِهِ l   يَكُنْ لِهَوْذَةَ فِيما نابَهُ تَبَعا

وَكُلُّ زَوْجٍ مِنَ الدِّيباجِ يَلْبَسُهُ   اَبُو قُدامَةَ مَحْبُوٌّ بِذاكَ مَعا

(43b) فَهذا يَدُلُّكَ عَلَى التّاجِ والكِسْوَةِ. وَقَدِمَ m عَلَى جَوَانَبَةَ لِيَنْفُذَ اِلَى اليَمامَةِ فَشَهِدَ يَوْمَ الصَّفْقَةِ

---

a) So Mfḍt: our MS عامله.

b) So Mfḍt; our MS apparently عداد.   c) Mfḍt بابَىْ.

d) So MS; Mfḍt جبان or حيبان (perhaps جنان is intended); جَبّارُ means lime-plaster, and may be the designation of a gate. Yāq. II, 169[7] gives جَبّارُ as the name of a place in Baḥrain. The following words, فِى اَنْفُسِهِمْ, are not in Mfḍt: they perhaps mean "among their own people".

e) Mfḍt وَكُلَّما.   f) Added from Mfḍt.   g) So Mfḍt; MS قام.

h) LA II, 291[3], with يَلْق for يَرَ; MbdKam. 239[18], with v. 2, as text.

i) Mfḍt تَعَصَّبَ.   j) Mfḍt زِيّنَها.

k) So MS; other texts صَوّاغُها.

l) This and the following verse are not in Mfḍt commy.

m) So Mfḍt; MS عليه.

a[فَكَلَّمَ هَوْذَةُ فى مائَةٍ مِن بَنى تَميم: فَوَهَبَهُم لَه: فَأَعْتَقَهُم . وكَانَت الصَّفْقَةُ] يومَ فِصْحِ النَّصَارَى : فقال الأَعْشَى

b لَمَّا أَتَوْهُ أُسَارَى كُلُّهُمْ c ضَرَعَا	سَائِلْ تَميمًا بِهِمْ أَيَّامَ صَفْقَتِهِمْ
لَا يَسْتَطِيعُونَ e بَعْدَ الْيَوْمِ f مُنْتَقَعَا	وَسْطَ الْمُشَقَّرِ d فى عَيْطَاءَ مُشْرِفَةٍ
رِسْلًا مِنَ الْقَوْلِ مَخْفُوضًا وَمَا رَفَعَا	g فَقَالَ لِلْمَلِكِ أَطْلِقْ مِنْهُمْ مِائَةً
فَأَصْبَحُوا كُلُّهُمْ عَنْ غِلِّهِ خُلِعَا	h فَفَكَّ عَنْ مِائَةٍ مِنْهُمْ i وِثَاقَهُمْ
يَرْجُو الْإِلَهَ بِمَا أَسْدَى وَمَا صَنَعَا	بِهِمْ تَقَرَّبَ يَوْمَ الْفِصْحِ صَاحِبَةً

٧ لَعَمْرِى وَمَا عَمْرِى عَلَىَّ بِهَيِّنٍ   لَقَدْ شَانَ حُرَّ الْوَجْهِ j طَعْنَةُ مُشْهِر

٨ فَبِئْسَ الْفَتَى إِنْ كُنْتُ أَعْوَرَ عَاقِرًا   جَبَانًا فَمَا عُذْرِى لَدَى كُلِّ مَحْضَر

٩ وَقَدْ عَلِمُوا أَنِّى أَكُرُّ عَلَيْهِمْ   عَشِيَّةَ فَيْفِ الرِّيحِ كَرَّ الْمُدَوِّر

الْمُدَوِّرُ الَّذى يَطُوفُ بِالدُّوَارِ وهو صَنَمٌ: أراد أَعْبُدًا كَانُوا يَتَّخِذُونَهَا عِنْدَ أَوْثَانِهِمْ يُشَبِّهُونَ ذلك ١٠ بِالطَّوَافِ. والْكَرُّ الرُّجُوعُ الى القِتَال. ويقال كَرَّ الْمُدَوِّرُ أراد عبيدًا تَخْرُجُ البه الأَبْكَارُ: قال عامرٌ

k أَلَا [يَا] لَيْتَ أَخْوَالى غَنِيًّا   لَهُمْ فى كُلِّ ثَالِثَةٍ دَوَار

١٠ وَمَا رِمْتُ حَتَّى بَلَّ l صَدْرِى وَنَحْرَهُ   نَجِيعٌ كَهُدَّابِ الدِّمَقْسِ الْمُسَيَّر

وما رِمْتُ أى وما بَرِحْتُ: ويقال منه رِمْتُ أَرِيمُ: ويقال رَامَ يَرُومُ أى طَلَبَ وَرِمَّ يَرِمُّ أى أَكَلَ وَرَتَمَ

---

a) This sentence, which had fallen out of our text by *homœoteleuton*, has been restored from Mfḍt.

b) Mfḍt إِنْ بَايَعُوهُ: Ṭabarī I, 987 as text.

c) MS ضَرَعَا; see Ṭabarī.

d) MS فى غَبْرَاءَ مُظْلِمَةٍ; Ṭab. مِنْ عَيْطَاءَ; Mfḍt as text.

e) Mfḍt, Ṭab. بَعْدَ الضَّرِّ.   f) Mfḍt مُمْتَنَعَا.

g) Here Mfḍt (*q. v.*) inserts an interesting verse not in our text or Ṭab.

h) Mfḍt commy. omits the last two vv.; Ṭabarī has them.

i) Ṭab. إِسَارَهُمْ.

j) MS ضَرْبَةُ; Mfḍt, BDur, BA, Bakrī, BQut, Yāq, all as text; see the story in the commy. to the Mfḍt; no other authority supports ضربة.

k) See fuller scholion and quotation in Mfḍt, and *post*, Supplt. No. 8.

l) Mfḍt نَحْرِى وَصَدْرَهُ.

يَرْأَمُ رِئْمَانًا اذا عَطَفَ. والنَّجِيعُ الدَّمُ الطَّرِيُّ الأَحْمَرُ. وكِهْدَاب اى كَهُدْبِ الثَّوْبِ. والدِّمَقْسُ القَزُّ. والمُسَيَّرُ المُخَطَّطُ: يقال بَرْدٌ مُسَيَّرٌ ومُسَبَّبٌ اى مُخَطَّطٌ ۞

١١ أَقُولُ لِنَفْسِى أَلَّا يُبجَادُ بِمِثْلِهَا　　　أَقِلِّى المِرَاحَ إِنَّنِى غَيْرُ مُقْصِرِ

١٢ (44a) فَلَوْ كَانَ b جَمْعًا مِثْلَنَا c لَمْ يَبِزْنَا　　　وَلٰكِنْ أَتَتْنَا أُسْرَةٌ ذَاتُ مَفْخَرِ

لم يَبِزْنَا لم يَسْلُبْنَا ولم يَغْلِبْنَا. وأُسْرَةُ الرَّجُلِ رَهْطُهُ الأَدْنَوْنَ مِنْهُ ۞

١٣ d أَتَوْنَا بِشَهْرَانَ العَرِيضَةِ كُلِّهَا　　　وَأَكْلُبَ طُرًّا فِى e جِيَادِ السَّنَوَّرِ

قد مَرَّ نَسَبُ شَهْرَانَ قَبْلَ ذلك. وطُرًّا كُلًّا. والسَّنَوَّرُ الدِّرْعُ: قال ذو الرُّمَّةِ f ۞ إِذَا اجْتَنِيبَ لِلْحَرْبِ

زِّنِ السَّنَوَّرُ ۞: وقال النابغة الجَعْدِىّ

نُحَلِّى بِأَرْطَالِ اللُّجَيْنِ سِيُوفَنَا　　　وَنَعْلُو بِهَا يَوْمَ اللِّقَاءِ g السَّنَوَّرَا

XII.

١ وَفَدْنَا فَآوَيْتَنَا بِأَشْرَافِ دَارِمٍ　　　غَدَاةَ جَزَيْنَا الجَوْنَ بِالجَوْنِ صَيْلَمَا

٢ وَلَمْ يَكْفِنَا قَوْمٌ مَّقَامًا وَلَمْ نَعُذْ　　　بِغَيْرِ القَنَا فِى خَشْيَةٍ أُوْ تَجَرُّمَا

يقول لم يَقُمْ أَحَدٌ مقامًا نقوم فيه نَحْنُ. ولم نَعُذْ اى لم نَسْتَعِنْ بِأَحَدٍ غيرِ القنا ولا h التَّجَأْنَا إِلَّا اليها فى خَوْفٍ من عَدُوٍّ او تَجَرُّمٍ او ذَنْبٍ فى جِنَايَةٍ ۞

٣ وَلَمْ أَرَ قَوْمًا يَّرْفَعُونَ لِوَاءَهُمْ　　　لِغَايَتِنَا فِى المَجْدِ مِمَّنْ تَكَلَّمَا

اللِّوَاءُ للأمير ممدود: يقال أَلْوَيْتُ لِوَآءً اى عَقَدْتُهُ: وأمّا لِوَى الرَّمْلِ فمقصور: ويقال أَلْوَيْنَا اى وَقَعْنَا فى لِوَى الرَّمْلِ. والمَجْدُ الشَّرَفُ. والماجِدُ الشريفُ ۞

---

a) MS تُبجَاد (points perhaps by later hand).

b) So MS; the construction is permissible (لَوْ كَانَ [الجَمْعُ] جَمْعًا; Mfḍt مِثْلَنَا جَمْعٌ, and cf. ante, No. X, 3.

c) Mfḍt لَمْ نُبَالِهِمْ.　　　　d) Mfḍt فَجَاؤُوا بِفُرْسَانِ الْعَرِيضَةِ.

e) Mfḍt لِبَاس.　　　　f) Dh. R., Dīw. XXX, 48.

g) MS السَّنَوَّرُ (sic). This verse should belong to the poem at pp. 145—148 of the *Jamharah*, but it is not found there.

XII. *Ṭawīl*; no citations found.　　　h) MS اللجِينَا(!)

٤ a مَنِ النَّـاسِ إِلَّا يَعْرِفُونَ عَلَيْهِـمْ   لَنَـا فِى جَسِيمِ الْأَمْـرِ أَنْ نَتَكَـرَّمَا

٥ وَنَحْـنُ الْأُولَى قُدْنَا الْجِيَادَ عَلَى الْوَجَا   كَمَـا لَـوَّحَ الْقَـوَّاسُ نَبْعًا وَسَاسَمَا

الْجِيادَ الْأَقْرَاسِ الْكَرِيمَة الْوَاحِد جَوَادٌ. وَالنَّبْعُ وَالشَّوْحَطُ سَوَاءٌ فَمَا نَبَتَ فِى الْجَبَلِ فَهُوَ نَبْعٌ وَمَا نَبَتَ فِى

السَّهْلِ فَهُوَ شَوْحَطٌ. وَالسَّاسَمُ شَجَرٌ مِنَ الْآبَنُوس: قَالَ النَّمِر بْنِ تَوْلَبٍ: (44b) b *[تَرَى] حَوْلَهَا النَّبْعَ

وَالسَّاسَمَا*. وَالْوَجَا أَنْ يَنْشَكَّى الْفَرَسُ حَافِرَهُ: وَالْحَفَا اَن يَرِقَّ الْحَافِرُ. وَقَوْلُهُ: كَمَا لَـوَّحَ اى أَنَّ الْخَيْلَ ٥

ضُمَّرٌ كَالْقِسِىِّ فِى يُبْسِهَا: فَطَوَّلَ الْكَلَامَ فِيهِ كَمَا قَالَ امرُؤ القيس

c لَهَا مَتْنَتَانِ خَظَاتَا كَمَا   أَكَبَّ عَلَى سَاعِدَيْهِ النَّمِرْ

اراد بِهَٰذَا التَّطْوِيل كَسَاعِدَى نَمِرٍ بَارِكٍ ۞

٦ وَنَحْـنُ صَبَحْنَا حَىَّ أَسْمَاءَ بِالْقَنَا   وَنَحْنُ تَرَكْنَا حَىَّ مُرَّةَ مَأْتَمَا

حَىَّ أَسْمَاءَ يعنى بنى قَرَارَة: وَمُرَّةَ ابن عَوْف بن سَعْد. وقوله مَأْتَمَا اى جَمَاعَةً: وَالْمَأْتَمُ النساء يَجْتَمِعْنَ ١٠

فِى سُرُورٍ أَوْ غَمٍّ: قَالَ الشاعر

d عَشِيَّةَ قَامَ النَّائِحَاتُ وَشُقِّقَتْ   خُدُودٌ بِأَيْدِى مَأْتَمٍ اَىِّ مَأْتَمِ

٧ بَقَرْنَا الْحَبَالَى مِنْ شَنُوءَةَ بَعْدَمَا   حَبَطْنَ بِفَيْفِ الرِّيحِ نَهْدًا وَحَثْعَمَا

بَقَرْنَا اى شَقَقْنَا: يقال بَقَرَ بَطْنَهُ وَبَعَجَ بَطْنَهُ يَبْقُرُهُ وَيَبْعَجُهُ بِمَعْنًى وَاحِدٍ. وَنَهْدٌ وَخَثْعَمُ حَيَّانِ ۞ e

٨ مُجَنَّبَةً قَدْ لَاحَهَا الْغَزْوُ بَعْدَمَا   تُبَارِى مَرَاخِيهَا الْوَشِيجَ الْمُقَوَّمَا ١٥

مُجَنَّبَة يعنى الخيل: وَكَانُـوا يَجْنُبُون الْخَيْل وَيَرْكَبُون الْإِبِل لِلوَقْتِ الَّذِى يَحْتَاجُون اليها فِى الْحَرب:

وَمِثْلُهُ قول لَبِيدٍ

f يَطُرُدُ الزُّجَّ يُبَارِى ظِلَّهُ   بِأَسِيلٍ كَالسِّنَانِ الْمُنْتَخَلْ

---

a) MS النَّاسِ مِنْ.

b) LA XV, 178[17]; Aḍdād 34[13]; MS omits تَرَى (accidentally in turning the page).

c) I. Q. XIX, 30; Lane 769b.

d) This verse appears to be compounded of parts of two verses of different meanings: see LA XIV, 269[2] and [4]; see also Aḍdād, p. 67. Perhaps the confusion is due to error of the copyist.

e) Yāq. IV, 336[8] has a verse which may come in before v. 8 (or perhaps be a substitute for it): —

وَنَحْنُ جَلَبْنَا الْخَيْلَ مِن بَطْنِ لَابَةٍ   فَجِئْنَ يُبَارِينَ الْأَعِنَّةَ سُهَّمَا

f) Dīw. XXXIX, 46.

والمَراخِى السِّراع ۞

٩ وَنَحْنُ صَبَحْنَا حَىَّ نَجْرَانَ غَارَةً　　تُبِيلُ حَبَالَاهَا مَخَافَتَنَا دَمَا

نَجْرَانُ أرضٌ باليَمَن. وتُبِيل اى تَرْمِى بِأَوْلَادِها مِن مَخَافَتِنا. فلمّا حُذِفَ مِن نَصَبْتَهُ: تُبِيل يعنى الغَارة

وَدَمًا مفعول به كأنّه قال: تُبِيلُ الحَبَالَى دَمًا مَخَافَتَنَا ۞

XIII.

١ تَجَنَّبْ نُمَيْرًا وَّلَا تُوطِهَا　　فَإِنَّ بِهَا عَامِرًا حُضَّرُ ٥

٢ (45a) وَإِنَّ رِمَاحَ بَنِى عَامِرٍ　　يُقَطِّرْنَ a مِلْ عَلَقِ الْأَحْمَرِ

بنو عامر يعنى رَهْطُهُ. والعَلَق الدَّم. والعَلَق ايضًا فى غير هذا الموضع دُودَةٌ تكون فى الماء تَنْشَب فى

حَلْقِ الشّارب: والعَلَق عَلَق البَكْرة. وقال عُجَيْر السَّلُولِىّ: سَلَالِيمَ العَلَق: وأراد b مِن العَلَق فوصَّل

الكلام وأَدْغَمَ: ومِثْلُه كثير جائزٌ ۞

٣ هُمُ الْجَبَّابِرُونَ عِظَامَ الْكَسِيرِ　　إِذَا مَا الْكَسَائِرُ لَـمْ c تُجْبَرِ ١٠

يعنى يُغْنُون ويُعْطُون مَن أَقْعَدَهُ الدَّهْرُ عن التَصَرُّف: فهو كالكَسِير اى المكسور. وقوله * اذا ما الكَسائِرُ

لم تُجْبَرِ * مَثَلٌ: اى حِينَ لا يُوأسِى أَحَدٌ أَحَدًا ۞

٤ وَهُمْ يَضْرِبُونَ غَدَاةَ الصَّبَا　　ح أَنْفَ الْمُدَجِّجِ ذِى الْمِغْفَرِ

غَدَاةَ الصَّباح اى غدَاةَ الغارة لِأَنَّ الغارة لا تَقَع إلّا فى وَقْتِ الصباح. والمُدَجِّج الداخل فى السلاح:

ومثله المُقَنَّع: وقال عَنْتَرة ١٥

d ومُدَجِّجٍ كَرِهَ الْكُمَاةِ نِزَالَهُ　　لَا مُمْعِنٍ هَرَبًا وَّلَا مُسْتَسْلِمِ

والمِغْفَر البَيْضَة سُمِّىَ مِغْفَرًا e لِأَنّه يُغَطِّى الرَّأسَ والعُنُق: ومنه يقال غَفَرْتُ مَتَاعِى اى جَعَلْتُهُ فى الوِعَاءِ:

XIII. *Mutaqārib*; no citations found.

a) MS مِلْ عَلَقٍ أَحْمَرٍ.　　b) MS مِن عَلَقٍ.

c) MS يَجْبَرِ, but correctly in scholion.

d) Muʿall. 48.

e) MS الَّا أَنّه (*sic*).

وقال لَبِيدٌ a* فى لَيْلَةٍ غَفَرَ النُّجُومَ غَمَامُهـا* اى غَطّاها: وغَفَرَ الجُرْحَ اذا بَرَأَ ثم رأْسَه وقال أَسْقَلَه: والغَفْرُ

الزِّئْبِرُ: والغِفارة وقايةٌ كالخِرْقةِ تُوقَى المرأةُ مِقْنَعَتها: وقولهم غُفْرانَكَ اللهُمَّ اى تَغْطِيتَكَ وسِتْرَكَ: والغَفيرة

من الشَّعَرِ والجَمْعُ الغَفائِر وهى الذَّوائِب ☾

٥   يُقِيمُونَ لِلْحَرْبِ أَصْعارَها   إِذَا ثُـوِّرَ القَسْطَلُ الأَغْبَـرُ

الأَصْعار جمع صَعَرٍ وهو المَيَلُ: ويقال: واللهِ لأُقِيمَنَّ صَعَرَكَ: (45b) اى مَيَلَكَ. وثُوِّرَ هُيِّجَ. والقَسْطَلُ ٥

الغُبار وجَمْعه قَساطِل. يقول يُقِيمُونَ أَوَدَ الحَرْبِ فى هذا الوقت الذى ثار فيه القَسْطَلُ الأَغْبَرُ ☾

٦   كُماةٌ حُماةٌ إِذَا ما الشِّفا   ﻩ يَعْجِزُ عَن ضَيِّهَا المِشْفَرُ

كُماة جمع كَمِيٍّ وهو الشُّجاع. والحُماة الذين يَحْمُون الحَقائِقَ ويَحْفَظُون الدُّبُرَ. والمِشْفَر اراد الشِّدْقَ

فاسْتَعار كما قال الحُطَيْئَةُ

١٠   b سَقَى جارَكَ العَيْمانَ لَمّا جَفَوْتَهُ   وقَلَّصَ عَن بَرْدِ الشَّرابِ مَشافِرُهْ

يقول هم حُماةٌ فى مثل هذا الوقت الذى تَنْكَشِر فيه الشِّفاه وتَكْلَحُ فيه الوُجُوه: وهو مثل قول لَبِيدٍ

c رَقَمِيّاتٍ عَلَيْها نَاهِضٌ   تُكْلِحُ الأَرْوَقَ مِنْهُم والأَيَلّ

والأَرْوَق الطَّوِيل الأَسْنان والأَيَلُّ القَصِيرُها: يقول تُكْلِحُ الجَمِيعَ ☾

٧   يُطِيلُونَ لِلْحَرْبِ تَكْرارَها   إِذَا أَلْهَبَتْ لَهَبًا تُسْعَـرُ

ويروى: يُطِيلُونَ فى الحَرْبِ. واللَّهَبُ النـار. وتُسْعَر تُشْعَل: يقال سَعَرَتِ النـارُ تَسْعَرُ سَعْرًا وأَسْعَرْتها ١٥

أَنـا إِسْعارًا ☾

٨   وَإِنَّ الَّذِى قَـدْ أَتَيْتُمْ بِهِ   سَيَكْذِبُهُ عَنْكُمُ d المُخْبَرُ

[اى] انَّ الخَبِيرَ يَعْرِفُ أَيّامَنا وأَيّامَكم وآتاءَه للجميع ويَعْلَم مَن لَه الفَضْلُ على الآخَرِ ☾

٩   سَتَعْلَمُ e أَىْ رُمْتُمُوهُمْ إِذَا   تَلَقَّى كَتائِبَها الحُسَّـرُ

---

a) Muʿall. 42; our MS has كَفَرَ, which is the reading of Tibrīzī, and the only one which
appears to be known to the commentators; on the other hand, the quotation would be inappro-
priate here unless we read غَفَرَ.

b) Dīw. II, 26.   c) Lab. Dīw. XXXIX, 72.

d) MS المُخبِر without vowels: the scholion points to the passive form.

e) So MS; probably we should read إِنْ for أَىْ.

رُمْتُمُوهُ اى طَلَبْتُمُوهُ. والكَتائِبُ جميعُ كَتيبَةٍ وهى الجَيْشُ المُتَكَتِّبُ المُجْتَمِعُ: يقال تَكَتَّبَ الجَيْشُ

اذا تَجَمَّعَ ويقال سُمِّيَتِ الكَتابَةُ كِتابَةً لِاجْتِماعِ الحُروفِ (46a) وضَمِّ بعضها الى بعضٍ: ويقال كَتَبْتُ

البَغْلَةَ اذا جَمَعْتَ حَياءَها بِحَلْقَةٍ: قال الشاعرُ

a لا تَأْمَنَنَّ فَزارِيًّا خَلَوْتَ بِه   عَلَى قَلُوصِكَ وَٱكْتُبْها بِأَسْيارِ

٥ والحُسَّرُ جَماعَةُ حاسِرٍ وهو الـذى لا سِـلاحَ مَعَـه: فاذا كانَ مَعَـهُ سِلاحٌ فهو مُقْنَعٌ: قال مُتَمِّم بن

نُوَيْرَةَ فى أَخِيهِ مالِكٍ

b ولَا بِكَهامٍ بَزُّهُ عَـنْ عَـدُوِّهِ   إِذَا هُوَ لاقَى حاسِرًا أَوْ مُقْنَعا

والحَسيرُ المُعْيِى والحَسَرُ الأَعْياءُ ۞

١٠ تَبَيَّنْ فِى شُبُهاتِ الْأُمُورِ   فَإِنَّ التَّجارِبَ قَدْ تُؤْثَرُ

١١ لَقَدْ كَانَ فِيما خَلَا عِبْرَةٌ   وَّبِالْعِلْمِ يَعْتَبِرُ الْمُبْصِرُ

١٢ يُلَامُ الْمُفَرِّطُ فِى أَمْرِهِ   إِذَا صَرَّحَ الْأَمْرُ لِلْمُعْذِرِ

المُفَرِّطُ المُضَيِّعُ والتَّفْرِيطُ التَّضْيِيعُ: يقال فَرَّطَ فلانٌ فى أَمْرِهِ اى ضَيَّعَ: وأَفْرَطَ اذا جاوَزَ المِقْدارَ:

وفِى المَثَلِ: رُبَّما وَقَعَ الإِفْراطُ مَوْضِعَ التَّفْرِيطِ: اى تُريدُ أَنْ تُفْرِطَ c فِى إِحْكامِ الشَّىْءِ فَتُبالِغَ فيه

والمُبالَغَةُ فيه تَضْيِيعٌ ۞

XIV.

١ لَقَدْ تَعْلَمُ الْحَرْبُ أَنِّى ٱبْنُها   وَأَتَّى الْهُمامُ بِهَا الْمُعْلِمُ

٢ وَأَنِّى أَحُلُّ عَلَى رَهْوَةٍ   مِنَ الْمَجْدِ فِى الشَّرَفِ الْأَعْظَمِ

أَحُلُّ أَنْزِلُ يقال حَلَلْتُ بِمَنْزِلٍ كَذَا وَأَلْمَمْتُ بِمَعْنًى. والرَّهْوَةُ المَكانُ المُرْتَفِعُ: قال ذو الرُّمَّة

---

a) LA II, 195[10], with بَعيرِكَ: see Ḥam. 193[4-6]; poet Sālim b. Dārah of ʿAbdallāh b. Ghaṭafān.

b) Mfḍt LXVII, 10.

c) MS تُفَرِّطَ. The proverb quoted is not in Maidānī. This view of the difference between

تَفْرِيط and إِفْراط accords with the saying attributed to ʿAlī b. Abī Ṭālib in LA IX, 243[9], TA,

V, 198[15], Lane 2378a لَا تَرَى الْجَاهِلَ (LA لَا يُرَى الْجَاهِلُ) إِلَّا مُفْرِطًا أَوْ مُقَرِّطًا.

XIV. *Mutaqārib*; vv. 7 and 8 cited.

a   نَظَرْتُ كَمَا جَلَّى عَلَى رَأْسِ رَهْوَةٍ   مِنَ الطَّيْرِ أَقْنَى يَنْفُضُ الطَّلَّ أَزْرَقُ

واما رَهْوَةٌ بلا أَلِف ولام فهو جَبَلٌ: قال عمرو بن كُلْثوم

b   نَصَبْنَا مِثْلَ رَهْوَةَ ذَاتَ حَدٍّ   نُطَاعِنُ دُونَهُ حَتَّى يَبِينَا

والرَّهْوُ المكان الواسع والرَّهْو الطريق والرَّهْو الكُرْكِيُّ (46b) والرهو المُسْتَرْخِى المُتَثَنِّى الأَحْمَقُ: قال المُخَبَّلُ

c   فَأَنْكَحْتَهُ رَهْوًا كَأَنَّ عِجَانَهَا   مَشَقُّ إِهَابٍ أَوْسَعَ السَّلْخَ نَاجِلُهْ

والمَجْدُ والشَّرَفُ واحد فجاء بهما لمّا اخْتَلَفَ لَفْظَاهُما ۞

٣   وَأَنِّى أُشَمِّضُ بِالـــدَّارِعِيـــنَ فِى ثَـوْرَةِ الرَّهَجِ الْأَقْتَمِ

أُشَمِّضُهُ أَزُجُّهُ. وثَوْرَةُ الرَّهَجِ ارتفاع الغُبار. والأَقْتَمُ الغُبار الكَدِرُ فيه قُتْمَةٌ أى سَوَادٌ: والقَتَمُ الغُبار: قال رُوبَةُ يصف طريقًا أغبَرَ: * وَقاتِمِ الْأَعْماقِ خَاوِى الْمُخْتَرَقِ *

٤   وَأَنِّى أَكُرُّ إِذَا أَحْجَمُوا   بِأَكْرَمَ مِنْ عَطْفَةِ الضَّيْغَمِ

أَكُرُّ أَرْجِعُ الى الكَرِّ. اذا أَحْجَمُوا جَبُنوا: يقال أَحْجَمَ فلان عن الأَمْرِ اذا لم يُقْدِمْ عليه ولم يَجْسُرْ والاحْجام التأخير. وقوله بِأَكْرَمَ من عَطْفَةِ الضَّيْغَمِ اى كَرِّى أَكْرَمُ من كَرِّ الضَّيْغَمِ وهو الأَسَدُ: وأَصْلُ الضَّغْمِ العَضُّ ۞

٥   وَأَضْرِبُ بِالسَّيْفِ يَوْمَ الْوَغَى   أَقُدُّ بِهِ حَلَقَ الْمُبْرَمِ

الوَغَى للحرب والجَلَبَة: قال الهُذَلِيّ

e   كَأَنَّ وَغَى الْخَمُوشِ بِجَانِبَيْهِ   وَغَى رَكْبٍ أُمَيْمَ ذَوِى زِيَاطِ

---

a) LA XIX, 62⁹ and XX, 66⁴, as text: XVIII, 164²² with أَوْرَقُ; Dīw. LII, 45.

b) This verse is made up of the first hemist. of v. 40 and the second of v. 29 of ʿAmr's *Muʿallaqah* (Tibrīzī's text).

c) MS corruptly أَنْكَحْتَهَا and والسَّلْخَ نَاجِلُهْ; إِهَابِ for the verse see LA XIV, 170¹¹ and XIX, 59¹⁹; also Agh. XII, 42⁵, and No. 112 of Mr Krenkow's MS of Selections from the Mfḍt and Aṣmt., v. 42 (last mentioned and Agh فَأَنْكَحْتُمْ, LA فَأَنْكَحْتَهُ).

d) Dīw. XL, 1.

e) LA IX, 180⁷ (as text), and XX, 277²⁰ (with هِيَاطِ; latter reading in Ḥam. 57¹⁻²); poet al-Mutanakhkhil; see Jamharah 120¹³.

وَأَقُدّ أَقْطَعُ a وَالقُدّ القَطْعُ وَالقَدِيد المَقْطُوع. وَالمُبْرَم المُحْكَم: يَعْنِى بِه الدُّرُوع وَالجَوَاشِنَ الَّتِى أُحْكِمَ

صُنْعُها وَعَمَلُها: وَيُقال أَبْرَمْتُ الحَبْلَ اذا أَحْكَمْتَ قَتْلَه وَحَبْلٌ مُبْرَمٌ b وَسَحِيلٌ وَمُحَدْرَجٌ وَمَشْزُورٌ اى

مُحْكَمُ القَتْلِ ✸

٦   فَهَذَا عَتَادِى لَوَ أَنَّ الْفَتَى   يُعَمَّرُ فِى غَيْرِ مَا مَهْرَمِ

ويروى: *فَهَذَا أَوَانِى لَوَ أَنَّ الْفَتَى*: اى وَقْتِى وَحِينِى. وَالعَتَاد العُدّة. وَالاِسْتِعْداد لِمَا يُحْتاجُ إِلَيْه:

وَقال الشاعر: c *وَتَقْوَى الْإِلَه خَيْرُ الْعَتَادِ*. وَما هُنا صِلَةٌ وَصَّلَ بِها كَلَامَهُ ✸ (47a)

٧   d وَقَدْ عَلِمَ الْحَىُّ مِنْ عَامِرٍ   بِأَنَّ لَنَا ذِرْوَةَ الْأَجْسَمِ

ذِرْوَة كُلِّ شَىْءٍ أَعْلَاه: وَذِرْوَة وَعُرْوَة واحد. وَالأَجْسَم الأَضْخَم الأَعْظَم ✸

٨   e وَأَنَّا الْمَصَالِيتُ يَوْمَ الْوَغَى   إِذَا مَا الْعَوَاوِيرُ لَمْ تُقْدِمِ

المَصَالِيت جمع مِصْلَات وهو الماضِى فى الأُمُور: وَيُقال سَيْفٌ صَلْتٌ وَإِصْلِيتٌ اذا كان ماضِيًا فى الضَرِيبَة:

وَانْصَلَتَ السَّيْفُ مِن الغِمْد اذا أُجْرِدَ: وَيُقال أَصْلَتَ سَيْفَهُ اذا جَرَّدَه: وَجَبِين صَلْتٌ اى مُشْرِق: وَرَجُلٌ

صَلْتٌ وَصَلَتٌ اى صادِق اللِقاء: وَحَجَرٌ صَلْتٌ وَصَلْتٌ اى شَدِيد صُلْب: وَيُقال صَلَدَ الزَّنْد وَأَصْلَدَ اذا

لَمْ يُورِ نارًا. وَالعَوَاوِير جمع عُوّار وهو الجَبَان: قال الاعشى

f غَيْرُ مِيلٍ وَلَا عَوَاوِيرَ فِى الْهَيْـــــجَا وَلَا عُزّلٍ وَلَا أَكْفَالِ

العُزّل جمع أَعْزَل وهو الذى لا سِلاحَ مَعَه. وَالعَوَاوِير الجُبَناء. وَالأَكْفال جمع كَفِلٍ وهو الذى لا يَثْبُت

على ظَهْر الدابّة: وَقِيل لِأَعْرابِيّ راكِب وَأَبُوهُ يَمْشِى مَعَهُ: لِمَ رَكِبْتَ وَأَبُوكَ راجِلٌ: فَقال: إِنَّ أَبِى لَكَفْلٌ:

اى لا يَثْبُت على ظَهْر الدابّة

---

a) MS القُدّ.

b) So our MS; سَحِيلٌ however means "of single strand", not twisted; see Lane, s. v., and

Zuhair, Mu‘all. 18.

c) MS وَتَقْوَى اللّه; the half-verse is in met. *Khafīf*: a syllable is wanting at the beginning.

d) In LA XIV, 366[21], TA VIII, 228 foot, this v. is cited with a different rhyme: —

بِأَنَّ لَنَا الذِّرْوَةَ الْأَجْسَمَا

e) Cited LA II, 358[18], with الْمَغَاوِيرُ لَمْ تَقْدَمِ.

f) al-A‘shà, *Mā bukā'u*, 57; LA VI, 294[19], XIV, 108[15], etc. (MS incorrectly الأَكْفَال).

XV.

١ لِلْمُقْرَبَاتِ غُدُوٌّ حِيـنَ نُحْضِرُهَا   وَغَارَةٌ تَسْتَثِيرُ النَّقْعَ فِى رَهَـجِ

الْمُقْرَبَاتُ لِلْخَيْلِ الَّتِى تُدْنَى مِن اصحابها لكرامتها عَلَيْها: تُرْبَطُ عند البُيوتِ لا تَسْرَحُ مع غيرها : الواحِدَة
مُقْرَبَة. وتُحْضِرُها تَحْمِلُها على الْحَضْرِ وهو عَدْوٌ: يقال أَحْضَرَ الرَّجُلُ والفَرَسُ اذا عَدَوَا. والنَّقْعُ ✿ الغُبَار

٢ فَـمَا يُفَارِقُنِى الْمَزْنُوقُ مُحْتَـمِـلًا   رِحَالَـةً شَدَّهَا الْمِضْمَارُ بِالتَّبَجِ

٥
(47b) الْمَزْنُوقُ فَرَسُه. والرِّحَالَةُ السَّرْجُ: ومنه قول الشاعر:

a إِنْ لَا أَزَالُ عَلَى رِحَالَةِ سَابِحٍ   نَهْدٍ مَرَاكِلُهُ نَبِيلِ الْمَحْزِمِ

والمِضْمَار التَّعَهُّد والاقَامَةُ عَلَيْها: قال النابغة: * b وُرْقٌ مَرَاكِلُه مِنَ الْمِضْمَارِ *. والتَّبَجُ الصَّدْر وجَمْعه أَتْبَاجٌ ✿

٣ إِذَا نَعَى الْحَرْبَ نَاعُوهَا بَدَتْ لَهُمْ   أَبْنَاءُ عَامِرَ تُرْجِى كُلَّ مُحْتَرَجِ

ويروى: ناعُوها بَدَتْ أَصْلًا: اى عَشِيًّا الواحد أَصِيلٌ. وقوله تُرْجِى اى تَسُوق: والتَّرْجِيَةُ d أَصْلُها أَنْ
تَدْفَعَ الظَّبْيَةُ غَزَالَها بِصَدْرِها اذا أَرَادَتْ أَنْ تُرْشِحَهُ. e وَمُحْتَرَجٌ خَارِجِيٌّ قد خَرَجَ من الضَّمَّةِ وهو السابق: قال أَوْسُ بن حَجَرٍ

f وَخَارِجِيٌّ يَوْمَ الأَرْضِ مُعْتَزِمًا   وَقَيْنَةٌ ذَاتُ شِمْرَاخٍ وَأَحْجَالِ

والخَارِجِيُّ من الناسِ الذى يَسُودُ بِغَيْرِ إِرْثٍ. g وقوله نَعَى [الْحَرْبَ] ناعوها اى ذَكَرُوها ذاكِرُوها ✿

٤ عَلَيْهِمُ الْبَيْضُ وَالأَبْدَانُ سَابِغَةً   يُقَحِّمُونَ كَأَنَّ الْقَوْمَ فِى رَهَـجِ

١٥
الْبَيْضُ جمع بَيْضَة وهى المِغْفَر وهى القُرْدُمَانِىّ: قال لَبِيدُ بن رَبِيعَةَ

h فَخْمَةٌ ذَفْرَاءُ تُرْتَى بِالْعُرَى   قُرْدُمَانِيًّا وَتَرْكًا كَالْبَصَلْ

XV. *Basīṭ*; no citations found.

a) This verse is made up of the first hemist. of v. 45 and the second hemist. of v. 21 of 'Antarah's *Mu'allaqah*.

b) Dīw. X, 24 (Ahlw. وُرْقًا).   *c*) This explanation is not correct; see Lane.

d) MS أَصْلُه.   *e*) MS وَمُسْتَخْرِج.

f) This v. is not in the Dīw., ed. Geyer; it may belong to No. XXXII in that Collection.

g) MS وقوله نَعَاهَا اى.   *h*) Dīw. XXXIX, 59.

وَالأَبْدانِ جمع بَدَنٍ وهو الدِّرْعُ. والسابِغَةُ القَضّافَضَةُ. ويُقَاحِمُونَ اى a يَحْمِلُونَها على دُخُولِ الرَّهَجِ

وَاقْتِحامِ القوم. والرَّهَجِ الغُبارِ ۞

٥ صَبَّحْنَ عَبْسًا غَدَاةَ الرَّوْعِ آوِنَةً   وَهُنَّ عَالِيَنَ بِٱبْنِ الجَوْنِ فِى دَرَجِ

صَبَّحْنَ يعنى الغارة لأنّها لا تَقَعُ اَلَّا فى الصباحِ. والرَّوْعُ الفَزَعُ وَأَرْتَعَ وراعَ فَزِعَ. وآوِنَةً اى وَقْتنا جَمْعُ

٥ أَوانٍ. والدَّرَجُ المَشَقَّةُ ۞ (48a)

٦ وَٱنْقَضَّتِ الخَيْلُ مِنْ وَّادِى الذِّنَابِ وَقَدْ   أَصْغَتْ b أَسِنَّتَها حُمْرًا مِّنَ الوَدَجِ

اِنْقَضَّتْ هَبَطَتْ كَٱنْقِضاضِ العُقابِ. وَأَصْغَتْ أَمالَتْ والصَّغَا المَيْلُ: يقال صَغا الى كذا اى مالَ اليه:

ومنه c فَقَدْ صَغَتْ قُلُوبُكُما. والوَدَجُ اراد دَمَ الأَوْداجِ كأنَّه خَضَّبَها بالدمِ فصارَتْ حُمْرًا بِهِ. وانّما قال

أَصْغَتْ لأَنَّها تريد ان تَطْعُنَ بها فقد d أمالَتها للطَّعْنِ: وقال الشاعر فى معناه: *e خَفَضُوا أَسِنَّتَهُمْ فَكُلُّ

١٠ نَاعِى*. اراد بالوَدَجِ الأَوْداجِ: ومِثْلُه: *f فِى حَلْقِكُمْ عَظْمٌ وَقَدْ شَجِينَا* ۞

٧ إِنْ تَسْأَلِى الخَيْلَ عَنَّا فِى مَوَاقِفِها   يَوْمَ المُشَقَّرِ وَالأَبْطَالِ فِى زَعَجِ

يوم المشقَّر يعنى g يوم الصَّفْقَةِ وكان قد أَبْلَى h فيه. والأَبْطالِ الأَشِدَّاءُ الذين تَبْطُلُ الدِّماءُ عندهُم فلا

يُؤْخَذُ منهُم ثَأْرٌ. وزَعِجَ قَلِقَ وشِدَّةٌ: ويقال زَعَجٌ فَزِعٌ. وقد مَرَّ ذِكْرُ المُشَقَّرِ ۞

٨ تُنْخَبِرُكِ أَنِّى أُعِيدُ الكَرَّ بَيْنَهُمُ   إِذَا القَنَا حُطِّمَتْ فِى يَوْمِ مُعْتَلَجِ

١٥ تُنْخَبِرُكِ جوابُ إِنْ تَسْأَلِى. وحُطِّمَتْ كُسِرَتْ والحَطْمُ الكَسْرُ: ومنه ما يقال: حَطَمَ اللهُ ظَهْرَ عَدُوِّكَ.

وَيَوْمٌ مُعْتَلَجٍ يَوْمُ اعْتِلاجِ وازْدِحامٍ ۞

a) MS يَحْمِلُونَهُ.   b) MS أَسِنَّتَها.

c) Qur LXVI, 4.   d) MS أَمالَها.

e) LA XX, 208[20]; poet الأَجْدَعُ الهَمْدانِىّ.

f) LA XIX, 150[19]; poet المُسَيَّبُ بنِ زَيْدِ مَناةَ.

g) It is scarcely probable that the Mushaqqar mentioned here means the fortress in al-Baḥrain; it seems more likely that it is the valley in Mount Aja' mentioned in Yāq. IV, 542[3].

h) MS فيها.

XVI.

١ أَلَا مَنْ مُّبْلِغٌ عَنِّي زِيَادًا *a*   غَدَاةَ الْقَاعِ إِذْ أَزِفَ الضِّرَابُ

٢ غَدَاةَ تَثُوبُ خَيْلُ بَنِي كِلَابٍ   عَلَى لَبَّاتِهَا عَلَقٌ يُشَابُ

الْقَاعُ الْأَرْضُ الْحُرَّةُ الطِّينِ تُمْسِكُ الْمَاءَ وَلِلْجَمْعِ أَقْوَاعٌ وَقِيعَانٌ: وَقِيعَةٌ وَقْعٌ بِمَعْنًى. وَأَزِفَ قَرُبَ: يُقَالُ أَزِفَ

خُرُوجُ الْحَيِّ اى دَنَا: وَالْأُزُوفُ الدُّنُوُّ وَالْقُرْبُ لِلشَّيْءِ الرَّاحِلِ. وَتَثُوبُ تَرْجِعُ. وَاللَّبَّاتُ الصُّدُورُ. وَالْعَلَقُ

الدَّمُ الطَّرِيُّ: وَيُشَابُ اللَّحْمُ بِالدَّمِ مِنْ عَقْرِهِ ۞ (48*b*)

٣ فَإِنَّ لَنَا حُكُومَةَ كُلِّ يَوْمٍ   يُبَيِّنُ فِي مَفَاصِلِهِ الصَّوَابُ

٤ *b* وَإِنِّي سَوْفَ أَحْكُمُ غَيْرَ عَادٍ   وَلَا قَدِعٍ إِذَا الْتُمِسَ الْجَوَابُ

الْقَدْعُ الْكَلَامُ الْقَبِيحُ. وَيُرْوَى: وَلَا قَدِعٍ: *c* وَالْقَدْعُ الْهَيُّوبُ لِلشَّيْءِ وَفَاعِلُ ذَلِكَ قَادِعٌ وَالِاسْمُ الْقَدْعُ ۞

٥ حُكُومَةَ حَازِمٍ لَّا عَيْبَ فِيهَا   إِذَا مَا الْقَوْمُ كَظَّهُمُ الْخِطَابُ

كَظَّهُمْ غَلَبَهُمْ وَمَلَأَهُمْ غَيْظًا: وَيُقَالُ *d* كَظَظْتُ الْبَابَ اى سَدَدْتُهُ. وَالْخِطَابُ الْمُخَاطَبَةُ ۞

٦ فَإِنَّ *e* مَطِيَّةَ الْحِلْمِ التَّأَنِّى   عَلَى مَهَلٍ وَلِلْجَهْلِ الشَّبَابُ

الْمَطِيَّةُ كُلُّ مَا رُكِبَ ظَهْرُهُ: وَإِنَّمَا هَذَا مَثَلٌ ۞

٧ وَلَيْسَ الْجَهْلُ عَنْ سِنٍّ وَلَكِنْ   غَدَتْ بِنَوَافِذِ الْقَوْلِ الرِّكَابُ

يَقُولُ مَا قُلْنَاهُ مِنَ الشِّعْرِ تَحْمِلُهُ الرُّوَاةُ إِلَى كُلِّ فَجٍّ عَلَى رِكَابِهِمْ اى إِبِلِهِمْ: اى هُوَ مِثْلُ نَوَافِذِ السَّهْمِ اذا

خَرَجَ عَنِ الْفُوقِ لَمْ يَرُدَّهُ أَحَدٌ ۞

٨ فَإِنَّ بَنِى بَغِيضٍ قَدْ أَتَاهُمْ   رَسُولُ النَّاصِحِينَ فَمَا أَجَابُوا

بَنُو بَغِيضٍ عَبْسٌ وَذُبْيَانُ وَأَنْمَارُ بَنُو بَغِيضٍ بْنِ رَيْثِ بْنِ غَطَفَانَ. يَقُولُ: قَدْ أَتَاهُمْ رَسُولٌ مِمَّنْ نَصَحَهُمْ

فَمَا قَبِلُوا النُّصْحَ ۞

٩ وَلَا رَدُّوا *f* مَحْزُورَةَ ذَاكَ حَتَّى   أَتَانَا *g* الْحِلْمُ وَانْصَرَقَ الْعِجَابُ

XVI. *Wafir*; v. 4 cited.   *a*) Ziyād is an-Nābighah of Dhubyān; see next piece.

b) Cited in LA X, 132[19], with قَدِع.   *c*) MS الْقَدْع ,قَادِع ,الْقَدَع.   *d*) MS كَظَمْت.

e) Cf. No. XVI*a*, v. 1; either مَطِيَّة here should apparently be corrected to مَظِنَّة, or the reverse correction be made in the other passage; the scholia however show that the commentator read the text as printed.   *f*) MS مَحُورَة.   *g*) Prof. Nöldeke suggests that for الْحِلْم

الْمَحُورَة وَالْمُحَاوَرَة وَالْإِحَارَة وَالْحَوَارُ وَالْحَوِيرُ كُلُّهُ الْجَوَابُ: قَالَ طَرَفَةُ

a وَأَصْفَرَ مَضْبُوحٍ نَظَرْتُ حَوِيرَهُ   عَلَى النَّارِ وَاسْتَوْدَعْتُهُ كَفَّ مُجْمِدِ

وَيُرْوَى: نَظَرْتُ حَوَارَهُ عَلَى النَّارِ ۞

١٠ فَإِنَّ مَقَالَتِي مَا قَدْ عَلِمْتُمْ   وَخَيْلِي قَدْ يَحِلُّ لَهَا النِّهَابُ

٥ اى قَوْلِي الَّذِي أَقُولُهُ قَدْ عَلِمْتُمْ أَنِّي لَا يَفْتُونِي عَمَّا أُرِيدُهُ (49a) شَىْءٌ وَلَا أَهَابُ أَحَدًا يَثْنِي عَزْمِي

وَقَوْلِي. وَالنِّهَابُ جَمْعُ نَهْبٍ ۞

١١ إِذَا يَمَّمْنَ خَيْلًا مُسْرِعَاتٍ   جَرَى بِمَنْحُوسٍ طَيْرِهِمُ الْغُرَابُ

يَمَّمْنَ قَصَدْنَ: يُقَالُ يَمَّمْتُكَ وَتَأَمَّمْتُكَ اى قَصَدْتُكَ ۞

١٢ وَإِنْ مَرَّتْ عَلَى قَوْمٍ أَعَادٍ   بِسَاحَتِهِمْ فَقَدْ خَسِرُوا وَخَابُوا

XVIa.

فَأَجَابَهُ النَّابِغَةُ الذُّبْيَانِيُّ   10

١ b أَلَا أَبْلِغْ عُوَيْمِرَ عَنْ زِيَادٍ   فَإِنَّ مَظِنَّةَ الْجَهْلِ الشَّبَابُ

وَيُرْوَى * أَبْلِغْ عَامِرًا عَنِّي رَسُولًا * فَإِنَّ مَظِنَّةَ الْجَهْلِ الشَّبَابُ *. وَمَظِنَّةُ الرَّجُلِ حَيْثُ يَأْوِيهِ وَلَا يَبْرَحُ

مِنْهُ: وَيُقَالُ: اطْلُبُوا الْعِلْمَ فِي مَظَانِّهِ ۞

٢ c فَإِنَّكَ سَوْفَ تَحْلُمُ أَوْ تَنَاهَى   إِذَا مَا شِبْتَ أَوْ شَابَ الْغُرَابُ

١٥ اى أَنْتَ لَا تَحْلُمُ كَمَا أَنَّ الْغُرَابَ لَا يَشِيبُ: وَهَذَا مَثَلٌ ۞

٣ فَكُنْ كَأَبِيكَ أَوْ كَأَبِي بَرَاءٍ   تُوَافِقْكَ الْحُكُومَةُ وَالصَّوَابُ

(which is quite clear in the MS) we should read الْحُكْم; this view is supported by v. 3 of No. XVIa and its scholion, and, it may be added, by vv. 3—5 of our poem. (It appears probable that, instead of No. XVIa being the answer to No. XVI, the latter is the answer to the former: this seems best to explain v. 1 of XVIa and vv. 6—7 of XVI).   a) Muʿall. 101.

XVIa. *Wâfir*. This poem is No. IV of Nab. Dîw. (ed. Ahlw.); see the occasion explained in Ahlw., p. 209. Vv. 1, 2, 3, 4 are in BAthîr, Kam. 483.

b) Cited and rendered, Lane 1925c, LA XVII, 145⁶: both as in Dîw., where first hemist. is فَإِنْ يَكُ عَامِرٌ قَدْ قَالَ جَهْلًا, and so BA; the Lexx. mention السِّبَابُ as alternative reading in hemist. 2.

c) In the Dîw. this verse comes after vv. 3—4; BA agrees with our order. MS has تُنَاهَى. Ahlw. misprints شِبْتَ for شِبْتَ.

ابو بَراءٌ عَمُّهُ عامر بن جَعْفَرٍ. اى كُنْ كَعَمَّكَ فَتَأْتَى لَكَ الْحُكْمُ كما كان يَتَأْتَى لَهُ ☙

٤ وَلَا تَذْهَبْ بِحِلْمِكَ a هَافِيَاتٌ مِّنَ الْخُيَلَاءِ لَيْسَ لَهُنَّ بَابُ

هَافِيَاتٌ ما يَسْتَخْفُّكَ فَتَطِيشُ لَهـا. من الخُيَلَاءِ اى من الْكِبْرِ. وقولهُ لَيْسَ لَهُنَّ بابٌ اى اذا طَلَبْتَ
مَخْلَصًا لم تَجِدْ بابَهُ ☙

٥ فَاِن يَكُ رَبُّ أَذْوَادٍ بِحِسْمَى أَصَابُوا فِى لِقَائِكَ مَـا أَصَابُوا

أَذْوَادٌ اِبِلٌ وهو جمع ذَوْدٍ وهو ما بَيْنَ الثَلٰثَةِ الى الْعَشَرَةِ. وحِسْمَى موضِعٌ. ورَبُّ الشّىءِ صاحِبُهُ ورَبُّ
الدارِ صاحِبُها ورَبُّ الضَّيْعَةِ صاحِبُها ومالِكُها: ومنه رَبُّ السَّماواتِ اى مالِكُها ☙

٦ فَمَا اِنْ كَانَ مِنْ نَسَبٍ بَعِيدٍ وَلَـٰكِنْ أَدْرَكُوكَ وَهُمْ غِضَابُ

ذَكَرَ ابو الْعَبّاس ثعلب انّ حِسْمَى يومٌ لِبَنِى بغيض على بنى عامر (49b) فُتِلَ فيه حَنْظَلَةُ بن الطُّفَيْلِ
اخو عامر بن الطُّفَيْل ☙

٨ فَوَارِسُ مِـنْ مَّنُولَةَ غَيْرُ مِيلٍ c وَمُـرَّةَ فَـوْقَ جَمْعِهِمُ الْعُقَابُ

مَنُولَةُ d اُمُّ مازِنٍ وشَمْخٍ ابْنَى فَزَارَةَ: ومُرَّةُ ابْنُ عَوْفِ بن سَعْدٍ. وقولهُ غير مِيلٍ e جمع أَمْيَلَ وهو الذى
لا تُرْسَ معهُ. والْعُقابُ الرَّايَةُ وجمعها عِقْبانٌ ☙

XVII.

١ يَا رُبَّ قِرْنٍ قَـدْ f تَرَكْتُ مُجَدَّلًا ضَخْمِ السَّبِيعَةِ رَأْسُ حَيٍّ جَحْفَلِ

يقال هُوَ قِرْنُهُ فى القِتالِ والحَرب اذا كان شَجاعَتُهما واحدَةً: وهو قِرْنُهُ فى السِّنِّ اذا كان مِيلادُهُما واحدًا.
مُجَدَّلًا اى مَصْرُوعًا على الْجَدالَةِ وهى الارضِ: قال الراجز

g وَقَدْ أَرْكَبُ الْآلَةَ بَعْدَ الْآلَةِ وَأَتْـرُكُ الْعَـاجِـزَ بِالْجَدالَـةِ

a) Dīw. طَامِيَاتٌ, BA طامثاتٌ.

b) Dīw. مِنْ لِقَائِكَ, and فَاِنْ تَكُنِ الْفَوارِسُ يَوْمَ حِسْى.

c) Dīw. وَمُرَّةَ. d) MS أَمْرَأَة sic!

e) For the meanings of أَمْيَل see LA XIV, 161[1] ff.; that given in the scholion does not suit here.

XVII. Kāmil; no citations.

f) MS تَرَكْنَ: all the following verbs are in the 1st pers. sing. g) See ante, p. 103[1].

وقوله ضَخْم a الدَّسيعَة اى الخَلْق. جَحْفَل غَليظ: ورَجُل جَحْفَل وجَحَنْفَل اذا كان غَليظ الشَّفَة ✿

٢   وَتَرَكْتُ نِسْوَتَهُ لَهُنَّ تَفَجُّعٌ   يَنْدُبْنَهُ أُصُلًا بِنَوْحٍ مُعْوِلِ

تَفَجُّع وتَوَجُّع واحد. أُصُلًا عَشِيًّا. والمُعْوِل الَّذى يرفَع صَوْتَهُ فى البُكاء والاعْوال: يقال أَعْوَلَتِ المرأةُ
تُعْوِلُ إعْوالًا ✿

٣   مِن آلِ عَبْسٍ قَدْ شَفَيْتُ حَرارَتى   وَغَنِمْتُ كُلَّ غَنيمَةٍ لَـمْ تَضْهَلِ

تَضْهَل تَجْتَمِع: يقول فَرَّقْتُها حين جَمَعْتُها: يقال ضَهَل للرجُل مالٌ وضَهَل فى ضَرْعِ الناقةِ لَبَنٌ اى
اجْتَمَع: وبِئْر ضَهُولٌ ✿

٤   وَنَجا بِعَنْتَرَةَ الأَغَرِّ مِنَ الرَّدَى   يَهْوِى عَلَى عَجَلٍ هُوِىَّ الأَجْدَلِ

الأَغَرُّ فرسه والأُنْثَى غَرّاء وهى التى فى وَجْهِها غُرَّة: والغُرَّة فوق القُرْحَة. والرَّدَى الهَلاك. كأنَّه قال: فَرَّ
على فرسه (50a) فكأنَّه نَجا به: وهو يَهْوِى قُوَيْبًا اذا أَحَطَّ فى المَضِيّ. والأَجْدَل الصَّقْر والجميع الأَجادِل
ويقال للصَّقْر ايضًا قَطامِيٌّ وقُطامِيٌّ ✿

٥   وَتَرَكْتُ عَبْلَةَ فى السَّواءِ لِفِتْيَةٍ   باتُوا عَلَى كُتُفِ الخُيُولِ الجُوَّلِ

عَبْلَة صاحبَة عَنْتَرَة. والسَّواء والسِّوَى الوَسَط اى تَرَكْتُ بَيْنَهُم. وكُتُف c الخُيُول اى يَبيتُونَ عَلى
أَكْتاف خُيُولِهِم. الجُوَّل من الجَوَلانِ ✿

٦   راحوا بِهِنْدٍ وَالوَجيهَةِ عَنْوَةً   يَّوْمَ الوِقاعِ عَلَى نَجائِبَ ذُمَّلِ

نَجائِب إبِلٌ كِرامٌ. d[وذُمَّلٌ] من الذَّميل وهو ضَرْب من السَّيْرِ سريع. عَنْوَةً اى e غُلْبَةً: ويقال من عنا
يعنو. والوِقاع مَصْدَر وأَقَعْتُه مُواقَعَةً ووِقاعًا ✿

_____

a) This explanation of ضَخْمُ الدَّسيعَة appears to be incorrect; see LA IX, 439[1] ff, and Lane 879c.

b) The mention of ᶜAntarah and his mistress ᶜAblah (v. 5) in this poem seems to make it impossible that it can be by Āmir: for the latter was born in the year of the Battle of Shiᶜb Jabalah, when ᶜAntarah was already a mature warrior of full age; he must have been old while ᶜĀmir was still a youth.

c) MS الخَيْل.

d) Accidentally omitted in MS.

e) MS غَفْلَةً(!)

XVIII.

١ صَبَحْنَا الْحَيَّ مِنْ عَبْسٍ صَبُوحًا   بِكَأْسٍ فِى جَوَانِبِهَا التَّمِيلُ

التَّمِيلُ وَالْمُثَمَّلُ وَالْمُثَمَّنُ الشَّمُّ. وَالصَّبُوحُ شُرْبُ الْغَدَاةِ: وَالْقِيلُ شُرْبُ نِصْفِ النَّهَارِ وَالْغَبُوقُ شُرْبُ الْعَشِيِّ

وَالْجَاشِرِيَّةُ شُرْبُ السَّحَرِ. وَالتَّمِيلُ الَّذِى أُنْقِعَ وَبَقِىَ فِى ٱلٱنْقِاعِ حَتَّى يُدْرِكَ فِيهِ وَيَجْرِى الشَّمُّ فِى أُصُولِهِ.

وَمِنْهُ تَمِيلَةُ النَّاقَةِ لِلْعَلَفِ [الَّذِى] يَبْقَى فِى جَوْفِهَا ۞

٢ وَأَبْقَيْنَا لِمُرَّةَ يَوْمَ نَحْسٍ   وَإِخْوَتِهِمْ فَقَدْ ذَهَبَ الْغَلِيلُ

يَوْمُ نَحْسٍ يَوْمُ رِيحٍ وَعَبْرَةٍ: وَإِنَّمَا أَرَادَ يَوْمًا صَعْبًا. وَالْغَلِيلُ حَرَارَةٌ فِى الصَّدْرِ مِنْ عَطَشٍ أَوْ غَيْظٍ: وَالْغُلَّةُ

وَالْغَلِيلُ وَاحِدٌ. اى ٱشْتَفَيْنَا مِنْهُمْ لِأَنَّا قَدْ نِلْنَا مِنْهُمْ وَأَبْكَيْنَا فِيهِمْ فَقَدْ زَالَ الْغَلِيلُ ۞

٣ تَرَكْنَا دُورَهُمْ فِيهَا دِمَاءٌ   وَأَجْسَادٌ فَقَدْ ظَهَرَ الْعَوِيلُ

الْعَوِيلُ الْبُكَاءُ وَالصِّيَاحُ: يُقَالُ أَعْوَلَتِ الْمَرْأَةُ تُعْوِلُ (50b) إِعْوَالًا: وَامْرَأَةٌ مُعْوِلَةٌ اى بَاكِيَةٌ صَيَّاحَةٌ

فِى بُكَاءِهَا ۞

٤ فَذَلَّ الْأَبْلَخُ الْمُخْتَالُ إِنَّا   نُخَيِّسُهُ وَعَزَّ بِنَا الدَّلِيلُ

الْأَبْلَخُ الْمُتَكَبِّرُ. وَالْمُخْتَالُ ذُو الْخُيَلَاءِ. نُخَيِّسُهُ اى نُذَلِّلُهُ: وَمِنْهُ سُمِّىَ الْمُخَيِّسُ a بِالْبَصْرَةِ: b وَالْخِيسُ

الْأَجَمَةُ يَرْتَبِطُ فِيهِ الْأَسَدُ: وَيُقَالُ خَاسَ الْبَيْعُ يَخِيسُ خَيْسًا اذا بَقِىَ وَكَسَدَ ۞

٥ قَتَلْنَا مَالِكًا وَأَبَا رَزِينٍ   غَدَاةَ الْقَاعِ إِنْ لَمَعَ الدَّلِيلُ

لَمَعَ الدَّلِيلُ [اى] لَمَّا رَآهُمْ رَبِيعُنَا وَدَلِيلُنَا لَمَعَ إِلَيْنَا بِثَوْبِهِ. وَالْقَاعُ الْأَرْضُ الْحُرَّةُ الطِّينِ تُمْسِكُ الْمَاءَ

وَجَمْعُهُ قِيعَانٌ وَأَقْوَاعٌ: قَالَ الشَّاعِرُ: *وَأَقْفَرَ أَقْوَاعُ اللِّوَى وَخَمَائِلُهُ* وَالْخَمَائِلُ جَمْعُ خَمِيلَةٍ وَهِى رَمْلٌ

يَنْبِتُ الْحَشِيشُ ۞

٦ لَعِنَا فِى الرَّوْعِ أَبْطَالٌ كِرَامٌ   إِذَا مَا الْخَيْلُ جَدَّ بِهَا الصَّهِيلُ

الرَّوْعُ الْفَزَعُ وَالرَّائِعُ الْفَزِعُ. وَالْأَبْطَالُ الْأَشِدَّاءُ تَبْطُلُ عِنْدَهُمُ الْأَثْآرُ لَا يُقْدَرُ عَلَيْهِمْ لِعِزِّهِمْ وَامْتِنَاعِهِمْ: فَمَنْ

قَتَلَهُ بَطَلَ ذَهَبَ دَمُهُ هَدَرًا ۞

_____

XVIII. *Wafir*; no citations found.

a) This prison, buil!t by the Caliph ʿAlī, and used by al-Ḥajjāj, is generally said to have been

at al-Kūfah: LA VII, 377[3].   b) So LA VII, 378[2]; MS الخَيِّس.

٧   عَلَى جُرْدٍ مُسَوَّمَةٍ عِتَاقٍ   تَوَقَّصُ بِالشَّبَابِ وَبِالْكُهُولِ

الجُرْدُ لِلخَيل القِصار الشُّعور: وطُولُ الشَّعر هُجْنة والواحد أَجْرَدُ والانثى جرداء. ومُسَوَّمَة مُعْلَمَة. عِتاقٌ

كِرامٌ يقال فرس عتيقٌ اى كريم. aوتَوَقَّصُ اى تَوَقَّلُ وهو أَشَدُّ العَدْوِ حتى يكاد يَضْرَعُ ۞

٨   إِذَا مَا الرَّكْضُ أَسْهَلَ جَانِبَيْهَا   وَجَدَّ السَّيْرُ وَانْقَطَعَ النَّقِيلُ

أَسْهَلَ جانِبَيْها أَسالَ بالعَرَق. والنَّقِيل الواحدة نَقِيلة وفى النِعال التى تُتَّخَذُ لِلخَيل والابل تُحذاها.

يقول تُقْطَع نِعالُها من شِدَّة السَّير. والنَّقِيلُ ما خُصِفَ من النِعال: (51a) والنَّقْلُ ضَرْبٌ من السَّيْر ۞

٩   وَيَوْمَ الشِّعْبِ غَادَرْنَا لَقِيطًا   بِأَبْيَضَ صَارِمٍ عَضْبٍ صَقِيلِ

غَادَرْنا تَرَكْنا: ومِنه سُمِّى الغَدِير لِأَنَّ السَّيلَ غَادَرَهُ اى تَرَكَهُ. والصارِم السَّيف القاطع. والعَضْبُ ايضًا

القاطع: ويقال لِسانٌ عَضْبٌ اى حادٌّ ۞

١٠   غَدَاةَ أَرَادَ أَنْ يَسْمُو إِلَيْنَا   بِأُسْرَتِهِ وَأَخْلَفَهُ الْقَبِيلُ

يَسْمُو يَرْتَفِع والسُّمُوُّ الارتِفاع. بِأُسْرَتِه بِقَوْمِه الذى أَسَرَ بِهِمْ اى شَدَّدَ بِهِمْ: والأَسْرُ وَثاقَةُ الخَلْق وإحْكامُه:

ويقال أَسَرْتُ القَتَب: وقال الله تَبارَك وتَعالى: bوَشَدَدْنَا أَسْرَهُمْ: اى خَلْقَهُم والله أَعْلَم ۞

١١   فَأُبْنَا غَانِمِينَ بِمَا اسْتَفَأْنَا   نَسُوقُ الْبِيضَ دَعْوَاهَا الْأَلِيلُ

أُبْنا رَجَعْنا والأَوْبُ الرُجوع والأَوْبَة الرَجْعَة والإِيابُ الرجوع ايضًا: قال الغَنَوِيُّ cوَالْإِيَابُ حَبِيبٌ. واسْتَفَأْنا من

الفَيْءِ. والأَلِيل والأَنِين من الصُراخ وأَنْ تَتَوَلْوَلَ وتَتَمَرَّحَ لِأَنَّها قد أُسِرَتْ فهى غريبَةٌ تَبْكى ۞

XIX.

١   بَنِى عَامِرٍ غُضُّوا الْمَلَامَ إِلَيْكُمْ   وَهَاتُوا فَعُدُّوا الْيَوْمَ [فِيكُمْ] dمَشَاهِدِى

٢   وَلَا تَكْفُرُوا فِى النَّائِبَاتِ بَلَاءَنَا   إِذَا عَضَّكُمْ خَطْبٌ بِإِحْدَى الشَّدَائِدِ

٣   سَلُوا تُخْبَرُوا عَنَّا غَدَاةَ أُقَيْصِرٍ   وَأَيَّامَ حِسْمَى أَوْ ضَوَارِسَ حَاشِدِ

حِسْمَى موضع او بَلَد. ويروى أَيَّامَ بالجَرِّ والنَصْب. وحاشِدٌ من هَمْدان. وضَوارِسَ ما ضَرَّسَهُم من الحَرب:

ويقال فلانٌ ضَرِسٌ شَكِسٌ اى سَيِّىءُ الخُلُق. وكذا أُعْرِب ۞

---

a) This does not agree with the explanations of al-Aṣmaʿī and Abū ʿUbaidah in LA VIII, 376⁵ ff.; see Lane 2961c, and Aṣm., *Khail*, 269ff.

b) Qur. LXXVI, 28; and see Lane, 58a.

c) Not found in Ṭufail's *Dīwān.*   XIX. *Ṭawīl.*   *d)* Omitted by copyist: conj.

٤ وَبِالْكَوْرِ إِذْ ثَابَتْ حَلَائِبُ جَعْفَرٍ   إِلَيْكُمْ وَجَاءَتْ خَثْعَمٌ لِّلتَّحَاشُدِ

(51b) الْكَوْرُ جَبَلٌ. وَثَابَتْ رجعت تَئُوبُ ثَوْبًا. وَالْحَلَائِبُ الجماعات: يَجْتَمِعُونَ لِلتَّعَاوُنِ. وَالتَّحَاشُد من

الْإِحْشَادِ لِلْأَمْرِ وهو الاجتماع وَالْإِلْتِفَافِ: يقال تَحَاشَدَ عَلَيَّ بنو فلان اى تَعَاوَنُوا عَلَيَّ ☞

٥ لِيَمْتَرِعُوا عِلْقَاتِنَا ثُمَّ ^a يَرْتَعُوا   فَأَرَدَتْ قَنَاتِى مِنْهُمْ كُلَّ مَاجِدِ

الْعِلْقَةُ وَالْعِرْقَةُ الْمَعَاشُ وَالْقِوَامُ. أَرَدَتْ أَهْلَكَتْ وَالرَّدَى الهلاك. وَالْمَاجِدُ الشَّرِيفُ ☞

٦ فَأَنْفَذْتُ عَبْدَ اللَّهِ ثَمَّ بِضَرْبَةٍ   وَقَدْ حَامَ عَنْهَا كُلُّ حَامٍ وَّذَائِدِ

خَامَ جَبُنَ وَضَعُفَ يَخِيمُ. وقوله كُلُّ حَامٍ اى كُلُّ من يَحْمِى على إِنْسَانٍ قد جَبُنَ لِشِدَّةِ الْأَمْرِ. وَالذَّائِدُ

الْمَانِعُ: يقال قد ذُدْتُهُ عن كذا وكذا اى مَنَعْتُهُ ^c وَالْمَذُودُ الْمَمْنُوعُ ☞

٧ تَرَكْتُ صَرِيعًا بِالْعَرَاءِ مُجَدَّلًا   ضُبَيْعَةَ إِذْ نَجَّى شُتَيْرَ بْنَ خَالِدِ

ضُبَيْعَةُ رجلٌ من بَنِى عَبْسٍ. مُجَدَّلًا مَصْرُوعًا مُلْقًى فِى الْجَدَالَةِ. وَالْعَرَاءُ الْقَفْرُ من الْأَرْضِ ☞

٨ طِمِرٌّ وَزَيْدُ الْخَيْلِ قَدْ نَالَ طَعْنَةً   إِذِ الْمَرْءُ زَيْدٌ جَائِرٌ غَيْرُ قَاصِدِ

أراد نَجَّى شُتَيْرًا طِمِرٌّ وهو الفرس الْوَثُوبُ يقال طَمَرَ اى وَثَبَ: وَيُسَمَّى ^d الْبُرْغُوثُ طَامِرَ بْنَ طَامِرٍ. وَالْجَائِرُ

وَالْجَائِضُ وَلْجَائِدُ وَالْعَادِلُ الْمُنْحَرِفُ عن الطريق ☞

٩ فَذَلِكَ مَا أَعْدَدْتُ فِى كُلِّ مَأْقِطٍ   كَرِيهٍ وَعَامٍ لِّلْعَشِيرَةِ آئِدِ

الْمَأْقِطُ مَضِيقُ لِلْحَرْبِ. وَآئِدٌ مُثْقَلٌ من قول الله جلّ وعزّ ^e وَلَا يَئُودُهُ حِفْظُهُمَا: اى لا يُثْقِلُهُ: يقال

آدَنِى الشىْءُ اذا أَثْقَلَنِى: وَالْأَيْدُ وَالْآدُ الْقُوَّةُ وَالشِّدَّةُ ☞ (52a)

XX.

١ قَتَلْنَا يَزِيدَ بْنَ عَبْدِ الْمَدَانِ   عَلَى غَيْرِ جُرْمٍ وَّلَمْ نَظْلِمِ

٢ بِأَعْوَى وَيَوْمَ لَقِينَاهُمْ   بِأَرْعَنَ ذِى لَجَبٍ ^fمُبْهِمِ

---

a) MS تَرْتَعُوا.   b) MS فَأَنْقَذْتُ.   c) MS الممدود(!)

d) MS الْبَرَاغِيثُ.   e) Qur. II, 256.

XX. *Mutaqārib*; v. 2 cited (without name) in Yāq. I, 317³.

f) So in MS, and also in scholion; but the second time مُبْهَم (قُفْل); Lane has only مُبْهَم,
but the active form seems better where the subject is not a manufactured article.

الْأَرْعَنُ الْجَيْشُ الَّذِى لَهُ رَعْنٌ مِثْلُ رَعْنِ الْجَبَلِ وَهُوَ أَنْفٌ يَتَقَدَّمُ مِنْهُ. وَذِى لَجَبٍ ذِى صَوْتٍ

وَجَلَبَةٍ. وَمُبْهَمٌ مِنَ الْبُهَمِ: يُقَالُ فَارِسٌ بُهْمَةٌ اذَا كَانَ لَا يُدْرَى كَيْفَ يُؤْتَى لَهُ: وَمِنْهُ يُقَالُ قُفْلٌ مُبْهَمٌ

اى عَسِرٌ عِنْدَ الْافْتِتَاحِ ۞

XXI.

أَغَارَ عَامِرُ بْنُ الطُّفَيْلِ عَلَى بَنِى عَبْسٍ فِى a خَيْلٍ: وَزَيْدُ الْخَيْلِ بْنُ مُهَلْهِلٍ مُجَاوِرٌ فِى بَنِى عَبْسٍ. فَأَخَذَ

5 طَائِفَةً مِنْ إِبِلِهِمْ. فَأَدْرَكَهُ زَيْدُ الْخَيْلِ: فَقَالَ لَهُ وَهُوَ حَامِيَةُ الْقَوْمِ: مَا تُرِيدُ. فَقَالَ زَيْدٌ: لَقَدْ عَلِمْتَ ذُو

أُرِيدُ (يَعْنِى الَّذِى أُرِيدُ: قَالَ الزُّبَادِىُّ هِىَ لُغَةُ طَيِّئٍ: قَالَ رَجُلٌ مِنْهُمْ

فَإِنَّ بَيْتَ تَمِيمٍ ذُو سَمِعْتَ بِهِ   فِيهِ تَنَمَّتْ وَأَرْسَتْ عِزَّهَا مُضَرُ

وَأَنْشَدَ لِبَعْضِ الْأَسَدِيِّينَ *أَلَا أَنْظُرَاهَا فِى الْقَطِيعِ ذُو مَضَى* وَأَنْشَدَ غَيْرُهُ

b فَإِنَّ الْمَاءَ مَاءُ أَبِى وَجَدِّى   وَبِئْرِى ذُو حَفَرْتُ وَذُو طَوَيْتُ

10 اى الَّذِى حَفَرْتُ وَطَوَيْتُ). وَقَالَ لَهُ عَامِرٌ: مَا كَانَتْ بَنُو عَبْسٍ c لِنَتْرُكَكَ وَسَلَبِى وَمَا أَظُنُّكَ تَنَالُ ذٰلِكَ

حَتَّى أُذِيقَكَ بَعْضَ مَا تَكْرَهُ. قَالَ لَهُ زَيْدٌ: أَلَا تَرَى تَعْلَبَ رُمْحِكَ مُنْهَضِمًا. قَالَ لَهُ عَامِرٌ: لٰكِنَّ السَّيْفَ لَيْسَ

بِهِ بَأْسٌ. قَالَ زَيْدٌ: أَفَلَا أُعْطِيكَ رُمْحِى هٰذَا. قَالَ: بَلَى فَأَدْرَكَهُ فَتَنَحَّ عَنْهُ. فَفَعَلَ. وَلَحِقَهُ ضُبَيْعَةُ بْنُ

الْحَارِثِ فَقَالَ: يَا زَيْدُ دُونَكَ وَالرَّجُلَ. فَقَالَ زَيْدٌ: إِنِّى أَرَى فِيهِ ذُو تَرَى (اى أَهَابُهُ كَمَا d تَهَابُهُ]). (52b)

فَحَمَلَ ضُبَيْعَةُ فَطَعَنَ عَامِرًا فَمَارَ الرُّمْحُ. وَحَمَلَ عَلَيْهِ فَطَعَنَهُ: فَقَالَ عَامِرٌ

15 ١ فَإِنْ تَنْجُ مِنْهَا يَا ضُبَيْعُ فَإِنَّنِى   وَجَدِّكَ لَمْ أَعْقِدْ عَلَيْكَ التَّمَائِمَا

التَّمَائِمُ الْعُوَذُ e الْوَاحِدَةُ تَمِيمَةٌ: وَهِىَ مَا تُنَاطُ عَلَى الْفَرَسِ وَالصَّبِىِّ خِيفَةَ الْعَيْنِ ۞

٢ فَأَنْزَلْتُهُ إِنْزَالَ إِنْزَالَ مِثْلِى مِثْلَهُ   بِنَجْلَاءَ بَلَّتْ ظَهْرَهُ وَالْمَآكِمَا

نَجْلَاءُ طَعْنَةٌ وَاسِعَةٌ: وَسِنَانٌ مِنْجَلٌ اذَا كَانَ وَاسِعَ الطَّعْنِ: وَعَيْنٌ نَجْلَاءُ وَعُيُونٌ نُجْلٌ: وَأَنْشَدَ تَعْلَبُ

نَوَاتُ الشِّفَاهِ f الْحَوِّ وَالْأَعْيُنِ النُّجْلِ وَالْمَآكِمُ لَحَمَاتٌ ۞

XXI. *Ṭawīl*; verses 4 and 9 cited.

a) MS جَبَلٍ.   b) Ḥam. 292¹⁶.   c) MS لنتترك.

d) Accidentally omitted between two pages.   e) MS الواحد.   f) MS الجَوّ.

٣ وَأَدَّيْتَ زَيْدًا بَعْدَ مَا كَانَ ثَاوِيًا   إِلَى أَهْلِهِ يَوْمَ الثَّنِيَّةِ سَالِمَا

٤ a فَأَصْبَحْتُمُ لَا فِى سَوَامٍ فِدَائِهِ   وَأَصْبَحَ فِى تَيْمَانَ يَخْطِرُ نَاعِمَا

السَّوَامُ مَا رَعَى مِنَ المَالِ. وَتَيْمَانُ مَوْضِعٌ. يَخْطِرُ نَاعِمًا لِأَنَّهُ سَلِمَ مَتَى لَمْ أَقْتُلْهُ فَهُوَ نَاعِمُ البَالِ لِسُرُورِهِ بِنَجَائِهِ ۞

٥ يُرَجِّى جِيَادَ الخَيْلِ نَحْوَ دِيَارِكُمْ   وَقَدْ كَانَ فِى جِلْدٍ مِنَ القِدِّ آزِمَا

يُرَجِّى يَسُوقُ. وَآزِمٌ ضَيِّقٌ. يَزْعُمُ عَامِرٌ أَنَّ زَيْدَ الخَيْلِ كَانَ أَسِيرًا فِى أَيْدِيهِمْ وَأَنَّهُمُ اسْتَنْكَرُوهُ عَلَى قِتَالِ ٥

عَامِرٍ: فَلَمَّا أَعْطَاهُ الرُّمْحَ اسْتَنْقَذَهُ مِنْهُمْ وَهُوَ قَوْلُهُ: فِى سَوَامٍ فِدَائِهِ. يَقُولُ: b لِمَ تَأْخُذُوا فِدَاءَهُ سَوَامًا:

فَأَصْبَحَ يَغْزُوكُمْ وَقَدْ كَانَ فِى قِدِّكُمْ وَأَسْرِكُمْ ۞

٦ فَلَا تَعْجَلَنْ وَانْظُرْ بِأَرْضِكَ فَارِسًا   يَهُزُّ رُدَيْنِيًّا وَأَبْيَضَ صَارِمَا

رُدَيْنِيٌّ رُمْحٌ مَنْسُوبٌ إِلَى رُدَيْنَةَ وَهِىَ امْرَأَةٌ كَانَتْ تُقَوِّمُ الرِّمَاحَ بِالخَطِّ: وَالخَطُّ قَرْيَةٌ بِالبَحْرَيْنِ وَمِنْهُ يُقَالُ ١٠

رُمْحٌ خَطِّىٌّ وَرِمَاحٌ خَطِّيَّةٌ: وَكَانَتْ سُفُنُ البَحْرِ تَرْفَأُ إِلَيْهَا فِى القَدِيمِ ۞

٧ (53a) لَهُ كُلَّ يَوْمٍ غَارَةٌ عُرِفَتْ لَهُ   إِذَا قَادَهَا لِلْمَوْتِ جُرْدًا سَوَاهِمَا

إِذَا قَادَهَا يَعْنِى الخَيْلَ وَإِنْ لَمْ يَأْتِ بِذِكْرِهَا. وَجُرْدًا قِصَارَ الشَّعَرِ وَالوَاحِدُ أَجْرَدُ وَطُولُ الشَّعَرِ هُجْنَةٌ فِى

الخَيْلِ. وَقَوْلُهُ سَوَاهِمَ أَىْ ضَوَامِرُ مُتَغَيِّرَةٌ: يُقَالُ c سَهَمَ وَجْهُهُ أَىْ تَغَيَّرَ ۞

٨ وَعَبْدَ d بَنِى بَرْشَا تَرَكْنَا مُجَدَّلًا   غَدَاةَ ثَوَى بَيْنَ الفَوَارِسِ كَازِمَا

مُجَدَّلًا مَصْرُوعًا يُقَالُ جَدَّلَهُ وَقَطَّرَهُ وَجَعْفَلَهُ إِذَا صَرَعَهُ. وَثَوَى أَقَامَ أَىْ مَاتَ فَبَقِىَ هُنَاكَ. وَكَازِمًا ١٥

يُقَالُ e كَزَمَ بِأَنْفِهِ ۞

٩ f تَنَاوَلْتُهُ فَاخْتَلَّ سَيْفِى ذُبَابُهُ   شَرَاسِيفَهُ العُلْيَا وَجَدَّ المَعَاصِمَا

اخْتَلَّ انْتَظَمَ. وَذُبَابُ السَّيْفِ مَوْضِعُ المَضْرَبِ مِنْهُ. وَشَرَاسِيفُهُ الوَاحِدُ شُرْسُوفٌ وَهُوَ مَقَاطُّ الأَضْلَاعِ مِمَّا

يَلِى الصَّدْرَ. وَالمِعْصَمُ مَوْضِعُ السِّوَارِ وَلِلْجَمْعِ المَعَاصِمُ ۞

١٠ وَأَنْتَ قَرِيبٌ قَدْ رَأَيْتَ مَكَانَهُ   تُنَادِى شَتِيرًا يَوْمَ ذَاكَ وَعَاصِمَا ٢٠

---

a) Cited as text in Bakrī 210⁶; Bakrī appears to be in error in bringing this verse as evidence that Taimān was in the country of ʿAbs; the verse implies that Zaid was in his own country, that of Ṭaiyiʾ.

b) MS لَمْ يَأْخُذْ sic.   c) MS سَهَمَ وَجْهُهُ مَا تَغَيَّرَ.

d) The name بَنُو البَرْشَاء occurs as that of a sub-tribe in Nāb. Dīw. XXI, 11: LA VIII, 151²⁴.

e) So LA vocalizes: MS كَزَمَ.   f) Cited ʿAskarī, Kit. aṣ-Ṣināʿatain 82, as على غِابَةِ التَّكَلُّفِ.

XXII.

١ أَفْرَاسَنَا بِالسَّهْلِ بَدَّلْنَ مَذْحِجًا　　　ذُرَى شَعَفٍ شَثًّا وَّبَانًا وَّعَرْعَرَا

ذِرْوَةُ كُلِّ شَىْءٍ أَعْلَاهُ. وَالشَّعَفُ رُوُوسُ الجِبَالِ الوَاحِدَةُ شَعَفَةٌ: يُرِيدُ لَحَقَتْهُمْ بِالجِبَالِ. وَهَـذِه كُلُّهَا شَجَرٌ۞

٢ فَأَصْبَحْنَ لَمْ يَتْرُكْنَ حَظًّا لِّعَامِرٍ　　　مِّنَ النَّاسِ إِلَّا لَاحِقًا قَدْ تَغَبَّرَا

5 يُقَالُ قَدْ لَحَقْتُ حَقِّى اذَا أَدْرَكْتُهُ. وَتَغَبَّرَ أَخَذَ غُبْرَهُ وَهُوَ وَاحِدُ الأَغْبَارِ وَفِى البَقِيَّةِ مِنْ كُلِّ شَىْءٍ: قَالَ لِلْحَارِثِ بن حِلِّزَةَ البَشْكُرِى

a) لَا تَكْسَعِ الشَّوْلَ بِأَغْبَارِهَا　　　إِنَّكَ لَا تَدْرِى مَنِ النَّاتِجُ

اى b بَقَّ فِيهَا وَلَا تَسْتَقْصِ عَلَيْهَا فَإِنَّكَ مَيِّتٌ۞

XXIII.

١ لَعَمْرِى لَقَدْ أَهْدَى زِيَادٌ مَّقَالَةً　　　c عَلَيْنَا فَهَلْ إِنْ كَانَ ذَا مِرَّةٍ ضَرَرْ

10 (53b) زِيَادٌ يَعْنِى النابغةَ الذبيانِيَّ. وَالمِرَّةُ الإِحْكَامُ: يُقَالُ حَبْلٌ مُمَرٌّ اى مفتولٌ مُحْكَمٌ: وَقد أَمَرَّ فَتْلَهُ اذا أَحْكَمَهُ۞

٢ تُعَيِّرُنَا يَوْمَ d المَرَوْرَاةِ سَادِرًا　　　وَّعِنْدَكَ مِنْ أَيَّامِنَا قَبْلَهَا غِيَرْ

سَادِرًا رَاكِبًا رَأْسَهُ جَهْلًا. وَالمَرَوْرَاةُ يَوْمٌ ظَفَرَتْ بنو ذُبيانَ بِبَنِى عامِرٍ. ويروى عِبَرْ۞

٣ فَمَنْ مُّبْلِغٌ ذُبْيَانَ عَنِّى رِسَالَةً　　　مُّغَلْغَلَةً مِنِّى وَمَا تَنْفَعُ الْعِذَرْ

XXII. Ṭawīl; no citations found.

a) Mfḍt No. CXXVII, 2; LA X, 185[6]. MS corruptly الشَّوَكَ.

b) MS بَقَّى and تَسْتَقْصِى. The explanation here given does not agree with that in LA, l. c.

XXIII. Ṭawīl; no citations traced.

c) MS عَلَيْهِ; the correction seems necessary.

d) MS المَرَوْرَات, and so often elsewhere; the reasons for preferring the spelling in the text are stated in Yāqūt IV, 505[20] ff.

الْمُغَلْغَلَة الرسالة a يُتَغَلْغَلُ [بها] حتى تَصِلَ الى صاحبها. والعُذُر جمع عُذْرَة وهي العُذْرَة ايضًا: قال النابغة

$$b \quad \text{هَا اِنَّ تَا عُذْرَةٌ اِلَّا تَكُنْ نَفَعَتْ} \qquad \text{فَاِنَّ صَاحِبَهَا مُشَارِكُ النَّكَدِ}$$

٤ وَقَدْ عَلِمَتْ عُلْيَا هَوَازِنَ أَنَّـنَا   بَنُو الْحَرْبِ لَا نَعْبَا بِوِرْدٍ وَّلَا صَدَرْ

٥ نَشُقُّ عِصَابَ الْحَرْبِ حَتَّى نُدِرَّهَا   اِذَا مَا نُفُوسُ الْقَوْمِ طَالَعَتِ الثُّغَرْ

قال نَشُقُّ عِصَابَ للحرب مَثَلٌ: وأَصْلُ ذلك ان الناقةَ اذا امْتَنَعَتْ من الحَلَبِ عُصِبَ فَخِذاها فَتَدِرُّ: قال ومثله قول الحُطَيْئَة

$$c \quad \text{تَدِرُّونَ اِنْ شُدَّ الْعِصَابُ عَلَيْكُمُ} \qquad \text{وَنَأْبَى اِذَا شُدَّ الْعِصَابُ فَلَا نَدِرْ}$$

ويقال في مَثَل: لَأُعْصِبَنَّكَ عَصْبَ السَّلِمَةِ اى لَأُضَيِّقَنَّ عَلَيْكَ. والثُّغَرُ جمع ثُغْرَة وهي نُقْرَة النَّحْرِ ☙

٩ تَرَى رَائِدَاتِ الْخَيْلِ حَوْلَ بُيُوتِنَا   أَبَابِيلَ تَـرْدِى بِالْعَشِيِّ وَبِالْبُكْرِ

الرائدات التى d تَرُودُ تَجىءُ وتَذْهَبُ: ويقال e الرائدُ لا يَكْذِبُ أَهْلَهُ: وهو f الذى يَذْهَبُ فى طَلَبِ الكَلَأَ يَتَقَدَّمُ القومَ فَيَنْظُرُ مَوَاقِعَ الكَلَأَ. وأَبابِيلُ جماعاتٌ واحدها اِبِّيلٌ وإِبَّوْلٌ. وتَرْدِى من الرَّدَيانِ وهو ضَرْبٌ من العَدْوِ: g وقيلَ للمُنْتَجِع بن نَبْهانَ: ما الرَّدَيانُ. فقال: الذَّهابُ بين آرِيِّه الى مُتَمَعَّكِه: يقال رَدَى يَرْدِى رَدْيًا h [وَرَدَيَانًا] (54a) ☙

XXIV.

١ لَعَمْرُكَ مَا تَنْفَكُّ عَنِّى مَلَامَةً   بَنُو جَعْفَرٍ مَّا هَيَّجَ الضِّغْنُ جَعْفَرَا

٢ اِذَا قُلْتُ هَذَا حِينَ رَاجَعَ وُدَّهَا   أَبَى حِقْدُهَا فِى الصَّدْرِ اِلَّا تَذَكُّرَا

٣ لِمَهْلَكِ أَفْرَاسٍ أُصِبْنَ وَرُبَّـمَا   أَصَابُوا بِهَا أَمْثَالَهَا ثُمَّ أَكْثَرَا

٤ مِنَ الْأَرْضِ أَهْلًا بَعْدَ مَالٍ وَّجِيرَةٍ   وَأَبْقَتْ لَهُمْ مِنِّى مَآتِمَ حُسَّرَا

---

a) MS يَتَغَلْغَلُ; بها added conj.

b) Mu'all. 50; usual text قَدْ تَاهَ فِى الْبَلَدِ; Tibrīzī mentions our reading as variant.

c) Dīwān, XIX, 19.   d) MS تَرُدُّ.

e) For this proverb see Lane 1185c, and Ḥam. 547²⁴.

f) MS has يَطْلُبُ in place of الذى.   g) See Lane 1071a b.

h) Added conj.; probably dropped between two pages.

XXIV. Ṭawīl; no citations.

الْمَآتِمُ اجْتِمَاعُ النِّسَاءِ وَتَقَابُلُ بَعْضِهِنَّ بَعْضًا فِى فَرَحٍ او تَرَحٍ وللجمع الْمَآتِمُ: قَالَ الْأَعْشَى

a وَأَقْسِمُ بِاللهِ الَّذِى أَنَا عَبْدُهُ　　　لَيَصْطَفِقَنْ يَوْمًا عَلَيْكِ الْمَآتِمُ

يَعْنِى النِّسَاءَ. والْحُسَّرُ جمع حاسِر وهو الْمَكْشُوفُ عن رَأْسِهِ ۞

XXV.

١　يَا لَهْفِى عَلَى مَا ضَلَّ سَعْيِى　　　وَسَيْرِى فِى الْهَوَاجِرِ مَا أَقِيلُ

5　٢　فَإِنَّ الْحَىَّ خَثْعَمَ أَحْرَزَتْهُمْ　　　رِمَاحُهُمُ وَتُنْذِرُهُمْ سَلُولُ

سَلُولُ يريد بنى سَلُولَ: [وهم] بَنُو مُرَّةَ بنِ صَعْصَعَةَ بنِ هَوَازِنَ: وأُمُّهُم سَلُولُ بِنْتُ ذُهْلِ بنِ شَيْبَانَ.

b وكانوا احْتَمَلُوا من خَثْعَمَ أَنْ يُنْذِرُوكُمْ من كِلَابٍ إِنْ أَرَادَتْكُم وَأَنْ يَكْتُمُوا عَلَيْكُمْ إِنْ أَرَدْتُمُوهُم ۞

٣　بِمَخْرَجِنَا فَلَا نَخْفَى عَلَيْهِمْ　　　وَيَأْتِيهِمْ بِعَوْرَتِنَا الدَّلِيلُ

الْعَوْرَةُ موضع الْوُصُولِ الى القوم وهو الثَّغْرُ: ومنه يقال. فلانٌ يُحَامِى عَوْرَةَ آلِ فلانٍ. يقول نَحْنُ لا نَخْفَى

10　علَيْهِمْ لِكَثْرَتِنَا ۞

٤　وَلَوْ أَنِّى أُطِعْتُ لَكَانَ مِنِّى　　　لِمُدْرِكَ أَكْلُبٍ يَوْمٌ طَوِيلُ

مُدْرِكُ أَكْلُبٍ ابو أَنَسِ بن مُدْرِكٍ فارِسُ خَثْعَمَ. وقوله يَوْمٌ طَوِيلٌ من الشَّرِّ فهو أَطْوَلُ ما يكون عِنْدَهُم ۞

٥　وَلَكِنِّى عُصِيتُ وَكَانَ جَهْلًا　　　بِهِمْ أَلَّا يُبَالُوا مَا أَقُولُ

٦　(54b) يَلُومُنِىَ الَّذِينَ تَرَكْتُ خَلْفِى　　　وَيَعْصِينِىَ الَّذِينَ بِهِمْ أَصُولُ

15　صُلْتُ أَصُولُ من الصَّوْلَةِ: وهو أَنْ يَعْتَرِكَا الفَحْلَانِ من الجِمَالِ ۞

---

a) al-Aʿshà, Dīw. Escorial MS fol. 42a, with فَأَقْسِمُ and لَتَصْطَفِقَنْ; a somewhat different reading of first hemistich in MbḍKām. 396[10].

XXV. *Wāfir*; no citations.

b) i.e. "They had taken upon them the duty, or office, by agreement with Khathʿam".

c) MS broken away: restoration certain.

XXVI.

١ إِذَا شِئْتَ أَنْ تَلْقَى الْمَنَاعَةَ فَاسْتَجِرْ خِذَامَ بْنَ زَيْدٍ إِنْ a أَجَارَ خِذَامْ

الْمَنَاعَةُ الْعِزُّ وَالْمَنَعَةُ. وَخِذَامُ بْنُ زَيْدٍ مِن بَنِى زَيْدٍ۞

٢ دَعَوْتُ أَبَا الْجَبَّارِ b أَخْتَصُّ مَالِكًا وَلَمْ يَكُ قِدْمًا مَّنْ أَجَرْتَ يُضَامْ

أَبُو الْجَبَّارِ مَالِكُ بن حِمَارٍ الشَّمْخِىُّ من فَزَارَةَ. يُضَامُ يَنْتَقِصُ: وَالضَّيْمُ وَالذُّلُّ وَاحِدٌ وَهُو ايضًا النُّقْصَانْ۞

5 ٣ فَقَامَ أَبُو الْجَبَّارِ يَهْتَزُّ لِلنَّدَى كَمَا اهْتَزَّ عَضْبُ الشَّفْرَتَيْنِ حُسَامْ

الشَّفْرَتَانِ حَدَّا السَّيْفِ وَشَفْرَةُ السِّكِّينِ حَدُّهُ. وَحُسَامٌ قَاطِعٌ: وَالْعَضْبُ ايضًا الْقَاطِعُ۞

٤ وَكُنْتُ سَنَامًا مِّن فَزَارَةَ d تَامِكًا وَفِى كُلِّ قَوْمٍ ذِرْوَةٌ وَسَنَامْ

ذِرْوَةُ كُلِّ شَىْءٍ أَعْلَاهُ وَمِنْهُ ذِرْوَةُ الْجَبَلِ وَلِلْجَمْعِ ذُرًى۞

٥ فَنَكَّبْتَ عَنِّى الشَّارِعِينَ وَلَمْ أَكُنْ e مَخَافَةَ شَرِّ الشَّارِعِينَ أَنَامْ

يُقَالُ نَكَبَ عَنِّى فُلَانٌ اى عَدَلَ عَنِّى: وَنَكَبَ عَنِ الطَّرِيقِ اى انْحَرَفَ عَنْهَا: وَالنَّكِيبُ الَّذِى يَطْلَعُ: 10

قَالَ لَبِيدٌ: *f بِنَكِيبٍ مَعِرٍ دَامِى الْأَظَلّ* اى نَكَبَتْهُ الْحِجَارَةُ۞

XXVII.

١ أَلَسْنَا نَقُودُ الْخَيْلَ قُبًّا عَوَابِسًا وَنَخْضِبُ يَوْمَ الرَّوْعِ أَسْيَافَنَا دَمَا

عَوَابِسُ كَوَالِحٌ اى عَبَسَتْ وُجُوهُهَا لِكَرَاهِيَةِ الْحَرْبِ. وَالْقُبُّ مِن الْخَيْلِ الضَّوَامِرُ الْبُطُونِ وَالْوَاحِدُ أَقَبُّ۞

٢ وَنَحْمِى الذِّمَارَ حِينَ يَشْتَجِرُ الْقَنَا وَنَثْنِى عَنِ السَّرْبِ الرَّعِيلَ الْمُسَوَّمَا

XXVI. *Ṭawīl*. This poem occurs in the account of the Day of Raqam given in the commentary to the *Mufaḍḍalīyat*, p. 33[15], where it is stated by Ibn al-Kalbī to have been copied from «the Book of Ḥammād ar-Rāwiyah». The version there given enables some corrections to be made in the text of our MS.

a) MS أَجَابَ; Mfḍt as text.   b) So Mfḍt; MS فَاخْتَصَّ.

c) MS وَكُنْتُ.   d) Mfḍt نَامِيًا, with تَامِكًا as *v. l.*

e) Mfḍt فَنَكَّلْتَ.   f) Labīd Dīw. XXXIX, 7.

XXVII. *Ṭawīl*. Vv. 3, 4, 5 cited.

a [الذمار الـذى] يَحِقُّ أنْ يَحْمِيَه. واشْتِجَارُ القَنا اختلافه بالطعن (55a). والسَرْبُ مَذْهَبُ الحَىّ
والسَرْبُ ايضًا ما رَعَى من المال. قال الأصمعى: الرَعِيل للجماعة من الخيل b [والجمع] أَراعيلُ. وقوله المُسَوَّمَا
اى المُعْلَم من السِمَة⁕

٣ c وَنَسْتَلِبُ الْحَـوَّ الْعَوَابِسَ كَالْقَنَا   سَوَاهِمَ يَحْمِلْنَ الْوَشِيجَ الْمُقَوَّمَا

٥ الحَوّ الواحد أَحْوَى والأنْثَى حَوّاءُ والاسم الحُوَّة: وهى كُدُورة تَضْرِبُ الى السَواد: يقال فرسٌ أَحْوَى
وكُمَيْت أَحْوَى وخَيْل حُوّ: وهى أَصْلَب للخيل. وسَواهم مُتغيِّرة قد أَضَرَّت الغارة والحَرْبُ بها فقد
أَقْوَرَت. والوَشِيجُ الرِماحُ. وشَبَّه الخَيْلَ بالقنا لدِقَّتها وضُمُورها وطولها. والمُقَوَّم والمُثَقَّف واحد⁕

٤ d وَنَحْنُ صَبَّحْنَا حَىَّ أَسْمَاءَ غَارَةً   أَبَالَتْ حَبَالَى الْحَىِّ مِنْ وَقْعِهَا دَمَا

٥ وَبِالنَّقْعِ مِنْ وَادِى e أُبَيْدَةَ جَاهَرَتْ   أُنَيْسًا وَقَدْ أَرْدَيْنَ سَادَةَ خَثْعَمَا

١٠ أُبَيْدَة أرض خَثْعَم. يريد f أُنَس بن مُدْرِك الخَثْعَمى. وأَرْدَيْنَ يَعْنى للخيل أَهْلَكْنَ والرَدَى الهلاك⁕

٦ وَيَوْمَ عُكَاظٍ أَنْتُـمْ تَعْلَمُونَهُ   شَهِدْنَا فَأَقْدَمْنَا بِهَا الْحَىَّ g مُقْدَمَا

بها يعنى حَرْبَ الفِجَار التى بين كنانَةَ وقَيْس⁕

٧ وَنَحْنُ فَعَلْنَا بِالْحَلِيفَيْنِ فَعْلَةً   نَفَتْ بَعْدَ h [هَا] عَنَّا الظَّلُومَ الْغَشَمْشَمَا

الحَلِيفَان أَسْدٌ وغَطَفان. i والغَشَمْشَم من الغَشْم وهو الظُلْم: يقال فلانٌ ظَلُومٌ غَشُومٌ⁕

١٥ ٨ وَمَا بَرِحَتْ فِى الدَّهْرِ مِمَّا عِصَابَةٌ   يَذُودُونَ عَنْ أَحْسَابِنَا مَنْ تَعَرَّمَا

وما بَرِحَتْ اى ما زالَتْ. وعِصابَة جماعة نحو من عِشْرِينَ وأَكْثَر. يَذُودون اى يَمْنَعُون والذِياد المَنْع.
وقوله مَنْ تَعَرَّمَا اى مَنْ جَهِلَ من j العُرَام وهو الشَرُّ⁕

---

a) MS broken away.

b) Omitted by copyist.

c) Vv. 3—4 in BQut. *Shiᶜr*, p. 191¹⁶; v. 3 there differs considerably from our text:

وَنَسْتَلِبُ الْأَقْرَانَ وَالْجُرْدُ كُلَّـهِ   عَلَى الْهَوْلِ يَعْسِفْنَ الْوَشِيجَ الْمُقَوَّمَا

d) Bakrī 63⁸, as text; second hemist. in BQut.: أَبَالَ الْحَبَالَى غِبَّ وَقْعَتِنَا دَمَا.

e) MS أُبَيْدَةَ; both Bakrī and Yāq. give the vocalization as text. This v. in Bakrī, *l.c.*

f) See *ante*, No. XXV, v. 4, scholion.

g) MS مُقْدَمَا.   h) Omitted in MS.

i) MS وَالْغَشُومُ.   j) MS الْعُرَّامِ.

٩ يَقُودُونَ جُرْدًا كَالسَّرَاحِينِ تَسْتَمِى   صُدُورَ الْعَوَالِى [---ᵕ-] وَأَدْهَمَا

(55b) الجُرْد للخيل [ال]قِصار الشَّعْرَة الواحد أَجْرَد وهو عَتِيق اذا كان قصير الشعر. والسراحين الذئاب
الواحد سِرْحان. وتَسْتَمِى تَصِيد. والعوالى عوالى الرماح ما دون السنان بِقَدْر ذراعٍ: وسافلتُهُ أَسْفَلُهُ

١٠ وَنَحْنُ أَبَرْنَا حَىَّ أَشْجَعَ بِالْقَنَا   وَنَحْنُ تَرَكْنَا حَىَّ مُرَّةَ مَأْتَمَا

أَبَرْنَا أَهْلَكْنَا واسْتَأْصَلْنَا. وأَشْجَعُ ابنُ الرَّيْثِ بنِ غَطَفَانَ بنِ سعد بنِ قَيْس بن عَيْلَانَ. ومُرَّةُ ابنُ
عَوْفِ بن سعد بن ذُبْيَانَ بن بَغِيضِ بن الرَّيْثِ

XXVIII.

١ رَهِبْتُ وَمَا مِنْ رَهْبَةِ الْمَوْتِ أَجْزَعُ   وَعَالَجْتُ هَمًّا كُمْتُ بِالْهَمِّ أُولَعُ

٢ وَلِيدًا إِلَى أَنْ خَالَطَ الشَّيْبُ مَفْرِقِى   وَأَبْسَنِى مِنْهُ الثَّغَامُ الْمُنَزَّعُ

الثَّغام شجرٌ أبيضُ يُشَبَّه به الشَّيْبُ: قال c ابو العبّاس: بَلْ له ثَمَرٌ أبيضُ كالقُطْنِ: اذا هَبَّتْ عليه
الريحِ طَيَّرتْهُ

٣ دَعَانِى سُمَيْطٌ يَوْمَ ذَلِكَ دَعْوَةً   فَنَهْنَهْتُ عَنْهُ وَالْأَسِنَّةُ شُرَّعُ
* * * * * *d

الذِمار الحُرْمَة. والسُّمَيْطَع السَّيّد الشَّريف ويَجْمَعُ السَّمَادِعِ

٤ وَلَوْلَا دِفَاعِى عَنْ سُمَيْطٍ وَكَرَّتِى   لَعَالَجَ قِدًّا قَفْلُهُ يَتَقَعْقَعُ

قَفْلُهُ ما يَبِسَ منه: يقال جِلْدٌ قافِلٌ اى يابِسٌ: يَتَقَعْقَعُ من الْيُبُوسَةِ: ومنه e الْمَثَلِ: فلا يَقْعَقَعُ لَهُ
بِالشِّنَانِ: اى لا يُفْرِعُهُ شىٌ. ويروى قَفْلُهُ بضَمِّ القاف وفَتْحِهِ

٥ وَأَقْسَمْتُ لَا يَجْزِى سُمَيْطٌ بِنِعْمَةٍ   وَكَيْفَ يُجَازِيكَ الْحِمَارُ الْمُجَدَّعُ

الْأَجْدَعُ والْمُجَدَّعُ الْمَقْطُوعُ الْأَنْفِ والْأُذُنِ: وقول ابى ذُوَيْبٍ الهُذَلِىّ fوَافِيَانِ وأَجْدَعُ: اراد بالْوَافِيَيْنِ اى
gوِلَهُمَا آذانٌ وأَجْدَعُ الْأُذُنِ: والجَدْعُ القَطْعُ

---

a) MS broken away. Perhaps we may read مِنْ كُمَيْت.   b) Cf. ante, No. XII, 6.
XXVIII. Ṭawīl. No citations found.   c) I.e. Thaʿlab.
d) Here follows a hiatus (not indicated in the MS), the scholion dealing, not with the verse
immediately above, but with one which has fallen out and ended with سَمَيْدَع.
e) For this phrase see MbdKām. 216⁷ (in Khuṭbah of al-Ḥajjāj), and Lane 1602c.
f) Mfḍt CXXVI, 40.   g) MS لها.

٦ ^a وَأَمْكَنَ مِنّى الْقَوْمَ يَوْمَ لَقِيتُهُمْ   نَوَافِذُ قَدْ خَالَطْنَ جِسْمِى أَرْبَعُ

٧ ^b فَلَوْ [شِئْتُ] نَجَّتْنِى سَبُوحٌ طِمِرَّةٌ   تَحُكُّ بِحَدَّيْهَا الْعِنَانَ وَتَمْزَعُ

(56a) سَبُوحٌ فَرَسٌ يَجْرِى جَرْىَ الْمَاءِ يَدْحُو بِيَدَيْهِ دَحْوًا يَتَلَقَّفُ بِهِمَا. وَطِمِرَّةٌ وَثَّابَةٌ. وَتَمْزَعُ مَزْعًا تَمُرُّ مَرًّا سَرِيعًا ۞

XXIX.

١ لَتَسْأَلَنَّ أَسْمَاءُ وَهْىَ ^cحَفِيَّةٌ   نُصَحَاءَهَا أَطُرِدْتُ أَمْ لَمْ أُطْرَدِ   ٥

حَفِيَّةٌ بَارَّةٌ مُشْفِقَةٌ تَسْأَلُ نُصَحَاءَهَا عَنّى وَتَتَعَهَّدُ أَحْوَالِى ۞

٢ قَالُوا لَهَا ^dإِنَّا طَرَدْنَا ^eخَيْلَهُ   ^fفَلَحْمَ الْكِلَابِ وَكُنْتُ غَيْرَ مُطَرَّدِ

٣ ^gفَلَأَبْغِيَنَّكُمُ الْمَلَا وَعُوَارِضًا   ^hوَلَأُورِدَنَّ الْخَيْلَ لَابَةَ ضَرْغَدِ

الْمَلَا مُتَّسَعٌ مِنَ الأرض. وَيُقَالُ إِنَّهَا مِنْ أرْض كَلْبٍ. وَعُوَارِضُ جَبَلٌ لِبَنِى أَسَدٍ. وَهُوَ الَّذِى ⁱقَالَهُ فِى شِعْرِهِ أَبُو مُحَمَّدٍ الْفَقْعَسِىُّ   ١٠

وَكَأَنَّهَا وَقَدْ بَدَا عُوَارِضُ   وَاللَّيْلُ بَيْنَ قَنَوَيْنِ رَابِضُ

٤ ^kوَالْخَيْلُ تَرْدِى بِالْكُمَاةِ كَأَنَّهَا   حِدَأٌ تَتَابَعُ فِى الطَّرِيقِ الْأَقْصَدِ

الْحِدَأُ جَمَاعَةُ الْحِدَأَةِ. وَزَعَمَ بَعْضُ النَّاسِ أنها كانت تَصِيدُ لِسُلَيْمَانَ بنِ دَاوُودَ صَلَّى الله عليه وسلَّم. وَالْكُمَاةُ الْأَشِدَّاءُ. وَتَرْدِى مِنَ الرَّدَيَانِ وَهُوَ ضَرْبٌ مِنَ الْمَشْىِ ^l۞

---

a) MS broken: word not quite certain.   b) Conj.; MS broken.

XXIX. *Kāmil*; this poem is No CVII of the *Mufaḍḍalīyat*, q. v. for other citations and various readings. Our version follows the text of al-Athram as cited in the scholia of the Mfḍt.

c) MS خَفِيَّةٌ; see *ante*, III, 1.   d) Mfḍt فَلَقْدُ.   e) MS خَبْلَةٌ (*sic*).

f) See *ante*, No VIII, 4.   g) Mfḍt فَلَأَنْعِينَّكُمْ.

h) Mfḍt وَلَأُقِيطَنَّ.   i) So MS; Mfḍt يقول له.

j) These lines are attributed to ash-Shammākh in his *Dīwan*, p. 113; and see Geyer, *Altarab. Diiamben*, p. 207.

k) Mfḍt بِالْخَيْلِ تَعْثُرُ فِى الْقَصِيدِ.

l) After v. 4 the Sh. Sh. M. 316 inserts the following:

فِى نَاشِئٍ مِنْ عَامِرٍ وَمُجَرَّبٍ   مَاضٍ إِذَا انْفَلَتَ الْعِنَانُ مِنَ الْيَدِ

٥ *a* فَلَأَثْأَرَنْ بِمَالِكٍ وَبِمَالِكٍ   وَأَخِى الْمَرْوَرَاةِ الَّذِى لَـمْ *b* يُوسَدِ

ويروى يُسْنَد: اى لم يُوارَ فى الْقَبْر: وهَاؤُلَاء قوْمٌ قُتِلوا من قوْمِه ۞

٦ *c* وَقَتِيلَ مُرَّةَ *d* أَثْأَرَنْ فَإِنَّـهُ فَـرْعٌ وَإِنْ أَخَاهُـمْ لَـمْ يُقْصَدِ

قَتِيلُ مُرَّةَ حَنْظَلَةُ بن الطُفَيْل أخوه. فَرْعٌ شريفٌ. واخاهُم لم يُقْصَدْ اى لم يُقْتَلْ: يقال أقْصَدَهُ السَّهْمُ

اى قَتَلَهُ: قال النابغَةُ

e فِى إثْرِ غَانِيَةٍ رَمَتْكَ بِسَهْمِهَا فَأَصَابَ قَلْبَكَ غَيْرَ أَنْ لَـمْ تُقْصَدِ

اى لم تَقْتُلْ ۞

٧ *f* يَا أَسْمَ أُخْتَ بَنِى فَزَارَةَ إِنَّنِى غَازٍ وَإِنَّ الْمَرْءَ غَيْرُ مُخَلَّدِ

٨ فِيئِى إِلَيْكِ فَلَا هَوَادَةَ بَيْنَنَا بَعْدَ الْفَوَارِسِ إِذْ ثَوَوْا بِالْمَرْصَدِ

(56*b*) فِيئِى اى أرْجِعِى من فَاء يَفِىءُ فَيْئًا اذا رجع والفَىءُ الرجوع: قال الله جَلَّ ذِكْرُه: *g* وَحَتَّى تَفِىءَ

إِلَى أَمْرِ اللهِ فَإِنْ فَاءَتْ فَأَصْلِحُوا بَيْنَهُمَا بِالْعَدْلِ. ونَوَوْا قُتِلوا فى الْمَعْرَكَة فتُرِكُوا هُنَاكَ ۞

٩ إِلَّا بِكُلِّ أَحَمَّ نَهْدٍ سَابِحٍ وَعَلَالَةٍ مِنْ كُلِّ أَسْمَرَ مِذْوَدِ

أَحَمُّ فرسٌ يَضْرِب الى السَّوَاد والنَّهْد الْعَظِيم الطويل. وقوله سابحٍ اى يَجْرِى جَرْيًا كَالْمَاءِ. وعَلَالَةٌ كُلِّ شىءٍ

شَىءٌ بعد شَىءٍ من جَرْىٍ او طَعْنٍ او غَيْرِهما. وأَسْمَرُ رُمْحٌ وإذا كان أَسْمَرَ كان أَجْوَدَ له وأَصْلَبَ لأَنَّه

نَصِيجٌ. ومِذْوَدٌ [ما] يُذادُ به اى يُمْنَع به والذِيادُ الْمَنْع والذائِد الْمانِع ۞

١٠ وَأَنَا ابْنُ حَرْبٍ لَا أَزَالُ أُشِبُّهَا *h* سَعْرًا وَأُوقِدُهَا إِذَا لَمْ تُوقَدِ

أُشِبُّهَا اى أُشْعِلُها. وسَعْرًا نارًا: ويسمَّى الْعُود الذى تُحَرَّكُ به النارَ الْمِسْعَر: ويسمَّى الرجُل الْمُتَحَرِّكُ الْيَقْظان

فى أُمورِه مِسْعَرًا مُشَبَّهًا بذلك الْعُود الذى *i* يُهَيِّجُ النارَ ۞

---

a) MS. وَلَأَثَائِرَنْ sic; Mfḍt فَلَاتَأَرَنْ.   *b*) Mfḍt يُسْنَد.

c) MS. وَقَتِيل.   *d*) MS. لَاثَأَرَنْ sic.   *e*) Nāb. Dīw. VII, 6.

f) This is the order of Mfḍt, which makes a much better sequence: in our MS. vv. 7 and 8 are transposed.

g) Qur. XLIX, 9.   *h*) Mfḍt سَمَرً.

i) Mfḍt has another verse, which however is not consecutive with v. 10:

وَإِذَا تَعَذَّرَتِ الْبِلَادُ فَأَمْحَلَتْ فَمَجَازُهَا تَيْمَاءُ أَوْ بِالْأَثْمَدِ

Yāq. I, 119 has the verse (with a differing first hemist., وَلَئِنْ تَعَذَّرَتِ الْبِلَادُ بِأَهْلِهَا) between vv. 2 and 3 of our text.

XXX.

١ a أَلَا مَنْ مُبْلِغٌ أَسْمَاءَ عَنِّى   وَلَوْ حَلَّتْ بِيَمْنٍ أَوْ جُبَارِ

٢ بِأَنَّ حَلِيلَهَا دَرَهَتْ عَلَيْهِ   خُطُوبٌ لَّا تُفَرَّجُ بِالسِّرَارِ

يَمْنٌ وجُبَارٌ بالحِجاز. والحَلِيل الزَّوج والحَلِيل المَرأَة: قال عَنْتَرَة

b وَحَلِيلِ غَانِيَةٍ تَرَكْتُ مُجَدَّلًا   تَمْكُو قَرِيصَتُهُ كَشِدْقِ الْأَعْلَمِ

٥ وَدَرَهَتْ وانْدَرَهَتْ وانْدَلَثَتْ بَمَعْنَى. والخُطُوب الأُمُور: يقول: لا أَقْدِرُ على إِسْرَارِها لِعِظَمِها ۞

XXXI.

١ وَيْلٌ لِّخَيْلٍ سَيْلِ خَيْلٍ مُّغِيرَةٍ   رَأَتْ رَغْبَةً أَوْ رَهْبَةً وَّهْىَ تُلْجَمُ

٢ c (58b) * * * * * *   صُدُورُ الْقَنَا قَالُوا جَمِيعًا تَقَدَّمُوا

XXXII.

وقال عامِرُ بن الطُّفَيْل يَرْثِى أَبَاهُ طُفَيْلًا d ويَذْكُرُ جَدَّهُ

١ أَلَا كُلُّ مَا هَبَّتْ بِهِ الرِّيحُ ذَاهِبٌ   وَكُلُّ فَتًى بَعْدَ السَّلَامَةِ شَاجِبُ

١٠ شاجِبٌ أى هالِكٌ والشَّجَبُ الهَلاك: يقال شَجِبَ فلانٌ يَشْجَبُ شَجَبًا اذا هَلَكَ۞

٢ e أَلَا إِنَّ خَيْرَ النَّاسِ رِسْلًا وَّنَجْدَةً   بِهِرْجَابَ لَمْ تُحْبَسْ عَلَيْهِ الرَّكَائِبُ

الرِّسْلُ الرَّخَاءُ والنَّجْدَةُ الشِّدَّةُ: قال الرَّاجِزُ

f لَوْ أَنَّ عِنْدِى مِنْ قُرَيْمٍ رَجْلًا   لَمَنَعُونِى نَجْدَةً أَوْ رِسْلَا

XXX. *Wafir*; first verse cited.

a) Bakrī 856[7], Yāq II, 15[9], and IV, 1037[18], as text.   b) Muʻall. 42.

XXXI. *Ṭawīl*; no citation found.

c) Head of page cut away so that nothing can be read.

XXXII. *Ṭawīl*; v. 2 cited.

d) *Sic*; the grandfather is nowhere mentioned in the text of our MS.

e) Bakrī 830[9], Yāq. IV, 960[9] (both incorrectly with رَسْلًا).

f) Poet Ṣakhr al-Ghaiy: see LA XIII, 299[15], Lane 1082c, Dīw. Hudh. No. 12, Qālī, Amālī I, 210.

ورَجُلٌ نَجُدٌ a وذو نَجْدَةٍ اى شُجاعٌ وقومٌ أَنْجادٌ: والنَّجَدُ بفتح للجيم العَرَقُ والكَرَبُ: رجلٌ مَنْجُودٌ اى مَكْرُوبٌ ۞

٣   وَهَوَّنَ وَجْدِى أَنَّنِى لَوْ رَأَيْتُهُ   يُسَاوِرُهُ ذُو لِبْدَتَيْنِ مُكَالِبُ

يُسَاوِرُهُ يُوَاثِبُهُ. وذو لِبْدَتَيْنِ أَسَدٌ: واللِبْدَةُ الشَعَرُ بَيْنَ كَتِفَىِ الأَسَدِ: قال زُهَيْرٌ

b لَدَى أَسَدٍ شَاكِ السِّلاحِ مُقَاذِفٍ   لَهُ لِبَدٌ أَظْفَارُهُ لَمْ يُقَلَّمِ

مُكَالِبٌ من الكَلَبِ على الشيءِ: يقال كَلِبَ يَكْلَبُ كَلَبًا إِذَا اشْتَدَّ حِرْصُهُ ۞

٤   لَمَارَسْتُ عَنْهُ الْخَيْلَ غَيْرَ مُهَلِّلٍ   لَعَمْرُ أَبِى أَوْ تَشْتَعِبْنِى الشَّوَاعِبُ

مَارَسْتُ عَالَجْتُ. مُهَلِّلٌ يقال قد هَلَّلَ الرَجُلُ اذا أَحْجَمَ وكَفَّ. وتَشْتَعِبْنِى تَجْذِبْنِى والشَّوَاعِبُ الجَوَاذِبُ: ويُسَمَّى الموت شَعُوبَ c ۞

XXXIII.

راهَنَ عامرُ بن الطفيل على فَرَسٍ له يقال له الكُلَيْبُ فَسُبِقَ: فقال عامرٌ فى ذلك

١   أَظُنُّ الْكُلَيْبَ خَانَنِى أَوْ ظَلَمْتُهُ   بِبُرْقَةِ d حِلِّيتٍ وَمَا كَانَ حَائِنَا

٢   وَأَعْـذِرُهُ e أَنِّى خَرِقْتُ وَإِنَّـمَا   لَقِيتُ أَخَا f حِبٍّ وَصُودِفْتُ بَادِنَا

XXXIV.

(58a) [وَقال عامر بن] الطفيل يَوْمَ لَقِىَ زَيْدَ الْخَيْلِ **** عامر بن الطفيل . فَحَمَلَ عَلَيْهِ ضُبَيْعَةُ فَقَتَلَهُ: فَتَشَاءَمَتْ بَنُو عامرٍ بعامرٍ:

---

a) The words وذو نَجْدَةٍ have been misplaced in the MS and entered by mistake in the next scholion.   b) Muʿall. 42.

c) The scholion omits to notice the use of أَوْ with the jussive in this verse, which is exactly parallel to its use in Labīd, Muʿall. 56: أَوْ يَرْتَبِطْ بَعْضَ النُّفُوسِ حِمَامُهَا; two more examples are cited in Nöldeke, *Zur Grammatik*, p. 72, top; أَوْ is equivalent to لَمْ إِنْ.

XXXIII. *Ṭawīl*; both vv. cited in Yāq. I, 580⁶⁻⁷, and the first in Bakrī 282⁷.

d) MS حِلِيب; the correct spelling is fixed by Yāq. and Bakrī.

e) Yāq. إِنِّى خَرِقْتُ مُوَزَّعًا.   f) Yāq. خُفّ(!).

XXXIV. *Ṭawīl*. The greater past of the first line on the page has been cut away, and the

١ أُنِّثْتُ قَوْمِى أَتْبَعُونِى مَلَامَةً   لَعَلَّ مَنَايَا الْقَوْمِ مِمَّا أُكَلَّفُ

٢ فَإِنْ تَكُ أَفْرَاسٌ أُصِبْنَ وَفِتْيَةٌ   فَإِنِّى لَجَرَّافٌ بِهِنَّ مُجَرَّفُ

XXXIVa.

فَأَحَابَهُ ضُبَيْعَةُ

١ زَعَمَ الْوُشَاةُ بِأَنَّ دُومَةَ أَخْلَفَتْ   ظَنِّى وَقَلَّصَ خَيْرُهَا الْمَوْعُودُ

٢ صَدَقُوا وَبَيَّنَ لِى شَوَاكِلُ أَمْرِهَا   وَجَرَى بِهِ حَرْقُ الْجَنَاحِ قَعِيدُ

القعيد الذى يَجِى، مِنْ خَلْفِكَ وهو يُتَفَأَّلُ بِهِ: والنَطِيحُ مِنْ أَمَامِكَ: والسَانِحُ ما لَقِيَتْ مَيَامِنُهُ مَيَامِنَكَ: والبَارِحُ [ما لَقِيتَ] مَيَاسِرُهُ مَيَاسِرَكَ. وشَوَاكِلُ مَشَابِه. حَرِقٌ قد سَقَطَ رِيشُه مِن الكِبَرِ ۞

٣ مُتَقَارِبُ الْحَنَكَيْنِ شَحَّاجُ الضُّحَى   أَرِنٌ كَأَنَّ جَنَاحَهُ مَشْدُودُ

يقال شَحَجَ الْغُرَابُ ونَعَقَ ونَغَقَ وصاحَ بمَعْنًى واحِد. وأَرِنٌ نَشِيطٌ مَصْوِتٌ ۞

٤ فَزَجَرْتُهُ أَنْ لَّا يُفَرِّخَ بَيْضَهُ   وَيُصِيبَهُ صَدِئُ الرِّصَافِ سَدِيدُ

الرِّصَافُ ما شُدَّ على نَصْلِ السَّهْمِ من العَقَبِ. وقوله سَدِيدٌ اى قاصِدٌ. ومنه سَدَّدَ السَّهْمَ ۞

٥ أَفَرِحْتَ أَنْ جُرْحٌ أَلَمَّ بِفَارِسٍ   لَمْ يَبْقَ مِمَّنْ سُدْتَّ غَيْرَ مَسُودِ

٦ أَوَكَأَنَّ هَادِيَهُ إِذَا اسْتَعْرَضْتَهُ   جِذْعٌ تَحَسَّرَ لِيفُهُ مَجْرُودُ

---

sense is obscure; but it is clear from the verses that one of ʿĀmir's tribe was slain, or possibly more, by Ḍubaiʿah b. al-Ḥārith of ʿAbs; see *ante*, No. XXI, and *cf.* also No. XXIV.

XXXIVa. *Kāmil*; the superscription of this piece is evidently incorrect: the poem cannot be an answer to the one before, (in itself a mere fragment), because it is not (as the laws of such a contest require) in the same metre and rhyme. The verses moreover contain nothing that has personal reference to ʿĀmir, unless it be v. 5; they are themselves but a fragment.

a) MS دُومَةُ, but no root دوم exists in the language.

b) MS شَجَّاج.   *c)* MS شَجَّمَ الْغُرَابُ وَلَعَقَ وَنَعَقَ.

d) MS شَدِيدٌ.   *e)* Words indistinct: apparently غَيْرَ مَسُودِ; meaning obscure.

f) This verse seems to be part of the description of a horse, and to have nothing to do with what precedes.

XXXV.

١ وَأَنْتَ لِسَوْدَاهِ الْمَعَاصِمِ جَعْـدَةٍ   وَّأَقْعَسَ مِـنْ نَسْلِ الْإِمَاهِ الْعَوَارِكِ

واحدُ الْمَعَاصِمِ مِعْصَمٌ وهو موضع السوار. والْأَقْعَسُ الذى (57a) فى ظَهْرِهِ اخْحِنَاءٌ. والْعَوَارِكُ الطَّوَامِثُ ۞

٢ تَبِيعٍ لِّقَوْمٍ لَّمْ يَكُنْ مِنْ صَمِيمِهِمْ   وَلٰكِنَّهُ مِـنْ نَسْلِ آخَـرَ هَالِكِ

a تَبِيعٌ اى مَتْبُوعٍ فعيل بمعنى مَفْعُولٍ مثل قَتِيلٍ ومقتولٌ وجَرِيحٍ وَمَجْرُوحٍ: ويجىءُ فعيلٌ بمعنى فَاعِلٍ: فَعِيلَةٌ بَيِّنٌ اى قَاعِدَةٌ قَدِيرٍ بمعنى قَادِرٍ وعَلِيمٌ عالِمٌ ورَضِيعٌ راضِعٌ اى يَخِيلُ. والصَّمِيمُ لِلخالِصِ الْمَحْضِ ٥ ويقال هو فى صَمِيمِ قومِه اى خالِصِهِمْ: وصَمِيمُ القَلْبِ حَبَّةُ القَلْبِ: والصَّمِيمُ القَارُورَةِ المَصْمُومَةِ: والصِّمَّةُ فى الشُّجاعِ وجَمْعُها صِمَمٌ: وبه سُمِّىَ الرجلُ صِمَّةً وهُوَ ابو دُرَيْدِ بن الصِّمَّةِ: ولَها الْأَكْبَرُ والْأَصْغَرُ ۞

٣ أَبُـوكَ ابو سَوْءٍ وَّخَالُكَ مِثْلُهُ   وَهَلْ تُشْبِهَنَّ إِلَّا أَبَاكَ وَخَـالَكَ

وفى هذه الْأَبْيَاتِ إِقْوَاءٌ ولكنها نُنْشَدُ مقَيَّدَةً. ولْخَالُ اخو أُمِّ الرجلِ: والْخَالُ التَّبَخْتُرُ والْكِبْرُ: قال الْعَجَّاجُ: b * وَالْخَالُ ثَوْبٌ مِنْ ثِيَابِ الْجُهَّالِ *: ولْخَالُ السَّحابُ الْمُخِيلَةُ لِلْمَطَرِ: ولْخَالُ من بُرُودِ الْيَمَنِ: ولْخَالُ المكان: ١٠ وخَالَ الشَّىْءَ ظَنَّهُ وحَسِبَهُ ۞

XXXVI.

١ تَرَكْتُ نِسَاءَ سَاعِدَةَ بْنِ مُرٍّ   لَـهُـنَّ c لَـدَى مَزَاحِفِهِ عَـوِيـلُ

الْعَوِيلُ الْبُكَاءِ. وساعِدَةُ رجلٌ من عَبْسٍ قَتَلَهُ عامِرٌ. مَزَاحِفُهُ حَيْثُ يَتَزَاحَفُونَ لِلْقِتَالِ وهو مُعْتَرَكُ الْقَوْمِ. والْعَوْلُ والْعَوِيلُ الصِّياحُ بالْبُكَاءِ والرَّنِينِ ۞

١٥   ٢ جَمَعْتُ لَـهُ يَـدَىَّ بِـذِى كُعُوبٍ   يُقَدِّمُ نَصْلَهُ أَظْمَى طَـوِيـلُ

XXXV. *Ṭawīl*; no citations.

a) This note suggests an impossible sense for تَبِيع in this place; it is evidently the equivalent of نَابِع, and means a follower (or member of another tribe in subordinate alliance), as opposed to a member of the tribe of full blood; see Qur. XVII, 71, Quṭāmī, Dīw. VI, 26.

b) Dīw. frag. 41, 11.

XXXVI. *Wāfir*. Vv. 1 and 2 in Abū Zaid, *Nawādir*, 148.

c) *Nawādir* عَلَى مَزَاحِفِ.

نَصْلُهُ سِنَانُه. وأَظْمَى رُمْحٌ أَسْمَرُ وقَناةٌ ظَمْيَاءُ: وإذا كان أَسْمَرَ فهو أَصْلَبُ له: ومنْهُ يقال شَفَةٌ

ظَمْيَاءُ اى سَمْرَاءُ ☙ a

٣   شَكَكْتُ بِهِ مَجَامِعَ رُحْبَيَيْهِ   b[فَصَارَا رِدَاوُهُ مِنْهُ طَمِيلُ

(57b)   رُحْبَيَاهُ c مِرْفَقاهُ (؟). وطَمِيلٌ d قِطْعَةٌ يُسَدُّ بِهِ نَقْبُ الحَوْضِ ☙

XXXVII.

١   لِلَّهِ غَارَتُنَا وَالْمَحْلُ قَدْ شَجِيَتْ   مِنْهُ الْبِلَادُ فَصَارَ الْأُفْقُ عُرْيَانَا   5

شَجِيَتْ امْتَلَأَتْ. والْأُفْقُ ولِلجَمع الآفاق النَّواحى من الارض ونَواحى السماء. وعُرْيان من الغَيم والنَّبات ☙

٢   حَتَّى صَبَبْنَا عَلَى هَمْدَانَ صَيِّقَةً   سُورَ الْكِلَابِ وَمَا كَانُوا لَنَا شَانَا

ويروى سُورَ السِّقَاءِ. وصَيِّقَةٌ ذاتُ e صيق وهو الغُبار: قال ابو النَّجْم *صيقٌ شَيَاطِينَ f رَفَتْهُ شَمْأَلُهُ* ☙

٣   فَظَلَّ بِالْقَاعِ يَوْمٌ لَّمْ نَدَعْ كَتَدًا   إِلَّا ضَرَبْنَا وَلَا وَجْهًا وَّلَا شَانَا

10   الْقَاعُ الارضُ الحُرَّةُ الطِّينِ الْمُسْتَوِيَة تُنْسِكُ الماءَ: ولِلجَمع قِيعانٌ وأَقْوَاعٌ وقِيعَةٌ. والشَّأنُ ولِلجَميع الشُّؤونُ وهى

مَجارِى الدُّموعِ وهى قَبائِلُ الرَّأسِ. وزَعَمُوا أَنَّ الدموع تَخْرُجُ من القَبائِل: وقال عَبِيدُ بن الأَبْرَصِ الأَسَدِىّ

g عَيْناكَ دَمْعُهُمَا سَرُوبُ   كَأَنَّ شَأْنَيْهِمَا شَعِيبُ

٤   ثُمَّ نَزَعْنَا وَمَا آنْفَكَّتْ شِقَاوَتُهُمْ   حَتَّى سَقَيْنَا أَنَابِيبًا وَّخِرْصَانَا

يقال ما آنْفَكَّ يَفْعَلُ كذا وما زَالَ وما بَرِحَ وما فَتِئَ بِمَعْنًى واحد. والخِرْصانُ الرِّماحُ هنا: والخِرْصُ

15   السِّنانُ أيضًا ☙

٥   وَمَا أَرَدْنَاهُمْ عَنْ غَيْرِ مَعْذِرَةٍ   مِنَّا وَلٰكِنَّهُ قَدْ كَانَ مَا كَانَا

---

a) After v. 2 the *Nawādir* adds:

فَإِنْ سِلْمًا بَنِي حَرْبٍ فَسِلْمًا   وَإِنْ حَرْبًا فَقَدْ شُفِيَ الْغَلِيلُ

b) Word cut away; conj.

c) Word partly cut away and indistinct.

d) This meaning of طَمِيلٌ does not appear in LA XIII, 434[15] ff., and does not seem to make

sense here.   XXXVII. *Basīt.* No citations found.

e) MS صَيِّقٌ *sic!*   f) MS رَفَتْهُ.   g) ʿAbīd, I, 7.

يقال عُذْرٌ ومَعْذِرَة وعِذْرَة وجَمْعُهُ عِذْرٌ: قال النابغة

a) فَـآتِهَا عِذْرَةٌ إِلَّا تَكُنْ نَفَعَتْ   فَإِنَّ صَاحِبَهَا قَدْ تَاهَ فى الْبَلَد

ويقال له العُذْرَى ايضا: [b قال الشاعر (وهو الجَمُوح الظَّفَرِيّ)

لَا دَرَّ دَرُّكِ إِنِّـى قَـدْ رَمَيْـتُـهُـمْ   لَوْ لَا حُدِدْتُ وَلَا عُذْرَى لِمَحْدُود]

(59a) c) والمَحْدُود ضدّ المَجْدُود ۝

٩ سِرْنَا نُرِيدُ بَنِى نَهْدٍ وَإِخْوَتَهُمْ   جَرْمًا وَّلَكِنْ أَرَادَ اللَّهُ هَمْدَانَا

d) كَمَلَ شِعْرُ عَامِرِ بْنِ الطُّفَيْلِ الْعَامِرِيّ عَمَلَ (sic) أَبِى بَكْرٍ (sic) محمد ابْنِ القَاسِمِ الأَنْبَارِيّ النَّحْوِيّ. وَالحَمْدُ لِلَّـهِ كَثِيرًا: وَصَلَّى اللَّـهُ عَـلَى مُحَمَّدٍ وَآلِـهِ وَسَلَّمَ. وَذَلِكَ فى شَهْرِ جمادى الآخِرة سَـنَـت (sic) ثَـلْـثِيـنَ وَأَرْبَـعَ (sic) مِـائَـةٍ ۝

---

a) Mu‘all. 50; see different reading in scholion to No. XXIII, 3, *ante.*

b) A line has here been cut away; apparently it contained the words within square brackets. For the verse see Dīw. Hudh. No. 232, 2 (Wellhausen, *Skizzen,* I), and LA VI, 219[10] (I owe this reference to Prof. Nöldeke).

c) See Lane 526*c* and 385*c,* LA IV, 119[3].

d) The blunders of the copyist in this colophon are given without correction in order that the character of the MS, where he had not the assistance of a good original, may be appreciated. The month in which he finished the transcript began on the 1st March 103$\frac{8}{9}$ A.D.

SUPPLEMENT

Verses attributed to ʿĀmir ibn aṭ-Ṭufail not contained in the *Dīwān*.

1.

Kamil of al-Mubarrad, 93—4; *ʿAinī* I, 242—3; Khiz. III, 528; SSM 322.

١ تَقُولُ ٱبْنَةُ الْعَمْرِيِّ مَا لَكَ بَعْدَ مَا   أَرَاكَ صَحِيحًا كَالسَّلِيمِ الْمُعَذَّبِ

السَّلِيمُ الْمَلْدُوغُ: وقِيل له سليم تَفَوُّلًا لَهُ بِالسَّلَامَةِ ۞

٢ فَقُلْتُ لَهَا هَمِّى الَّذِى *a* تَعْلَمِينَهُ   مِنَ الثَّأْرِ فِى حَيَّىْ زُبَيْدٍ وَأَرْحَبِ

زُبَيْدٌ وَأَرْحَبُ حَيَّانِ من الْيَمَنِ. والثَّأْرُ ما يَكُونُ لَكَ عند مَنْ أَصَابَ حَمِيمَكَ من النِّتْرَةِ: ومَنْ قال

٥ ثَأْرٌ فقد أَخْطَأَ ۞

٣ إِنْ آغْزُ زُبَيْدًا أَغْزُ قَوْمًا أَعِزَّةً   *b* مُرَكَّبُهُمْ فِى الْحَيِّ خَيْرُ مُرَكَّبِ

٤ وَإِنْ أَغْزُ حَيَّىْ خَثْعَمٍ فَدِمَاؤُهُمْ   شِفَاءٌ وَخَيْرُ الثَّأْرِ لِلْمُتَأَوِّبِ

الْمُتَأَوِّبُ الذى يَأْتِيكَ لِطَلَبِ ثَأْرِهِ عِنْدَكَ: يقال آبَ يَؤُوبُ اذا رَجَعَ: والتَّأْوِيبُ فِى غير هـذا السَّيْرُ

فِى النَّهَارِ بِلَا تَوَقُّفٍ ۞

٥ فَمَا أَدْرَكَ الْأَوْتَارَ مِثْلُ مُحَقِّقِ   بِأَجْرَدَ طَاوٍ *c* كَالْعَسِيبِ الْمُشَذَّبِ   10

الْأَوْتَارُ الْأَحْقَادُ واحدها وِتْرٌ وحِقْدٌ. والْأَجْرَدُ الْفَرَسُ الْمُتَحَسِّرُ الشَّعَرِ: والْأَجْرَدُ الضَّامِرُ أيضًا. والْعَسِيبُ

---

1. The text is that of the *Kamil* (copied in Khiz. III, 528); the scholia are those of al-Akhfash, as printed in Wright's edn. and copied in the Khiz. The *ʿAinī* has slight differences. For vv. 8—10 see ʿAskarī, *Kitāb aṣ-Ṣināʿatain* 298, Qālī, *Amālī, Dhail* 118—119.   *a)* *ʿAinī* تَعْرِفِينَهُ.

b) Both *ʿAinī* and Khiz. have مَرَاكِبُهُمْ and مَرَاكِب; for مُرَكَّبٌ see LA I, 416²⁵—417¹.

c) *ʿAinī* بِالْعَسِيبِ.

السَّعَفَة . وَالمُشَذَّب الطَّوِيل الذى قد أُخِذَ ما عليه من العُقَد والسُّلَّاء والخُوص: ومنه قِيل للطَّوِيل

المُعَرَّق مُشَذَّب ۞

وَأَسْمَرَ خَطِّىٍّ وَأَبْيَضَ بَاتِرٍ ۞ وَزَغْفٍ دِلَاصٍ كَالْغَدِيرِ الْمُتَوَّبِ

خَطِّىٍّ رُمْحٌ منسوب الى الخَطّ وهى جَزِيرَة بالبَحْرَيْن يقال إنَّها تُنْبِت عَصَى الرِّماح: وقال الاصمعىُّ:

لَيْسَتْ بها رِماحٌ ولكن سَفِينَة كانت وَقَعَتْ اليها فيها رِماحٌ وَأَرْفَتْ بها فى بعض السِّنِين المُتَقَدِّمة: ه

فقيل لتلك الرِّماح الخَطِّيَّة: ثُمَّ عَمَّ كُلَّ رُمْحٍ هَذَا النَّسَبُ الى اليَوْمِ. والزَّغْف الدِّرْع الرقيقة النَّسْجِ.

والمُتَوَّب a الذى تُصَفِّقُهُ الرِّياح فيَذْهَب ويَجىء: وهو مِنْ ثَابَ يَثُوب اذا رَجَع: وإنَّما سُمِّى الغَدِير غَدِيرًا

لأنَّ السَّيْلَ غَادَرَهُ اى تَرَكَهُ ۞

٧ b سِلَاحُ آمرِئٍ قَدْ يَعْلَمُ النَّاسُ أَنَّهُ ۞ طَلُوبٌ لِثَأْرَاتِ الرِّجَالِ مُطَلَّبِ

٨ c فَإِنِّى وَإِنْ كُنْتُ ابْنَ فَارِسِ عَامِرٍ ۞ وَفِى السِّرِّ مِنْهَا وَالصَّرِيحِ الْمُهَذَّبِ

٩ d فَمَا سَوَّدَتْنِى عَامِرٌ عَنْ وِرَاثَةٍ ۞ أَبَى اللَّهُ أَنْ أَسْمُو بِأُمٍّ وَلَا أَبِ

١٠ وَلَكِنَّنِى أَحْمِى حِمَاهَا وَأَتَّقِى ۞ أَذَاهَا وَأَرْمِى مَنْ رَمَاهَا e بِمِقْنَبِ

ويروى: مَنْ رَمَاهَا بمِنْكِب ۞

2.

LA XV, 276[1-3]; also X, 74[10-12]; TA VIII, 388 (first v. only): scholia from LA.

١ سُودٌ صَنَاعِيَةٌ إِذَا مَا أَوْرَدُوا ۞ صَدَرَتْ f عَتُومَتُهُمْ وَلَمَّا تُحْلَبِ

٢ صُلْعٌ صَلَامِعَةٌ كَأَنَّ أُنُوفَهُمْ ۞ بَعْرٌ يُنَظِّمُهُ الْوَلِيدُ بِمَلْعَبِ

ويروى: g يُنَظِّمُهُ وَلِيدٌ يَلْعَبُ . سُودٌ صَنَاعِيَةٌ يَصْنَعُونَ المَالَ h وَيُسَمِّنُونَهُ ولا يَسْقُون أَلْبَان إِبِلِهِم الأَضْياف.

والصَّلَامِعَة الدِّقَاق الرُّوؤُس. قال ثعلب: العَنُومَة النَّاقة الغَزِيرَة الدَّرِّ: وقال الأَزْهَرِىُّ: العَتُوم نَاقَة غَزِيرَة

يُؤَخِّر حِلَابُها الى آخِرِ اللَّيْلِ ۞

---

a) This explanation seems to require the form الْمُتَوَّب, which one of Wright's MSS gave together with the active form.   b) Omitted in ʿAinī.

c) ʿAinī agrees with text in Dīw. No. I; ʿAsk. agrees with text above in verses 8—10; so also Qālī, except that he has بِمِنْكِب in v. 10.

d) ʿAinī as text above.   e) ʿAinī بِمِنْكِب.

f) LA X, 74[10] and 79[6] عَنُومُهُمْ.   g) So LA X, 74[11].   h) LA X, 74 وَيُسَمِّنُون فِصْلَانَهُمْ.

٣ لَا يَخْطُبُونَ إِلَى الْكِرَامِ بَنَاتِهِمْ   وَتَشِيبُ [a] أُيِّمُهُمْ وَلَمَّا تُخْطَبِ

3.

Yāqūt III, 466[17]; LA X, 90[9]; scholion from LA.

١ لَا تَسْقِنِي بِيَدَيْكَ إِنْ لَمْ أَغْتَرِفْ   نِعْمَ الضَّجُوعُ بِغَارَةِ أَسْرَابِ

الضَّجُوعُ اسم موضعٍ: قال الاصمعى هو رَحَبَةٌ لِبَنِى أَبِى بَكْرِ بن كِلابٍ [b] ☞

4.

Yāqūt I, 527[6].

قال عامر بن الطفيل يَرْثِى ابن أَخِيهِ عَبْدَ عَمرِو بْنَ حَنْظَلَةَ بن الطُّفَيْل

١ وَهَـــلْ دَاعٍ فَيَسْمِعَ عَبْدَ عَمْرٍو   لِأُخْرَى الْخَيْلِ تَصْرَعُهَا الرِّمَاحُ

٢ فَـــلَا وَأَبِيكَ لَا أَنْسَى خَلِيلِى [c]   بِبَدْوَةَ مَا تَحَرَّكَتِ الرِّيَاحُ

٣ وَكُنْتَ صَفِيَّ نَفْسِى دُونَ قَوْمِى   وَوِرْدِى دُونَ [d] حَامِلَةِ السِّلَاحِ

5.

Yāqūt IV. 1024[6] (as amended in V, 506).

١ وَيَحْمِـلُ بَـزَّى ذُو جِرَاءٍ كَأَنَّهُ   أَحَـمُّ الشَّوَى وَالْمُقْلَتَيْنِ سَبُوحُ

٢ فَـرُوثٌ بِصَحْرَاءِ الْيَفَاعِ [e] كَأَنَّهُ   إِذَا مَا مَشَى خَلْفَ الظِّبَاءِ نَطِيحُ

٣ فَعَايَنَهُ قُنَّاصُ أَرْضٍ فَأَرْسَلُوا   ضِرَاءً بِكُلِّ الطَّارِدَاتِ مُشِيحُ

٤ إِذَا خَافَ مِنْهُنَّ اللِّحَاقَ ارْتَمَى بِهِ   عَنِ الْهَوْلِ حَمْشَاتُ الْقَوَائِمِ رُوحُ

---

a) LA X, 74[12] أُمَّهُمْ (corruptly). This verse occurs in Dīw. VIII, 3, to which the whole piece probably belongs.

b) This v. is printed as in LA, which reproduces it from the *Ṣiḥāḥ*; it is however incorrectly vocalised, and wrongly ascribed to ʿĀmir. The correct reading is

لَا تَسْقِنِى بِيَدَيْكِ إِنْ لَمْ أَلْتَمِسْ   نَعَمَ الضَّجُوعِ بِغَارَةِ أَسْرَابِ

and the verse belongs to a poem by Labīd (Khālidī p. 144). The construction نَعَمَ الضَّجُوعِ is grammatically impossible; a proper name cannot be the اسْم نَعَم (Nöldeke). In LA II, 58, TA I, 361 and VII, 340, and Muḥīṭ 1312 another verse from the same poem, ending in الْأَظْرَابِ, is ascribed to ʿĀmir.   c) So TA X, 33[11].   d) Yāq. حَامِلَهِ السِّلَاحِ.

e) This repetition of كَأَنَّهُ seems to be a corruption. Compare v. 2 with ʿAbīd VIII, 9, and vv. 3 and 4 with *id.*, vv. 10—11.

6.

LA I, 56²¹⁻²²; IV, 479²⁰ (second verse only); XVIII, 245⁴ (both verses). TA I, 60¹⁸; X, 110, bottom. Lane 2952b (second verse only). Ṣīrāfī, comm. to Sībawaihi (Jahn, transln. p. 46). The verses are sometimes cited as a portion of Ṭarafah's Muʻallaqah: see Seligsohn, Ṭarafa, p. ١٥٣, vv. 16—17.

١ a لَا يُرْهِبُ ابْنَ الْعَمِّ مِنِّيَ صَوْلَةٌ   وَّلَا أُخْتَتَى مِنْ صَوْلَةِ الْمُتَهَدِّدِ

٢ b وَإِنِّيَ إِنْ أَوْعَدْتُهُ أَوْ وَعَدْتُهُ   لَأُخْلِفُ إِيعَادِى وَأُنْجِزُ مَوْعِدِى

ويروى *لَمَخْلَفُ إِيعَادِى وَمُنْجِزُ مَوْعِدِى*✧

7.

Ḥamāsah, 342.

١ قَضَى اللّٰهُ فِى بَعْضِ الْمَكَارِهِ لِلْفَتَى   بِرُشْدٍ وَّفِى بَعْضِ الْهَوَى مَا يُحَاذِرُ

٢ أَلَمْ تَعْلَمِى أَنِّى إِذَا الْإِلْفُ قَادَنِى   إِلَى الْجَوْرِ لَا أَنْقَادُ وَالْإِلْفُ جَائِرُ

8.

Al-Anbārī, commentary to *Mufaḍḍalīyat*, No. CVI, v. 9.

١ c أَلَا يَا لَيْتَ أَخْوَالِى غَنِيًّا   عَلَيْهِمْ كُلَّمَا أَمْسَوْا دُوَارُ

ويروى: *لَهُمْ فِى كُلِّ ثَالِثَةٍ دُوَارُ*✧

٢ بِبِرِّ إِلَاهِهِمْ وَيَكُونُ فِيهِمْ   عَلَى الْعَافِينَ أَيَّامٌ قِصَارُ

9.

Ṭabarī I, 1747⁴⁻⁵; Agh. XV, 137²⁰⁻²¹.

١ بَعَثَ الرَّسُولُ بِمَا تَرَى فَكَأَنَّمَا d عَمْدًا نَشُدُّ عَلَى الْمَقَانِبِ غَارَا

---

a) So LA I, 56, and Ṣīrāfī. LA XVIII, 245 and TA X, 110 read first hemist. thus:

وَلَا يَخْتَتِى ابْنُ الْعَمِّ مَا عِشْتُ صَوْلَتِى

Seligsohn, Ṭarafa, reads لَا يُرْهِبُ ابْنُ الْعَمِّ مَا عِشْتُ صَوْلَتِى.

b) So LA IV, 479. LA I, 56 has second hemist. thus:

لَيَأْمَنُ مِيعَادِى (sic) وَمُنْجِزُ مَوْعِدِى

LA XVIII, 245, TA I, Lane, Ṣīrāfī, Seligsohn, all read, in first hemist. وَإِنِّى وَإِنْ, and the second hemist. as in the scholion.

c) This verse is cited in Naq. 950⁵, with the note: الدُّوَارُ عِيدٌ يَطُوفُونَ فِيهِ, and with the reading for the second hemist. given in our scholion above; it is also mentioned that Abū ʻAbdillāh (= Ibn al-Aʻrābī) read فِى كُلِّ نَائِبَةٍ.   d) Agh. أَشُدُّ.

٢ وَلَقَـدْ وَرَدْنَ بِمَـا الْمَدِينَةَ [a]شُرَّبًا   وَّلَقَـدْ قَتَـلْنَ بِجَوِّهَا الْأَنْصَارَا

10.

Yāqūt II, 502 (with corrections in V, 179—80).

١ هَلَّا [b]سَأَلْتِ إِذَا اللِّقَاحُ تَرَوَّحَتْ   هَرَجَ الرِّئَالِ وَلَمْ تَبُلَّ صِرَارَا

٢ إِنَّا لَنُعْجِلُ بِالْعَبِيطِ لِضَيْفِنَا   قَبْلَ الْعِيَالِ وَنَطْلُبُ الْأَوْتَارَا

٣ وَنَعُدُّ أَيَّامًا لَنَا وَمَآثِرًا   قِدْمًا نَبُذُّ الْبُدَّوَ وَالْأَمْصَارَا   5

٤ مِنْهَا [c]خُوَىٌّ وَّالذَّهَابُ وَبِالصَّفَا   يَوْمٌ تَمَهَّدَ مَجِّدُ ذَاكَ فَسَارَا

11.

Al-Anbārī, Commy. to *Mufaḍḍalīyāt*, No. V, p. 31. ("Day of ar-Raqam").

وَكَانَ عَامِرُ بن الطفيل لَقِيَ يَوْمَئِذٍ رَجُلًا من بني وَائِلَةَ او غَاضِرَةَ بن صَعْصَعَةَ يقال له عَبْسُ بن حِذَارٍ:

وَكَانَ يُكْنَى أَبَا أَبِيٍّ وَيُدْعَى ذَا الْعُنُقِ: وكان شُجَاعًا وهو الَّذِى قَتَل بِشْرَ بن أَبِى خَازِمٍ الْأَسَدِىِّ.

فَجَعَلَ يَرْتَجِزُ يَوْمَئِذٍ *** فَأَبْلَى يَوْمَئِذٍ بَلَاءً حَسَنًا. فقال عامرُ بن الطفيل   10

١ وَأَبُو أُبَىٍّ مَّا مُنِيتُ بِمِثْلِـهِ   يَا حَبَّذَا هُوَ مُمْسَيًا وَّنَهَارَا

٢ لَـقِـىَ الْخَمِيسَ أَبُو أُبَىٍّ بَـارِزًا   أَلْـوَائِـلِـىُّ وَحَرَّمَ الْإِدْبَـارَا

٣ يَحْمِى إِذَا جَعَلَتْ سَلُولُ وَعَامِرٌ   يَوْمَ الْـهِـيَـاجِ يُحَجِّبُونَ فَـزَارَا

يُقَالُ جَبَّبَ الْقَوْمُ اذا هَرَبُوا۞

12.

Umdah II, 167

وَأَنْشَدَ ابو زياد لعامرِ بْن الطفيل   15

١ وَبِالْفَيْفَا مِنَ الْيَمَنِ اسْتَثَارَتْ   قَبَائِلُ كَانَ أَلْبَهُمْ فِخَـارَا

---

a) Agh. سربا.

b) Yaq. سَأَلْتَ; in such cases the person invited to enquire is invariably a woman.

c) Probably we should read خُوَىّ; see Yāq. II, 373[10], and the verses of Labīd (Khālidī 104[4]) there quoted (Naq. 229[8], q. v., however, has Labīd's verse with خ). خُوَىّ was a Day between ʿĀmir b. Ṣaṣʿah and Khathʿam, in the territory of the latter; خُوَىّ is described as وَادٍ يَفْرُغ من فَلَجٍ من وَرَاء حَفَرِ أَبِى مُوسَى, and the fight there was between Bakr b. Wāil and Tamīm.

13.

Yaqūt I, 853[10]; LA X, 93[3] and XI, 151[24]; Bakrī 201[14]; TA V, 431 and VI, 198.

قال [(LA XI, 151) زُرْلا يَوْمَ الرَّقَمِ] فَرَسَهُ عامر بن الطفيل عَقَر به مَوضِع *** تَضَرُّعُ

١ وَنِعْمَ أَخُو الصَّعْلُوكِ أَمْسِ تَرَكْتَهُ a بِتَضَرُّعَ يَمْرِى بِالْيَدَيْنِ وَيَعْسِفُ

b قال ابن بَرِّى: اخو الصعلوك يعنى به فَرَسَهُ: ويَمْرِى بِيَدَيْهِ يُحَرِّكُهُما كالعابِثِ: ويَعْسِف تَرْجُف
حَنْجَرَتُهُ من النَّفَسِ ۞

5

14.

Aghānī XVI, 54.

١ قُلْ لِزَيْدٍ قَدْ كُنْتَ تُوَثِّرُ بِالْحِلْــمِ إِذَا سَفِهَتْ حُلُومُ الرِّجَالِ

٢ لَيْسَ هَذَا الْقَتِيلُ مِنْ سَلَفِ الْحَـــيِّ c كَلَاعٍ وَّيَحْصِــبٍ وَّكُلَالِ

٣ أَوْ بَنِى آكِلِ الْمُرَارِ وَلَا صِيْـــدِ بَنِى جَفْنَةَ الْمُلُوكِ الطِّوَالِ

٤ وَابْنِ مَاءِ السَّمَاءِ قَدْ عَلِمَ النَّاس وَلَا خَيْرَ فِى مَقَالَةِ غَالِى

٥ إِنَّ فِى قَتْلِ عَامِرِ بْنِ طُفَيْلٍ لَبَوَّأُوا لِطَـيِّءٍ الْأَجْبَالِ

٦ إِنَّنِى وَالَّذِى يَحُجُّ لَـهُ النَّا d سُ قَلِيلٌ فِى عَامِرَ الْأَمْثَالِ

٧ يَوْمَ لَا مَالَ لِلْمُحَارِبِ فِى الْحَرْب سِوَى نَصْلِ أَسْمَرَ عَسَّالِ

٨ وَلِجَامٍ فِى رَأْسِ e أَجْرَدَ كَالنِّـعـ عِ طُــوَالٍ وَّأَبْيَــضٍ قَصَّالِ

٩ وَدِلَاصٍ كَالنِّهْىِ ذَاتِ فُضُولٍ ذَاكَ فِى حَلْبَةِ الْحَوَادِثِ مَالِى

١٠ وَلَعَمْرِى فَضْلُ الرِّئَاسَةِ وَالسِّـنّ وَجِدٍّ عَلَى هَوَازِنَ عَالِى

١١ غَيْرَ أَنِّى أَوْلَى هَوَازِنَ فِى الْحَرْب بِضَرْبِ الْمُتَوَّجِ الْمُخْتَالِ

۱۳ وَبِطَعْنِ الْكَمِيِّ فِى حَمَسِ النَّقْعِ عَلَى مَتْنِ هَيْكَلٍ جَوَّالِ

---

a) TA VI, 198 يَكْبُو for يَمْرِى, and بِنَتَضْرُعَ for تَضَرُّعِ.

b) Scholion taken from LA X, 93[4]; Bakrī 201, against all the others, explains thus:

يَصِف رَجُلًا طُعِن فهو يَضْرِب بِيَدَيْهِ على الارض. وَالعَسْف ان يَرْتَفِع حَنْجَرَتُهُ عِنْد الْمَوْت ۞

14. These are an answer to some verses by Zaid al-Khail: see Agh. l. c., p. 53.

c) Names of princes of Ḥimyarite tribes; كَلَاعٍ stands for ذُو الْكَلَاعِ (BDur 307[15] and 312[7]).
For يَحْصُبُ see LA I, 311[5-6]. كُلَالٍ is for عَبْدُ كُلَالٍ (BDur 307[23]). All these names in Wüst. Tab. 3.

d) Probably we should read قَلِيلٌ فِى عَامِرِ أَمْثَالِى.   e) Agh. أَجْوَنَ.

15.

Naqā'iḍ 229¹⁵ and 408¹⁸ (for the story see p. 407).

[قال عامر بن الطفيل فى يوم رَحْرَحَانَ]

١   قَضَيْنَا الْجَوْنَ عَنْ عَبْسٍ وَّكَانَتْ   مَنِيَّةُ مَعْبَدٍ فِينَا هُزَالَا

16.

TA VIII, 134²⁰; first v. also in LA XIV, 182²¹, Bakrī 157 foot, Khiz. III, 44, Naq. 284¹³.

١   أَنَازِلَةً أَسْمَاءُ أَمْ غَيْرُ نَازِلَهْ   أَبِينِى لَنَا يَا أَسْمَ مَا أَنْتِ فَاعِلَهْ

٢   فَإِنْ تَنْزِلِى أَنْزِلْ وَلَا آتِ مَوْسِمًا   وَّلَوْ رَحَلَتْ لِلْبَيْعِ جَسْرٌ وَّبَاهِلَهْ

17.

LA XVIII 254¹⁵; second v. in TA X 116¹⁰, and Lane 769*b*.

١   وَأَهْلَكِنِى لَكُمْ فِى كُلِّ يَوْمٍ   تَعَوُّجُكُمْ عَلَىَّ وَأَسْتَقِيمُ

٢   رِقَابٌ كَالْمَوَاجِنِ خَاظِيَاتٌ   وَّأَسْتَاهٌ عَلَى الْأَكْوَارِ كُومُ

18.

'Umdah II, 171—2; the verses are said to have been uttered by 'Āmir b. aṭ-Ṭufail at the court of an-Nu'mān, when Bisṭām b. Qais of Shaibān was preferred before him for honour among the Arabs visiting the king.

١   كَانَ *a* التَّبَابِعُ فِى دَهْرٍ لَّهُمْ سَلَفْ   وَّابْنُ الْمُرَارِ وَأَمْلَاكٌ عَلَى الشَّامِ

٢   حَتَّى انْتَهَى الْمُلْكُ مِنْ لَّحْمٍ إِلَى مَلِكٍ   بَادِى السِّمَانِ لِمَنْ لَّمْ يَرْمِهِ رَامِى

٣   أَنْحَى عَلَيْنَا بِأَظْفَارٍ فَطَوَّقَنَا   طَوْقَ الْحَمَامِ بِإِتْعَاسٍ وَّإِرْغَامِ

٤   إِنْ يُّمْكِنِ اللَّهُ مِنْ دَهْرٍ *b* تُسَاءُ بِهِ   نَتْرُكْكَ وَحْدَكَ تَدْعُو رَهْطَ بِسْطَامِ

٥   فَانْظُرْ إِلَى الصَّيْدِ لَمْ يَحْمُوكَ مِنْ مُّضَرٍ   هَلْ فِى رَبِيعَةَ إِنْ لَّمْ تَدْعُنَا حَامِى

---

17. LA ascribes the verses to عامِرُ بْنُ الطُّفَيْلِ السَّعْدِىّ; no poet of this name can be found in the genealogies of the many tribes called Sa'd, and in TA this *nisbah* is not given against the name.

a) Edition has النتابع.

b) Edn. نساء.

19.

Ḥamāsah, 72 (but see commy. on v. 2 on p. 73, where the verse is ascribed to ʿAbd ʿAmr b. Shuraiḥ).

١   طُلِّقْتِ إِنْ لَمْ تَسْأَلِي أَىَّ فَارِسٍ   حَلِيلُكِ إِذْ لَاقَى صَدَاءً وَخَثْعَمَا

٢   أَكُرُّ عَلَيْهِمْ دَعْلَجًا وَلُبَانَهُ   إِذَا مَا آشْتَكَى وَقْعَ الرِّمَاحِ تَخَمْحَمَا

20.

Ibn Qutaibah, *Shiʿr*, 191.

١   وَمَا الْأَرْضُ إِلَّا قَيْسُ عَيْلَانَ أَهْلُهَا   لَهُمْ سَاحَتَاهَا سَهْلُهَا وَحُزُومُهَا

٢   وَقَدْ نَالَ آفَانَى السَّمَاوَاتِ مَجْدُنَا   لَنَا الصَّحْوُ مِنْ آفَاتِهَا وَغُيُومُهَا

21.

Agh. X, 146: vv. 1—5 and 9 again in Agh. XVIII, 161; a reply to a poem of self-praise by Yazīd b. ʿAbd al-Madān of the Bal-Ḥārith, who had contended with ʿĀmir as to rank and distinction when both were suitors for the hand of the daughter of Umayyah b. al-Askar of Kinānah. Abu-l-Faraj al-Iṣfahānī expresses the opinion (XVIII, 161, foot) that the whole story is one of the inventions of Ibn al-Kalbī, and that the verses are plainly of late origin, being weak and paltry, and quite unlike the genuine work of the age to which they are ascribed.

١   *a* عَجَبًا لِوَاصِفِ طَارِقِ الْأَحْزَانِ   وَلِمَا تَجِىءُ بِهِ بَنُو الدَّيَّانِ

٢   فَخَرُوا عَلَىَّ *b* بِجِبْوَةٍ لِمُحَرِّقٍ   وَإِتَاوَةٍ *c* سِيقَتْ إِلَى النُّعْمَانِ

٣   مَا أَنْتَ وَآبْنَ مُحَرِّقٍ وَقَبِيلَهُ   وَإِتَاوَةِ اللَّخْمِيِّ فِى *d* عَيْلَانِ

٤   *e* فَآقْصِدْ بِذَرْعِكَ *f* قَصْدَ قَوْمِكَ نَصْرَهُمْ   وَدَعِ الْقَبَائِلَ مِنْ بَنِى قَحْطَانِ

٥   *g* إِنْ كَانَ سَالِفَةُ الْإِتَاوَةِ فِيكُمُ   أَوْلَى فَفَخْرُكَ فَخْرُ كُلِّ يَمَانِى

٩   *h* وَأَفْخَرْ بِرَهْطِ بَنِى الْحِمَاسِ وَمَالِكٍ   وَبَنِى الْقِصَابِ وَرَعْبَلٍ وَقِيَانِ

٧   فَأَنَا الْمُعَظَّمُ وَآبْنُ فَارِسِ قُرْزُلٍ   وَأَبُو بَرَاءَ زَانِفِى وَنَمَانِى

---

a) Agh. XVIII يَا لَلرِّجَالِ لِطَارِقِ الْأَحْزَانِ.

b) Agh. (X and XVIII) جَبوة.   *c)* Agh. سَلَقَتْ مِنَ النُّعْمَانِ.

d) Agh. X غِيلان.   *e)* Agh. X فَآقْصِدْ بِفَخْرِكَ.

f) Agh. XVIII قصد أمرك قصدة.

g) Agh. XVIII (*sic*) أن كان سالفا زنا الاتاوة فيكم.

h) Some of these names in Wüstenfeld, Tab. 8; perhaps قَنَّان should be read for قيان.

٨   وَأَبُو جَرِيّ ذُو الْفَعَالِ وَمَالِكُ   مَنَعَا الذِّمَارَ صَبَاحَ كُلِّ طِعَانِ

٩   وَإِذَا تَعَاظَمَتِ الْأُمُورُ a هَوَازِنَا   كُنْتُ الْمُنَوَّهَ بِاسْمِهِ b وَالْبَانِى

22.

Yaqut IV, 493[12]; for some corrections see V, 428.

١   وَإِنَّكِ لَوْ رَأَيْتِ أُمَيْمَ قَوْمِى   غَدَاةَ قُرَاقِرٍ لَنَعِمْتِ عَيْنَا

٢   وَهُنَّ خَوَارِجٌ مِّنْ حَيّ كَلْبٍ   وَقَدْ شُفِىَ الْحَرَارَةُ وَاشْتَفَيْنَا

٣   c وَقَدْ صَبَّحْنَ يَوْمَ عُوَيْرِضَاتٍ   قُبَيْلَ الشَّرْقِ بِالْيَمَنِ الْحَصِينَا

٤   وَبِالْمَرْدَاتِ قَدْ لَاقَيْنَ غُنْمًا   وَمِنْ أَهْلِ الْيَمَامَةِ مَا بَغَيْنَا

23.

LA III, 172[20]; TA II, 88[20].

١   تَوَضَّحْنَ فِى عَلْيَاءَ قَفْرٍ كَأَنَّهَا   مَهَارِقُ فَلُّوجٍ يُعَارِضْنَ تَالِيَا

---

a) Agh. X هوازن :XVIII (sic) موارتا.   b) Agh. XVIII والثانى.

c) This v. in Yaq. III, 749[11], with قُبَيْلَ الصُّبْحِ. For Ḥuṣain see No. II, 18 and III, 3.

INDEX TO THE DĪWĀN OF ʿABĪD

The Roman numerals refer to Odes, the Arabic to fragments. The rhyme-words are those of the second hemistich of the first couplet; they are arranged alphabetically, the *muqayyad* rhyme being put first, then the others in order of the vowels of the *iʿrāb* — ', ‿, ⌐. The sign † after a rhyme ending in ' or ‿ indicates that the poem contains one verse or more exhibiting a change to ‿ or ', called *iqwā*. The asterisk after the name *Basīṭ* means that the poem is in a peculiar or rare form of this metre.

Rhyme.	Number of poem.	Metre.	Number of verses.	Page.
† الْغُرَاب	1	*Wāfir*	3	81
وَتَكَتَّبُوا	II	*Kāmil*	29	12
فَوَاهِب	XVIII	*Ṭawīl*	5	53
فَالذُّنُوب	I	*Basīṭ* *	45	5
كَالْكِتَاب	XXVII	*Khafīf*	18	73
مَغْلُوب	IX	*Ṭawīl*	16	31
بِالْأَرِيب	2	*Wāfir*	1	81
مُرِيب	VIII	*Ṭawīl*	14	29
إِصْبَاحِى	XXVIII	*Basīṭ*	15	75
اللَّاحِى	XXIV	*Basīṭ*	21	66
مَوْعِد	XIX	*Kāmil*	17	54
حَادِى	5	*Basīṭ*	3	82

Rhyme.	Number of poem.	Metre.	Number of verses.	Page.
لِمِيعَادِ	XXV	Basīṭ	12	69
الْمَسَاجِدِ	4	Ṭawīl	2	82
الْمَجَدَّدِ	XXX	Ṭawīl	36	78
أَسَّدِ	XIV	Basīṭ	12	46
وَلَدُودَا	3	Kāmil	8	81
غُرِّ	6	Munsariḥ	3	82
الْمُسْمِرِ	7	Munsariḥ	1	83
بِالْقَهْرِ	8	Ṭawīl	3	83
وَنَاجِزِ	9	Kāmil muraffal	3	83
دُرُوسِ	XII	Kāmil	22	41
وَأَضْرَاسَا	10	Basīṭ	16	84
† غِصَاصِ	XXIII	Wāfir	24	65
† غُمُوضُ	X	Ṭawīl	20	34
† عِبَيْطِ	XXII	Basīṭ	27	62
بَرَقْ	11	Ṭawīl	3	85
بُرُوقُهْ	VI	Kāmil muraffal	7	26
خَلَقَهْ	12	Munsariḥ	4	86
مَعَكْ	13	Ramal	1	86
سَوَاهِكَا	XVII	Ṭawīl	ʿ18	51
فَالرِّجَلِ	III	Munsariḥ	12	17

Rhyme.	Number of poem.	Metre.	Number of verses.	Page.
أَلْهَامِلُ	XXVI	Sarīʿ	21	71
أَلْبَالِي	V	Basīṭ	18	23
ٱلْمُحْتَالْ	15	Khafīf	3	86
أُنَالْ	XI	Khafīf	35	36
أَمْثَالِي	XV	Ṭawīl	17	47
ٱلْحَلَالْ	XX	Ramal muraffal	18	58
قَاتِلِي	14	Ṭawīl	2	86
عَلِمُوا	16	Basīṭ	2	87
نَنِيمُوا	17	Wāfir	1	87
بَرَامِ	IV	Kāmil	20	19
ٱلنَّدَامَهْ	XXIX	Kāmil muraffal	12	77
مَعْلُومَهْ	XXI	Basīṭ	14	60
زَمَانِ	XVI	Kāmil	10	49
لِينِ	XIII	Wāfir	18	44
وَحَيْنَا	VII	Kāmil muraffal	25	27

INDEX OF PERSONAL NAMES IN THE DĪWĀN OF ʿABĪD

(Names of commentators omitted: for them see Introduction, p. 9.)

حُجْر Prince of Kindah, 2[4], 16[13], 20[15], 21[2], 27[12], 52[14], 72[11], 81[2], 83[6,7].

خَالِدُ بن نَضْلَةَ الْقَعْقَسِيُّ boon companion of al-Mundhir, 27.

خُزَيْمَةُ tribe (father of Asad), 43[14].

دَارِمٌ tribe (section of Tamīm), 15[8].

دَاوُودُ 82[4].

دُودَانُ used for tribe of Asad, 73[4].

الرِّبَابُ group of tribes, 52[14] and 53 note *a*.

بنو الزِّنَّبَةِ sub-tribe of Asad, 1[4].

زُهَيْرٌ cited, 17[2].

آلُ زَبَّيْدٍ a house in Asad (?), 38[10].

بنو سَعْدِ بن ثَعْلَبَةَ ʿAbīd's sub-tribe in Asad, 54[1], 72[13].

سَعْدَةُ, سُعْدَى woman's name in *nasīb*, 78[7], 79[4].

سَلْمَى woman's name in *nasīb*, 63[1].

الْأَجْدَلَانِ two men of Kindah (one named Mālik) slain, 52[6].

أَسَدٌ tribe, 46[1], 47[9], 64[4], 70[12], 77[4], 78[1].

أَسْمَاءُ woman's name, 69[1].

الْأَعْشَى cited, 7[6].

أُمَامَةُ name of ʿAbīd's mother, 5[2].

أَمْرُو الْقَيْسِ 20[16], 53[1], 80[7] (in diminutive form مُرَيُّ الْقَيْسِ), 83[6].

أَبُو بَرَاءٍ عَامِرُ بن مَالِك Chief of ʿĀmir, 11[8].

تَمِيمٌ tribe, 16[1].

بنو جَدِيلَةَ من طَيِّءٍ tribe, 12[1], 13[11], 13[14], 17[1].

جُذَامٌ tribe, 87[3].

جُشَمُ name in ʿAbīd's genealogy, corruptly written حَنْتَمُ, 1[1] (note).

جَنْدَلٌ a man of Kindah slain, 53[2].

لحَارِثُ الْأَعْرَجِ King of Ghassān, 59[3].

كَعْبُ بن زُهَيْرِ cited, 20[16] (note h).

كِنْدَة tribe, 22[17], 28[1].

لَبِيدُ بن رَبِيعَةَ cited, 10[11], 11[8], 22[2].

لَخْمٌ tribe, 87[3].

مالِك one of the "Falcons" of Kindah, 52[6].

مالِك بن تَعْلَبَةَ a sub-tribe of Asad, 1[4].

ماوِيَّة name of ʿAbīd's sister, 1[3].

مَرَّةُ الْخَيْرِ a man of Kindah, 52[9].

مَعَدّ great division of the Arabs, 53[10].

الْمُنْذِرُ بن ماءِ السَّماءِ 2[6] ff.

مَهْدَد woman's name in nasīb, 55[1].

مَيَّة do.   17[6].

نَبَطٌ, نَبِيطٌ Nabaṭeans, 30[6].

نَصْرُ race of Kings of al-Ḥīrah, 82[3].

هِنْد woman's name in nasīb, 23[4], 61[7].

هَوازِنُ name of a large tribal group, 28[10].

يَعْبُوبُ name of a god or idol, 13[14].

يَهُودُ the Jews, 30[5].

سُلَيْمَى woman's name in nasīb, 72[2].

شَراحِيلُ a prince, probably of Kindah, 57[9].

عامِرُ tribe, 15[12], 16[1], 52[10], 72[17].

عَبِيد genealogy, 1[1] ff., 5[1].

عَدِى man of Ghassān, 59[6].

عِلْباءُ بن قَيْسٍ slayer of Ḥujr, 81[6].

عَمْرو man of Kindah, 52[14].

عَمْرو أَبُو كَرِبَ of Kindah, 70[3,6].

بنو عَمْرو ʿAbīd's sub-tribe (?), 48[6].

عَمْرو بْن مَسْعُودٍ الْأَسَدِى boon companion of al-Mundhir, 2[8].

غَسّانُ tribe, 28[3], 47[6,9], 54[2], 73[2].

فاطِمَة woman's name in nasīb, 41[3].

قُرْص Chief of Ghassān, killed, 52[9] (and note), 59[9].

ذُو الْقَرْنَيْنِ 82[4].

أُمُّ قَطامِ mother of Ḥujr, 16[23], 21[1], 27[12].

قَيْصَرُ 22[18], 23[2].

كاهِلُ sub-tribe of Asad, 72[13].

كَبِيشَة woman's name in nasīb, 19[12], 20[12].

INDEX OF GEOGRAPHICAL NAMES IN THE DĪWĀN OF ʿABĪD

(cited by number of poem and verse)

INDEX TO THE DĪWĀN OF ʿĀMIR

See remarks on p. 161.

Rhyme.	Number of poem.	Metre.	Number of verses.	Page.
الشَّبَابُ ✓	XVI A (by an-Nābighah)	*Wāfir*	8	130
الضِّرَابُ	XVI	*Wāfir*	12	129
شَاجِبُ	XXXII	*Ṭawīl*	4	146
أَسْرَابِ	3 (by Labīd)	*Kāmil*	1	154
الْمُعَذَّبِ	1	*Ṭawīl*	10	152
فَأَرْكَبِ	VIII	*Kāmil*	13	111
مَوْكِبِ	I	*Ṭawīl*	3	92
تُحْلَبِ	2	*Kāmil*	3	153
فَاسْتَقَرَّتِ	V	*Khafīf*	10	104
رَهَجِ	XV	*Basīṭ*	8	127
† الرِّمَاحُ ✗	4	*Wāfir*	3	154
سَبُوحِ	5	*Ṭawīl*	4	154
نَهْدُ	III	*Kāmil*	10	101
تَعُودُ	VII	*Wāfir*	12	109
الْمَوْعُودُ	XXXIV A (by Ḍubaiʿah)	*Kāmil*	6	148

Rhyme.	Number of poem.	Metre.	Number of verses.	Page.
أَلْمُتَهَدِّد	6	Ṭawīl	4	154
أُطَّرَد	XXIX	Kāmil	10	144
مَشَاهِدِى	XIX	Ṭawīl	9	134
أُسُودُقَا	VI	Ṭawīl	10	107
ضَرَرْ	XXIII	Ṭawīl	6	138
دَوَّارْ	8	Wāfir	2	155
يَتَحَانِرُ	7	Ṭawīl	2	155
† حُضَّرُ	XIII	Mutaqārib	12	122
جُبَّارِ	XXX	Wāfir	2	146
فَخَارَا	12	Wāfir	1	156
صِرَارَا	10	Kāmil	4	156
غَارَا	9	Kāmil	2	155
وَنِهَارَا	11	Kāmil	3	156
وَعَرْعَرَا	XXII	Ṭawīl	2	138
جَعْفَرَا	XXIV	Ṭawīl	6	139
النَّكِيرَا	IV	Wāfir	4	103
أُولَعُ	XXVIII	Ṭawīl	7	143
وَيَعْسِفُ	13	Ṭawīl	1	157
أُكَلَّف	XXXIV	Ṭawīl	2	147
الْعَوَارِكُ	XXXV	Ṭawīl	3	149

Rhyme.	Number of poem.	Metre.	Number of verses.	Page.
† التَّنِيلُ	XVIII	Wāfir	11	133
أَقِيلُ	XXV	Wāfir	6	140
عَوِيلُ	XXXVI	Wāfir	3	149
الرِّجَالِ	14	Khafīf	12	157
وَرِمَالِ	IX	Kāmil	4	114
جَحْفَلِ	XVII	Kāmil	6	131
وَأَئِلِ	X	Ṭawīl	4	115
هُوَزَالَا	15	Wāfir	1	158
فَاعِلَهْ	16	Ṭawīl	2	158
خِذَامُ	XXVI	Ṭawīl	5	141
تُلْجَمُ	XXXI	Ṭawīl	2	146
† الْمُعْلِمُ	XIV	Mutaqārib	8	124
وَأَسْتَقِيمُ	17	Wāfir	2	158
الشَّامِ	18	Basīṭ	5	158
نَظْلِمِ	XX	Mutaqārib	2	135
عَلَامَا	II	Wāfir	32	93
دَمَا	XXVII	Ṭawīl	5	141
خَتْعَمَا	19	Ṭawīl	2	159
صَيْلَمَا	XII	Ṭawīl	9	120
النَّمَائِمَا	XXI	Ṭawīl	10	136

Rhyme.	Number of poem.	Metre.	Number of verses.	Page.
حَزُّومُهَا	20	*Ṭawīl*	2	159
ٱلدَّيَّانِ	21	*Kāmil*	9	159
عُرْيَانَا	XXXVII	*Basīṭ*	6	150
خَائِنَا	XXXIII	*Ṭawīl*	2	147
عَيْنَا	22	*Wāfir*	4	160
تَالِيَا	23	*Ṭawīl*	1	160

INDEX OF PERSONAL NAMES IN THE DĪWĀN OF ʿĀMIR

الأَغَرُّ horse of ʿAntarah, 132[8].

الأَغْلَبُ العِجْلِيّ 102[12].

آكِلُ المُرَارِ 157[9], 158[13].

أَكْلُبُ, tribe, 101[7], 115[5], 120[6].

امرُؤُ القَيْس 93[15], 102[15], 115[11], 121[2].

أُمَيْمَة 160[4].

أُمَيّة بن ابى الصَّلْت 109[7].

(أُنَيْس) أَنَس بن مُدْرِك الخَثْعَمِيّ 142[9].

الأَنْصار 156[1].

الأَوْس 95[15].

أَوْس بن حَاجِر 115[3], 127[11].

الأَوْقَص 96[14].

باذان 117[9].

باهِلَة a tribe, 158[6].

بَحِير 104[9].

(أَبُو بَكْرِ بنُ كِلاب = ذُو البَرَزَى) 103[15,16].

بِسْطام بن قَيْس البَكْرِيّ 158[16]

إِبْراهِيمُ بن العَرَبِيّ 95[10].

الأَجْدَعُ الهَمْدانِيّ 128[9] (note).

الأَخْطَل 95[3], 112[10].

أَرْحَب (sub-tribe of Hamdān) 95[2], 152[3].

الأَزْدُ (شَنُوءَة) 95[13,16], 121[13].

أُسامَة 97[14].

أَسَد بن خُزَيْمَة 96[1,2], 142[14].

أَسْماء a woman of Fazārah, addressed by ʿAmir several times in the nasīb, 121[9], 142[6], 144[3], 145[8], 146[1], 158[5].

أَسْوَد (من عَبْد القَيْس) 110[18].

أَشْجَع tribe of Ghaṭafān, 111[12,15], 114[4], 143[4].

الأَصْمَعِيّ 142[2].

الأَعْشَى (من بنى قَيْس) 96[9], 99[1], 105[18], 106[3], 109[10], 113[3] (note), 118[9], 119[1], 126[13], 140[1].

بِشْرُ بن أَبِى خَازِمٍ الأَسَدِىّ .156[9]

ابن بِشْرٍ (من عبد القيس) .111[1]

بَشِيرٌ .103[15]

بنو بَغِيضٍ .129[16], 131[9]

بَكْرُ بن وَائِلٍ .115[4,5]

التَّبَابِعُ .158[13]

تَمِيمٌ .99[3], 100[11], 117[10], 119[1,2], 136[7]

ثَمُودُ .110[1]

جَبَّارُ بن سُلْمَى .91[3]

جُذَامٌ .95[8]

جَرْمٌ tribe, 101[6,7], 151[6]

أبو الجَبِرِى .160[1]

جَرِيرُ بن عَطِيَّةَ .93[13]

جَسْرٌ (= النَّخَع) tribe, 158[6]

جَعْفَرٌ ʿĀmir's house in Kilāb, 116[4], 135[1], 139[14]

بنو جَفْنَةَ .157[9]

الجَمُوحُ الضَّفَرِىّ الهُذَلِىّ .151[3]

جُوانَبِذ (= جُوَانُوَيْهِ) 117[15], 118[2,14]

الجَوْنُ , أبو الجَوْنِ 93[3], 100[15], 101[2], 120[10], ابنُ الجَوْنِ 128[3], 158[3]

حَا؟ tribe, 96[12] (see note).

حَاجِبُ بن زُرَارَةَ .98[4,16]

الحَارِثُ بن حِلِّزَةَ البَيَشْكُرِى .138[6]

الحَارِثُ بن كَعْبٍ tribe, 159[18]

الحَارِثُ بن وَعْلَةَ الجَرْمِىّ .97[3] (note).

حَاشِدٌ branch of Hamdān, 134[18,19]

حَامٌ tribe, 96[11]

الحِرْمَازِىُّ .104[10]

الحُصَيْنُ الحَارِثِىّ ذو الغُصَّةِ 97[14], 101[9,10], 160[6]

الحُطَيْئَةُ (جَرْوَلٌ) 93[1], 123[9], 139[6]

حَكَمٌ tribe, 96[11]

بنو الأَحْمَاسِ branch of the Banu-l-Ḥarith, 159[18]

حِمْيَرٌ .95[13]

حَنْظَلَةُ (brother of ʿĀmir) 131[9], 145[4], 154[6]

حَنِيفَةُ tribe, 96[11,14], 110[2], 118[3]

خَالِدُ بن الوَلِيدِ ابو سُلَيْمَانَ .106[2]

النُّعْمانُ ابو قٰبوس اللَّخْمِىّ king, 159[14,15].

النَّمِرُ بن تَوْلَب 121[4].

نَمِر tribe, 122[5].

نَهْد tribe of al-Yaman, 101[3,5], 121[13], 151[6].

نَهْشَلُ بن الحَرِّىّ 95[5].

ابن هَرْمَةَ poet, 100[3].

هَمْدانُ tribe, 95[17], 150[7], 151[6].

هِنْد 132[15].

هَوازِنُ group of tribes, 116[4], 139[3], 140[6], 157[16,17], 160[2].

هَوْذَةُ بن عَلِىٍّ الحَنَفِىُّ 117[9,15], 118[7,10,12], 119[1].

وائِلَةُ a subdivision of ʿĀmir, 156[8].

الوَجيهَةُ woman's name, 132[13].

وَرْدُ بن ناشِب العَبْسِىّ 103[12,13].

الوَليد (من عبد القيس) 111[1].

الوَليدُ بن عَبْدِ المَلِكِ Caliph, 95[11].

يُحابِر a name of Murād, a Yamanite tribe, 96 (note g).

يَحْصُب a prince of al-Yaman, 157[8].

يَزيدُ بن عَبْدِ المَدانِ 135[17].

مُدْرِكٌ ابو أَنَّسٍ الأَكْلُبِىّ 140[11,12].

مَذْحِجٌ tribe, 95[2], 107[11] ff., 138[1].

مُرَّةٌ a slain man of ʿAbd-al-Qais, 111[1].

مُرَّةُ بن عَوْفٍ a tribe of Dhubyān, 105[3], 111[12,15], 112[6], 121[9], 131[11], 133[5], 143[4], 145[3].

المَزْنوق name of a horse 104[15], 116[5], 127[4].

مُسْهِرٌ الحارِثِىّ 119[7].

المُسَيَّبُ بن زَيْدِ مَناةَ 128[10] (note).

مُضَرُ 118[1], 158[17].

مَعْبَدُ بن زُرارَةَ 158[3].

مُعَقِّرُ بن حِمار البارِقِىّ 113[10] (note).

بنو المُغيرَةِ family of Quraish, 106[9].

مَقْروق 104[9].

المُكَعْبِرُ 118[6].

المُنْتَجِعُ بن نَبْهانَ 139[12].

المُنْذِرُ بن ماءِ السَّماءِ 159[10].

مَنولَةُ wife of Fazārah, 131[11].

النابِغَةُ الجَعْدِىّ 94[1], 120[8].

النابِغَةُ الذُّبْيانِىُّ 94[17], 104[16], 112[15], 127[7], 130[10], 139[1], 145[5], 151[1], (see زِباد).

INDEX OF GEOGRAPHICAL NAMES IN THE DĪWĀN OF ꜤĀMIR

The names marked with an asterisk are the sites of battles or skirmishes (*Ayyām*).

حَلَّبِتْ (بِرَقَتْ) place of a race 147[11].

* الحَوْمانُ 97[16].

* حُوَى 156[6].

خَبْتْ (perhaps we should read (جَوْبْ) 109[5].

الْخَطُّ 137[9].

* خُوَى see حُوَى.

* الدَّنَابُ 128[6].

* الذُّهَابُ 156[6].

* ذُو نَجَبٍ 97[14].

* رَحْرَحانُ 158[2].

* الرَّقَمُ 157[2].

رَهْوَةٌ a mountain, 125[2].

* زَرُود (ذُو) 95[18,19].

سُوَيْقَةٌ 115[8].

الشَّامُ 95[15], 158[13].

* الشِّعْبُ ,شِعْبُ جَبَلَةَ 98[3,4,13], 100[11], 1347.

* أَبِيدَةٌ valley in KhathꜤam 142[9,10].

* أَعْوَى 135[18], (Yazīd b. ꜤAbd al-Madān killed).

* أَقْبِصِرُ 134[18].

* بَدْوَةٌ 154[8] (ꜤAbd ꜤAmr killed).

بَرَاقِش 94[2].

البَحْرانُ 97[13].

البَصْرَةُ 133[12].

تَضْروعٌ 157[2,3].

تَيْمانُ place in country of Ṭayyi', 137[2].

* الثَّنِبَّةُ 137[1].

تَهْلانُ 104[12].

جُبَارُ place in the Ḥijāz, 146[1].

* جَبَلَةَ (شِعْبُ) 98[3,4,13], 100[11], 1347.

جَيَّارُ 118[3] (and note).

* حِسْمَى (or حُسْمَى ?) 131[5,9], 134[18], (Ḥandhalah b. aṭ-Ṭufail killed).

INDEX OF SELECTED WORDS (BOTH DĪWĀNS)

صهب : أَصْهَب جـ صُهْب 30⁵,⁶, 33⁵

61⁹,¹⁰, 71¹⁰

صوح : مُنْصاح 76⁶,⁷.

صول : صُلْت أُصُول 140¹⁴,¹⁵.

صيد : أَصْيَد جـ صِيد 79¹¹, 157⁹

158¹⁷

صيق صَيِّق 150⁷,⁸.

ضبب : ضَباب 21¹⁷, 28⁷.

ضبث : ضَبُوث 109³,⁴.

ضبر : مُضَبَّر 9¹⁵, 24¹³,¹⁴.

ضجر 34⁷.

ضرب : ضَريب 10¹⁴,¹⁵. ضَريبَة 68¹.

ضرس : ضَرِس 134²⁰. ضَروس

52¹¹,¹²

ضرع 119².

ضرغامة 15⁵,⁷.

ضرم 27²,⁴. ضِرام 22¹⁵,¹⁶.

ضرو (tree) 93¹⁵, 94². ضَرى ضاريات

31¹⁰ ضَرو جـ ضِراء 75¹.

ضغم : ضَغم ضَيغَم 125¹⁰,¹²,¹³.

ضغو: ضَغا يَضْغُو 11¹⁰.

ضمر،ضامِزة،ضَمَر (emend.)62¹⁰,38¹³ note k.

ضهل 132⁵⁻⁷.

ضوى : ضاوِي 1⁸.

ضبر: لا صَبْر 111¹².

ضيق: ضاق ذَرْعًا 76⁶. ضاق ذَرْعُه

27⁵,⁸.

ضبل : ضالٌ (= سِدْرٌ) 25³,⁸.

طبب : طِبّ 37⁶,¹¹.

طبو: طَبا (= دَعا) 34⁸,⁹.

طَحْطَح 95¹³.

طرف 32¹¹,¹², 39⁵.

طلوب 10⁵.

طلق : لَبْلَة الطَّلَق 85¹⁹.

طلو: طَلاء 3¹⁰.

طَمَر ،طِمِر 15⁵,⁶, 110¹²,¹³, 135¹¹,¹²,

144².

طمل : طَميل 150³,⁴ and note d.

ضنب : مُطْنِب 13¹⁵,¹⁷.

طوح (طبح) مُنْطاح 77¹,².

طول : طُوال الـ 108³,⁵,⁶.

طوى انْطَوى 28³.

طيح : (a) يَطيح 31⁹.

طين : طِينَة 64⁸.

ظمى: أَظْمى ،ظَمْياء 149¹⁵ 150¹.

عبأ يَعبأ 79⁵.

عبط : عَبيط 31¹³, 156⁴.

عبقرى 61¹,² note a

عبل: عَبْل. عَبْلَة 15⁵,⁷. مُعْبَلة 25¹⁵,¹⁶.

جـ مَعابِل 16⁵ note e.

عنب : أَعْتَب 16³.

عَتَق الخَمْر 61¹⁰, 71¹⁰.

عتم 93¹⁵, 94². عَتوم ،عَتومة 153¹⁵,¹⁸.

عاجِلِزة 24¹³,¹⁵, 47¹.

عُدْمُلى 60⁵,⁶.

عدو: عَدا الْعَدَاء 55¹. عادى 110¹⁵,¹⁶.

عذب: أَعْذَب 13¹⁴,¹⁶. عَذوب 10⁹,¹⁰.

عذر: عُذْرى 151³,⁴. عِذار الْعَرب

118¹,².

عرب : عَريب 5⁵.

عرر: عُر 80¹. عِرار 47¹², 48¹.

---

a) Perhaps نَطيح should be
read: see emendanda et addenda.

عُنْوَانٌ ‎78[6].

عَهْدَةٌ ج عِهَادٌ ‎30[13], ‎31[3-6].

عور: تَعَاوَرَتْ فلانًا الرِّمَاحُ ‎21[2]. عُوّارٌ ج عَوَاوِيرُ ‎126[9,13,14].

عول: مِعْوَلٌ ج مَعَاوِلُ ‎19[10].

عَوْمُ السَّفِينِ ‎30[1,2], ‎44[4].

عون: حَرْبٌ عَوَانٌ ‎22[15,16].

عَيْبَةٌ ج عِيَابٌ ‎18[8].

عيث: عَاثَ الذِّئْبُ ‎110[16].

عيف: تَعَيُّفٌ ‎12[4], ‎13[1].

عين: مَعِينٌ ‎6[13].

غُبْرٌ ‎138[5].

غبط: غِبْطَةٌ ‎43[14], ‎48[5]. مُغْتَبِطٌ ‎63[2].

غبن: مُغَابَنَةٌ note h ‎45[7,9,10].

غَبِيٌّ ‎36[7,8].

غُدَافٌ ‎55[13].

غذمر: مُغَذْمِرٌ ‎63[12].

غَرْبٌ ‎34[15]. غَارِبٌ ج غَوَارِبُ ‎30[1-3].

غـــرر: أَغَــرُّ (of words) ‎35[6,7].
‎83[12] (of a man's face).

غُرْزٌ ‎34[12].

عضب: أَعْضَبُ ‎12[4], ‎13[1].

عضل: مُعَضَّلٌ ‎15[17,18].

عُطْبُولَةٌ ‎72[2,3].

عطو: تَعَاطَى ‎38[5], ‎47[6].

عَطَاءٌ ج عَطَايَا ‎13[6].

عفر: أَعْفَرُ ,عِفْرٌ ‎74[8].

عقب: عُقَابٌ ‎15[17,19].

عَقْدٌ ج أَعْقَادٌ ‎69[3].

عَقَرَ يَعْقِرُ ‎39[13].

عقص: عِقَاصٌ note d ‎66[7].

عَقْلٌ (embroidery) ‎60[9,10].

عقو: عَقًى ‎73[9,10].

عَكَفَ ‎21[9], ‎22[8], ‎35[10].

علد: عَلَنْدَى ‎62[9], ‎67[9].

عَلَقٌ ‎122[6,8]. عِلْقَاةٌ ‎129[2,4]. عِلْقَاةٌ ‎135[4,5].

علكز: عُلَاكِزٌ ‎83[12].

عَلَّلَ ‎79[9]. عُلَالَةٌ ‎145[12,13].

علو: عَلَاةٌ ‎24[2,3].

عَنْتَرِيسٌ ‎40[8].

عُنَاجُوجٌ ج عَنَاجِيجُ ‎39[2,3].

عَنَدٌ ‎47[1,2].

عنس: عَانِسٌ ‎34[4].

عَرِسَ ,عَرَّسَ ,أَعْرَسَ ‎108[10-12].

عَرِضَ ,عَرَّضَ ‎112[19].

عرض: عَرِيضٌ ‎34[11].

عرق: تَعَرَّقَ دَقْرَهُ ‎82[1]. عُرْقَاةٌ ‎135[4,5].

عُرْقُوبٌ ‎32[17].

عرك: عَارِكٌ (= طَامِثٌ) ‎149[1,2].

عرم: تَعَرَّمَ ,عُرَامٌ ‎142[15,17].

عرن: عَرِينٌ ‎35[9].

عرو: عَرَاءٌ ‎135[9,10].

عزب: مِعْزَابَةٌ note l ‎39[13].

عَزَفَ يَعْزِفُ ‎14[6,7]. عَازِفٌ ج عَوَازِفُ ‎47[12].

عزل: عَزْلَاءُ ج عَزَالٍ ‎27[7,8]. مِعْزَالٌ note m ‎39[13,14].

عزو: اعْتَزَى ‎28[7,10].

عسف: يَعْسِفُ ‎157[3,4]. عَسِيفٌ ‎27[1,3].

عَسَلَ ,عَسَّالٌ ‎157[13].

عَصَبٌ ‎139[8]. عَصَّبَ ‎98[12]. مُعَصَّبٌ ‎50[6,8]. عُصْبَةٌ ‎98[9,11]. عِصَابَةٌ ‎142[15,16]. عِصَابٌ ‎139[4-8]. عَصَبْصَبٌ ‎15[12,13].

عَصْمَرٌ ‎9[14].

عصل: أَعْصَلُ ج عُصْلٌ ‎28[9].
